CRIMINOLOGY

SECOND EDITION

CRIMINOLOGY:
A SOCIOLOGICAL
UNDERSTANDING

Steven E. Barkan

University of Maine

UPPER SADDLE RIVER, NEW JERSEY 07458

Library of Congress Cataloging-in-Publication Data

Barkan, Steven E.
  Criminology: a sociological understanding/Steven E. Barkan.—2nd ed.
    p. cm.
  Includes bibliographical references and index.
  ISBN 0-13-089643-8
    1. Crime—Sociological aspects.   2. Criminology.   I. Title.

HV6025.B78 2001
364—dc21   00-046492

VP, Editorial director: Laura Pearson
AVP, Publisher: Nancy Roberts
Senior acquisitions editor: Christopher DeJohn
Managing editor: Sharon Chambliss
Director of marketing: Beth Gillett Mejia
Editorial/production supervision: Kari Callaghan Mazzola
Prepress and manufacturing buyer: Mary Ann Gloriande
Electronic page makeup: Kari Callaghan Mazzola and John P. Mazzola
Interior design: John P. Mazzola
Director, Image Resource Center: Melinda Reo
Manager, Rights and Permissions: Kay Dellosa
Interior image specialist: Beth Boyd
Photo researcher: Melinda Alexander
Image permissions coordinator: Charles Morris
Cover director/cover design: Jayne Conte
Cover art: Sandra Dionisi/Stock Illustration Source, Inc.

This book was set in 10/12 Palatino by Big Sky Composition
and was printed and bound by Courier Companies, Inc.
The cover was printed by Phoenix Color Corp.

Criminology: A Sociological Understanding, Second Edition
Steven E. Barkan

© 2001, 1997 by Prentice-Hall, Inc.
A Division of Pearson Education
Upper Saddle River, New Jersey 07458

Printed in the United States of America
10 9 8 7 6 5 4 3 2

ISBN 0-13-089643-8

PRENTICE-HALL INTERNATIONAL (UK) LIMITED, *London*
PRENTICE-HALL OF AUSTRALIA PTY. LIMITED, *Sydney*
PRENTICE-HALL CANADA INC., *Toronto*
PRENTICE-HALL HISPANOAMERICANA, S.A., *Mexico*
PRENTICE-HALL OF INDIA PRIVATE LIMITED, *New Delhi*
PRENTICE-HALL OF JAPAN, INC., *Tokyo*
PEARSON EDUCATION ASIA PTE. LTD., *Singapore*
EDITORA PRENTICE-HALL DO BRASIL, LTDA., *Rio de Janeiro*

To Barb, Dave, and Joey,
and in memory of my parents

CONTENTS

4 VICTIMS AND VICTIMIZATION   78

PART II: EXPLAINING CRIME

5 EXPLAINING CRIME: EMPHASIS ON THE INDIVIDUAL   106

6 SOCIOLOGICAL THEORIES: EMPHASIS ON SOCIAL STRUCTURE 142

7 SOCIOLOGICAL THEORIES: EMPHASIS ON SOCIAL PROCESS 172

 8 SOCIOLOGICAL THEORIES: CRITICAL PERSPECTIVES 204

11   PROPERTY CRIME   298

14   PUBLIC ORDER CRIME AND ORGANIZED CRIME   396

PART IV: CONTROLLING AND PREVENTING CRIME

15   POLICING: DILEMMAS OF CRIME CONTROL IN A DEMOCRATIC SOCIETY   434

16 PROSECUTION AND PUNISHMENT   470

Welcome to this sociological introduction to the field of criminology! The successful first edition of this book emphasized the need to understand the social causes of crime in order to be able to significantly reduce crime. I liken this approach to that followed by the field of public health. If crime were a disease like cancer, we would naturally try to determine what was causing it so that we could prevent people from getting it. Although it's important to treat people who already have cancer, there will always be more cancer patients unless we discover its causes and then do something about these causes. The analogy to crime is clear: Unless we discover the causes of crime and do something about them, there will always be more criminals.

Unfortunately, this is not the approach the United States has taken during the past few decades. Instead it has relied on a "get tough" approach to the crime problem that relies on more intensive policing, longer and more certain prison terms, and the building of more and more prisons. The nation's prison and jail population soared and reached 2 million as the new century began. Although crime did decline during the 1990s, criminologists dispute whether this decline stemmed from this "get tough" approach or, instead, from an improved economy, a decline in illegal drug trafficking, and other factors. As the 1990s ended, many criminologists even began to warn that the surge in prisoners could be setting the stage for a crime increase down the line, as almost all of these prisoners, penniless and without jobs and embittered by their incarceration, will one day be returned to their communities.

In offering a sociological understanding of crime, this book suggests that the "get tough" approach is short-sighted since it ignores the roots of crime in the social structure and social inequality of society. To reduce crime, we must address these structural conditions and appreciate the role that factors such as race and ethnicity, gender, and social class play in criminal behavior. For criminology courses like my own, housed in sociology departments, it is especially important that criminology students acquire the sociological understanding that this book offers. But this understanding is also important for criminology students in courses housed in criminal justice departments. If crime cannot be fully understood without appreciating its structural context, then students in both sociology and criminal justice departments who do not develop this appreciation have only an incomplete understanding of the reasons for crime and of the most effective strategies to reduce it.

In presenting a sociological perspective on crime and criminal justice, this book highlights issues of race and ethnicity, gender, and social class in every chapter and emphasizes the criminogenic effects of the social and physical features of urban neighborhoods. This second edition continues to include certain chapters that remain uncommon in other criminology texts, including Chapter 2 on "Public Opinion, the News Media, and the Crime Problem," Chapter 13 on "Political Crime," and Chapter 17 on "How Can We Reduce Crime?" In addition, the book's criminal justice chapters, Chapter 15 on "Policing: Dilemmas of Law Enforcement in Democratic Society" and Chapter 16 on "Prosecution and Punishment," continue to address two central themes in the sociological understanding of crime and criminal justice: (1) the degree to which race and ethnicity, gender, and social class affect the operation of the criminal justice system, and (2) the extent to which reliance on the criminal justice system can reduce the amount of crime. These two themes in turn reflect two more general sociological issues: the degree to which inequality affects the dynamics of social institutions, and the extent to which formal sanctions affect human behavior.

The second edition of this book has been thoroughly revised. It includes the latest crime and criminal justice statistics available in early 2000 and discusses the latest research on crime and criminal justice issues that had appeared by that time. To improve readability, many in-text references have been deleted; at the same time, dozens of references appearing since the first edition have been added. This second edition also discusses several new crime topics, including computer crime, harm reduction and illegal drug use, workplace violence, police crime-reporting scandals, restorative justice, and control balance theory. In addition, every chapter now includes three new features: (1) chapter-opening "Crime in the News" vignettes that will engage students' attention and demonstrate the text's relevance to real-life events and issues; (2) end-of-chapter "Internet Exercises" that show how the Internet can be used to explore issues raised in each chapter; and (3) end-of-chapter "Study Questions" that help students understand and learn the key points of each chapter. This edition continues to include the "Crime and Controversy" and "International Focus" boxes that highlighted the first edition, with several new boxes added.

 ## SUPPLEMENTS

Instructor's Manual with Tests

This carefully prepared manual includes chapter outlines, chapter objectives, chapter overviews, teaching suggestions, discussion questions, and class exercises, along with over 800 test questions keyed to the text.

Prentice Hall Custom Test

Prentice Hall's testing software program permits instructors to edit any or all items in the Test Item File and add their own questions. Other special features of this program, which is available for Windows and Macintosh, include random generation of an item set, creation of alternative versions of the same test, scrambling question sequence, and test preview before printing.

Companion Website

In tandem with the text, students can now take full advantage of the World Wide Web to enrich their study of criminology through the Barkan Website. This resource correlates the text with related material available on the Internet. Features of the Website include chapter objectives, study questions, and links to interesting material and information from other sites on the Web that can reinforce and enhance the content of each chapter. Address: **www.prenhall.com/barkan**

Sociology on the Internet: A Critical Thinking Guide, 2001

This guide focuses on developing the critical thinking skills necessary to evaluate and use online sources effectively. The guide also provides a brief introduction to navigating the Internet, along with complete references related specifically to the Sociology discipline and how to use the companion websites available for many Prentice Hall textbooks. This brief supplementary book is free to students when shrinkwrapped as a package with any Prentice Hall Sociology title.

 ## ACKNOWLEDGMENTS

In the preface to the first edition I stated my personal and intellectual debt to Norman Miller and Forrest Dill, and I continue to acknowledge how much I owe them. Norman Miller was my first undergraduate sociology professor and quickly helped me fall in love with the discipline. He forced me to ask questions about society that I probably still haven't answered. I and the many other students he influenced can only say an inadequate "thank you" for caring so much about us and, to paraphrase a verse from a great book, for training us in the way we should go. Forrest Dill was my mentor in graduate school and introduced me to criminology and the sociology of law and to the craft of scholarship. His untimely death almost two decades ago continues to leave a void that will never be filled.

My professional home since graduate school has been the Sociology Department at the University of Maine. I continue to owe my colleagues there an intellectual debt for sharing and reaffirming my sense of the importance of social structure and social inequality for understanding crime and other contemporary issues. They continue to provide a warm, supportive working environment that often seems all too rare in academia.

I also wish to thank the editorial, production, and marketing staff at Prentice Hall for their help on all aspects of the book's creation. In particular, Sharon Chambliss's help on this edition was indispensable. I also wish to thank the reviewers who read various chapters and provided very helpful comments and criticism: Thomas E. Carroll, University of Missouri; Jon Darling, University of Pittsburgh—Johnstown; Jerry C. Jolley, Lewis-Clark State College; Richard Lundman, The Ohio State University; Nick Maroules, Illinois State University; J. William Spencer, Purdue University; James Spruill, Community College of Allegheny County; Lawrence

D. Weiss, University of Alaska, Anchorage; Thomas E. Allen, Jr., University of South Dakota; B. Keith Crew, University of Northern Iowa; Francis Y. Donkor, Cleveland State University. Any errors that remain, of course, are mine alone.

Finally, as in the first edition, I acknowledge with loving and heartfelt gratitude the joy and wonder that my wife, Barbara Tennent, and my sons, David and Joey, bring to my life. They put up with my need to write, my quirks, and my reactions to the success and failure of our favorite sports teams more than any husband and father has a right to expect.

The second edition of this book is again dedicated to my late parents, Morry and Sylvia Barkan, who instilled in me respect for learning and sympathy for those less fortunate than I. As I continue to think about them after so many years, I can only hope that somewhere they are smiling with pride over this latest evidence of their legacy.

Steven E. Barkan

ABOUT THE AUTHOR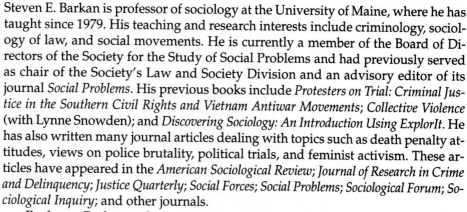

Steven E. Barkan is professor of sociology at the University of Maine, where he has taught since 1979. His teaching and research interests include criminology, sociology of law, and social movements. He is currently a member of the Board of Directors of the Society for the Study of Social Problems and had previously served as chair of the Society's Law and Society Division and an advisory editor of its journal *Social Problems*. His previous books include *Protesters on Trial: Criminal Justice in the Southern Civil Rights and Vietnam Antiwar Movements*; *Collective Violence* (with Lynne Snowden); and *Discovering Sociology: An Introduction Using ExplorIt*. He has also written many journal articles dealing with topics such as death penalty attitudes, views on police brutality, political trials, and feminist activism. These articles have appeared in the *American Sociological Review*; *Journal of Research in Crime and Delinquency*; *Justice Quarterly*; *Social Forces*; *Social Problems*; *Sociological Forum*; *Sociological Inquiry*; and other journals.

Professor Barkan welcomes comments from students and faculty about this book. They may e-mail him at barkan@maine.edu or send regular mail to the Department of Sociology, 5728 Fernald Hall, University of Maine, Orono, Maine 04469-5728.

CRIMINOLOGY AND THE SOCIOLOGICAL PERSPECTIVE

Crime in the News

"*Homicides Haunt Baltimore,*" the newspaper headline screamed. It was early December 1999, and city officials were hoping against hope that they could keep the number of homicides below 300. They lamented the fact that Baltimore's homicide rate was one of the worst in the nation and attributed the high rate to the city's deep-rooted poverty and active trafficking in crack and other drugs. As the clock clicked toward December 31, they knew that more people would be killed in Baltimore's homes and streets.

While Baltimore despaired, the rest of the country was still recovering from the shock of the April 1999 tragedy at Columbine High School in Colorado, where two students went on a shooting rampage and left more than a dozen dead. In the bloody aftermath, a distraught nation tried to understand why the United States was so violent and what we could do to have a safer society.

At a March conference on crime control strategies that year, the police chief of Fort Worth, Texas, observed that "you can arrest only so many people." A former police chief of Winston-Salem, North Carolina, agreed. "We can go on locking people up," he said, "but we have to start looking at the front end of the problem. We're fast becoming the No. 1 country for detention. We better start looking at kids. If you intervene at the earliest possible moment, you can reduce the number of people who wind up in the criminal justice system. The high chair, not the electric chair, is the answer."

Sources: Broder 1999:A27; Zuckoff 1999.

A s our new century begins, crime remains a major problem. Despite the Columbine shootings and Baltimore's homicide woes, crime actually declined during most of the 1990s but remained higher than its rate a generation ago. Meanwhile, the prison and jail population jumped last decade to almost two million, an increase of hundreds of thousands in just ten years. Why do we have so much violence and other crime? What can we do to reduce our crime rate? What difference do police and prisons make? Should we "start looking at kids" instead? How serious is white-collar crime? Is the war on drugs working? What role do race, social class, and gender play in the commission of crime and in the response of the criminal justice system to the crime problem? These are just a few of the questions this book tries to answer.

The rationale for this book is simple. Crime is one of our most important social problems and also one of the least understood. Most of our knowledge about crime comes from what we read in newspapers, watch on TV, or see in movie theaters. From all these sources we get a distorted picture of crime and we hear about solutions to the crime problem that ultimately will do little to reduce it. These are harsh accusations, to be sure, but they are ones with which most criminologists would probably agree.

A major reason crime is so misunderstood is also a major reason for my writing this book. Simply put, the popular sources from which we learn about crime say little about its social roots. By "social roots" I mean that crime is not only an individual phenomenon but also a social one. Individuals commit crime, but their likelihood of doing so is profoundly shaped by their social backgrounds. In this sense, crime is no different from other behaviors that sociologists study. This basic sociological understanding of crime has an important social policy implication: If crime is rooted in the way our society is organized, then crime reduction efforts will succeed only to the extent they address the structural roots of criminality.

This book presents a sociological understanding of crime and criminal justice, an approach commonly called sociological criminology. As we'll see later, for most of its history virtually all criminology was sociological criminology, and this two-word term would have been redundant. This criminology gave explicit attention to issues of poverty, race, and ethnicity as well as to the structure of communities and social relationships. As John Hagan (1994) a criminologist and former president of the American Society of Criminology, reminds us, a sociological criminology is thus a *structural* criminology. It takes account of the social and physical characteristics of communities and of the profound influence of race, ethnicity, class, and gender.

In the past few decades, criminology has moved away from this structural focus toward individualistic explanations (Dowdy 1994). Sociologists worry that sociology and criminology/criminal justice are becoming isolated from each other (Akers 1992; Berry 1994; Farrell and Koch 1995). Other fields, especially biology and psychology, are now vying with sociology for prominence in criminology. These fields enliven the discipline and have forced sociology to sharpen its theoretical and empirical focus. However, they ultimately fail to explain two of the most central questions in criminology: Why do crime rates differ across locations and over time? and Why do crime rates differ according to the key dimensions of structured social inequality: race, ethnicity, class, and gender? Only a sociological criminology can begin to answer these questions, which must be answered if we are to have any hope of seriously reducing crime.

A sociological criminology is not only a structural criminology. To be true to the sociological perspective, it should also be a criminology that debunks incorrect

◀ *SWAT team members escort freed students outside Columbine High School where two students went on a shooting rampage inside the school in Littleton, Colorado, on Tuesday, April 20, 1999.*

perceptions about crime and false claims about the effectiveness of various crime-control strategies. In addition, it should expose possible injustice in the application of the criminal label.

These several themes are addressed throughout the book. The first part of the book, Understanding Crime and Victimization, introduces the sociological perspective and discusses public beliefs about crime and criminal justice. It also discusses what is known about the amount and social patterning of crime and victimization. Part II, Explaining Crime, critically reviews the major biological, psychological, and sociological explanations of crime and criminality, and discusses their implications for crime reduction. These explanations are integrated into the chapters contained in Part III, Criminal Behaviors. These chapters discuss the major forms of crime and ways of reducing them. The fourth and final part of the book, Controlling and Preventing Crime, begins by exploring two important issues for a sociological understanding of the criminal justice system: To what degree does social inequality affect the chances of arrest, conviction, and imprisonment, and to what degree do legal sanctions reduce criminal behavior? The concluding chapter of the book presents a sociological prescription for crime reduction.

Let's begin our sociological journey into crime and criminal justice by reviewing the sociological perspective and discussing the mutual relevance of sociology and criminology. We'll look briefly at the development of sociological criminology and at its approaches to crime and criminal justice, and also review some key legal terms and concepts.

 ## THE SOCIOLOGICAL PERSPECTIVE

Above all else, the sociological perspective stresses that people are *social beings* more than individuals. This means that "society" profoundly shapes their behavior and attitudes. People growing up in societies with different cultures tend to act and think differently from one another. People within a given society growing up in various locations, in different networks of social relationships, and under diverse socioeconomic circumstances also tend to act and think differently. We cannot understand why people think and behave as they do without understanding their social location in society.

This perspective derives from the work of Emile Durkheim (1858–1917), a French sociologist and one of the founders of the discipline. Durkheim called social forces "social facts" and stressed how these forces influence our behavior and attitudes. Importantly, Durkheim drew heavily on deviance to illustrate this central view.

In perhaps his most famous study, Durkheim found that even suicide, normally regarded as the most individualistic act possible, has social roots (Durkheim 1952 [1897]). Examining data in France and elsewhere, he found suicide rates varying across locations and across different kinds of people. Protestants, for example, had higher suicide rates than Catholics. Durkheim explained these differences by focusing on the structural characteristics, in particular the level of social integration, of the locations and people he studied. People in groups with high social integration, or strong bonds to others within their group, have lower suicide rates. I'll return to Durkheim's work on suicide in Chapter 6, but for now simply cite it as a powerful piece of sociological, which is to say structural, analysis of individual behavior.

I've mentioned *social structure* several times by now, so it will help to define it and discuss its several dimensions. Social structure refers to how a society is organized in terms of social relationships and social interaction. It is both *horizontal* and *vertical*. Horizontal social structure refers to the social and physical characteristics of communities and the networks of social relationships to which an individual belongs. Vertical social structure is more commonly called *social inequality* and refers to how a society ranks different groups of people.

Whether members of a society rank at the top or bottom of this hierarchy depends on which social characteristics a society values. You might recall Dr. Seuss's® classic story *The Sneetches*, in which stars were the major dimension of stratification: The "best" Sneetches had stars; the "worst" Sneetches did not (Seuss 1961). In the United States and most other industrial nations, race, ethnicity, social class, and gender are, of course, the key determinants of where one ranks. These dimensions profoundly affect people's behavior, attitudes, and, perhaps most importantly, life chances. In the Sneetches' world, those without stars became very frustrated as they were treated with disdain. In the real world, inequality is a bit more complex, but the consequences for the people on the bottom are much worse than those for the starless Sneetches. Further, although the Sneetches decided that stars no longer mattered, humans, unfortunately, are not as smart as the Sneetches: We're not about to decide that race, ethnicity, social class, and gender no longer matter.

In 1959 sociologist C. Wright Mills (1959) emphasized that social structure lies at the root of *private troubles*. If only a few individuals, he wrote, are unemployed, then their private troubles are their own fault. But if masses of individuals are unemployed, structural forces must account for their bad fortune. What people may define as private troubles are thus more accurately described as public issues, wrote Mills. Their personal troubles result from the intersection of their personal biography and historical and social conditions. Mills referred to the ability to understand the structural and historical basis for personal troubles as the *sociological imagination*. Once people acquire a sociological imagination, they're better able both to understand and to change the social forces underlying their private troubles.

As Mills's comments suggest, sociology's emphasis on the structural basis for individual behavior and personal troubles often leads it to challenge conventional wisdom. Max Weber (1864–1920), another founder of sociology, echoed this theme when he noted that one of sociology's most important goals was to uncover "inconvenient facts" (Gerth and Mills 1946). As Peter Berger (1963) observed in his classic book, *Invitation to Sociology*, the "first wisdom" of sociology is that things are not always what they seem.

This fundamental insight of the sociological perspective is captured in the classic children's fable by Hans Christian Andersen, "The Emperor's New Clothes." As you might recall, the Emperor marched through town supposedly wearing ornate, regal attire, for which he had paid handsomely, but in fact was wearing nothing at all. Not trusting their eyes, all the townspeople pretended to admire his attire until one small but wise child blurted out, "But he's not wearing any clothes at all!" Like the small child, sociology often exposes false claims about reality and taken-for-granted assumptions about social life and social institutions.

Peter Berger (1963) referred to this sociological tendency as the *debunking motif*. Inevitably, he wrote, sociologists end up debunking the topics they study. As a discipline, sociology refuses to accept "official interpretations of society" and "carries with it a logical imperative to unmask the pretensions and the propaganda" of everyday life (p. 38). One implication of this imperative, Berger added, is that sociologists often study so-called "unrespectable" elements of social life. In the United States, this usually means people and behaviors outside of the "world of middle-class propriety" (p. 44). Since its inception in the United States, sociology has often studied the poor and the deviants among us, especially in urban communities, and the problems they face.

The Mutual Relevance of Sociology and Criminology

With this brief discussion of the sociological perspective in mind, the continuing relevance of sociology for criminology immediately becomes clear. Perhaps most important, crime, victimization, and criminal justice cannot be fully understood without appreciating their structural context. Using Mills's terminology, crime and victimization are public issues rather than private troubles. They are rooted in the social and physical characteristics of communities, in the network of relationships in which people interact, and in the structured social inequalities of race, ethnicity, social class, and gender. Reflecting this point, most of criminology's important concepts, including anomie, relative deprivation, and social conflict, draw from concepts originally developed in the larger body of sociology. Moreover, research methodology originating in sociology provides the basis for most criminological research.

Criminology is just as relevant for its parent field. As Ronald L. Akers (1992:9), a sociologist and former president of the American Society of Criminology, notes, "Some of the most exciting and significant theoretical and methodological advances in sociology have come directly from or have been enhanced by theory and research in criminology."

A major reason for this connection is the structural basis of criminality. If crime and victimization derive from community characteristics, social relationships, and inequality, criminological insights both reinforce and advance sociological understanding of all these areas. Crime, victimization, and legal punishment are certainly important, negative "life chances" for African-Americans and others at the bottom of the socioeconomic ladder. More than most other subfields in sociology, criminology shows us how and why social inequality is, as Elliott Currie (1985:160) puts it, "enormously destructive of human personality and of social order." By the same token, positions at the top of the socioeconomic ladder contribute to a greater probability of white-collar crime and of little or no punishment. Again, perhaps more than most other sociological subfields, criminology illuminates the privileges of those at the top of the social hierarchy.

The other major dimension of inequality, gender, also has important consequences for criminality and victimization and, perhaps, legal punishment. Although criminology lags behind some other sociological subfields in considering the importance of gender, its findings have still contributed to the larger body of sociological knowledge about this topic.

More generally, as Bonnie Berry (1994:11) notes, the study of crime "has advanced such standard sociological concepts as norms, social definitions, cultural and other relativity, alienation, inequality, status, roles, social boundaries, notions of formal and informal social control responses, the variance between stated and achieved goals, Durkheim's social functions of deviance, and so on." In doing their research, criminologists have further devised new methodological techniques that enhance sociological methodology in general.

 ## THE RISE OF SOCIOLOGICAL CRIMINOLOGY

Many of the themes just outlined shaped the development of sociological criminology in the United States earlier in this century. Because Part II of this book discusses the development of criminological theory in greater detail, for now I simply sketch this history to underscore the intellectual connection between criminology and sociology.

For much of recorded history, people attributed crime and deviance to religious factors. Individuals were said to commit these behaviors because God, or, in polytheistic societies, gods, were punishing or testing them. During the Middle Ages, deviance was blamed on demonic possession. As we moved into the eighteenth century, the so-called classical school of criminology began to stress that criminals rationally choose to commit crime after deciding that the rewards of doing so outweigh the risks of punishment. In view of this, said classical scholars, legal punishment needed to be only severe enough to deter would-be criminals from breaking the law. The classical scholars were in effect legal reformers and disapproved of the harsh punishment so common then.

The nineteenth century saw the rise of a more "positivist" approach to criminal behavior as scholars began to investigate the causes of crime through scientific investigation. Perhaps the first positivist criminologist was Adolphe Quetelet (1796–1874), a Belgian astronomer and mathematician who gathered and analyzed crime data in France. Quetelet found that crime rates in France remained fairly stable from one year to the next and, further, were higher for adults in their early twenties than for other age groups and higher among men than among women. He also found the rates higher among the poor than the nonpoor.

Later in the century Emile Durkheim began providing his major contributions to the new discipline of sociology. As noted earlier, he stressed the primacy of social structure over the individual and thus established the sociological paradigm. He also considered deviance a normal phenomenon of healthy societies and stressed its functions for social stability. The punishment of deviance, he said, clarifies social norms and reinforces social ties among those doing or watching the punishing. Durkheim further argued that deviance is necessary for social change to take place. A society without deviance, he said, would be one with no freedom of thought; hence, social change would not be possible. A society thus cannot have social change without also having deviance.

Quetelet's and Durkheim's interest in the social roots of crime was eclipsed in the second half of the nineteenth century by growing interest in biological roots of crime. Physicians and other biological researchers began to investigate the biological basis for criminal behavior. Although their methodology was seriously flawed and many of their views racist and xenophobic, their perspective influenced public and scholarly thinking on crime. The recent surge in biological explanations of crime indicates the continuing popularity of this way of understanding criminal behavior.

In the United States, the discipline of sociology began developing at the University of Chicago after the turn of the century. Not surprisingly, much of the focus of these early Chicago sociologists was on urban life. As they looked outside their offices, they saw a huge city with much poverty, many racial and ethnic groups, and, like cities today, much crime. They noticed that crime rates in Chicago's various neighborhoods stayed stable from one year to the next, even as certain immigrant groups moved out and others moved in. Something about the social and physical conditions of these neighborhoods, these sociologists reasoned, must be contributing to their crime rates. That something they called "social disorganization," or the breakdown of conventional institutions, which they attributed to the stark poverty of the neighborhoods and the high mobility of their residents. Although this perspective eventually went out of favor, it's now making an important comeback.

One of the students of the Chicago sociologists was Edwin Sutherland, who soon became a towering figure in the development of sociological criminology. Sensitive to the *criminogenic* (crime-causing) conditions of urban neighborhoods, Sutherland was especially interested in how and why these conditions promote criminality. His explanation centered on peer influences, which formed the heart of his famous *differential association* theory. Sutherland also criticized biological explanations of crime still popular in the 1930s and 1940s. He further developed the concept of "white-collar crime" and was sharply critical of the illegal and harmful practices of the nation's biggest corporations. At the heart of his sociological criminology was a "critical humanism" marked by a concern for issues of race, poverty, and political and economic power (Farrell and Koch 1995:60).

At about the same time, Robert K. Merton, a Columbia University sociologist, developed his *anomie theory* of deviance. Borrowing heavily from Durkheim, Merton attributed deviance to the poor's inability to achieve economic success in a society that highly values such success. His theory was perhaps the most "macro" of all the early structural theories of crime and was quite influential for many years until it, too, fell out of favor before making a recent comeback. In its place rose a new *control theory* of criminal behavior that, like Durkheim, emphasized the criminogenic effects of weak bonds to social institutions. Although this theory focused on social relationships, it was less of a macro, structural theory than its social disorganization and anomie forebears.

The 1960s were a turbulent era marked by intellectual upheaval in several academic disciplines, perhaps, most of all, sociology. Scholars questioned the consensus tradition that was Durkheim's legacy and asserted that society was rooted in conflict between dominant and subordinate groups. In the study of crime and deviance, *labeling* and then *conflict theories* quickly captured scholarly interest. These theories called attention to disparities in the application of criminal labels and to the politics of law formation. Shortly thereafter, new feminist understandings of gender and society began to make their way into criminology, as feminists criticized the male bias of traditional criminological theories and called attention to the gendered nature of crime and victimization.

Today all these sociological theories continue to vie for scholarly popularity. The renewal of social disorganization and anomie theories suggests that criminologists are beginning to rediscover U.S. criminology's structural origins and its early concern with race and poverty. In this textbook I hope to contribute to this rediscovery.

 ## CONSENSUS AND CONFLICT IN THE CREATION OF CRIMINAL LAW

Consensus and conflict views of crime, law, and society derive from analogous perspectives in the larger field of sociology. A brief outline of these views (discussed further in Chapter 8) will help illustrate this connection.

Consensus or functionalist theory in sociology derives from Durkheim's work. It assumes a consensus of opinion among different members of the public on what the social norms of behavior are and should be. Formal norms, or laws, represent the interests of all segments of the public. People obey these laws not because they're afraid of being punished but because they've internalized the norms and regard them as appropriate to obey. When crime and deviance occur, they violate these widely accepted norms, and punishment of the behavior is necessary to ensure continuing social stability.

Conflict theory derives from the work of Karl Marx and Friedrich Engels and is virtually the opposite of consensus theory. It assumes that members of the public disagree on many of society's norms, with their disagreement reflecting their disparate positions based on their inequality of wealth and power. Laws represent the views of the powerful, not the powerless, and help them stay at the top of society's hierarchy and keep the powerless at the bottom. Behavior labeled criminal by laws is conduct by the poor that threatens the interests of the powerful. The latter may commit quite harmful behaviors, but since they determine which laws are created their behaviors are usually legal, as they make sure no laws are passed to ban their activities.

These two theories have important implications for how we define and understand crime. In consensus theory, crime is defined simply, if somewhat tautologically, as any behavior that violates a criminal law. Criminal law in turn is thought both to represent and to protect the interests of all members of society.

In conflict theory, the definition of crime is more problematic: It's just as important to consider why some behaviors don't become illegal as to consider why others are illegal. Many laws represent the interests of the powerful by prohibiting behaviors in which the poor tend to engage and which threaten the powerful. Other behaviors may be quite harmful but also legal, if they are behaviors in which the powerful engage or otherwise favor. Here white-collar crime, especially corporate crime, and political crime by governments are prime examples. A conflict view of crime, law, and society thus defines crime more broadly than does a consensus view. In particular, it's willing to consider behaviors criminal in the larger sense of the word if they're harmful, even if they're not illegal.

Both theories have their merits. The greatest support for consensus views of law formation involves laws banning the criminal behaviors we call street crime, which all segments of society condemn and which victimize the poor more than the wealthy. Although the historical roots of some of these laws lie in the conflict between rich and poor, today they can't be said to exist for the protection of the wealthy and powerful. The greatest support for conflict views of law creation involves laws banning behaviors that some segments of society favor and others deplore. We'll discuss examples of both kinds of behavior in the chapters ahead.

Research Methodology in Criminology

Theory and research lie at the heart of any natural, physical, or social science. Theories and hypotheses must be developed and then tested. The beauty of Durkheim's theory of social integration and suicide was that he was able to test it by gathering and analyzing suicide rate data in France. The fact that several kinds of data all supported his theory gave it considerable power. Although research methodology and data analysis in sociology and criminology have advanced considerably since Durkheim's day, his study of suicide remains a classic application of the sociological perspective to an important social problem.

I've taught research methods and data analysis for many years, and consider research a fundamental part of the sociological and criminological enterprises. Throughout this book, I discuss criminological research to indicate the latest research findings but also to illustrate the complexity of data and the difficulty of drawing firm conclusions from research. This section briefly reviews the major types of research in criminology and discusses the nature of causal analysis in criminological and other social science research.

Types of Research

Surveys

One of the most important types of research in criminology and sociology is survey research. A survey involves the administration of a questionnaire to some group of respondents. Usually the group is a random sample of an entire population of a particular location, either the whole nation, a state, a city, or perhaps a campus. In a random sample, everyone in the population has an equal chance of being included in the sample. The process of picking a random sample is very complex but is functionally equivalent to flipping a coin or rolling two dice to determine who is in, and not in, the sample. The familiar Gallup Poll is a random sample of the adult population of the United States. Even though the size of the Gallup sample can be as small as 400, sampling theory allows us to conclude that the sample's results would accurately reflect the opinions and behaviors of the entire population, if we could ever measure them. This means we can generalize the results of the sample to the population.

Other surveys are carried out with nonrandom samples. For example, a researcher might hand out a questionnaire to a class of high school seniors or first-year college students. Although we can't safely generalize from these results to the population, some very well-known studies in sociology and criminology rely on such "captive audience" surveys.

◄ *Telephone surveys are be-coming more popular in criminology and other social sciences.*

The three most common kinds of surveys are face-to-face interviews, mailed surveys, and telephone surveys. To conduct a face-to-face survey of a random sample of respondents, researchers must first draw a random sample of individuals or households. Interviewers then visit these potential respondents to solicit their participation in the survey. If the respondents agree, the interviewers sit down with them for up to an hour or so and ask them many questions, most of which have fixed responses, such as "strongly agree" or "strongly disagree." Face-to-face surveys can be quite expensive and time-consuming but can gather more information on a greater variety of items than the other two kinds of surveys. They also tend to have higher response rates (referring to the proportion of potential respondents who agree to be interviewed) than the other two types.

Mailed questionnaires cost less time and money than face-to-face interviews but have lower response rates and yield information on fewer questions. People often throw out questionnaires they get in the mail. Despite this problem, mailed questionnaires remain a viable survey option when face-to-face interviews are not feasible, but they are losing popularity to telephone surveys.

Because of computer advances in random-digit dialing, telephone surveys are becoming more popular. Random-digit dialing automatically yields random samples of respondents. Once they're on the phone, interviewers can ask them to take the time to answer a few questions. Usually, these phone interviews last no more than 10 to 20 minutes. Phone surveys take less time and cost less money than face-to-face interviews but yield less information and have lower response rates. Despite these problems, the advantages of telephone surveys outweigh their disadvantages, and they have become very common in sociology, criminology, and political science. Many Gallup, Harris, and other national polls also rely on telephone interviews.

In criminology, surveys are a popular way of gathering "self-report" data on crime and delinquency. Most of these surveys are either telephone surveys of random samples or "captive audience" surveys of nonrandom samples of high school or college students. Respondents, usually adolescents, are asked to indicate how many times in the past they have committed various kinds of offenses. Chapter 3 discusses self-report studies in further detail.

EXPERIMENTS

Experiments are very common in psychology but less so in sociology and criminology. Typically there is an experimental group, which is subjected to an experimental condition, and a control group for comparison. A common type of experiment with criminological implications concerns the effects of violent pornography. An experimental group of subjects may watch violent, pornographic films, while a control group watches nonviolent films. Researchers test both groups before and after the experiment to see whether the subjects in the experimental group became more violent in their attitudes toward women than those in the control group. If they find such evidence, they can reasonably conclude that watching the pornographic films prompted this shift in attitudes.

One problem with experiments is that they're not generalizable. Most experiments in psychology and other fields have been done with college students in psychology courses. Yet these students are not typical of the larger population. Among other things, they're younger and more educated than the average U.S. resident. Although conclusions from these experiments are often assumed to apply to people in general, such conclusions may be premature.

OBSERVATIONAL STUDIES

Many classic sociological and criminological studies have resulted from researchers spending much time and effort observing various groups. One of the most famous observational, or field, studies in sociology in the last several decades is the late Elliott Liebow's *Tally's Corner* (1967), a study of urban African-American men. Shortly before he died, Liebow published another ethnographic work, *Tell Them Who I Am: The Lives of Homeless Women* (1993), which provides a rich account of urban women living in the streets. In criminology and deviance, classic field studies include William Foote Whyte's *Street Corner Society* (1943), a study of leadership in a Chicago gang, and Laud Humphreys' *Tearoom Trade* (1970), a study of male homosexual sex in public bathrooms. More recent field studies of other offenders are discussed in later chapters.

Observational studies can't readily be generalized to other segments of the population, but over the years they have provided richer accounts than any other methodology could yield. Several ethnographic studies of urban areas, such as Elijah Anderson's (1999) sensitive account of inner-city culture, don't touch on crime directly but still provide important perspectives that help us understand why street crime is so common in these areas.

RESEARCH USING EXISTING DATA

Criminologists often gather and analyze data that have been recorded or gathered by government agencies and other sources. For example, they may code data from the case files of criminal defendants to determine whether defendants' race, ethnicity, social class, or gender affects their likelihood of conviction and imprisonment. The U.S. government does extensive data collection of the rates and dynamics of crime and victimization. Sociologists and other criminologists have analyzed these data repeatedly. Sometimes they combine these data with census data when they do "aggregate-level" research on how the social characteristics of states, counties, or cities affect such criminological variables as crime and imprisonment rates.

Analysis of any of these data is only as good as the reliability of the data. Chapter 3 discusses measurement issues in the kinds of data the government gathers.

COMPARATIVE AND HISTORICAL RESEARCH

Two final types of research that combine several of the kinds already mentioned are comparative and historical research. Comparative research usually means cross-cultural or international research. Different nations' varying rates of crime and other behavior reflect differences in the nations' social structure and culture. By examining other nations' experience, we can better understand our own situation. International Focus boxes throughout this book highlight the comparative approach.

Historical research is also important. Much of the work of the three so-called founders of sociology—Emile Durkheim, Max Weber, and Karl Marx—was historical. Societies change over time, as do their rates of criminal and other behavior. For example, murder rates in Western nations were much higher a few centuries ago than they are now. By looking at crime in history, we can better understand our own situation today and the possibilities for change. Most chapters in this book discuss historical research.

Criteria of Causality

In criminology we often ask whether one variable influences another variable (e.g., whether attachment to one's parents influences delinquency). The variable that does the influencing is called the independent variable, while the variable that is influenced is called the dependent variable. Before we can conclude that an independent variable in fact does influence a dependent variable, several "criteria of causality" must be demonstrated (Babbie 1999).

The first criterion is that the independent variable (A) and the dependent variable (B) must be statistically related. At a minimum, that means that where one ranks on the independent variable makes a difference in how much of the dependent variable happens. Using our delinquency example, if 40 percent of adolescents with weak parental attachment in a national sample are delinquent compared to only 22 percent of adolescents with strong parental attachment, then A (parental attachment) and B (delinquency) are statistically related. Note that to have such a relationship we don't need an "all-or-nothing" situation, that is, 100 percent of the adolescents with weak attachment versus 0 percent of those with strong attachment.

The second criterion of causality is that A must precede B in time. Even if A and B are statistically related, that doesn't necessarily mean that A influences B. It could just as well mean that B influences A. This familiar "chicken-and-egg" question (sometimes called the "causal order" problem) will be noted throughout the book as I discuss criminological research findings. In our delinquency example, although the data might suggest that parental attachment affects delinquency, they could also suggest that delinquency affects parental attachment. Delinquent adolescents may end up having conflict with their parents, reducing the parental attachment they feel.

The third criterion of causality is that the relationship between A and B is not spurious. This means that no other variable, or "third factor," is influencing both A and B in such a way as to have A and B appear to be statistically related if this variable is not held constant. My favorite example of spuriousness is the relationship you'd find if you studied listening to rock music and having acne. I can guarantee you that a survey of a random sample of the U.S. population would find that people who often listen to rock music have worse acne than those who hardly ever listen to rock music. Therefore, listening to rock music causes acne. Or perhaps having bad acne leads one to stay at home a lot and listen to rock music!

Obviously neither situation is true, because we've failed to control for an important variable that affects both the likelihood of listening to rock music and, for different reasons, the likelihood of having acne. This variable, of course, is age. Younger people are more likely to listen to rock music and also, for different reasons, to have acne. If you simply determine the statistical relationship between listening to rock music and having acne without holding age constant, you'd end up with a relationship that is definitely spurious.

Returning to our delinquency example, several variables might render our attachment-delinquency relationship spurious. One such variable is income. For the sake of argument, let's say that because of the stress of poverty, poor adolescents are more likely than middle-class adolescents to have weaker parental attachment and also to commit delinquency. If so, the initial, bivariate (two-variable) relationship noted earlier for parental attachment and delinquency might in fact be spurious.

As we'll be seeing throughout the book, issues of causal order and spuriousness plague criminological (and also sociological) research. These problems were especially true of earlier research, before the 1970s, but are still worrisome today, as even the best-designed criminological research of recent decades has been challenged on methodological grounds.

Even if all three criteria of causality are satisfied, the explanation offered for why A affects B still has to make sense. Accordingly, a fourth criterion of causality is that no other explanation of the relationship makes more sense than the researcher's explanation. Consider here the fact that shortly after Ronald Reagan took office in 1981, the official U.S. crime rate data began to decrease. The Reagan White House quickly claimed credit for this decrease. Supporting their claim, this relationship satisfied our first three criteria of causality. First, there was a relationship between President Reagan taking office and the crime rate going down. Second, he took office before the crime rate began decreasing, so that causal order was not at issue. Third, there is no apparent third factor that would affect both the likelihood of Reagan winning the presidency and the crime rate going down.

However, as we'll see in a later chapter, there was a better explanation of this apparent relationship. While Ronald Reagan won the election for a lot of reasons, demographic changes were a prime reason for the decrease in the crime rate that occurred after he took office. The number of people in the 15 to 25 age group that commits a disproportionate amount of crime declined in the 1980s. Anticipating this demographic change, criminologists had predicted before Mr. Reagan won the presidency that crime rates would decline in that decade. They most likely would have declined even if his opponent, President Jimmy Carter, had won reelection. Thus the Reagan-crime rate relationship does not satisfy the fourth criterion of causality.

 ## AN OVERVIEW OF CRIMINAL LAW

Before concluding this chapter, let's review some important concepts and elements of the criminal law. All societies have norms, or standards of behavior. In most traditional societies, these norms remain unwritten and informal, and are called customs. There is no law as conventionally defined. Instead, as anthropologists point out, customs are enforced through informal social control such as ostracism and ridicule. People obey these norms because they believe in them and because they fear the society's informal sanctions.

In contrast, larger, more modern societies are also more heterogeneous and more characterized by diversity of opinion and of experience. As a result, informal norms and informal social control have less power over individual behavior. Norms tend to be more formal, meaning that they tend to be written, or codified. We call these formal norms laws. Social control is also more formal and takes the form of specialized groups of people whose chief tasks are to create laws, to interpret them, and to apprehend and punish law violators.

Law in the United States has its origins in English common law, which began during the reign of Henry II in the twelfth century. Over the centuries, England developed a complex system of law that specified the types of illegal behaviors, the punishment for these behaviors, and the elements that have to be proven before someone could be found guilty of a crime. English judges had great powers to interpret the law and in effect to make new, so-called "case law." As a result, much of English law derived from judges' rulings rather than from, as in most continental European nations, legislatures' statutes.

During this time, the jury was also developed to replace ordeals as the chief way of determining a defendant's guilt or innocence. The jury's power was quite limited, however, because jurors could be punished if they found a defendant innocent. The jury's power and importance grew considerably in 1670 after William Penn was arrested and tried for preaching about Quakerism. When the jury acquitted him, the judge imprisoned and starved them. In response, an English court ruled that juries could not be punished for their verdicts. This ruling allowed juries to acquit defendants with impunity and strengthened their historic role as protectors of defendants against arbitrary state power (Barkan 1983).

When English colonists came to the new world, beginning with the Pilgrims, they naturally brought with them English common law. Several of their grievances that led to the Revolutionary War centered on England's denial of jury trials for colonial defendants, its search and seizure of colonial homes and property, and its arbitrary use of legal punishment. After the Revolution, the new nation's leaders wrote protections from these and other legal abuses into the Constitution and Bill of Rights.

Legal Distinctions in Types of Crime

Most U.S. jurisdictions still retain common-law concepts of the types of crime and the elements of criminal law violation that must be proven before a defendant can be found guilty. One distinction is made between *mala in se* crimes and *mala prohibita* crimes, with the former considered more serious than the latter. *Mala in se* (evil in themselves) crimes refer to behaviors that violate traditional norms and moral codes. This category includes the violent and property crime with which the public is most concerned. *Mala prohibita* (wrong only because prohibited by law) crimes refer to behaviors that violate contemporary standards only; examples include illegal drug use and many white-collar crimes (Klotter and Edwards 1998).

Roughly corresponding to this distinction is another one between *felonies* and *misdemeanors*. Felonies are crimes punishable by more than one year in prison, while misdemeanors are crimes punishable by less than one year. Most people convicted of felonies and then incarcerated are sent to state prisons (or if convicted of a federal crime, to federal prisons), while most people convicted of misdemeanors and then incarcerated serve their sentence in local jails, which also hold people awaiting trial.

Criminal Intent

For a defendant to be found guilty, the key elements that must be proven are *actus reus* and *mens rea*. *Actus reus* (actual act) refers to the actual criminal act of which the defendant is accused. For a defendant to be found guilty, the evidence must indicate beyond a reasonable doubt that he or she committed a criminal act. *Mens rea* (guilty mind) refers to criminal intent. This means that the state must show that the defendant had intended to commit the act. Although the concept of criminal intent is complex, it generally means that the defendant committed a criminal act knowingly. If the defendant is too young or mentally incapable of understanding the nature and consequences of the crime, criminal intent is difficult to prove.

By the same token, the defendant must have also broken the law willingly. This generally means that the defendant was not under duress at the time of the crime. Duress is usually defined narrowly, and usually means that the defendant was in fear of her or his life or safety at the time of the crime. If someone holds a gun to your head and forces you to shoplift (admittedly an unlikely scenario), you did not have criminal intent.

The concept of *mens rea* also covers behaviors in which someone acts recklessly or negligently and injures someone else even though he or she did not intend the injury to happen. If you accidentally leave an infant inside a car on a hot day and the infant becomes ill or dies, you can be found guilty of a crime even though you did not intend the infant to suffer. If you try to injure someone but end up accidentally hurting someone else instead, you can still be found guilty of a crime even though you did not intend to hurt that person.

Legal Defenses to Criminal Liability

Defendants may offer several types of excuses or justifications as defenses against criminal accusations (Robinson 1984). One possible defense is that the defendant committed the act by accident. If you're driving a car in the winter at a safe speed but skid on the ice and hit a pedestrian, your act is tragic but probably not criminal. If, however, you were driving too fast for the icy conditions and then skidded and hit a pedestrian, you might very well be held responsible.

Another defense is that the defendant committed a criminal act out of ignorance. Here it's generally true, as the popular slogan says, that "ignorance of the law is no excuse," as people are assumed to be aware of the law generally. However, the law does exempt "mistakes of fact" that occur when someone engages in an illegal activity without being aware it's illegal. If someone gives you a package to mail that, unknown to you, contains illegal drugs or stolen merchandise, you commit a mistake of fact when you mail the package and, thus, are not criminally liable.

Duress is another defense to criminal prosecution. As noted earlier, it's usually narrowly defined to mean fear for one's life or safety. During the Vietnam War, several antiwar protesters arrested for civil disobedience claimed in their trials that they were acting under duress of their consciences. However, judges almost always excluded this defense from the jury's consideration (Barkan 1983).

A common defense to prosecution is self-defense to prevent an offender from harming you or someone nearby. However, if you injure your would-be attacker more than legitimate self-defense would reasonably have required, you may be held liable.

◄ *Bernhard Goetz is interviewed in the hallway of the Bronx State Supreme Court in New York on Tuesday, April 23, 1996, hours before the jury returned a verdict in the $50 million civil suit filed against Goetz by Darrell Cabey, one of his victims in a December 22, 1984, subway shooting. Twelve years after he shot four black youths in a subway car, Goetz was ordered to pay $43 million to Cabey, the man left paralyzed by his final bullet.*

How much force someone is allowed to use in *self-defense* remains a controversial issue. Here the case of Bernhard Goetz is widely cited. In December 1984, Goetz, a white man, was riding a New York subway when he was approached by four young black males who demanded money. None of the youths displayed a weapon. In response, Goetz pulled out a gun and fired four bullets, one at each of the youths. He wounded three of the youths and missed the fourth. A few moments later he shot a fifth bullet at this last youth, who was sitting down some feet away, and severed his spinal cord. During his trial, Goetz claimed that he was in fear of his life and safety. The prosecutor insisted that he overreacted. The jury acquitted Goetz of attempted murder and assault but convicted him of possessing an illegal handgun. Some observers applauded the verdict, saying it sent a message to muggers everywhere, while others warned of vigilante justice against young black males and speculated that Goetz's actions were racially motivated (Fletcher 1988).

The issue of self-defense has also arisen in cases of battered women who kill their husbands or other male partners who have been battering them for years. Often, such a killing occurs when the husband is sleeping, turned the other way, or otherwise not threatening the woman at that moment. Several women who killed their batterers in these circumstances have claimed they were acting out of self-defense, even if they were not afraid for their lives at the moment they committed the homicide. Traditionally, the law of self-defense does not apply to this situation, and many judges still refuse to permit this defense. However, some courts have expanded the self-defense concept to cover these circumstances.

Another possible defense is *entrapment*. The law here is again complex, but basically entrapment refers to a situation where law enforcement agents induce someone to commit a crime, but the defendant wouldn't have committed the crime had he or she not been so induced.

A final, very controversial defense is the *insanity* defense. Despite the attention it receives, few criminal defendants plead insanity, diminished capacity, or related mental and emotional states, and abolition of the insanity defense would not affect the operation or effectiveness of the criminal justice system (Walker 1998). This issue aside, if a defendant does not have the capacity (e.g., knowing right from wrong) to have criminal intent at the time he or she committed a criminal act, the person is not assumed to have the necessary *mens rea*, or guilty mind, for criminal liability.

Although the insanity defense is rare, when it's used it can be quite controversial. One of the most notorious insanity defenses in the last two decades was that of John Hinckley, Jr., who shot President Ronald Reagan in 1981 and claimed that he did so to win the attention of actress Jodie Foster. The jury's verdict of not guilty by reason of insanity outraged the public and prompted several states to revise their insanity laws.

 ## SUMMARY AND CONCLUSION

Viewed from a sociological perspective, crime is a public issue rooted in the way society is organized, not a private trouble rooted in the personal failures of individuals. Accordingly, a sociological criminology highlights the role played by social structure, broadly defined, in criminal behavior, victimization, and the legal response to crime. It emphasizes the criminogenic social and physical conditions of communities and stresses the impact of social inequalities based on race, ethnicity, social class, and gender. It also challenges common-sense perceptions of crime and the legal order and offers prescriptions for dealing with crime that address its structural roots.

My primary aim in this book is to develop your sociological imagination, to allow you to perceive perhaps a little more than you do right now the structural basis for crime, victimization, and criminal justice. As you develop your sociological imagination, perhaps you will understand yourself, or at least your friends and loved ones, a little better than you do now. As C. Wright Mills (Mills 1959:5) observed forty years ago, the idea that individuals can understand their own experience only by first understanding the structural and historical forces affecting them is "in many ways a terrible lesson [and] in many ways a magnificent one." It is terrible because it makes us realize that forces affecting our behavior and life chances are often beyond our control; it is magnificent because it enables us to recognize what these forces are and perhaps, therefore, to change them.

I welcome your entry into the world of sociological criminology and envy the journey you are about to make.

 ## KEY TERMS

actus reus	duress
causal order	felony
common law	generalize
conflict	independent variable
consensus	*mala in se*
criminal intent	*mala prohibita*
criminogenic	*mens rea*
debunking motif	misdemeanor
dependent variable	private troubles

public issues	sociological imagination
self-defense	sociological perspective
social inequality	spurious
social structure	surveys
sociological criminology	

 ## Study Questions

1. What do we mean by the "sociological perspective?" How does this perspective help us to understand the origins of crime and possible ways of reducing crime?
2. In what ways are the disciplines of sociology and criminology relevant for each other?
3. What are the advantages and disadvantages of using surveys to understand crime and other social phenomena?
4. What are any three legal defenses to criminal liability? Do you think these defenses should exist, or do you think they have been exploited by criminal defendants?

 ## Internet Exercises

In this and later chapters you'll find a series of Internet exercises that are designed to help you discover the wealth of crime and criminal justice information on the Web. This exercise introduces you to just two excellent Web sites. The first site is **http://www.apbnews.com**. This is a wonderful collection of news articles, opinion columns, and statistics about crime and criminal justice in the United States and elsewhere. It also includes video and sound clips and information on unsolved mysteries, fugitive criminals, video and sound clips, and a host of other topics. Go to this site to see what it has to offer. Once there, click on **Video Center** to see the site's latest video and sound clips on recent crimes and news items about the criminal justice system.

The second site is the government-sponsored Sourcebook of Criminal Justice Statistics, edited at the State University of New York at Albany. This Sourcebook is published annually and updated regularly on the Web. It contains more than 600 tables of data on crime, victimization, public opinion about crime, jail and prison statistics, and many other topics. These data are culled from more than 100 sources. To access its Web site, go to **http://www.albany.edu/sourcebook**. Notice that the opening page briefly describes the Sourcebook and then lists its various sections, ranging from Section 1, Characteristics of the Criminal Justice Systems, to Section 6, Persons under Correctional Supervision.

Sourcebook data are in Adobe Acrobat format. Before you can access the data, you need to have the Adobe Acrobat reader, which reads Portable Document Files (PDF files) on your computer. If you don't already have it, go to the Adobe Web site at **http://www.adobe.com/products/acrobat/readstep.html** to download the appropriate reader for your computer—it's free! Once you're at this site, just follow the instructions.

Now that you have the Adobe Acrobat reader, go back to the Sourcebook Web site listed above and click **Section One** to open this section. You'll see a brief description of the section's contents and then, toward the bottom of its opening page, a list of each topic in the section. Click **Expenditures for criminal justice activities**. You'll see a list of various tables of data that you can open; under each table is its Acrobat file that you click to open the table. Click on the file for Table 1.1. to access "Justice system direct and intergovernmental expenditures, by level of government, United States," for various fiscal years. This table lists, in millions of dollars, the amount of money that various levels of government spend on justice. Thus the 1990 figure of $79,434 for all governments stands for $79,434,000,000. How much did all levels of government spend on justice for the latest year listed in the table? How much did this figure rise since 1990?

Now go back to the previous page on **Expenditures for criminal justice activities**. Scroll down this page until you reach the subsection on **Corrections expenditures**. Click on the file for "Direct expenditures for correctional activities of State governments …"; at the time of this writing this was for Table 1.8. Now you'll see how much money has been spent by state governments for corrections over the years. This time the dollar figures are in thousands, so that the $15,842,063 for 1990 stands for $15,842,065,000. How much did the states spend on corrections for the latest year listed in the table? How much did this figure rise since 1990?

PUBLIC OPINION,
THE NEWS MEDIA,
AND THE CRIME PROBLEM

Crime in the News

Halloween was not a happy day in 1999 in Wellesley, Massachusetts, an affluent community of 27,000 people near Boston with less than two dozen violent crimes a year. On October 31, 1999, a 58-year-old Wellesley woman was stabbed and beaten to death with a hammer on a trail near a town pond. Because her death resembled recent murders in nearby towns, Wellesley residents feared that a serial killer was at work. Four months later their fears were allayed when the woman's husband was arrested for the crime. Although he and his children vigorously protested his innocence, most of the townspeople were relieved. "It's sort of perverse, but there's a sense of relief knowing that it probably wasn't random," said one resident. "I feel terrible for their family, but I feel better knowing that it probably wasn't some psychotic killer on the loose." Another resident, who had once been mugged in a different town, was not as reassured. "That's not like murder," she said, "but it taught me that you're never completely safe anywhere, including Wellesley. I think safety is an illusion. Just because the police have charged the husband that doesn't make it any less likely that I or anyone else walking on this street isn't going to be a victim of some random violent act."

Sources: Hart and Latour 1999; Lewis 2000:B4.

*T*hink about why you're taking this criminology course. If you're like my own students, you might be taking it simply because you needed some credits and this course fit into your schedule. Or you might be interested in becoming a probation officer, a juvenile caseworker, a police officer, a prison guard, or a lawyer. Perhaps you even want an academic career in crime and criminal justice. Some students may be taking the course because they broke the law in the past (hopefully not in the present!). Conversely, some may be victims of crime themselves, or friends or relatives of crime victims. Still others may be simply interested in and even fascinated by crime and criminals. A final group may consider crime a serious social problem and even be worried about becoming crime victims themselves.

Now think about why you've taken courses in other subject areas: math, biology, English or African literature, or even many of the social sciences. It may have been to fulfill general education or major requirements; to prepare you for a career; to help you learn more about an interesting topic; or—let's be honest—to fill a convenient time slot in your schedule.

It's doubtful that you took these courses because you were concerned about their subject matter or because you were worried about the subject matter somehow affecting you. A criminology course differs in this sense as its subject matter is very real to students. They hear a lot about crimes like the one in Wellesley from the news media and see many crimes portrayed in TV programs and the movies. As a result, students come into their criminology courses with real concerns about crime and even fears that they or their friends and relatives will become crime victims. Like the residents of Wellesley, they worry about not being safe no matter where they live.

In all these respects, students are no different from average citizens. We all hold strong opinions about crime and criminal justice, and these opinions have important implications for public policy on crime. But where do these opinions come from? How accurate are the sources of our beliefs and, for that matter, our beliefs themselves? What does social science research reveal about these matters? To return to some themes introduced in Chapter 1, how does our location in society affect our beliefs? This chapter attempts to answer these questions and to indicate the major findings on public opinion about crime.

 ## PUBLIC OPINION AND PUBLIC POLICY

As you undoubtedly learned long before you entered college, the most defining feature of a democracy is that citizens elect their leaders by majority vote. Extending this concept of "government of the people, by the people, and for the people," scholars of democratic theory have further postulated that decisions by public officials should reflect public opinion, which is said to reflect a consensus on the major issues of the day (Held 1991).

Critics have challenged this view on several grounds. A first criticism is that public officials are influenced more by a small, wealthy, powerful elite than by the general public. The elite's influence might be acceptable if its views reflect those of ordinary citizens. However, critics say this isn't always the case (Domhoff 1998). Although democratic theorists dispute this criticism, let's assume that elite views sometimes do exert greater influence on policy decisions. To the extent this is true, public policy development in the United States differs from the idealized version of democratic theory.

A second criticism of democratic theory lies in what might be termed the "tyranny of the majority." Under democratic theory, the majority rules. Ideally, majority opinion adheres to democratic principles of fairness, equality, and justice. In reality, however, critics say that the majority's views may violate these principles. Consider, for example, the classic book (and also the classic movie starring Henry Fonda) *The Ox-Bow Incident*, which involved the lynching of three men mistakenly accused of cattle rustling and murder (Clark 1940). Simplistically put, the book's message is that majority opinion may result in severe injustice.

U.S. history is filled with similar examples, the most notorious being the popular support for slavery before the Civil War. In an instance involving political crime, dislike by U.S. citizens and public officials of socialist and other dissenters to World War I led to a virtual abolition of the First Amendment to the Constitution during that time. Dissenters were jailed simply for writing letters to the editors of newspapers challenging the justness of U.S. participation in the war. Many historians now regard this period as an unfortunate episode in U.S. history (Brock 1968; Peterson and Fite 1957). To the extent, then, that majority opinion violates democratic principles, and that such opinion may influence public policy, democratic theory again comes under attack.

A corollary to this criticism is that the reasons for the public's view of a particular issue may violate democratic principles even if the view itself does not. To take a hypothetical example, suppose that public opinion polls show strong sentiment for reducing federal spending on urban areas. There may be several legitimate reasons for feeling this way: The federal deficit is too large; federal taxes are already too high; the federal government needs to spend more money on the environment. But suppose further research discovers that many white people want to reduce spending on large cities because they're racially prejudiced against the many urban residents who are African-Americans and other people of color. Such racial prejudice is anti-democratic. To the extent that public sentiment against urban spending is based on racial prejudice, it's inappropriate in a democratic society for this sentiment to influence public policy.

A final challenge to democratic theory is that public opinion is often inaccurate. As I often remind my students, Europeans used to believe that the earth was flat. In today's world, many people get their information from the news media, but the news media often distort reality (Glassner 1999). Studies of rumor and mass hysteria further remind us that what everyone "knows to be true" may in fact not be true. So-called expert opinion may also be inaccurate. A century ago some of the most respected U.S. physicians believed that women shouldn't go to college: The rigors of higher education would upset their menstrual cycles, and they couldn't be expected to do well on exams during "that time of the month" (Ehrenreich and English 1979). Fortunately, we've moved beyond this foolish belief, but the damage it did at the time to women's opportunities for higher education was real.

What relevance does all this have for public opinion about crime? As we shall see shortly, people have many strong opinions about the causes of crime and the punishment of criminals. Public opinion on these topics and concern about crime often influence criminal justice policy decisions: Penalties for serious criminal behaviors are increased, laws banning other behaviors as criminal are enacted, and funds for new prison construction are authorized.

But what if public views about crime topics are in some cases misinformed? Although public concern about crime is real—and therefore, to paraphrase sociologists

Dorothy and W. I. Thomas (1928), is real in its consequences—what if at least some of this concern is the result of sensational news media coverage of violent crime and alarmist statements by politicians? Moreover, what if anti-democratic attitudes affect public views about crime? If these possibilities turn out to be true, they raise some troubling questions for the influence of public opinion on criminal justice policy in a democratic society.

The remainder of this chapter examines some important public beliefs about crime and criminal justice and their implications for policy. Although a major theme of the discussion is the possible inaccuracy of these public beliefs, the goal here is not simply to muckrake. Rather, the aim is to emphasize the problems involved in allowing public opinion on a complex topic like crime to influence policy without careful evaluation of all available evidence.

 ## THE ACCURACY OF PUBLIC BELIEFS ABOUT CRIME AND CRIMINAL JUSTICE

To stimulate your thinking about these issues, please take a moment to answer the following questions about crime in the United States:

1. What percentage of convicted felony defendants is found guilty by a jury instead of by a judge? Answer: _____%

2. How much of the average police officer's time is spent fighting crime (i.e., questioning witnesses, arresting suspects) as opposed to other activities? Answer: _____%

3. About how many people die each year from taking illegal drugs? Answer: _____

4. What percentage of all felonies in a given year leads to someone being convicted of a felony and imprisoned? Answer: _____%

5. In terms of race and social class, who is the typical criminal in the United States? Answer: _____

If your answers are similar to my own students' answers, you would have said the following: (1) 30 to 60 percent of convicted felons are found guilty at a jury trial; (2) 30 to 60 percent of police officers' time is spent fighting crime; (3) 50,000 or more people die annually from illegal drugs; (4) 30 to 35 percent of all felonies in a given year lead to someone being imprisoned for committing the felony; and (5) the "typical" criminal, despite many exceptions, is probably poor and nonwhite.

Now compare your answers to what the best available evidence tells us: (1) Less than 10 percent of convicted felons are found guilty at jury trials, with most found guilty as a result of plea bargaining (Barlow 2000); (2) only about 10 to 20 percent of police officers' time is spent fighting crime, the remainder being spent on directing traffic, responding to traffic accidents, and other much more mundane matters (Kappeler, Blumberg, and Potter 2000); (3) about 9,000 to 10,000 people a year die from illegal drugs (Dorsey and Zawitz 1999); (4) well under 10 percent of all felonies in a given year lead to someone being imprisoned for committing the felony (Walker 1998); and (5) the profile of the "typical" criminal, if one includes very common crimes like employee theft and other kinds of white-collar crime, is certainly not restricted to those who are poor and nonwhite (Reiman 1998).

Most students have some trouble believing these findings. While I don't pretend that what I have presented as the best available evidence is the only evidence, each of these five findings is based on sound evidence that later chapters will discuss. For now, let us assume that these findings are accurate and that public opinion and perceptions on these and other crime and criminal justice matters may sometimes be incorrect.

The News Media and Public Opinion on Crime

Where do perceptions, accurate or inaccurate, about crime and criminal justice come from? Where did you acquire the information that led to your answers? Research suggests that the major source of your information is probably the news media and that politicians and law enforcement officials also influence your thinking (Potter and Kappeler 1998; Surette 1998). In one poll, 65 percent of respondents named the media as having the greatest influence on their views about crime, while only 21 percent mentioned personal experience (Kurtz 1997).

Pretend for a moment that you're either a newspaper editor, a TV news director, a politician, or a law enforcement official. Why might it be in your interest to call attention to a growing crime and drug problem? If you're a newspaper editor or TV news director, crime coverage holds the potential of capturing readers' or viewers' attention and even increasing their numbers (Chermak 1994): The higher your newspaper's circulation or your TV station's ratings, the more successful your career. If you're a politician, a "tough" posture on crime promises to increase your popularity and therefore your chances for reelection. If you're a law enforcement official, emphasis on the growing danger of crime may lead to increased funding for your police force or prison.

Similar considerations influence programming decisions for prime-time TV shows. To return to some of the items that were included in our mini-survey: Jury trials, for example, make for much more dramatic programming than plea bargains; violent street crime is more exciting for viewers than white-collar crime; police chases of criminals capture viewers' interest a bit more than traffic citations. If most of us get our knowledge of crime and criminal justice from the news media and TV programs, which tend to cover or portray only the most sensational kinds of crime and criminal justice activities, it's no surprise that many of us develop perceptions that may not reflect what's really happening in the world of crime and the criminal justice system (Surette 1998).

◀ *Like other media, television programs (such as NYPD Blue) tend to portray the most sensational kinds of crime and criminal justice activities.*

In this regard, consider media coverage about crime just a few years ago. From 1993 through 1996, the U.S. homicide rate dropped by 20 percent. Despite this drop, murder stories on the TV networks' evening newscasts jumped by 721 percent during that time compared to the preceding three-year period. Many of the murder stories were about the O. J. Simpson case, but a sizable increase occurred even without these stories (Kurtz 1997). In 1993 alone, the networks' evening newscasts aired 1,632 stories about crime, more than double the 785 appearing on the newscasts in 1992; the 1993 stories included 329 about murders, compared to only 104 in 1992 (Freeman 1994). Reflecting this media focus, 87 percent of U.S. residents in a 1993 poll said that crime was higher than a year earlier (Meddis 1993), 88 percent in a 1994 poll agreed that crime was at an all-time high (Jackson 1994), and 52 percent in another 1994 poll named crime as the "most important problem" (topping all other concerns) facing the United States. This last figure was only 9 percent 18 months earlier and only 1 percent in 1990 (see Figure 2.1).

But how true were these perceptions? Although many people "knew" that crime was rising rapidly, is it possible that what they thought was true may not have been true at all? Let's look at the evidence. The best available data offer a picture very different from what the media implied in 1993, and what people perceived, as reported crime in 1993 was slightly lower than in 1992 (Freeman 1994). Even though the crime rate actually fell from 1991 through 1994, the U.S. Congress passed legislation in 1994 that provided billions of dollars for new prison construction and additional police, increased the number of federal crimes punishable by death, and mandated life imprisonment for persons convicted of a third felony. And even though crime continued to fall for the rest of the decade, a 1998 Gallup poll found that 56 percent of U.S. residents thought there was more crime than five years earlier, while only 35 percent thought there was less crime (Jackson 1999).

In short, the growing alarm over crime in the last decade occurred even though crime was declining. As one television news reporter said in 1994, "The myth of rapidly rising crime is so widespread that almost every report[er] believes it's true. I'm as guilty as anyone" (quoted in Williams 1994:72). Unfortunately, the media's promotion of this myth helped fuel the growing public concern over crime in the early 1990s.

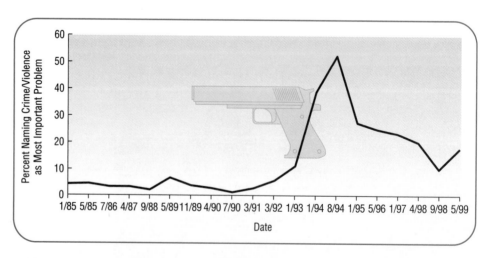

▲ FIGURE 2.1 CRIME/VIOLENCE AS MOST IMPORTANT PROBLEM
Source: Gallup Polls, 1985–1999. Copyright © 1999 by the Gallup Organization. Reprinted with permission of the Gallup Organization.

This wasn't the first time U.S. media coverage and politicians' warnings about crime have increased despite stable or declining crime rates. In the mid-1980s the press and public officials began to warn the nation about the rising use of cocaine and crack. Front-page newspaper articles and magazine cover stories discussed the dangers these drugs posed to our cities and to the nation's youth. Illegal drugs became a daily topic of conversation, and national opinion polls indicated growing public concern that quickly came to a crescendo.

This concern didn't match reality, however. Various surveys during this period found that use of cocaine, crack, and other illegal drugs was in fact declining. The decline didn't result from the increased attention given to illegal drug use, as it started before the media coverage began to increase. The increased attention to cocaine and crack in the mid-1980s thus was out of proportion to what was really happening in the world of illegal drug use (Beckett 1994; Orcutt and Turner 1993). This conclusion isn't meant to suggest that illegal drug use is of no concern, only that media coverage, politicians' pronouncements, and public opinion sometimes don't fit the facts about crime and criminal justice.

Overdramatization of Crime in the News Media

As these two examples from the recent past suggest, press coverage and public concern often have little to do with actual crime rates. Scholarly investigations of media crime coverage support this conclusion, with documentations of "crime waves," in which news media devote considerable attention to a small number of crimes, providing perhaps the most striking evidence of the problem.

In one of the earliest studies of crime waves, Felix Frankfurter, later to become a justice of the U.S. Supreme Court, and Roscoe Pound, then dean of the Harvard Law School, examined the manufacture of a crime wave in the last two weeks of January 1919, when the Cleveland newspapers sharply increased their number of crime stories even though police reports of crime had increased only slightly (Frankfurter and Pound 1922). Frankfurter and Pound criticized the press for alarming the public and for pressuring Cleveland officials to ignore the rights of due process guaranteed to criminal defendants by the U.S. Constitution. A more recent study by Mark Fishman (Fishman 1978) examined a media-manufactured crime wave in 1976 by New York City newspapers, which extensively covered a few crimes against the elderly. Although evidence did not indicate that crimes against the elderly were increasing, the media coverage of these crimes alarmed the public.

In addition to manufacturing crime waves, the news media also *overdramatize* crime by reporting so many stories about it (Wright 1985). On TV, crime is a staple of the nightly news: As the old saying goes, "If it bleeds, it leads." A recent study of thousands of local TV news stories in 13 U.S. cities found that crime was the most common topic (20 percent of all stories), easily outpacing weather (11 percent), accidents and disasters (9 percent), and human interest stories (7 percent). Crime stories accounted for 4 minutes in a typical 30-minute local news show, tied with sports and led only by commercials (8 minutes) (Reports 1998).

The news media further overdramatize crime by focusing on violent crime, even though most crimes are not violent (see Chapter 3). This emphasis on violent crime thus leads the news media to cover most the crimes that occur the least (Warr 2000). As Mark Warr, a noted scholar of public opinion about crime, puts it, "If I were an alien and I came to this planet and I turned on the television, I would think that most crimes were ... violent crimes, when in fact those are the least common crimes in our society" (quoted in Williams 1994:72).

Several studies support this view. In one study, 26 percent of all crime articles in the *Chicago Tribune* concerned homicides, compared to only 0.2 percent of all felonies known to the Chicago police (Graber 1980). Another study in New Orleans found that 68 percent of the crime stories in the city's newspapers and more than 80 percent of the stories on its TV stations concerned violent crime, even though only 20 percent of all serious crime during that period was violent crime (Sheley and Ashkins 1981). Although homicide represented only 0.4 percent of all felonies known to the police in the three months, it accounted for 12 percent of all crime stories in the newspapers and about 50 percent of all crime stories on the TV stations. An investigation of crime stories in newspapers in 26 major U.S. cities found a similar disparity (Liska and Baccaglini 1990). Of all the crime stories contained in a sample of the newspapers over a one-year period, 30 percent concerned homicides, even though homicides amounted to only .02 percent of all felonies in those cities during that period.

Nor is the disproportionate attention given to violent crimes confined to U.S. news media. In Toronto, England, and Scotland, newspapers and radio and TV shows have been found to overreport crime, and especially violent crime (Ericson, Baranek, and Chan 1991; Schlesinger, Tumber, and Murdock 1991). While the coverage of violent crime varies among the news media, and in particular depends on whether the news outlet is a "quality" one or a more "popular" or "tabloid" type, one inescapable conclusion is that "images of crime which reach the public through the print [and electronic] media are grossly distorted" (Sheley and Ashkins 1981:492).

A Brief Look Back

Another problem with media coverage of crime is that it typically lacks any historical context (Surette 1998). In particular, it overlooks the fact that crime has been considered a serious problem throughout U.S. history. Although this may be of small comfort to people who are increasingly worried about crime, it does remind us that perhaps there never were the "good old days" in which crime wasn't a problem. As the President's Commission on Law Enforcement and Administration of Justice reported in 1967, "There has always been too much crime. Virtually every generation since the founding of the Nation and before has felt itself threatened by the spectre of rising crime and violence" (quoted in Pepinsky and Jesilow 1984:21).

In the nineteenth century, for example, the major cities on the East Coast were scenes of repeated mob violence in the 1830s, 1840s, and later decades, hastening the development of the modern police force (see Chapter 15). Teenage gangs roamed the streets and attacked innocent bystanders, and wealthy citizens in many cities worried about burglary and robbery. Many of these crimes were attributed to what were called the "dangerous classes" (Adler 1994).

Newspaper headlines and stories calling attention to crime were common. During the week before and after July 4, 1876, the editions of the *New York Times* contained many crime reports. Consider the brutal murder of William Schroeder, who was attacked in a public park June 25, 1876, at 2:00 A.M. by six "youthful ruffians." Schroeder had the misfortune of being one of a group of men and boys asleep in the park at the time. Two members of the youth gang carried sticks and began to beat the sleeping people. One of the gang members shoved his stick into Schroeder's left eye, causing a brain injury that killed him three days later.

Other violent crimes abounded in this one week. For example, James McDonnell, 11, was shot in the face by "a pistol ball fired by some unknown person." Still another youth, John Reiger, 18, was seriously injured after being hit in the head by a stone while driving a wagon; his assailant was arrested. While sitting in front of his store, Ferdinand Schiff was shot in the head from a roof opposite his store by two boys. Patrolman Ford was attacked with an axe as he attempted to arrest some "disorderly persons." During another fight, Thomas Phillips was stabbed in the chest. The *Times* reported that about 2,000 people were arrested in this week.

The quaintness of some of these crime descriptions aside, they don't sound very different from those we read today. Although firearms were much less powerful back then, the crimes reported in the *Times* for this one week in the summer of 1876 do paint a dismaying picture. One historian estimates that five people were murdered for every 100,000 people in New York City in 1876 (Butterfield 1994). This rate more than a century ago was higher than that for other Western nations today, even if it was less than New York's current rate. Moving ahead a half century, Wright (1985:14–16) observes that the 1920s were a "crime boom" decade, with periodicals displaying headlines such as "Cities Helpless in the Grip of Crime" and "The Rising Tide of Crime." As a special committee of the American Bar Association declared in 1922, "Since 1890 there has been, and continues, a widening, deepening tide of lawlessness in this country, sometimes momentarily receding, to swell again into greater depth and intensity." A New York newspaper observed about the same time, "Never before has the average person, in his place of business, in his home or on the streets, had cause to feel less secure. Never before has a continuous wave of crime given rise to so general a wave of fear" (quoted in Wright 1985:16).

These observations remind us that crime has always been thought a serious problem. Although we worry about it today, people have always worried about it, with their concern fueled by media coverage that at least sometimes distorts what's really happening in crime and criminal justice. This coverage often includes crime myths, to which we now turn.

Crime Myths

A myth may be defined as "a person or thing having only an imaginary or unverifiable existence" or as "an ill-founded belief held uncritically" (Webster's 1983). False beliefs about crime are therefore called *crime myths*. We have already discussed several such myths: the perception of rising crime rates in the early 1990s and rising drug use in the late 1980s; the media's depiction of crime as mostly violent; and media-generated crime waves. Crime myths are generated by the media, elected officials, and law enforcement officials. Once generated, they take on a life of their own and increase public concern about crime, especially violent crime (Kappeler, Blumberg, and Potter 2000; Pepinsky and Jesilow 1984; Wright 1985). The media's tendency to depict crime victims as particularly virtuous reinforces this effect (Kappeler, Blumberg, and Potter 2000). One media observer put it this way:

> Reporters, like vampires, feed on human blood. Tales of tragedy, mayhem, and murder are the daily stuff of front-page headlines and breathless TV newscasts. But journalists rarely restrict their accounts to the sordid, unadorned facts. If the victims of such incidents are sufficiently wealthy, virtuous or beautiful, they are often turned into martyred saints in the epic battle between good and bad (Cose 1990:19).

Crime myths often focus on unpopular groups in society. In the United States such groups are often chosen because of their national origin or race (Kappeler, Blumberg, and Potter 2000). As railroad construction slowed in the 1870s, for example, whites began to fear competition from Chinese immigrants for scarce jobs. As a symbolic attack on these immigrants, labor unions and newspapers began to call attention to the use of opium, then a legal drug, by Chinese immigrants in opium dens. The Chinese were said to be kidnapping white children and turning them into opium fiends. A few decades later, the press began to feature reports concerning the use of cocaine, then also a legal drug, by blacks, saying that its use would make blacks more "cunning," cause them to become extraordinarily strong, and make them invulnerable to bullets (Musto 1999). We may laugh at such beliefs now, but back then they had important implications for perceptions of these citizens and for public policy on drugs.

In a modern example of a racial crime myth, TV news broadcasts sometimes give disproportionate attention to African-Americans in their crime stories. Although 70 percent of illegal drug users in the United States are white and 15 percent black, one study found that television news stories about drugs depict blacks 50 percent of the time and whites only 32 percent of the time (Reed 1991).

Teenagers comprise another unpopular group today that is the focus of crime myths (Males 1999). During the 1990s, mass shootings at secondary schools helped fuel public concern over juvenile crime, even though youth violence was in fact declining for much of the decade. Helping to fuel this concern, TV news broadcasts aired many stories on youth violence. In one study of thousands of news stories on local news broadcasts, 68 percent of the stories about violence focused on youth violence, and 55 percent of the stories about youths focused on their violence. In reality, however, only about 14 percent of violent crime is committed by teenagers, and less than 1 percent of all teenagers are arrested annually for violent crime (Jackson 1997). The TV news thus gave a distorted picture of youths heavily involved in violent crime, when the truth was quite the opposite.

In addition to emphasizing the virtuousness of victims and focusing on unpopular groups, the media help create crime myths in other ways (Kappeler, Blumberg, and Potter 2000). These include (1) selecting people to be interviewed who support the reporter's point of view; (2) using value-laden language when referring to criminals ("preying on their victims" instead of more neutral terms); (3) presenting data that are misleading (e.g., reporting increases in the number of crimes without noting increases in population size); (4) emphasizing, as we have already seen, violent crime while neglecting far more common property crimes and various forms of white-collar crime (Mintz 1992); and, finally, (5) failing to provide the social and/or historical context for the information presented in a crime story. As one scholar puts it, "Individual crimes very rarely occur without being part of a broader context.... In current crime reporting there's little indication that crime is part of a larger societal pattern. The view we get is of highly atomized events unique to a specific location" (quoted in Bishop 1993:13).

Crime myths have several effects. They are especially likely to prompt politicians to urge tougher treatment of criminals. As one media critic puts it, "Crime rhetoric has become desperate to the point of it being unthinkable for a candidate for major political office to dare pander to facts instead of fear" (Jackson 1994:15). Because they tend to focus on individual crimes and criminals, crime myths also obscure underlying social and cultural forces (which are the subject of much of the rest of this book). They further divert attention from crimes that are not often the subject of myths, particularly white-collar crimes, which arguably are more harmful than street crimes (see Chapter 12). To the extent that crime myths focus on street crimes, they reinforce negative feelings about poor people, by whom street crimes are typically committed, and thus also about poverty (Reiman 1998). And to the extent that crime myths feature African-Americans and other minorities, they reinforce negative stereotypes about these groups (Peffley, Shields, and Williams 1996).

Kappeler and associates (2000) describe several criminal events that took on mythical proportions and passed into the national consciousness as fact. No doubt you've heard of children taken sick or even killed on Halloween by poisoned candy. Such stories surfaced in the mid-1970s when the media reported that several children had died from poisoned Halloween candy. Subsequent investigation, however, confirmed only two such deaths, neither involving a stranger giving poisoned candy to a trick-or-treater. In one death, a five-year-old boy had died after supposedly eating Halloween candy laced with heroin, but it was later discovered that he had found the drug in his uncle's home. The second death occurred after an eight-year-old boy ate candy laced with cyanide by his father. The truth of both boys' deaths received far less coverage than the initial reports of trusting trick-or-treaters murdered by strangers.

To consider another myth: You've probably seen faces of missing children, believed to be kidnapped, on milk cartons and on flyers posted at post offices, convenience stores, and other public places, or you may have seen some of the many TV movies devoted to the subject. Stories of missing and presumably abducted children accelerated in the early 1980s. Various government reports indicate that between 1.5 million and 2.5 million children are reported missing from their homes each year, with some 50,000 never heard from again. However, most children reported missing are in fact runaways. Of the relatively few that are abducted, almost all are abducted by a parent as part of a divorce-induced custody battle, and perhaps fewer than 300 annually are abducted by strangers (Kappeler, Blumberg, and Potter 2000). While even one child abducted by a stranger is one too many, the real number of such children appears to be much smaller than is usually thought.

◀ *Despite widespread views and media publicity, most missing children are runaways, not victims of child abductors, and most of the children who are abducted are taken by a parent rather than a stranger.*

A third crime myth discussed by Kappeler and associates (2000) is termed the "serial killer panic of 1983–1985." During that period, numerous stories appeared in the media about serial killers, men who roam from state to state and murder people, often brutally, at random. The preeminent newspaper in the United States, the *New York Times*, featured a front-page article in January 1984 that called serial killing a national epidemic, accounting for roughly 20 percent, or 4,000, of all homicides each year in the country (Lindsey 1984). During the next two years, many other news reports repeated the *Times*'s estimate. However, a later study put the annual number of serial killings at no more than 400 and perhaps as few as 50 (Jenkins 1988). The higher end of the estimate is still only one-tenth the size of the 4,000 figure that was widely circulated in the 1980s. Rather than accounting for 20 percent of all homicides, then, serial killers probably account for at most 2 percent. Serial killers do exist and must be taken seriously, but upon inspection they do not appear to pose as great a menace as the media would have us believe (Kappeler, Blumberg, and Potter 2000).

The Effects of Media Coverage

Like many social scientists, I've been assuming that media coverage affects public perceptions of crime and criminals and in particular causes the public to perceive rising crime rates, to be more afraid of crime, and to view the typical criminal as poor and nonwhite. Although these effects might seem obvious, systematic research indicates they don't always occur (Surette 1998). However, since several studies do point to a media effect, they're worth reviewing briefly.

In one study, Mary Holland Baker and her colleagues (1983) surveyed random samples of Phoenix, Arizona residents in September 1979 and in July 1980. Although the two samples reported similar levels of crime victimization, the 1980 sample was more likely than the earlier one to think that crime was increasing in its neighborhoods and in the city of Phoenix. Baker and colleagues attributed the 1980 sample's perceptions and its increased fear of crime to intensified newspaper coverage—in short, a perceived crime wave—in early 1980 of homicides, robberies, and other serious crimes in Phoenix.

In another study, Allen E. Liska and William Baccaglini (1990) examined the effects of newspaper coverage of felonies in 26 U.S. cities on fear of crime among those cities' residents. Articles about local homicides tended to increase fear of crime among the residents, while articles about nonlocal homicides tended to decrease fear, as readers evidently felt safer knowing that these crimes were happening elsewhere. These effects held true regardless of the race, gender, and age of the residents and were especially strong for articles appearing in the first fifteen pages of the newspapers.

A recent study suggested that TV coverage of crime can also have an effect. In a survey of Philadelphia residents, respondents who watched TV news shows at least four times a week were 40 percent more likely than respondents who didn't watch the TV news to be concerned about crime (Bunch 1999).

An additional study asked a few hundred college students in an Introduction to Criminal Justice class how many homicides occur annually in the United States. Because of the heavy attention the media give to violent crime, the authors hypothesized that the students would greatly exaggerate the number of homicides. This was indeed the case. In the year the study was done, 1994, 23,305 homicides occurred in the United States. *Yet almost half of the students estimated that at least 250,000 occur each year!* The authors concluded that "these misperceptions must be

CRIME AND CONTROVERSY

Media Coverage of Violence against Women

One particularly controversial aspect of media coverage concerns the issue of violence against women. In recent years, scholars and anti-rape activists have criticized the way the media depict rape and battering and cover celebrated rape trials. According to media critic Tiffany Devitt, this coverage too often suggests that women asked or wanted to be raped by wearing "provocative" clothing and being careless in their behavior. As a result, she says, the media lose sight of "the commonness of rape and the ease with which men perpetrate this crime without punishment." This was especially true, she says, in the coverage of the 1991 trial of William Kennedy Smith, a member of the famous Kennedy family, for allegedly raping a young woman at a party. Several months before the trial, one of the nation's leading newspapers published the name of Smith's accuser and details of her previous sexual activity, speeding tickets, and the like. After the trial, a magazine cover story charged that the accusation against Smith symbolized a larger feminist attack on men and was part of a "sweeping repudiation of the male sex." Devitt terms this view close to "paranoia" and says it turns "victims into perpetrators."

Two other media critics, Paula Kamen and Steve Rhodes, note that the rapes that the media cover "are almost always stranger rapes," even though most rapes are committed by nonstrangers. One reason for the focus on stranger rapes, they say, is that reporters rely on the judgment of police, who are more skeptical of reports of nonstranger rapes than of reports of stranger rapes. Another reason is that reporters accept the "commonly held rape myth" that women falsely accuse men of raping them. Kamen and Rhodes urge that reporters who cover sexual assaults receive training from rape-crisis centers and other programs on the nature and extent of rape. Rape-crisis centers, they note, often have more reliable data than the police on the extent and nature of rape. As one example, a rape-crisis hot line in the town of a major midwestern university answered 570 calls in a recent year, even though students reported only 31 completed and attempted rapes to the university or local police in the same period.

Similar problems exist in the reporting of battering, which, as Tiffany Devitt and Jennifer Downey note, results in more hospital emergency room visits by women than "auto accidents, muggings, and rape combined." Devitt and Downey continue, "Despite its prevalence, domestic abuse remains a gravely undercovered story. When it is covered, it is often treated as a bizarre spectacle rather than an all-too-common social crisis."

Another problem, they note, is that reporters "use language that is euphemistic or evasive on the issue of blame." Although, as Chapter 10 discusses, the most serious violence between spouses is committed by men, reporters usually use terms like spouse abuse or marital disputes, which obscure the gendered nature of battering and imply that women may also be at fault: "Abusive relationships are euphemistically termed 'a stormy relationship' or 'a marriage gone sour,' as though no one were to blame."

A third problem is that reporters often wonder in print about why the woman did not try to leave her batterer. This speculation ignores the fact that women usually do try to leave or call the police and, when they don't, often have many sound reasons for not doing so. The media's speculation thus implies, as with rape, that battered women are somehow responsible for their victimization and helps "draw attention away from the issue of the abuser's behavior."

In recent years, Devitt and Downey add, the media have been quick to publicize the very few cases where women abuse their husbands: "Media that have underreported the damage caused by violence against women in the home are now rushing to explore the potential lethality of domestic violence against men." When governors have released women imprisoned for killing abusive partners out of desperation, these cases have received much media attention. Ironically, this coverage hurts battered women in two ways, say Devitt and Downey. First, some of the press stories note that the women whose sentences were commuted were living apart from their husbands at the time they killed their abusers—the implication being that the women had no more reason to live in fear. In reality, this is a time of great peril for battered women. Second, the media coverage of the commuted sentences stresses the hope they give battered women. Devitt and Downey observe, "Such comments are a cruel joke to millions of battered women, who cannot be helped by commutations unless they have reached the awful point of having killed their partners."

Sources: Devitt 1992; Devitt and Downey 1992; Kamen and Rhodes 1992.

corrected so that students can understand the nature of the crime problem and critically evaluate proposed solutions" (Vandiver and Giacopassi 1997:141).

If media coverage can at least sometimes influence public perceptions, including fear, about crime, can it also influence public policy? The answer again seems to be yes. The New York City media's focus on crimes against the elderly, discussed earlier, prompted new legislation and other measures (Fishman 1978). In a comprehensive study, media analysts David Pritchard and Dan Berkowitz (1993) documented the influence of press coverage on legislative decision making about crime between 1950 and 1980. Pritchard had earlier found that press coverage heavily influenced prosecutors' decisions in homicide cases (Pritchard 1986). Although these studies aren't the final word on the subject, they do indicate that the news media often influence public opinion and public policy on crime.

To the extent this is so, it's important that media coverage of crime be objective and accurate. Yet we've seen it's often inaccurate and misleading instead. If so, the media's influence on public opinion and public policy on crime raises troubling questions for key beliefs of democratic theory.

 ## RESEARCH ON PUBLIC ATTITUDES ABOUT CRIME AND PUNISHMENT

A growing body of research addresses the sources of public attitudes about crime and punishment and their influence on daily behaviors and public policy. This research raises several issues for the themes of social inequality and social structure that Chapter 1 introduced. Let's look first at fear of crime.

Fear of Crime

Take a moment and write down the things you do in your daily life to reduce your chances of becoming a crime victim. If you're like my students, you probably wrote that you usually lock the doors of your dormitory room, apartment, or house and also of your car (if you have one). You might also have written, especially if you are a woman, that you're careful where you walk alone at night or that you refuse to walk alone at night. And you might have even written that you or your family has a gun at home or that you carry a weapon or some sort of protection device in case you're ever attacked.

Most of us take some of these precautions, and some of them are probably so much a part of our daily lives that we don't even think about them. On some lofty intellectual level, we may realize that something like air pollution or price fixing by large corporations might ultimately pose more danger to us than street crime or cost us more money. But we don't lock our doors to keep out air pollution and we don't carry any devices to protect ourselves from price fixing.

We worry about crime because crime is so directly and personally threatening. And we especially worry about crime by strangers, even though, as Chapter 4 will indicate, we often have more to fear from those we know than from those we don't know.

In addition to the presence of strangers, other situational factors contribute to our fear of crime. Mark Warr (1990) asked a sample of Dallas residents about various kinds of hypothetical crime scenarios. For each vignette, respondents were asked to indicate how fearful they would be in each situation. They were most afraid in scenarios where they were (1) in an unfamiliar location, (2) in a setting at

Perceptions of Crime and Criminal Justice in Canada

In 1988 the Canadian General Social Survey polled almost 10,000 Canadians about their attitudes about crime and criminal justice and about whether they had been victims of various crimes. Although Canada has less crime than the United States (see Chapter 9), many people in the survey were nonetheless concerned about crime. Almost one fourth said they had installed locks, bars on windows, or burglar alarms in the past year to protect themselves or their property. Almost three fourths said sentences handed down by the courts were not severe enough.

Only 2 percent of the Canadian sample felt unsafe walking alone in their neighborhood during the day, but 26 percent felt unsafe walking alone in their neighborhood at night. As in the United States, there were significant subgroup differences in concern about walking alone at night. For example, 40 percent of Canadian women said they felt unsafe, versus only 12 percent of men. Women were thus three times more likely than men to feel unsafe. There was a significant ethnic difference as well: Thirty-six percent of native French-speaking respondents said they felt unsafe at night versus only 21 percent of native English-speaking respondents. As in the United States, the elderly, those aged 65 and older, were more likely to feel unsafe (41 percent) than other age groups (under 28 percent). Urban residents (28 percent) were 10 percent more likely than rural residents to say they felt unsafe.

These brief comparisons indicate that the sources of fear of crime in Canada are similar to those found in the United States and discussed in the text. Although Canada has less crime than the United States, gender, ethnicity, age, and urban/rural residence all appear to affect how safe Canadians feel walking alone in their neighborhoods at night. Analysis of data from other nations would be necessary to determine whether similar subgroup differences are found in societies outside of North America.

Source: Author's analysis of 1988 Canadian General Social Survey data.

night, and (3) alone. In vignettes involving the presence of others, fear was higher if the other people were young men the respondents didn't know than if they were older and/or women.

It shouldn't surprise you to learn that many people are afraid of becoming a victim of crime, with some more afraid than others. A standard question included in the General Social Survey (GSS), a random sample of the non-institutionalized U.S. population that has been conducted almost annually since 1972, asks, "Are there any areas around here—that is, within a mile—where you would be afraid to walk alone at night?" In 1998, 42 percent of the GSS sample responded "yes." Striking figures like this, along with recognition of the measures people take because of their worry over becoming crime victims, have made fear of crime probably the most studied attitude or perception in the criminological literature (Warr 2000).

Some studies note certain problems in measuring fear of crime (Williams, McShane, and Akers 2000). The standard GSS question cited previously has been criticized, for example, for focusing only on crime in the immediate neighborhood and for not asking about fear for one's safety during the daytime. (Pointing out that the question does not even mention "crime," one of my students, a rural resident, noted that he was afraid to walk in his neighborhood at night because his neighborhood was mostly woods where bears could be lurking!)

What makes some people more afraid of crime than other people? To answer this question, researchers have focused on both structural factors and individual characteristics. Structural factors concern the social and physical characteristics of the locations in which people live, while individual characteristics include demographic variables such as age, gender, and race, and crime-related factors such as personal victimization and vicarious victimization, that is, knowing someone who has been a crime victim. Let's turn first to the structural factors.

STRUCTURAL FACTORS

Research on these factors focuses on the population size of the town or city in which respondents live, the crime rate of these communities, the quality of the living conditions of respondents' neighborhoods (i.e., whether the neighborhood is filled with abandoned buildings), and the proportion of nonwhites in respondents' neighborhoods. As might be expected, population size is a fairly strong predictor of fear of crime: Generally speaking, the larger the population size, the greater the fear of crime (Liska, Lawrence, and Sanchirico 1985). Figure 2.2 indicates this with 1998 GSS data: Urban residents are almost three times as likely as rural residents to be afraid to walk alone at night.

Why are big-city inhabitants more afraid of crime than those living in smaller towns or rural areas? First, big-city residents may be more likely to perceive a higher risk of victimization—that is, a higher crime rate—in their immediate neighborhoods and in their cities as a whole. Since people who discern a higher risk of victimization are more afraid of crime than those who perceive a lower risk, big-city residents are thus more likely to fear crime (Warr 1990).

Second, big-city inhabitants are more likely than others to recognize poor living conditions in their neighborhoods. This perception strongly increases fear of crime, as people associate abandoned buildings, dilapidated housing, and graffiti on public buildings with a heightened risk of victimization (Bennett and Flavin 1994).

A third reason for this urban-rural difference has to do with the racial make-up of large cities. Regardless of their own race, residents of locations with high proportions of nonwhites, especially blacks, are more likely to fear crime than inhabitants of locations that are mostly white (Taylor and Covington 1993). In one study that didn't find this general effect, whites who perceived themselves as being in the racial minority were still more afraid of crime than whites who perceived themselves in the majority (Chiricos, Hogan, and Gertz 1997). Since large

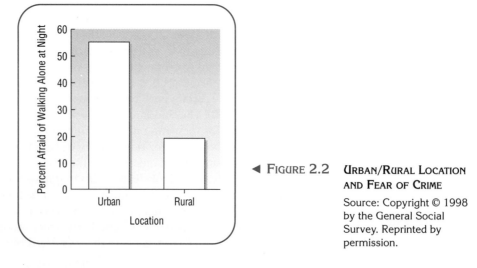

◀ FIGURE 2.2 URBAN/RURAL LOCATION AND FEAR OF CRIME

Source: Copyright © 1998 by the General Social Survey. Reprinted by permission.

urban areas typically have higher proportions of nonwhites than rural areas, the racial makeup of place of residence is yet another reason why urban residents fear crime so much.

The previously discussed research on the media and fear of crime suggests one further reason. When urban residents read or hear about violent crimes in their newspapers or on television, the crimes typically are local ones, raising the inhabitants' fear of crime. But when rural residents read about violent crimes, the crimes are more likely to be nonlocal. Local coverage of nonlocal crimes in turn decreases the rural residents' fear of crime.

Surprisingly, at this "ecological" level of analysis, actual crime rates are only weakly related, if at all, to fear of crime. That is, when we look at people in cities or towns of similar sizes but with different crime rates, fear of crime in a given location doesn't seem to depend on the rate of crime found there. Residents living in large cities do perceive higher crime rates than those living in smaller towns, and, as noted earlier, this perception helps to account for their heightened fear of crime. But inhabitants of locations of any size generally don't know the actual crime rate of their place of residence. As a result, residents of one large city may be more afraid, perhaps because of media coverage or neighborhood conditions, than those of another large city even though the second city might actually have the higher crime rate (Skogan and Maxfield 1981). In the Philadelphia study discussed earlier, people in one neighborhood, Germantown, were relatively unconcerned about crime even though their crime rate was rather high, while people in a South Philadelphia neighborhood were very concerned about crime even though their crime rate was only average. This discrepancy might have reflected the impact of TV news coverage, as the South Philadelphia residents watched TV news much more often than the Germantown residents (Bunch 1999).

INDIVIDUAL CHARACTERISTICS

Demographic and other characteristics of individuals may also influence their fear of crime. Before turning to these characteristics, let me first note one that, very surprisingly, does not make much of a difference at all. If you asked your friends whether victims of crime (personal victimization) should be more likely than nonvictims to fear crime, your friends would probably say yes. If you asked them whether people who know crime victims (vicarious victimization) should be more likely than those who don't know victims to fear crime, they would probably say yes again. A large body of research, however, indicates that both personal and vicarious victimization are only weakly related, if at all, to fear of crime (Baumer 1985; Miethe and Lee 1984; Stafford and Galle 1984). (For a contrary view, see Skogan 1987.)

Part of the reason for victimization's weak effect is that some of the demographic groups that are most afraid of crime are those with relatively low victimization rates. Consider the demographic variable of age, for example: The elderly feel physically vulnerable to attack and thus are more apt than younger people to fear crime, even though they're actually less likely than the young to be crime victims (LeGrange and Ferraro 1989; Lichtblau 2000).

Gender also affects fear of crime, with women far more fearful than men (Gardner 1990; LaGrange and Ferraro 1989; Ortega and Myles 1987). GSS data (see Figure 2.3 on page 38) indicate that women are twice as likely as men to report being afraid of walking alone at night in their neighborhoods. Fear is even higher among women in urban areas (see Table 2.1 on page 38). In the 1998 GSS, 70 percent of

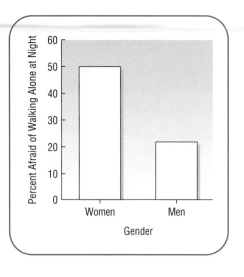

◀ FIGURE 2.3 GENDER AND FEAR
OF CRIME

Source: Copyright © 1998
by the General Social
Survey. Reprinted by
permission.

urban women reported being afraid of walking alone at night. Even in rural areas, where fear of crime is much lower overall, women are still more likely than men to report being afraid. Women fear crime more than men do even though, as Chapter 4 will indicate, they're less likely than men to be victims of various crimes besides rape. The primary reason for this apparently paradoxical finding is that women, like the elderly, perceive themselves as physically vulnerable to crime, especially rape. Women's high fear of crime thus reflects their fear of rape (Gordon and Riger 1989; Young 1992). A study of Seattle women found that they judged rape to be as serious as homicide and that young women feared rape more than any other crime (Warr 1985).

A third demographic variable influencing fear of crime is race (Ortega and Myles 1987). As the GSS data in Figure 2.4 (on page 39) indicate, blacks are somewhat more fearful than whites. This racial difference results largely from the fact that people of color are more likely than whites to live in large cities, which have high crime rates. Because of this, they are more likely than whites to see themselves at risk for crime, and they are thus more fearful (Clemente and Kleiman 1977; Skogan and Maxfield 1981).

Although fear of crime is highest among the age and gender subgroups least likely to be victimized, that pattern doesn't hold true for racial subgroups. As we'll see in Chapter 4, nonwhites' fear of crime does square with harsh reality, since they are indeed more likely than whites to be crime victims.

TABLE 2.1 GENDER, RESIDENCE, AND FEAR OF CRIME
(% AFRAID OF WALKING ALONE AT NIGHT)

URBAN		RURAL	
Women	Men	Women	Men
70	44	32	12

Source: Copyright © 1998 by the General Social Survey. Reprinted by permission.

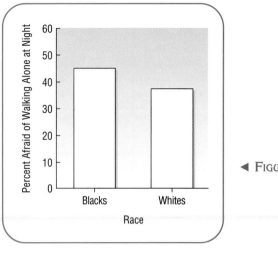

◀ FIGURE 2.4 **RACE AND FEAR OF CRIME**

Source: Copyright © 1998 by the General Social Survey. Reprinted by permission.

If gender and race both affect fear of crime, then black women should be especially concerned about victimization. To illustrate this, Figure 2.5 reports fear of crime results from the GSS for the race/gender intersection of black women, black men, white women, and white men: Black women are much more likely than white men to be afraid of walking alone in their neighborhoods at night. This difference illustrates a "double burden" that African-American women face from being both black and female.

Social class is one final demographic variable that is linked to fear of crime, with the poor more likely to be fearful because they're more likely to live in high-crime areas (Baumer 1985; Skogan and Maxfield 1981). If we allow annual family income to be a rough measure of social class, Figure 2.6 (on page 40) portrays the relationship in the GSS between social class and fear of crime. As expected, the lowest income group in the figure is the most afraid of crime.

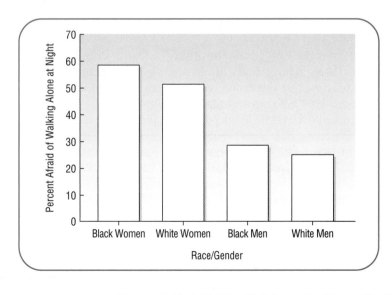

◀ FIGURE 2.5 **GENDER, RACE, AND FEAR OF CRIME**

Source: Copyright © 1998 by the General Social Survey. Reprinted by permission.

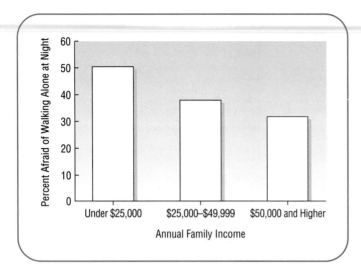

◀ Figure 2.6 **Annual Family Income and Fear of Crime**

Source: Copyright © 1998 by the General Social Survey. Reprinted by permission.

The Consequences of Fear

Now that we have some idea of the sources of fear of crime, let's turn to its consequences. Observers often assert that fear of crime paralyzes our society, especially urban areas, undermines traditional feelings of community, weakens social ties within communities, and threatens the economic viability of whole neighborhoods (Lewis and Salem 1986; Skogan 1986). Other observers caution against exaggerating these effects (Warr 2000).

Despite this caution, there are many heartbreaking accounts of the difference crime makes in the lives of urban residents. Consider the words of a fifth-grade girl living in a high-crime neighborhood of Boston: "Every night, I hear sirens. And I wonder: Who got killed now? Why did that person have to get killed?" Or the concern of a small restaurant owner in the same neighborhood, whose business is declining because of the crime and who worries over leaving his five children alone in the afternoon: "If I don't rush home from work, the drug dealers might get to them. I've got to make sure they stay inside. And I can't be there all the time, no way. It's very scary." Or the views of yet another resident of the neighborhood, who worries constantly about just walking down the block to the subway or automated teller machine: "It really takes a toll. You're constantly on alert. You're always on edge" (Grunwald 1994:19,22).

While we should indeed not exaggerate the effects of fear of crime, we must also avoid understating them. A large body of research documents how concern about crime affects the way we live our daily lives and influences criminal justice policy-making (Scheingold 1984; Skogan and Maxfield 1981).

As noted earlier, concern over crime leads people to take many precautions. A Gallup poll found that 43 percent of U.S. residents said they no longer shop at night (Neuborne 1994). Fear of rape controls women's daily behavior in ways that men never have to experience (Gordon and Riger 1989; Griffin 1971; Warr 1985). Fear of crime prompts many people to buy handguns and others to move out of their communities (Lizotte, Tesoriero, Thornberry, and Krohn 1994; Morenoff and Sampson 1997). It has also led to the development of neighborhood watch groups and a burgeoning home security industry involving millions of dollars of products and services. In the area of criminal justice policy, public concern over crime underlies legislative decisions to increase the penalties for crime and to build new prisons.

◄ *Fear of crime has serious consequences, such as prompting many people to buy handguns.*

In sum, fear of street crime has important consequences. This is true even if this fear is exaggerated by sensational media coverage and thus does not always reflect actual levels of crime. To paraphrase again Dorothy and W. I. Thomas (1928), if things are considered real, then they are real in their consequences. The consequences of fear of crime thus are very real for most of us, and especially for women, for the elderly, and for the residents, most of them people of color, of high-crime urban neighborhoods.

The Seriousness of Crime

Which of the following crimes seems more serious to you: turning in a false fire alarm or taking $35 from an unlocked dormitory room? How about taking a tape deck from a locked car versus stabbing a stranger with a knife? Attracting increased scholarly attention in the last two decades, public judgments of crime seriousness are important for several reasons (Warr 2000). First, these judgments are part of a society's ways of thinking, feeling, and acting that we call, as you may have learned in other courses, its culture. To a large extent, judgments of crime seriousness reflect the value placed on human life and the value placed on personal property. Anthropologists have studied small, traditional societies where personal property isn't held nearly as sacred as it is in Western societies and where strong norms exist for sharing one's property with others. In these small societies, theft, to the extent it takes place at all, is considered relatively harmless and perhaps not even a "crime" (Edgerton 1976).

Second, and perhaps most important for our discussion, public judgments of crime seriousness help determine appropriate penalties for criminal offenders. More specifically, they influence the penalties stipulated by legislators for violations of criminal codes and the sentences judges give to convicted offenders: The more serious the crime is judged, the more serious the penalty or sentence (Sellin and Wolfgang 1964; Warr 2000).

Third, people's perceptions of crime seriousness affect their own views of appropriate punishment for criminal offenders and also, to some extent, their own fear of crime (Warr, Meier, and Erickson 1983).

Thorsten Sellin and Marvin Wolfgang initiated the study of crime seriousness in 1964 with the publication of their book, *The Measurement of Delinquency* (Sellin and Wolfgang 1964). The book featured a survey given to samples of judges, university students, and police, with each group of respondents asked to assign a seriousness score to almost 150 offenses (the more serious the crime, the higher the score). Though obviously different in other respects, the three groups of respondents assigned roughly similar seriousness scores to the various offenses. A decade later, Wolfgang and other colleagues developed a national survey of crime seriousness that was administered in 1977 to a random sample of some 60,000 U.S. residents (Wolfgang et al. 1985). More than 200 offenses were included in this survey. Table 2.2 presents the average seriousness scores the sample assigned to some of the offenses.

These seriousness scores allow us to realize, among other things, that the public considers selling marijuana more serious than simply smoking the drug and, perhaps in a bit of sexism, a woman engaging in prostitution slightly more serious than a customer employing her services. Wolfgang and his colleagues used the scores to determine why the public judges crimes as more or less serious. Violent crimes were considered more serious than property crimes, crimes against individuals more serious than crimes against businesses, and street crimes more serious than white-collar crimes.

Another important conclusion of the work on crime seriousness is that different demographic subgroups—for example, blacks and whites, women and men, the poor and nonpoor—generally agree on the seriousness of most crimes. When differences between subgroups are found (e.g., seriousness ratings by blacks are lower than those by whites for some crimes), they are usually small or inconsistent (Cullen, Link, and Polanzi 1982; Rossi et al. 1974).

TABLE 2.2

SERIOUSNESS SCORES FOR SELECTED OFFENSES

OFFENSE	SCORE
A person plants a bomb in a public building. The bomb explodes and twenty people are killed.	72.1
A man forcibly rapes a woman. As a result of her physical injuries, she dies.	52.8
A man stabs his wife. As a result, she dies.	39.2
A person runs a narcotics ring.	33.8
A person robs a victim of $1,000 at gunpoint. The victim is wounded and requires hospitalization.	21.0
A person breaks into a bank at night and steals $100,000.	15.5
A person steals a locked car and sells it.	10.8
A person sells marijuana to others for resale.	8.5
A person steals $1,000 worth of merchandise from an unlocked car.	6.5
A person turns in a false fire alarm.	3.8
A woman engages in prostitution.	2.1
A person is a customer in a house of prostitution.	1.6
A person smokes marijuana.	1.4
A person under 16 years old plays hookey from school.	0.2

Source: Wolfgang, Figlio, Tracy, and Singer 1985.

The picture emerging from studies of crime seriousness is thus quite different from that emerging from studies of fear of crime, where demographic subgroups differ substantially. Thus, although research provides strong evidence for the impact of race, class, and gender on fear of crime, research indicates these dimensions have little effect on crime seriousness. Whereas the research on fear of crime supports a conflict view of crime and society, the research on crime seriousness supports consensus perspectives.

Although several methodological problems in seriousness research suggest we take such a conclusion cautiously (Cullen et al. 1985; Miethe 1982), it's interesting to note that studies of people in other nations find cross-cultural agreement on the seriousness of various crimes (Evans and Scott 1984; Newman 1976). If consensus on judgments of crime seriousness can be assumed, then it's appropriate to base sentencing decisions and other aspects of criminal justice policy on these judgments.

Attitudes toward the Punishment of Criminals

A final public perception concerns judgments of appropriate punishment for convicted criminals. The GSS includes a standard item: "In general do you think the courts in this country deal too harshly or not harshly enough with criminals?" In the 1998 GSS, 79 percent of the respondents replied "not harshly enough" versus only 66 percent of the respondents in the very first GSS in 1972. This trend and other findings in the last two decades suggest that U.S. residents think criminals are treated far too leniently, and that public views have become more punitive over time. As discussed earlier, these views underlie "get tough" calls by elected and judicial officials.

As you might expect, several studies measure public judgments about sentences for people convicted of various kinds of crimes. Perhaps the most important conclusion to be drawn from these is that, like judgments of crime seriousness, public sentencing preferences are fairly similar among blacks and whites, women and men, and the poor and nonpoor. This similarity of attitudes again supports consensus perspectives on crime and society and indicates that legislative and judicial officials may appropriately consider the high degree of public punitiveness in making policy on crime and criminal justice (Blumstein and Cohen 1980; Thomas, Cage, and Foster 1976).

However, recent evidence suggests that conclusions of consensus in public sentencing preferences may be premature. For example, although the public may generally hold a punitive orientation, religious fundamentalists, who interpret the Bible literally as the actual word of God, hold especially punitive views. Because religious fundamentalism has recently been an important force in the U.S. political arena, it's also "potentially a powerful force in shaping crime control policy" (Grasmick and McGill 1994:39). But if religious fundamentalists are even more punitive than other people, a consensus on punitiveness among people of different religious beliefs cannot be assumed.

More importantly, significant racial differences also exist in certain views on the treatment and punishment of criminals. Using national polling data, John Hagan and Celesta Albonetti (1982) found strong racial and class differences in perceptions of bias in the criminal justice system: Blacks were more likely than whites, and the poor more likely than the nonpoor, to perceive such bias. Before and during the 1994–1995 criminal trial of football star and TV personality O. J. Simpson

◄ *Racial prejudice fuels the strong support by whites for harsher treatment of criminals. It also raises support by whites for the use of excessive force by police against criminal suspects.*

for allegedly murdering his ex-wife, Nicole Brown Simpson, and her friend Ron Goldman, most whites in the United States thought he was guilty, while most blacks thought he was innocent (Saad and McAneny 1995). In another area, Sandra Lee Browning and Liquin Cao (1992) found that blacks were more likely than whites to subscribe to a "liberal" ideology on criminal justice that emphasizes social factors as causes of crime and stresses the need for rehabilitation of criminals. On at least one form of punishment, the death penalty, there is also a strong racial difference. In the 1998 GSS, 73 percent of respondents with an opinion said they favored "the death penalty for persons convicted of murder." This overwhelming support for the death penalty, however, masks a large racial difference in support: Only 50 percent of blacks said they favored the death penalty, versus 78 percent of whites.

Blacks and whites also differ in the principles they use to judge how severe prison sentences should be. Whites tend to base their sentencing principles on judgments of crime seriousness, while blacks tend to base theirs on attributes of the offender and concern for the victim (Hamilton and Rytina 1980; Miller, Rossi, and Simpson 1986).

One additional set of findings also challenges conclusions of racial consensus in punitiveness. It's possible for people to hold similar views for very different reasons. For example, although feminists and religious fundamentalists both dislike pornography, they dislike pornography for quite different reasons. You would thus not expect one group to attend an anti-pornography rally sponsored by the other.

Similarly, blacks and whites appear to have very different reasons for holding similar views on the proper punishment of criminals. In particular, racial prejudice fuels the strong support by whites for harsher treatment of criminals, including the death penalty for persons convicted of murder (Barkan and Cohn 1994; Cohn, Barkan, and Halteman 1991). It also raises support by whites for the use of excessive force by police against criminal suspects (Barkan and Cohn 1998).

If racial prejudice does affect sentencing preferences among whites, then sentencing policy based on these preferences may be misguided. To return to the discussion that began this chapter, to the extent that public support for harsher sentencing, including the death penalty, is motivated by racial prejudice, it's inappropriate in a democratic society for public and judicial officials to be influenced by such support. Since the public associates violent street crime with African-Americans (Doleschal 1979), it's also possible that racial prejudice underlies judgments by whites of the seriousness of such crime. To the extent that this is true, it's also inappropriate to base criminal justice policy on rankings of crime seriousness.

SUMMARY AND CONCLUSION

We've now come full circle. The chapter began with a critical discussion of decision making in a democratic society. We saw then that traditional views neglect the possibilities of elite influence, tyrannical public views that may violate democratic principles, and inaccuracy in public beliefs. The next section of the chapter examined distortion in news media coverage about crime. While emphasizing that crime is a very serious problem, I suggested that the media nonetheless often give a false picture of rising crime rates and a false impression of most crime as violent crime. Enough evidence exists on the effects of media coverage on public perceptions of crime to call into question the appropriateness of blindly basing criminal justice policy on public opinion. In saying this, I certainly don't mean to sound anti-democratic—far from it. I simply mean to suggest that the available evidence on public opinion and criminal justice policy departs substantially from the ideals of democratic theory.

We next reviewed the major findings on fear of crime and emphasized the effects on fear of dimensions of social inequality and social structure. Although the public appears to be more afraid of crime by strangers than crime statistics warrant, fear of crime is a social fact and thus has real and in many ways sad consequences for how we live our daily lives. Women and the urban poor are especially fearful, and perhaps it's not too much of an exaggeration to say that such fear can affect their actions so profoundly that they become virtual prisoners of their own society.

The complementary literatures on crime seriousness and appropriate punishment for criminals were also reviewed. Since both sorts of judgments are essential elements of public opinion on crime, they both have important implications for legislative and judicial policy. Initial findings of consensus in these judgments thus underscored the appropriateness of grounding policy in public opinion. But more recent evidence of differences between blacks and whites on the punishment of criminals calls into question the appropriateness of basing policy on these judgments.

A final issue involves measurement problems in assessing public opinion on crime and punishment. Although democratic theory doesn't address this point directly, it assumes we can gauge public opinion accurately, for otherwise policy makers cannot be sure of public views on important issues. But measurement problems sometimes call into question our ability to gauge public opinion accurately enough for it to be used as a basis for criminal justice policy.

To illustrate this, let's return for a moment to attitudes on the death penalty. As noted earlier, the standard GSS item on the death penalty, which is used with only slightly different wording in other public opinion surveys, indicates very strong support for capital punishment, even if blacks support it less than whites. A recent body of research suggests, however, that methodological problems in measuring death penalty opinion may artificially inflate estimates of public support (Bowers 1993). For example, items giving respondents a choice between the death penalty or life imprisonment without parole yield much lower support for capital punishment than items like the GSS's question that mention only the death penalty.

This is a potentially important finding for public policy, since the wide public support for the death penalty has influenced recent U.S. Supreme Court decisions upholding its constitutionality (Bowers 1993). To the extent, however, that the Court has been influenced, as recent work suggests, by artificially inflated estimates of public support, its conclusions may not have been justified.

As this chapter has tried to show, public opinion about crime and punishment is often an elusive target. But it is also a fascinating target, precisely because public sentiment about crime and punishment reflects our hopes and fears for society. As a product of our location in society, these hopes and fears further reflect the influence of our race, class, and gender and of various aspects of the social structure and organization of the communities in which we live.

For better or worse, then, public opinion will continue to affect public policy on crime and criminal justice. If that is true, enlightened policy making demands that social scientists continue their research on the sources and consequences of public opinion and that they continue to improve its measurement. It also requires accurate measures of the nature and incidence of crime itself. Appropriately, the next chapter turns to the measurement of crime.

KEY TERMS

crime wave	public policy
crime myth	punitiveness
democratic theory	racial prejudice
fear of crime	religious fundamentalism
individual characteristics	sentencing preferences
news media	seriousness of crime
overdramatization	structural factors
public opinion	

STUDY QUESTIONS

1. What are three criticisms or challenges to democratic theory? What is the relevance of these challenges for public opinion about crime?

2. In what ways do the news media overdramatize crime? What effect does the media treatment of crime have on public opinion?

3. In what ways do the news media help create and reinforce crime myths? What are the effects of crime myths?

4. What are the structural and individual correlates of fear of crime? What are the consequences of fear of crime?

5. Why might conclusions of consensus in public sentencing preferences be premature?

INTERNET EXERCISES

The Sourcebook of Criminal Justice Statistics Web site has lots of information on public opinion about crime and the criminal justice system. To access this information, go to **http://www.albany.edu/sourcebook**. Click Section 2 to open up this section on **Public attitudes toward crime and criminal justice-related topics**. Scroll down until you reach, just under **Contents**, the **Most important problems for country and neighborhoods**. Click on this heading.

Near the top of the table that appears you'll see the percent of the public who named "crime; violence" as the most important problem. Notice how this percent has fluctuated over the years. Drawing on the text's discussion, what do you think accounts for this fluctuation?

Further down in the table is the percent who named "drugs; drug abuse" as the most important problem. Notice that this percent has also changed over the years. Drawing on the text's discussion, what do you think accounts for this change?

Now go back to the Contents section on a previous Web page and scroll down until you reach **Death penalty**. Click on **Attitudes toward the death penalty, by demographic characteristics....** Answer the following questions: Which gender is more opposed to the death penalty? Which racial/ethnic group is most opposed to it? Which region of the country is most in favor of the death penalty? What reasons account for the answers you just gave?

THE MEASUREMENT
AND PATTERNING
OF CRIMINAL BEHAVIOR

Crime in the News

*I*n November 1999 the FBI reported that serious crime had plummeted by 10 percent in the first half of the year, continuing a nationwide crime decline since the early 1990s. One criminologist called the 10 percent drop "enormous and encouraging," while another exclaimed, "This is astounding. No one could have predicted the drops would have been this deep." Experts contacted by the Associated Press attributed the drop to several factors, including a thriving economy, the aging of the baby boom generation, a stabilizing of the crack market, and various crime control strategies. One also cited a value shift in the United States. "Lawfulness is becoming the norm, and it's contagious. Cities around the country are investing in crime programs as never before. Rather than huddling behind double-locked doors, citizens are getting involved in their communities."

Source: Sniffen 1999.

ow accurate are crime statistics anyway? When the U.S. Congress investigated the 1970s Watergate scandal that forced President Richard Nixon to resign, Republican Senator Howard Baker of Tennessee became famous for repeatedly asking about the president, "What did he know and when did he know it?" Of the measurement of crime, a similar question might be asked: "What do we know and how do we know it?" Accurate answers to this question are essential for criminal justice policy and criminological theory. For example, we can't know whether crime is increasing unless we first know how much crime occurs now and how much occurred in the past. Similarly, if we want to be able to explain why more crime occurs in urban areas than in rural areas, we first need to know the amount of crime in both kinds of locations.

Unfortunately, crime is very difficult to measure, since it's usually a private event known only to offender and victim. Unlike the weather, crime can't be observed merely by looking out the window. On TV police shows or in crime movies, crimes are always discovered, since otherwise there would be no plot. But real life is never that easy: Because crime often remains hidden from the police, it can't easily be measured. Thus, we can never know with 100 percent accuracy how much crime there is or what kinds of people or organizations are committing crime and who their victims are.

At best we can measure crime in different ways, with each one giving us a piece of the puzzle. When we put all these pieces together, we begin to come up with a more precise picture of crime. Like many jigsaw puzzles you may have, however, some pieces might be missing. We can guess at the picture of crime, sometimes fairly accurately, but we can never know whether our guess is completely correct. Fortunately, the measurement of crime has improved greatly over the last few decades, and we know much more about crime than we used to (Warr 2000). This chapter reports the state of our knowledge.

Measuring Crime

The Uniform Crime Reports (UCR)

The primary source of U.S. crime statistics is the Uniform Crime Reports (UCR) of the Federal Bureau of Investigation (FBI). Begun in the 1930s, the UCR involve massive data collection from almost all the police precincts in the United States. Each precinct regularly reports to the FBI various crimes known to the police. The most extensive reporting is done on what are called "Part I" offenses or "Index" crimes, which the FBI considers to be the most serious: homicide (murder and nonnegligent manslaughter), forcible rape, robbery, and aggravated assault, classified as violent crimes; and burglary, larceny, motor vehicle theft, and arson, classified as property crimes. The police tell the FBI whether each Index crime has been "cleared by arrest." A crime is considered cleared if anyone is arrested for the crime or if the case is closed for another reason (e.g., the death of the prime suspect). If someone has been arrested, the person's race, gender, and age are reported. The FBI also gathers data from the police on "Part II" offenses, which include fraud, embezzlement, vandalism, prostitution, gambling, disorderly conduct, and several others offenses (see Table 3.1).

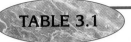

TABLE 3.1

PART I OFFENSES

Criminal Homicide: (a) murder and nonnegligent manslaughter: the willful killing of one human being by another (deaths caused by negligence, attempts to kill, assaults to kill, suicides, accidental deaths, and justifiable homicides are excluded); (b) manslaughter by negligence: the killing of another person through gross negligence (traffic fatalities are excluded)

Forcible Rape: the carnal knowledge of a female forcibly and against her will: includes rapes by force and attempts to rape (excludes statutory offenses: no force used and victim under age of consent)

Robbery: the taking or attempting to take anything of value from the care, custody, or control of a person or persons by force or threat of force and/or by putting the victim in fear

Aggravated Assault: an unlawful attack by one person upon another to inflict severe bodily injury: usually involves use of a weapon or other means likely to produce death or great bodily harm (simple assaults are excluded)

Burglary: unlawful entry, completed or attempted, of a structure to commit a felony or theft

Larceny-Theft: unlawful taking, completed or attempted, of property from another's possession that does not involve force, threat of force, or fraud: examples include thefts of bicycles or car accessories, shoplifting, pocket-picking

Motor Vehicle Theft: theft or attempted theft of self-propelled motor vehicle that runs on the surface and not on rails (excluded are thefts of boats, construction equipment, airplanes, and farming equipment)

Arson: willful burning or attempt to burn a dwelling, public building, personal property, etc.

PART II OFFENSES

Simple Assaults: assaults and attempted assaults involving no weapon and not resulting in serious injury

Forgery and Counterfeiting: making, altering, uttering, or possessing, with intent to defraud, anything false in the semblance of that which is true

Fraud: fraudulent obtaining of money or property by false pretense: included are confidence games and bad checks

Embezzlement: misappropriation of money or property entrusted to one's care or control

Stolen Property: buying, receiving, and possessing stolen property, including attempts

Vandalism: willful destruction or defacement of public or private property without consent of the owner

Weapons: All violations and attempted violations of regulations or statutes controlling the carrying, using, possessing, furnishing, and manufacturing of deadly weapons or silencers

Prostitution and Commercialized Vice: sex offenses such as prostitution and procuring

Sex Offenses: statutory rape and offenses against common decency, morals, etc. (excludes forcible rape and prostitution and commercial vice)

Drug Abuse: unlawful possession, sale, use, growing, and manufacturing of drugs

Gambling

Offenses against the Family and Children: nonsupport, neglect, desertion, or abuse of family and children

Driving Under the Influence

Liquor Laws: state/local liquor law violations (except drunkenness and driving under the influence)

Drunkenness

Disorderly Conduct: breach of the peace

Vagrancy: vagabonding, begging, loitering, etc.

All Other Offenses: all violations of state/local laws, except as above and traffic offenses

Suspicion: no specific offense: suspect released without formal charges being placed

Curfew and Loitering Laws: persons under age 18

Runaways: persons under age 18

Source: Federal Bureau of Investigation 1999.

In turn, each year the FBI reports to the public the "official" number of Index crimes (i.e., the number the FBI hears about from the police) that occurred in the previous year for every state and major city in the United States. (Because of incomplete reporting of arson by police, the total number of arsons is not included in the UCR.) The FBI also reports the number of crimes cleared by arrest, and the age, race, and gender distribution of people arrested for these crimes. Because of this information, UCR data are especially valuable for understanding the geographical distribution of Index offenses and certain demographic characteristics of those who get arrested for committing them. For Part II offenses, the FBI reports only the number of people arrested. Table 3.2 presents UCR data for Index crimes. Note that violent crime comprises about 13 percent of all Index crimes, and property crime about 87 percent.

For about three decades after the beginning of the UCR in the 1930s, the UCR and other official statistics (e.g., arrest records gathered from local police stations) were virtually the only data in the United States about crime. But in the 1960s and 1970s, scholars of crime began to question their accuracy. Before reviewing the criticism, let's first see how crimes become known to the police.

HOW A CRIME BECOMES "OFFICIAL"

Most importantly, a crime usually becomes known to the police only if the victim (or occasionally a witness) reports the crime, usually by calling the police and talking to a dispatcher (911 operator). Yet close to two-thirds of all victims don't report their victimization to the police. Since the police discover only 3 to 4 percent of all crimes themselves, many crimes remain unknown to the police and don't become part of the official UCR crime count.

When the police do hear about a crime, they decide whether to record it. Sometimes they don't believe the victim's account or, even if they do believe it, they may not feel that it describes actual criminal conduct. Even if the police do believe a crime has occurred, they may be too busy to do the paperwork to record it, particularly if the crime isn't that serious. If the police don't record an event as a crime, they don't report it to the FBI, and it isn't included in the UCR crime count. Some evidence suggests that police record only about 65 percent of all calls (Warner and Pierce 1993).

TABLE 3.2

SELECTED UCR DATA, 1998

TYPE OF CRIME	NUMBER KNOWN TO POLICE	% CLEARED BY ARREST
Violent Crime	1,531,044	49.1
Murder and nonnegligent manslaughter	16,914	68.7
Forcible rape	93,103	49.9
Aggravated assault	974,402	58.5
Robbery	446,625	28.4
Property Crime	10,944,590	17.4
Burglary	2,329,950	13.6
Larceny-theft	7,373,886	19.2
Motor vehicle theft	1,240,754	14.2
Total Crime Index	12,475,634	21.3

Sources: Federal Bureau of Investigation 1999; Rennison 1999.

◄ *UCR and other data sources show that most crime is property crime, not violent crime.*

Even when the police do record a crime, an arrest is the exception and not the rule. Unless a victim or witness identifies the offender or the police catch him (or, much less often, her) in the act, they probably won't be able to make an arrest. Unlike their TV counterparts, police don't have the time to gather evidence and interview witnesses, unless the crime is very serious. As Table 3.2 indicated, the proportion of all Index crimes cleared by arrest is thus shockingly small. This proportion does vary by the type of crime and is higher for violent crimes. Yet even for homicides, where there is the most evidence (a corpse), only about two-thirds are cleared by arrest.

CRITIQUE OF UCR DATA

Because so few crimes become known to the police and thus included in the UCR, the UCR drastically underestimate the actual number of crimes. And because so few offenders are arrested, UCR demographic data on arrestees apply only to a small proportion of all Index offenders. Increased recognition some thirty years ago of these problems led to several critiques of the validity of the UCR and other official measures and, in turn, evaluations of these critiques. Let's review the critiques briefly (O'Brien 2000).

First, and as already noted, the UCR severely underestimate the actual number of crimes committed in the United States and in the individual states and cities every year. We'll explore the extent of this underestimation later in this chapter.

Second, in focusing primarily on Index crimes, the UCR emphasize these crimes as the most serious ones facing the nation and divert attention away from white-collar crimes. As a result, the seriousness of white-collar crime is implicitly minimized (Reiman 1998).

Third, UCR data may be more valid indicators of the behavior of police than that of offenders. If so, the characteristics the UCR present for the people who do get arrested may not accurately reflect those of the vast majority who escape arrest. This possibility is especially likely if police arrest practices discriminate against the kinds of people—typically poor, nonwhite, and male—who are frequently arrested. In this regard, some research suggests that police personnel and funds are concentrated in nonwhite neighborhoods and that police make proportionally more arrests in poor than nonpoor neighborhoods, even when we adjust for the seriousness of the crimes in these poor areas (see Chapter 15) (Liska and Chamlin 1984). To the extent that such bias exists, arrest data yield a distorted picture of the "typical" offender. To compound the problem, since white-collar criminals are even less likely than Index criminals to get arrested, arrest data again mischaracterize the "typical" offender and divert attention away from white-collar criminals.

Fourth, the official number of crimes may change artificially if citizens become more or less likely to report offenses committed against them. For example, if the introduction of the 911 emergency phone number across the United States has had its intended effect, more crime victims may be calling the police. If so, more crimes become known to the police and thus get reported to the FBI, artificially raising the official crime rate. Similarly, the increased number of reported rapes since the 1970s in the United States may partly reflect growing awareness by women and police of rape. This awareness may be prompting more women to call the police and more police to record the incident as a rape (Jensen and Karpos 1993).

The official number of crimes may also change artificially because of changes in police behavior. This can happen in two ways. One way is through police crackdowns on prostitution and illegal drug trafficking involving sweeps of neighborhoods thought to be centers of these crimes. The number of crimes known to the police and the number of people arrested for them rise dramatically, artificially increasing the official rate of these crimes, even though the actual level of criminal activity might not have increased (Sheley and Hanlon 1978). The second way is more ominous: The police can change how often they record offenses reported to them as crimes. They can decide to record more offenses to make it appear the crime rate is rising, with such "evidence" providing a rationale for increased funding, or they can decide to record fewer offenses to make it appear the crime rate is falling, with such evidence indicating the local force's effectiveness at fighting crime (Seidman and Couzens 1974). This happened in Chicago in the early 1980s, when police classified almost 40 percent of that city's burglaries, robberies, and other thefts as "unfounded" and thus did not report them to the FBI. When the FBI learned of the practice and told Chicago to recount these crimes, its crime rate jumped 25 percent (Warner 1997).

Police recording scandals also rocked several other cities just a few years ago. In New York, a Bronx police commander was given a desk job in 1996 after he allegedly downgraded some felonies to misdemeanors; his action was attributed to pressure from city officials to lower the crime rate. He also was suspected of upgrading some misdemeanor arrests to felony arrests in an apparent effort to increase his precinct's clearance rate (Krauss 1996). In Philadelphia, the FBI decided it had to throw out that city's crime statistics for 1996 and 1997 after it learned that Philadelphia police were recording crimes in ways that artificially lowered the city's crime rate. For example, they counted crimes based on when they were recorded into computers rather than when they actually occurred, usually two months but sometimes as much as one year earlier. Thus, crimes committed in 1996 were included in the crime rate for 1997 (Brown 1997). Worse yet, Philadelphia police for several years had been downgrading major crimes to minor ones to make the crime rate again look lower than it really was. Burglaries and other stolen property cases were made into "missing" or "lost" property cases; car break-ins were redefined as vandalism; and beatings and stabbings were called "hospital cases." This downgrading involved about 10 percent, or 10,000 offenses, of all serious crime in the city (Matza, McCoy, and Fazlollah 1998).

After Philadelphia made its reporting practices more accurate, its crime rate rose 9 percent in 1998, an increase observers attributed to the more accurate reporting rather than to an increase in the actual number of crimes. As one put it, "It's kind of like throwing out a scale that has been showing you underweight for years. It doesn't mean you're gaining weight just because you've finally got an accurate scale" (Matza, McCoy, and Fazlollah 1999:A1). Other reporting scandals were exposed in the late 1990s in cities such as Atlanta, Baltimore, and Boca Raton, Florida. In Boca Raton, a police captain downgraded 385 felony property crimes to misdemeanors like trespassing and thus artificially reduced the city's crime rate by almost 11 percent in 1997. In one case he classified a burglary, in which someone broke into a house and stole a purse at 1:00 A.M. while the residents slept, as a mere act of vandalism (Butterfield 1998).

Crime reporting practices have also been less than accurate at college and university campuses. Critics say that some campuses hide evidence of rapes and other crimes in internal judicial proceedings to avoid alarming the public and reducing admissions applications. When students and campus employees are victimized near a campus, their crimes are included in the tallies of some campuses but not in those of others (Chacón 1998; Goldberg 1997). In 1997, U.S. Department of Education officials decided to audit crime figures at several campuses in the wake of reports that they had failed to officially report rapes and other crimes—including some off campus but in areas patrolled by campus police—that students had themselves reported to campus police (Matza 1997).

A fifth problem with UCR data is that police in various communities may have different understandings and definitions of certain crimes. As a result, police in one area may be more likely than police elsewhere to record a given event as a crime. Even when they do record an event, police forces also vary in the degree to which they record the event as a more serious or a less serious crime (e.g., a simple assault instead of an aggravated assault). One study found that Los Angeles police recorded any attempted or completed sexual assault as a rape, even if it didn't involve sexual intercourse, while Boston police recorded a sexual assault as a rape only if it involved completed sexual intercourse, the UCR's definition. Perhaps not surprisingly, Boston's official rape rate was much lower than that for Los Angeles (Chappell et al. 1971).

Finally, although UCR information on the number of Index crimes typically appears in the press, the press often fails to report the rate of crime. A crime rate is obtained by dividing the number of crimes in a given location by the population of that location, and, by convention, multiplying the result by 100,000 to eliminate decimals. Thus 100 homicides in a population of 5 million is equal to a crime rate of 2 per 100,000. Crime rates allow us to compare the risk of crime in locations of different population sizes and to assess whether crime is becoming more or less of a problem over time. Since the population rises year to year, you'd expect the number of crimes to rise as well, even though the crime rate might remain stable. Thus, an increase in the number of crimes in a given year may be taken to mean that "crime is up" even though the crime rate may not have changed.

To gather more information on Index crimes, the FBI has recently begun the National Incident-Based Reporting System (NIBRS) and is gradually converting the UCR to the NIBRS. Under the NIBRS, the police provide the FBI extensive information on each crime incident for the eight Index crimes and fourteen other Part II crimes, including drug offenses, gambling, prostitution, and weapons violations. The information includes the relationship between offenders and victims and the use of alcohol and other drugs immediately before the offense (Chilton, Major, and Propheter 1998). Previously, such detailed information had been gathered only for homicides in what are called the Supplementary Homicide Reports (SHR). Because of the information it provides on every crime incident in the categories it covers, the NIBRS promises to greatly increase our understanding of the causes and dynamics of many types of crimes.

To avoid the problems in the UCR associated with police practices and interpretations, some researchers advocate using "calls to police" to indicate the number and nature of crimes in a given community (Warner and Pierce 1993). When crime victims call the police to report a crime, a dispatcher records their calls. Although, as discussed earlier, these calls don't always find their way into police records submitted to the FBI, they may still provide a more accurate picture of the number and kinds of crimes.

The National Crime Victimization Survey (NCVS)

Another source of crime data is the National Crime Victimization Survey (NCVS). Formerly called the National Crime Survey, it was begun in the early 1970s by the U.S. Department of Justice with the aid of the U.S. Bureau of the Census. The Justice Department initiated the NCVS to avoid UCR problems just noted and to gather information not available from the UCR. This includes the context of crime, such as the time of day and physical setting in which it occurs, and the characteristics of crime victims, including their gender, race, income, extent of injury, and relationship with their offenders. Over the years, the NCVS has provided government officials and social scientists an additional, important source of crime data to determine whether the rates of various crimes are increasing or decreasing and to test various theories of crime.

Every six months the Census Bureau interviews about 80,000 residents, age 12 and older, of some 43,000 randomly selected households, with a response rate of 94–95 percent. Respondents are asked whether they or their household had been a victim in the past half year of any of the following crimes: aggravated and simple assault, rape and sexual assault, robbery, burglary, various kinds of larcenies (including purse snatching and household larceny), and motor vehicle theft. The crimes are described rather than just listed. Notice that these crimes correspond to the Part I crimes included in the UCR, except that the UCR classify simple assault as a Part II crime. The NCVS excludes the two remaining Part I crimes, homicide and arson—homicide victims obviously cannot be interviewed, and too few household arsons occur—and all Part II crimes besides simple assault. The NCVS also doesn't ask about commercial crimes, such as shoplifting and burglary in a store or other business, which the UCR include. Finally, NCVS includes sexual assaults short of rape, while the UCR exclude them.

For each victimization, the NCVS then asks respondents additional questions, including the age, race, and gender of the victim and whether the victimization was reported to the police. For crimes such as robbery, assault, and rape where the victim may have seen the offender, the resident is also asked to identify the race and gender they perceived the offender to be.

The NCVS estimates that 31,300,000 offenses of the kinds it covers took place in 1998. Table 3.3 reports three kinds of data: (1) NCVS estimates of the number of incidents of victimization in the United States for 1998; (2) the proportion of these incidents reported to the police; and (3) the number of corresponding official crimes identified by the UCR for that year. Because of the differences noted in the coverage of the NCVS and the UCR, comparisons of crime frequency data between them are inexact and must be made cautiously.

As you can easily see, many more incidents of victimization take place than the UCR would have us believe, since only a surprisingly small proportion, some 38 percent overall, are reported to the police. The crimes not reported are "hidden" crimes and are often referred to as the "dark figure" of crime (Biderman and Reiss 1967). If, as most researchers feel, NCVS data are more reliable than UCR data, the NCVS confirms earlier suspicions that the U.S. street crime problem is much worse than official data indicate.

Why do so many crime victims not report their victimizations? Although specific reasons vary by the type of crime, in general many victims feel their victimization wasn't harmful or serious enough to justify the time and energy in getting involved with the police. Some also feel that the police wouldn't be able to find the offender anyway. Victims of rape, family violence, and other crimes in which they may well know the offender also fear further harm by the offender if they report what happened. Moreover, people suffering these crimes often don't want other parties knowing about their victimization, and the best way to avoid publicity is to avoid talking to the police (Rennison 1999).

Although the number of victimizations reported in Table 3.3 is in the tens of millions, the U.S. population is in the hundreds of millions, and the chances of becoming a crime victim thus might be fairly low. In some ways this is true for violent

TABLE 3.3

NUMBER OF OFFENSES, NCVS AND UCR DATA, 1998

TYPE OF CRIME	NCVS	% REPORTED TO POLICE	UCR
Violent Crime	8,117,000	45.9	1,531,044
Homicide	—	—	16,914
Forcible rape[a]	333,000	31.6	93,103
Aggravated assault	1,674,000	57.6	974,402
Simple assault	5,224,000	40.3	—
Robbery	886,000	62.0	446,625
Property Crime	23,191,000	35.4	10,944,590
Burglary	4,054,000	49.4	2,329,950
Larceny-theft[b]	17,999,000	29.3	7,373,886
Motor vehicle theft	1,138,000	79.7	1,240,754
Total Crimes	31,308,000	38.0	12,475,634

[a]NCVS number for "rape" includes sexual assaults
[b]Includes NCVS category of "personal theft"
Source: Federal Bureau of Investigation 1999.

crime, because the NCVS estimates that your chances of becoming a victim of a violent crime in any given year are "only" about 3.8 percent (i.e., 3.8 percent of the 12 and older population each year is the victim of a violent crime). Your chances of becoming a victim of a property crime, however, are much higher, about 22 percent (Rennison 1999).

These numbers obscure other figures. First, the risk of victimization varies greatly for the demographic subgroups of the population; depending on your race, class, gender, and area of residence, you may be much more likely than average (or, if you're lucky, much less likely than average) to become a crime victim in any given year (see Chapter 4). Second, the annual risk of victimization "adds up" and over the course of a lifetime can become quite high. In 1988, for example, the NCVS estimated the following lifetime risks of victimization: robbery, 30 percent (i.e., 30 percent of the public would one day be robbery victims); assault, 74 percent; personal larceny, 99 percent; burglary, 72 percent; household larceny, 90 percent; and motor vehicle theft, 19 percent (Koppel 1987). As these figures indicate, most of us will become a victim of at least one violent or property crime during our lifetime, and many of us will become the victim of more than one such crime.

EVALUATING NCVS DATA

Scholars continue to discuss the relative merits of NCVS and UCR data (O'Brien 2000). The NCVS has at least three major advantages. First, it yields a much more accurate estimate of the number of crimes in the United States. Since it involves a random sample of the U.S. population, estimates of the number of victimizations in the population can be made. Second, because the NCVS's data avoid potential police biases and inconsistencies, they provide a potentially more accurate portrait than UCR data of demographic characteristics of offenders. Finally, NCVS information on the characteristics of victims and the context of victimization has furthered the development of theories of victimization (see Chapter 4).

Other observers point to problems with NCVS data, a major one being that the NCVS itself underestimates the number of crimes. Recall that the NCVS doesn't ask about commercial crimes such as shoplifting and burglary. Further, just as crime victims often don't report their crimes to the police, they sometimes also don't tell NCVS interviewers about their victimizations. The potential for such underreporting is especially high if they know their offenders. Victims of multiple crimes may also forget about some of the crimes they've suffered. Some studies suggest that respondents reveal only about 75 to 85 percent of their victimizations by property crime to NCVS interviewers, and only about half of their victimizations by violent offenses (Turner 1981).

The potential for underreporting in the NCVS is especially high for rape and family violence. Women who have been raped may be reluctant to tell an interviewer about it, particularly when the offender is someone the woman knows. For similar reasons, women who have been beaten by husbands or boyfriends may also underreport their victimization to NCVS interviewers. Reflecting traditional attitudes, some women may consider their rape or battering more of an unfortunate episode than a crime and thus, again, not reveal the crime to an interviewer (Allison and Wrightsman 1993). Although a few years ago the NCVS improved its way of asking about rape and family violence (Bachman and Taylor 1994), the potential for underreporting of these crimes still remains.

Although the NCVS underestimates some crimes, it might overestimate others (Levine 1976). Respondents might mistakenly interpret some noncriminal events as crimes. They might also be guilty of "telescoping" by reporting crimes that occurred before the six-month time frame for the NCVS. Further, many of the assaults and larcenies they report are relatively minor in terms of the injury suffered or property taken (Gottfredson 1986). Despite the potential for overestimation, most researchers feel that underestimation is the more serious problem, and that the NCVS data on robbery, burglary, and motor vehicle theft provide a reasonably accurate picture of the actual number of these crimes in the nation (Gove, Hughes, and Geerken 1985).

One final problem with the NCVS recalls a similar problem with the UCR. Because the NCVS solicits information only on street crimes, not on white-collar crimes (Simpson, Harris, and Mattson 1995), it again diverts attention from the seriousness of white-collar crime.

Self-Report Studies

A third source of information on crime comes from studies asking respondents about offenses they may have committed in a given time period, usually the past year. Some of these self-report studies use interviewers, while others use questionnaires that the respondents fill out themselves. Self-report studies can be used to demonstrate the *prevalence* of offending: the proportion of respondents who have committed a particular offense at least once in the time period under study, and the *incidence* of offending: the average number of offenses per person in the study (Elliott, Huizinga, and Ageton 1985).

Although some self-report studies involve adult inmates of jails and prisons, most involve adolescents, often high school students, who are asked not only about their offenses but also about various aspects of their families, friends, schooling, and other possible influences on their delinquency. High school students are often studied because they comprise a "convenience sample" (or "captive audience," as it's also called) that enables researchers to gather a lot of information without having to spend too much time and money. High school samples also yield a high response rate. (Wouldn't you have wanted to fill out an interesting questionnaire in high school instead of listening to yet another lecture?)

THE HISTORY OF SELF-REPORT STUDIES

The first known self-report survey was carried out in Fort Worth, Texas, in the 1940s by Austin Porterfield (1946). Porterfield gathered data from two groups of adolescents and young adults: some 2,000 who had been in juvenile court for various delinquent offenses, and 337 college students with no juvenile court record. After asking each group about the extent of their involvement in a series of delinquent offenses, Porterfield found that the college students had been as delinquent as the youths with court records. He speculated that the college students' higher social class status led police and other officials to overlook their misbehavior.

At about the same time, Eleanor and Sheldon Glueck of Harvard University conducted what has since become a classic, longitudinal study of 500 male delinquents and 500 male nondelinquent control subjects matched on age, ethnicity, and other factors (Glueck and Glueck 1950). The Gluecks gathered data on the boys from legal and school records and from interviews with the boys, their relatives, neighbors, and employers, and studied both groups of subjects from childhood through adulthood. They found that inadequate parenting (such as poor supervision and faulty discipline) contributes to antisocial behavior early in childhood and that such behavior predicts adult criminality. Although the Gluecks' study received considerable attention, it was criticized for methodological deficiencies and eventually forgotten until two scholars, John Laub and Robert Sampson, discovered sixty boxes of the Gluecks' data in the basement of the Harvard Law School Library. With the aid of modern computers and other analytical advances, Laub and Sampson reconstructed and reanalyzed the Gluecks' data. Their exhaustive efforts have paid off with some illuminating studies of the "life course" development of delinquency and adult criminality (Laub and Sampson 1988; Sampson and Laub 1993) (see Chapter 8).

The impetus for self-report studies increased as the 1960s approached because of concern, discussed earlier, over the accuracy of official crime and delinquency data. In one of the most influential self-report studies in this early period, James F. Short, Jr. and F. Ivan Nye (1957) surveyed a few thousand high school students and a smaller sample of youths in reform schools. Like Porterfield (1946), Short and Nye found that a surprising amount of delinquency had been committed by their "nondelinquent" sample and concluded that delinquency was not confined to youths from lower- or working-class backgrounds.

Because of the information it provides on offenders and the influences on their offending, self-report research has permitted major developments in our understanding of delinquent and criminal behavior. One of its most important findings is the amount of delinquency that remains hidden from legal officials. Self-report studies thus underscore the extent of the dark figure of crime that the NCVS demonstrates. They remain very common today and are becoming even more popular, with some important longitudinal efforts underway.

Perhaps the most well-known such effort is the National Youth Survey (NYS), begun in 1976 under the direction of Delbert Elliott and his colleagues at the University of Colorado (Elliott, Huizinga and Ageton 1985). That year they directed interviews of a random, national sample of some 1,700 youths, who were reinterviewed every year until 1980, and every three years since 1980. Because of its longitudinal nature and variety of survey questions, the NYS has been the source of some very important studies by Elliott and his colleagues and by other researchers.

CRITIQUE OF SELF-REPORT STUDIES

Scholars have debated the advantages and disadvantages of self-report data at length. Perhaps the most common criticism is that self-report studies focus on minor and trivial offenses: truancy, running away from home, minor drug and alcohol use, and the like (Cernkovich, Giordano, and Pugh 1985). This focus was indeed true of most early self-report research, but recent studies, including the NYS, have asked their subjects about more serious offenses such as rape and robbery. The inclusion of these offenses has increased self-report research's ability to help us understand the full gamut of criminal behavior.

A second criticism is that respondents in self-report studies may not always tell the truth about offenses they've committed (Bridges 1987). However, investigations using lie detectors and police records verify the overall accuracy of respondents' answers (Hardt and Peterson-Hardt 1977).

A third criticism is that several self-report studies have included only boys. As I discuss in this and later chapters, research limited to males neglects the origins and dynamics of female offending. Because females have much lower rates of offending than males, the lack of female samples makes it difficult to learn what leads to their lower rates and limits our understanding of what accounts for nonoffending.

A final criticism of self-report studies is that they, like the UCR and NCVS, ignore white-collar crime, since their subjects—usually adolescents or, occasionally, adult jail and prison inmates—don't commit this type of crime.

Evaluating UCR, NCVS, and Self-Report Data

None of the three major sources of street crime data is perfect, but which is the best depends on what you want to know (O'Brien 2000). For the best estimates of the actual number of crimes, NCVS data are clearly preferable to UCR data. Keep in mind, however, that NCVS data exclude homicide, arson, commercial crimes, and most of the Part II offenses in the UCR.

For the best estimates of offender characteristics such as race and gender, self-report data and victimization data may be preferable to UCR arrest data, which include few offender characteristics and may be affected by the racial, class, and/or gender bias of police. As we'll see later, however, comparisons of offenders "identified" in all three data sources suggest that arrest data provide a fairly accurate portrait of offenders despite any bias affecting police arrest decisions.

UCR data, despite their flaws, are superior for understanding most fully the geographical distribution of street crime. Although the NCVS sample is extremely large, it's still too small to tell us much about regional variations in U.S. crime, although it does permit some comparisons of larger and smaller communities.

Short of a super spy satellite circling the earth and recording each of the millions of crimes taking place every year, or a video camera in every household and on every street corner recording every second of our behavior, the measurement of crime will necessarily remain incomplete. To return to our earlier metaphor, some pieces of the crime puzzle will always be missing, but we think we have enough of it assembled to figure out the picture. Together, the three major sources of crime data we've discussed provide a reasonably accurate picture of the amount of crime and the social distribution, or correlates, of criminality.

 # RECENT TRENDS IN U.S. CRIME RATES

In Chapter 2's discussion of news media coverage of crime, I emphasized that the media increased their coverage of crime during the 1990s even though the crime rate was falling. Figure 3.1 (on page 62) shows the trend since the 1960s according to UCR data. For both violent and property crime, these data depict a sharp increase in crime from the 1960s into the 1970s, a leveling off and decrease in the early to mid-1980s, another increase in the late 1980s into the early 1990s, and a sharp decrease during the rest of the 1990s. Figure 3.2 (also on page 62) presents NCVS data for the period since 1973, when the NCVS began for both violent and property crime; the violent crime data also include homicide data from the UCR. In contrast to the UCR, the NCVS depicts a stable violent crime rate through the 1970s, but like the UCR shows a rate that first declined in the early 1980s and then rose. In contrast to the UCR, the NCVS also shows a property crime rate that has

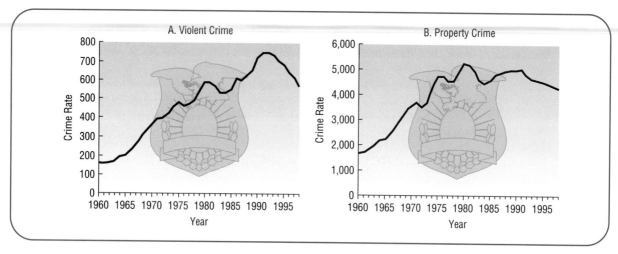

▲ FIGURE 3.1 OFFENSES KNOWN TO THE POLICE, 1960–1998, UCR
(NUMBER PER 100,000 INHABITANTS)
Source: Maguire and Pastore 1999.

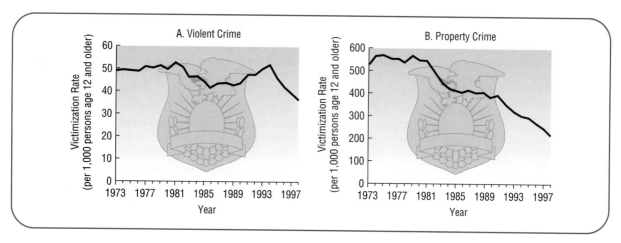

▲ FIGURE 3.2 VICTIMIZATION RATES FOR VIOLENT AND PROPERTY CRIME, 1973–1998
(NUMBER PER 1,000 PERSONS 12 OR OLDER OR 1,000 HOUSEHOLDS)
NOTE: THE VIOLENT CRIMES INCLUDED ARE HOMICIDE, RAPE, ROBBERY, AND SIMPLE AND AGGRAVATED
ASSAULT; PROPERTY CRIMES INCLUDE BURGLARY, THEFT, AND MOTOR VEHICLE THEFT. HOMICIDE DATA ARE
FROM THE UCR WHILE RAPE, ROBBERY AND ASSAULT, AND ALL PROPERTY CRIME DATA ARE FROM THE
NCVS. BECAUSE THE NCVS WAS REDESIGNED IN 1992, DATA BEFORE 1992 REFLECT ESTIMATES BASED
ON THIS REDESIGN AND SHOULD BE INTERPRETED CAUTIOUSLY.
Source: UCR and NCVS statistics 1999.

steadily declined since the early 1970s. Both crime sources show violent and property crime declining sharply for most of the 1990s. The differences depicted in the
two figures result from the different methodologies used (Biderman and Lynch
1991). The fact that both data sources showed declining crime through most of the
1990s gives us confidence that crime really was declining, despite the fact that neither data source yields a perfectly accurate picture of the amount of crime.

THE PATTERNING OF CRIMINAL BEHAVIOR

Crime is patterned, meaning it's not just committed randomly by individuals but instead occurs according to certain predictable patterns stemming from the characteristics of regions, communities, people, and even the climate and seasons of the year. Let's review briefly some of the spatial patterns concerning characteristics of locations, and then turn to social patterns regarding characteristics of people.

Geographical Patterns

INTERNATIONAL COMPARISONS

International comparisons of crime data are inexact. (See International Focus box on page 64.) We've already seen that U.S. crime data aren't totally reliable. Across the world, different nations have varying definitions and interpretations of criminal behavior and alternate methods of collecting crime data. These problems suggest caution in making international comparisons. That said, these comparisons still provide striking evidence of the ways in which crime is patterned geographically.

Simply put, some nations have higher crime rates than others. In this regard, the United States has the highest homicide rate of any Western industrial nation, and has one of the highest rates of other violent crimes. Its property crime rate, however, seems about average (Lynch 1995; Zimring and Hawkins 1997). Scholars often attribute nations' crime rates to their cultures. In Japan, for example, one of the most important values is harmony; the Japanese are expected to be peaceable in their relations with each other and respectful of authority. Conflict is frowned upon, and even lawsuits are relatively uncommon. Since such a culture inhibits people from committing criminal offenses against each other, Japan's crime rates remain relatively low despite its economic growth and industrialization since World War II (Thornton and Endo 1992; Westermann and Burfeind 1991). Harmonious relations are also thought to be valued in Switzerland, helping to account for that country's low street crime rate (Clinard 1978).

In contrast to these two nations, the United States is thought to be more individualistic and disrespectful of authority (Bellah et al. 1985; Messner and Rosenfeld 1997). With the familiar phrase "look out for number one" as a prevailing philosophy, there's less emphasis in the United States on peaceable relations and less sense of social obligation. People thus don't care as much about offending others and become more likely to do so. The United States is also thought to have higher rates of violence than other industrial nations because of its higher degree of inequality (Krahn, Hartnagel, and Gartrell 1986). Chapter 6 discusses the inequality-violence linkage further.

COMPARISONS WITHIN THE UNITED STATES

Crime rates within the United States also vary geographically. According to the UCR, the South and West have the highest rates of violent crime, while the Midwest has the lowest; the West also has the highest rate of property crime. Community size also makes a huge difference, as crime rates are much higher in urban than in rural areas. Figure 3.3 (on page 65) presents UCR data for crime rates per 100,000 broken down by community size. As you can see, violent and property

Measuring Crime in Other Nations

Although international crime data are gathered by the United Nations and other organizations, the measurement of crime across the world is highly inconsistent. In some countries, such as the United States and Canada, the government systematically gathers crime data through police reports and victimization surveys. In other nations, especially those that are very poor, crime reporting is haphazard and even virtually nonexistent. Some nations gather and provide arrest and conviction data, while others do not. Another problem is that various crimes are defined differently by different nations. What constitutes a rape, for example, in some nations, may be very different from what constitutes one in the United States. Because of its nature, homicide is probably the crime most uniformly defined, and homicide data are believed to be the most consistent international data available about crime. In addition, several nations have begun to conduct victimization surveys. Although social and cultural differences make comparisons of international victimization data somewhat inexact, these data have nonetheless yielded valuable information on international differences in victimization rates.

The four major sources of international crime data include the International Criminal Police Organization (INTERPOL); the Comparative Crime Data File (CCDF), gathered by Dane Archer and Rosemary Gartner; the World Health Organization (WHO); and the United Nations. Although these four sources differ in the crimes they cover and the definitions of crime they use, Richard R. Bennett and James P. Lynch conclude that they yield similar results for certain types of investigations, but not for others.

One particularly important question is whether the factors influencing citizens' decisions to report crimes to the police vary from one nation to the next. In developed nations, the seriousness of the crime is the key determinant of victims' decisions to report the crime, while individual-specific factors such as the victim's age and race play a smaller role. To see whether these factors operate in less developed nations, Richard R. Bennett and R. Bruce Wiegand conducted a victimization survey of a random sample of households in Belize in Central America. The authors' findings were "surprisingly similar to those found in the United States and Europe" (p.146), as factors relating to the crime itself played the most important role in victims' decisions to report the crime, followed by individual-specific factors.

Sources: Archer and Gartner 1984; Bennett and Lynch 1990; Bennett and Wiegand 1994; van Dijk and Kangaspunta 2000).

---

crime rates in our largest cities (MSAs, or Metropolitan Statistical Areas) and other cities are much higher than the rates in rural communities. I should stress here that urbanization does not automatically lead to high crime rates. Some of the largest non-U.S. cities (e.g., London and Tokyo) have much lower homicide rates than those in much smaller U.S. cities.

Seasonal and Climatological Variations

Some of the most interesting crime data concern seasonal and climatological (weather-related) variations in crime rates. For many people, summer can be quite grim, as assaults, rapes, and homicides are generally higher in the warmer months. Turning to property crimes, burglary and larceny tend to be summer crimes, while robbery seems to be more a winter crime (Federal Bureau of Investigation 1999).

Because few scholars have studied these patterns, explanations for them are speculative but seem to make sense. As you might know from your own experience,

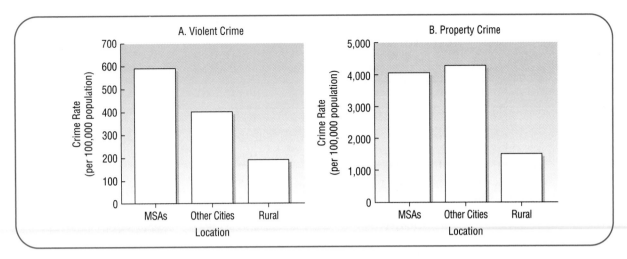

▲ Figure 3.3   **Urbanization and UCR Crime Rates, 1998**
(number of crimes per 100,000 population)
Source: Federal Bureau of Investigation 1999.

the heat of summer can cause tempers to flare, perhaps violently (Baron and Bell 1976). Also, people often go on vacation in the summer and leave their empty homes attractive targets for burglars. Even when they're not away, people are more apt to leave windows open in the summer to let in fresh air, again making burglary more likely. Perhaps one reason for the high crime rates in the South and West is the generally warmer weather there than in the Midwest and East.

In one particularly exhaustive study, Steven F. Lab and J. David Hirschel (1988) gathered police and weather data on over 20,000 assaults, burglaries, and larcenies occurring in Charlotte, North Carolina, in 1983. For daytime crimes, higher temperatures were related to higher rates of all three offenses. For nighttime crimes, however, higher temperatures were related only to assaults. Higher levels of humidity were linked to lower levels of all three crimes, regardless of when they occurred. To explain this finding, the authors speculated that people spend more time indoors on humid, sticky days and are generally less physically active.

A more recent crime study in Israel found homicide rates higher in December and August, but relatively low in July, another hot month. Robberies were most frequent in the winter months, perhaps because unemployment rates are higher in the winter, creating more motivation to commit robbery, and because potential robbers realize there are fewer people on the streets then to notice criminal activity (Landau and Fridman 1993).

Social Patterns of Criminal Behavior

Gender and Crime

One of the key social correlates of criminal behavior is gender: Women's crime rates are much lower than men's. Figure 3.4 (on page 66) displays UCR arrest data broken down by gender. As you can see, men account for about 83 percent of violent crime arrests and 71 percent of property crime arrests.

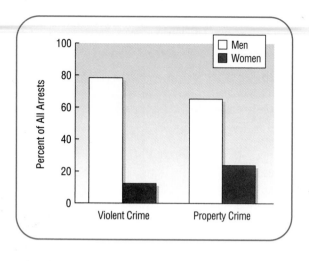

◀ FIGURE 3.4 GENDER AND ARREST, 1998
(PERCENT OF ALL INDEX CRIME ARRESTS)

Source: Federal Bureau of Investigation 1999.

There's always the possibility of bias in police arrest practices: Perhaps the police are more likely to arrest men because of notions of "chivalry" toward women (see Chapter 15). However, victimization and self-report data reinforce the UCR's large gender difference. In the NCVS, victims' reports on the gender of offenders indicate that men account for 86 percent of all violent offenders (Greenfeld and Snell 1999). Although the gender difference in some self-report studies is smaller than the UCR's, the difference for the most serious self-reported crimes approaches the UCR's (Steffensmeier and Allan 2000).

In the past, many scholars of crime ignored female criminality. Some did discuss it, but their explanations emphasized female physiology and women's "natural" child-rearing role (Klein 1973). For example, one of the first scholars of crime, physician Cesare Lombroso, attributed women's low criminality to their natural, biologically induced passivity that results from the "immobility of the ovule compared with the zoosperm" (Lombroso 1920 [1903]:109) (see Chapter 5).

Other scholars said that girls and women commit crime out of frustration over not having a boyfriend. Female offenses were thus said to be primarily sexual (e.g., prostitution), while male criminality was said to be much more diverse (Cohen 1955). In another explanation, followers of the great psychoanalytic thinker, Sigmund Freud, thought that women commit crime because of "penis envy": Jealous over not having penises, they strive to be more like men by committing crimes (and also by working outside the home). In an interesting twist, another scholar, Otto Pollak (1950), argued that women's crimes often never show up in official statistics. The reason? Women are naturally deceitful and thus are good at hiding their behavior. The "proof" of such deceit? Women learn to hide evidence of their menstrual periods and also to fake orgasms.

While now considered outmoded, this early emphasis on women's biology and child-rearing role was quite popular at the time in many fields of thought. For example, in 1873 the U.S. Supreme Court ruled that a woman, Myra Bradwell, had no right as a woman to practice law in Illinois (Friedman 1993):

Man is, or should be, woman's protector and defender. The natural and proper timidity and delicacy which belongs to the female sex evidently unfits it for many of the occupations of civil life. The constitution of the family organization, which is found in the divine ordinance, as well as in the nature of things, indicates the domestic sphere as that which properly belongs to the domain and function of women.... The paramount destiny and mission of women are to fulfill the noble and benign offices of wife and mother. This is the law of the Creator. (*Bradwell v. Illinois*, 86 U.S. [16 Wall.] 130 [1873])

Beginning in the 1970s, women began to enter the field of criminology in greater numbers and, along with some male scholars, raised important questions about the origins and nature of female criminality and of crimes such as rape and family violence that especially victimize women (Daly and Chesney-Lind 1988; Simpson 1989). These scholars criticized biological views of female criminality and in their research found that it stemmed from the same factors underlying male criminality. With the aid of self-report research, the new generation of researchers also found that women commit the same diversity of criminal behaviors as do men, even if their overall rates are much lower.

EXPLAINING WOMEN'S LOW CRIME RATES

If women's low rates don't stem from their biological nature, then from what do they derive? A first explanation concerns the way we socialize girls and boys. Put briefly, we raise boys to be active, assertive, dominant, and to "fight like a man." Since all these traits are conducive to criminal behavior, especially violence, the way we raise our boys increases their odds of becoming criminals (Miedzian 1991). Conversely, we raise our girls to be less assertive, less dominant, and more gentle and nurturing. Since these traits are not conducive to criminal behavior, we in effect are raising our girls not to be criminals.

A second explanation concerns the different opportunities provided to girls and boys to commit crime. Because of the traditional "double standard," parents typically monitor their daughters' behavior more closely than their sons', permitting sons to stay out later at night than daughters. Boys thus have more opportunity than girls to commit crime (Heimer and Coster 1999).

A third explanation addresses the degree to which girls and boys feel attached to their families, schools, and other social institutions. Some research indicates that the strength of these bonds is stronger for girls than for boys because of socialization. Girls, for example, feel more strongly attached than boys to their parents and thus are more likely to value their parents' norms and values. Girls also place more importance on schooling and are more likely than boys to emphasize obedience to the law (Rosenbaum 1987). These attachments and beliefs lead to lower rates of female offending (see Chapter 7).

Finally, peer influences may also matter less for girls than for boys. Girls' greater attachment to parents and schools makes them less vulnerable to peer influences, and thus less likely to commit delinquency (Giordano, Cernkovich, and Pugh 1986; Mears, Ploeger, and Warr 1998). Since boys feel less attached to parents and schools, they are more susceptible to the pressure of their peers, most of them boys themselves, to commit delinquency.

These basic differences in the way we raise girls and boys are key to understanding the origins of crime and how crime might be reduced. Put simply, *we are already doing a good job of raising our girls not to be criminals*. If men's crime rates were as low as women's, crime in the United States would *not* be a major problem. Most of the theories explored later in this book ignore this basic fact. Although these theories stress such things as the effects of inequality and peer influences on criminal behavior, the fact remains that men have much higher rates of crime than women. Thus any effort to reduce criminality must start with the difference that gender makes. The more we know about the origins of both female criminality and law-abiding behavior, the greater our understanding of what it will take to lower the rate of male criminality.

IS FEMALE CRIMINALITY RISING?

Before moving on, let's review an important controversy that arose in the mid-1970s, when magazines and scholarly books began to stress that women's arrest rates were rising much faster than men's (Adler 1975; Deming 1977; Simon 1975). This rise of the "new female criminal" was greeted with alarm and blamed, especially in the popular press, on the new women's liberation movement. Because of this movement, some observers said, females were behaving more like males and working more outside the home, giving them greater opportunities to commit crimes in the workplace. This blame represented a more general backlash against the women's movement (Faludi 1991) and reflected a similar phenomenon a century earlier when similar charges were made about the post-Civil War women's rights movement (Marks 1990).

The 1970's research led other criminologists to study whether female crime was in fact rising and, if it was, whether the women's movement should be blamed. Most concluded that female crime wasn't soaring and that any possible rise could not be due to the women's movement (Cernkovich and Giordano 1979; Steffensmeier 1980; Weis 1976).

Let's review the reasons for their conclusions. Although women's arrests were rising during this period, for example, so were men's. The percentage increase in women's rates was greater than that for men, but only because women had relatively few arrests to begin with. A better statistic to consider is the percentage of all arrests that are of women: This percentage rose only very slowly from the 1960s into the 1970s, and then leveled off. Moreover, because the increase in this percentage began in the late 1950s, it couldn't have stemmed from the women's movement, which didn't begin until the late 1960s. Instead, the increase in women's arrests is best seen as a result of their increasing poverty in the 1960s due to rising divorce

◀ *Research in the 1970s led criminologists to conclude that the female crime rate was not soaring, contrary to popular opinion. Although women's arrests were rising during the 1970s, so were men's. The percentage increase in women's rates was greater than that for men, but only because women had relatively few arrests to begin with. The percentage of all arrests of women rose only very slowly from the 1960s into the 1970s, and then leveled off.*

rates and changes in the U.S. economy. Finally, the women being arrested were typically poor and often nonwhite. They weren't the kinds of women involved in the women's movement and did not hold feminist beliefs. To the extent that they weren't part of the women's movement, then, it was unfair to blame the movement for any increases in their criminality.

Race and Crime

One of the most sensitive but important issues in criminology is the disproportionate involvement of African-Americans in street crime. Even though blacks comprise only 12–13 percent of the U.S. population, they represent 34 percent of all Index crime arrests, and 40 percent of all Index violent crime arrests (see Figure 3.5). Another way of understanding racial differences in Index arrests is to examine racial arrest rates, or the number of each race arrested for every 100,000 members of that race. Figure 3.6 displays these rates for blacks and whites. As you can see, the black arrest rate for violent and property crime is much higher than the white rate. This racial difference is even greater if we look only at murder and nonnegligent manslaughter. As you can see in Figure 3.7 (on page 70), the black arrest rate for homicide is about eight times greater than the white rate.

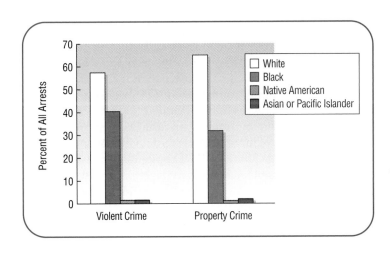

◀ FIGURE 3.5   RACE AND ARREST, 1998
(PERCENT OF ALL INDEX CRIME ARRESTS)
Source: Federal Bureau of Investigation 1999.

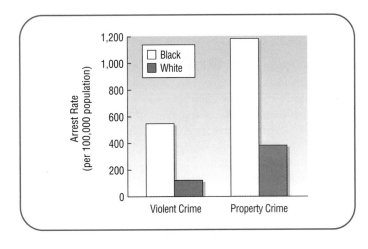

◀ FIGURE 3.6   RACE AND ARREST RATES, 1998
(NUMBER OF INDEX CRIME ARRESTS PER 100,000 POPULATION)
Source: Federal Bureau of Investigation 1999.

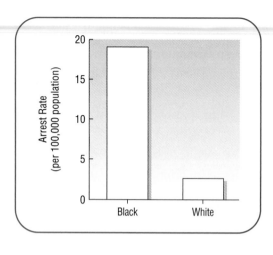

◀ FIGURE 3.7   RACE AND ARREST RATES FOR MURDER AND
NONNEGLIGENT MANSLAUGHTER, 1998
(NUMBER OF INDEX CRIME ARRESTS PER 100,000
POPULATION)

Sources: U.S. Bureau of the Census 1998; Federal
Bureau of Investigation 1999.

As with gender, these arrest statistics may reflect bias in police arrest practices more than racial differences in actual offending (Hawkins 1994; Mann 1993). Once again, however, NCVS data tend to support the UCR portrait of higher black crime rates. Recall that NCVS respondents are asked to report the perceived race of offenders for crimes—assault, rape, robbery—in which they saw their offender. Suggesting that African-Americans do have higher crime rates, the proportion of offenders identified by NCVS data as black is similar to the black proportion of UCR arrests (Hindelang 1978; Walker, Spohn, and DeLone 2000).

Self-report data are more ambiguous. Although early self-report studies found only small black-white differences, this research focused on minor types of offenses. Then an influential analysis of National Youth Survey (NYS) data for serious offenses found larger black-white differences and concluded that UCR arrest data reflect actual racial differences in offending rather than racial bias in arrest (Elliott and Ageton 1980). However, analyses of more recent NYS data find only very small racial differences in serious offending (Elliott 1994). Despite the inconsistent self-report data and notwithstanding possible racial bias in the criminal justice system (see Chapters 15 and 16), most scholars today agree that African-Americans are more heavily involved in serious street crime (Hagan and Peterson 1995; Harris and Shaw 2000; Sampson and Wilson 1995; Walker, Spohn and DeLone 2000). For more minor offenses, however, the actual racial difference in offending may be less than the racial difference in arrests would suggest.

EXPLAINING AFRICAN-AMERICAN CRIME RATES

Explanations of African-American criminality have proven very controversial. Earlier in this century, racist explanations emphasized the supposed biological inferiority of blacks (LaFree and Russell 1993) (see Chapter 5). Beginning in the 1960s, explanations focusing on a subculture of violence (e.g., attitudes approving violence) and on deficiencies in black family structure (e.g., absent fathers) in black communities became popular (Moynihan 1965; Wolfgang and Ferracuti 1967).

Debate continues on both these explanations. Many scholars consider the evidence for an African-American subculture of violence weak at best, but others favor this explanation (see Chapter 6). Although explanations focusing on African-American family structure remain popular, evidence that father-absent households produce lawbreaking children is in fact inconsistent (see Chapter 7). Some recent studies even suggest that father-absent households increase delinquency by whites but not by blacks (LaFree, Drass, and O'Day 1992; Smith 1992).

Critics further charge that these explanations "blame the victim" by ignoring the dire effects of poverty, inequality, and other structural conditions of African-American neighborhoods (Hawkins 1983; Mann 1993). Research since the 1980s has focused on these problems (Harris and Shaw 2000; Walker, Spohn, and DeLone 2000). In his influential work, William Julius Wilson (Sampson and Wilson 1995; Wilson 1987) argues that the movement of large manufacturing industries from U.S. cities in the 1960s and 1970s led to economic dislocation and a growing urban "underclass," characterized by persistent unemployment and composed mostly of blacks. The frustration and social disorganization associated with such economic dislocation and concentrated poverty help account for much of the increased crime by blacks during that time (see Chapters 6 and 9).

Before leaving the issue of race and crime, several more points are worth mentioning (LaFree and Russell 1993). First, race is a "social construction," meaning something that we make up rather than something real. How, for example, do we determine whether someone is black? In the United States, we usually consider someone black if they have any African ancestry at all, even if most of their ancestry is white. Other countries follow different practices. This ambiguity in measuring race may lead to "faulty conclusions regarding the relationship between race and involvement in crime" (Hawkins 1994:48).

Second, most of what we know about race and crime concerns black-white differences. Unfortunately, there are relatively few studies of crime by people who are neither white (non-Hispanic) nor black.

Third, studies of black-white differences in crime rates are talking about street crime, not white-collar crime. If street criminals are disproportionately African-American and other people of color, white-collar criminals are typically white. Despite the explanations of black criminality stressing a violent subculture, family structure deficiencies, or economic deprivation and neighborhood conditions, whites are quite capable of committing white-collar crime despite growing up in intact families and living in advantaged communities.

Regardless, we must not shy away from acknowledging and explaining African-American street crime and from trying to reduce it. As several scholars have recently observed, social scientists avoid studying race and crime because they don't want to contribute to negative attitudes toward blacks (Hagan and Peterson 1995; LaFree and Russell 1993; Sampson and Wilson 1995). However admirable this concern, scholarly silence on African-American offending nonetheless limits the prospects for reducing crime in the very African-American neighborhoods where it causes the most distress (see Chapter 4). As Gary LaFree and Katheryn K. Russell (1993:281) put it, "[W]e must face the problem of race and crime directly, forthrightly, and with the most objective evidence we can muster collectively. Ignoring connections between race and crime has not made them go away." It is both possible and important to explain the race-crime connection in a non-racist manner. In this regard, structural explanations, to which I've alluded, are especially promising (see Chapters 6 and 9).

Class and Crime

Most people arrested and imprisoned for street crime are poorly educated with low incomes: About two-thirds of prisoners lack even a high school diploma (Maguire and Pastore 1999). Sociologists have long been interested in the association between social class and criminality, and they developed several theories of crime from the 1920s through the 1950s to explain why poor people have higher crime rates (see Chapters 6 and 7).

In the 1960s many sociologists began to argue that the overrepresentation of the poor in the criminal justice system stemmed more from class bias than from real differences in offending. The new self-report studies during this time reinforced this belief, as they usually found that middle-class youths committed the same kinds of offenses at the same rates as their poorer counterparts. Echoing Porterfield's (1946) earlier speculation, researchers concluded that class bias hid middle-class delinquency from the juvenile justice system. Several scholars, most notably Tittle, Villemez, and Smith (1978), proclaimed the long-assumed relationship between social class and criminality a myth.

While conceding the possibility of class bias, other scholars challenged this new view (Braithwaite 1981; Clelland and Carter 1980; Hindelang, Hirschi, and Weis 1979). Addressing the debate, a president of the American Society of Criminology warned that a failure to recognize the importance of class would leave criminology impoverished (Hagan 1992). Some scholars argued that the self-report evidence of no class-crime relationship resulted from the emphasis on minor offenses in early self-report research. In the National Youth Survey, higher rates of serious offending exist among poorer youths, although the class difference here is still less than official data suggest (Elliott 1994; Elliott and Ageton 1980).

If the way we measure delinquency affects whether we find a social class-delinquency relationship, so does the way we measure social class. What exactly is social class? How should we measure it? Should we divide people on the basis of their incomes, occupations, or education, or perhaps some combination of the three? Should we look only at the poorest of the poor? As these questions imply, it's surprisingly difficult to define and measure social class, and studies of its relationship with criminality have used different measures (Farnworth et al. 1994). The most common come from the "status attainment" literature and involve occupational prestige and educational achievement: People are ranked on whether they're in more or less distinguished occupations and/or have more or fewer years of education. Studies measuring the social class of adolescents' families this way usually find little or no relationship with delinquency (Farnworth et al. 1994).

In response to this problem, some scholars have begun using measures more closely approximating Wilson's (1987) important concept, discussed earlier, of the underclass. If class has any association with delinquency and crime, that association should be clearest when people in the underclass are compared with those outside it. In a recent study of youths in Rochester, New York, class was only inconsistently related to delinquency when status-attainment measures of class were used, and strongly related to delinquency when underclass measures were used. The underclass-delinquency link existed only for serious offenses—burglary, robbery, and the like—but not for minor offenses. The persistence of underclass membership also mattered: Youths whose families had been in the underclass (e.g., unemployed) the longest were more delinquent than those with less persistent membership. Researchers Margaret Farnworth and colleagues concluded that scholars "have prematurely dismissed the relationship between social class and crime" (1994:56).

If we consider white-collar crime along with street crime, there probably is no relationship between social class and criminality. Although underclass members have higher rates of serious street crime, middle- and upper-class persons clearly have the monopoly on white-collar crime. Explanations of underclass involvement in street criminality that focus on poverty, unemployment, and related structural conditions cannot account for white-collar criminality.

◀ *Young people have high rates of street crime and other kinds of deviant behavior.*

Age and Crime

As you've probably realized by now, criminologists disagree on all sorts of issues involving the measurement and patterning of crime. Age, however, is one area where there is widespread agreement: "The view that involvement in crime diminishes with age is one of the oldest and most widely accepted in criminology" (Steffensmeier and Allan 2000:106). Simply put, street crime is disproportionately committed by young people: As Figure 3.8 shows, the 10–25 age bracket accounts for only 21 percent of the population but almost 55 percent of all arrests. Crime peaks at ages 17 or 18 and then declines, especially beyond young adulthood. Despite minor variations depending on the type of crime, this pattern holds true whether one looks at UCR arrests, the perceived age of offenders reported to NCVS interviewers, or self-report data (Farrington 1986). It also generally holds true regardless of gender (Steffensmeier and Streifel 1991). White-collar crime is once again a different matter, as it tends to be committed by older people: Teenagers and young adults are too young to be in a position to commit such crime.

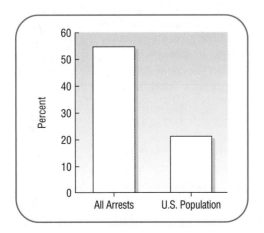

◀ FIGURE 3.8 **AGE AND ARREST, 1998** (FOR AGES 10–24)

Sources: U.S. Bureau of the Census 1998; Federal Bureau of Investigation 1999.

Why is street crime primarily a young persons' phenomenon, and why does it decline after adolescence and young adulthood (Steffensmeier and Allan 2000)? First, adolescence is a time when peer influences are especially strong. To the extent that peers influence one's own delinquent behavior, it's not surprising that adolescence is a peak time for offending. As we move into adulthood, peer influences diminish, and our peers become more law-abiding than they used to be. As a result, we become more law-abiding as well (Warr 1998). This change might be more apt to happen for middle-class youths than for working-class youths, which may be one reason for the higher rates of offending found in young, working-class adults (Hagan 1991).

Second, adolescents have an increasing need for money that part-time jobs or parental allowances may not satisfy. For some adolescents, crime provides money (Agnew 1994; Greenberg 1977). If this is true, one reason crime declines when people move into adulthood might be that full-time employment and greater financial resources ensue. The particularly bleak prospects for good employment in young adulthood that African-Americans face may be one reason for their relatively high street crime rates at this stage of their lives (Steffensmeier and Allan 2000).

Third, our ties to society rise as we become young adults. We acquire full-time jobs, usually get married and have children, and in general start becoming full-fledged members of society. These bonds to society give us an increasing sense of responsibility and stake in conformity and thus reduce our likelihood of committing crime (Laub and Sampson 1993).

We also become more mature as we leave adolescence. We're no longer youthful rebels who think that everything our parents say and want us to do is stupid. We begin to realize that many of the indiscretions of our youth may have been fun and daring but were clearly illegal. What we were ready to excuse back then, we cannot excuse now. "Yes, I did _____ (fill in the blank) when I was a teenager," you might tell your own children, "but I don't want you doing that!" They'll inevitably see this remark as a sign of your hypocrisy; you'll regard it as a sign of your maturity.

An understanding of the age-crime relationship helps us understand shifts in a nation's crime rate. An increased birth rate will, some fifteen years later, begin to lead to an increased number of people in the 15–25 crime-prone age group. All other things equal, the nation's crime rate should rise as the number of people in this age group rises. If the birth rate later declines, then as these young people move into their less crime-prone middle age and are replaced by fewer numbers of youths, the crime rate should decline.

A major reason for the rise of U.S. crime rates in the 1960s and leveling off of crime rates in the 1980s was the entrance of the "baby boom" generation born after World War II into the 15–25 age group (Ferdinand 1970). In the 1970s, demographers projected that, as the baby boom generation aged and the birth rate slowed, there would be fewer people in this age group by the 1980s. These projections led criminologists to predict that the crime rate in the 1980s would level off and perhaps even decline, which is apparently what happened (Steffensmeier and Harer 1991).

 ## CHRONIC OFFENDERS AND CRIMINAL CAREERS

One of the most important findings of self-report studies, especially those studying the same people over time, is that a few adolescents commit most of the offenses, especially serious offenses (Visher 2000). A study of almost 10,000 males born in

Philadelphia in 1945 found that about 6 percent of the sample committed more than half of all serious crimes committed by the whole group by the time they all turned 18 (Wolfgang, Figlio, and Sellin 1972). A similar study of close to 1,400 males born in 1955 in Racine, Wisconsin, found that 6.5 percent of the sample accounted for 70 percent of all felonies committed by the entire group (Shannon 1988). While many young people break the law, their offenses are usually minor ones. As these studies indicate, however, a small number commit many offenses each, particularly the more serious offenses, and persist in their offending over time (Tracey, Wolfgang, and Figlio 1990).

These chronic offenders often continue their offending into adulthood as they enter criminal careers (Blumstein et al. 1986; Elliott 1994). Career criminality is more common among those with low education and bleak job prospects, characteristics most common of the urban underclass (Sampson and Wilson 1995). Although some scholars feel that offending does not continue long into adulthood and thus dispute the existence of criminal careers (Gottfredson and Hirschi 1988), most accept the concept as a valid characterization of a small number of offenders (Blumstein, Cohen, and Farrington 1988).

CRIME AND CONTROVERSY

Criminal Potential and Life Events after Childhood

The new focus on chronic offenders and criminal careers has alerted scholars to the prime importance of early childhood problems for later criminality. Echoing the Gluecks' earlier findings (see this chapter), scholars now highlight inadequate parenting and negative school experiences (see Chapter 7), but differ on whether these experiences can be offset by later life events.

Taking a skeptical view, Michael Gottfredson and Travis Hirschi believe that later life events do not diminish the likelihood of criminal behavior. In their view, early childhood problems lead to low self-control, which in turn leads to antisocial behavior during childhood, delinquency during adolescence, and crime during young adulthood. This pattern, they say, persists despite any changes in an individual's life, including marriage and employment.

Other scholars assert that later life events do matter. In their reanalysis of the Gluecks' data, Robert J. Sampson and John Laub highlighted the effects of adult social bonds, most notably marriage and employment, on reducing criminality, and concluded that "childhood pathways to crime and deviance can be significantly modified over the life course by adult social bonds" (p. 611). Specifically, young men who marry or join the labor force are more likely to desist from crime than those who do not develop these adult social bonds.

In a recent study, Julie Horney and two colleagues extended Sampson and Laub's work by analyzing changes in life events over short periods of time. They interviewed 658 newly convicted male offenders incarcerated in Nebraska during 1989 and 1990. The authors found that offending was higher for those offenders living with a girlfriend but lower for those living with a wife. It was also lower when they were attending school and higher when they were using illegal drugs. The authors concluded that "social events during adulthood are related to crime" (pp. 671–672).

Findings like those of Sampson and Laub and of Horney and her colleagues indicate that life events after childhood can inhibit criminality, and suggest that Gottfredson and Hirschi erred in assuming otherwise. To acknowledge the importance of adult life events does not, of course, mean we must minimize the effect of negative experiences during early childhood. Both periods seem very important in explaining the onset and cessation of criminal behavior.

If adult life events do matter for criminal potential, social policies to reduce crime should take this period of life into account. For example, increased employment opportunities during young adulthood should reduce crime rates by people in this age group. Similarly, if marriage reduces a man's criminal potential outside the marriage, then policies aimed at preventing marital breakup and divorce should also prevent crime.

Sources: Gottfredson and Hirschi 1990; Gottfredson and Hirschi 1986; Horney, Osgood, and Marshall 1995; Sampson and Laub 1993; Sampson and Lauritsen 1990.

Knowledge of the age patterning of crime and of the existence of career criminals is important for efforts to reduce crime. The "three strikes and you're out" legislation popular a few years ago required life imprisonment for people convicted of a third felony. Since imprisonment would continue long after the criminality of most offenders would have declined anyway (after they left young adulthood), critics charged that this legislation would increase prison overcrowding but do little to reduce crime (see Chapter 16). In another area, criminal justice officials and social scientists have begun to try to predict the likelihood of career criminality in order to identify and target career criminals for innovative means of punishment and treatment (Visher 2000). However, such prediction has been less than accurate, with many "false positives" resulting (people falsely predicted to be career criminals), and efforts to target career criminals remain beset by various legal and ethical dilemmas.

 ## SUMMARY AND CONCLUSION

I hope this chapter has shown the importance and complexity of measuring crime. The way we measure crime is critical for understanding its origins and reducing it. If we don't measure crime accurately enough, we may miss important factors that underlie it, and thus we cannot hope to reduce crime to any appreciable degree.

All the major sources of crime statistics have their advantages and disadvantages. The UCR provide us the best data for understanding the geographical distribution of crime but greatly underestimate the actual number of crimes and are subject to possible police bias. They also tell us relatively little about the social context of crime and victimization and about the characteristics of victims. NCVS data give us the best estimate of the actual number of crimes, but even they underestimate certain crimes. They also include many relatively minor offenses and exclude commercial crimes and homicide, as well as most Part II offenses. NCVS data provide solid information on the context and consequences of victimization and the characteristics of victims. The third major data source, self-report research, supplies comprehensive information about offenders, including the many influences on their behavior, but is generally limited to adolescents. Inclusion of serious offenses in the most recent self-report studies has made them even more valuable.

Because the three major sources of crime statistics don't cover white-collar crime, they tell us little about it and reinforce impressions that white-collar crime is not as serious or as common as street crime. But together they provide a reasonably good picture of street crime in the United States. The picture is of a relatively small number of violent crimes and a much larger number of property crimes. Despite continuing debate, it is also one of offenders who tend to be male, nonwhite and especially black, poor, and young.

The gender distribution of street crime alerts us to two related phenomena: Something about being a female in our society inhibits criminality, and something about being a male promotes it. Continued research on the reasons for this gender difference thus holds great promise for crime reduction. The racial and class distribution of street crime alerts us not only to the effect of race and class on criminality but also to the structural factors accounting for this effect. These factors can and must be explored without resorting to explanations that smack of racial or class prejudice.

Now that we have some idea of the extent of street crime and of the characteristics of offenders in the United States, it's almost time to turn to explanations of such crime. But first we explore further in the next chapter the characteristics of crime victims and the theories and consequences of victimization.

KEY TERMS

chronic offenders

climatological

criminal careers

differential opportunities

international comparisons

life events

measurement

National Crime Victimization Survey

patterning

property crime

seasonal

self-report studies

subculture of violence

underclass

underreporting

Uniform Crime Reports

victimization

violent crime

 ## STUDY QUESTIONS

1. What are any four criticisms of Uniform Crime Reports data? In what ways are the UCR superior to and inferior to victimization and self-report data?

2. Why does the United States have higher crime rates than Japan and several other nations? How do international comparisons of crime rates reflect the sociological perspective?

3. Why do women have lower crime rates than men? To what degree are changes in women's crime rates related to the contemporary women's movement?

4. Why do African-Americans have higher crime rates than whites? Is it racist to claim that this racial difference in crime exists?

INTERNET EXERCISES

As the text notes, the FBI's Uniform Crime Reports is a major source of crime data. You can look at these data yourself by going to **http://www.fbi.gov/ucr.htm**. Scroll down just a bit until you see **Crime in the United States**. Under this click **1999**. Now click **Section II—Crime Index Offenses Reported**. (*Note:* you'll need the Adobe Acrobat reader, discussed in the Internet exercise for Chapter 1, to access UCR information. If you don't already have this reader on your computer, you should download it now by going to the Adobe Acrobat Web site at **http://www.adobe.com/products/acrobat/readstep.html**). The first page you see for Section II—Crime Index Crimes Reported should say **Crime Index Total** at the top. What is the number of offenses reported for 1999? What percent increase or decrease was this from 1998? Scroll down further until you see some information on regional differences in the total crime rate. Which region of the United States had the highest crime rate? Which had the lowest? You'll also see some information on the **Law Enforcement Response**. How many arrests for Index crimes occurred in 1999? What was the clearance rate? Further down you should see a pie chart indicating the percent distribution of all Index crimes. What percent of the total is accounted for by larceny-theft?

VICTIMS
AND VICTIMIZATION

Crime in the News

*T*he headline of the newspaper article is poignant: "Robbery threatens a lifetime of memories: 84-year-old woman terrorized in home." The subsequent story is equally moving. The attacker forced open a door of the victim's home in the early afternoon, woke her from her nap, hit her in the face with his fist, and broke several facial bones. After shouting "Give me your money or I'll kill you!" the thief took several hundred dollars from the social security check the grandmother had recently cashed and left as quickly as he had come.

The victim, who had lived in her home for more than 70 years, doesn't want to move in with her son in a safer neighborhood: "I don't like to move," she says from her hospital bed. "I've been there all these years. My father built it and gave it to me and said, 'Take good care of it.' I'll still stay there." But her son is not so sure: "It's no place for her to be alone." A few years ago someone else had broken into her house, and several months earlier a purse snatcher had broken her arm. The son does not want his mother to return to her home.

Source: Coakley 1994.

*B*efore the 1960s, we knew little about crime victims. With criminals monopolizing the attention of social scientists and government officials, victims remained hidden from the public agenda and from the scrutiny of social science. When they were discussed, the focus was on how they helped cause their own victimization (Hentig 1948).

Crime victims began to attract more attention in the late 1960s as the growing crime rate and urban unrest in the United States heightened interest in "law and order." The courts, it was said, were giving too many rights to criminals and not enough to their victims. This concern helped put victims on the public agenda. At about the same time, feminists began to address rape as a major crime. Bringing new attention to rape survivors in particular and to crime victims more generally, this focus emphasized the perspective of women who had been raped and challenged views that they bore any blame for their victimization. It also addressed the psychological and other consequences of rape and women's experiences in the criminal justice system. Somewhat later, family violence against women began to receive similar attention. The study of victims, or victimology, had begun (Karmen 2000).

The growing interest in victims led to the initiation of the National Crime Survey, now known as the National Crime Victimization Survey (NCVS). As Chapter 3 noted, the NCVS has significantly increased our understanding of victims and victimization. Several other victimization surveys in the United States and other nations have added to this understanding, and today the field of victimology is flourishing. This chapter discusses what we know about victims and victimization.

 # DEFINING VICTIMS AND STUDYING VICTIMIZATION

No doubt you or someone you know has worried about becoming a victim of a crime such as a robbery, burglary, assault, rape, or theft of something from your car or dorm room. Have you ever worried about becoming a victim of price fixing or false advertising? Would you even know if you had been a victim? Have you worried about being a victim of air or water pollution? You might know that the air and water aren't as clean as they could be, but does that make you a victim of a crime? Have you ever worried about eating bacteria-laden poultry or meat, taking unsafe medicine, or driving an unsafe car? If you, or someone you know, has ever taken ill or been injured in the workplace, did it occur to you that this might constitute crime victimization?

What exactly is a crime victim? Presumably, one definition is someone who suffers because of a crime. But what if someone or, worse yet, many someones suffer from behavior that doesn't violate the law and thus isn't a crime? To take one example, U.S. pharmaceutical companies routinely export (usually to Third World nations) dangerous drugs that are prohibited in the United States. Because no U.S. law prohibits the drug companies from sending their products elsewhere, they don't commit any crime. But this noncriminal behavior still causes death and illness, especially in children, every year (Braithwaite 1984; Henry and Chomicki 1990).

Another example involving children concerns various corporations that sent infant formula to Third World nations, where it was sold or distributed as free samples to new mothers. Seeing a potential source of great profit, these corporations stressed the ease of formula feeding. Unfortunately, the mothers were often illiterate

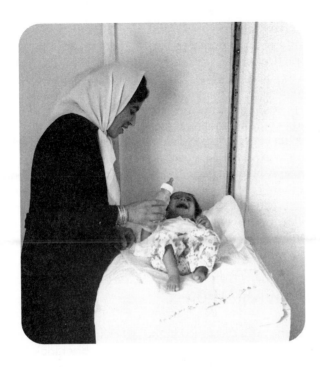

◄ *Not long ago several corporations marketed infant formula in Third World nations. The companies stressed the ease of formula feeding but failed to ensure that the Third World consumers were able to understand the directions for preparing and using the formula. Many babies became malnourished and even died from starvation as a result of improper use of the formula. Despite the consequences, no laws were broken, and the corporations committed no crimes in distributing the formula.*

and couldn't understand the directions for preparing formula. They mixed it with dirty water that hadn't been boiled and sterilized and, to save money, often gave their babies less formula than required. Thinking the baby bottle had magical properties, some mothers even let their infants suck on empty bottles. Many infants acquired intestinal ailments, became severely malnourished, or even died. An international protest campaign and boycott began and lasted several years until the companies finally ceased "their lucrative but deadly practices" (Viano 1990:xvi). In the larger sense of the word *victim*, these children were clearly victims—though technically not crime victims, since no official crime had been committed.

As this brief discussion suggests, people can be victimized in many ways, but only sometimes are they victims of actual legally defined crimes. They can be victims of legal behavior by the kinds of multinational corporations mentioned earlier, but that does not make them *crime victims*. They can also be victims of illegal behavior by corporations. That does make them victims of criminal behavior, but they are not the kinds of victims to whom our hearts go out. We certainly don't hear about them in the news media, and *they* might not even be aware of their victimization. Finally, people can be victims of violations of civil liberties and human rights, including government surveillance, torture, and genocide. If we expand the definition of victims and victimization even further, we may talk about people as victimized by poverty, institutional racism, and/or institutional sexism. The term *institutional* implies that the very structure of society is one that inherently oppresses, subtly or more overtly, the poor, women, and people of color.

When we move away from individual victims of street crimes to mass victims of white-collar crime, human rights violations, and the like, we are talking about "collective victimization," much of it international in scope. Unfortunately, as Viano (1990:xvii) points out, such collective victimization "has generally been neglected as a field of study and research." Because victimology has focused on street crimes, we know far more about victimization by such crimes than we do about victimization by other kinds of crimes and by legal but harmful behaviors (Levi 1992).

No universally accepted definition of *crime victim* exists. Defining *victims* as people suffering from street crimes or, more broadly, as those hurt by harmful corporate practices or institutional racism is ultimately a matter of personal viewpoint. As Karmen (1990:11) observes, "The key question becomes 'Which suffering people get designated as victims, and which don't, and why?' The answer is important, since it determines whether or not public and private resources will be mobilized to help them out, and end their mistreatment."

Since the beginning of victimology almost four decades ago, the answer has been that victims are those people suffering from street crimes. Since street crime is a serious problem, especially in poor urban neighborhoods, the victimization it causes certainly merits scholarly attention. Reflecting the victimology literature, this chapter deals mostly with street crime. But keep in mind that victimization by white-collar crime also deserves the concern of the public, elected officials, and social scientists.

THE PATTERNING OF VICTIMIZATION

Like the crime rates discussed in the last chapter, victimization rates are patterned geographically and socially. Let's start with a brief look at geographical patterns.

Geographical Patterns

Victimization rates as measured by the NCVS differ across the United States. For violent crime, the West has the highest victimization rate, and the Northeast and South the lowest. (Recall from Chapter 3, however, that the South has a high violent crime rate according to UCR data; differences in the two data sources probably account for this discrepancy.) For property crime victimization, the West again has the highest rate, and the Northeast the lowest. Meanwhile, cities have higher victimization rates than rural areas (Figure 4.1).

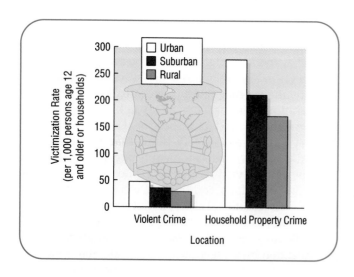

◀ FIGURE 4.1   **VICTIMIZATION RATES AND PLACE OF RESIDENCE, 1998** (NUMBER PER 1,000 PERSONS 12 OR OLDER OR 1,000 HOUSEHOLDS)

Source: Rennison 1999.

▲ *Urban areas have higher crime victimization rates than do rural areas.*

Social Patterns

Victimization rates also vary by the demographic characteristics of people. Table 4.1 (on page 84) displays the relevant data for violent crime (aggravated and simple assault, rape and sexual assault, and robbery) and for household property crime (burglary, motor vehicle theft, and other, miscellaneous thefts). Our discussion centers on these data and also on other information not reported in the table.

GENDER, RACE, AND ETHNICITY

For the combined measure of violence reported in Table 4.1, males have a higher victimization rate than females and, indeed, are twice as likely as females to be victimized by aggravated assault. Males are especially likely to be homicide victims, as there are about 3.5 male homicide victims for every 1 female victim. However, women experience almost all the rape victimization reported to NCVS interviewers and almost all of the assaults by family members and other intimates (see Chapter 10).

Blacks are slightly more likely than whites to be violent crime victims, but non-Hispanics (which include most blacks) are slightly more likely than Hispanics to be such victims. The black-white difference is much greater for homicides, as blacks are almost seven times as likely as whites to be homicide victims (see Figure 4.2 on page 84). For household property crime, black households have an appreciably higher rate of victimization than either white households or those of members of other races.

American Indians are also vulnerable to crime victimization. From 1992 to 1996, the average annual violence victimization rate for this group was 124 per 1,000 persons twelve and older, compared to only 50 per 1,000 for the entire nation. American Indians are thus more than twice as likely as people in general to be violent crime victims, and their rate of violence victimization is much higher than that for any other racial or ethnic subgroup. They're also more likely than the other subgroups to be victimized by someone of a different race (Greenfeld and Smith 1999). In the last decade there were signs that violence on Indian reservations was

TABLE 4.1 — VIOLENT VICTIMIZATION RATES AND DEMOGRAPHIC CHARACTERISTICS, 1998
(RATE PER 1,000 PERSONS 12 OR OLDER)

VARIABLE	VIOLENCE	HOUSEHOLD PROPERTY CRIME
Sex		
Male	43	—
Female	30	—
Age		
12–15	83	—
16–19	91	—
20–24	67	—
25–34	42	—
35–49	30	—
50–64	15	—
65 or older	3	—
Race		
White	36	213
Black	42	248
Other	28	224
Ethnicity		
Hispanic	33	268
Non-Hispanic	37	212
Family Income		
Less than $7,500	64	209
$7,500–$14,999	49	230
$15,000–$24,999	39	211
$25,000–$34,999	42	233
$35,000–$49,999	32	222
$50,000–$74,999	32	249
$75,000 or more	33	249

Source: Rennison 1999.

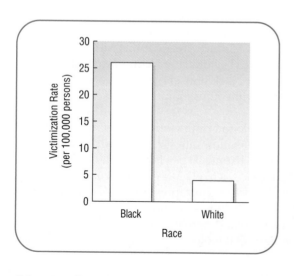

◀ FIGURE 4.2 RACE AND HOMICIDE VICTIMIZATION, 1997
(NUMBER OF VICTIMS PER 100,000 PERSONS)
Source: Maguire and Pastore 1999.

Cross-National Victimization Patterns

Chapter 3 noted that the United States has the highest rate of serious violent crime in the Western world. This is the conclusion of police statistics gathered by Interpol and the United Nations and also, perhaps more reliably, of victimization surveys conducted in many nations in the last fifteen years or so. Just behind the United States in violent victimization are Australia and Canada. European nations such as England, Germany, France, and Sweden have violent victimization rates only about half the U.S. rate. Homicide victimization in the United States exceeds that in other nations by an even greater margin: at least three to four times greater. However, the U.S. rate for minor violence does not exceed that in other industrialized, common-law nations (Britain and its former colonies). In property victimization, the U.S. rate is about average for democratic nations.

Despite the different victimization rates and other differences among these nations, the demographic victimization patterns reported for the United States are also found in other countries. For example, higher victimization rates exist for urban residents than for rural residents, for young people than for older people, and for men (excluding rape) than for women. The international similarity of these patterns underscores the impact of residence, age, and gender on the risk for victimization.

Police and victimization survey data from the Netherlands reinforce this point. Since the early 1990s, public concern about crime there has increased, especially over burglary and robbery. The Netherlands' highest crime rates are found in the four most urbanized regions in the western part of the country; cities in these regions have much higher crime rates than other areas. Young people are much more likely than older people to be victimized, especially by bicycle theft (an extremely common crime in the Netherlands) and assault. Repeat victimization (more than once a year) is more common in the Netherlands among young people, minorities, and big-city residents. These demographic patterns resemble those found in the United States.

Like U.S. residents, the Dutch take many precautions to prevent crime. Two-thirds of all homes have extra locks, and in almost two-thirds of all homes a light is left on when the house is empty. Other "private security" measures appear to have risen dramatically since the early 1980s. In another similarity, the early 1980s also saw an increase in efforts to aid crime victims. In 1984 the Dutch started a national network of seventy-two agencies called the Association of National Victim Support, which has since helped more than 100,000 victims.

Sources: Eijken 1995; Lynch 1995; van Dijk and Kangaspunta 2000; van Dijk and Mayhew 1993.

becoming even worse. Although the U.S. homicide rate declined dramatically during most of the 1990s, the rate on reservations rose 87 percent from 1992 to 1996. At a Navajo reservation in Arizona, the rate was four times greater than the U.S. rate (Sahagun 1998).

FAMILY INCOME

Table 4.1 shows some important differences in violent crime victimization rates for people with different family incomes. Generally, the lower the income, the higher the rate of victimization. Figure 4.3 (on page 86) displays this trend graphically. For household property crime, however, this relationship is reversed, as the victimization rate generally increases as income increases. This trend bears further scrutiny, however. It holds true for the miscellaneous thefts that are one of the three types of household property crime (and by far the largest type), but not for the other two types, burglary and motor vehicle theft. For burglary, victimization rates

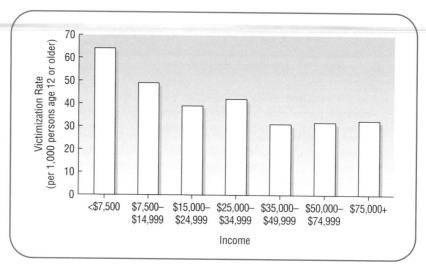

▲ FIGURE 4.3   FAMILY INCOME AND VIOLENT VICTIMIZATION, 1998
(NUMBER PER 1,000 PERSONS 12 OR OLDER)
Source: Rennison 1999.

are higher for households with lower incomes, and are twice as high for those in the lowest income bracket than for those in the highest. For motor vehicle theft, income is not related to the rate of victimization (Rennison 1999).

AGE

Figure 4.4 (on page 87) displays the striking difference that age makes in violent victimization. Paralleling age differences in crime rates discussed in the previous chapter, young people are much more likely than older people to be violent crime victims. Recall from Chapter 2 that although people 65 and older are more fearful of crime than their younger counterparts, their victimization rates are much lower (Klaus 2000). We noted the likely reasons for this apparent paradox: The elderly feel more vulnerable because of their slower physical movement; however, because of their fear, they are more likely than younger people to stay at home and otherwise avoid possible places of victimization. These explanations notwithstanding, a recent study suggests that older people's fear of crime may be justified. Fox and Levin (1991) examined data indicating whether robberies had ended in homicides. Although most robberies don't lead to homicide, they found that, to the extent that homicide does result, it's more likely to happen to the elderly than to younger people.

RACE, GENDER, AND AGE COMBINED

In Chapter 2 we saw how race and gender interact to produce especially high fear of crime among black women, and in Chapter 3 we saw how race, gender, and age combine to produce higher crime rates among young black men. So far in this chapter we have seen that victimization rates are higher for blacks than for whites, for men than for women, and for the young than for the old. Is it possible that race and

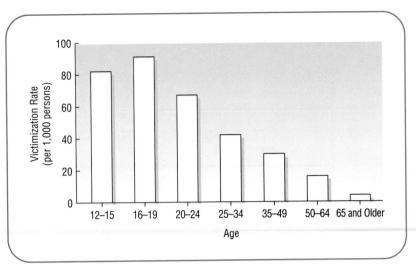

▲ FIGURE 4.4   AGE AND VIOLENT VICTIMIZATION, **1998**
(NUMBER PER 1,000 PERSONS 12 OR OLDER)
Source: Rennison 1999.

gender, along with age, also interact to produce especially high victimization rates for young black men and especially low ones for older white women? The answer is yes. To illustrate, Table 4.2 reports homicide victimization rates for various age, race, and gender categories. In each age group, black males are the most likely and white females the least likely of the four race-gender categories to be homicide crime victims. The highest rate, 143 for black men 18–24 years old, is about 72 times greater than the lowest rate, 2.1, for white women 25 and older.

TABLE 4.2   AGE, RACE, GENDER, AND HOMICIDE VICTIMIZATION, **1997**
(RATE PER 100,000 PERSONS)

CATEGORY	RATE
Age 18–24	
Black males	143.4
Black females	15.9
White males	15.1
White females	3.5
Age 25 and older	
Black males	47.1
Black females	10.1
White males	6.0
White females	2.1

Source: Maguire and Pastore 1999.

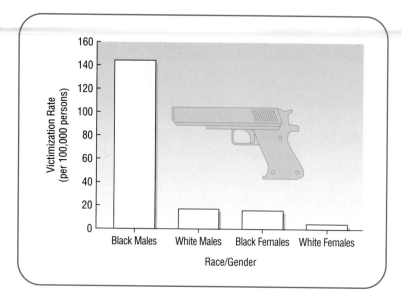

◀ FIGURE 4.5 RACE, GENDER, AND HOMICIDE VICTIMIZATION, AGES 18–24, 1997 (NUMBER OF VICTIMS PER 100,000)

Source: Maguire and Pastore 1999.

To reinforce the difference race and gender make in victimization, Figure 4.5 displays the homicide victimization rates for the 18–24 age group. Within each gender, blacks are much more likely than whites to be killed; within each race, males are much more likely than females to be killed. Race and gender certainly affect our chances of dying a violent death.

The Victim–Offender Relationship

STRANGERS VERSUS NONSTRANGERS

Recall that the NCVS asks respondents who report assault, rape, or robbery victimization whether they knew the offender. This information yields a valuable portrait of the victim-offender relationship. Although this might surprise you, strangers commit less than half of these offenses combined, with the remainder committed by family members, friends, and acquaintances. When we examine the victim-offender relationship by gender, some important differences emerge (Table 4.3). In short, although men are more likely than women to be victims of violent crime,

TABLE 4.3	PERCENT OF LONE-OFFENDER VICTIMIZATIONS INVOLVING STRANGERS (BY TYPE OF CRIME AND GENDER)		
TYPE OF CRIME		FEMALE	MALE
Aggravated assault		30	51
Simple assault		19	45
Robbery		48	69
Rape/sexual assault		18	—
Total Victimizations		23	49

Source: Bachman and Saltzman 1995.

women are much more likely than men to be attacked by someone they know. In fact, women are three times as likely to be attacked by someone they know (77 percent) than by a stranger (23 percent). A similar gender difference in victimization has been found in England (Mawby and Walklate 1994).

The NCVS has also determined whether the extent of stranger involvement in violent victimization differs by race and by urban-rural residence. Although no substantial racial differences have been found, victimization by strangers is more common in urban and suburban areas than in rural areas (Bastian and DeBerry 1994).

PERCEIVED RACE, GENDER, AND AGE OF OFFENDERS

As noted in the previous chapter, NCVS respondents who have been crime victims report that the race, gender, and age distribution of offenders is similar to that found in UCR arrest data: disproportionately young, nonwhite, and male. Table 4.4 includes the relevant NCVS data for race. Although whites account for the majority of all offenses, the proportion of offenders perceived as nonwhite exceeds their proportion in the national population. This is especially true for robbery, where blacks are perceived as committing 43 percent of all single-offender robberies.

Again paralleling UCR arrest data, NCVS respondents perceive that most offenders (more than 85 percent) in lone-offender crimes are male. Although NCVS respondents' perceptions of offenders' ages are inexact, they do report that most of their offenders are young, once more replicating what UCR arrest data tell us: For all violent crimes involving one offender, almost two-thirds are perceived as being under 30 years old.

Some of the most important NCVS data concern the race of the offender and of the victim. One of the central myths of the public perception of crime today is that black offenders prey on white victims. NCVS data reveal a quite different pattern, however, as they show that most crime is *intraracial*, meaning that it occurs within the same race. In about 80 percent of all violent crimes, offenders and victims are of the same race. Figure 4.6 (on page 90) illustrates this dynamic for homicide. A full 85 percent of all homicides are intraracial: Whites tend to kill whites, and blacks tend to kill blacks. Homicides involving black offenders and white victims account for only 7 percent of the total. Robbery is the most interracial (i.e., between the races) crime, as about one-third involve black offenders and white victims.

TABLE 4.4

PERCEIVED RACE OF OFFENDER IN SINGLE-OFFENDER VICTIMIZATIONS, 1997

TYPE OF CRIME	WHITE	BLACK	OTHER
All violent crimes	62%	25%	10%
Rape/sexual assault	63	21	16
Robbery	38	43	15
Assault	64	24	10

Source: Maguire and Pastore 1999.

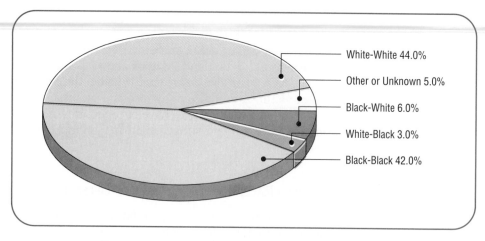

▲ FIGURE 4.6   RACE OF OFFENDER-VICTIM FOR SINGLE OFFENDER/SINGLE VICTIM
HOMICIDES, 1998
Source: Federal Bureau of Investigation 1999.

Crime Characteristics

In addition to the demographic data just presented, the NCVS also contains much information on various crime characteristics, including the use of alcohol and other drugs, the time and place of occurrence of crime, the use of weapons, and the extent of self-protection and resistance by victims.

THE USE OF ALCOHOL AND OTHER DRUGS

Chapter 14 discusses this topic in greater detail, but it's worth noting here that crime victims report rather heavy involvement of alcohol and drugs in the commission of violent crimes: Victims perceive that offenders were under the influence of alcohol or drugs in about 44 percent of all the violent crimes in which they could distinguish whether these substances had been used. Alcohol was the lone drug used in 29 percent of these offenses; and drugs other than alcohol were used in 8 percent; both alcohol and drugs were used in 6 percent (Greenfield 1998).

TIME AND PLACE OF OCCURRENCE

Whereas a majority of all violent crimes and about 60 percent of all household thefts occur at night, the majority of personal thefts occur during the day. The largest single proportion of violent crime, 20 percent, occurs on the street away from the victim's home (Table 4.5), with the next most common site the victim's home. About 25 percent of all crimes involving nonstrangers occur in the victim's home, compared to only 3 percent of crimes involving strangers.

USE OF WEAPONS

According to NCVS respondents, weapons are used in about 24 percent of all violent crimes, including 22 percent of assaults, 9 percent of rapes and sexual assaults, and 39 percent of robberies. Strangers are more likely than nonstrangers to use

TABLE 4.5

PLACE OF OCCURRENCE FOR VIOLENT CRIME
(% OF ALL INCIDENTS)

PLACE	PERCENTAGE
On street away from victim's home	20
At victim's home	15
School building/property	13
Near victim's home	10
Parking lot or garage	9
In or near someone else's home	8
Other commercial building	7
Restaurant, bar, nightclub	5
Park, field, playground	3
Other	9

Source: Bastian 1995.

weapons. About one-third of the weapons are firearms, most of them handguns, and about 25 percent are knives. The remainder includes blunt objects such as clubs or rocks (Rennison 1999).

VICTIM SELF-PROTECTION AND RESISTANCE

NCVS findings indicate that most violent crime victims do not passively let the crime occur, as almost 75 percent try to keep the crime from being completed. About 20 percent struggle with the offender, and about 15 percent try to run away or hide. About 10 percent try to persuade the offender not to go through with the crime; and almost 15 percent attack or threaten the offender with bodily injury. Women and men are about equally likely to take at least one of these measures. Victims who do use such measures say they helped the situation about 67 percent of the time, hurt the situation 8 percent of the time, both helped and hurt the situation 8 percent of the time, and neither helped nor hurt the situation 12 percent of the time (Maguire and Pastore 1999).

Intimate Violence

The NCVS and other victimization surveys have provided important information on the nature and extent of *intimate violence*. We'll look further at such violence in Chapter 10, but for now comment briefly on what the NCVS and other studies tell us about it. *Intimate violence* involves any rape, robbery, or sexual or physical assault committed by spouses, ex-spouses, partners (boyfriends/girlfriends) and ex-partners. The NCVS estimates that 956,200 intimate violent offenses occurred in 1998, with about 85 percent of these, or about 810,000, committed against women (Rennison 1999). Women are thus much more likely than men to suffer violence at the hands of intimates: accounting for 21 percent of the violent crime women suffer but only 2 percent of the violence men suffer. To put that another way, about 7.5 of every 1,000 women experience a violent victimization by an intimate every year, compared to only 1 of every 1,000 men. Paralleling the overall drop in street crime during the middle and late 1990s, the 810,000 intimate victimizations women experienced in 1998 were lower than the 1.1 million they experienced in 1993 (Greenfeld et al. 1998).

Table 4.6 presents the demographic correlates of intimate violence against women. Higher rates are found against blacks than whites and, reflecting our earlier look at the age pattern for violent victimization, against younger females than older ones. Again reflecting our earlier look at violent victimization, intimate violence is more common against poorer women than wealthier ones, and more common against urban women than their suburban or rural counterparts.

NCVS data on sexual violence are illuminating. The NCVS estimates that about 333,000 rapes and sexual assaults (including attempts) occurred in 1998. Almost all of these (93 percent) were committed against women, whose victimization rate for rape and sexual assault was 2.7 per 1,000 persons, compared to a male rate of 0.2 per 1,000 persons. Most of the rapes and sexual assaults reported to

---

TABLE 4.6 CORRELATES OF INTIMATE VIOLENCE AGAINST FEMALES
(RATE PER 1,000 FEMALES AGE 12 OR OLDER)

VARIABLE	RATE
Race	
White	8.2
Black	11.7
Other	5.6
Ethnicity	
Hispanic	7.2
Non-Hispanic	8.7
Age	
12–15	2.6
16–19	20.1
20–24	20.7
25–34	16.5
35–49	7.2
50–64	1.3
65 or older	0.2
Annual Household Income	
Less than $7,500	21.3
$7,500–$14,999	12.3
$15,000–$24,999	10.4
$25,000–$34,999	7.2
$35,000–$49,999	5.8
$50,000–$74,999	4.4
$75,000 or more	2.7
Location of Residence	
Urban	10.0
Suburban	7.9
Rural	8.0

Source: Greenfeld et al. 1998.

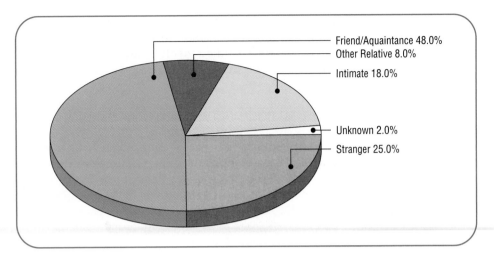

▲ **Figure 4.7** **Victim-Offender Relationship for Rape/Sexual Assault, 1998 NCVS**
Source: Rennison 1999.

NCVS interviewers were committed by someone the victim knew, and only 25 percent by a stranger (Figure 4.7).

Other studies have also focused on intimate violence, particularly rape. The 1996 National Violence Against Women Survey (NVAW) of 8,000 women 18 and older found that almost 18 percent had experienced a completed or attempted rape at some point in their lifetime and 0.3 percent (almost identical to the 0.27 percent NCVS finding just noted) had been raped (2.9 times each on the average) in the previous year. These percentages yielded the following estimates: Close to 18 million U.S. women have been raped (including attempts) in their lifetime; 300,000 were raped in 1996; and almost 900,000 rapes occurred in 1996. Of the women in the survey who had been raped since turning 18, about 17 percent had been raped by a stranger; 62 percent had been raped by an intimate partner (husband/ex-husband, boyfriend/ex-boyfriend, or date); and 28 percent by another relative or an acquaintance (Tjaden and Thoennes 1998). (These percentages exceed 100 percent because some victims had multiple offenders.)

The NCVS, NVAW, and related studies yield a striking conclusion: The popular perception of rape involving a stranger attacking a woman is a myth. In the NCVS, women are three times as likely to be raped by someone they know as by a stranger, and, in the NVAW, they are about six times as likely to be raped by someone they know as by a stranger.

 ## EXPLAINING VICTIMIZATION

Now that we know something about crime victims, let's take a look at why they get victimized. When we attempt to explain crime, we are trying to explain two related phenomena: Why do some locations have higher crime rates than others, and why are some individuals more likely than others to commit crime? Theories of crime attempt to answer these questions and are presented in several of the following chapters. When we try to explain victimization, we ask similar questions:

Why do some locations have higher victimization rates than others, and why are some individuals more likely than others to become crime victims? The factors victimologists have studied involve the opportunities for criminal behavior and victimization. Let's see what they say.

Lifestyle and Routine Activities Theory

The most popular theory of victimization stems from two originally separate theories, *lifestyle theory* and *routine activities theory*, developed about the same time in the late 1970s. Although they have somewhat different emphases, they overlap considerably, as both assume that "the habits, lifestyles, and behavioral patterns of potential crime victims enhance their contact with offenders and thereby increase the chances that crimes will occur" (Miethe and Meier 1990:244). As a result, the theories today are often treated as components of one larger theory (Meier and Miethe 1993).

Lifestyle theory stresses that the lifestyles of some people put them more at risk than others for becoming crime victims (Garofalo 1987). These are people who spend a lot of time outside their homes in places such as bars and nightclubs or just out on the street. These lifestyles increase their chances of becoming crime victims: An argument may break out in a bar, a robber may see an easy target. Recognizing that victimization is often committed by nonstrangers, the theory further assumes that people are more likely to become victims if they spend a lot of time with the kinds of people who themselves commit high numbers of crimes. This helps explain why young people have the highest victimization rate for violent crime: Simply put, they spend so much time with other young people, who as a group commit the highest rates of violence.

Routine activities theory argues that some people engage in regular or routine activities that increase their risk for victimization (Felson 1998). For victimization to occur, three components must coincide: an attractive target (property or people), a motivated offender, and the absence of "guardianship" (e.g., people who might observe and stop the crime from being committed). Thus, as more attractive targets emerge over time (e.g., more empty homes because of increased vacation travel or a rise in single-person households), victimization should increase. As more motivated offenders emerge (perhaps because of increasing unemployment), victimization should also increase.

The convergence of targets, motivated offenders, and absent guardians necessary for victimization is more likely in some neighborhoods than others, and in certain specific locations within neighborhoods. These locations are "hot spots" for crime. Lawrence M. Sherman and his colleagues (Sherman, Gartin, and Buerger 1989) found these hot spots concentrated in a small proportion of all locations. They analyzed more than 300,000 calls to police about "predatory crime" (personal victimization) and commercial crime that occurred in Minneapolis from December 1985 to December 1986. Minneapolis contains about 115,000 "places": 109,000 street addresses of homes and commercial buildings, and 6,000 street intersections. Forty percent of these places generated no calls to the police. Of the remaining 60 percent that did have calls, half had only one call each. Only 3.3 percent of the 115,000 places accounted for a startling 50.4 percent of all calls.

When the researchers looked just at predatory crime, the concentration of calls to police from hot spots was even greater. All the robbery calls came from just 2.2 percent of all Minneapolis places; all calls for rape and other sexual crimes came from just 1.2 percent; and all the calls for auto thefts came from just 2.7 percent. All combined, the calls for robberies, auto thefts, rapes, and other sexual assaults came from only 5 percent of the 115,000 places. To turn that around, 95 percent of the places had no such calls.

The presence of bars and taverns helps turn some locations into hot spots. Because alcohol use promotes aggressive behavior, assaults in and outside bars are common. In addition, people going to bars tend to carry large amounts of money and thus make attractive targets for potential robbers, especially if they become more vulnerable by drinking too much. One study found that the number of taverns on 4,400 city blocks in Cleveland significantly affected the amount of crime on those blocks, even when controlling for other relevant factors (Roncek and Maier 1991).

Victimologists' investigations have become more sophisticated in their use of variables. Early studies inferred opportunity for crime from sociodemographic indicators of respondents and general measures of their activities. Recent research uses more precise measures of respondents' behavior (e.g., the average number of nights a week spent walking alone at night) and of the physical and social characteristics of the neighborhoods in which they live (e.g., the amount of trash and litter in the immediate area) (Lynch and Cantor 1992). This research shows that victimization depends both on people's routine activities and on neighborhood physical characteristics. However, several matters remain in dispute, including whether lifestyle better predicts violent or property victimization, whether target attractiveness and the absence of guardianship are more important for victimization than living near high-crime areas, and even whether time spent away from home predicts risk for burglary (Garofalo and Clark 1992).

Deviant Lifestyles and Victimization

An interesting idea emerging from lifestyle and routine activities theories is that some people increase their chances of becoming crime victims by committing crimes themselves. Their own involvement in crime leads them to visit high crime areas and to be with other offenders. Because offenders who get victimized are naturally reluctant to call police, they're particularly vulnerable to victimization.

Many studies of offending and victimization uncover a statistical connection but haven't shown that offending actually leads to victimization. For example, young people have high rates of both offending and victimization, but that doesn't necessarily mean that their offending puts them at risk for becoming victims. They might simply live in high-crime areas. However, recent research suggests the relationship is not spurious, and deviant lifestyles are now thought to play an important role in criminal victimization (Lauritsen, Sampson, and Laub 1991). For example, a study in California found that the chances of being murdered were greater for youths who were members of gangs and who had been arrested for violence or drugs than for youths who hadn't had such involvement (Lattimore, Linster, and MacDonald 1997). Another study in Columbus, Ohio, found that female gang members were also at risk for victimization by various crimes (Miller 1998).

Deviant lifestyles also make college students more vulnerable to being victimized. A study of college students surveyed at nine campuses found that those who smoked marijuana and had threatened other people were more likely to have had something stolen from them. Supporting routine activities theory, students who often ate out were also more likely to be victims of theft (Mustaine and Tewksbury 1998). Another study of students from twelve campuses reached similar conclusions. Violent victimization was more common for students who spent several nights a week partying and who used marijuana, hashish, or cocaine, while theft victimization was more common for students who spent more money on nonessential items and presumably thus made attractive targets for criminals (Fisher et al. 1998).

Physical Proximity and Victimization

A final explanation argues that if people live in or near high-crime areas, they're more likely to be victimized even if they don't have victimization-prone lifestyles (Garofalo 1987). In a study using British data, Sampson and Lauritsen (1990) also found that proximity to high-crime areas increased victimization even when controlling for various lifestyle factors. Thus offending and proximity both independently affect one's chances of becoming a crime victim. People with deviant lifestyles who also live in or near high-crime areas thus have an especially high risk of becoming crime victims themselves.

Explaining Demographic Variation in Victimization

The theories just discussed help explain the demographic patterns of victimization we saw earlier. If lifestyles, both deviant and nondeviant, affect victimization, then it's not surprising, for example, that young people have much higher rates of victimization than the elderly, as they're much more likely to spend time away from home, especially in bars, nightclubs, and other high-risk areas, and are also more apt to engage in deviant lifestyles. Men are also more likely than women to spend time away from home and to engage in deviant lifestyles. This similarity between young people and men underscores why young males have such particularly high rates of victimization. Turning to race, African-Americans are more apt than whites to live in high-crime areas and thus more likely to become crime victims. Their higher rate of offending for at least some crimes also increases their victimization risk. The same logic applies to people with low family incomes. Given all these factors, it's no surprise that young, black males have a high victimization rate, and that older white females have a low one.

Lifestyle and routine activities theories are less applicable, however, to violent crimes that happen in the home (Mawby and Walklate 1994). Given that these theories focus on predatory crime outside the home, they assume that activities outside the home increase the likelihood of such victimization: "Time spent in one's home generally decreases victim risk, while time spent in public settings increases risk" (Meier and Miethe 1993:466). Because intimate violence often occurs inside the home, however, it can't be attributed to routine activities or lifestyles conducive to victimization. If this is true, these theories of victimization apply less to women than to men, since a greater proportion of women's victimization is from intimate violence. For obvious reasons, the theories are also irrelevant for physical and sexual abuse of children, since children cannot be considered to engage in lifestyles or routine activities conducive to such abuse. Finally, these theories also don't apply to victimization by most white-collar crime.

The Issue of Victim Precipitation

Health-care experts emphasize that people who smoke cigarettes or eat too much fat greatly increase their chances for poor health and early death. They urge such people to stop smoking and to reduce their fat intake. To the extent that people ignore such advice, it's fair to say they bear some blame for any health problems that develop.

Is criminal victimization analogous? Are crime victims to blame for becoming victims? Since lifestyle and routine activities theories explain crime "not in the actions or numbers of motivated offenders, but in the activities and lifestyles of potential victims"(Meier and Miethe 1993:473), they imply that people would be less at risk for victimization if they changed their behavior. Taken to an extreme, they imply that we would all be a lot safer if we never left our homes. By venturing outside, we decrease our guardianship and make ourselves and our homes attractive targets for motivated offenders. People who engage in deviant lifestyles and commit crimes also increase their risk for victimization. It might be possible, of course, to change such lifestyles and cut back on criminality. But most of us don't really have anything to change in these areas. If that's the case, there's little else we can do to reduce our victimization. We have to go to work every day, and we have the right to engage in leisure activities, including vacations. We can't just hide under our beds. That said, it is true that we could be less careless at times. Leaving the keys in the car might be a mistake.

There are some crimes, however, in which victims do seem to play an active role in their own victimization. In 1958 Marvin Wolfgang developed the idea of "victim-precipitated" homicide (Wolfgang 1958), where the eventual victim is the one who was the first to use physical force, including a weapon. The person attacked fights back, perhaps using a weapon, and kills the victim. The victim, in short, precipitates his own death. If the victim hadn't initiated the violent encounter, he might not have been killed. While not meant to excuse the homicide, the concept of victim-precipitated homicide does point to an element of victim responsibility. In his study of 588 homicides, Wolfgang (1958) found that about one-fourth were victim-precipitated. Depending on how "precipitation" is defined, other evidence indicates that some victims also precipitate assaults, robberies, and other crimes (Karmen 2000). This is especially true when women kill their male partners: Almost half of such killings are precipitated by a physical attack by the man on the

◀ *Lifestyle and routine activities theories explain crime "in the activities and lifestyles of potential victims," implying that people would be less at risk for victimization if they changed their behavior. Taken to an extreme, they imply that we would all be a lot safer if we never left our homes. By venturing outside, we decrease our guardianship and make ourselves attractive targets for motivated offenders.*

woman (Felson and Messner 1998). In a recent example of another type of family killing that was victim-precipitated, in March 2000 a New Jersey father was arguing with his 10-year-old son about a missing container of chocolate cake frosting that the father accused the boy of taking. The father handed the boy a kitchen knife and dared him to use it; the boy stabbed his father to death (Associated Press 2000).

Wolfgang's student, Menachem Amir, applied the victim-precipitated concept to rape not too long after Wolfgang developed it for homicide (Amir 1971). Amir defined victim-precipitated rape as any rape that results when a woman engages in sexual relations and then changes her mind, or behaves in any way, including accepting a drink, that could be construed as indicating her interest in having sex. Using this definition, Amir concluded that about one-fifth of the rapes he studied in Philadelphia were precipitated by the victim.

Needless to say, as feminists began to study rape later in the 1970s, they found Amir's notion of victim-precipitated rape repugnant (Russell 1975). It implied that women were somehow at fault for being raped and that rapists simply couldn't control themselves. It also put the burden for avoiding rape on women and fed common myths about the nature of rape. These myths make it very difficult for a rapist to be convicted if there is any evidence that the woman was wearing attractive clothing, had previously been sexually active, or in any other respect could be construed as somehow consenting to sexual activity (see Chapter 10). It may well be true that some homicide victims start the chain of events leading to their death, but it's quite different to say that women precipitate, or bear any responsibility for, their rapes.

 ## The Costs and Consequences of Victimization

Crime victims suffer in many ways. Some are injured and require medical attention; some may even have to miss work or other major life activities. Victims of property crime obviously lose money and property. Yet victims may also suffer various psychological consequences. In the last twenty years, the field of victimology has extensively studied the consequences of victimization. Let's take a look at some of these.

Economic and Medical Costs and Consequences

The NCVS asks its respondents about the economic consequences of their victimizations and the extent of any possible injuries. The numbers the NCVS has compiled are rather impersonal but do indicate the serious impact of crime (Klaus 1994). The most significant economic and medical costs and consequences are as follows:

♦ The crimes the NCVS covers—robbery, rape, assault, personal and household theft, burglary, and auto theft—cost crime victims an estimated $17.6 billion in direct costs. This includes loss to the victim of any money or property stolen or damaged, medical expenses, and any wages lost because of missed work. About 12 percent of all personal crimes and 24 percent of all household crimes involve losses of at least $500.

♦ Only about 10 to 15 percent of victims who had money or property stolen can expect to recover it.

- About 8 percent of all violent crime victims and 6 percent of household crime victims lose time from work, usually a week or less.

- About one-third of all violent crime victims, or about 2 million to 3 million annually, are physically injured. Of those injured, about 84 percent receive cuts and bruises, 7 percent broken bones or teeth knocked out, 4 percent knife wounds, and 1 percent gunshot wounds. About half of those injured require medical treatment, with about two-thirds of this treatment involving professional attention, usually at a hospital. About 4 percent of all injured victims stay in the hospital for at least one night, with the average stay being nine days. A study of teenagers wounded by guns found that the hospitalization costs averaged $14,434 per victim (Connell 1993).

Psychological Consequences

Before the beginning of victimology, criminologists did not study the many psychological consequences suffered by crime victims. Over the last twenty years, psychologists and other scholars have conducted in-depth interviewing of crime victims to get a picture that goes far beyond the straight economic and medical data just discussed. For some people and for some types of crimes, victimization can be especially traumatic (Frieze, Hymer, and Greenberg 1987).

In this context, rape has probably been studied more than any other crime. One approach compares women who report their rapes to the police to other crime victims or to control groups of nonvictims. Although this method has proven useful, its samples might be biased, since most women who are raped, especially those raped by someone they know, don't report their crimes. Recognizing this problem, scholars have queried random samples of women to determine which ones are rape survivors, then asked these women about their experiences.

The picture that develops from both kinds of studies is one of serious consequences that can have a lifelong impact. We've already seen in Chapter 2 that rape plays a large role in women's high fear of crime. Women victimized by rape suffer additional psychological effects, including mild depression and loss of self-esteem. These symptoms begin to subside a few months after the rape for most women but can last much longer for others. Sexual dysfunction—the refusal or inability to engage in sexual relations—is also common, especially for women who were not sexually active before the rape. Several studies indicate that about 20 percent of rape survivors attempt suicide and 40 to 45 percent consider it. Drug abuse, including alcoholism, is also common, perhaps especially among women victimized as children by rape or other sexual abuse (Resick 1990).

Several rape studies address post-traumatic stress disorder (PTSD), defined as "a persistent reexperiencing of a traumatic event through intrusive memories and dreams and by a variety of anxiety-related symptoms" (Lurigio and Resick 1990:51). One study found that 60 percent of rape survivors experience PTSD at some time after the rape. Major depression and other very serious psychological disorders appear in a "significant minority" of women who are raped (Resick 1990:76).

Studies of victims of other types of crimes find similar psychological symptoms that, though serious, tend not to be as severe as those in rape survivors. Victims of burglary, robbery, and nonsexual assault exhibit higher levels than control group nonvictims of fear, vulnerability, anxiety, loss of confidence, sleep difficulties, and other similar symptoms. They also can develop PTSD (Kilpatrick et al.

1987). Along with more major symptoms such as depression, these traits also develop in family violence survivors. Because such violence tends to be repeated, survivors are likely to develop feelings of powerlessness and negative self-concept. Whereas other crime victims are helped greatly by a social support network of relatives, friends, and neighbors, family violence survivors often become socially isolated (Andrews 1990).

Do the psychological consequences of victimization vary by gender, race, social class, and age? Here the results are mixed. Although some studies find women suffering more serious consequences than men for the same kinds of crimes, one study of robbery victims found no such differences. Male victims of sexual assault appear to suffer consequences similar to women's. Turning to race, some studies find black victims suffering more serious consequences than whites, while others find no racial differences. However, social class does appear to make a consistent difference, as people with low incomes and education suffer more serious consequences for the same crimes than people of higher socioeconomic status. In addition, symptoms of wealthier victims subside more quickly than those of their poorer counterparts. Finally, the psychological consequences of crime tend to be less serious for young victims than for older ones, although there is again some evidence to the contrary (Lurigio and Resick 1990).

Finally, one additional line of research investigates whether crimes committed by strangers have more serious consequences than those committed by non-strangers. Most of these studies have examined rape and find that rapes committed by strangers or nonstrangers generally have the same type of impact. However, the evidence is again a bit mixed, and some research suggests that rapes are especially traumatic when committed by nonstrangers (Lurigio and Resick 1990).

Recent research has begun to examine "indirect victimization" among relatives of homicide victims and among partners and husbands of rape victims. In addition to suffering the grief that accompanies any loved one's death, relatives of homicide victims, as well as partners of rape victims, have been found to experience symptoms similar to those of victims of violent crimes, including PTSD (Riggs and Kilpatrick 1990).

 ## Victims in the Criminal Justice System

A growing body of literature addresses the experiences of victims in the criminal justice system. Most of this literature concerns women who have been raped, who are said to be assaulted a second time in the criminal justice system. Such "second victimizations" stem from popular myths about rape. In the past, many police, prosecutors, and judges believed these myths (LeDoux and Hazelwood 1985). Although their attitudes have improved somewhat, criminal justice professionals still greet women's reports of rape with some skepticism (Horne 1993). If anything, jurors believe these myths even more fully. Although many states have passed laws to protect women during prosecutions and trials of their offenders, the burden is still on women to prove they didn't give consent.

Women who have been battered by their current or ex-husbands/boyfriends face similar problems (Bannister 1993). Criminal justice professionals have been slow to recognize that family violence isn't just a private matter. Myths about battering still abound (see Chapter 10), and as they still influence criminal justice professionals to some extent, battered women continue to have trouble getting help from the criminal justice system.

More generally, scholars, elected officials, and criminal justice officials have begun to recognize that crime victims of all stripes feel shut out of the criminal justice process and otherwise have needs that must be addressed (Karmen 2000). As a result, several kinds of services and programs for victims have begun across the United States. Several jurisdictions have developed "victim-witness advocate programs" involving court professionals to help steer victims through the morass of the criminal justice system. Many areas have also begun social service and victim restitution programs to help victims deal with the economic and psychological impact of their victimization.

In another innovation, judges have begun to ask victims to submit *victim-impact statements* to help the judges decide on the appropriate sentence for convicted offenders. Victim involvement in sentencing is meant to increase victims' satisfaction with the criminal justice process. A study of 500 prosecutions of felonies in Ohio found that 62 percent of the victims filled out victim-impact statements. Completion of such statements did not increase victims' satisfaction with the way their case was handled but did make it more likely that judges would imprison defendants. In an interesting twist, some victims who filled out the statements felt that the sentence was not serious enough and became more dissatisfied with the criminal justice process (Erez and Tontodonato 1992). Another study of prosecutions, this time in New York City, found that victim-impact statements did not even affect the likelihood of incarceration (Davis and Smith 1994).

Despite these efforts, victims of all types of crimes continue to feel forgotten, especially when they think offenders have been treated too leniently. In one case, a 17-year-old high school student and budding artist was permanently disabled by a former boyfriend, who later received a prison sentence that was reduced by one year in a plea bargain. The victim's mother was shocked: "It doesn't matter even if it is an hour. Can any court tell her, "'We're going to reduce your pain and suffering?' Can any court give her back the gift of being an artist? No, they can't." Her daughter, confined to a wheelchair, felt no better. "I am now unable to do the simple things that we all take for granted," she told the judge. "I cannot even use the bathroom without an aide. I am now trying to put the pieces of my life back together. But I will never fully recover, at least not emotionally" (Marks 1994:B5).

 ## VICTIMIZATION BY WHITE-COLLAR CRIME

Earlier I stressed the lack of research on white-collar crime victims' experiences. Since the NCVS doesn't ask about white-collar crime, the wealth of information available on the injuries, economic costs, and psychological suffering of street crime victims is lacking for their white-collar crime counterparts. The inattention to white-collar crime victims is unfortunate, as the financial losses, injuries and illnesses, and even deaths that people suffer from white-collar crime are greater than those suffered from street crime (Reiman 1998) (see Chapter 12).

A few recent studies have aimed to fill the gap. One research team interviewed 47 people, many of them elderly, who lost funds when a savings and loan company collapsed because of criminal conduct by its officers and employees (Shover, Fox, and Mills 1994:86–87). Forty percent of the sample lost large sums of money and remained angry about their victimization several years later; a few remained very depressed. One victim said she has thought about it "every day. Every day for eight years. I go to bed with it. I get up with it. I think of it through the day. And my husband ... I haven't seen my husband smile in eight years....

Really, it destroyed our life. We're not happy people anymore." Another victim said, "It's destroying us. It's destroying us. Especially my wife, especially my wife. She ... [is] a walking bag of nerves, very short tempered [and] despondent. And I've been the same way, by the way. I've had my ups and downs." Ironically, many victims blamed themselves for what happened as much as they blamed the savings and loan officials. The researchers called for further research on white-collar crime victims, concluding that "some victims of white-collar crime endure enormous long-term pain and suffering" similar to that experienced by victims of street crime (Shover, Fox, and Mills 1994:96).

VICTIMIZATION OF THE HOMELESS

Another group of victims only recently studied is the homeless. Although there have been many newspaper accounts of attacks on homeless, social science research on their victimization has been lacking. Routine activities theory predicts particularly high victimization rates among the homeless, as they tend to live in high-crime areas and, given their common mental and physical weaknesses, can't defend themselves and thus lack guardianship. A study of 150 homeless adults in Birmingham, Alabama, confirmed their high risk of becoming crime victims (Fitzpatrick, Gory, and Ritchey 1993).

CRIME AND CONTROVERSY

The Politics of Victimization

Several critics argue that government efforts to help crime victims have three undesirable goals: (1) to reduce criticism about ineffective law enforcement; (2) to strengthen public support for the existing political order; and (3) to deflect attention away from white-collar crimes and institutional racism and poverty.

Robert Elias is perhaps the leading proponent of this critique of "the politics of victimization," as he calls it. He observes that the many state and federal government victim-support programs remain woefully underfunded and that crime victims remain irrelevant to the outcomes of most criminal prosecutions. As a result, "victims have gotten far less than promised" (Elias 1990:230). Existing programs perpetuate the idea that violence and other crime is the fault of deviant individuals rather than rooted in the larger society. For example, rape and other sexual assaults are "viewed as a problem of lax enforcement and victim indiscretions, never as a problem of male society," while "the elderly are viewed as victimized

mostly by crime, not by the persistent poverty they often live in" (1990:244). The news media also adopt this individualistic approach to understanding victimization and neglect larger social forces at work, emphasizing the victims of street crime more than those of white-collar crime.

Elias's critique is well taken, but it does not lessen the importance of victimization by street crime or the value of programs to help its victims. As I pointed out at the outset of this chapter, street crime is a serious problem in the United States, especially in poor, nonwhite, urban neighborhoods. If a greater understanding of street crime victimization can help reduce it, then continued research in this area is necessary. Yet, as Elias points out, it is also important to study other kinds of victimization and to address the larger social forces at work.

Sources: Elias 1986; Elias 1990; Elias 1993; Mawby and Walklate 1994.

Homelessness itself may be such an "ultimate state of victimization" that criminal victimization doesn't add substantially to the problems that homeless people already experience.

The researchers found that 35 percent of the sample had been victims of violence or personal theft in the preceding year, a proportion about four times higher than the NCVS's estimate for the general population and three times higher than that for the poorest income bracket. Compared to the homeless nonvictims, homeless victims were more likely to be afraid of being on the street and to suffer various physical and mental health problems. However, these effects of victimization were minimal when other factors were held constant, suggesting that homelessness itself may be such an "ultimate state of victimization" that criminal victimization doesn't add substantially to the problems the homeless already experience (Fitzpatrick, Gory, and Ritchey 1993:366).

A study of homeless youths in Seattle also found them at increased risk for victimization. But even in this high-risk group, the chances of victimization varied. Youths who spent more time living in the streets were at greater risk, as were those who used illegal drugs more often (Hoyt, Ryan, and Cauce 1999). These latter findings supported predictions drawn from routine activities and lifestyle theories.

Another study, this time of 200 homeless women in New York City, found troubling racial differences in victimization and fear of crime (Coston 1992). The sample included 102 "minorities" (95 African-Americans, 4 Hispanics, 2 Haitians, 1 Asian-American) and 98 "nonminorities" (whites). Sixty percent of the minorities had been victims of crime, usually robbery or assault, while living on the street, compared to only 48 percent of the nonminorities. The minority homeless were also more likely to feel highly vulnerable to future victimization.

 ## SUMMARY AND CONCLUSION

Victims of street crime remain a prime subject for social science research and for government action. A growing body of research has greatly advanced our knowledge of victims' sociodemographic characteristics and experiences during and after their victimization. The social pattern of victimization is disturbingly similar to the pattern we saw in Chapter 3 for criminality, as it's concentrated among the poor, nonwhite, and young sectors of society. As a result, just as the most common street criminal in the United States is poor, nonwhite, and young, so is the most common victim of street crime. Although women are less likely to be victimized than men overall, they face the threat of rape and intimate violence as a daily social fact and generally are more likely than men to be victimized by intimates and other people they know.

NCVS and other victimization data have furthered the development of theories of victimization. The most popular theories emphasize the role played by people's daily lifestyles and routine activities and imply that changes in our behavior would reduce our risk for victimization. That's true to an extent, but some behaviors are easier to change than others. We can reduce our visits to bars and taverns, which seem to be a special location for victimization, but we can't simply shut ourselves in our homes and hide under our beds.

These theories of victimization imply that victims are responsible for their victimization. Taken to an extreme, victims might even be said to precipitate their victimization. That may be true for some homicides, but it's an antiquated and even dangerous concept when applied to rape. Unless we want to say that women precipitate their rapes by simply knowing men and spending time with them—an absurd notion—the idea of women's involvement in their rapes must be abandoned. Views that battered women are somehow responsible for being beaten and otherwise injured deserve a similar fate. Unfortunately, these views about rape and battering still guide much public thinking on crime and affect the prosecution of rapists and batterers and the experiences of women in the criminal justice system.

In looking, in the last three chapters, at public opinion about crime, the extent and patterning of criminal behavior, and the patterning and consequences of criminal victimization, one theme that emerges is inequality. It is the groups at the bottom of the socioeconomic ladder—the poor, people of color, the young—who are most likely to fear crime and have the highest rates of both criminality and victimization. Gender presents somewhat of an exception to this link: Although women, who have less social and economic power than men, are much more likely to fear crime, they have a much lower offending rate and a lower victimization rate. The way we socialize females and males explains much of this pattern.

The last three chapters have also stressed the importance of white-collar crime. The focus of media, scholarly, and government attention on street crime is certainly important and well deserved, but the neglect by all three sources of white-collar crime is very unfortunate.

Finally, I've alluded several times in the last three chapters to the effects of social structure, broadly defined, on public opinion, criminality, and victimization. As the next few chapters turn to theories of criminal behavior, the importance of social structure will again receive special emphasis.

KEY TERMS

crime characteristics	lifestyle theory
crime victim	politics of victimization
demographic variation	psychological consequences
inequality	routine activities theory

victim precipitation   victimization

victim-impact statement   victimology

victim-offender relationship

 ## STUDY QUESTIONS

1. Does it make sense to consider people who suffer from the legal behavior of corporations and from poverty to be crime victims? Why or why not?

2. How do violence victimization rates differ by gender, age, race, and family income? Why do these different rates exist?

3. Are victims of violence harmed more by nonstrangers or by strangers? What does this pattern imply for efforts to reduce criminal victimization?

4. How does routine activities theory help us understand why criminal victimization occurs? What does this theory imply for efforts to reduce crime?

 ## INTERNET EXERCISES

As the text notes, the National Crime Victimization Survey (NCVS) is the major source of data for victims and victimization in the United States. You can access the data from this survey by going to the Bureau of Justice Statistics (BJS) Web site at **http://www.ojp.usdoj.gov/bjs/**. This is an invaluable site for all kinds of information on crime and justice, but for now we'll just focus on victimization data.

To do so, click on **Crime and victims** at the top of the page. Take a moment to scroll through this page to see some basic information on victimization. Now click on **Criminal victimization, general** at the top of the page. You'll see some "summary findings" and links to various BJS publications. According to the summary findings, how many crimes did U.S. residents suffer in the year covered by these findings? What percent of these crimes were violent crimes?

Now go back to the previous Web page and click on **victim characteristics**. You'll again see summary findings and links to BJS publications. According to the summary findings, people from which social backgrounds were most vulnerable to violent crime? Which race was most vulnerable? Which income group was most vulnerable?

EXPLAINING CRIME:
EMPHASIS ON
THE INDIVIDUAL

Crime in the News

In 1999 a controversy erupted when two economists proposed that almost half of the 1990s crime decline was the result of the large increase in abortions two decades earlier in the wake of the U.S. Supreme Court's famous Roe v. Wade decision. The drop in crime began, they said, when the children who were not born because of the abortion increase, much of it found among poor, unmarried teenagers, would have reached their late teenage years, when offending reaches its peak. The states that first legalized abortion before Roe v. Wade were also the first to see their crime rates drop. States with the highest abortion rates after Roe v. Wade also had larger crime decreases than states with lower abortion rates.

The economists' claims met with skepticism from criminologists and provoked concern from both sides of the abortion debate. Criminologists said the 1990s crime rate decline stemmed from factors far more important than the rise in abortions two decades earlier. These included the thriving economy during the 1990s, a stabilizing in gang wars over the sale and distribution of crack that began in the mid 1980s, and perhaps more effective policing and community-based crime control strategies. One leader of the anti-abortion movement said the study was "so fraught with stupidity that I hardly know where to start refuting it. Naturally, if you kill off a million and a half people a year, a few criminals will be in that number. So will doctors, philosophers, musicians and artists." A leader in the pro-choice movement said of the economists' report, "I don't think it has any policy implications whatsoever." A newspaper columnist observed, "I've seen a lot of far-fetched and dangerous ideas passed off as 'social research,' but none more shallow and potentially malicious than the claim that the drop in crime in the United States can be attributed to legalized abortions." Some observers warned that the abortion study could revive the belief of the eugenics movement, popular in the 1920s and 1930s, that certain kinds of people should not be allowed to "breed."

Sources: Goldstein 1999; Goode 1999; Goodman 1999.

*E*xplanations of crime and of rises and declines in crime rates are a central task of the field of criminology. Yet very different views on these issues exist. For example, I once had a student who said the Devil caused most crime. Upon hearing this, several other students in the classroom snickered. When I asked the student how she would reduce crime, she said the Devil needed to be exorcised from the bodies it possessed. More snickers. Coming to the student's defense, I said I respected her religious beliefs but added that modern criminological theory doesn't blame the Devil for crime and thus doesn't think exorcism would reduce it.

As this story illustrates, our assumptions of what causes crime affect what we think should be done to reduce it. If we think the Devil is to blame, our crime-reduction efforts will center on removing the Devil's influence. If we hold biological or psychological problems in individuals responsible, our efforts will focus on correcting these problems. If we attribute crime to things such as poverty and inadequate parenting, our efforts will center on reducing poverty and improving parenting skills. If we instead attribute crime to a criminal justice system that is too "soft" on criminals, our efforts will focus on adding more police, increasing prison terms, and building more prisons. To develop the most effective approach, we must first understand why crime occurs.

Contemporary theories of crime differ widely in their assumptions and emphases. While evidence exists to support all the theories, each one has its proponents and detractors. Although the folk societies studied by anthropologists often blame deviance on angry gods or fiendish demons (Edgerton 1976), modern societies stress scientific explanations. In the social and behavioral sciences, sociologists and psychologists have contributed the most to understanding crime, with economists a distant third. Of scholars in the remaining sciences, biologists and medical researchers have long been interested in crime.

The next few chapters discuss the major biological, psychological, and sociological theories of crime. Although I discuss the strengths and weaknesses of all three disciplines' approaches, as a sociologist I favor sociological theories over their biological and psychological counterparts. To help you understand why I feel this way, let's discuss some differences in the three disciplines' perspectives.

Theories of crime try to answer at least one of three questions: (1) Why are some individuals more likely than others to commit crime? (2) Why are some categories or kinds of people more likely than others to commit crime? (3) Why is crime more common in some locations than in others? (Short 1997). Biologists, medical researchers, and psychologists tend to focus on the first question, while sociologists and most criminologists tend to concentrate on the last two. As a rough way of understanding the differences among the theories, biological and psychological explanations place the causes of crime inside the individual, while sociological explanations place the roots of crime in the social environment outside the individual. Put another way, biology and psychology focus on the micro or smaller picture, while sociology focuses on the macro or larger picture. That doesn't necessarily make biology and psychology wrong and sociology right, or vice versa. It simply reflects longstanding differences among these disciplines in understanding human behavior. As a sociologist I'm interested in the larger picture, which I feel provides a more penetrating analysis of crime and society.

This basic difference between these approaches has important implications for efforts to reduce crime. If the fault for crime lies within the individual, then to reduce crime we must change the individual. If the fault instead lies in the social environment, then to reduce crime we must change that environment.

To understand further the differences between micro and macro levels of analysis, let's leave criminology for a moment and consider two eating disorders, anorexia and bulimia. As you probably know, anorexia involves undereating or starvation, while bulimia involves cycles of binging and purging. What causes these disorders? Psychologists and medical researchers both cite problems in individual anorexics and bulimics. Psychologists emphasize low self-esteem, feelings of inferiority and lack of control, and other difficulties, while medical researchers stress possible biochemical defects (Huebner 1993; Shapiro et al. 1993). These individual-level explanations are valuable, and you might well know someone with an eating disorder who was helped by a psychologist or physician.

A sociological explanation would utilize a different approach. Starting with the observation that anorexia and bulimia almost always affect *young women*, sociologists would ask, "What is it about U.S. society that makes anorexia and bulimia *young women's* problems? Why don't men suffer these problems?" In answering these questions, sociologists stress the standards of female beauty dominating U.S. culture. The pictures of women in the magazines read by young women emphasize again and again that women who are beautiful are, perhaps above all else, slender. The Barbie® dolls that most girls play with provide the same image. Because of this cultural view, women are more likely than men to feel they are too heavy and to diet. Given this cultural emphasis on female thinness, it is inevitable that some women will always feel they're too heavy, even if objective evidence indicates they are not. Some of these women will further diet to an extreme and perhaps not even eat, or force themselves to regurgitate after eating (Bordo 1993).

This sociological explanation suggests that the roots of eating disorders lie more in society than in individual anorexics or bulimics. No matter how often psychologists and physicians cure women with these problems, there will always be new women taking their place as long as the cultural emphasis on the slender female body continues. To my sociological mind, this understanding of eating disorders provides a more in-depth analysis of society, as it indicates that micro efforts to cure eating disorders might help individual anorexics or bulimics but ultimately can have only a limited effect in reducing the overall eating disorder problem.

That said, it's also true that most women don't suffer eating disorders despite the cultural emphasis on female slenderness. To understand why certain women do suffer these disorders, psychological or perhaps biological explanations are necessary. Whether you favor micro or macro explanations of eating disorders or crime depends on whether you think it's more important to understand the smaller picture or the larger one.

It is time now to turn to the many theories of crime. When I begin to talk about theories to my students, their eyes often glaze over—and you may be feeling the same way. That's why I started this chapter by stressing the need to understand *why* crime occurs if we want to *reduce* it. When I say the same thing to my students, they usually nod in agreement and begin to see the importance of theory. I hope you'll feel the same way. As you read about the various theories, try to think what they imply for successful efforts to reduce crime. Although we have a lot of material to cover in the next few chapters, I think you'll find the discussion clear, concise, and, if we're lucky, even exciting. Before we continue our excursion into the world of theory, let's first review the historical change from theology to science in the understanding of crime.

FROM THEOLOGY TO SCIENCE

God and Demons as Causes of Crime and Deviance

Like many tribal societies studied by anthropologists today, Western societies long ago had religious explanations for behavior that violated their norms (Einstadter and Henry 1995). People in ancient times were thought to act deviantly for several reasons: (1) God was testing their faith in Him; (2) God was punishing them; (3) God was using their behavior to warn others to follow His rules; and (4) they were possessed by demons. In the Old Testament, the prophets communicated God's unhappiness to the ancient Hebrews with behavior that today we would call mad and even violent. Yet they, and Jesus after them in the Temple, were regarded as divinely inspired. Ancient Greeks and Romans, who believed in multiple gods, had similar explanations for madness.

From ancient times to the Middle Ages, witches—people who supposedly had associated with or been possessed by the Devil—were a special focus of attention. The Old Testament mentions witches several times, including the commandment in Exodus (22:18), "Thou shalt not suffer a witch to live." Witches also appear in ancient Greek and Roman literature. Biblical injunctions against witches took an ominous turn in Europe from the 1400s to the 1700s, as some 300,000 "witches," most of them women, were burned at the stake or otherwise executed. Perhaps the most famous witch-hunting victim was Joan of Arc, a military hero for France in its wars with England, whom the English burned at the stake in May 1431. Other witches put to death, often by the Roman Catholic Church that dominated continental Europe, were what we would today call healers, midwives, religious heretics, political protesters, and homosexuals. In short, anyone, and especially any woman, who violated Church rules could have been branded a witch (Hoyt 1981).

The Age of Reason

Although, as my student's comment illustrates, some people still blame the Devil for crime, religious views began to give way in the 1700s to scientific explanations. This century marked the ripening in Europe of the Age of Reason, or the Enlightenment, which challenged medieval beliefs that God directly controlled all human behavior and that the Church's authority should be accepted without question. Enlightenment philosophers such as René Descartes, John Locke, and Jean Jacques Rousseau instead felt that God had left people to govern their own affairs through the exercise of free will and reason. In their view, people rationally calculate the advantages and disadvantages of potential actions and undertake behavior promising the greatest pleasure and least pain. To ensure that people not act too emotionally, Enlightenment thinkers stressed the need to acquire an education to develop reasoning ability (Durant and Durant 1961).

Despite this more "enlightened" way of thinking, Europeans suspected of crimes during this time were often arrested on flimsy evidence and imprisoned without trial. Torture was commonly used in continental Europe to force people to confess to their alleged crime and to name anyone else involved. In England the right to jury trials for felonies lessened the use of torture. However, English defendants convicted by juries risked losing their land and property to the king. Many defendants thus refused jury trials, only to suffer a form of torture known as "pressing" (finally abolished in 1772), in which a heavy weight was placed on the body of the accused. Some were crushed to death right away, while others lasted a few days until they either confessed or died. If they managed to die without confessing, their families kept their land and property (Jones 1986).

Despite the use of pressing, torture was less common in England than on the Continent, although the death penalty was often used, with more than 200 crimes, including theft, punishable by death. Common citizens could be found guilty of treason for plotting the death of the king, servants for plotting the death of their master, and women for plotting the death of their husband. Execution was a frequent punishment for such "treason," with the "traitors" sometimes disemboweled or dismembered before they were killed.

The Classical School of Criminology

Against this frightening backdrop, Italian economist Cesare Beccaria (1738–1794) wrote a small but pathbreaking book on crime, *Dei Delitti e Delle Pene* (*On Crimes and Punishments*), in 1764 (Beccaria 1819 [1764]). Essentially a plea for justice, Beccaria's treatise helped found what is now called the *classical* school of criminology. Beccaria was appalled by the horrible conditions in the European criminal justice system in the 1700s. Like other Enlightenment thinkers, he believed that people acted rationally and with free will, and calculated whether their behavior would cause them more pleasure or more pain. He argued that the law needed only to be punitive enough to deter people from committing crime, and condemned the treatment of criminals, especially torture, for being much crueler than this humane standard. He also opposed executions for most crimes (Jones 1986).

▲ *Cesare Beccaria and Jeremy Bentham founded the classical school of criminology. They felt that the severity of legal punishment should be limited to what was necessary to deter people from committing crime.*

Beccaria is often regarded as the founder of modern criminology, and his treatise credited with leading to many reforms in the prisons and criminal courts (Vold, Bernard, and Snipes 1998). One admirer calls him a "prophet" of an enlightened approach to crime prevention and crime control (Mueller 1990). However, several critics claim this praise is undeserved. They note that although Beccaria has been lauded for opposing torture and the death penalty, his treatise actually contains many ambiguous passages about these punishments. Moreover, the criminal justice reforms with which he has been credited were actually already being implemented before he wrote his treatise (Newman and Marongiu 1990). Yet even these critics concede Beccaria's views greatly influenced continued reforms, thanks in large part to their adoption by other reformers: "There is little doubt that Beccaria's ideas were used and promulgated by many other reformers at the time.... In that sense [they] had an enormous effect" (Newman and Marongiu 1990:339). Several European nations adopted criminal justice reforms suggested by Beccaria. His views also influenced the thinking of John Adams, Benjamin Franklin, Thomas Jefferson, and the writers of the U.S. Constitution, and are reflected in contemporary debates over the rationality of criminals and the deterrent effect of the law (Mueller 1990).

The other great figure of the classical school was English philosopher Jeremy Bentham (1748–1832). Like Beccaria, Bentham felt that people weigh whether their behavior is more apt to cause them pleasure or pain, and that the law was far more severe than it needed to be to deter such rational individuals from behaving criminally. His writings inspired changes in English criminal law in the early 1800s and affected the development of the first modern police force in London in 1829. They also influenced the creation of the modern prison. Before the time of Bentham, Beccaria, and other legal reformers, long-term incarceration did not exist; jails were intended only for short-term stays for suspects awaiting trial, torture, or execution. The development of the prison in the early 1800s thus represented a major and still controversial change in the punishment of criminals.

Although the classical school of criminology led to important reforms in the criminal justice system throughout Europe, critics then and now have said its view of human behavior was too simplistic (Jones 1986). Even though individuals sometimes weigh the costs and benefits of their actions, other times they act emotionally. Also, although people often do act to maximize pleasure and to reduce pain, they do not always agree on what is pleasurable. Classical reformers assumed the legal system treats all people the same and overlooked the possibility that suspects' race, class, and gender might affect their treatment. Finally, classical scholars failed to recognize that forces both outside and inside individuals might affect their likelihood of breaking the law. We'll examine this last critique when we discuss positivism.

THE REVIVAL OF THE CLASSICAL PERSPECTIVE

The classical school's views are reflected in a set of theories gaining prominence in criminological thinking. These theories are sometimes called the *neoclassical perspective* but are more often grouped under the rubric of *rational choice theory*. Echoing the classical view, they all assume that individuals choose to commit crime after calculating whether its potential rewards outweigh its potential risks (Cornish and Clarke 1986). In this regard, the routine activities theory discussed in Chapter 4 on victimization can be seen as a rational choice theory, as it assumes criminals are more active when there are attractive targets and little guardianship. Although rational choice theory's roots lie in the classical school, its modern inspiration comes from economic models of rational decision making and more generally from a growing emphasis in sociology and other fields on the rationality of human behavior (Collins 1994).

Since rational choice theory assumes criminals weigh the risks of their actions, it also assumes they can be deterred from committing crime if the potential risks seem too certain or too severe. To turn that around, belief in the law's deterrent impact is based on a rational choice view of potential criminals. For that reason, rational choice theory is closely aligned with *deterrence theory*, which assumes that potential and actual punishment can deter crime, and the two theories are often considered synonymous. Their assumptions underlie current efforts to fight crime with a get-tough approach involving harsher punishment and more prisons.

In addressing the deterrent effect of the law, scholars distinguish between *general* and *specific deterrence*. General deterrence occurs when members of the public decide not to break the law because they fear legal punishment. To take a traffic example, we may obey the speed limit because we don't want to get a speeding ticket. Specific deterrence occurs when offenders already punished for breaking the law decide not to commit another crime because they don't want to face legal consequences again. Sticking to our traffic example, if we've already received a speeding ticket or two and are close to losing our license, we may obey the speed limit because we don't want to suffer further consequences.

Most research on rational choice and deterrence theory addresses the general deterrent impact of legal punishment. Here scholars distinguish *objective* from *subjective deterrence*. Objective deterrence refers to the impact of actual legal punishment, while subjective deterrence refers to the impact of people's perceptions of the likelihood and severity of legal punishment. Deterrence theory predicts that people are deterred from crime by actual legal punishment that is certain and severe, and also by their own perceptions that legal punishment will be like this. We'll discuss both the objective and subjective deterrent effect of legal punishment later in this book (Chapters 15 and 16). Suffice it to say here that the evidence on either effect is inconsistent and controversial, with many scholars feeling that actual and perceived punishment have only a weak or perhaps no effect on crime and delinquency, and others finding a more substantial effect (Nagin 1998; Paternoster 1987).

Some research also documents the deterrent effect of internal punishment (e.g., guilt, shame, embarrassment, and conscience) and of informal sanctions such as disapproval by friends and loved ones (Grasmick, Bursik, and Arneklev 1993). However, as Ronald L. Akers observes, such evidence says nothing about the deterrent effect of legal punishment: "The question to be answered about deterrence theory is not whether punishment of any kind from any source deters, but whether the threat of punishment *by law* deters" (Akers 1997:23; emphasis in original).

Other research on rational choice and deterrence theory addresses the degree to which criminals calculate their behavior. While some crimes, such as corporate crime, involve careful planning and weighing of all risks (Paternoster and Simpson 1993), other crimes, particularly violent ones, typically don't involve such efforts. The picture of property crime is especially mixed. A study of "active residential burglars" found them less willing to commit hypothetical burglaries if they perceived a high risk of arrest (Decker, Wright, and Logie 1993). However, another study of "chronic property criminals" found they "simply do not think about the possible legal consequences of their criminal actions before committing crimes" (Tunnell 1990:680). Instead they thought mainly of the potential reward from committing crime and put possible risks "out of their minds," as most believed they wouldn't be caught. They thus commit their crimes "with little concern for the law, arrest, or imprisonment" (p. 687). Overall, rational choice theory might accurately describe the decision making of some criminals for some types of crimes, but it appears to be more limited in scope than assumed by its proponents.

The Rise of Positivism

Notice that in discussing the classical school of criminology I said nothing about its proponents' views on the causes of crime, other than their belief that some people commit crime when they decide the benefits outweigh the risks. It didn't occur to them that crime might result from forces beyond the control of the individual. This view was the key belief of a new way of thinking, *positivism*, which came to dominate the nineteenth century and derived from the great discoveries in the physical sciences of Galileo, Newton, and others (Jones 1986). These discoveries indicated to social philosophers the potential of using science to understand not only the physical world but also the social world.

French social philosopher Auguste Comte (1798–1857) founded the positive school of philosophy with the publication of his six-volume *Cours de Philosophie Positive* (*Course in Positive Philosophy*) between 1830 and 1842. Comte argued that human behavior is determined by forces beyond the individual's control. As noted earlier, biologists and psychologists generally find these forces inside the individual, while sociologists find them outside the individual. Research in biology, psychology, and sociology that attempts to explain what causes crime is all positivist in its orientation, even though these disciplines' theories differ in many other ways.

The rise of science as a mode of inquiry was cemented in 1859 with the publication of Charles Darwin's *Origin of Species*, in which he outlined his theory of evolution, and in 1871 with the publication of his book on human evolution, *Descent of Man*. The idea that science could explain the origin and development of the human species was revolutionary. It spawned great controversy at the time of Darwin's publications and is still attacked today by people accepting the biblical story of creation. However, Darwin's theory came to dominate the study of evolution and also established the credibility of science for understanding human behavior and other social and physical phenomena.

Since the time of Comte and Darwin, positivism has guided the study of crime and other human behaviors. While positivist research has greatly increased our understanding of the origins of crime, critics charge it with several shortcomings (Taylor, Walton, and Young 1973; Vold, Bernard, and Snipes 1998). First, positivism accepts the state's definition of crime and ignores the possibility that the ruling groups in society define what's criminal and what's legal. Positivism thus accepts the legitimacy of a political and legal order that may contain serious injustices. Second, in criticizing the classical view of individuals acting with free will and determining their own behavior, positivism sometimes goes too far in the other direction by painting an overly deterministic model of human behavior and denying free will altogether. Third, positivism assumes there are two categories of people, criminals and noncriminals, and that criminals are different from the rest of us not only in their behavior but also in the biological, psychological, or social characteristics that determine their behavior. We noncriminals are thus considered normal and the criminals considered abnormal and even inferior. As the self-report studies discussed in Chapter 3 indicate, however, the line between criminals and noncriminals might be quite thin, with noncriminals very capable of breaking the law.

These criticisms of positivism notwithstanding, positivism remains the dominant approach in criminology today. This is true for virtually all biologists and psychologists who study crime, but also true, despite notable exceptions, for most sociologists. Let's turn now to biological explanations of criminality to see what they might offer to the understanding of crime.

BIOLOGICAL EXPLANATIONS

The first positivist research on crime was primarily biological. Today biological explanations enjoy a renewed popularity but remain controversial because of their social policy implications and occasional methodological shortcomings. We'll examine several types of biological explanations from over the years and then review the controversy.

Phrenology

One of the earliest biological explanations of crime, phrenology, concerned the size and shape of the skull and was popular from the mid-1700s to the mid-1800s (Jones 1986). An Austrian physician, Franz Gall (1758–1828), was its major proponent. Gall thought that three major regions of the brain (intellectual, moral, and lower) govern three distinct types of behavior and personality characteristics. The lower region was associated with criminal behavior and would be largest in criminals. Since phrenologists could not directly measure the size of the three brain regions, they reasoned that the size and shape of the skull corresponded to the brain's size and shape. They thus thought that skull dimensions provided good evidence of criminal tendencies.

As an explanation of crime, phrenology was popular for a while but never really caught on. We now know, of course, that its assumptions were mistaken: The brain neither works as compartmentally as phrenologists thought nor can be measured by measuring the skull. But perhaps the most important reason phrenology faded was that its biological determinism clashed with the classical emphasis on free will, still popular in the early 1800s. The determinism of positivism didn't become widely accepted until much later that century.

Cesare Lombroso: Atavism

If Cesare Beccaria was the founder of the classical school of criminology, then Cesare Lombroso (1835–1909), an Italian physician, was the founder of the positivist school (Wolfgang 1972). Influenced by Darwin's work on evolution, Lombroso thought criminals were *atavists*, or throwbacks to an earlier stage of evolution, and saw criminality as the result of atavism. In essence, criminals were evolutionary accidents who resembled primitive people more than modern (i.e., nineteenth-century) people. Lombroso felt that atavistic criminals needed to be executed since any other punishment would not work. After doing extensive research, Lombroso published his atavist theory in 1876 in his famous book, *L'Uomo Delinquent* (*The Criminal Man*) (Lombroso 1876). What was Lombroso's evidence for his theory of atavism? He measured the bodies of men in Italian prisons and decided that they looked more like primitive men than modern men. Among other things, their arms were abnormally long, their skulls and jaws abnormally large, and their bodies very hairy.

◄ *Cesare Lombroso believed that criminals were atavists, or evolutionary accidents. His views were influenced by Darwin's theory of evolution and in turn led other scholars to study whether criminals are biologically different from noncriminals.*

Given the intense interest in evolution generated by Darwin's work, Lombroso's "discovery" attracted much attention and his atavist theory of crime became quite popular. Unfortunately, Lombroso's research was methodologically flawed (Vold, Bernard, and Snipes 1998). Because the Italian criminal justice system at the time was hardly a fair one, it's likely that many of his prisoners had not actually committed crimes. His control groups probably included people who *had* committed crimes without being imprisoned, as is still true today. Many differences he found between his prisoners and control group subjects were too small to be statistically significant. It's also possible that Lombroso unconsciously measured his subjects in ways that fit his theory. Even if we were to assume that his prisoners did look different from how men in a proper control group would have looked, it's possible that their imprisonment resulted more from fear of, and bias against, their unusual appearance than from their criminality. Finally, some of the traits Lombroso described characterize Sicilians, who have long been at the bottom of Italy's socioeconomic ladder. Lombroso's prisoners might have looked like atavists not because his theory made any sense but because his atavistic traits happened to be ones belonging to Sicilians.

By the end of his career, Lombroso had modified his view of atavism. While he continued to think that the most serious criminals were atavists, he reasoned that this group comprised only about one-third of all offenders. The remainder were criminals who developed brain problems long after birth, and a large category of "occasional" criminals whose behavior stemmed from problems in their social environment. Two of Lombroso's students, Raffaele Garofalo (1852–1934) and Enrico Ferri (1856–1929), carried on his views and made their own contributions to criminology's development. Garofalo continued to emphasize biological bases for crime, while Ferri stressed that social conditions also play a role. Both scholars attacked the classical view of free will and crime, and argued for a more positivist, determinist view of crime causation.

As the founder of modern positivist criminology, Lombroso left a lasting legacy, as his assumption that criminals were biologically different continues to guide today's biological research on crime (Vold, Bernard, and Snipes 1998). It should come as no surprise, however, that his atavist theory has long been discredited. In 1913 English psychiatrist Charles Goring (1870–1919) published his book *The English Convict*. Goring measured the body dimensions of 3,000 English prisoners and of the members of a large control group. He didn't discover the differences between the two groups that Lombroso uncovered and thus found no support for atavism. Goring did find, however, that the criminals he studied were shorter and less heavy than control group subjects and thought this indicated a hereditary basis for crime. This possibility notwithstanding, Goring's critique of Lombroso's research struck home, and Lombroso's theory soon fell out of favor.

LOMBROSO ON WOMEN

In Chapter 3 I noted that until recently few criminologists studied women criminals. Lombroso was one of these few. That's the good news. The bad news is that his explanation of female criminality, reflecting the sexism of his time, rested on antiquated notions of women's biology and physiology. Lombroso published *The Female Offender* in 1895. In it he wrote that women were more likely than men to be atavists and that "even the female criminal is monotonous and uniform compared with her male companion, just as in general woman is inferior to man" (Lombroso 1920 [1903]:122). He also thought that women "have many traits in common with children," that their "moral sense is deficient," and that "they are revengeful, jealous."

In view of these terrible qualities, how did Lombroso explain why women commit so little crime? He reasoned that women were naturally passive and viewed their "defects [as] neutralized by piety, maternity, want of passion, sexual coldness, weakness and an undeveloped intelligence." A woman who managed to commit crime despite these crime-reducing traits must be, thought Lombroso, "a born criminal more terrible than any man," as her "wickedness must have been enormous before it could triumph over so many obstacles" (Lombroso 1920 [1903]:150–152). Although most modern criminologists consider Lombroso's views hopelessly outdated, his emphasis on women's physiology and supposed biological nature remains influential in the study of women's crime and other behaviors (Chesney-Lind 1997; Klein 1995).

Earnest Hooton: Biological Inferiority

After Goring's 1913 refutation of Lombroso's atavism theory, criminologists temporarily abandoned the idea that criminals were physiologically different. Then in 1939 Harvard University anthropologist Earnest Hooton (1887–1954) revived interest in physiological explanations with the publication of two books, *The American Criminal: An Anthropological Study* (1939a) and *Crime and the Man*; (1939b). In these books Hooton reported the results of his measurement of 14,000 male prisoners and 3,200 control group subjects. Compared to the control group, Hooton said, prisoners tended to have, among other things, low foreheads, crooked noses, narrow jaws, small ears, long necks, and stooped shoulders. Not one to mince words, Hooton labeled criminals "organically inferior" and "low-grade human organisms" and concluded that the "primary cause of crime is biological inferiority.... The penitentiaries of our society are built upon the shifting sands and quaking bogs of inferior human organisms" (Hooton 1939b:130). He further concluded that criminals' body shapes influenced the types of crime they committed. Murderers tended to be tall and thin, for example, while rapists were short and heavy. Men with average builds did not specialize in any particular crime because they, like their physical shape, had no specific orientation.

Hooton's belief in the biological inferiority of criminals led him to urge the government to reduce crime by undertaking "the extirpation of the physically, mentally, and morally unfit, or ... their complete segregation in a socially aseptic environment" (Hooton 1939a:309). Put more simply, Hooton was advocating that the government sterilize criminals or exile them to reservations.

Hooton's research suffered from the same methodological flaws as Lombroso's, including the assumptions that all his prisoners had committed crimes and accurately represented criminals, and that all his control group subjects were noncriminals. It's also doubtful that Hooton's control group adequately represented the general population, since a majority were either firefighters or members of the Massachusetts militia. Given their occupations, their physical fitness, size, and so forth may well have differed from those of the population at large. Because of these and other weaknesses, Hooton's work did not become popular, especially with the onset of World War II and the "extirpation" of the millions of people whom the Nazis considered biologically inferior.

William Sheldon: Body Shapes

Although assumptions of biological inferiority grew less fashionable, interest in physiology and criminality continued. In 1949 William Sheldon (1898–1977) published his book, *Varieties of Delinquent Youth*, in which he outlined his theory of somatology (Sheldon 1949). This theory assumes that people's body shapes affect their personalities and hence the crimes they commit. Sheldon identified three such body types (see Figure 5.1). *Endomorphs* are heavy with short arms and legs; they

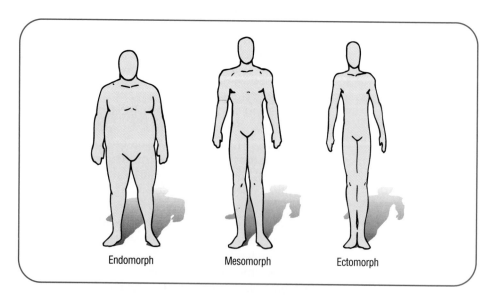

▲ FIGURE 5.1   **WILLIAM SHELDON'S THREE BODY SHAPES**

WILLIAM SHELDON ATTRIBUTED CRIME TO PEOPLE'S BODY SHAPES, WHICH HE THOUGHT INFLUENCED THEIR PERSONALITIES AND THUS THE CRIMES THEY COMMITTED.

Source: Adapted from Sheldon 1949.

tend to be relaxed and extroverted, and relatively noncriminal. *Mesomorphs* are athletic and muscular; they tend to be aggressive and particularly apt to commit violent crimes and other crimes requiring strength and speed. Finally, *ectomorphs* are thin, introverted, and overly sensitive. Sheldon compared 200 male delinquents in an institution to a control group of some 4,000 male college students. Compared to the students, the delinquents tended to be mesomorphic, as Sheldon predicted.

Despite some appeal to his theory, Sheldon's research suffered from the same methodological flaws of the work of Lombroso, Hooton, and other early biologists (Curran and Renzetti 1994; Vold, Bernard, and Snipes 1998). In addition, even if Sheldon's delinquent subjects were more mesomorphic, he couldn't rule out the possibility that their muscular, athletic bodies made it more probable that they worried juvenile justice officials and hence more likely that they would be institutionalized. These many flaws, coupled with memories of the Holocaust, minimized the popularity of Sheldon's somatological theory of crime.

Family, Heredity, and Genes

Biologists and medical researchers have long noticed that crime tends to "run in families" and naturally assume that criminal tendencies are inherited (Rowe and Farrington 1997). To these researchers, crime is analogous to disease and illness. Just as many cancers, heart disease, and other medical problems are often genetically transmitted, so, they say, is crime and, for that matter, other behavioral problems such as alcoholism and schizophrenia. Work on heredity and crime now occupies a central place in biology and crime research. Let's review early and current efforts in this area.

THE JUKES AND THE KALLIKAKS

The first notable study of family transmission of crime was *The Jukes: A Study in Crime, Pauperism, Disease, and Heredity*, published in 1877 by Richard Dugdale (Dugdale 1877). Noticing that six members of the Jukes family were behind bars in rural New York, Dugdale researched their family tree back 200 years and found that about 140 of 1,000 Jukes during that time had been imprisoned. Unfortunately, Dugdale had no control group and thus could not determine whether the Jukes' level of criminality was higher than other families'. Henry H. Goddard's 1912 study, *The Kallikak Family: A Study in the Heredity of Feeblemindedness*, was sounder in this regard (Goddard 1912). Goddard examined the descendants of one Martin Kallikak, who fathered children through two different women in the late 1700s. Goddard found a higher proportion of crime and other problems in one set of Kallikak's descendants than in the other. Despite the interesting control group, learning and environmental factors explain Goddard's findings better than heredity. The "deviant" set of Kallikak's descendants, for example, lived in poverty, while the "normal" set lived in wealth.

TWIN STUDIES

The ideal way to study heredity and crime would be to take individuals at birth, clone them genetically, and randomly assign them and their clones to families (one individual or clone per family) living in various kinds of circumstances across the country. You would then monitor the individuals' and clones' behavior for the next forty years or so. At regular intervals throughout this long study, you would determine whether individuals and clones tend to act alike. If crime is inherited, then individuals who commit crime should have clones who also commit crime. For each individual-clone pair, you would thus determine whether (1) both members of the pair commit crime, (2) both members do not commit crime, or (3) one member commits crime and the other doesn't. When both members of a pair act alike, as in (1) or (2), we have *concordance*; when they don't act alike, as in (3), we have *discordance*. If crime is inherited, you would find a higher level of concordance than discordance in all your individual-clone pairs; if crime is not inherited, you would find similar levels of concordance and discordance.

For better or worse, in the real world we can't do such an "ideal" study. *Jurassic Park* and other science fiction notwithstanding, we can't yet clone whole dinosaurs or humans, despite recent advances in cloning involving other animals. Even if we could clone humans, we wouldn't be allowed to assign babies and their clones randomly to families across the land. The same holds true for identical twins, who are the genetic equivalent of clones.

One way to approximate this ideal study of heredity and crime is to compare identical twins who continue to live with their natural parents with siblings who are not identical twins and thus not genetically the same. We can then determine whether the level of concordance between the identical twins is higher than that between non-twin siblings. Researchers have performed several such studies and usually find higher concordance among the identical twins than among the other siblings. This evidence is widely interpreted as supporting a genetic basis for crime (Jacobson and Rowe 2000).

However, critics argue that other reasons may account for the concordance. Compared to other siblings, identical twins spend more time together, tend to have the same friends, are more attached to each other, and tend to think of themselves as alike. They are also more likely than other siblings to be treated the same by their parents, friends, and teachers. All these likenesses produce similar attitudes and behaviors among identical twins, including delinquency and crime (Walters 1992; Walters and White 1989).

Adoption Studies

To rule out these possibilities, some researchers study identical twins separated shortly after birth and raised by different sets of parents. Because the twins do not live together, any concordance must stem from genetic factors. However, identical twins separated at birth are very rare, and too few studies exist to infer a genetic basis for crime. Their results are also mixed: Some find a high level of concordance, while others do not. Moreover, most of the identical twins in these studies who were reared "separately" were usually raised by parents who were close family members or neighbors. The twins thus lived in roughly the same environments, with many of them even spending a lot of time with each other. Since the twins were not really raised that separately after all, any concordance found may simply reflect their similar environments and not their genetic sameness (Lewontin, Rose, and Kamin 1984).

Other researchers look at non-twin siblings who through adoption are raised by different sets of parents. In this kind of study, researchers determine whether natural parents who are criminals tend to have children, though adopted and raised by other parents, who also become criminals (Carey 1994). These studies usually find that the criminality of natural parents is statistically related to the criminality of their adopted children. For example, a study of almost 1,000 adopted boys born in Denmark between 1927 and 1941 found that 49 percent of boys with criminal records had natural fathers with criminal records, versus only 31 percent of boys without such records (Hutchings and Mednick 1977). A similar study of some 4,000 adopted Danish males found criminal conviction rates of 24.5 percent among those with natural parents who had been convicted, versus only 14.7 percent among those with natural parents who had not been convicted (Mednick et al. 1987).

Although many researchers interpret such evidence as support for a genetic basis for crime, others argue that many siblings in adoption studies are adopted several months after birth and thus experience similar environmental influences before adoption at a critical stage of their development. These influences might thus account for any similarity found later between their behavior and their natural parents'. Another problem is that adoption agencies usually try to find adoptive parents whose socioeconomic status and other characteristics match those of the natural parents. The resulting lack of random assignment in adoption studies creates a bias that may account for the statistical relationships found (Walters and White 1989).

Despite the methodological problems in heredity and crime research, many biologists and some criminologists continue to feel that the "heritability of aggression and nonviolent offending is substantial," to quote a recent review (Jacobson and Rowe 2000:341). Others are optimistic that the research will one day prove a genetic link but concede that it hasn't yet done so (Fishbein 1996). Still other scholars criticize any rush to judgment on heredity and crime. As another review put it, "Current genetic research on crime has been poorly designed, ambiguously reported, and exceedingly inadequate in addressing the relevant issues" (Walters and White 1989:478). Even if crime does "run in families," socialization and role modeling, not heredity, may well be the reasons (Widom 1992). Given the methodological problems in heredity and crime research, a genetic basis for crime cannot yet be assumed. Even if a strong genetic link is one day established beyond a doubt, the social environment also plays an important role in crime, as biological proponents readily point out (Jacobson and Rowe 2000).

CHROMOSOMAL ABNORMALITIES

Before leaving the world of genetics, we should touch briefly on the issue of abnormal chromosomes. As you might remember from your biology classes in high school and college, each person normally has 23 pairs of chromosomes, or 46 chromosomes altogether. The twenty-third pair determines the sex of the child at the moment of conception. Two X chromosomes (XX) mean the fetus will be female, while one X chromosome and one Y chromosome (XY) mean it will be male. Although sperm usually carry either one X or one Y chromosome, occasionally a sperm will carry two X's, two Y's, neither an X nor a Y (designated "O"), or both an X and a Y. The chromosome pattern that results in a fertilized egg will thus be either XXX, XYY, XO, or XXY respectively.

The pattern that most interests some criminologists is XYY, which was discovered in 1961 and is found in fewer than 1 of every 1,000 men. Compared to normal, XY men, XYY men are more likely to be tall with long arms and severe acne and to have low intelligence. The relatively few studies of XYY men find that they are considerably more likely than normal XY men to be arrested or imprisoned, mainly for petty thefts (Carey 1994). Because the XYY abnormality is so rare, however, sample sizes in these studies are quite small. Some who view the XYY abnormality as a cause of crime attribute this link to the low intelligence of XYY men. However, others feel that their arrests and imprisonment are more the result of bias against their unusual and even menacing appearance. In any event, because the XYY abnormality is so rare, at most it explains only a very minuscule fraction of crime (Ellis 1982).

Neurochemical Mechanisms

The human body is filled with many kinds of substances that act as "chemical messengers" to help its various parts perform their functions. Since these functions include behavior, biologists have tried to determine the role chemical substances might play in crime. Two substances that have received considerable attention are hormones and neurotransmitters.

HORMONES: TESTOSTERONE AND MALE CRIMINALITY

In the human body, endocrine glands secrete hormones into the blood, which then transports them throughout the body. After arriving at the various organs or tissue for which they're intended, hormones enable certain functions to occur, including growth, metabolism, sex and reproduction, and stress reaction. One of the most popular modern biological explanations of crime centers on testosterone, the so-called male hormone. As Chapter 3 indicated, men commit much more crime than women. As you undoubtedly already know, men also have more testosterone than women. Combining these two basic sex differences, many biologists and other scholars interested in crime argue that testosterone, or, to be more precise, variation in the amount of testosterone, is an important cause of male criminality. Testosterone differences explain not only why men commit more crime than women but also why some men commit more crime than other men.

Ample evidence exists of a correlation between testosterone level and aggression or criminality. In the animal kingdom, testosterone has often been linked to aggression; among humans, the sex difference both in testosterone and in crime is obvious. Many studies also find that male adolescents and adults with records of violent and nonviolent offending have higher testosterone than males with no such records (Brain 1994; Dabbs and Morris 1990). A recent study of 4,462 Vietnam-era male veterans found a testosterone-criminality relationship. After measuring men's testosterone levels and interviewing them about their offending at various stages in their lives, the researchers found "a moderately strong and significant relationship between testosterone and adult deviance" (Booth and Osgood 1993).

What accounts for the relationship between testosterone and offending? Biologists and other scholars cite several mediating factors that increase the chances of juvenile and adult crime (Booth and Osgood 1993). In particular, higher testosterone is thought to increase aggression and perhaps risktaking and impulsiveness, and thus also low self-control, all important components of delinquency and crime. These effects may also reduce the interpersonal bonds that inhibit offending (see Chapter 7), again leading to higher rates of deviance. As you can see, testosterone is thus thought to interact with many social factors in producing criminality. In conjunction with the evidence of a testosterone-criminality correlation, this interaction of the biological and the social makes a hormonal explanation of criminal behavior very appealing.

However, several methodological problems indicate the testosterone explanation may well be a Trojan horse that is appealing on the outside but flawed upon closer inspection. Consider, for example, the common assumption that testosterone produces aggression throughout the animal kingdom. Although this link is commonly found, it's also true that in many animal species, among them guinea pigs and lions, females are more aggressive than males, although they have lower testosterone. Moreover, neuroendocrinologists who study hormones and behavior caution against extrapolating from animal studies to human behavior. Although it's true that hormones strongly affect many behaviors of lower animals, including primates, the human central nervous system is so complex that simple endocrine influences cannot be assumed.

The evidence among humans of testosterone-induced offending is also open to question. Although many studies have found a link between testosterone and aggression or offending, other studies have found no such link. As you know from Chapter 1, moreover, correlation does not mean causation. A correlation among human males between high testosterone and high offending does not necessarily mean that testosterone affects offending. Methodologically, it is just as plausible that offending affects testosterone, or that some third factor leads to both high testosterone and high offending. In the animal kingdom, for example, aggression and dominance lead to high testosterone in certain species. Although this has not been widely investigated among humans, it's possible that delinquency and adult criminality lead to feelings of dominance and thus to higher testosterone (Miczek et al. 1994).

The sex difference in testosterone and criminality is also obviously subject to other interpretations. As Chapter 3 discussed, sex-role socialization produces different behaviors in girls and boys and different opportunities for offending. To most sociologists, a testosterone-based explanation of the gender difference in crime seems much less plausible than one based on social and structural factors.

In view of these problems, a significant effect of testosterone on human aggression cannot be assumed. A recent review commissioned for the National Academy of Sciences concluded that the testosterone-aggression correlations often found among human males "are not high, they are sometimes difficult to replicate, and importantly, they do not demonstrate causation. In fact there is better evidence for the reverse relationship (behavior altering hormonal levels).... [W]inning—even in innocuous laboratory competitions—can increase testosterone" (Miczek et al. 1994:6–7).

HORMONES: PMS AND CRIME BY WOMEN

One final hormonal explanation of criminality focuses on women. In some women, hormonal changes in the days before menstruation appear to be linked to increased stress, tension, lethargy, and other problems. These women are said to suffer from premenstrual syndrome, or PMS. Thinking this emotional condition might lead to aggression and other offending, some researchers study whether crime by women tends to occur in their premenstrual phase. If PMS were not related to women's crime, their offending would occur randomly throughout their menstrual cycles. If PMS did lead women to offend, their deviance would tend to occur in their premenstrual phase (see Figure 5.2 on page 124).

To study this possibility, researchers have asked women in prison to think back to when they committed the offense for which they were arrested and to remember the dates of their menstruation. From this information researchers can determine whether offenses occurred randomly throughout the women's cycles or instead were concentrated in their premenstrual phase. A leading researcher in this field, Katharina Dalton, has found such a concentration, with about half of the prisoners she studied reporting they committed their offenses in the eight-day period immediately preceding and during menstruation (Dalton 1961).

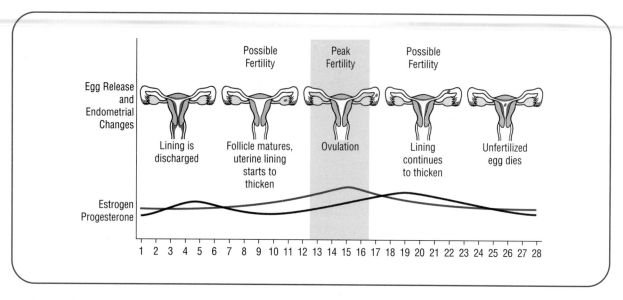

▲ FIGURE 5.2   THE MENSTRUAL CYCLE
SOME STUDIES ATTRIBUTE CRIMES BY WOMEN TO PREMENSTRUAL SYNDROME, BUT METHODOLOGICAL
PROBLEMS CAST DOUBT ON THIS CONCLUSION.

Dalton attributed their criminality to their emotional condition and increased lethargy and clumsiness during this time: Their emotional condition prompted them to commit the crimes, and their lethargy and clumsiness made it more difficult for them to avoid detection and arrest. To support her view of women's physical ineptitude, Dalton noted that half of women drivers involved in serious auto accidents are also in the eight-day premenstrual-menstrual phase. Dalton's and other researchers' findings have led some criminal defense attorneys to claim PMS as a defense when women have been tried for various crimes. In England in 1980, for example, one woman murdered her boyfriend by driving her car into him, and another killed a co-worker in a London pub. Both claimed that PMS led to their violence, and both received probation instead of imprisonment.

As you might expect, the PMS explanation for women's crime is quite controversial. Many scholars feel that it takes us back to the myths of "raging hormones," when women were considered unfit to be airplane pilots, president of the United States, and other positions because they could not be trusted to act rationally during "that time of the month."

Beyond these ideological concerns, the PMS research is also methodologically flawed, perhaps fatally (Horney 1978; Katz and Chambliss 1995). It assumes that women can accurately remember when menstruation occurred, since even a few days' error can place their crime outside of their premenstrual phase. Some women are very regular and can remember the dates of their menstruation but others cannot. More important, it is well known that stress and other problems can disrupt women's cycles, with menstruation occurring either sooner or later than expected. If the stress of committing crime, or the stress leading up to the crime, hastens menstruation, it may appear artificially that the crime occurred in a woman's premenstrual phase only because menstruation occurred sooner than normal. In recalling Dalton's finding that half of all women drivers in serious accidents were in the eight-day premenstrual-menstrual phase of their cycles, consider that half of all women passengers involved in accidents are in the same phase (Horney 1978). As

Janet Katz and William J. Chambliss (1995:290) aptly put it, "Unless we wish to argue that the passenger's lethargy somehow caused the accident, it would appear that the trauma of the accident triggered menstruation, not vice versa."

NEUROTRANSMITTERS

The human nervous system consists of billions of cells called neurons and bundles of neurons called nerves. Nerves carry messages from the brain throughout the body and messages from the body back to the brain and spinal cord. Certain neurons called receptors are found in the sense organs of the body, such as the eye. Receptors send messages, or impulses, through nerves back to the brain. After obtaining these messages, the brain sends instructions for particular actions back to various parts of the body. Neurons transmit impulses to each other across synapses with the aid of chemical substances called *neurotransmitters*. In studying aggression, scientists have been particularly interested in one particular neurotransmitter, serotonin (Jacobson and Rowe 2000).

In animal studies, low levels of serotonin are linked with higher levels of aggression. Many studies of humans have found low levels of serotonin in violent offenders (Moffitt et al. 1998). Although some researchers find the serotonin research particularly interesting, it suffers from several of the methodological problems already discussed, including inconsistent measurement of offending and the possibility that serotonin levels result from aggression rather than the reverse, which make it premature to assume a strong role for serotonin in human aggression. Some studies even find *higher* levels of serotonin in aggressive individuals. A recent review concluded that "serotonin is not a very discriminating marker for violence" (Wallman 1999:24).

Diet and Nutrition

In late 1978 a San Francisco city supervisor named Dan White allegedly murdered George Moscone, the city's mayor, and Harvey Milk, a city supervisor and gay activist. I lived near San Francisco at the time and will never forget how much the murders shocked the Bay Area. People even stopped shopping for Christmas presents for several days, as the whole community shared in collective grief. When White was tried for the two murders, his attorney claimed he had been eating too much junk food. The sugar and various additives in the food supposedly deepened his depression and reduced his ability to tell right from wrong. White's "Twinkie defense" worked, as he was convicted only of manslaughter, not first-degree murder. His conviction on the lower charge outraged Bay Area residents (Weiss 1984).

As this example indicates, diet and nutrition are popularly thought to play a role in aggression and crime (Kanarek 1994). Researchers investigate this role with two kinds of studies. In the first kind, they control the levels of various nutrients given to animal or occasionally human subjects in the laboratory and then compare the behavior of these subjects to control groups. In the second kind, they compare the diet and nutrition of offenders, usually juveniles, to those of nonoffenders. From this body of evidence several diet and nutritional factors have been identified as producing aggression and other forms of offending. High amounts of sugar and refined carbohydrates, excessive levels of chemical additives, and deficiencies in vitamin B and other vitamins have received the most attention.

Despite the common-sense appeal of this research, it, too, suffers from several methodological problems that cast doubt on its findings, including small samples, possibly spurious findings, and ambiguity in defining offending. Moreover, several studies of diet and nutrition do not find them linked to antisocial behavior. A review of the research concluded that diet and nutrition have at most a "relatively minor" effect on criminality (Kanarek 1994:535).

Pregnancy and Birth Complications

Some of the most interesting biological research concerns the effects of pregnancy and birth complications. These complications are often referred to as *perinatal* problems. Poor nutrition or the use of alcohol and drugs during pregnancy are thought to harm fetal development, with potentially long-lasting effects on central nervous system (CNS) functioning that in turn can lead to antisocial behavior. For example, a recent study found that boys born to women who smoked during pregnancy were twice as likely as those whose mothers did not smoke to be arrested for a violent crime by age 34 (Conlon 1999). CNS functioning can also be impaired by complications during difficult births. Although the evidence is mixed, some studies find such neurodevelopmental problems to be linked to later onset of childhood and adolescent behavioral problems, especially violent aggression. A recent review noted that "delivery complications appear to be more predictive of later criminal behavior than pregnancy problems or low birthweight" (Brennan, Mednick, and Volavka 1995:76).

Although this body of research suggests a biological role in offending, other interpretations are possible. In particular, pregnancy and birth complications may often be the fault of mothers who don't observe standard advice for promoting fetal health and development. As biological researchers Elizabeth Kandel and Sarnoff A. Mednick (1991:526) observe, "Such poor prenatal mothering might be related to poor mothering after birth, which would render the birth complications-violent behavior association spurious." To rule out this possibility, postnatal parenting would have to be observed, or adopted babies with perinatal complications studied.

◄ *Smoking during pregnancy may impair fetal development, causing potentially long-lasting effects on central nervous system functioning. Although the evidence is mixed, some studies find that such neurodevelopmental problems are linked to the later onset of childhood and adolescent behavioral problems, especially violent aggression.*

CRIME AND CONTROVERSY

Race and Biological Research

Efforts to explain crime through genetic or other biological explanations continue to spark racial controversy. Three events from the 1990s underscore the racial passions aroused by such explanations.

The first controversy engulfed the appointment of a prominent psychiatrist to the head of the National Institute of Mental Health (NIMH). In a February 1992 meeting, Frederick K. Goodwin, then head of the U.S. Alcohol, Drug Abuse and Mental Health Administration, had likened the violence of urban youths to the behavior of young monkeys. In his remarks, Goodwin noted that half of young male monkeys die by violence, and those that survive are not only "hyperaggressive" but also "hypersexual." They thus "copulate more and ... reproduce more to offset the fact that half of them are dying." Then, he added, "Maybe it isn't just the careless use of the word when people call certain areas of certain cities jungles."

When his comments became known, critics attacked them as racially insensitive, and Goodwin resigned his post, only to be appointed head of NIMH. The American Psychological Association and the National Association of Social Workers criticized his appointment, and the American Orthopsychiatric Association (AOA), a national society of mental health professionals, called for his removal. However, many other groups, including the American Psychiatric Association, supported the appointment.

Goodwin's critics further charged that his policies stressed biological approaches to violence while neglecting social and environmental explanations. As one example, he had urged scientists to discover biological markers that would identify violence-prone children as young as age five. The president of the AOA said this approach would ignore social causes of urban violence, including childhood abuse and poverty: "This kind of identification program would label and stigmatize poor five-year-olds and reify the very behavior that the policy would hope to squelch. It could also be a harbinger to the development of a repressive social policy."

The second controversy came the next year, when a scheduled conference on genetics and crime sponsored by the National Institutes of Health (NIH) was canceled at the last moment after critics condemned its racial implications. The conference, "Genetic Factors in Crime: Findings, Uses, and Implications," was originally scheduled for October 1992 at the University of Maryland. NIH had promised $78,000 to support the conference but became alarmed by the criticism. NIH officials were particularly concerned by a conference brochure which declared that "genetic research holds out the prospect of identifying individuals who may be predisposed to certain kinds of criminal conduct, of isolating environmental factors which trigger those predispositions, and of treating some predispositions with drugs and unintrusive therapies." When they learned of the conference, several African-American organizations and social science scholars reacted with outrage.

The third controversy surrounded a major research project in Chicago funded by the National Institute of Justice and the MacArthur Foundation. Still ongoing, the $32 million project, titled the Project on Human Development in Chicago Neighborhoods, is an ambitious longitudinal effort to study 11,000 randomly selected subjects ranging in age from babies still in their mothers' wombs through young adults. The subjects are being monitored through personal interviews and questionnaires and academic, criminal, and medical records. The aim is to determine the social, psychological, and biological differences between offenders and nonoffenders.

One of the project's major hypotheses is that children with certain antisocial personality traits, including stubbornness, defiance, and fearlessness, are more likely than other children to become serious delinquents and adult criminals. The project aims to identify these children so that crime prevention programs can target them.

Several African-American scholars fear that the targeted children will be mostly African-Americans. One scholar said, "They say they're not looking at black children and violence, but it's real clear who's being focused." The project's researchers reply that these charges are groundless, and that the project promises to yield an enormous amount of knowledge on the causes of urban violence that can provide the basis for effective prevention programs.

Sources: Bass 1992; Coughlin 1994; Holden 1992; Jeffery 1993; Leary 1992; Montgomery 1995.

Critique of Biological Explanations

Many biologists and some criminologists are enthusiastic about the potential of biological theories to explain crime (Fishbein 1998; Jeffery 1994; Moffitt et al. 1998). Most sociologists and other criminologists are more wary (Akers 1997; Curran and Renzetti 1994; Vold, Bernard, and Snipes 1998). Let's look at some of their concerns.

One problem is that crime is simply too diverse. Even if biological factors account for some violent aggression, they wouldn't explain the vast majority of criminality. Among other problems, they can't easily account for the "relativity" of deviance; that is, they can't explain why someone with a biological predisposition to violence turns to street crime instead of, say, football or any other activity involving physical force. As McCaghy and Capron (1994:43) point out, violence "in a bar brawl" makes you a criminal; violence "on a battlefield" makes you a hero. A biological explanation of violence is thus not the same thing as a biological explanation of *criminal* violence.

Another problem is methodological. As our review of biological explanations indicated, several methodological problems—including small, unrepresentative samples of offenders, inadequate control groups, and correlations between biological factors and offending that are subject to many interpretations—make it difficult to infer any firm conclusions from biological research.

A third problem concerns what I call "group rate differences." As we saw earlier in this chapter, sociologists are interested in different crime rates from one group or setting to another. Thus we are less interested, for example, in why a particular individual in a big city commits a crime than in why urban areas have higher crime rates than rural areas. Biological explanations cannot easily account for group rate differences. Take the fact that the United States has a much higher homicide rate than Western European nations. How would you explain this biologically? Is it really conceivable that U.S. residents are different biologically from residents of England, Germany, or Denmark in a way that leads to more crime in the United States? Can the high crime rates of big cities as compared to rural areas really be attributed to biological problems in big-city residents? Can biological explanations account for why street crime rose in the United States during the 1960s and fell in the 1990s? Even if they might explain why some individuals commit crime, they cannot easily account for different crime rates among groups or locations or for changes in crime rates. As one observer notes, the explanation of these kinds of trends "will come not from research in neurobiology but from understanding economic forces, variation in cultural mores regarding the acceptability of violence, diversity in the kinds and efficacy of means of informal and formal social control, and availability of firearms" (Wallman 1999:24).

A final concern about biological explanations addresses their social policy implications. One implication is that to reduce crime we have to do something about the biological deficiency that causes it. However, short of some science-fiction world that, thankfully, does not yet exist, we can't easily change biology. And if we can't change biology, we can't reduce crime. Say, for example, that biochemical deficiencies explain why people commit crime. If so, what can we do to reduce crime? Perform some genetic engineering? Give them drugs to correct the deficiencies? Given the rapid rise in scientific advances, some of these measures are quickly becoming possible but remain rather frightening. Perinatal research is a notable exception. If it turns out to be true that perinatal problems predict later offending, then it may be possible to reduce crime with social policies aimed at better prenatal health care and nutrition, especially among the poor, where pregnancy and birth complications are more common.

Responding to the concern that biological explanations imply little chance for reducing crime, some researchers stress that biological traits interact with environmental influences to produce crime: Biological factors may predispose individuals to crime, but the extent and timing of their influence depends on environmental factors (Fishbein 1996; Tibbetts and Piquero 1999). Efforts to change the social environment thus hold much promise for reducing crime. Although this "softer" position is more compatible with a sociological framework, it still suggests the need to do something about the biological traits. Thus some scholars recommend, for example, that children be screened for biological traits that may lead to later criminality (Jeffery 1994; Nelkin 1993). Proposals like this raise several ethical and other concerns, including the possibility that children targeted in this fashion may be "labeled" as potential criminals (see Chapter 8) and treated that way.

A related problem with biological explanations centers on their potential justification for appalling acts committed against people regarded as biologically different. It's a short step from considering people biologically different to viewing them as biologically inferior (Rafter 1997; Shipman 1994). History is replete with acts of genocide, lynchings, hate crime, and other actions taken against people deemed biologically inferior to some ruling group, with their supposed inferiority justifying the inhumane treatment. Hundreds of thousands of Native Americans were murdered in what came to be called the United States by white Europeans who considered them subhuman. Millions of Africans were brought to the New World in chains and kept for two centuries in slavery. In the early decades of this century, the eugenics movement in the United States led to the involuntary sterilization of some 70,000 people, almost all of them poor and many of them African-American (Rafter 1997). Not too long after, Nazi Germany slaughtered millions of Jews and others who were thought inferior to the Aryan race. The "evidence" gathered by American eugenicists of biological inferiority reinforced Nazi ideology (Kuhl 1994).

If, then, we find that a biological trait makes certain people more likely to be criminals, history tells us it's very easy for these groups to be considered biologically inferior and in need of special, even inhumane, treatment, even if no biologists today advocate such treatment. These groups are usually the poor and people of color, as biological research on crime has centered on street crimes committed by the poor, ignoring the white-collar crimes by wealthier people. It might sound silly to you even to suggest that a defective gene or hormonal imbalance leads corporate executives to engage in price fixing or to market unsafe products. Yet, given our society's prejudices, it might not sound as silly to suggest that a biological problem leads poor people to commit acts of common violence. Many of the early biological researchers were prejudiced against the poor, immigrants, and people of color and interpreted their findings as "proof" of these groups' biological inferiority (Gould 1981). Given continuing racial and ethnic prejudice, we must be very careful in interpreting the findings of contemporary research on biology and crime.

One sociologist wrote a decade ago, "In my opinion, criminologists ultimately must come to grips with biological hypotheses and findings" (Gibbons 1992:7). As we've just seen, however, many sociologists continue to be critical of these same hypotheses and findings. The value of biological explanations will undoubtedly remain a major source of controversy in criminology for some years to come.

Psychological Explanations

As discussed earlier, psychology offers valuable understanding of individual behavior but says little about the larger social and structural forces also at work. In the area of crime, sociology and psychology together provide a more comprehensive explanation than either discipline can provide separately. Sociology tries to explain why certain groups and locations have more crime than others, while psychology may be able to tell why a few people with these backgrounds commit serious crime while most do not (Andrews and Bonta 1999; Bartol 1999). Let's look at the major psychological explanations for criminal behavior, leaving learning approaches, which are more compatible with a sociological framework, for a later chapter (Chapter 7).

Psychoanalytic Explanations

Modern psychoanalytic explanations see delinquency and crime rising from internal disturbances developing in early childhood because of interaction problems between parents and children. These explanations derive from the work of Sigmund Freud (1856–1939), the founder of psychoanalysis (Freud 1935 [1920]; 1961 [1930]). Although Freud focused more on mental disorders than on criminality per se, his work provided a logical foundation for extensions into delinquency and crime by later theorists. Freud and his followers see mental disorders arising from a conflict between society and the instinctive needs of the individual. The individual personality consists of three parts: the *id*, the *ego*, and the *superego*. The id, present at birth, consists of instinctual desires that demand immediate gratification: Infants get hungry and don't take no for an answer if they're not fed soon enough. Eventually the ego develops and represents the more rational part of personality. A child learns that he or she can't always expect immediate gratification of his or her needs. The superego comes later and represents the internalization of society's moral code. This is the individual's conscience and leads the individual to feel guilty or ashamed for violating social norms. The development of these three parts of the personality is generally complete by about age 5.

Freud thought that people are inherently pleasure-seeking because of the id, but that too much pleasure-seeking can translate into antisocial behavior. The ego and superego thus need to restrain the id. This happens in mentally healthy individuals as the three parts of the personality coexist harmoniously. A lack of balance can result when a child's needs for food, emotional comfort, and the like are not met because of parental deprivation, neglect, or overly harsh discipline. According to psychoanalytic theory, if the superego becomes too weak to control the id's instinctive impulses, delinquency and crime result. They can also result if the superego is too strong, when individuals feel overly guilty and ashamed. The rational part of the personality, the ego, realizes that if individuals commit a crime they will be punished and thus reduce their guilt. Given this realization, the ego leads the person to break the law.

Psychoanalytic explanations have been valuable in emphasizing the importance of early childhood experiences for later behavior, but their value for understanding crime is limited for several reasons (Vold, Bernard, and Snipes 1998). First, they suggest that antisocial behavior is mentally disordered behavior, which isn't true for most individuals. Second, they neglect social factors and overemphasize childhood experiences; while these are undoubtedly important, later life-cycle influences are also important (Laub and Sampson 1993). Finally, psychoanalytic research relies on case histories of individuals under treatment or on samples of offenders in juvenile institutions, adult prisons, or mental institutions. Such methodology ignores the possibilities that the subjects might not represent the vast majority of offenders not under treatment or institutionalized and that any mental or emotional problems in the institutionalized subjects may be the result, and not the cause, of their institutionalization.

Before we leave psychoanalytic explanations, a comment on their view of women's criminality is in order. Although Freud is widely regarded as one of the three or four greatest thinkers of the last two centuries (along with Marx, Darwin, and Einstein), his views on women reflected the sexism of his day (Klein 1973). Freud viewed child rearing as women's natural role in life and thought that females who could not adjust to this role suffered from "penis envy" and hence mental disorder. To compensate for the lack of a penis, some women, he thought, tried to act like men in desiring careers. Extending Freud's views to delinquency and crime, Freudian scholars later attributed most girls' delinquency to their sexual needs. In a traditional Freudian framework, then, women and girls with mental disorders or histories of crime and delinquency need to be helped to adjust to their natural child-rearing roles. Thanks to critiques by feminist scholars, this view of female criminality lost popularity in the 1970s but hasn't disappeared.

Moral Development and Crime

Since the time of Jean Piaget (1896–1980), psychologists have been interested in children's mental and moral development. Piaget thought that children experience four stages of mental development. The *sensorimotor* period lasts until the age of two and involves learning about their immediate environment and developing their reflexes. The *preoperational* period lasts from ages two to seven and consists of learning language, drawing, and other skills. A stage of *concrete operations* lasts from ages seven to eleven and involves learning logical thinking and problem solving. The final *formal operations* stage occurs during ages eleven to fifteen and concerns dealing with abstract ideas (Pulaski 1980).

Following in Piaget's footsteps, psychologist Lawrence Kohlberg (1969) developed his theory of *moral development*. This is the development of the ability to distinguish right from wrong and to determine the ethically correct course of action in complex circumstances. Kohlberg theorized that individuals pass through several stages in which they develop their ability to reason morally. In the early stages, children's moral reasoning is related solely to punishment: Their view of what is correct behavior is equivalent to behavior that keeps them from getting punished. In later stages they begin to realize as adolescents that society and their parents have rules that deserve to be obeyed in and of themselves, not just to avoid punishment. They also realize that exhibiting the behaviors expected of them will lead others to view them positively. In the final stages of moral development during late adolescence and early adulthood, people recognize that universal moral principles supersede the laws of any one society. Individuals reaching this stage may decide to disobey the law in the name of a "higher" law.

Kohlberg further theorized that not everyone makes it through all the stages of moral development. In particular, some people's moral development stops after only the early stages. Because their view of right and wrong is limited to what avoids punishment, they haven't developed what many of us would call a conscience and may well engage in harmful behavior as long as they think they won't get punished for it. Kohlberg thus thought that incomplete moral development was a major reason for criminal and other antisocial behavior. Studies by Kohlberg and others of the level of moral reasoning in samples of offenders and nonoffenders support his theory (Henggeler 1989; Kohlberg 1969).

One problem with tests of Kohlberg's theory is the familiar chicken-and-egg question of causal order. Even if offenders do have a lower level of moral reasoning than nonoffenders, it's possible their offending affected their moral reasoning rather than the reverse. They might have begun to violate the law for other reasons, such as peer pressure or hostility toward their parents, and then adjusted their moral reasoning to accommodate their illegal behavior to minimize any guilt or shame.

Intelligence and Crime

Researchers have long blamed crime on low intelligence. Studies early in this century by Goddard and others found low IQs among prisoners and juveniles in reform schools. Scholars later criticized this research for using small, unrepresentative samples and unreliable tests, and it lost popularity by the 1930s (Gould 1981). In the late 1970s, however, an article by Travis Hirschi and Michael Hindelang in a preeminent sociology journal renewed interest in the IQ-crime issue (Hirschi and Hindelang 1977). They reviewed many studies using both self-report and official data and found that delinquents' IQ scores were about eight points lower than nondelinquents' scores. The authors concluded that low IQ is an important cause of delinquency.

Although findings are not always consistent, later studies also link delinquency to low IQ. Some scholars go as far as to say that IQ is a stronger predictor of delinquency than either race or social class and that blacks' low native intelligence is the major reason they commit more street crimes than whites (Herrnstein and Murray 1994).

Most research on IQ and offending focuses on adolescents, for whom several reasons are thought to explain the apparent causal link between IQ and delinquency. First, youths with low intelligence do poorly in school. Poor school performance in turn leads to less attachment to school and more alienation from it, and thus to higher rates of delinquency. Second, low intelligence leads to a lower ability to engage in moral reasoning and to delay gratification, increasing the likelihood of offending. Third, adolescents with low intelligence are thought to be less able to appreciate the consequences of their actions and to be more susceptible to the influence of delinquent friends (Hirschi and Hindelang 1977; Lynam, Moffitt, and Stouthamer-Loeber 1993).

If some studies link low intelligence to crime, other research proposes that low intelligence is inherited. Dugdale's early study of the Jukes and Goddard's study of the Kallikaks both assumed that low intelligence is passed biologically from one generation to the next. Research on heredity and intelligence became more sophisticated early in this century with the development of the IQ test and its administration to different groups of people. Finding different average IQ scores among these groups and assuming that IQ tests measure natural intelligence, many researchers concluded that IQ is an inherited trait and that different kinds of people differ in natural intelligence. For example, the low scores of Polish and Russian immigrants to the United States who took the test in the early 1900s indicated to researchers that they were innately less intelligent than whites from Anglo-Saxon backgrounds (Gould 1981).

Over the years, black-white differences in IQ scores have also been found, with the average scores of blacks about 10 to 15 points below those for whites (Wilson and Herrnstein 1985). Some researchers interpret blacks' lower scores as evidence that they are naturally less intelligent than whites, while others think the scores stem from poor prenatal care among blacks, which leads permanently to lower intelligence (Herrnstein and Murray 1994; Jensen 1969; Wilson and Herrnstein 1985).

Suppose we accept the assumptions guiding the research linking IQ, race, and crime: (1) IQ tests are valid measures of natural intelligence; (2) blacks are intellectually inferior to whites; (3) low natural intelligence produces higher rates of delinquency and crime; (4) low natural intelligence is an important and perhaps the major reason for high rates of street crime by blacks. What do these beliefs imply about efforts to reduce such crime?

Since they discount social factors, they suggest, first of all, that efforts to reduce social inequality and other structural problems would do relatively little to reduce black crime rates. Since they emphasize blacks' low natural intelligence as a primary cause of their criminality, they also imply that to reduce black crime rates we have to improve their innate intelligence. But to say that intelligence is innate or natural suggests that efforts to raise it will probably be useless; given this futility, we can do little to reduce African-American crime. Since we cannot reduce it, perhaps all we can do is to deter blacks from committing crime by putting even more of them in prison. Some might even say we should sterilize blacks because their low intelligence poses a menace to the rest of society.

This is certainly a pessimistic appraisal, and perhaps a bit simplistic, but is it warranted? Not if the assumptions turn out to be questionable or even false, which is precisely what many critics charge (Gould 1981; Lewontin, Rose and Kamin 1984; Menard and Morse 1984). Without question, the early IQ research was rife with methodological problems; much of it was carried out by researchers with views we would now call racist. Recent IQ studies are more carefully designed, with many using twins and adopted children, but still suffer from the same problems affecting heredity and crime research. As a result, their findings on IQ, race, and crime are suspect. In one particular problem, IQ studies often use samples of offenders in adult prisons or juvenile institutions. Because incarcerated offenders represent only a very small proportion of all offenders, we cannot safely generalize these studies' findings to the entire offender population.

Perhaps more important, many critics charge, IQ tests are culturally biased and less a measure of intelligence than of white, middle-class background or of school achievement. Instead of reflecting low natural intelligence, then, blacks' low IQ scores may simply reflect their poorer schooling and the fact that they are not white and usually not middle class.

In sum, race-IQ-crime assumptions are highly questionable at best and patently false at worst, with dangerous racial and class overtones. Although it's too early to rule out the assumed intelligence-criminality link in the race-IQ-crime chain, history tells us we must tread very cautiously in this area.

Personality and Crime

Some of the most important work today in psychology and crime focuses on temperament, or personality, and aggressive and other antisocial behavior. In an early study, Eleanor and Sheldon Glueck administered Rorschach (ink blot) tests to 500 delinquents and the same number of nondelinquents matched on several characteristics, and found greater personality problems in the delinquents (Glueck and Glueck 1950). Other research began to use personality inventories, most often the Minnesota Multiphasic Personality Inventory (MMPI) and the California Psychological Inventory (CPI), administering them to samples of incarcerated juvenile and adult offenders. These inventories list several hundred true/false and other items (e.g., "I would do almost anything on a dare") to which subjects respond; the CPI includes about one third of the MMPI items. These studies found personality differences between offenders and nonoffenders that are assumed to be responsible for the offending.

Much of the current research focuses on childhood temperament, as many studies, some of them longitudinal, link temperament problems during infancy and childhood with behavioral problems during this time and also with later delinquency during adolescence. The long list of temperament problems includes such things as attention deficits, impulsiveness, hyperactivity, irritability, coldness, and suspiciousness. Children with temperament problems are more likely to become delinquent in unstable families marked by inadequate parenting than in stable ones where parents are loving and supportive. Although most children with temperament problems do not commit serious delinquency during adolescence, the ones with the worst problems are more likely to become delinquent. Further, most serious delinquents are thought to have had childhood temperament problems (Caspi et al. 1994; Farrington 1998).

This body of work has important implications for reducing crime. If early childhood temperament problems do matter, then attempts to reduce them may reduce delinquency and crime (Zigler, Taussig, and Black 1992). Such efforts include preschool and early family intervention programs. If we wait until adolescence to work with juvenile offenders, it's often too late. As Cathy Spatz Widom and Hans Toch (Widom and Toch 1993:263) observe, "By the time [juveniles] are treated, often after referral by court personnel, typically they have been involved in a long history of antisocial behavior and conduct problems that are not reversed easily."

Although the personality research is appealing, several problems limit its applicability (Einstadter and Henry 1995; Tennenbaum 1977). Perhaps most important,

◀ *Although most children with temperament problems do not commit serious delinquency during adolescence, the ones with the worst problems are more likely to become delinquent. Furthermore, children with temperament problems are more likely to become delinquent in unstable families marked by inadequate parenting than in stable ones where parents are loving and supportive.*

several studies of personality and offending find no differences between offenders and nonoffenders. Also, because most of the research examines juvenile offenders in institutions, the offenders' personality problems may be the result of their institutionalization and not the cause. The personality-offending link may even result from an effect of offending on personality traits rather than the reverse. Because many studies don't control for socioeconomic status, education, and other characteristics, their correlation between personality and criminality may also be spurious. In one further methodological problem, the validity of the MMPI and other inventories for assessing the effects of personality on criminality is also open to question, since some of their items ask subjects about their offending. Thus a respondent who admits to offending automatically provides an answer indicating a personality problem.

A recent study of youths in Pittsburgh and New Zealand sought to overcome these problems by measuring personality without regard to criminality and by using random samples and self-reports of offending (Caspi et al. 1994). The researchers found personality differences linked to delinquency. Youths expressing negative emotionality—a tendency to react to stress with fear and anger—and/or high impulsiveness were more likely to be delinquent than youths with neither trait. Despite its methodological sophistication, however, this study didn't deal adequately with the question of causal order and did not eliminate the possibility of spuriousness.

A final problem with personality research is that personality explanations of crime, like their biological counterparts, can't adequately account for the "relativity" of deviance: They cannot explain why individuals psychologically predisposed to thrill-seeking or violence undertake criminal actions instead of legal ones (McCaghy and Capron 2000). Some people with the impulsiveness trait mentioned previously, for example, may pursue car racing or parachute jumping as careers or hobbies; others may choose crime. Personality explanations do not help us understand why one behavior instead of the other is chosen.

Taken together, these problems mean we must be cautious in drawing conclusions from the personality-crime research. As a recent review noted, "While it might be comforting to think that the criminal is a special type of person that can be distinguished from noncriminals through [psychological] testing, in reality it appears that ... there are few if any differences between these groups" (Curran and Renzetti 1994:109). Many psychologists, of course, disagree with this assessment, and personality research will no doubt continue to challenge conventional criminological thinking. In this regard, the research project in New Zealand mentioned previously has been extremely valuable, as it has followed subjects from childhood through age 21. Its longitudinal design allows it to assess whether various problems during childhood predict delinquency and other problems several years later. As the International Focus box on page 136 discusses, this project's findings provide a powerful case for the argument that personality and other problems during childhood do help lead to delinquency and other problems later on. It also underscores the need to try to prevent these problems from emerging in the first place.

Critique of Psychological Explanations

Some psychologists criticize the "antipsychological bias" they see in sociological criminology (Andrews and Bonta 1999). While true to some extent, this charge is also too severe. Although sociologists certainly look beyond the individual, many

Psychological Research in New Zealand

New Zealand has been the site of some of the best-designed research on the biological, psychological, and developmental (family-based) causes of delinquency and crime. The researchers involved are Avshalom Caspi and Terrie A. Moffitt, psychology professors at the University of Wisconsin-Madison, and several colleagues there and in New Zealand.

The basis for their research is the Dunedin Multidisciplinary Health and Development Study, a longitudinal investigation begun in the 1970s. The researchers began studying more than 1,000 children born in 1972 and 1973 in New Zealand's province of Dunedin when they were three years old, and studied them again every two years thereafter into early adulthood, gathering several kinds of medical, psychological, and sociological information each time. At the outset of the study, they also obtained perinatal data for when the subjects were born.

As reported earlier in this chapter, Caspi, Moffitt and colleagues found correlations in one study between various personality characteristics and delinquency among their subjects and also a sample of Pittsburgh youths. For both sexes, delinquency (as measured by self-reports) was higher in youths with the following traits: aggression (feels willing to hurt or frighten others); alienation (feels victimized and betrayed); stress reaction (feels nervous and vulnerable or worries a lot); and social potency (feels forceful and decisive). It was also lower in youths with these traits: traditionalism (favors high moral standards); harm-avoidance (dislikes excitement and danger); and control (is reflective and cautious). As noted in the chapter, this study did not deal with the usual problems of causal order and spuriousness, rendering the correlations it found subject to different interpretations.

In other research, the New Zealand researchers have taken advantage of their study's longitudinal design and have found that behavioral, personality, and other problems during childhood predict several types of problems by adolescence and then young adulthood, including conflict in interacting with others, delinquency, employment problems, and domestic violence. They have also found that boys at age 13 with neuropsychological problems such as poor language processing, poor memory, and difficulty in linking visual information to motor skills ended up with the highest rates of delinquency, even after controlling for socioeconomic status. They concluded that neuropsychological problems are an important risk factor for male delinquency. Such problems, they feel, impair communication between children and their parents, teachers, and peers, and hamper school performance. These problems in turn promote delinquency (see Chapter 7).

According to Caspi, Moffitt, and their colleagues, their findings have important implications for preventing crime, since childhood neuropsychological, personality, and behavioral problems often stem from issues in the social or family environment that can be prevented. These issues include poor nutrition during pregnancy, alcohol or drug use during pregnancy, birth complications, childhood head injuries, exposure to lead and other toxic substances, and inadequate parenting. Thus "public health interventions that improve the home and community environments in which children develop may ultimately trickle down to help alleviate the problem of persistent crime."

Sources: Caspi 2000; Caspi et al. 1995; Caspi et al. 1994; Caspi et al. 1998; Moffitt and Caspi 1999; Moffitt, Lynam, and Silva 1994; Silva and Stanton 1996.

of their structural explanations for crime rest on social-psychological states such as frustration and alienation (see Chapter 6). Many of the social process theories favored by sociologists (see Chapter 7) also rest on psychological concepts such as learning and role-modeling.

In certain respects, psychological explanations complement sociological ones in explaining crime. By highlighting the importance of negative childhood experiences, especially within the family, for later delinquency and criminality, they begin to fill in the smaller picture of crime that sociology's structural approach leaves empty. As we'll be seeing in the next two chapters, moreover, several psychological concepts play an important role in sociological theories of crime.

Despite the contributions that some psychological approaches make to our understanding of crime, several issues remain (Curran and Renzetti 1994; Vold, Bernard, and Snipes 1998). First, psychological studies often use small, unrepresentative samples of offenders in prisons or mental institutions. Even if these offenders are psychologically different, the difference may be the result of their institutionalization and not the cause. Second, psychological studies generally disregard structural factors such as poverty and cannot easily account for variations in crime by group and location or for changes in crime rates.

Third, although they offer interesting statistical correlations, their causal order remains unclear. In this regard, the recent longitudinal studies of early childhood temperament and later delinquency have been very valuable, as their research design allows us to conclude that temperament problems precede initial delinquency, even if delinquency might later in turn affect temperament. The key is to discover why young children have temperament problems. Biologists think many of these are genetic in origin and trace them to biochemical defects. In a recent example of such research, two sets of scientists from the United States and Israel identified a genetic basis for a personality trait they called "novelty-seeking." People with this trait tend to be extroverted, impulsive, and quick to anger (Angier 1996). We can expect that future research will seek to discover whether the gene the scientists found is disproportionately present in criminal subjects. For their part, as we have seen, many psychologists trace personality problems to early childhood experiences. While acknowledging the influence of these experiences, sociologists would stress that the most negative experiences occur amid poverty and other structural problems conducive to crime (see Chapter 6).

In an additional problem, psychologists of crime join their biological counterparts in rarely studying crimes by white-collar offenders, even though these crimes may involve injury and death. That researchers and the public continue to be attracted to suggestions of psychological abnormality in common criminals may reflect popular views of the poor and people of color more than the actual existence of abnormality.

ABNORMALITY OR NORMALITY?

Psychological approaches also suggest that crime and criminals are both psychologically abnormal. Normal people don't commit crime; abnormal people do. Emile Durkheim (1962 [1895]), one of the founders of sociology (Chapter 1), wrote that crime and deviance are indeed normal, meaning that they occur in every healthy society because people will always violate the norms of any society. Building upon Durkheim's perspective, sociological criminology sees crime and deviance arising from normal social structures, institutions, and processes. Since psychological explanations feel that individuals have problems that lead them to commit crime, they suggest the way to reduce crime is to cure the few aberrant individuals who commit it. As we saw with eating disorders, a sociological perspective suggests there will always be other deviants to take their place given the social and structural forces at work.

It may also be mistaken to view most criminals as psychologically abnormal. It's very possible to commit horrible violence and still be psychologically normal in other respects. Studies after World War II of prison guards in Nazi concentration camps found them to be good husbands and fathers who performed well on various psychological tests. Despite their apparent psychological normality, they were able to commit some of the worst crimes known to humanity.

Two famous psychological experiments are telling in this regard. The first took place in the early 1960s when Yale University psychologist Stanley Milgram recruited Yale students and residents of Bridgeport, Connecticut, to administer electric shock in a learning experiment (Milgram 1974). Subjects were asked to apply electric shock to "learners" who performed poorly in word-pair tests. The inspiration for Milgram's experiment was the Nazi Holocaust, which was attributed to an "authoritarian personality" that was said to be the result of German culture, history, and socialization. Milgram planned to conduct his experiment in both Germany and the United States but was stunned to find his U.S. subjects all too ready to administer electric shock to learners who were screaming in pain and pleading for them to stop. Unknown to the subjects, no electric shock was actually used. The learners they saw were all actors, and the learners they heard over the loudspeaker were all part of a tape recording. Because it indicated that psychologically normal U.S. residents were quite capable of inflicting serious injury on innocent people, Milgram's experiment attracted wide attention and remains controversial to this day.

The other experiment was conducted at Stanford University, where psychologist Philip Zimbardo constructed a mock prison in the basement of a psychology building (Zimbardo 1972). He recruited volunteers from male Stanford students and, after eliminating those with histories of illegal drug use or mental and emotional problems, randomly assigned the remainder to be either guards or prisoners in the mock prison. The "prisoners" were "arrested" by real police, booked, and fingerprinted, and then taken to the mock prison. In the prison they wore uniforms and stockings on their heads to remove their individuality, and were each given a number to replace their names.

By the end of the first day of the experiment, the "guards" were already treating the prisoners harshly, verbally abusing them and forcing them to stand at attention hours on end, do calisthenics, and the like. Within another day or so the prisoners refused to come out of their cells (revamped laboratory rooms). The rebellion prompted further abuse by the guards. At the end of a few more days, one of the prisoners suffered a nervous breakdown and had to be convinced he wasn't really a prisoner. With more prisoners suffering similar symptoms, Zimbardo decided to end his experiment prematurely. Zimbardo later wrote that the behavior of both the guards and the prisoners was pathological in many ways but could not be due to preexisting problems in the individuals comprising both groups, since he screened them for such problems and then randomly assigned them to the groups. Instead the behavior was due to the structural conditions and role expectations of the mock prison experience that led normal people to behave unacceptably.

 ## SUMMARY AND CONCLUSION

All the major theories discussed in this chapter focus on the individual. Classical and neoclassical perspectives (rational choice) assume that individuals commit crime when they decide the potential gains outweigh the potential costs. Biological and psychological theories attribute crime to individual biological or psychological attributes.

Ultimately, your view of the world influences the value you find in these explanations. If you think that people are responsible for their own behavior, then you'll probably prefer rational choice views. If you think that social problems arise primarily from individual faults and problems, then you will probably prefer biological and/or psychological theories. If instead you think that social problems derive primarily from problems in the larger social structure, then you will probably prefer sociological explanations. While there's certainly room for more than one way to understand criminality, the explanation we adopt has important implications for efforts to reduce crime.

Rational choice views attribute crime to the choices individuals make about their own behavior. Crime policies based on these views aim to affect these choices by making punishment more certain and more severe. It's unclear, however, whether the decision making of potential criminals follows the rational choice model, as well as whether increasing the certainty and severity of punishment can reduce crime rates significantly. The world of rational choice and deterrence theory is, further, largely devoid of social inequality and social structure. To the extent these social facts generate criminality, the rational choice model ignores important sources of crime.

Biological and psychological explanations both ultimately locate the genesis of crime inside the individual. They suffer from common methodological problems, including small sample sizes, difficulties in distinguishing offenders from nonoffenders, and, despite some recent longitudinal studies, ambiguity in causal order. Hence, these interpretations have not yet established a strong role for biological or psychological factors in criminality. Several explanations in the two disciplines also minimize the importance of social and structural factors for delinquency and crime. Even if the biological evidence were more conclusive, sociologists would continue to be troubled by its implications for social policy on crime. Several psychological approaches are more compatible with a sociological framework but still miss the larger crime picture on which sociology focuses.

Historically, biological research and, in its work on intelligence, psychological research have had damaging consequences for women, the poor, and people of color. Recent writings on intelligence and heredity indicate that views on the inferior intelligence of certain groups have not yet lost favor. Sensitivity to the dangers of these and similar views demands that biological and psychological evidence of criminality be interpreted cautiously.

Despite the limitations of biological and psychological research from a sociological standpoint, this research has been valuable in stressing the importance of early childhood for later delinquency and criminality. Certain approaches in both fields focus on childhood medical and psychological problems stemming from poor prenatal health and nutrition and inadequate parenting. These approaches suggest that programs focusing on families at risk for both sets of problems can achieve significant crime reduction.

Because this risk is greatest for families living in poverty, this line of biological and psychological work complements sociological attention to the criminogenic effects of poverty and other structural conditions in the social environment that we'll explore in the next chapter. Chapter 7 examines social process theories in sociology that stress negative childhood social experiences, which again are more common for families living in poverty. Notwithstanding their differences, contemporary efforts in biology, psychology, and sociology thus all underscore the crime-reduction potential of well-designed and well-funded efforts that address the causes and consequences of poverty.

 ## KEY TERMS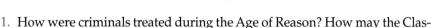

abnormality	neurotransmitter
atavism	personality
classical school	phrenology
concordance	positivism
deterrence theory	premenstrual syndrome
discordance	psychoanalytic
ego	rational choice theory
Enlightenment	somatology
heredity	superego
id	temperament
IQ	testosterone
moral development	

 ## STUDY QUESTIONS

1. How were criminals treated during the Age of Reason? How may the Classical School of Criminology be considered a reaction to this treatment?

2. What concerns do many sociologists and criminologists have about biological explanations of criminal behavior? How valid do you think these concerns are?

3. What does the research on intelligence and crime tell us? What are the methodological and other critiques of this line of research?

4. The question of abnormality versus normality lies at the heart of much psychological research on criminal behavior. Do you think many criminals are psychologically abnormal?

 ## INTERNET EXERCISES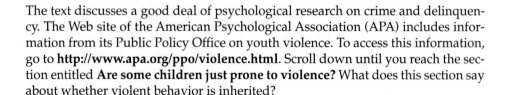

The text discusses a good deal of psychological research on crime and delinquency. The Web site of the American Psychological Association (APA) includes information from its Public Policy Office on youth violence. To access this information, go to **http://www.apa.org/ppo/violence.html**. Scroll down until you reach the section entitled **Are some children just prone to violence?** What does this section say about whether violent behavior is inherited?

Now scroll down until you reach the section on **preventing violence in children who seem most vulnerable**. What are the "three primary characteristics" of effective prevention programs? What are some of the methods that can be used to achieve what the site calls "enduring effects" on children?

Scroll down further and you'll see a list of the experiences that help keep children from becoming violent. What are any three of these experiences?

SOCIOLOGICAL THEORIES:
EMPHASIS ON
SOCIAL STRUCTURE

Crime in the News

In neighborhoods in Washington, D.C. where tourists don't go, live thousands of poor people. In early 2000 the city announced it would crack down on "slumlords," landlords who own apartment buildings in these neighborhoods and who fail to keep their buildings from meeting even minimal standards for human habitation. The city threatened to close some of the buildings and to bring criminal charges against the slumlords. According to one official, the targeted buildings included "some of the most dangerous and unsanitary conditions in the city, including rat and roach infestations, broken windows, inadequate toilet and kitchen facilities, exposed wiring, holes in floors and walls, trash accumulations and other filth." Washington's mayor, Anthony A. Williams, said, "We're distressed by the conditions these people are being forced to live in ... while deadbeat landlords are turning a huge profit. The kind of neglect [tenants] face every day is illegal, immoral, and we're here to say it's going to stop." In one of the buildings, three families shared a three-room apartment and paid $625 a month in rent. One of the tenants said that rats roamed the apartment, that the ceiling leaked, and that there was often no heat. She added, "If they close the building, I'll have to find somewhere to move, and I don't know where. Of course, we're worried. I have a six-year-old daughter. Where will we go?"

Sources: Pan 2000a; Pan 2000b.

*L*et's begin this chapter with two mental exercises. (A) Pretend that you could wave a magic wand and create a community that would have a lot of street crime. What kind of community would this be? How would it look? Write down four or five characteristics that immediately come to mind. (B) Now pretend that you could take an individual and clone him or her at birth. One grows up in a poor urban area and the other in a wealthy suburb. Who would be more likely to commit street crimes?

If you're like my own students, your list for exercise A looks something like the neighborhoods in our nation's capital: poverty, overcrowding, unemployment, rundown housing and schools. Am I correct? If so, notice that your list describes poor urban areas much more than wealthy suburbs. As a result, your answer to exercise B was undoubtedly the individual in the urban area. Am I correct again? If these were your answers, you recognize that there's something about poor urban areas that leads to more street crime. This "something" is what sociologists call structural conditions or structural problems. While we must avoid stereotyping urban areas as evil and suburbs as angelic, the sociological evidence on the structural problems of urban areas supports your hypotheses.

As we saw in the last chapter, individual-level theories of crime can't easily account for why some locations and groups have higher crime rates than others. Given their more macro-level orientation, sociologists highlight the role played by social structure or, as it is more popularly called, social environment, in these differences. As Chapter 1 indicated, social structure refers not only to the physical features of communities but also to the way society is organized: the distribution of social and economic power, and the nature of relationships among individuals and groups. Specific aspects of the social structure are sometimes called structural conditions and include such things as the level of unemployment and the extent of nuclear versus extended-kin families. Structural conditions are social forces external to the individual that affect behavior and attitudes. These forces explain why crime and other behaviors vary across locations and groups.

A structural approach helps us understand why poor urban areas have higher street crime rates than wealthy suburbs. While individual-level explanations must attribute this difference to biological or psychological abnormalities of urban residents, structural explanations instead emphasize structural conditions that make street crime more likely in urban areas. Although most urban residents still do not commit street crimes, structural problems like the ones you listed help account for what crime does result. Given such conditions, street crime is more likely there than in communities where wealthy people live in comfortable houses spread far apart. All other things equal, individuals growing up in poor urban environments are more likely to commit street crime than ones raised in more affluent locations. The structural conditions of the community matter more than the particular individuals living in it.

Recall the last chapter's discussion of Philip Zimbardo's prison experiment where the student "guards" acted brutally and the "prisoners," after an initial rebellion, reacted passively and then suffered emotional problems. Since Zimbardo screened his subjects for any history of drug use or mental disorder and then assigned them randomly to be either guards or prisoners, the different but still "deviant" behaviors of the two groups couldn't have stemmed from the individual characteristics of their subjects, who, by definition, were as "normal" as you or I. Instead the behavioral patterns are best seen as the result of the structure of the prison experience: the arbitrary power that the guards wielded over the prisoners and the physical features of the mock prison itself. Zimbardo's experiment thus dramatically suggests the influence of social structure on individual behavior. Milgram's electric shock experiment, also discussed in the last chapter, makes the same point: The social environment can pressure normal people to commit serious offenses. The analogy to crime in poor urban areas, if not exact, is nonetheless telling: It's very possible that the structural problems of such settings make high rates of street crime likely and even inevitable.

 ## THE LEGACY OF DURKHEIM

Sociologists have recognized the impact of social structure on deviance and crime since Emile Durkheim's work a century ago. As the last chapter noted, Durkheim considered deviance a normal phenomenon of all healthy societies. He further emphasized the influence of structural forces on individual behavior. Durkheim was a member of the conservative intellectual movement in Europe that arose after the French Revolution and other traumatic changes in the late 1700s and early 1800s. As such, he felt that human nature is basically selfish. He thus thought that individuals have unlimited aspirations that, if left unchecked, would result in chaos: "To achieve any other result, the passions first must be limited.... But since the individual has no way of limiting them, this must be done by some force exterior to him" (Durkheim 1952 [1897]:274). This force is the moral authority of society.

In virtually all his work Durkheim emphasized two related mechanisms, socialization and social ties, by which society was able to limit individual impulses and prevent chaos. Through socialization, we learn social norms and become good members of society instead of selfish individuals. The social ties we have to family, friends, and others further help socialize us, integrate us into society, and control our aspirations. Thus a strong set of norms—or, to use Durkheim's term, a strong collective conscience—and solid social ties are both necessary for a stable society. A weakening in either element of the social structure destabilizes society and leads to chaos. This view lies at the heart of the "Durkheimian tradition" in sociology (Collins 1994).

Durkheim's most notable application of this theory was to suicide. Although suicide is commonly considered the result of individual unhappiness, Durkheim found suicide rates influenced by external forces. For example, they tended to be higher in times of rapid social change, such as sudden changes in the economy. During these periods, the norms that traditionally govern our behavior and attitudes become less clear as new circumstances arise to which these norms might not apply. Normlessness, or anomie, sets in. Aspirations that previously were controlled now become unlimited, leaving people feeling more adrift and finding it more difficult to deal with their problems. They also realize that not all their aspirations can be fulfilled, and the resulting frustration leads some to commit suicide (Durkheim 1952 [1897]).

Durkheim used a similar argument to explain why Protestants have higher suicide rates than Catholics. It's not that Catholics are any happier than Protestants, which an individual-level explanation might propose. Instead, said Durkheim, Catholic doctrine is stricter than Protestant belief, with many more rules for behavior and attitudes. The aspirations of Catholics are thus more controlled than those of Protestants. Moreover, Catholics also have clearer norms on which to rely for comfort in times of trouble, while Protestants are left more to fend for themselves. Finally, Catholic doctrine condemns suicide in no uncertain terms, while Protestant doctrine is less clear on the subject. Because of these several factors, suicide rates are higher among Protestants than among Catholics.

Durkheim also found that unmarried people have higher suicide rates than married people. Rejecting the idea that the unmarried are any less happy than the married, Durkheim attributed this to their lack of social ties or of social integration. He reasoned that people with fewer ties have fewer sources of support in times of personal trouble, and so have higher suicide rates.

Thus two structural conditions, anomie and low social integration, contribute to higher suicide rates. Obviously not everyone in a society marked by anomie or low integration commits suicide. Individual-level explanations remain necessary to explain the particular suicides that do occur, but they cannot explain why suicide rates are higher for some groups and locations than others. Although Durkheim focused on suicide and only tangentially on crime, we'll see in this and the next chapter that theorists have since applied his views to various kinds of criminal behavior.

A modern literary application of Durkheim's (and the nineteenth-century conservative movement's) view of human nature and society appears in William Golding's famous novel, *Lord of the Flies*, which you might have read in high school (Golding 1954). To summarize a complex story far too simplistically, a group of young boys from England is stranded on an island after a plane crash. They have left their society behind and with it the norms, institutions, and social bonds that governed their behavior. Not sure how to proceed, they begin to devise new norms to deal with their extraordinary circumstances, but their backgrounds as well-behaved youngsters do them no good after the ripping away of their society. Slowly but surely they become savages, as the book calls them again and again, and the story ends in murder. An adult who rescues them at the end of the book remarks in surprise, "I should have thought that a pack of British boys—you're all British, aren't you?— would have been able to put up a better show than that—I mean." One of the boys replies, "It was like that at first, before things—. We were together then—" (Golding 1954:186). Echoing the view of Durkheim and other conservative intellectuals, Golding's bleak vision of human nature remains compelling, if controversial, and is reflected in many contemporary treatments of crime.

 ## SOCIAL DISORGANIZATION AND SOCIAL ECOLOGY

Durkheim and other members of the conservative intellectual movement were concerned by industrialization and the rapid growth of large cities in the nineteenth century. To these thinkers, society was quickly changing from small, rural communities characterized by close, personal relationships to larger, urban communities marked by impersonal relationships. In rural societies, people are similar to each other in backgrounds and interests; they know each other well and look out for each other. Social norms in such societies are clear to all inhabitants and are generally followed by everyone. In contrast, people in industrialized, urban societies are more different from each other. Their social relationships are more impersonal, and social norms are less clear. Thus these communities are able to exert less social control over individual behavior, leading to more deviance, crime, and other problems. Although Durkheim thought the impersonal nature of urban society could be overcome by the "organic solidarity" resulting from interdependence fostered by the division of labor, he still recognized, as noted earlier, the greater potential in modern society for anomie and low social integration (Collins 1994).

This basic pessimism about social order in industrial society guided the work of U.S. sociologists and other social scientists who began to study crime and deviance in the late 1800s and early 1900s. These scholars lived and worked in Chicago and other large cities. They looked at the world around them (e.g., large cities) and quite naturally found a lot of deviance and crime that concerned and even appalled them. Many of these scholars had grown up in small, rural communities with a strict Protestant upbringing condemning various acts of deviance as sins. In Chicago and elsewhere they saw drinking, prostitution, and other deviance being committed by poor people, many of them Catholic immigrants. The social scientists' concern over urban crime was thus heightened by their bias against urban areas, against Catholics, and against immigrants, and by their religious beliefs that viewed drinking and other acts as sins. Unlike Durkheim, they didn't view deviance as a normal phenomenon of all healthy societies. Instead they thought it symptomatic of a sickness in society stemming from the moral failings and mental problems of individual deviants, and condemned it as immoral. These social pathologists, as they're now called, were guilty of a "sacred provincialism" that substituted moral and religious judgment for careful social science reasoning (Mills 1943; Schwendinger and Schwendinger 1974).

Although the social pathology school faded by the 1930s, a new approach emerged at the University of Chicago that continued to address crime in urban communities. In contrast to the social pathology school, this approach emphasized structural causes of urban crime over individual failings. Whereas the social pathology school attributed crime to personal problems in the people committing these behaviors, the new approach attributed it to the social disorganization of certain neighborhoods in urban areas. Taking a cue from Durkheim, social disorganization theorists blamed crime in these neighborhoods on a breakdown in social bonds and social control and on the accompanying "uncertainty and confusion concerning appropriate behavior" (Shoemaker 1996:81). (In this sense, the "society" in *Lord of the Flies* suffered from extreme social disorganization.) These were neighborhoods in transition, with poor immigrants and others moving in and longstanding residents moving out. High divorce rates, dilapidated housing, and other problems characterized these neighborhoods. In such conditions, these theorists thought, high crime rates were inevitable.

The concept of social disorganization first appeared in the work of W. I. Thomas and Florian Znaniecki, whose book, *The Polish Peasant in Europe and America*, documented the troubles that Polish immigrants to Chicago faced in the different society they found there (Thomas and Znaniecki 1927). The huge environs of Chicago were very different from the small, rural farms of Poland. The latter were stable areas where little change took place. The bustling city of Chicago was undergoing rapid upheaval in the early 1900s. In such a setting, the immigrants found their "old ways" not working as well; their children faced new, alien influences and weakened familial and other traditional sources of social control. As a result, delinquency and crime became much more common in Polish neighborhoods in Chicago than they had been in the old country.

At about the same time, other sociologists at the University of Chicago, most notably Robert E. Park and Ernest W. Burgess, developed an ecological analysis of Chicago neighborhoods. Just as the relationship of plants and animals to their physical environment can be studied, said Park and Burgess, so can that of people to their environment. Their type of analysis has since been called a social ecology approach. Park and Burgess divided Chicago into a series of five concentric circles or zones, radiating from the inner city to the outlying areas. They found these zones differing widely in their physical and social characteristics. The outer areas had wealthier homes and more spacious streets, for example,

◀ *A social ecology approach recognizes that cities can be divided into different neighborhoods or zones that vary according to their physical and social characteristics. These characteristics in turn lead to different crime rates. Generally, the inner zones of cities have higher crime rates than the outer zones.*

while the inner zones had poorer, more crowded housing and other symptoms of social disorganization (Park, Burgess, and McKenzie 1925).

Clifford R. Shaw and Henry D. McKay

Park and Burgess's ecological model in turn influenced the work of Clifford R. Shaw and Henry D. McKay, who studied delinquency rates in Chicago from 1900 to 1933. Shaw and McKay noted that the ethnic and racial backgrounds of inner zone residents changed during this time. In the early 1900s, inner zone residents came from English, German, and Irish backgrounds. By the 1920s, these residents had given way to Polish and other Eastern European immigrants, who in turn began to be replaced in the 1930s by African-Americans migrating from the South. After painstakingly compiling data from some 56,000 juvenile court records on male delinquency in Chicago for the three decades, Shaw and McKay found that delinquency remained highest in the inner zones regardless of which ethnic groups lived there. They also found that the ethnic groups' delinquency fell after they moved to the more outlying areas (Shaw and McKay 1942).

Shaw and McKay concluded that personal characteristics of the ethnic groups could not logically explain these two related phenomena. Instead, structural conditions in the inner zones had to be at work: While Shaw and McKay acknowledged that individual-level factors help explain whether particular adolescents commit delinquency, they argued that these adolescents would commit much less delinquency if they were living in more advantaged communities.

Echoing Park and Burgess, Shaw and McKay found the inner zones characterized by dilapidated housing, high rates of poverty and divorce, and other problems, all symptoms, they said, of social disorganization, the breakdown of norms and social bonds. Social disorganization, then, accounted for the high rates of offending in the inner zones. In such a climate, deviant values emerge to flourish alongside conventional values. Adolescents grow up amid these conflicting values and behaviors. Most adopt the conventional ones, but some adopt the deviant ones, especially when influenced by delinquent peers. Although Shaw and McKay recognized that different parts of cities have different crime rates, they still felt that the impersonality and diversity of urban life was responsible for the high rates as a whole.

Critique of Social Disorganization Theory

Shaw and McKay's social disorganization theory was popular for some time, but later gave way to several methodological critiques (Bursik 1988; Kornhauser 1978). The most devastating criticism concerned their reliance on official records for measuring delinquency rates. As Chapter 3 noted, middle-class delinquents may escape detection and not show up in official records. Conversely, because bias against the poor and people of color may raise their chances of being labeled deviant, the race and class differences found in official delinquency records may be exaggerated. This methodological critique rendered Shaw and McKay's findings of higher delinquency rates in the inner zones very suspect. In a related criticism, scholars also noted that social disorganization theory cannot explain middle-class delinquency, since the middle classes do not, almost by definition, live in conditions of social disorganization.

Shaw and McKay were also faulted for imprecision in their concept of social disorganization. At times they engaged in circular reasoning by taking criminality as an indicator of disorganization. This made it difficult for subsequent research to test their theory and, indeed, later investigations found only mixed support (Lander 1954). Another criticism is that Shaw and McKay, succumbing to stereotyping, underestimated the amount of social *organization* in cities' inner zones. Rich, ethnographic studies of inner-city neighborhoods find they can have high amounts of social order and social integration (Suttles 1968; Whyte 1943). Conclusions by Shaw, McKay, and other social disorganization theorists may thus reflect middle-class biases.

Further, despite Shaw and McKay's view that the social disorganization of inner zones leads to criminality, it's also true that most people in these zones do not commit crime. In a related problem, some critics allege that Shaw and McKay underestimated the ability of some U.S. ethnic groups (e.g., Asians) living in inner-city areas to maintain low crime rates because of cultural emphases on strong family ties and respect for authority. Although Shaw and McKay acknowledged this possibility, they didn't discuss it in detail. Conversely, some neighborhoods have high crime rates despite being stable in other respects. In view of these many problems, the causal power of the social disorganization model eventually came to be considered rather weak (Kornhauser 1978).

The Revival of Social Disorganization Theory

Since the mid-1980s, however, sociologists have rediscovered social disorganization theory and found it a powerful tool for explaining variation in crime and victimization across groups and locations (Bursik 1988; Krohn 2000). In response to the methodological critiques of Shaw and McKay's work, recent research uses self-report and victimization data (to avoid the problems of official crime measures), calls to the police (see Chapter 3), and more sophisticated, neighborhood-level measures of social disorganization than were available to Shaw, McKay, and other early theorists.

Although the results of the new research depend on the type of crime examined and the way variables are measured, it generally finds crime and victimization highest in communities with: (1) low participation in voluntary organizations; (2) few networks of friendship ties; (3) low levels of "collective efficacy," or community supervision of adolescents and of other informal social control mechanisms; and (4) high degrees of residential mobility, population density, single-parent homes, dilapidated housing, and poverty (Bellair 1997; Peterson, Krivo, and Harris 2000; Sampson 1997). In related research, studies in countries as diverse as England, Ghana, and Uganda find crime and delinquency rates highest in communities resembling the inner-city zones studied by Shaw and McKay, while studies of U.S. neighborhoods undergoing rapid economic or racial change in the 1960–1990 period find them marked by increasing delinquency (Bursik 1984; Clinard and Abbott 1976; Taylor and Covington 1988). Taken together, these diverse findings provide new empirical support for Shaw and McKay's sixty-year-old theory. Reviews of the theory say it "continues to have important ramifications for modern criminology" and provides a strong structural underpinning for the cultural and social processes that explain criminality (discussed later in this chapter and in Chapter 7) (Bursik 1988:519; Curran and Renzetti 1994).

Other Ecological Work

The revival of social disorganization theory has spawned a more general interest in ecological studies examining other sorts of factors (Hagan 1993; Sampson 1995). Drawing on routine activities and lifestyle theories of victimization (see Chapter 4), some studies include individual-level indicators of the degree to which respondents expose themselves to possible victimization by motivated offenders, possess attractive targets for would-be criminals, and take "guardianship" measures to prevent crime. "Multi-level" studies of these factors and social disorganization measures find the former predicting victimization among individuals and the latter predicting victimization across communities. These studies nicely integrate social disorganization and routine activities theories and suggest that macro and micro factors are both important for understanding crime and victimization (Rountree et al. 1994).

ECONOMIC DEPRIVATION AND CRIME

Some of the most important contemporary ecological work examines the effects of economic deprivation on community crime rates. Austin T. Turk (1993:355) notes that this line of research represents a marked departure from the focus of biological and psychological explanations: "Instead of looking for what is wrong with people, these researchers are looking for what is wrong with society."

Two possible reasons explain why economic deprivation might increase neighborhood criminality. Shaw and McKay thought that poverty fostered crime at the community level only because it first generated social disorganization and hence undermined traditional social control mechanisms. In this sense they considered the ecological effect of poverty on crime to be indirect. While not rejecting this assumption, recent scholars have maintained that economic deprivation also has direct ecological effects on crime. As Chapter 3 noted, sociologist William J. Wilson (1987) and others argue that social and economic changes in the past four decades have taken hundreds of thousands of manufacturing and other jobs from northern

Crime Rates Rise as Norms Break Down

Emile Durkheim thought that deviance rises when normlessness, or anomie, increases. During times of rapid social change, norms become more unclear, and society's hold over individuals lessens. Their aspirations become less limited than before, and suicide and other forms of deviance rise. Social disorganization theory would make the same prediction. When conventional social institutions weaken, as in times of rapid social change, deviance and crime should increase.

In the last decade we had several real-life tests of these predictions, as nations emerged from decades of authoritarian rule and underwent dramatic social change. The available evidence indicates that crime in these nations also rose dramatically, leading to calls for harsh punishment of criminals.

In early 1994, for example, South Africa had its first free elections, as its notorious system of apartheid finally crumbled. Eighteen months later, said one report, "crime has continued to soar in South Africa, increasing in some areas and categories by as much as 75 percent in one year." Crime, the report continued, "is the subject of the hour in any neighborhood." Although the murder rate had dropped during this time, it remained about four times higher than that in the United States, and other violent crimes had increased dramatically. The apparent rise in crime was cited as the main reason for an increase in the number of South Africans who wanted to leave the country. One woman planned to emigrate to New Zealand because of her fears about her family's safety. Sleeping with two guns by her side, she would wake up every morning at 3:30. "I get out of bed, I take the big gun. I check every window. Every door. I make sure all my kids are in bed because I would hate to shoot one of them by mistake."

Other South Africans organized vigilante groups to hunt down and beat suspected criminals. The rise in vigilantism occurred because these citizens distrusted the police, who had often beaten and killed blacks to bolster white rule during apartheid. They also thought the police were corrupt, undertrained, and hardly capable of doing a good job even if they were called.

A half decade earlier, the Soviet Union had broken up. In its wake rose a crime wave in Russia and other former Soviet countries that left their inhabitants reeling. Between 1990 and 1994, the number of crimes in Moscow doubled, and in 1994 Moscow had 1,820 murders, about 240 more than New York City. Sixteen Moscow police officers were killed in 1994, compared to only one in New York City. Russia's crime wave continued through the rest of the decade, rising more than 16 percent in 1999 alone, and has threatened foreign investment in the country.

Not surprisingly, many Russians began calling for extremely punitive measures to fight crime. A former Russian prosecutor said, "This is a time of total lawlessness. People don't go to the police because they think it's not only useless but dangerous." One Russian journalist wrote, "Unfortunately for our weak little country, if it wishes to reestablish law and order, the only principle can be: 'The only good bandit is a dead bandit.'" A police official added, "We have to act harshly and decisively. That's the only way the bandits are going to respect us." Other commentators warned that such measures would bring back to Russia the brutal excesses suffered under Communist rule.

Crime also rose in the Czech Republic after it was freed from Communist rule in 1989. The crime increase "spread alarm throughout the country," says one scholar, with reported crime rising 30.5 percent from 1990 to 1991. The number of illegal firearms also rose and, with that, an initial, large jump in homicides.

Although the rise of crime in South Africa and the former Soviet nations apparently supports the predictions of Durkheim and social disorganization theorists, other factors are also at work. Citizens in these nations might feel they have less to fear from the police now then when police ruled by terror. Also, as the former Communist countries moved toward capitalism, it's likely that they began to adopt capitalist ideologies, including, as Robert Merton and other anomie theorists note, an emphasis on individual economic success. If these values underlie crime in the United States, the adoption of these values in the former Soviet nations may also have helped raise crime rates there. Other reasons for the rising crime rates are more economic. The end to Communist rule in the former Soviet nations meant that new trade markets opened up, and with them the prospects for great financial gain. With so much money to be had, more crime in pursuit of this money was inevitable. Meanwhile, the rise in South African crime may have resulted in part from its growing unemployment rate, which reached 34 percent by the mid-1990s.

Sources: Bartlett 1995; Dailey 1995; Filipov 1995; ITAR/TASS 2000; Nelan 1995; Parker 1996; Ransdell 1995; Serio 1997.

cities and left behind increasing economic deprivation for urban residents, most of them African-American. This deprivation makes it nearly impossible for people to leave the cities, trapping them through a continuing cycle of severe poverty into what Wilson calls an "underclass." Because of the simultaneous stresses of such concentrated poverty, urban living, and racial and ethnic discrimination, members of the underclass commit violence and other crime out of frustration, anger, or economic need (Bernard 1990; Phillips 1997; Sampson and Wilson 1995).

To illustrate this view, suppose two people start to play the familiar Monopoly board game. Reflecting the egalitarian ideology of our society, the rules require that everyone be given $1,500 to start the game. Suppose instead we make the game a little more realistic and give one person $30,000 at the outset, and the other only $100. Even if both players land on Boardwalk, Park Place, and other desirable properties, who can better afford them? Who will win the game? How will the loser feel? In the real world (or maybe even in the game), what behavior might result?

The findings of research testing the alternative explanations of economic deprivation's effect on crime depend on the ecological unit studied (neighborhood, city, census tract, or state) and how economic deprivation is measured. Some studies use simple measures of the average socioeconomic status of community residents; others calculate the degree of economic inequality by measuring the differences among incomes in a given community; still others include measures of extreme poverty that more closely capture Wilson's underclass concept.

Most of the studies find the expected economic deprivation-crime relationship. In some, an initial relationship disappears when social disorganization factors are held constant, supporting Shaw and McKay's view of how poverty generates crime. In other studies, economic deprivation continues to be linked to crime even when social disorganization is taken into account, supporting Wilson's view of the causal process. Studies using measures of severe economic deprivation find this direct effect more often than studies using income measures that relate less to Wilson's underclass concept (Bursik and Grasmick 1993a). Although these new ecological studies do not agree on how economic deprivation generates crime, they nonetheless underscore its importance for community differences in criminality (Kovandzic, Vieraitis, and Yeisley 1998; Parker and McCall 1999; Peterson, Krivo and Harris 2000; Phillips 1997).

One reason the poor become angry and frustrated might be their realization that other people in society are much richer. This realization leads them to experience relative deprivation: It's one thing to be poor if everyone else is; it's another to be poor if many others are not (Blau 1982). Relative deprivation should be higher in poor neighborhoods located near affluent ones than in poor neighborhoods farther away, since people in the former neighborhoods see the wealth and possessions of richer residents much more often than do their counterparts in the latter neighborhoods. If this is true, they should also be more angry and frustrated and, as a result, more likely to commit crime. Crime rates should thus be higher in poor neighborhoods bordering affluent areas than in poor neighborhoods farther away. Although their results are not always consistent, some studies find this is indeed the case (Sampson 1985).

Scholars have also begun to address the role played by political and economic forces outside neighborhoods in generating the ecological link between economic deprivation and crime. Robert J. Bursik, one of the leading ecological scholars, argues that the poorest neighborhoods lack contacts and influence with political officials and economic leaders outside the neighborhoods and thus face much greater difficulty in acquiring external financial and human resources (e.g., police, social service agencies) that could improve neighborhood conditions and help control crime. Conversely, they may be less able than wealthier neighborhoods to resist policies that may drive up criminality. For example, Bursik found that certain Chicago neighborhoods were unable to resist the establishment of public housing projects. These projects were built against the wishes of the neighborhoods' residents and soon led to increased delinquency, in part by increasing residential turnover (Bursik 1989; Bursik and Grasmick 1993b).

Reflecting the emphasis on economic deprivation, John Hagan (1994:98), former President of the American Society of Criminology, calls for "a new sociology of crime and disrepute" that focuses on "the criminal costs of social inequality." Echoing Wilson (1987), Hagan argues that the urban underclass has faced several serious and intensifying problems since the 1960s: decreasing economic opportunities and increasing poverty, and increasing residential segregation stemming from housing discrimination. This last problem, termed "American apartheid" by Douglas S. Massey and Nancy A. Denton (1993), exacerbates the economic deprivation of nonwhite urban residents. In short, "structural changes have brought increasing inequality into the American economy and into the lives of individuals who live in its most distressed communities" (Hagan 1994:98). This inequality, Hagan says, underlies much of the violence and other crime, including drug trafficking and drug use, found in these communities.

Rodney Stark (1987:905) observes that social scientists "have been almost unwilling to discuss the question of why black crime rates are so high." As I noted in Chapter 3, it's possible to acknowledge and explain these rates without resorting to biological and other racially biased explanations. The new ecological work on economic deprivation and crime provides one such explanation, suggesting that a primary reason is the economic deprivation of African-Americans, the seriously disadvantaged communities in which many live, and their resulting frustration and hostility. All these factors in turn generate violent crime and other offenses (Harris and Shaw 2000; Krivo and Peterson 1996; Paschall, Flewelling, and Ennett 1998; Phillips 1997). A complementary explanation has to do with the *kinds of places* in which many African-Americans live. Let's discuss this view in some detail.

KINDS OF PLACES VERSUS KINDS OF PEOPLE

The revival of ecological theories reflects the belief of many scholars that "kinds of places" matter more than "kinds of people" (Sampson 1995; Stark 1987). Recalling Shaw and McKay's central finding that neighborhoods can continue to have high crime rates despite changes in the kinds of people who live there, Rodney Stark (1987:893) observes that *"there must be something about places as such* that sustains crime" (emphasis his). Stark says it's irrelevant to the ecological approach to note that most urban residents are not criminals, since this approach claims only that crime is more likely in urban areas than elsewhere, not that all urban residents commit crime. Drawing on various ecological and other approaches, Stark then advances thirty propositions, many of them focusing on neighborhood physical features, that offer a compelling ecological explanation for the high crime and delinquency of particular urban neighborhoods and more generally of the cities containing them. His view has since been referred to as the *theory of deviant places*.

In one proposition, Stark assumes that the more dense a neighborhood, the greater the likelihood that "good kids" will come into contact with "bad kids," increasing the pressures on the former to break the law. This helps explain why cities have more serious delinquency than other areas because adolescents who step out the door can easily find other teenagers. In suburbs and especially rural areas where

◀ *Rodney Stark's theory of deviant places highlights the criminogenic impact of physical and other characteristics of urban neighborhoods.*

housing is much more spread out, it's more difficult to get together with friends, especially if a car ride is necessary.

In another set of propositions, Stark notes that poor urban neighborhoods contain many overcrowded homes, which generate family conflict and lead their inhabitants, especially adolescents, to spend extra time outside the home to have some "elbow room." Once outside, they're freer to associate with delinquent peers, with more delinquency resulting. The presence of convenience stores and other places to "hang out" in urban neighborhoods aggravates this problem, as these places can become targets for crime or at least foster communication about committing crime elsewhere.

In other propositions, Stark notes that the dilapidation and deviance of urban neighborhoods cause their residents to feel stigmatized. This stigmatization prompts nondeviant residents to leave the neighborhoods, reduces the willingness of those who remain to report crimes to the police, and attracts other deviants. All these factors in turn increase these neighborhoods' criminality.

Taken together, Stark's propositions and other research on kinds of places provide a powerful ecological basis for the high crime rates of urban neighborhoods. They suggest that normal people get caught in a vicious cycle of structural conditions that generate delinquency and crime, just as the normal people in Zimbardo's and Milgram's experiments (Chapter 5) committed abnormal behavior. Crime in turn worsens neighborhood conditions and leads to even more criminality (Bursik 1986). Stark's and other ecological perspectives thus explain why neighborhoods can continue to have high crime rates even when some people move from the neighborhoods and others move in.

They also provide yet another racially unbiased explanation of the high African-American crime rates in the United States. As Stark notes (1987:905–906), the particularly high crime rates of non-Southern blacks can be seen as "the result of *where* they live," for example, the inner zones of cities. These areas, says Stark, are "precisely the kinds of places explored in this essay—areas where the probabilities of *anyone* committing a crime are high" (emphasis his). In the South, blacks tend to live in rural areas and thus have lower crime rates than their northern counterparts. Kinds of places, as noted earlier, matter more than kinds of people.

A recent experiment underscores this point: Since 1994, the Moving to Opportunity program in Baltimore has moved more than 200 randomly-selected families from high-poverty neighborhoods to low-poverty areas. Their children have been compared to those in a like number of families in the program from high-poverty areas that did not move. The violent offending rate of the teenagers who moved to the low-poverty neighborhoods became substantially lower than that of the teenagers who did not move, even though both groups of teenagers had similar offending rates before the first group moved. The study's authors concluded that the improved neighborhood conditions accounted for the drop in violent crime they observed (Ludwig, Duncan, and Hirschfield 1999).

Notice I'm not saying that kinds of people make no difference. Ecological theories do not mean we should "stop seeking and formulating 'kinds of people' explanations" (Stark 1987:906) to explain why some individuals in damaging ecological conditions commit crime while most do not. The low crime rates of some other nations and of certain U.S. ethnic groups indicate that cultural and individual differences also matter.

Whether you prefer kinds of places or kinds of people explanations depends on which level of analysis makes the most sense to you. Ecological theories remind us that no matter what kinds of people we have in mind, their criminality would be lower if they grew up and lived in communities lacking the many structural conditions generating crime. We don't have to be stranded like the boys in *Lord of the Flies* to realize that where we live strongly affects our values and behavior, including crime. To return to one of the mental exercises that began this chapter, a clone growing up amid overcrowding, extreme poverty, and other disadvantaged structural conditions will often turn out very different from its match growing up in a more advantaged area.

Before moving to the next structural theory of crime, I should note that the new emphasis on ecological characteristics is also guiding the study of the social control of criminals. Several structural features of communities, including their degree of economic deprivation, affect the nature of policing and the legal treatment of offenders (Jacobs and O'Brien 1998; Myers 2000). Chapters 15 and 16 discuss this work in greater detail.

Anomie/Strain Theory

As discussed previously, Durkheim felt that anomie or strain results when people's aspirations become uncontrolled and unfulfilled. Although Durkheim discussed how anomie can lead to suicide, it remained to Columbia University sociologist Robert K. Merton more than sixty years ago to connect anomie to other forms of deviance. In the paper "Social Structure and Anomie," perhaps the most famous in the criminology literature, Merton discounted the assumption, popular then and still today, that criminality is rooted in biological impulses. He argued instead that "certain phases of social structure generate the circumstances in which infringement of social codes constitutes a 'normal' response" (Merton 1938:672). Assuming that most crime is committed by poor people, he intended his anomie theory to explain the high rates of crimes by the poor.

Merton reasoned as follows. Every society includes cultural goals and institutional means (norms) about how to reach those goals. These two dimensions are usually in harmony, meaning that, more often than not, members of society can reach the cultural goals, or at least have some hope of reaching them, by following certain socially defined means. A lack of harmony, or anomie, between the goals and the means results when either too much emphasis is given to goals or the means are inadequate to reach the goals. An example of the former, says Merton, is when the philosophy in athletics of "winning is not everything, it's the only thing" becomes more important than sportsmanship, leading to improper behavior on the field and illegal behavior off it. A similar emphasis on winning at all costs, Merton adds, prompts dealers in poker games to give themselves four aces and even leads people to cheat at solitaire.

In U.S. society, Merton reasons, there is, similarly, too much emphasis on economic success. As a result, in their efforts to fulfill "the American Dream," U.S. residents often find that they can't do so unless, like athletes or card players, they commit illegal activity.

This problem is greatest for the poor in the United States, says Merton. They not only live in a society stressing economic success above all else but also lack the ability to achieve this success through the institutional means of education, working, and the like. The strain they feel is heightened because they live in a society stressing the egalitarian ideology that all people can pull themselves up by their bootstraps. Given this ideology, they're especially likely to feel frustrated. As they then respond to their strain, the poor may either accept or reject the cultural goals of economic success and the institutional means—working—of becoming economically successful. These possibilities result in the logical adaptations to anomie depicted in Table 6.1, where "+" means accept, "−" means reject, and "±" means reject and substitute new goals and means.

The first adaptation is *conformity*. Even given anomie, most poor people continue to accept the goal of economic success and the means of working; in short, they continue to be law-abiding members of society. Merton says it's not surprising that so many people continue to conform, because otherwise there could be no social order. Conformity is, of course, not deviant behavior but a logical and by far the most common adaptation to anomie.

The second adaptation is *innovation*. Here people continue to accept the goal of economic success but reject the means of working and undertake new means, or innovate, to achieve success. Unlike conformity, innovation thus involves illegal behavior, of which theft, fraud, and other economic crimes are prime examples. If

TABLE 6.1

MERTON'S ADAPTATIONS TO ANOMIE

ADAPTATION	CULTURAL GOALS	INSTITUTIONAL MEANS
1. Conformity	+	+
2. Innovation	+	−
3. Ritualism	−	+
4. Retreatism	−	−
5. Rebellion	±	±

we were to think about good grades as another kind of success, then cheating would be an example of innovation.

The third adaptation is *ritualism*. Here people reject the goal of economic success but continue to accept the means of working. Examples include bureaucrats who come to work day after day as a ritual, not to achieve economic success. Though a logical adaptation to anomie, ritualism is not deviant per se and certainly not illegal, and Merton spends little time discussing it.

Retreatism is the fourth adaptation. Here people reject both the goal of economic success and the means of working. They in effect have given up. Merton includes in this category alcoholics, drug addicts, and hobos.

The fifth and final adaptation is *rebellion*. People undertaking this adaptation not only reject both the goal of economic success and the means of working but also try to bring about a new society with different, more egalitarian goals. These are the radicals and revolutionaries of society who often break the law in an attempt to transform it.

Like social disorganization theory, Merton's anomie theory provides a structural explanation of criminality that assumes that problems in the way society is set up produce deviance among normal but poor people. In social disorganization theory, these problems involve structural conditions at the neighborhood level that generate deviance by weakening traditional social control mechanisms. In anomie theory, these issues involve a disjunction at the societal level between the goal of economic success and the means of working that generates deviance by creating strain. Although the theories disagree on how and why economic deprivation leads to deviance, they nonetheless locate the roots of deviance in the social structure, not in the properties or failings of individuals. A 1964 review of anomie theory called it "the most influential single formulation in the sociology of deviance in the last twenty-five years" (Clinard 1964:10).

Critique of Anomie Theory

Since that time, however, critics have faulted anomie theory for several shortcomings (Kornhauser 1978; Taylor, Walton, and Young 1973; Vold, Bernard, and Snipes 1998). The most common criticism concerns Merton's assumption that the poor commit more crime than the nonpoor, which many scholars question, as I noted in discussing Shaw and McKay. Their criticism mounted in the 1960s and 1970s as evidence began to accumulate from self-report studies that middle-class adolescents were as delinquent as lower-class youths.

Because Merton's theory aims to explain deviance by the poor, it doesn't address either middle-class delinquency or the many serious white-collar offenses, both violent and property crimes, committed by the "respectable" elements of society. Although Merton acknowledged that the wealthy could feel anomie by wanting more economic success than they already have, he still felt that anomie was far more common among the poor.

Anomie theory also doesn't explain the violent crimes of homicide, assault, and rape, which do not readily fit into any of Merton's logical adaptations. Innovation applies to crimes such as theft that are committed for financial gain. Thus, one violent crime, robbery, could be considered an example of innovation. But the motivation for the other violent crimes is usually not financial. Instead it's anger, jealousy, or the thrill of "doing evil" (Katz 1988). For rape it's also hatred of women and perhaps sexual gratification (Brownmiller 1975; Felson and Krohn 1990). Even

◄ *Research shows that much alcohol and drug use occurs from noneconomic factors such as peer influences.*

much theft is done more for thrills than for money. Since the power of a theory of crime depends to a large degree on the number of different crimes it can explain, anomie theory's inability to explain most violent crimes and other noneconomic offenses is a serious failure.

Merton's retreatism adaptation is also problematic. He assumed that most alcoholism, drug addiction, and vagrancy occurs when poor people reject both economic success and working. They are "double failures" who give up on society and withdraw from it. However, research since Merton's time finds that much alcohol and drug use occurs from noneconomic factors such as peer influences (Venturelli 1994). Merton's explanation also overlooks the alcohol and drug abuse found among the nonpoor, including very successful occupational groups such as physicians. Friends of yours who have used marijuana, cocaine, and other illegal drugs might disagree with Merton's assumption that they've given up on making money by getting a good education and working.

Anomie theory also fails to explain why people choose one adaptation over another, a point Merton himself conceded. Although anomie theory provides a structural basis for several adaptations, some of them deviant, to anomie, its inability to discuss why one or another adaptation might be chosen limits its explanatory value. More generally, the theory cannot explain why, given anomie, some people commit crime while others do not. Like social disorganization and other structural theories, it disregards the influence of individual-level factors on variation in criminality among the poor.

Finally, several tests of anomie theory haven't supported it. In these studies, researchers measure adolescents' aspirations and expectations. Anomie theory predicts that strain and thus delinquency should be highest among juveniles with high aspirations and low expectations, and among juveniles with the largest gap between their aspirations and expectations. However, empirical tests do not support these hypotheses (Elliott, Huizinga, and Ageton 1985; Johnson 1979).

In sum, anomie theory (or strain theory, as it's often called) provides an important structural explanation for some crimes by the poor in the United States but falls short in other respects. Many scholars even say the theory should be abandoned and prefer instead the social process theories discussed in the next chapter.

Defense and Extension of Anomie Theory

In response, anomie theory's supporters have revised and extended it to explain some of the crimes that Merton's original formulation did not cover. They have also defended the theory against its criticism (Adler and Laufer 1995; Agnew 2000). Let's review what the supporters say.

One of their arguments focuses on the issue of social class and offending. Even if Merton may have exaggerated class differences in delinquency by relying on official records, his assumption of these differences appears to be supported at least for serious offenses (see Chapter 3). The anomie concept can also be extended, as Merton himself observed, to cover white-collar crime by corporate executives who feel intense pressure to maximize profits even if it means breaking the law (Passas 1990). A similar argument may explain middle-class delinquency: Given the importance in the United States of economic success, middle-class adolescents may still feel they don't have enough wealth and possessions and thus break the law.

This view forms the basis for a recent extension of Merton's theory by Steven F. Messner and Richard Rosenfeld (1997), who argue that crime in the United States results from several values thought to characterize U.S. society as whole. These values include achievement, individualism, universalism, and the fetishism of money. To achieve the American Dream, people must be ambitious and ready to compete with others for individual gain. Their pursuit of economic success occurs in a society whose universal, or egalitarian, ideology is that anyone, rich or poor, has a chance for success. Because money matters above all else, "success" means economic success, and U.S. residents often judge one another's worth by how much wealth and possessions they have. Rich or poor, many people might feel they don't have enough and turn to crime. At the same time, the exaggerated emphasis on monetary success undermines traditional social control institutions such as the family and schools, making crime even more possible.

As Messner and Rosenfeld (1997:10) point out, "The American Dream thus has a dark side that must be considered in any serious effort to uncover the social sources of crime." It creates intense pressures for financial success that only some people can achieve. The remainder sometimes turn to crime as a result. U.S. society, in short, is *criminogenic*, or crime-causing. It is, as Messner and Rosenfeld (1997:1) put it, a "society organized for crime." The same values that make the American Dream attainable also make crime not only possible but likely.

In a related view, Charles Derber (1996:8) says the United States has fallen prey to *wilding*, or excessive, "degraded American individualism," in which the pursuit of individual gain and pleasure has led to all sorts of social harms, both legal and illegal, by rich and poor alike. Derber adds that the "wilding epidemic" has increased in the last two decades because of financial and political corruption by U.S. business and political leaders. To reduce wilding, he says, the United States must strive for a "civil society," in which feelings of trust and mutual responsibility replace excessive individualism.

A second argument of anomie theory's supporters addresses the empirical tests of the theory. They say most of these tests focus on individuals, even though anomie theory should be tested as a structural theory, with aggregate (e.g., community or society) data (Bernard 1987). In this regard, the work discussed earlier on communities and economic deprivation is a logical extension of Merton's emphasis on the strain produced by poverty in an egalitarian society. Even if individual data have some merit, the empirical tests do not concentrate on the most economically deprived people, who, as we saw earlier, might be the most likely to feel strain and thus commit crime (Bernard 1984).

When individual data are used, strain is typically measured by examining the difference between expectations and educational or occupational aspirations. These aspirations, the theory's supporters say, are not the same as the *economic* aspirations that Merton addressed. Eventual economic success might be more important to adolescents than their eventual education or occupational status (Bernard 1984). Supporting this view, a study of Seattle adolescents by Margaret Farnworth and Michael J. Leiber found delinquency more related to the imbalance between economic goals and educational expectations than to the imbalance between their educational goals and expectations. The authors concluded that "the apparent failure of strain theory in recent empirical study might well be a function of inappropriate" measurement of strain (Farnworth and Leiber 1989:272).

It's also true that adolescents have immediate goals in addition to eventual socioeconomic success; for example, popularity with peers, doing well in school, and the like. Since they often consider these goals more important than longer-range socioeconomic ones, adolescents may give little thought to the possibility they might not achieve socioeconomic success. If so, it's not surprising that the studies focusing on the gap between socioeconomic aspirations and expectations fail to support anomie theory.

The immediate goal for adolescents of having money is particularly important. Several scholars contend that adolescents are much more concerned about having money now, as adolescents, than about having it later as adults (Greenberg 1977). If so, the best measure of strain would focus on their present desire for money, and this type of strain should predict delinquency. Two recent studies that test this hypothesis find different results. In a study of middle-class students in a midwestern high school, Velmer S. Burton, Jr. and R. Gregory Dunaway (1994) found delinquency higher among students who felt they had less money and fewer possessions than their friends than among those who didn't feel this way. However, in a study of a national sample of tenth-grade boys, Robert Agnew (1994) found no differences in delinquency between those who wanted "more money per week than they actually receive" (p. 415) and those who were satisfied with the money they had. Agnew suggested that adolescents who have less money than they'd like adjust to this problem, and thus reduce the strain they feel, by placing less emphasis on money. In another study, however, Agnew and colleagues (Agnew et al. 1996) found that money may matter for adults as well. Cincinnati adults who desired a lot of money but had low expectations for becoming rich were more likely to commit theft than those who felt otherwise. The authors concluded that "classic strain theory may have been dismissed prematurely by many quantitative researchers" (p. 700).

General Strain Theory

A recent but already influential formulation is Agnew's (1992) "general strain theory" of delinquency, which broadens anomie theory's focus beyond economic goals and success. Agnew argues that adolescent strain results not only from failure to achieve economic or other goals but also from the removal of positive stimuli (e.g., the death of a loved one, the ending of a romantic relationship) and the introduction of negative stimuli (e.g., arguments with parents, insults by teachers or peers). Events occurring closely in time cause more stress than events occurring far apart. Repeated stress leads to several negative emotions, including anger, frustration, and unhappiness. Of these, anger is particularly likely to occur when adolescents

Crime in Families: Social Environment or Biological Problem?

The last chapter noted that crime might "run in families" not because of heredity but because children learn from their parents and use them as role models. The current chapter suggests yet another explanation: Crime might run in families because all family members live in the same social environment. If that environment fits the criminogenic environment outlined in this chapter—economic deprivation, urban conditions, and so forth—the external influences that lead parents to violate the law, either as adults or as adolescents, may have the same impact on their children. A recent report on research on family tendencies to crime illustrates the continuing controversy between biological and structural explanations.

The report concerned a set of studies by Allen Beck, a demographer for the Bureau of Justice Statistics of the U.S. Department of Justice, who found data suggesting that crime does run in families. In a survey of 2,600 juvenile offenders detained in high-security youth centers, 25 percent said their father had been imprisoned; 25 percent reported a sibling had been imprisoned; 9 percent said their mother had been imprisoned; and 13 percent reported another relative had been imprisoned. In a survey of a large sample of adult inmates in local jails, 35 percent said a close relative had been imprisoned. A third survey of state prisoners found 37 percent reporting an immediate family member had been imprisoned.

These proportions might mean that crime runs in families, but do they indicate a biological link? In reacting to these findings, several biologically inclined scholars answered yes. The late Richard J. Herrnstein, a Harvard University psychology professor and a leading advocate of a genetic basis for criminality, commented that these "stunning statistics" suggest both a genetic and an environmental basis for criminal behavior. As a result, "kids brought up in criminal families get a double exposure. That accounts for this enormously dramatic statistic." Another scholar, Deborah W. Denno of Fordham University, attributed the findings to the genetic transmission of hyperactivity across generations. Hyperactive children have problems in school and often become delinquent, she noted. When they later become parents, their families tend to be unstable and their children thus more vulnerable to delinquency.

However, many sociologists would respond that Beck's data could be explained by the social environment (e.g., poverty and urban living conditions) in which both the offenders and their families were raised and now live. As the late Marvin E. Wolfgang, a leading criminologist at the University of Pennsylvania, observed upon hearing of Beck's data, "I'm not denying the statistics, but you should remember that most of these people come from low socioeconomic backgrounds, disadvantaged neighborhoods, where a high proportion of people will be sent to jail whether they are related or not."

As these disparate comments indicate, very different conclusions can be reached from the same research findings. The debate between sociological and other explanations for criminal behavior will undoubtedly continue for some time to come.

Source: Butterfield 1992.

---

blame others for their misfortune. Because anger increases the desire for revenge and inhibits self-control, it, along with some other negative emotions, can increase delinquency and drug use.

In short, as Agnew points out, general strain theory "is very simple. It argues that if we treat people badly, they may get mad and engage in crime" (Agnew 2000:356). Whether someone does engage in crime depends on a variety of factors, including the individual's social support networks, relationships with delinquent friends, and personal characteristics such as self-esteem and self-efficacy (the sense that you're in control of your life). Agnew argues that most tests of strain theory examine the effects of only one or two of the types of strain adolescents experience, and don't consider the cumulative impact of stressful events. This weakness helps account for the tests' failure to support the theory. Agnew thus feels that Merton's version of strain theory needs to be supplemented by recognizing the noneconomic strains facing adolescents.

Tests of general strain theory generally support it. Agnew and Helene Raskin White studied 1,380 New Jersey adolescents and found general strain linked to delinquency and drug use. As hypothesized by the theory, they also found the link between strain and both delinquency and drug use stronger for youths with delinquent friends. Agnew and White (1992:495) concluded that general strain theory "has the potential to serve as a major explanation of delinquency" and urged that it be tested among different demographic subgroups. A test of the theory with National Youth Survey data also supported it. Strain affected delinquency directly, perhaps because it increased anger and resentment, and also indirectly by weakening conventional social bonds and strengthening ties to delinquent peers. The authors concluded that general strain theory "makes an important contribution to delinquency theory" (Paternoster and Mazerolle 1994:235). Another study also supported the theory. It found that adolescents who had experienced various stressful life events, including death or serious illness of a family member or friend and a change in school or residence, were more likely to be delinquent (Hoffmann and Cerbone 1999).

In view of other work suggesting that strain is particularly likely in the urban underclass that suffers severe economic deprivation, it's particularly important that general strain theory be tested in this group, since the theory doesn't explicitly consider the difference that economic deprivation might make. An important area of convergence between general strain theory and economic deprivation research is that the two approaches both link strain and crime/delinquency through anger, frustration, and other social-psychological states. Their attention to these states underscores the importance of social-psychological factors for the genesis of crime and delinquency.

The recent defense, revisions, and extensions of strain theory have revived it as an important explanation of crime and delinquency (Adler and Laufer 1995). Additional research is needed to assess the importance of strain at the aggregate and individual levels for crime and delinquency.

Subcultural Theories

Recall that Merton's anomie theory doesn't explain why some people unable to achieve economic success turn to crime, while others do not. Shaw and McKay gave an early clue to one of the processes involved when they noted that juveniles in socially disorganized neighborhoods grow up amid conflicting values, some of them law-abiding and some of them lawbreaking. Delinquency results when juveniles adopt the latter values. Beginning in the 1950s, scholars began to discuss various kinds of subcultures through which adolescents and others learn it's okay to break the law. Explicitly or implicitly, most of these theorists trace these subcultures' origins to poverty and other kinds of strain.

Albert K. Cohen: School Failure and Delinquent Subcultures

Extending Merton's anomie theory into noneconomic behavior, Albert K. Cohen developed the notion of a delinquent subculture in his influential book, *Delinquent Boys* (Cohen 1955). Like Merton, Cohen assumed that lower-class boys have high

◀ *Albert Cohen wrote that delinquency stems from the failure to do well in school.*

delinquency rates. He observed that much and perhaps most delinquency, such as fighting and vandalism, is noneconomic or nonutilitarian, and that even delinquency involving theft—shoplifting, burglary, and the like—is often done more for thrills than for economic reasons. As a result, this delinquency cannot result from anomie as Merton defined it.

Working within anomie theory's general framework, Cohen adapted Merton's concept of strain but reasoned that a major adolescent goal involves looking good to others, including teachers and friends, and thus feeling good about oneself. Typically, the school experience of lower-class boys makes it difficult to achieve this goal. Cohen thought that schools are dominated by middle-class values such as courtesy, hard work, and deferred gratification. Having not been raised with these values, lower-class boys do poorly in school and experience status frustration, or strain. To reduce their frustration, they turn to a delinquent gang subculture to regain status and respect. This subculture includes values that conflict with middle-class norms conducive to lawfulness.

Two of the most important of these values are short-run *hedonism* and *maliciousness*. Hedonism, or pleasure-seeking, involves the immediate, impulsive gratification of the need for fun and excitement, while maliciousness involves a desire and even delight in hurting others. For obvious reasons, both values can lead gang members to pursue illegal activities. Their primary motive isn't to acquire money or possessions but rather to gain status from their peers and to improve their self-esteem by defying authority.

Notice that Cohen's book was entitled *Delinquent Boys*. What about girls? For the most part, Cohen ignored them because he considered delinquency primarily a lower-class male phenomenon. He thought girls weren't delinquent because they care less than boys about how well they do in school. Instead they attach more importance to romantic relationships because they consider marriage their major goal in life. Girls' delinquency, Cohen thought, stems more from a poor romantic life than from poor school performance.

CRITIQUE OF COHEN'S STATUS FRUSTRATION THEORY

When Cohen wrote his book in 1955, relatively little research on gang delinquency had been done since Shaw and McKay's work. Cohen's book helped change that, and delinquency research burgeoned in the ensuing years. Ironically, much of this research challenged Cohen's assumptions and conclusions (Curran and Ren-zetti 1994; Vold, Bernard, and Snipes 1998).

A first criticism is similar to one lodged against Merton's theory and involves Cohen's assumption that delinquency is concentrated in the lower classes. Cohen overlooked middle-class delinquency, which his theory can't explain. A second criticism concerns his assumption that most delinquency is nonutilitarian. Some re-searchers argue that delinquency is much more utilitarian, or economically moti-vated, than Cohen assumed. The heavy involvement of many urban gangs these days in drug trafficking is certainly aimed more at making money than at finding cheap thrills. Critics espousing social process views (see Chapter 7) also take issue with Cohen's explanation of why school failure leads to delinquency. While the association between school failure and delinquency is a common finding in the lit-erature, processes other than status frustration might be at work.

Another criticism is that Cohen failed to explain why many boys doing poor-ly in school don't become delinquent. Critics also charged that by placing more emphasis on delinquent subcultures than on the structural conditions in which poor adolescents live, Cohen implicitly blamed lower-class adolescents for their problems. A final criticism is that Cohen's view of girls and their delinquency was based on outmoded, sexist views. As Chapter 3 indicated, there's little evidence that girls' delinquency is more sexual than boys' or is more motivated by poor roman-tic relationships. There's also little evidence that girls care less than boys about doing well in school.

An interesting empirical test of Cohen's theory concerns the effects of dropping out of school on delinquency. Since he thought delinquency arises from poor school performance that leads to status frustration, a logical prediction from his theory is that dropping out of school should reduce this frustration and thus reduce delin-quency. Testing this hypothesis, some studies find less delinquency after dropping out of school, but some find more (Elliott and Voss 1974; Thornberry, Moore, and Christenson 1985). G. Roger Jarjoura (1993) faults these studies for not considering students' reasons for dropping out of school (poor grades, problems at home, fi-nancial problems, etc.) and for not controlling for important variables such as prior delinquency. Taking all these factors into account in a study of violence, theft, and selling drugs, Jarjoura found that dropping out usually had no independent effect on delinquency. When it did have an effect, it increased subsequent delinquency, opposite to what Cohen's theory would predict, perhaps because dropping out worsens parental relationships.

Walter B. Miller: Focal Concerns

Three years after Cohen's book, Walter B. Miller published an influential article on lower-class subcultures and delinquency that was based on three years of study-ing delinquent gangs in Massachusetts (Miller 1958). Like Cohen, Miller empha-sized that juveniles learn values conducive to delinquency from their subculture, but his views differed on the nature of the subculture. Whereas Cohen attributed delinquency to involvement in a delinquent gang subculture after failure in school, Miller attributed it to the lower-class subculture itself, which serves as a "generat-ing milieu" for the learning of values conducive to delinquency. Miller thus thought that lower-class juveniles are exposed to this subculture, and hence likely to com-mit delinquency, whether or not they do well in school.

Miller termed the values of the lower-class subculture *focal concerns* and viewed them as conflicting with the values of the larger culture of U.S. society. Together they

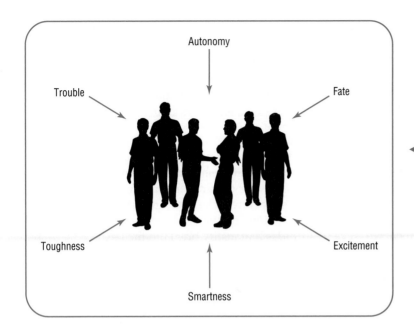

Autonomy

Trouble

Fate

Toughness

Excitement

Smartness

◀ FIGURE 6.1 FOCAL CONCERNS

WALTER MILLER FELT THAT LOWER-CLASS BOYS GROW UP AMID SEVERAL FOCAL CONCERNS THAT THEY LEARN FROM THEIR SUBCULTURE. THESE FOCAL CONCERNS, HE THOUGHT, HELP EXPLAIN THEIR HIGH RATES OF DELINQUENCY.

Source: Based on Miller 1958.

produce delinquency among boys growing up in the lower class and learning these focal concerns. In order of importance, Miller presented the focal concerns as follows (see Figure 6.1).

1. *Trouble.* Miller writes that "concern over 'trouble' is a dominant feature of lower class culture." Trouble most usually represents unwanted involvement by the criminal justice system. Adults want their children to stay out of trouble, while adolescents sometimes gain prestige by getting into trouble. Parents thus evaluate friends of their children on the basis of their "trouble potential."

2. *Toughness.* This concern evokes the John Wayne image of the strong, silent, brave cowboy adept at fighting and involves, Miller said, an "almost obsessive" preoccupation with masculinity and extreme homophobia (hatred of homosexuals). Miller feels it arises from the fact that many lower-class boys are raised in female-headed households and thus lack adequate male role models.

3. *Smartness.* To be "smart" in the lower-class subculture is to outwit others and to avoid being outwitted yourself. It involves the ability to achieve some goal "through a maximum use of mental agility and a minimum use of physical effort." Boys grow up outwitting each other in card games and other activities, including the mutual trading of insults, sometimes called giving each other "the dozens."

4. *Excitement.* Miller writes that many aspects of lower-class life revolve around "the search for excitement or 'thrill.'" On weekends people typically drink, gamble, go out on the town, and have sex. "Men seek to 'pick up' women, and women play the risky game of entertaining sexual advances. Fights between men involving women, gambling, and claims of physical prowess" are common. Miller feels the concern with excitement on weekends arises in part from the boring lives led the rest of the week.

5. *Fate*. Lower-class people have a particularly fatalistic outlook on life, says Miller. Whether they succeed or fail is due less to their own efforts than to good luck or bad luck. This helps account for their high amounts of gambling.

6. *Autonomy*. This focal concern involves a rejection of authority and a distaste for anyone trying to control one's behavior. Autonomy helps justify the violation of laws and other rules.

If adolescents grow up in a subculture valuing trouble, toughness, smartness, excitement, fate, and autonomy, says Miller, it shouldn't be surprising that they often end up being delinquent: "Following cultural practices which comprise essential elements of the total life pattern of lower-class culture automatically violates certain legal norms." Delinquents are thus normal adolescents who have learned from their subculture several attitudes that justify breaking the law.

CRITIQUE OF MILLER'S VIEW

Miller's analysis has been subject to some withering criticism (Vold, Bernard, and Snipes 1998). The most pointed critique is that his characterization of lower-class culture "blames the victim" by ignoring the dire effects of economic deprivation (Ryan 1976). Much, if not all, research since Miller's article finds that poor parents raise their children with values similar to those taught by middle-class parents, and that poor and middle-class adolescents have similar values and attitudes. Middle-class boys appear to value excitement, toughness, autonomy, and other focal concerns as much as their poorer counterparts (Cernkovich 1978). To the extent that middle-class delinquency exists, Miller's theory can't readily account for it, since it places the focal concerns conducive to delinquency in the lower class.

Critics have also accused Miller of engaging in circular reasoning. He identified delinquent boys' focal concerns by observing their behavior and then used these concerns to explain their behavior. A final criticism is that Miller's thesis, like Cohen's work, ignores female delinquency and thus is necessarily incomplete.

Marvin Wolfgang and Franco Ferracuti: The Subculture of Violence

About the time that Miller published his influential article, Marvin Wolfgang advanced the idea of a *subculture of violence* to explain the high level of spontaneous violence among lower-class, nonwhite and especially black, urban males. This subculture "does not define personal assaults as wrong or antisocial." Instead it's a subculture in which "quick resort to physical aggression is a socially approved and expected concomitant of certain stimuli" (Wolfgang 1958:329). Wolfgang expanded on this view nine years later in a book with Franco Ferracuti that presented their subculture of violence theory, which sought to explain the high level of violence committed by young men in poor urban neighborhoods (Wolfgang and Ferracuti 1967). Wolfgang and Ferracuti reasoned that when insults and other interpersonal conflicts occur, lower-class males often respond with physical force, whereas middle-class males tend to walk away. They attributed the lower-class reaction to a subculture of violence that expects a physical response to insults and other interpersonal problems. Echoing Miller's emphasis on lower-class males' obsession with masculinity, Wolfgang and Ferracuti thought that such physical aggression results from the need of lower-class males to defend their honor and masculinity. Boys growing up in a subculture of violence thus learn attitudes conducive to violence and, as a result, commit violence themselves.

As Chapter 3's discussion of race and crime indicated, the subculture of violence theory is very controversial. Early research found that the urban poor didn't approve of violence more than other demographic subgroups, and more recent research using national survey data finds that black males are no more likely than white males to favor the offensive use of violence and are even less likely than white males to support the defensive use of violence (Cao, Adams, and Jensen 1997). A study of Chicago neighborhoods similarly found that blacks were more likely than whites to say that fistfights by teenagers were "extremely wrong." The authors of the study concluded that "there is no race- or ethnicity-based subculture of violence" (Sampson and Bartusch 1999:2). Furthermore, there is also much more violence, especially family violence, among the middle class than Wolfgang and Ferracuti realized. Although the disproportionate involvement of young, urban, nonwhite males in street violence is beyond dispute, it doesn't automatically mean that their behavior stems from a subculture of violence, as Wolfgang and Ferracuti argue. Like Miller's, their reasoning is a bit circular: They infer a subculture of violence from the high level of violence among young, urban men and then attribute the violence to the subculture they've inferred.

These criticisms notwithstanding, a growing body of work now supports Wolfgang and Ferracuti's basic theme but places it squarely in the context of the structural problems discussed earlier in this chapter. According to this view, urban violence stems from the combined stresses of economic deprivation, urban living, and racial discrimination, all of which lead to a "subculture of exasperation" involving angry aggression and a need for greater self-respect (Harvey 1986). These factors in turn increase the willingness to use violence in interpersonal confrontations (Anderson 1999; Bernard 1990). We'll return to this view in Chapter 9.

Richard Cloward and Lloyd Ohlin: Differential Opportunity Theory

We saw earlier that Merton's anomie theory fails to explain why people facing anomie turn to one or another of several logical adaptations. In 1960 Richard Cloward and Lloyd Ohlin tried to extend Merton's formulation to address this problem (Cloward and Ohlin 1960). Merton stressed that society provides "differential access" to legitimate means—working—to achieve monetary success. The nonpoor have such access; the poor often do not. Extending Merton's view and drawing on Shaw and McKay's work on social disorganization, Cloward and Ohlin argued there is also differential access to illegitimate means, or illegitimate opportunity structures. Given anomie, the type of adaptation one pursues depends on which illegitimate opportunities are available. They applied their theory to the activities of poor urban males in delinquent gangs.

The deviant activities of the neighborhoods in which adolescents live determine the nature of the illegal activities they pursue. Where organized crime is a powerful presence, adolescents will naturally tend to become involved in it. In especially deprived areas where drug use and addiction are already rampant, adolescents will start using drugs.

The neighborhoods' deviant activities in turn reflect their social organization. Some neighborhoods are characterized by a *criminal* subculture. These tend to be well-organized, highly integrated neighborhoods with adults who have become well-to-do through illegitimate means (e.g., organized crime) and who spend a lot of time with adolescents. Cloward and Ohlin say that the latter look up to these adults as role models and turn to various forms of property crime themselves, just as middle-class youths who spend time with businesspeople may desire a business career. Delinquent gangs in these communities thus specialize in highly organized, well-planned criminal activities.

Other adolescents live in disorganized neighborhoods where a *conflict* subculture exists. Organized crime doesn't flourish, and there are few successful adult criminals to befriend impressionable adolescents. As a result, youths in these communities lack both legitimate and illegitimate opportunities. Delinquent gangs in these communities thus engage in high amounts of random, often spontaneous violence.

In some neighborhoods, regardless of their social organization, some youths find it difficult to gain access either to criminal gangs or to conflict gangs, or fail to do well in such gangs and drop out. These youths are "double failures," and among them a *retreatist* subculture develops that involves heavy drug and alcohol use.

Cloward and Ohlin's theory was immediately influential and helped prompt many of the antipoverty programs of the 1960s. Its emphasis on differential access to illegitimate opportunities remains important in helping to explain various types of deviance and crime. However, it, too, has been criticized for neglecting middle-class delinquency and white-collar crime (Curran and Renzetti 1994). While some research supports Cloward and Ohlin's idea that gangs specialize in various illegitimate activities determined by neighborhood social organization, the type of specialization doesn't always correspond with their criminal, conflict, and retreatist typology. Many gangs also combine several different kinds of illegitimate activities (e.g., drug use and theft) and thus are unspecialized (Short and Strodtbeck 1965). In another criticism, urban adolescent drug users often don't appear to be the "double failures" depicted by Cloward and Ohlin. Instead, as I remarked in regard to Merton's view, they use drugs for other reasons.

 ## STRUCTURAL THEORIES AND GENDER

What if the stranded children in William Golding's *Lord of the Flies* had been girls instead of boys? Would they have become as savage as the boys? Would they have committed murder? If not, is Golding's view of human behavior really only a view of male behavior? Could he have written the same book with girls as the protagonists?

As these questions indicate, Golding's neglect of gender limits the value of his book, however powerful it is in other respects. The same neglect characterizes the structural theories of crime discussed in this chapter. Careful readers will note that although social class and race lie at the heart of these theories, gender remains invisible. The work of the many scholars of social disorganization, anomie, and subcultural theories was limited not only to lower-class delinquency and crime but also to *male* delinquency and crime. Hence, these theories are explanations of only male offending.

Because they neglect female offending, social disorganization, anomie, and subcultural theories cannot easily explain gender differences in offending (e.g., why women commit less crime than men) or variation in female offending (e.g., why some women are more likely than others to commit crime). As one example, since women's average incomes are only about two-thirds those of men, they should experience more anomie than men and thus, if Merton is correct, be more

◀ *Structural theories of crime fail to explain why females in poor urban areas have lower crime and delinquency rates than males in these same areas.*

likely than men to commit crime (Leonard 1995). We know, however, that this isn't the case.

Scholars have begun to test the theories with samples of female offenders. Tests of strain theory generally find it explaining female offending as well as male offending, although they differ on whether strain is more important for one gender's offending than the other's. For example, one study examined the relationship between perceptions of future opportunities and delinquency and found perceived lack of opportunity more related to girls' delinquency than to boys' (Datesman, Scarpitti, and Stephensen 1975). A later study found perceptions of blocked opportunities related to delinquency for both females and males, with no substantial gender difference in the strength of the relationship (Cernkovich and Giordano 1979). General strain theory may also be useful for understanding female crime. Agnew and a colleague (Broidy and Agnew 1997) recently argued that the theory helps to explain why some females are more likely than other females to commit crime and also why males commit more crime than females overall.

Gender remains missing in the contemporary ecological work focusing on urban conditions, economic deprivation, and racial discrimination. As I stressed earlier, this new body of work provides an important structural understanding of the high crime rates in poor, nonwhite, urban areas. These areas' residents experience cumulative stress from three sources—the dilapidated conditions and other problems of urban neighborhoods, intensive economic deprivation, and continuing racial prejudice—which produce angry aggression and, as a result, violent and other crime. Yet most of the serious violent and property crime in these neighborhoods is still being committed by males even though females experience the same stress-producing conditions (and, some would argue, are even more economically deprived). While some research does suggests that deprivation and other structural conditions help explain variation in urban female offending (Baskin and Sommers 1993; Simpson 1991), gender differences in offending remain unexplained by the new ecological work.

SUMMARY AND CONCLUSION

The structural theories presented in this chapter are distinctively sociological. They invoke Durkheim's century-old view that external forces affect individual behavior and attitudes and remind us that quite normal people may be compelled to commit criminal behavior. This doesn't mean we should excuse such behavior, but it does mean that we should be sensitive to the structural conditions underlying crime as we try to reduce it.

Social disorganization theory, an early structural effort to explain crime, has recently been revived and with good reason. Its focus on the criminogenic conditions of urban neighborhoods is perhaps more timely than ever, and its emphasis on kinds of places over kinds of people is an important corrective to continuing beliefs that crime is due to moral or other failings of individual offenders. Its recent revival in contemporary ecological work represents a major theoretical development with significant policy implications. Perhaps most important, it provides a nonracist explanation for the high crime rates of poor urban areas. In calling attention to weakened social controls resulting from poverty and rapidly changing environments and to the transmission of deviant values, social disorganization theory also anticipated the core concepts of theories discussed in the next chapter.

Merton's anomie theory also went through a period of popularity, decline, and revival. Despite several problems, it calls attention to the strain and subsequent deviance produced by failure to reach economic and other goals. Such strain is heightened in a society whose ideology stresses equal opportunity for all. Anomie theory thus allows us to see that certain values of U.S. society are ironically criminogenic. The very ideology that drives many people to seek their fortunes legally drives others, poor or rich, to seek theirs illegally.

Subcultural theories were developed to help explain how and why structural conditions lead to crime and delinquency. Although they remind us that crime is a learned behavior, they come close to stereotyping the poor and blaming them totally for their behavior.

Social disorganization, strain, and subcultural theories all attempt to explain crime and delinquency by the poor. This focus is both their blessing and their curse. While it's important to explain why poor people disproportionately commit serious street crime, it's also important to recognize that wealthier people commit serious crimes themselves and to explain why they do so. Strain theory begins to provide part of the explanation for white-collar crime, but the other theories do not. Finally, all three theories suffer from their neglect of gender. Although females and males both experience social disorganization and anomie and both live in deviant subcultures (if those truly exist), males remain far more likely than females to commit serious crime and delinquency. None of the structural theories discussed in this chapter adequately accounts for this fact.

A final problem is that most people experiencing the structural problems presented in this chapter still don't commit serious crime and delinquency, while some not experiencing these problems do commit them. Structural theories cannot easily explain such individual variation. Several sociological theories have been developed to help us understand the more *micro* social processes by which some individuals are led into crime and deviance. The next chapter discusses these theories.

KEY TERMS

anomie	economic deprivation
aspirations	focal concerns
concentric zones	kinds of people
differential opportunity	kinds of places

relative deprivation	socialization
social disorganization	status frustration
social ecology	strain
social integration	subculture
social pathology	subculture of violence
social structure	underclass
social ties	

 ## STUDY QUESTIONS

1. How and why did Durkheim's work contribute to a structural under-standing of deviance and crime? How does the book *Lord of the Flies* reflect this understanding?

2. What does the new ecological work on crime and victimization generally tells us about the factors that make crime more common?

3. Why should anomie theory be considered a structural theory? How does general strain theory build upon anomie theory?

4. In what ways do structural theories ignore gender differences in criminal offending? Do you think these theories help us understand why these gen-der differences exist?

 ## INTERNET EXERCISES

Several of the theories discussed in this chapter, including Stark's theory of deviant places, help us to understand why urban areas generally have higher crime rates than suburban or rural areas.

To reinforce this point, go to the Uniform Crime Reports at **http://www.fbi.gov/ucr.htm**. Open up the 1999 UCR by clicking on **1999**. Scroll down the page that opens until you find the total Index Crime rate for metropolitan areas and for rural areas. What are the rates you find? How much lower is the rural rate?

Now click on **Violent Crime Total** in the left window. Scroll down the page that opens until you find the rate of violent crime for metropolitan areas and for rural areas. What are the rates you find? How much lower is the rural rate?. Di-vide the rural rate into the metropolitan rate. How many times greater is the vio-lent crime rate in metropolitan areas compared to that in rural areas?

Next, use your browser to go back to the previous Web page. Click on **Proper-ty Crime Total** in the left window. Scroll down the page that opens until you find the property crime rate for cities or metropolitan areas and for rural areas. What are the rates you find? How much lower is the rural rate?

Using the explanations for crime presented in this chapter, how would you ex-plain why rural areas have such lower crime rates than urban areas?

SOCIOLOGICAL THEORIES:
EMPHASIS ON
SOCIAL PROCESS

Crime in the News

Little Kayla Rolland, age 6, had her life cut short in March 2000 by a bullet fired by another 6-year-old in a classroom at their school near Flint, Michigan. Her assailant was a boy who had an argument with Kayla the day before. He decided he wanted to get even by scaring her, so that night he found a gun at his home under a pile of blankets in a bedroom. The next morning he took the gun to school. When he saw Kayla, he pulled out the gun, said "I don't like you," and pulled the trigger. A report noted that the boy "was the product of an environment and family that the word dysfunctional does not begin to capture." He lived in a run-down, two-bedroom house with vodka bottles strewn in the yard. Strangers routinely went in and out of the house to buy, sell, and use crack. He lived there with his uncle and another man and slept on a couch in the living room. His mother had left him with the men after she was evicted from her nearby house; his father was in jail for violating probation after he got out of prison for burglary and drug charges. A neighbor said of the boy's parents, "They trashed that house. The parents were always in the yard cussing and fighting and drinking."

Source: Naughton and Thomas 2000.

*T*he last chapter argued that the behavior of the boys in *Lord of the Flies* arose from the extreme anomie and social disorganization they faced. There are other ways to explain their behavior. We could talk instead about how they influenced each other to be violent. Or we could say their island lacked the law-abiding influence of parents, schools, and religion. The explanation in the last chapter emphasized social structure. The ones just listed emphasize social processes such as learning, socialization, and social interaction, and help to explain the tragic death of little Kayla (described in the "Crime in the News" vignette).

Such social process explanations see crime arising more from the interaction of individuals than from the way society is organized. Although structural and social process explanations both make sense, some scholars favor the macro view of structural approaches, while others favor the micro view of social process perspectives. Although the sociological study of crime began, as we saw in the last chapter, with a structural focus, in the last few decades a focus on social interaction and processes has dominated the field. Its popularity stems from scholarly recognition that most people living in criminogenic structural conditions do not commit serious crime. If this is true, then it's important to understand the social processes leading some people in these conditions to commit crime and others not to do so.

While conceding the importance of criminogenic social processes, structural theorists still stress the underlying influence of structural problems in society or in particular neighborhoods. Echoing Shaw and McKay, they argue that poor individuals would commit less street crime were they living in more advantaged circumstances. Today a healthy tension exists between the two approaches' proponents. Some scholars even favor *integrated* theories combining factors from both views. Although integrated theories are not the final word, I do think that both structural and social process factors are necessary for a comprehensive explanation of crime. We would have less crime if not for the structural conditions producing it, and we would have less crime if not for certain social processes increasing individuals' potential to commit crime. Efforts to reduce crime will not succeed unless they keep in mind these basic facts.

This chapter reviews the major social process theories of criminal behavior. While many scholars consider them psychological theories (Widom and Toch 1993), their focus on interaction among individuals normally places them under a sociological rubric. Whatever we call them, they incorporate ideas compatible with both sociological and psychological explanations, helping to explain their popularity today.

LEARNING THEORIES

From the time we're born, we all learn how to behave. Since the time of Emile Durkheim a century ago, sociologists have considered *socialization* critical for social order. In the 1600s the great political philosopher Thomas Hobbes (1588–1679), who considered human nature selfish, asked his famous question, "Why is there not a war of all against all?" (Hobbes 1950 [1651]) Durkheim's response some 200 years later was that we internalize the norms and values of society and thus learn how to get along with each other. As Randall Collins (1994:190) points out, Durkheim thought that society forms a "moral cocoon" around individuals that makes them "less individualistic, more a member of the group." No longer just individuals, we become social beings who care about the welfare of others and the well-being of society as a whole. Socialization makes this possible.

Following Durkheim, just about every Introduction to Sociology text has an early chapter extolling the virtues of socialization and emphasizing its importance during childhood and adolescence. If you've read such a text, you probably remember its socialization chapter talking about "agents of socialization": the family, school, friends, and the mass media. All these agents influence our values and behavior in critical ways. If Durkheim is right, they also help turn us into cooperative, law-abiding members of society.

Just as most people learn to obey society's norms, however, others learn that it's okay to violate these norms. They learn these "deviant" norms and values from their peers and immediate environments, and perhaps also from the mass media. Learning theories of crime see criminality as the result of the socialization process we all experience. Because of their individual circumstances, quite normal people learn and practice behaviors that the larger society condemns. Not surprisingly, children growing up in neighborhoods rife with crime often end up committing crime themselves. Middle-class kids often engage in shoplifting, vandalism, and other delinquency because of the influence of delinquent friends. White-collar executives learn to consider price fixing and other financial crimes a normal and necessary part of doing business.

Learning theories start where structural theories leave off. Structural theories tell us why various attitudes and feelings arise that promote criminality. Learning theories tell us how people come to adopt these views and how and why they result in crime. Several learning theories exist, and certain nuances distinguish them from one another. But they agree much more than they disagree, and all view crime and delinquency as an unfortunate consequence of "wrong" socialization. In showing how individuals are socialized to commit crime, learning theories join with structural approaches in presenting a positivist view of crime that stresses the influences of external forces on the individual.

Edwin H. Sutherland: Differential Association Theory

About sixty years ago sociologist Edwin Sutherland (1883–1950) presented the most famous and influential learning theory of crime, which he termed *differential association theory*. As Chapter 1 noted, Sutherland is a towering figure in the sociological study of crime. In addition to his differential association theory, he also wrote extensively about white-collar crime, particularly corporate crime, and helped make it a legitimate subject for scholarly investigation.

As a sociologist, Sutherland was critical of biological and psychological approaches. He thought they presented a false picture of crime and criminals as abnormal and suffered from the other failings outlined in Chapter 5. The work of Shaw, McKay, and other Chicago sociologists on social disorganization and criminogenic values had sensitized Sutherland to the consequences of growing up in neighborhoods abounding in crime and delinquency. As first presented in his text, *Principles of Criminology*, in 1939, Sutherland's differential association theory aimed to explain why poor individuals have high rates of criminality and included several propositions on how they learn to be deviant. Shaw and McKay's theory aimed to explain why poor urban areas have high crime rates, while Sutherland's tried to explain why and how some people in such areas develop criminal attitudes and turn to crime.

Sutherland later applied his theory to professional thieves, and argued that differential association with different types of thieves—for example, shoplifters, professional burglars, or pickpocketers—influences what kind of thief someone becomes. He also applied it to white-collar criminals, who learn that it's okay to violate the law from a business climate justifying lawbreaking to maximize profit (Sutherland 1937; 1939; 1940).

Sutherland's perspective reflected the views of French social psychologist and magistrate Gabriel Tarde (1843–1904). Tarde wrote several works from 1886 through the early 1890s, with his best-known work probably his 1890 book *La Philosophie Penale* (*Penal Philosophy*) (Tarde 1912 [1890]). In these writings he set forth his *imitation theory* of crime that individuals imitate each other in proportion to the amount of close contact they have. Critical of the biological work of Lombroso and others, Tarde believed that crime was not inherited or otherwise caused by biological traits but instead was learned through interaction with deviant friends. The fate of "street urchins," he said, is "often decided by the influence of their comrades," with a "child who was the most normally constituted ... [more] influenced by half a score of perverse friends by whom he is surrounded than by millions of unknown fellow-citizens" (Tarde 1912 [1890]:252–253).

Building on the work of Tarde and the Chicago sociologists, Sutherland presented his final version of differential association in a 1947 revision of his text. His theory contained nine propositions that have appeared in most criminology textbooks in the last half century (Sutherland 1947).

1. *Criminal behavior is learned.* Sutherland declares that criminal behavior is not inherited biologically nor otherwise the result of any biological traits.

2. *Criminal behavior is learned in interaction with other persons in a process of communication.* Here Sutherland says that the learning of criminal behavior occurs through interpersonal interaction.

3. *The principal part of the learning of criminal behavior occurs within intimate personal groups.* Following Tarde, Sutherland asserts that people learn crime from people who are close to them emotionally. He implies that criminal behavior is not learned from the mass media.

4. *When criminal behavior is learned, the learning includes (a) the techniques of committing the crime, which are sometimes very complicated, sometimes very simple; and (b) the specific direction of motives, drives, rationalizations, and attitudes.* This proposition says that the learning of criminal behavior involves mastering how to commit the crime and also deviant attitudes that justify committing it.

5. *The specific direction of motives and drives is learned from definition of the legal codes as favorable or unfavorable.* Gaining knowledge of criminal behavior also involves learning whether to define laws as worthy of obedience or deserving of violation.

6. *A person becomes delinquent because of an excess of definitions favorable to violation of law over definitions unfavorable to violation of law.* This is the heart of Sutherland's differential association theory. People will break the law if they develop more lawbreaking attitudes than law-abiding attitudes.

7. *Differential association may vary in frequency, duration, priority, and intensity.* Associations do not affect your views equally. Police come into frequent contact with criminals but do not usually adopt these criminals' attitudes (Shoemaker 1996). In this proposition, Sutherland notes that the effects of associations vary according to four dimensions. *Frequency* simply means how often you spend time with your friends. *Duration* means how much

◄ *Differential association and other learning theories emphasize that people learn criminal behavior through interpersonal interaction, especially interaction with people who are close to them emotionally.*

time on the average you spend with them during each association. *Priority* refers to how early in life the associations occur, while *intensity* means how much importance you place on your associations. While these dimensions often overlap, associations will likely have the greatest impact on your views if they are of high frequency and duration, take place early in life, and involve people whose views and friendship you value highly.

8. *The process of learning criminal behavior by association with criminal and anticriminal patterns involves all of the mechanisms that are involved in any other learning.* Here Sutherland emphasizes that socialization into crime includes the same processes involved in socialization into law-abiding behavior.

9. *While criminal behavior is an expression of general needs and values, it is not explained by these general needs and values, since noncriminal behavior is an expression of the same needs and values.* Sutherland says here that motives are not sufficient to explain crime. For example, the desire for money motivates some people to break the law, but motivates most of us to try to move up the socioeconomic ladder legally by acquiring a good education, working hard, and the like. Similarly, jealousy may lead some people to commit murder, but most people who are jealous do not commit murder. Thus other forces must also be at work.

Along with Merton's anomie theory, Sutherland's theory of differential association is the most notable historically in the sociological study of crime (Matsueda 1988; Vold, Bernard, and Snipes 1998). By explicitly linking crime to learning and socialization, Sutherland emphasized its social nature and thus countered explanations centering on biological abnormalities. By stressing the importance of differential associations, he helped to explain variation in offending among people experiencing similar structural conditions. And by extending his theory to white-collar crime, Sutherland emphasized that it's not only the poor who commit crime and helped to explain how the wealthy come to commit their crimes.

Since its inception, Sutherland's theory has also received much empirical support (Akers 1997). As a review noted, "Perhaps the most consistent finding in the literature on the causes of delinquency is that adolescents with delinquent peers are more likely to be delinquent themselves. In most research, the relationship of delinquent peers to delinquency exceeds that of any other independent variable" (Agnew 1991:47).

CRITIQUE OF DIFFERENTIAL ASSOCIATION THEORY

Despite its important contributions, differential association theory eventually came under attack. Since every other theory covered so far in this book has been heavily criticized, this fact shouldn't surprise you.

A first criticism, and also one of the most important, concerns the problem of causal order (Tittle, Burke, and Jackson 1986): the familiar chicken-and-egg question encountered in previous theories. Which comes first, criminal behavior or differential associations with offenders? Staying for a moment with the study of delinquency, which comes first, associating with delinquent peers or one's own delinquency? Although many studies find a statistical correlation between the two, it's possible that someone's delinquency produces friendships with delinquent peers rather than the reverse. You become delinquent for reasons other than differential association, but once you do, you may well find yourself spending more time with other delinquents. It might be true in the world of love that "opposites attract," but in the world of delinquency it is also true that "birds of a feather flock together" (Curran and Renzetti 1994). To the extent this is so, Sutherland and other learning theorists may misinterpret the real causal order at work.

In response to this criticism, scholars have begun to untangle the causal order in the delinquent peers-delinquency relationship that is so often found (see the Crime and Controversy box). Although Sutherland neglected the possibility that delinquency produces friendships with delinquents, this body of work nonetheless supports his central thesis that associations with delinquent peers produce delinquency.

In a second criticism, Sutherland may have erred in talking about the influence of friends' definitions or attitudes favorable to violating the law while neglecting the influence of the friends' behavior itself. We might do what our friends do *not* because we've adopted their attitudes, but simply because we want them to like us and be with us, or because we find their behavior rewarding. We can adopt their behavior without necessarily adopting any deviant attitudes they might have. This view of the learning of crime supports other learning theories more than it does Sutherland's (Warr and Stafford 1991).

A third criticism concerns Sutherland's implication that crime is committed in groups or, if done alone, is still influenced by "intimate personal groups." Differential association theory applies well to many crimes, and especially to juvenile offenses such as shoplifting, vandalism, and drug use, where peer influences loom large. But many criminal behaviors don't fit this pattern: They're committed by lone individuals and also don't stem from attitudes and techniques learned from intimate friends. For example, most murders are committed by people acting alone, who cannot be said to have learned from their friends that it's okay to commit murder. Differential association theory might help explain murders committed by members of gangs and organized crime groups, but these murders aren't the most typical (see Chapter 9). Most rapes are similarly committed by lone offenders who can't be said to have learned attitudes approving rape from their close friends. Rape might derive from attitudes in the larger culture condoning rape (see Chapter 10),

Delinquent Peers and Delinquency: The Causal Order Debate

Although many studies find that teenagers with more delinquent friends are themselves more likely to be delinquent than teenagers with fewer such friends, it's difficult to know how to interpret this statistical relationship. Does having delinquent friends help make you more likely to be delinquent, as differential association and other learning theories assume (the socialization perspective)? Or is it possible that the reverse is true: that involvement in delinquency increases your selection of other delinquents as the people with whom you spend time (the selection perspective)? A third possibility is that delinquent peers and delinquency influence each other in a reciprocal relationship (the interactional perspective).

Although they purported to test differential association and other learning theories, early studies of the delinquent peers-delinquency relationship couldn't adequately determine the causal order involved. They used cross-sectional data, or data taken at one point in time. A typical questionnaire would ask respondents how many of their friends were involved in delinquency and how often, or whether, in the past they themselves had committed delinquency. Although these studies found the delinquent peers-delinquency relationship presumed by differential association theory, the cross-sectional nature of their data prevented them from knowing which comes first.

To address this problem, some recent studies have used longitudinal data, and generally find that having delinquent peers influences one's own delinquency, and that one's own delinquency increases your involvement with delinquent peers. One such study by Terence P. Thornberry (the developer of interactional theory) and his colleagues analyzed data on Rochester, New York youths. The authors found a reciprocal relationship between delinquent peers and delinquency: Associating with delinquent peers leads to greater delinquency, and greater delinquency leads in turn to more associations with delinquent peers. These associations then lead to even further delinquency.

Thornberry and his colleagues concluded that neither the socialization perspective nor the selection perspective is adequate by itself to explain their results. Instead, their findings more nearly fit the assumptions of interactional theory. They further concluded that their findings reinforce the importance of doing longitudinal research, and that "the causal processes among variables central to traditional theories of delinquency are much more complex than those theories have depicted them to be" (p. 75).

In a more recent study, Ross L. Matsueda and Kathleen Anderson analyzed data from the National Youth Survey. Although, as expected, they found a reciprocal relationship between delinquent peers and delinquency, they also found that the effect of delinquency on delinquent peer associations was greater than that of the associations on delinquency. They concluded that the "latter effect has likely been overestimated in previous research" (p. 301). As their study suggests, the exact relationship between delinquent peers and delinquency remains an important one for criminology in the years ahead.

Sources: Matsueda and Anderson 1998; Thornberry et al. 1994.

---

but the focus of this sort of explanation differs from Sutherland's emphasis on intimate personal groups.

A related criticism concerns Sutherland's claim that the mass media have little effect on crime and delinquency. Writing in the 1930s and 1940s, Sutherland couldn't have anticipated the development of television and the increase of violence in films. A rich literature now exists on the impact of TV, violent films, pornography, and other aspects of our popular culture on crime in general and violent crime in particular. Although the findings are very complex, the literature at least indicates a correlation between exposure to violence in the mass media and the actual commission of violence (Surette 1998). If the media do increase criminality, then Sutherland's disavowal of a media effect was mistaken. That said, it's not yet clear whether the correlation between media violence and the commission of violence means that the former actually causes the latter. Chapter 9 discusses media and violence further.

Some critics also point to difficulties in testing differential association theory. As mentioned earlier, empirical tests of the theory usually examine the effects of the number of delinquent friends. To measure this variable, scholars might ask, "In the last year, how many of your friends have engaged in" shoplifting, marijuana use, and the like. But this focus differs from Sutherland's emphasis on the number of definitions favorable and unfavorable to violating the law. This concept is much more difficult to measure than the number of delinquent friends (Vold, Bernard, and Snipes 1998). Further, since we discover offenders only after they commit their offenses, we can never be sure of their attitudes preceding their offenses, as a valid test of Sutherland's theory requires (Shoemaker 1996).

In another area, a study by Mark Warr of data from the longitudinal National Youth Survey (see Chapter 3) found that "recent rather than early friends have the greatest effect on delinquency" (Warr 1993:35). This finding suggests that Sutherland got his "priority" dimension backward, since he thought that earlier friendships have the greatest effect.

Finally, since Sutherland's focus was on male delinquency, he didn't consider whether differential association works the same for females. Recent evidence suggests it may not. Although girls often have more intimate relationships than boys, their friends tend to be less delinquent than boys' friends. Their relationships are thus less likely than boys' to promote delinquency (Morash 1986). To put it another way, peer relationships may be a stronger determinant of male delinquency than female delinquency. To the extent this is true, Sutherland's theory applies more to males than to females. Despite this problem, differential association theory may nonetheless help explain the gender difference in criminality, as Sutherland himself speculated, since it "reminds us that women are not permitted the same associations as men" because of greater supervision by their families (Leonard 1995:61). Supporting this view, a recent study found that girls are less violent than boys in part because they're less apt than boys to learn "violent definitions" (Heimer and Coster 1999).

Despite the criticisms of differential association theory, it remains a compelling explanation of many forms of delinquency and adult crime. Notice that Sutherland did not say much about the processes by which individuals adopt deviant attitudes through differential associations. Other subsequent learning theories discuss some of these processes. We turn briefly to these theories.

Other Learning Theories

DANIEL GLASER: DIFFERENTIAL IDENTIFICATION THEORY

Sociologist Daniel Glaser extended differential association theory in 1956 when he presented his own theory of *differential identification* (Glaser 1956). Glaser's theory rested on the notion of *reference groups*, or groups whose values, attitudes, and behavior you admire and wish to copy. These can be groups to which you already belong, such as your circle of friends, or groups to which you don't belong, such as the clique of high school students who are the well-dressed school leaders, or even a popular music group. If your reference groups happen to be ones engaging in criminal or deviant behavior, you're apt to engage in such behavior yourself.

As Glaser summarizes his central thesis, "A person pursues criminal behavior to the extent that he identifies himself with real or imaginary persons from whose perspective his criminal behavior seems acceptable" (Glaser 1956:440). In contrast to differential association theory and the other learning theories discussed later, differential identification theory stressed that learning of criminal behavior can occur without actually interacting with the group influencing you. However, it doesn't explain why you might admire some reference groups more than others.

ALBERT BANDURA: SOCIAL LEARNING THEORY

About forty years ago, psychologist Albert Bandura developed his *social learning* theory of aggression (Bandura 1973). Like other social scientists interested in the learning of behavior, Bandura rejected the idea that humans are born naturally aggressive. Instead he argued that aggressive tendencies are learned later in life. We may see our friends or parents act aggressively, and we may see violence on TV and in other aspects of our popular culture. All these influences help us learn that aggression is acceptable behavior. In developing his theory, Bandura drew upon a rich body of psychological research on classical and operant conditioning. As advanced by Ivan Pavlov, John Watson, B. F. Skinner, and others, this tradition stresses that learning occurs because of the association of a stimulus with a response (*classical conditioning*) or because of the rewarding of a particular behavior (*operant conditioning*). Although Bandura recognized the importance of rewards for learning behavior, he also stressed that learning can occur just through modeling, or imitating behavior, without any rewards being involved.

◀ *Psychologist Albert Bandura was one of the first social scientists to investigate whether media violence leads to more violent behavior in society.*

Bandura was one of the first social scientists to investigate the effects of the mass media on aggression. In the early 1960s, he and some colleagues had a group of children watch a TV program in which actors engaged in various aggressive acts, including striking an inflated "Bobo doll," as it was called. The experimenters later frustrated these children, who then engaged in aggression themselves. Children in a control group who *did not* see the program were much less likely to be aggressive when frustrated by the experimenters (Bandura, Ross, and Ross 1963).

ROBERT L. BURGESS AND RONALD L. AKERS: DIFFERENTIAL REINFORCEMENT THEORY

In a 1966 article, Robert L. Burgess and Ronald L. Akers (1966) presented their *differential reinforcement* theory of crime. Akers developed this theory further in later work and, borrowing Bandura's term, named it a *social learning* approach (Akers 1977). Adapting the views of B. F. Skinner and other psychologists on operant conditioning and integrating them with Sutherland's differential association concept, Burgess and Akers argued that criminal behavior and attitudes are more likely to be learned when they're reinforced, or rewarded, usually by friends and/or family. When the rewards for criminal behavior outweigh the rewards for alternative behaviors, differential reinforcement occurs and the criminal behavior is learned.

Echoing the classical view of Beccaria and Bentham, Burgess and Akers thought that people decide whether to commit crime after calculating whether the potential rewards will outweigh the potential risks. Although much learning of criminal behavior occurs within the intimate personal groups emphasized by Sutherland, Burgess and Akers observed it can also stem from the influence of school authorities, police, the mass media, and other non-primary group sources. These sources all provide rewards and punishments that influence the learning of behavior. Although Burgess and Akers stressed the social context of differential reinforcement, they also recognized that criminal behavior can provide its own rewards, such as excitement, increased wealth, and the like.

 ## CONTROL THEORIES

Theories of behavior, including theories of crime and deviance, are often based on assumptions about human nature. As we saw in this and the last chapter, conservative thinkers of the 1800s thought that human nature was selfish and that society needed to restrain individual impulses. Thus Durkheim thought that suicide rises without effective social norms and ties. Similarly, psychoanalytic thinkers, following Freud, assumed the need to restrain the pleasure-seeking id from engaging in antisocial behavior. In *Lord of the Flies*, William Golding gave his view of what might happen without society's constraints.

Over the centuries, other thinkers have presented a much more optimistic appraisal of human nature. The most notable statement is probably that of English philosopher John Locke in his 1690 work, *An Essay Concerning Human Understanding* (Locke 1979 [1690]). Locke believed that humans were not predisposed at birth to be either good or bad. Instead, he argued, the mind is a *tabula rasa*, or blank slate, into which ideas are placed by experience. If anything, he said, society is more likely to make people turn out bad than good. His view of human nature was thus much more optimistic and his view of society more negative than the views advanced by Durkheim and other conservative thinkers.

Learning theories of crime share Locke's view of human nature. Recall their basic assumption that individuals learn to be criminals. This view implies that individuals would not commit crime unless they first learn criminal attitudes and behaviors. This in turn implies that the individual is a *tabula rasa* who would generally not become a criminal without first learning about crime from society. With this assumption of human nature, learning theories thus ask, "Why do people become criminals?"

Control theories of crime take a different view of human nature and thus ask a different question about crime. Their view of human nature resembles that of Durkheim, the novelist Golding, and other pessimistic appraisers. Control theories assume that people are naturally selfish and very capable of committing antisocial behavior, including crime. Given this view, control theories find it surprising that people do not commit crime. The key question they try to answer is not "Why do people become criminals?" but rather "Why do people not become criminals?" (Kornhauser 1978).

In answering this question, control theorists discuss two kinds of controls, personal and social (Reiss 1951). *Personal controls* concern such things as individual conscience, commitment to law, and a positive self-concept. *Social controls* concern attachments to and involvement in conventional social institutions such as the family, schools, and religion. Weak personal controls often result from weakened social controls. The basic argument is that a positive self-concept and other personal controls combine with strong attachments to conventional social institutions to keep individuals from becoming criminals. When either or both of these types of control weaken, individuals are freer to become criminals. In this regard, *Lord of the Flies* is a vivid example of the effects of weakened social attachments. We'll first look at some personal control theories and then at social control theory.

Walter Reckless: Containment Theory

In the 1950s and 1960s, sociologist Walter C. Reckless developed his *containment theory* of delinquency, which stressed that *inner and outer containments*, but particularly inner containments, help prevent juvenile offending (Reckless 1961; Reckless, Dinitz, and Murray 1956). Reckless identified several inner containments, including a positive self-concept, tolerance for frustration, and an ability to set realistic goals, that help ward off negative environmental influences that might ordinarily foster delinquency. But he saw a positive self-concept as having the greatest preventive effect. He further identified several outer containments, particularly the family, that also help prevent delinquency.

Both inner and outer containments were necessary, said Reckless, to keep juveniles from succumbing to *internal pushes* and *external pressures and pulls* that would otherwise prompt them to break the law. Internal pushes are social-psychological states and include such things as the need for immediate gratification, restlessness, and a hostile attitude. External pressures are structural problems and include poverty, unemployment, and other social conditions. External pulls are forces like delinquent peers that pull individuals into crime and delinquency.

In support of containment theory's emphasis on a positive self-concept, Reckless et al. (1956) studied 125 nondelinquent boys from a neighborhood with a high rate of delinquency and compared them with boys with official records of delinquency. The nondelinquents had more positive self-concepts than the delinquents; to turn this around, the delinquents had more negative self-concepts than the nondelinquents.

Critics of containment theory raise the familiar chicken-and-egg question. Although studies by Reckless and others have found lower self-concepts among boys with delinquent records, it's possible that their negative self-concepts were the result of their being officially labeled delinquent (see Chapter 8) and not the cause of their delinquency. Critics also say it's difficult to demonstrate that a positive self-concept is the most important factor preventing delinquency, as containment theory asserts. Other factors, such as peer relationships and family influences, may be more important (Shoemaker 1996). Finally, although some research finds self-concept differences between delinquents and nondelinquents, other studies find no differences. Supporting containment theory, however, other research finds that a poor self-concept fosters delinquency, especially when adolescents are also experiencing troubles at home or in school. Participating in delinquency may raise these adolescents' self-esteem (Kaplan 1980).

Gresham M. Sykes and David Matza: Neutralization and Drift Theory

Let's assume you believe there should be speed limits for cars. Now consider all the times you and your friends drive a car past the speed limit. Why do you do so? As you're about to exceed the speed limit, do you realize you're going to violate the traffic law? You might be worried about getting a ticket, but do you ever feel a tiny twinge of guilt now and then? If you do feel some guilt, why do you exceed the speed limit? Do you justify to yourself that it's acceptable to do so? If you don't feel any guilt, why not? Whether or not you feel guilty, do you reason that the speed limit is too low, and that no one, especially you, will get hurt if you exceed it? Do you simply like flouting the law? As these questions suggest, law-abiding people may accept the validity of laws but violate them anyway. Part of this process involves justifying to themselves why it's okay to break the law, especially when they would otherwise feel guilty or ashamed for disobeying the law.

Despite the possible need for many offenders to justify their criminality, the theories we've discussed so far spend little time discussing any guilt or qualms individuals might feel before they commit crime. Differential association theory paints a view of a rather passive individual pushed and pulled by delinquent friends into delinquency and crime. Differential reinforcement and some other learning theories give a more active role to the individual, who calculates whether potential rewards for crime outweigh the risks. Yet even these theories don't consider at length the guilt individuals may feel as they perform such calculations. Since control theories assume that people are naturally selfish, they, too, allow little or no role for guilt.

Focusing on guilt, Gresham M. Sykes and David Matza challenged the notion of Albert Cohen and others of a lower-class, delinquent subculture in their 1957 article, "Techniques of Neutralization: A Theory of Delinquency" (Sykes and Matza 1957). If such a subculture existed, poor adolescents wouldn't feel guilt or shame for committing delinquency. Because delinquents often do feel guilty or ashamed, Sykes and Matza argued, they thus must subscribe to middle-class values. According to the authors, evidence for delinquents' belief in these values also comes from their admiration of law-abiding persons such as their parents or clergy and from the fact that they distinguish between justifiable and unjustifiable victims, with examples of the latter being their own friends or place of worship. Since they've also internalized the law-abiding norms of their family and other conventional institutions, they can't easily violate these norms without feeling some remorse.

Given these assumptions, said Sykes and Matza, a fundamental question to answer is why people violate laws whose legitimacy they accept. Regarding delinquency, Sykes and Matza argued that adolescents must "neutralize" any guilt they feel before they commit delinquency, and thus must develop rationalizations about why it's okay to break the law. Sykes and Matza presented five common such rationalizations, or, as they called them, *techniques of neutralization*. These justifications precede delinquency and comprise an important part of the definitions favorable to law violation stressed by differential association theory. The five techniques of neutralization follow:

1. *Denial of responsibility.* Here adolescents rationalize that they're not responsible for the delinquent acts they're about to commit. Their behavior is due to forces beyond their control, such as abusive parents or deviant friends. If you're a teenager who drinks or uses illegal drugs with your friends, you may say that peer pressure made you do it.

2. *Denial of injury.* Here adolescents reason that no one will be hurt by their intended illegal behavior. Borrowing a car for a joy ride is just fun-loving mischief, not a crime; the owner will get the car back or at least has insurance, so no one gets hurt. A large department store won't miss any items that are shoplifted.

3. *Denial of the victim.* Even if offenders realize they're about to harm someone or something, they may reason that their target deserves what's about to happen. Robin Hood and his Merry Men felt it acceptable to rob from the rich and give to the poor. Shoplifters might reason that the store has "ripped them off," so now it's their turn to rip off the store. People about to commit hate crimes might reason that their targets are less than human and thus deserve to be beaten. Rapists might figure the victim "asked for it" by the way she dressed or acted. Batterers say their wives and girlfriends should have kept the children more quiet, should not have looked at another man, should have had dinner ready on time. To the batterers, these "transgressions" mean that these women deserve to be beaten.

4. *Condemnation of the condemners.* Here offenders question the motives and integrity of police, parents, teachers, and other parties who condemn the offenders' behavior. The police are corrupt, so it's okay for me to break the law. My parents used marijuana when they were my age, so why can't I?

5. *Appeal to higher loyalties.* Here offenders reason that their illegal behavior is necessary to help people dear to them. Members of gangs may conclude that loyalty to the gang justifies their taking part in illegal activities committed by the gangs. Poor people may steal food to help their starving families.

In later work, Matza (1964) expanded the idea of neutralization as he developed his *drift theory* of delinquency. Matza argued that delinquents aren't necessarily committed to delinquent values, as subcultural theories would assert, and thus aren't constantly delinquent. He felt instead that adolescents drift into and out of delinquency in an episodic fashion. Techniques of neutralization make their delinquency possible but so do *subterranean values*, which are part of the larger culture but also conflict with other values in the larger culture. They include an emphasis on daring and excitement, a belief that aggression is sometimes necessary, and the desire for wealth and possessions. While these values often underlie conforming behavior, they can also lead to deviant behavior, especially when peer influences help channel these values into illegal activity.

Although Sykes and Matza's ideas have been popular, they've also been criticized. Some scholars question Sykes and Matza's assumption that adolescents accept conventional values. If they don't hold conventional beliefs, then they don't feel guilty and thus have nothing to neutralize (Hindelang 1974). In addition, few studies have tested the theory empirically, in part because it's very difficult to test. Because we don't know when adolescents will break the law, we can never know for sure whether they engage in techniques of neutralization before they break the law. They may report afterward that they had done so, but we cannot know for certain whether a rationalization reported at this time stems from the offense or instead actually preceded it. Techniques of neutralization may thus be "after-the-fact rationalizations rather than before-the-fact neutralizations" (Hirschi 1969:207) that help soothe the guilt that offenders would otherwise feel. Thus, although several studies find that offenders from all walks of life do rationalize their behavior, they do not demonstrate that such rationalization occurs before illegal behavior, as Sykes and Matza assume (Pogrebin, Poole, and Martinez 1992).

Another criticism concerns Sykes and Matza's belief that delinquents aren't really committed to deviant values and, because they drift into and out of delinquency, are not chronic, or constant, offenders. Instead they leave the world of delinquency and crime as they mature into their twenties, find employment, and get married. Although most delinquents are not chronic offenders and thus end their delinquency as they leave their teens, some chronic offenders do pursue criminal careers later (see Chapter 3) and do hold different values from those of nondelinquents. While Sykes and Matza's theory thus applies to most adolescent offenders, it doesn't help us understand this small group of chronic offenders (Curran and Renzetti 1994).

A further criticism targets Sykes and Matza's characterization of their theory as consistent with differential association, as adolescents learn to justify their illegal behavior. Other scholars instead see their theory as more consistent with the perspective of control theories. Adolescents drift into delinquency when their bonds to conventional institutions weaken. Techniques of neutralization help weaken these bonds (Minor 1981).

A final criticism is one we've seen before. The work of Sykes and Matza's, and the empirical tests of their views, once again are limited to males. Because moral development might differ by gender (Gilligan 1982), neutralization and drift theory may apply more to males than to females. Tests of the theory with samples of girls and women are therefore necessary (Curran and Renzetti 1994). The tests of neutralization and drift theory also don't investigate whether it's generalizable across other sociodemographic categories, including race and social class.

Although many scholars criticize neutralization and drift theory, others defend it. Supporting Sykes and Matza's view, some studies find that most adolescents do disapprove of violence and other offending. An analysis of data from the National Youth Survey found that over 90 percent of respondents said that it's "wrong" or "very wrong" for someone of their age to hit or threaten to hit someone without any reason." Larger proportions supported the use of violence in certain situations, such as when someone insults you. Robert Agnew, the author of this study, claimed that these figures support Sykes and Matza's view on the importance of neutralization. Because his data were longitudinal, Agnew was also able to determine whether neutralization precedes violent offending, as Sykes and Matza assumed. Supporting their assumption, his analysis found that "neutralization may be a relatively important cause of subsequent violence" (Agnew 1994:572). Noting that his was the first longitudinal study of neutralization involving a national sample, Agnew (1994:573) concluded that his study "does much to provide support for the arguments of Sykes and Matza."

Most reviews say the evidence for neutralization and drift theory is a bit scanty, with one concluding that the theory "has received rather weak empirical support" (Curran and Renzetti 1994:226). However, Agnew's longitudinal study indicates that the dismissal of neutralization and drift theory may be premature. Further research on the theory is clearly needed.

Travis Hirschi: Social Control Theory

Have you ever refused to join your friends or acquaintances in illegal behavior because you were worried about what your parents might think, or because you were worried about how it might affect your school record? Do you know people whose religious beliefs have led them to avoid drinking, using illegal drugs, or having sex? As these examples suggest, our bonds to conventional social institutions such as family, schools, and religion may keep us from committing deviant behavior. This is the central view of Travis Hirschi's *social control theory*, which is perhaps the most popular and influential of all criminological theories today and certainly the most popular control theory. First presented in his 1969 book, *Causes of Delinquency* (Hirschi 1969), Hirschi's theory has spawned many investigations in the last three decades. It has many enthusiastic supporters and also some critics. Let's look at this theory in some detail.

Hirschi began his book by setting forth his view of a selfish human nature. Given this view, he said, the important thing to explain is why people don't commit crime. Their bond to society and its moral order is what keeps them from breaking the law. When that bond is weakened, crime results. Basing this view on Durkheim's own thinking, Hirschi quoted Durkheim's ideas about why this happens: "The more weakened the groups to which [the individual] belongs, the less he depends on them, the more he consequently depends only on himself and recognizes no other rules of conduct than what are founded on his private interests" (Durkheim 1952 [1897]:209).

Durkheim's use of male pronouns notwithstanding, the argument here is that all people feel freer to deviate when their ties to conventional social institutions weaken. In many ways Hirschi's control theory presents a social process or micro counterpart to the structural or macro view of social disorganization theory. If the latter theory says crime flourishes in *neighborhoods* with weakened social institutions, control theory argues it's more common among *individuals* with weakened bonds to the same institutions. Hirschi thought this would be true across all social classes.

◀ *Travis Hirschi's social control theory assumes that strong attachment between parents and children helps prevent delinquency.*

Social Bonding and Crime in Japan

According to Hirschi's social control theory, the stronger an individual's bonds to conventional social institutions such as the family and schools, the less likely the individual will be to break the law. Does Hirschi's view help us understand why whole nations differ in crime rates? Japan's experience provides some fascinating evidence for a positive answer to this question.

Japan, as you know, is an industrial nation that advanced rapidly since its defeat in World War II. In other ways it also resembles the United States. Its popular culture—films, TV shows, and so on—depicts a great deal of violence, and its history is filled with war, murders of peasants, political assassinations, and other violence. Despite these similarities, the rates in the United States of homicide, assault, rape, and robbery are many times higher than those in Japan. In explaining Japan's lower rates, several scholars emphasize the Japanese culture, in particular the value it places on "group-belonging."

From birth the Japanese are taught that the group is more important than the individual. The family, the school, and the workplace are the subjects of great respect and authority in Japanese culture. In school, individual achievement is not as important as a whole classroom's achievement. At home, Japanese families are known for their high levels of love and harmony. Children sleep with their parents from birth until they're about five years old. When they misbehave, parents punish them by locking them out of the house, whereas U.S. children are often punished by being "grounded," or kept within the house. As scholar David H. Bayley has said, "The effect is that American children are taught that it is punishment to be locked up with one's family; Japanese children are

taught that punishment is being excluded from one's family" (p. 10).

The emphasis on group-belonging in Japan promotes two other emphases: harmonious relationships and respect for authority. All three emphases contribute to especially strong social bonding in Japan and hence to its lower crime rates. Children there grow up strongly attached to their parents and teachers and very committed to obeying social norms. In contrast, U.S. children grow up much more independently, as U.S. culture emphasizes individualism rather than group-belonging. The ties U.S. children feel to parents, schools, and other conventional social institutions are weaker than those of their Japanese counterparts. With weaker bonds, U.S. adolescents are thus freer, as Hirschi's control theory predicts, to violate social norms, freer to commit crime and delinquency.

Japan's experience underscores the value of the social bond for reducing crime. It suggests that significant crime reduction could be achieved in the United States if children were more respectful of their parents and teachers, and if family relationships were more harmonious. Are these qualities beyond the scope of social policy? For better or worse, the U.S. culture is not likely to become more similar to the Japanese culture. Japan's example thus suggests that it's quite possible to have an industrial society with much lower crime rates, but it also implies the difficulty of implementing the Japanese model in the United States. In this regard, early family intervention programs for those families at greatest risk for conflict may be an effective strategy for reducing crime.

Sources: Bayley 1996; Fishman and Dinitz 1989; Thornton and Endo 1992; Westermann and Burfeind 1991.

Hirschi discussed the following four elements of the ties that individuals have to society.

1. *Attachment.* This refers to the degree to which we care about the opinions of others, including parents and teachers. We may care about their opinions because we love them or respect them or feel some other bond to them. The more sensitive we are to their views, the less likely we are to violate norms, both because we have internalized their norms and because we don't want to disappoint or hurt them. The opposite, of course, is also

true: The less sensitive we are to their views, the more likely we are to break the law.

2. *Commitment*. This refers to the amount of importance an individual places on conventional pursuits, such as getting a good education. The more committed you are in this sense, the more you have to lose if you break the law. People with low commitment to conventional pursuits thus are more likely to deviate.

3. *Involvement*. This is the amount of time an individual spends on some conventional pursuit. The argument here is that the more time spent, the less the opportunity to deviate: Some people may be too busy doing legitimate activities to have the time to break the law. Hirschi notes that this argument underlies the use of recreation programs in high-crime neighborhoods to prevent delinquency: The more time youths spend in these programs, the less time they have to be delinquent.

4. *Belief*. This refers to acceptance of the norms of conventional society. In contrast to neutralization theory, control theory believes that many people do not accept these norms. Those who do believe in these norms are less likely to deviate than those who reject them. Hirschi notes that all four elements are related, so that someone with a strong tie in one element tends to have strong bonds in the others. People who are strongly attached to conventional others, for example, also tend to believe in the norms of conventional society.

Hirschi tested his hypotheses with a sample of about 4,000 California male junior and senior high school students from the San Francisco Bay area. He asked them many questions about their delinquency and the four social bond elements outlined above, including their feelings about their parents and teachers; the amount of time they spent on various school activities; and what they thought about conventional pursuits such as getting a good education. To measure attachment to parents, for example, Hirschi asked several questions, including "Do you share your thoughts and feelings with your mother (father)?" and "Would you like to be the kind of person your father (mother) is?"

Supporting his theory, Hirschi found high degrees of attachment, commitment, and belief all correlated with low delinquency, regardless of social class. For example, youths who felt very close to their parents were less likely to be delinquent than youths who felt more distant. Although Hirschi also thought that attachment to friends would lower delinquency regardless of whether the friends themselves were delinquent, he didn't find this relationship in his data, and much later research confirms the influence of delinquent peers on one's own delinquency. In another unexpected result, youths busy with conventional pursuits (*involvement*) such as working, dating, and playing sports were *more* likely to be delinquent. A recent study suggests that the *type* of conventional pursuit matters here: Unsupervised social activities with friends were associated with higher delinquency in this study, while supervised activities with friends, activities with one's family, and solitary activities (e.g., reading) were related to lower delinquency (Agnew and Petersen 1989).

Since its inception, Hirschi's control theory has attracted much attention and won wide praise (Kornhauser 1978). Recent reviews note its dominance in the study of crime and delinquency (Akers 1997). At least seventy-one tests of the theory were published in the two decades following its own publication in 1969 (Kempf 1993).

Much of the theory's appeal stems from its straightforward presentation and apparent logic and "testability." Compared, for example, with Sutherland's emphasis on the number of definitions favorable and unfavorable to violating the law, Hirschi's four elements of the social bond are simpler to measure, making it easier to test his theory. In addition, Hirschi's emphasis on individuals freed to commit crime by weakened families and other social institutions complements growing official and public concern since the 1960s on the weakened social fabric, especially the "breakdown" of the family. Hirschi's theory thus provides a scientific explanation of crime that fits well with recent social and political currents.

The large number of empirical tests, most of them using self-report data, supporting control theory have only reinforced its popularity, as they generally find several elements of the social bond Hirschi identified related to delinquency. Specifically, they find delinquency lower among children who feel close to their parents; who like their teachers, value their schooling, and take part in school activities; and who believe in the conventional rules of society (Krohn and Massey 1980; Wiatrowski, Griswold, and Roberts 1981).

Much of the research inspired by Hirschi's theory focuses on the family, school, and religious context of delinquency. Let's look at these contexts briefly and spend most of our time on the family in view of its importance in current debates.

THE FAMILY

The role played by the family in delinquency and crime remains a controversial scholarly and public policy topic. Many social scientists and mass media commentators blame crime and delinquency on various family problems. What does the research say?

Scholars distinguish between family *structure* and family *functioning* (Rosen 1985). Family structure refers to the way the family is set up or organized, while family functioning refers to the nature of interaction and relationships within the family. Regarding family structure, the most studied and debated component is the "broken home," or a household headed by a single parent, usually the mother. Most such households result from a divorce or birth out of wedlock, but some result from the death of a parent or abandonment by a parent. Many people fear that broken homes contribute to delinquency, since in these homes there is only one parent to supervise the children and father role models are lacking for sons.

Early research used official records of delinquency and found that children from broken homes were more likely to have delinquent records (Wilkinson 1974). As concern increased four decades ago over bias in official criminal statistics (see Chapter 3), many scholars wondered whether these findings reflected official bias against children in broken homes and in favor of children from intact homes. For example, police officers and juvenile caseworkers may send delinquents from intact homes back to their parents but send delinquents from one-parent homes into the juvenile justice system (Johnson 1986).

The advent of self-report data during that same time permitted investigations of this possibility. For better or worse, however, these studies disagree on the importance of family disruption for delinquency. On the one hand, many studies generally find little or no relationship between the broken homes and delinquency. Relationships that *are* found are generally limited to status offenses (minor offenses such as truancy and running away from home) or to drinking and drug use (Johnson 1986; Rankin and Wells 1994). Yet other studies continue to find the presumed link between family disruption and juvenile offending (Thornberry et al. 1999). Firm conclusions in this area of research thus remain premature.

That said, most scholars believe that family functioning is more important than family structure for delinquency. Many studies over the years find positive family relationships, particularly strong parent-child attachment, linked to lower delinquency (Cernkovich and Giordano 1987; Loeber and Stouthamer-Loeber 1986). In two-parent households, strong attachment to both parents appears to reduce delinquency more than strong attachment to only one parent (Rankin and Kern 1994). To turn all this around, delinquency is more often found among children whose relationship with their parents is cold and distant. More generally, delinquency is more common in homes that are not happy and harmonious, including those where the parents might get along well with their children but not with each other.

Hirschi thought that poor attachment to parents contributes directly to delinquency by prompting children to reject their parents' values and influence. Other scholars think this effect is indirect and mediated by peer relationships. The argument here is that poor relationships with parents make children more vulnerable to the delinquent influences of their peers. If good parental relationships help protect children from "the outside world," including bad peer influences, then bad parental relationships permit these outside influences to have some effect (Warr 1993). Hirschi also thought that effective parental supervision of children results in less delinquency. Evidence from other studies again supports his view, as delinquency is generally higher in families lacking effective supervision (Wells and Rankin 1988).

Hirschi's 1969 book did not discuss parental discipline of children in great detail, but his theory certainly implies that effective discipline of children should reduce delinquency. The key here is to discover which kind of discipline is most effective. Child experts identify at least four kinds of discipline (Loeber and Stouthamer-Loeber 1986; Wells and Rankin 1988).

1. *Punitive* discipline involves harsh rules and frequent spanking, often for trivial offenses.
2. *Lax or permissive* discipline is the opposite of punitive; it involves few rules and allows children to do almost whatever they want.
3. *Erratic* discipline is inconsistent: It might be punitive sometimes and other times permissive.
4. *"Firm but fair"* discipline means an assertive but not overbearing parenting style. Parents set clear rules for their children's behavior but at the same time give them considerable autonomy. Reasoning and positive feedback replace spanking, which is rare or nonexistent. If you've ever seen the popular 1980s' TV comedy, "The Cosby Show," you saw parents practicing a firm but fair style of discipline.

Research on discipline and delinquency finds that firm but fair discipline is most effective in preventing delinquency, perhaps because it leads to greater internalization of parental values (Rankin and Wells 1990). This explanation complements social control theory nicely. In fact, the other three kinds of discipline all appear to promote delinquency. Parents can be too permissive, but they can also be too harsh. Although we've all heard the familiar adage, "spare the rod and spoil the child," research suggests that routine spanking and, more generally, harsh discipline tend to increase delinquency (McCord 1991b; Straus 1994). Instead of following the rules because they accept their parents' beliefs and values, children obey only to avoid a spanking or other harsh discipline, and might disobey another time if they think they can get away with it. Following Hirschi, it's also possible that harsh discipline can lower children's affection for their parents, again increasing their potential for delinquency. Finally, frequent spanking may teach children that violence is an acceptable solution to interpersonal conflict, especially among people who are close to each other. For all these reasons, many scholars think that corporal punishment contributes to adolescent and later violent aggression, and that this effect is especially great for harsh and even abusive punishment (Widom 2000).

SCHOOLS

A large literature on schooling and delinquency also exists. Supporting Hirschi's views, adolescents with poor grades and negative attitudes about their teachers, their schools, and the importance of education are more likely to be delinquent than youths with good grades and positive attitudes (Jenkins 1997). Adolescents who are less involved in school extracurricular activities are also more likely to be delinquent. Control theory's explanation of these relationships is different from strain theory's. As you might recall from the previous chapter, Albert Cohen's status frustration theory argued that school failure leads to frustration and hence to delinquency to resolve that frustration. Control theory instead argues that failure in and negative attitudes about school prompt youths to reject the conformist values of school and the legitimacy of school authorities to tell them how to behave.

RELIGION

Religion is another social institution that has been considered an important force for social stability. Durkheim thought that religious rituals strengthen the internalization of social norms and increase social bonds by allowing people to interact (Durkheim 1947 [1915]). Against this theoretical backdrop, some scholars think that religious belief and practice (*religiosity*) might also help to prevent delinquency and crime.

Early studies of the religiosity-delinquency relationship were inconclusive. Using religious attendance as a measure of religiosity, some studies found high religiosity linked to low delinquency, although the relationship was usually small. But other studies found no relationship. The issue lay dormant for several years until a 1969 study by Hirschi and Rodney Stark found no relationship in a sample of California students (Hirschi and Stark 1969). The article's negative findings on religion and delinquency spurred further research.

One of the problems in investigating the presumed religiosity-delinquency relationship lies in the difficulty of measuring religiosity. Should we ask adolescents how often they go to religious services? How often they pray or read the Bible? How important God is to them, or whether they believe in the Bible as the word of God? As these possibilities suggest, religiosity has several dimensions, and scholars of religion and society disagree on the best way to define and measure it. Most of the religiosity-delinquency studies have continued to focus on the effects of religious attendance.

The recent research on religiosity and delinquency generally finds that youths who are less religious are more likely to be delinquent. However, these results appear to depend on the type of delinquency studied. The religiosity-delinquency relationship is most often found for drinking, drug use, and sexual behavior, and it is not usually found for other kinds of delinquency, although a recent study of high school students did find that religiosity lowered their rate of criminal behavior

◀ *Criminologists continue to debate whether religious faith and practice inhibit crime and delinquency.*

(Brenda 1997). The religiosity-delinquency relationship is also found more often among adolescents in the South than in other regions of the United States (Stark and Bainbridge 1996). Some evidence even suggests the religiosity-delinquency relationship is spurious once "arousal" factors are taken into account (Cochran, Wood, and Arneklev 1994). In this view, adolescents who are restless and crave excitement tend to be bored with religion, and hence less religious, and also more likely to commit delinquency.

T. David Evans and colleagues (1995) note that almost all of the religiosity-crime research has focused on juveniles, whose religiosity may reflect parental and peer influences. For example, their religious attendance may result more from their parents' desires than from their own religious belief. Evans and his associates thus argue that studies of adults provide better tests of the presumed religiosity-crime relationship. In a study of white adults from a midwestern city, they found that involvement in religious activities (religious services, reading religious material, and listening to religious broadcasts) reduced adult criminality.

Given all these findings, it's fair to say the jury is still out on the religiosity-crime relationship. Much of the research only partially supports control theory's expectations, and the relationship might actually be spurious when other relevant factors are considered. However, a 1995 study by Evans et al. suggests that more consistent results might be found if adults were studied more often.

Gender, Race, Class, and Age

Although Hirschi assumed his theory applied to all adolescents regardless of their gender, race, social class, and age, his 1969 book didn't adequately address this assumption. For example, the 4,000 respondents studied were all boys. Noting this limitation, Hirschi said in a footnote that "the girls disappear" (Hirschi 1969:36). Given their disappearance, it wasn't clear whether control theory applies to girls as well as to boys. Of the over seventy tests of control theory that had appeared by the early 1990s, less than half studied girls, and even fewer included any blacks or other people of color (Kempf 1993). The majority of these studies, then, concerned only white males. Studies of other kinds of respondents are therefore important to determine the generalizability of control theory.

GENDER   Despite the low number of studies of girls, these studies are valuable. They address two major questions: Does control theory help explain why girls have lower delinquency rates than boys, and does it explain variation in girls' delinquency as much as it explains variation in boys' delinquency (Simpson and Elis 1995)?

The answer to the first question appears to be yes. Several studies find girls less delinquent than boys in part because they are more attached to family and school and are more likely to hold conventional beliefs. These gender differences stem from gender differences in socialization. As I noted in Chapter 3, girls are also more closely supervised by their parents. Because of their greater bond to conventional social institutions and greater parental supervision, girls are less likely than boys to be delinquent (Heimer and Coster 1999).

The answer to the second question is less clear. Since girls are probably more attached to their families and school, it stands to reason that problems at home or in school should be especially troubling for girls and thus have a greater effect on their delinquency than on boys' delinquency. Some studies find this to be the case, but other studies report that problems at home and/or in school affect boys' delinquency more than girls' (Canter 1982). Still other research finds that some dimensions of parental attachment and other social bonds matter more for girls, while others matter more for boys (Cernkovich and Giordano 1987). A study of 1,500 Seattle high school students found a relationship, for boys but not for girls, between delinquency and both positive attitudes about school and school achievement. But it also found positive attitudes about teachers and involvement in school activities both more related to girls' delinquency than to boys' (Rosenbaum and Lasley 1990). Gender differences in the effect of family conflict on delinquency may also depend on the type of delinquency. One study found the effect of family conflict on violent and property offenses to be greater for males than females, but the effect of family conflict on status offenses to be greater for females than males (Norland et al. 1979).

These complex findings indicate the need for more research on social bonds and female criminality, because control theory seems to have great potential for understanding gender differences in delinquency and crime. As one scholar puts it, "Control theory offers the best possibility for explaining both female delinquency and even more important, why it is less frequent than male delinquency" (Box 1981:144).

RACE AND CLASS   Relatively few studies investigate whether control theory explains race and class differences in delinquency, or whether the relationship between the social bond and delinquency differs by race and/or social class. Let's begin with the issue of broken homes. Early studies reported mixed findings on whether broken homes had a greater effect on black or white delinquency. Some found a greater effect among blacks, some found a greater effect among whites, and some found no racial difference (Austin 1978). Although many observers now attribute the high African-American crime rate to the predominance of broken homes among blacks (see Chapter 3), these mixed results, and especially the more recent evidence of no broken home-delinquency relationship, call this interpretation into question. That said, one study did find broken homes slightly more related to delinquency by African-Americans than by whites, but found this effect much smaller than that of structural and differential association factors (Matsueda and Heimer 1987).

Complicating things further, some studies even find that the presence of fathers *increases* delinquency among poor black adolescents, perhaps because the employment problems facing many of their fathers are so stressful (Farnworth 1984; Harris and Shaw 2000). Other studies find a relationship between criminality and family problems (including broken homes) among whites, but not among blacks, with one study finding female-headed households linked to lower crime by blacks but increased crime by whites (LaFree, Drass, and O'Day 1992). These complex findings underscore the need to avoid hasty conclusions on African-American family structure and crime and reinforce many scholars' view that family *interaction* and *relationships* matter much more than family *structure*.

Turning to family interaction and race, the few studies we have indicate that family relationships affect delinquency for people of various races. One study of African-American adolescents found family and school problems both affecting delinquency. In an interesting finding, school problems were more related than family problems to girls' delinquency, but family problems were more related than school problems to boys' delinquency (Farnworth 1984). Two studies of delinquency by Mexican-American and Puerto Rican male adolescents found strong effects of family bonds (Buriel, Calzada, and Vasquez 1982; Sommers, Fagan, and Baskin 1994). Some evidence indicates that Asian-Americans of various nationalities traditionally have particularly strong family bonds, and that these bonds normally insulate their children from delinquency. However, their experience as immigrants in the United States has for several reasons weakened these ties. Along with the economic deprivation and other structural problems faced by Asian-Americans, these weakened family bonds help account for delinquency in their families (Pao-Min 1981).

Is the effect of social bonds on delinquency greater for one race than another? Unfortunately, we have too little research to answer this question. Two studies of Toledo, Ohio youths found the family relationship-delinquency influence greater for whites than for blacks, but they also found no racial difference in the effect of school bonding on delinquency (Cernkovich and Giordano 1987; 1992). Other studies report inconsistent results on whether family factors affect white delinquency more than black delinquency (Simpson and Elis 1995). More research on the relative importance of social bonds for delinquency by different races is certainly needed.

We have virtually no research on whether social bond effects on delinquency vary for the different social classes. However, some research on social class and parental discipline has implications for delinquency. Some, but not all, studies find lower-income parents more likely than middle-income parents to use harsh physical punishment (Wauchope and Straus 1990). Because, as discussed earlier, such discipline appears to increase delinquency, this may be one reason, though not a strong one, for the greater involvement of poor adolescents in serious delinquency (Straus 1991). There is also some evidence that poor students feel less attached to schools and teachers than middle-class students do. If so, this may be another reason for social class differences in serious delinquency.

AGE Control theory helps explain why people usually reduce their criminality as they age and move out of adolescence. Their entrance into young adulthood means that they often marry, join the work force, and otherwise become more involved in conventional society. Since control theory predicts that this involvement should reduce their criminality, the lower rate of offending for young adults nicely supports the theory (Laub and Sampson 1993). An interesting question is whether variation in adult criminality is still explained by changes in elements of the social bond. Supporting this possibility, some research finds that crime is lower among young white men who are married and employed than among those who are single and jobless (Laub and Sampson 1993).

A related question is whether the social bond matters more at some points in adolescence than at others. Some research suggests this is the case. Family factors appear to be more important for delinquency beginning in early or middle adolescence than in later adolescence, while school factors are more important for delinquency beginning in middle adolescence than at other times (Simons et al. 1994). It's also possible that mothers and fathers have different effects on offending at different times in a child's life. A longitudinal study of 232 males born between 1926 and 1933 found that mothers' child rearing was a stronger predictor than fathers' child rearing of adolescent offending, while fathers' child rearing was a stronger predictor than mothers' of adult offending (McCord 1991a).

CRITIQUE OF HIRSCHI'S CONTROL THEORY

Despite the popularity of Hirschi's control theory, several problems limit its applicability. First, the correlations between social bonding and delinquency found by Hirschi and other scholars tend to be rather low, with the strongest results found for the quality of family interaction. The overall weakness of the reported relationships suggests that although attachment and other elements of the social bond may matter, they may not matter a great deal (Curran and Renzetti 1994). Some research also finds that social bond variables are even less related to serious delinquency than they are to minor delinquency. These results lead some scholars to conclude that social control theory explains minor offending more than serious offending (Agnew 1985).

Another problem concerns the familiar chicken-and-egg question of causal order. Take the common finding that youths with weak attachment to their parents are more delinquent than those with strong attachment. Does this finding mean that parental attachment influences delinquency or that delinquency influences parental attachment? It's possible, for example, that after you engage in delinquency for any number of reasons, your parents find out and reprimand you, you argue back, and your relationship with them suffers. The parental attachment-delinquency relationship might even be spurious because of the effects of some third factor. Just as age accounts for why you'll find a statistical relationship between listening to rock music and having acne (see Chapter 1), perhaps some third factor, such as religiosity, leads adolescents to have both high parental attachment and low delinquency. In that case, no causal relationship at all exists between attachment and delinquency.

Most recent tests of control theory use various *multivariate* statistical analysis to help rule out spuriousness. Because they continue to find the relationships predicted by control theory, spuriousness is probably not a serious issue, unless there are unknown factors whose effects need to be controlled. But because most of these studies analyze cross-sectional data (taken at one point in time), they can't easily rule out the possibility that the causal order at work is the opposite of that assumed by control theory. As Rankin and Kern (1994) point out, social bond variables such as parental attachment are usually measured at the time of the interview (e.g., "I feel close to my mother/father"), while delinquency is measured as the number of acts occurring in the past year or more. Because this means researchers "are using present measures of attachment to explain past delinquent behaviors"

(Rankin and Kern 1994:512), it's difficult to infer from a relationship between these measures that attachment affects delinquency. It might be more likely that delinquency affects attachment.

Several studies have investigated the causal order of the social bond-delinquency relationship with longitudinal data (Liska and Reed 1985; Matsueda 1989). Significantly, they often find delinquency worsening adolescents' relationships with their parents, their involvement in school, and their belief in conventional rules. More generally, they find delinquency sometimes affects social bond elements at least as much, and sometimes more than, the social bond affects delinquency. The extent to which this is true might depend on which social bond element is studied. One longitudinal study found that delinquency reduced school attachment, but that parental attachment reduced delinquency (Liska and Reed 1985). While the findings are complex, it does appear that, at a minimum, a reciprocal relationship often exists between the social bond and delinquency. As a result, these longitudinal studies question Hirschi's interpretation of his findings and suggest that "cross-sectional studies have greatly exaggerated the importance of Hirschi's control theory" (Agnew 1985:58).

A few other criticisms of the theory can be summarized more briefly. Several scholars note that Hirschi's concepts of commitment and involvement cannot easily be distinguished from each other: It's difficult to imagine someone spending a lot of time on a conventional pursuit who's not also committed to it (Krohn 2000). As one example, is time spent on homework best seen as a measure of involvement in school or commitment to the importance of education? Other scholars point out that attachment has been measured in so many ways over the years that the concept has become a bit fuzzy (Curran and Renzetti 1994). We also still know fairly little about the relationships among the various social bond elements. Some research, for example, suggests that problems at home produce delinquency, delinquency then impairs school performance, and poorer school performance then reduces parental attachment (Liska and Reed 1985). More studies of this sort are needed to understand the exact ways in which weakened social bonds may generate criminality.

In sum, Hirschi's control theory has been very influential for several reasons, and appears to account for gender, race, and class differences in delinquency and crime. It also appears to explain variation in criminality within each of these categories. At the same time, several problems exist, including questions about the direction of the social bond-criminality relationship that is so often found. A recent review notes that the theory's weaknesses "are serious, but not fatal. The theory, in fact, may be a very good one, but with limited utility" (Curran and Renzetti 1994:212).

Michael Gottfredson and Travis Hirschi: Self-Control Theory

In 1990 Hirschi coauthored a book with Michael Gottfredson that revised social control theory to present a "general theory of crime," as the book was entitled (Gottfredson and Hirschi 1990). They argued that *all* crime stems from one problem: the lack of self-control. People with low self-control act impulsively and spontaneously, value risk and adventure, and care about themselves more than others. They're thus more likely than people with high self-control to commit crime, since all types of crime, say the authors, are spontaneous and exciting, often hurt others, and require little skill. This is as true for white-collar crime as for petty theft and assault. Self-control, or more precisely, low self-control, thus "explains all crime, at all times" (p. 117) and accounts for gender, age, regional, and other patterning of criminal behavior. Men, for example, in this view commit more crime because they have less self-control than women do.

Low self-control comes from ineffective child rearing. Children whose parents are too permissive fail to develop adequate self-control. Low self-control often continues into adulthood and thus not only explains juvenile delinquency but also adult criminality. In stressing low self-control, Gottfredson and Hirschi explicitly minimize or rule out the effects of other problems such as economic deprivation and peer influences. They thus declare that the only hope to reduce crime lies in improving child rearing. Policies focusing on structural causes of crime and on criminal opportunities will, they say, have little effect.

Self-control theory has generated much research, most of which finds that individuals with low self-control are indeed more likely to commit various kinds of offenses and to have other kinds of problems as well (Evans et al. 1997; Grasmick et al. 1993). For example, a recent study of Canadian secondary school students also used self-control theory to help explain gender differences in delinquency. It found that male students had less self-control then female students and that this difference helped to explain why the males had committed more delinquency (LaGrange and Silverman 1999). Some research also finds that low self-control helps make people more vulnerable to being victimized by crime (Schreck 1999).

Although this body of research has made self-control theory popular, some scholars criticize it (Krohn 2000). A major problem is that it engages in circular reasoning: Since crime and other behaviors such as smoking and drinking are considered evidence of low self-control, crime is being used to explain itself (Akers 1991). Although some tests of the theory suffer from this problem, recent studies using more valid measures of low self-control, including thinking about short-term rather than long-term consequences and losing one's temper, support the theory.

In another problem, several studies use cross-sectional data (taken at one point in time). These studies can't adequately address the causal order issue: The associations found between low self-control and crime could simply mean that crime generates low self-control. Given this possibility, a recent longitudinal study of New Zealand residents followed from birth through age 21 was significant. Children who exhibited low self-control in childhood were more likely to commit delinquency when they reached adolescence (Wright et al. 1999).

A final criticism of self-control theory focuses on Gottfredson and Hirschi's assumption that all crime, including white-collar crime, is spontaneous and unskilled. Kenneth Polk (1991) argues that this assumption is far too simplistic and that many crimes don't fit this description. In fact, says Polk, so many crimes don't fit it that self-control theory is not of much use. In this regard, Gottfredson and Hirschi's description and thus their explanation of white-collar crime seem especially faulty. In their book and other work, they assumed that most white-collar crime involves fraud, forgery, and embezzlement, all of which they say fit their general description of crime and thus their self-control theory. Critics charge that this assumption ignores the vast amount of corporate and other business crime that involves much planning, skill, and specialized knowledge (Steffensmeier 1989).

In sum, although self-control theory may help explain some crimes, it doesn't seem to offer the general theory of crime that its authors intended. One scholar even calls it "a general theory of some instances of some forms of crime" (Gibbons 1994:194). While this might be a harsh assessment, more research on the theory is clearly needed.

Charles R. Tittle: Control Balance Theory

The most recent addition to the plethora of control theories is Charles R. Tittle's (1995) control balance theory, which a recent review applauds as "one of the most important theoretical contributions to the sociology of deviance" (Braithwaite 1997:77). Tittle observes that some people by virtue of their roles, statuses, and personal attributes can exercise considerable control over other people. At the same time, another set of people by virtue of their roles, statuses, and personal attributes are more easily controlled by others. When people are either very controlling or very controlled, Tittle says, they are more likely to engage in deviance than when their "control ratio"—the degree to which they exercise control versus the degree to which they experience control—is in balance. Thus people with a "control surplus," such as corporate executives, tend to commit crime, albeit of the white-collar variety, and those with a "control deficit," such as the urban poor, also tend to commit crime (Braithwaite 1997).

Why does the control ratio make a difference? Tittle assumes that people want to be as autonomous as possible. If they have a control deficit, they break the law to achieve more control over their lives, if only by victimizing someone else, and to lessen the humiliation and inferiority they normally experience because of their control deficit. If they have a control surplus, they break the law because they greedily want even more control than they already exercise and because they realize the risk they incur by lawbreaking is low precisely because of the control they exert.

One macro implication of Tittle's theory is that societies with large control imbalance will have more crime than societies with greater control balance. Thus a society with greater economic inequality should experience more crime than a society with less inequality (Braithwaite 1997). As we'll see in Chapter 9, research on international variation in homicide supports this view.

The few tests to date of control balance theory have so far supported it. In one study, 146 college students were asked to read several scenarios in which individuals engaged in various acts of deviance and then to indicate the likelihood that they would do what these individuals did. The students were also asked several questions to measure the amount of control they exercised and the amount of control they experienced. Supporting Tittle's theory, students with control surpluses and control deficits were both more likely than those with a control balance to indicate they would engage in the deviance recounted in the scenarios. However, the study also found that the types of deviant acts—e.g., predatory and defiant—associated with control surpluses and deficits differed from what Tittle's theory would have predicted. While the authors concluded that their study provided only mixed support for the theory, they also called for further tests of its assumptions (Piquero and Hickman 1999).

INTEGRATING SOCIAL PROCESS AND STRUCTURAL EXPLANATIONS

As you've been reading in this and the last two chapters, many explanations of crime and delinquency have been offered over the years. Together they point to the importance of biological, psychological, structural, and social process factors. We've seen that each explanation has been sharply debated. Scholars assert that this or that theory can explain only a limited number of crimes or ignores the significance of other factors. As I've noted, neither a social process nor a structural approach can adequately explain crime by itself. Social process theories cannot easily account for structural variation in criminality, and structural theories cannot easily account for individual variation in crime among people living in similar structural conditions.

I've also suggested that a more comprehensive understanding of crime might be achieved by integrating social process and structural factors. In the last two decades, several scholars have formulated integrated theories of crime to achieve such an understanding. (See Figure 7.1.) Let's look briefly at some of this work (Bernard and Snipes 1996).

Delbert S. Elliott and his colleagues formulated one of the most popular integrated theories (Elliott, Ageton, and Canter 1979; Elliott, Huizinga, and Ageton 1985). They integrated strain, social learning, and social control theories into what they considered a more comprehensive explanation of delinquency than any of the three theories offers by itself. In their view, childhood socialization affects whether bonds to society become weak or strong. Weak bonds are more likely for children living in socially disorganized areas, for example, poverty. During adolescence, youths achieve success or failure in schooling and other conventional activities, with failure causing further strain. Peer influences become very important during this time. Adolescents with weak bonds to their parents and schools and experiencing strain from failure in conventional activities are particularly vulnerable to the criminogenic influence of delinquent peers.

To this basic model, Terence P. Thornberry's *interactional theory* (Thornberry 1987; Thornberry et al. 1994) adds that delinquency and association with delinquent peers can further weaken parental and school bonds in a type of vicious cycle that increases delinquency even further. Other models add social psychological factors such as self-esteem (Shoemaker 1996). The argument here is that poor relationships with parents or poor performance in school can lower self-esteem, and that low self-esteem can lead to more delinquency.

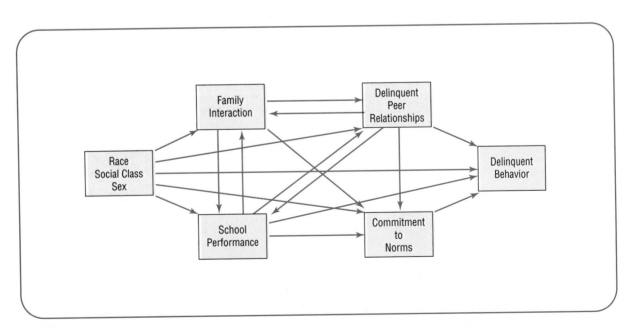

▲ FIGURE 7.1   A SAMPLE OF AN INTEGRATED MODEL OF DELINQUENCY

◀ *Integrated theories say that a poor relationship with parents is one of several factors that help to explain delinquency.*

Other integrated theories focus more on the onset and termination of delinquency and crime at different ages over the life course (Laub and Sampson 1993; Loeber and LeBlanc 1990). This research attempts to answer a question introduced in Chapter 3: Why are delinquency and crime highest in middle adolescence and why do they decline thereafter? In explaining the onset of delinquency, this research identifies many of the factors we've already reviewed: poverty, harsh or erratic parental discipline, poor family relationships, poor school performance, delinquent peers, and unemployment. In a departure from previous work, it also discusses the "turning points" that lead delinquency and crime to decline in late adolescence and early adulthood, which include increased ties to conventional institutions, especially the family and the world of work. In short, people tend to marry by young adulthood and also to work at a steady job. As social control theory would predict, involvement in the conventional institutions of family and work reduces the potential for criminality by affecting individuals' beliefs and increasing their stake in conformity.

Surprising as it might seem, some scholars dispute the value of integrated theories. Control theory proponent Travis Hirschi (1979), for example, believes that theoretical integration does more harm than good. In his view, some theories are so different that to integrate them yields a "theoretical mush" (Akers 1989:24) that does no one any good. Even interactional theory proponent Thornberry notes that integration may reduce the "clarity and strength" of the theories that are integrated (Thornberry 1989:56). In contrast, learning theorist Ronald L. Akers sees theoretical integration useful if the theories to be integrated complement each other. This is particularly true, he says, for structural theories and social learning theory, since "social learning is the basic process by which the structural variables specified in the macro-level theories have an effect on deviant behavior" (Akers 1989:28). He also notes the compatibility of social learning and social control theories.

As this summary makes clear, theoretical integration holds much promise but isn't without some risk. Future work will determine if theoretical integration in criminology leads to useless "mush" or instead to a more comprehensive explanation of crime and delinquency.

 ## SUMMARY AND CONCLUSION

Social process theories of crime emphasize learning, socialization, human interaction, and other social processes. They help us understand why some individuals are more likely than others to commit crime even if they live in similar circumstances. As such, they are an important complement to structural theories, which tell us much about the social and economic roots of crime but little about the mechanisms through which structural conditions generate crime.

But if structural theories err by forgetting about the individual, then it's also fair to say that social process theories err by forgetting about social structure and social inequality (Miller 1993). They might tell us why some individuals are more likely than others to commit crime, but they don't explicitly tell us why individuals living in disadvantaged economic, geographical, or other structural conditions are also more likely to commit crime than individuals living in more advantaged conditions. It may be, for example, that street crime is more common in poor communities because family relationships suffer from the stresses of poverty, but such an explanation traces the *ultimate* cause of crime to a structural condition instead of a social process mechanism. Debate between the two camps will certainly continue, as well it should: Both have much to offer, but both are also deficient in important respects.

Learning theories remind us that deviance is often the result of a social process, socialization, without which social order isn't possible. Most of us learn to be fairly conforming members of society, but some of us learn to be criminals. Different learning theories discuss different mechanisms by which such learning occurs. While questions still remain about the causal sequence involved and other important problems, the emphasis of learning theories on socialization and on peer influences is one of the most important themes in criminology today.

Control theories assume a pessimistic view of human nature. People are basically selfish and hedonistic and thus will deviate unless controlled by society. While different control theories focus on different kinds of constraints, all assume that without these constraints we'd have social chaos. Hirschi's social control theory has been the most influential formulation, with his emphasis on the parent-child bond receiving the most attention. Although the theory has been criticized, it has greatly expanded our knowledge of the micro origins of criminal behavior and seems to offer a convincing explanation of the gendered patterning of criminal behavior.

We now turn to our final chapter on theory, in which we look at "critical" perspectives that challenge fundamental ideas in criminology and that also spend much more time than any of the theories already discussed on the social reaction to crime. Social inequality and social structure lie at the heart of these perspectives, so they'll be of special interest to the themes of this book. At the same time, these perspectives have been criticized by traditional criminologists at least as much as theorists with critical perspectives have criticized traditional criminology, and we'll explore the controversy they generate.

KEY TERMS

attachment	reinforcement
containment	self-control
conventional social institution	social bond
delinquent peers	social control
differential association	social learning
drift	socialization
family interaction	*tabula rasa*
family structure	theoretical integration
learning	

STUDY QUESTIONS

1. What are the key assumptions of Sutherland's differential association theory? What are some criticisms of this theory?

2. What are the five techniques of neutralization discussed by Sykes and Matza? How have some scholars criticized their view of deviance and crime?

3. How does Hirschi's view of human nature relate to his social control theory of crime and deviance? In his theory, what are the four elements of the bonds that individuals have to their society?

4. If parents want to reduce their children's chances of growing up to be delinquents, what type of discipline should they practice? Why?

INTERNET EXERCISES

Many and probably most of the theories discussed in this chapter focus on delinquency. An excellent source of information on juvenile delinquency and juvenile justice is the U.S. Office of Juvenile Justice and Delinquency Prevention. Go to its Web site at **http://www.ojjdp.ncjrs.org/**. Clock on **JJ Facts and Figures** on the left side of the screen. Now click on **Statistical Briefing Book**. Next click on **Juveniles as Victims**.

We've seen that child abuse helps lead to delinquency later on, so now click on **Child Maltreatment**. Finally, click on **What is known about substantiated or indicated child maltreatment?** Now you'll see some basic information on child abuse in the United States. What percent of child victims are girls? Are the majority of child victims white or members of other racial and ethnic backgrounds? What percent are age two or younger? What percent of the abusers of children are their parents?

Why do you think child abuse is a risk factor for delinquency? What do you think our society could and should do to reduce child abuse?

Chapter 8

SOCIOLOGICAL THEORIES: CRITICAL PERSPECTIVES

Crime in the News

On March 16, 2000, Patrick M. Dorismond, 26, was waiting for a taxi after completing his shift as a security guard for a business district in New York City. Suddenly three undercover narcotics police came up to him and asked if he knew where they could buy marijuana. He reacted angrily at their assumption that he was selling drugs. A scuffle broke out, a backup officer rushed in, and then one of the officers fired a bullet into Dorismond's chest, killing him. In the aftermath, observers wondered whether the undercover police had assumed that Dorismond was selling drugs because he was black.

Source: Haberman 2000.

*D*espite their many differences, the sociological theories we've examined so far are similar in several ways. They are all *positivist* theories: They try to explain why crime occurs and locate its causes in the immediate social environment or in the whole society. These theories don't ask how particular behaviors and people come to be defined as crimes and criminals, and they disregard how social networks and institutions respond to crime. Although many of them suggest the need for social reforms to reduce crime, none urges the drastic overhaul of society's social and economic foundations. In these various ways, these sociological theories might all be called traditional theories.

Critical perspectives on crime take a different view. Because they highlight the ways in which people and institutions respond to crime and criminals, they are often called *social reaction* theories. Although critical perspectives differ from one another in many respects, they all consider the definition of crime *problematic*, meaning that the definition of a behavior as a crime and the defining of individuals as criminals are both something to explain. In explaining how these definitions originate, critical perspectives emphasize the concept of power and the inequality based on differences in power. Depending on the theory, power differences are based on social class, race or ethnicity, or gender. Whatever the source of the difference, the theories hold that behaviors by people or groups with power are less likely to be considered crimes than behaviors by those without power. The tragic killing of Patrick Dorismond illustrates the importance of understanding how certain people come to be defined as criminals.

The various critical perspectives reflect longstanding views, though they became more popular in the 1960s and 1970s, a turbulent era highlighted by the Southern civil rights movement, the Vietnam antiwar movement, and the beginning of the contemporary women's movement. Many sociology graduate students and younger sociology faculty took part in these movements, all of which questioned the status quo and emphasized the discriminatory and other damaging practices of social institutions. The civil rights movement and black power movements called attention to the racism pervading all aspects of society. The antiwar movement charged the U.S. government with committing genocide abroad and lying to its own citizens at home. The women's movement began to challenge the many inequities based on gender. "Question authority" and "don't trust anyone over 30" became rallying cries for a whole generation.

Against this backdrop, it was perhaps inevitable that younger sociologists would begin to question traditional views of society, including those of crime. As we saw in Chapter 3, they questioned the accuracy of official crime statistics and thus the validity of traditional theories. They wondered whether the chances of arrest and imprisonment had less to do with the crime itself and more to do with the suspect's race, social class, and gender. And they began to take up Edwin Sutherland's (1949) earlier focus on white-collar crime and to highlight the harm of corporate and other white-collar criminality.

This chapter discusses the major critical perspectives on crime. Labeling theory was the first critical perspective of the 1960s and was soon followed by various conflict theories. Feminist views on crime developed in the mid-1970s, in part because labeling and conflict theories neglected gender. Although all these theories stress the social reaction to crime, they also aim to explain the origins of crime. However, their explanations differ in important ways from those advanced by traditional theories. Let's turn first to labeling theory.

LABELING THEORY

Labeling theory addresses three major issues: (1) the definition of deviance and crime, (2) possible discrimination in the application of official labeling and sanctions, and (3) the effect of labeling on continued criminality.

The Relativist Definition of Crime and Deviance

Let's start with labeling theory's definition of deviance. Traditional theories of deviance and crime adopt an *absolutist* definition of deviance as something real that's inherent in behavior. In contrast, labeling theory adopts a *relativist* definition by assuming that nothing about a given behavior automatically makes it deviant. In this view, deviance is not a property of a behavior but rather the result of how others regard that behavior. Howard S. Becker (1963:9), one of the originators of labeling theory, presents the theory's definition of deviance in perhaps the most widely quoted passage in the deviance and criminality literature in the last forty years:

> Social groups create deviance by making the rules whose infraction constitutes deviance, and by applying those rules to particular people and labeling them as outsiders. From this point of view, deviance is not a quality of the act the person commits, but rather a consequence of the application by others of rules or sanctions to an "offender." The deviant is one to whom that label has been successfully applied; deviant behavior is behavior that people so label.

To illustrate this view, consider murder, widely regarded as the most serious crime because it involves the taking of a human life. Labeling theory would say there's nothing inherent in the killing involved in murder that makes it deviant. Rather, murder is considered deviant because society regards it as deviant due to the circumstances in which it occurs. Much killing occurs in wartime, but people who do the most killing in wars get medals, not arrest records. We deem it acceptable and even necessary to kill in wartime, so we don't call it murder, as long as the rules of war are followed. A police officer who kills an armed criminal does not murder. Capital punishment also involves killing, but, again, most of society doesn't consider an execution a murder.

The Imposition of the Deviant Label

In addition to defining deviance in an unusual way, labeling theory also discusses how official labeling occurs. Traditional theories accept the accuracy of official labeling such as arrest and imprisonment. Labeling theory challenges this view and says that some people and behaviors are more likely than others to be labeled deviant. Simply put, people in power impose definitions of deviance on behaviors committed by people without power. We saw examples of this in Chapter 2's discussion of how racial prejudice helped lead to the laws banning opium, cocaine, and marijuana. Most tests of labeling theory focus on the effects of race, social class, and, more recently, gender, on the chances of being labeled, with the argument

being that official labeling discriminates against people of color, the poor, and women.

William Chambliss's (1973) widely cited discussion of "the Saints and the Roughnecks" provides a classic example of labeling theory's view of the "the production of deviance." The Saints were eight extremely delinquent male high-school students in a particular town: They drank routinely, committed truancy, drove recklessly, and engaged in petty theft and vandalism. One of their favorite activities was going to street construction sites at night and removing warning signals; they would then hide and watch cars "bottom out" in potholes and other cavities. As their name implies, the Saints, despite their behavior, were considered "good kids." They came from middle-class families on the "right side of the tracks" and were never arrested, as their offenses were dismissed as harmless pranks. When they grew into adulthood, they went to graduate and professional schools and became doctors, lawyers, and the like.

The six Roughnecks fared much differently. They were also very delinquent and got into many fights but didn't cause as much monetary damage as the Saints did. They came from poor families on the "wrong side of the tracks" and were often in trouble with the police because everyone viewed them as troublemakers. When they grew into adulthood, they ended up in low-paying jobs and even prison.

Chambliss's analysis suggests that our impressions of people affect how likely we are to regard them as deviant. Although these notions often depend on people's race, class, and gender, other factors, including celebrity, also matter. In this regard, a primary task of the prosecution in the 1994–1995 O. J. Simpson murder case was to convince the jury that the former football star and TV and film personality was capable, despite his public image, of committing a monstrous crime (Pertman 1995).

Since the 1960s, many studies have examined whether extralegal factors such as race, class, gender, and appearance do affect the chances of arrest, imprisonment, and other official labeling. Overall, the evidence is inconsistent. Early studies found these variables having the effects predicted by labeling theory, but later research found official labeling affected primarily by legal factors such as the weight of the evidence and the seriousness of the offense. Debate on the importance of extralegal factors continues to be among the most heated in the criminology literature. (Chapters 15 and 16 discuss this debate in more detail.) My own view, shared by many but not all scholars, is that race, class, and gender do make a difference, with nonwhites, the poor, and sometimes women more likely to be officially labeled, but in more variable and subtle ways than depicted by labeling theory (Curran and Renzetti 1994:261–265). Other scholars concede that "differential processing" sometimes occurs but conclude that legal factors matter far more than extralegal ones (Akers 1997).

These mixed findings lead many critics to dismiss labeling theory, as they say that most people officially labeled have, in fact, committed the behavior for which they're labeled. Labeling proponents just as quickly point to the evidence in support of the theory (Wellford and Triplett 1993). Regardless of where the weight of the evidence lies, it's fair to say that labeling theory generated a new focus in the 1960s on the social reaction to crime and the operation of the legal system that continues to influence the study of crime and juvenile delinquency.

The Negative Consequences of Labeling

In the beginning of the 1944 film *Gaslight*, Gregory Anton, played by Charles Boyer, marries Paula Alquist, played by Ingrid Bergman, who won an Academy Award for Best Actress for the picture. The debonair Gregory and the younger and more naive Paula are very much in love. Their marriage after a whirlwind courtship seems made in heaven, and after a two-week Italian honeymoon, the new couple lives in the London home of Paula's wealthy aunt, who was mysteriously murdered some twenty years earlier.

Before too long, Paula's happiness begins to fade as evidence grows that she is losing her mind. Again and again her husband finds important objects that she apparently misplaced. After finding some of his own missing possessions, he accuses her of stealing and hiding them. One night Gregory notices his wife hasn't dressed for an important social function, and asks her in an astonished voice how she could have forgotten. As she apologizes virtually in tears, he angrily declares that it's now too late to attend the party. Things only get worse, as Paula continues to misplace things and forget other important events. Then she begins to notice the gaslights in the house flickering and dimming. Her husband says she's hallucinating. Just weeks before a happy and lively bride, Paula is now quiet, depressed, and unsure of herself, on the verge of a nervous breakdown.

Just when all seems lost, Scotland Yard detective Brian Cameron, played by the dashing Joseph Cotten, hears Gregory scold Paula at a party. Suspicious, he begins to find evidence that Gregory has been driving his wife mad by hiding the objects she has been supposedly hiding or losing, by making up invitations that never existed, and by secretly adjusting the gaslights. It turns out that Gregory is attempting to find some expensive jewels once owned by Paula's aunt and needs his young wife out of the way. I've already given away too much of the plot, but suffice it to say that the film comes to a thrilling climax.

When I first saw this film as an undergraduate, I said to myself, "That movie's about labeling theory!" Gregory makes his wife believe that she's going mad by treating her as if she were mad. She comes to accept this definition of herself and begins to lose her sanity. She's acting as she has been treated: She has accepted the label of madness that has been thrust upon her.

One of the most important sociological and social-psychological principles is that our interaction with others shapes our conception of ourselves. Recognizing this principle, childhood experts remind parents to praise their children in order to enhance their self-esteem and self-confidence, and they caution against rebuking children too often, lest they become sullen, defensive, and lacking in self-esteem.

More than thirty years ago, Robert Rosenthal and Lenore Jacobson (1968) performed a classic experiment illustrating the powerful effects of negative labels. At the beginning of the school year, schoolchildren were tested, and their teachers informed them which ones were "bright" and which were "dull." At the end of the school year, the children were tested again, and their scores were compared with their earlier scores. As you might expect, the bright students learned more that year than the dull students.

However, it turned out that there were *no* differences between the bright and dull students at the beginning of the study. Although the investigators did test the students, they assigned them randomly to either the bright or the dull group. Since the supposedly bright students did better during the year, this difference must have been due to the way they were treated by their teachers rather than to any extra ability. The teachers spent more time with them and praised them more and, in short, treated them as more intelligent. Conversely, they treated the dull students as less intelligent. In a "self-fulfilling prophecy" (Merton 1957), the bright students learned more than the dull students, even though there was no difference in intelligence or ability between the two groups. Although questions exist about the statistical accuracy of Rosenthal and Jacobson's analysis and replications haven't always found a "Pygmalion effect" (Sutton and Woodman 1989), their suggestion that people live up or down to the expectations others have of them remains compelling (Eden 1990).

Labeling theorists build on this view, part of the *symbolic interactionist* approach in sociology (Collins 1994), to present a similar view. They stress that labeling someone deviant can produce a deviant self-image, which prompts the person to commit even more deviance (Lemert 1951). Just like Ingrid Bergman in *Gaslight*, people labeled and treated as deviant come to accept that definition of themselves. Having accepted this self-image, they begin to act the role others now expect of them. Although it may be true that "sticks and stones may break my bones but names will never hurt me," labeling theory asserts that names—deviant labels—do hurt by affecting our self-image and promoting continued deviance.

More than fifty years ago, Frank Tannenbaum (1938:21), a historian of crime, called this process "the dramatization of evil" and said it "plays a greater role in making the criminal than perhaps any other experience." A person labeled deviant, said Tannenbaum, "becomes the thing he is described as being." Howard S. Becker (1963:31) highlighted a similar view in his 1963 book *Outsiders: Studies in the Sociology of Deviance.* Becker noted that the "experience of being caught and publicly labeled as a deviant" is "one of the most crucial steps" leading to a deviant career, with "important consequences for one's further participation and self-image."

Although *Gaslight* portrayed the effect of *informal* labeling by significant others, in this case a husband, labeling theory stresses the negative consequences of *official* labeling by the legal system. In this view, arrest, detention, and imprisonment all have the ironic effect of increasing deviance by generating a deviant self-image. The person labeled not only comes to accept the label but also finds others treating him or her like a criminal. As a result, conventional opportunities and friendships are blocked: Jobs are hard to get with a criminal record, and friendships with law-abiding people are difficult to achieve. The social-psychological and practical consequences of official labeling thus lead to *deviance amplification*, or the commission of continued deviance and the adoption of a deviant lifestyle, in a self-fulfilling prophecy.

Labeling theory's focus is not on the initial act or two leading someone to be officially labeled, and labeling theory does not try to explain why these initial acts occur. In Edwin Lemert's (1951) term, these acts are examples of "primary deviation" and occur among wide segments of the population. We all transgress now and then: Some youths shoplift, others commit vandalism, and still others use illegal drugs. But suppose a youth, say a 15-year-old male, is caught vandalizing or using an illegal drug. His arrest, fingerprinting, and treatment by the authorities make him think of himself as a young criminal. Parents, friends, teachers, and even the whole neighborhood hear about his crime. He's now labeled a troublemaker, and people look at him differently. Perhaps some of his friends are even told not to spend time with him. If some other offense occurs in the neighborhood, the youth might be suspected. He becomes angry and resentful, and figures if they're all going to treat him this way, why not act this way? "Secondary deviation," or continued deviance, follows.

Although this is admittedly a melodramatic and even simplistic scenario, it lies at the heart of labeling theory and emphasizes yet another social process by which people might come to break the law. A classic study showed how a record of deviance can reduce opportunities to succeed in the law-abiding world. Richard D. Schwartz and Jerome H. Skolnick (1962) mailed fictitious job applications to 100 potential employers. The applications were all the same, with one notable difference. In one set, the "applicant" listed that he had been imprisoned for assault. Another set mentioned that he had been tried and acquitted. A third set included a letter from a judge stating the applicant had been acquitted, while a final set did not mention any arrests.

As you might expect, Schwartz and Skolnick found that the potential employers were less likely to favor the applications listing the arrest, and even less likely to favor the ones listing the imprisonment. The researchers noted that if official labeling reduces law-abiding opportunities like employment, it ironically may force

◀ *According to labeling theory, arrest and other legal sanctions may increase deviance by generating a deviant self-image.*

someone into continued criminality. In line with their view, recent studies find that a record of juvenile delinquency hurts employment chances into young adulthood (Hagan 1993).

In arguing that official labeling increases future criminality, labeling theory is directly at odds with deterrence theory's view (see Chapter 5) that official labeling reduces future criminality (specific deterrence). The two theories also disagree on the effects of official labeling on the offender's perceptions. Labeling theory argues that labeling causes or increases a deviant self-image, while deterrence theory argues that it increases the offender's perceived risk of arrest and aversion to arrest and punishment. Many tests of labeling theory have addressed these contradictory expectations. Some studies investigate whether official labeling is more likely to increase or decrease future criminality, while others investigate whether official labeling increases deviant self-images or increases perceptions of risk.

The evidence on either effect of official labeling is highly inconsistent (Wellford and Triplett 1993). Some research finds that labeling does increase future deviance, other research finds the opposite effect, and still other studies find no effect in either direction. The majority of self-image research on juveniles finds that official labeling does not increase deviant self-images. Many youths already have deviant self-images before arrest, while the remainder seem able to keep their positive self-images intact despite arrest. A more negative self-image is likely to occur among youths involved in only minor delinquency (Thomas and Bishop 1984). The lack of empirical support for labeling theory's predictions leads many observers to dismiss the theory. Commenting on these inconsistent findings, a recent review noted, "The soundest conclusion is that official sanctions by themselves have neither a strong deterrent nor a substantial labeling effect" (Akers 1997:106–107).

Critique of Labeling Theory

As should be clear, labeling theory has generated much controversy over the years, and scholars have criticized it since its inception (Akers 1968; Gove 1980). As noted previously, empirical research fails to consistently support its arguments on the influence of extralegal factors on labeling and the effect of labeling on continued deviance. Regarding the latter argument, critics say that labeling theory paints an overly passive view of the individual as quietly succumbing to the effects of the deviant label. Labeling theorists reply that the theory's view of the individual is not nearly as passive as its critics charge (Paternoster and Iovanni 1989).

Scholars also challenge labeling theory on other grounds. Perhaps the most important is that the theory fails to explain primary deviance and thus ignores the effects of family and peer relationships and more macro factors. In another area, some versions of labeling theory strongly imply that a life of crime, or secondary deviance, doesn't develop unless official labeling first occurs. Disputing this view, critics say that people are quite capable of becoming career criminals without having first been labeled and also point to the large amount of hidden crime and delinquency committed by those who have never been arrested and thus never labeled. Labeling theorists concede the theory's irrelevance for primary deviance but note it was developed specifically to explain secondary deviance. They again accuse their critics of oversimplification.

Critics also take issue with labeling theory's prescription for reducing crime and delinquency. Since the theory stresses that official labeling—arrest, imprisonment, and the like—promotes continued deviance, many labeling theorists urge caution in using the law to fight crime except for the most serious offenders. In the early 1970s, for example, Edwin Schur (1973) urged a policy of "radical nonintervention" for most delinquents in which we would "leave kids alone wherever possible" and avoid using incarceration even for serious juvenile offenses. Critics, especially deterrence theory proponents, charge that such a policy would increase rather than reduce crime and delinquency. This concern notwithstanding, labeling theory's view led in the 1970s to a "diversion" movement that kept many juvenile offenders out of juvenile courts and youth centers (Lundman 1993).

Radical criminologists have also criticized labeling theory. While liking its general perspective, they nonetheless charge it with focusing on "nuts, sluts, and perverts," or deviance by the powerless, and ignoring crimes by the powerful. They also criticize the theory for ignoring the sources of the power inequalities that affect the making of laws and the likelihood of official labeling for criminal behavior (Liazos 1972; Taylor, Walton, and Young 1973).

Revising and Renewing Labeling Theory

The withering attack from all sides has reduced labeling theory's popularity. As Akers (1997:110) notes, "It no longer generates the interest, enthusiasm, research, and acceptance it once did as a dominant paradigm two or three decades ago." In response, the theory's proponents have attempted to revise it. Given the inconsistent evidence on the effects of official labeling, recent work has begun to return labeling theory to its symbolic interactionist roots by addressing the negative effects of informal labeling by social networks of friends, relatives, and loved ones (Wellford and Triplett 1993). As in *Gaslight*, such labeling can be very influential for adults, but its influence is even greater during childhood and adolescence, when self-concepts are forming. Some studies find that informal labeling can result in many negative consequences, including resentment, a deviant self-image, and continued deviance (Matsueda 1992; Triplett and Jarjoura 1994). Thus, even though labeling theory may overstate the effects of official labeling, refocusing the theory on unofficial labeling may illuminate the informal social processes leading to deviance and crime.

Other scholars note that official labeling promotes deviance for some people and deters it for others. If this is true, they say, then research must clarify the circumstances under which deviance amplification or deterrence occurs after labeling (Paternoster and Iovanni 1989). In this regard, John Braithwaite's (1989) work on shaming, or social disapproval, is especially promising. Braithwaite distinguishes between *disintegrative shaming* and *reintegrative shaming*. Disintegrative shaming, or stigmatization, occurs when offenders are treated like outcasts and no effort is made to forgive them and to involve them in community affairs. Braithwaite says that disintegrative shaming promotes continued deviance because it humiliates and angers offenders, denies them legitimate opportunities, and forces them to associate with criminal peers. A famous literary example of disintegrative shaming is Nathaniel Hawthorne's novel *The Scarlet Letter*, in which a young woman, Hester Prynne, is forced to wear the letter *A* to signify her adultery. (Contrary to Braithwaite's expectations, however, Prynne's shunning did not prompt her to commit continued adultery.)

Reintegrative shaming occurs when efforts are made to bring offenders back into the community. Such shaming reduces continued deviance, partly because it encourages offenders to feel ashamed, and is most common in *communitarian*

How Should We Deal with Juvenile Offenders?

As noted in the text, labeling theory spawned new concern over the negative consequences of labeling, especially for adolescents who get into trouble with the law. Edwin Schur and other sociologists warned that treating juveniles like common criminals would only make them more likely to continue breaking the law. During the 1970s, states across the nation heeded this warning, and began to "divert" from the juvenile justice system adolescents who had committed minor delinquency or status offenses (running away from home, truancy, etc.). Instead of going into juvenile court and youth centers, these offenders stayed out of the system and instead experienced other sanctions such as undergoing counseling, making restitution to their victims, or having their behavior strictly monitored by juvenile probation officers or sometimes by their parents.

A rough consensus of studies since the 1970s is that diversion produces modest decreases in recidivism (repeat offending). Because it costs much less money to divert juvenile offenders than to place them in youth centers, diversion remains a popular legal sanction for adolescents, especially those charged with minor offenses. That said, one problem with diversion is that it "widens the net," as juveniles who previously would not have been involved in the juvenile justice system at all now experience diversion. Ironically, then, diversion might have increased the number of juveniles officially labeled as delinquent.

As the public became more concerned about juvenile crime in the late 1970s, sentiment about juvenile delinquency began to change. Thinking that juvenile court sentencing is generally much less severe than that in the adult criminal justice system, many observers urged that serious juvenile offenders be tried as adults. Critics replied that even serious juvenile offenders are still too young to be able to fully comprehend their actions and, if treated like adults, would turn out even worse than if they were processed through the juvenile justice system.

Reinforcing the critics' views, later research suggested that the assumption of less severe sentencing of juvenile offenders may well be a myth. In one study, juveniles in California suspected of violent crimes were more likely to be petitioned (prosecuted) than adults suspected of these crimes. In another study also involving Californians accused of violent crimes, juveniles sentenced to the California Youth Authority received longer terms of incarceration than adults sent to prison.

As the treatment of juvenile offenders during the 1990s became even more punitive, criminologists warned that this trend would do more harm than good by punishing such offenders rather than trying to reform them. They also pointed out that juvenile crime declined during the decade despite the celebrated shootings by adolescents at Columbine High School and elsewhere. The punitive trend against juvenile offenders was thus a response to a myth of increasing juvenile violence. Certainly the controversy over how serious juvenile offenders should be treated will continue well into the new century.

Sources: Krisberg and Austin 1993; Lundman 1993; Males 1999; Schur 1973; Zimring 1998.

societies marked by a high degree of concern for the welfare of others. In the industrialized world, says Braithwaite, the key communitarian society stressing reintegrative shaming is Japan. In Japan, shame is keenly felt by all, including offenders. The Japanese are much more likely than their U.S. counterparts to feel that offenders can change and much less likely to favor harsh punishment. As a result, Japanese social networks readily support offenders and try to reintegrate them into the community. These efforts help generate a lower rate of recidivism, or repeat offending, in Japan than in the United States (Vincentnathan 1995).

Although Braithwaite recognizes that the United States and other industrialized nations are very different from Japan, he still feels that more reintegrative shaming could occur in these countries if they were to adopt more informal social control processes. For example, in Australia and New Zealand some programs have juvenile offenders and their families meet with the offenders' victims and their families (Braithwaite and Mugford 1994). As *The Scarlet Letter* suggests, however, disintegrative and reintegrative shaming may not always have the effects Braithwaite predicts, and we need much more research to test his theory.

Despite many pessimistic assessments of labeling theory's value, the new emphasis on informal labeling and on the conditions under which labeling increases or decreases deviance promises to reinvigorate the theory and increase its importance for contemporary criminology. In a recent review, Charles F. Wellford and Ruth A. Triplett (1993:18) concluded, "We consider the future of labeling theory to be quite promising," and urged its integration with other theories to present a more comprehensive explanation of crime and delinquency.

RESTORATIVE JUSTICE

Labeling theory's views in general, and Braithwaite's views in particular, are reflected in a new, *restorative justice* movement that has been gaining popularity in recent years (Quinn 1998; Turpin 1999). Reflecting a philosophy that goes back to ancient times, restorative justice focuses on restoring the social bond between the offender and the community. In contrast to the *retributive model* guiding U.S. crime policy that emphasizes punishment of the offender, restorative justice emphasizes the needs of the victim and of the community and, perhaps above all, the need to reintegrate the offender into the community. Often involving meetings between offenders, their victims, and community members, restorative justice is a more personal process that encourages offenders to take responsibility for their actions.

Criminal justice scholar Thomas Quinn (1998:10) says that restorative justice "focuses on restoring the health of the community, repairing the harm done, meeting victims' needs, and emphasizing that the offender can—and must—contribute to those repairs." The retributive model, he says, does none of these things. Although offenders are imprisoned, such punishment does little to "reduce citizen fear of crime, heal victims, or increase citizen satisfaction with the criminal justice system."

Restorative justice has been tried in some areas of the United States and also, as noted earlier, in nations such as Australia, Canada, Japan, and New Zealand. It is also popular among native peoples in the United States and Canada and in some socialist nations. Although restorative justice practices differ, they include such things as *victim impact panels*, in which victims talk with offenders about their feelings as victims; *family group conferences* involving family members of both offenders and victims; *sentencing circles* involving offenders' and victims' relatives, friends, and other associates; and *citizen reparative boards* that determine the conditions of probation for convicted offenders.

As should be evident, restorative justice emphasizes Braithwaite's goal of reintegrative shaming. The objective here is to maximize the chances that offenders will be rehabilitated, in contrast to the embitterment that often occurs with the retributive model's focus on punishment and imprisonment (or, in Braithwaite's term, disintegrative shaming). Restorative justice also puts much more emphasis than the retributive model on the needs of victims. Their offenders not only meet with them but also in many cases compensate them with money and compensate their communities with public service work.

The key question, of course, is whether restorative justice works. Does it reduce repeat offending, does it reduce community fear of crime, and does it enhance victim satisfaction with the criminal justice system? Unfortunately, restorative justice is still too new for us to have definitive answers to these questions. However, restorative justice does seem to increase victim satisfaction with the justice process and reduce their fear of revictimization by the same offender. Some studies also indicate that offenders who participate in restorative justice procedures are less likely to reoffend than control groups of offenders who experience more typical criminal justice outcomes. In the United States, restorative justice has probably been used most often for juvenile offenders who committed relatively minor offenses. Whether it would work for more serious juvenile offenders and for their adult counterparts remains an important question.

CONFLICT AND RADICAL THEORIES

Conflict and radical theories of crime take up where labeling theory leaves off. They argue that law is a key part of the struggle between powerful interests and the powerless. To preserve their position at the top, the powerful use the law to control the behavior of the powerless. This argument applies to both the formation of law and the operation of the criminal justice system.

In contrast, traditional theories of crime stress the positive functions of law. They believe law is needed by every modern society to maintain social order, given that there will always be people deviating. Law and the criminal justice system are thus designed to benefit all of us, not just the powerful. Traditional theories of crime thus advocate a "consensus" view of law, crime, and criminal justice, while conflict and radical theories advocate a "conflict" view (Hopkins 1975).

Consensus and Conflict Perspectives in Sociology

These views reflect a more general division in sociology between functional or consensus perspectives and conflict perspectives (see Chapter 1). Reflecting the Durkheimian sociological tradition, consensus perspectives stress that social institutions help create social stability (Collins 1994). For example, the family socializes its children and provides them emotional support, food, clothing, and shelter. Religion socializes us with the "golden rule" and other principles of behavior and strengthens social bonds by bringing people together at religious services. In the functional perspective, even social inequality is considered necessary. In this view, some occupations require more skills and talent than others, and only a few people have these skills and knowledge. To induce them to enter these occupations, society thus needs to promise high salaries. By definition, other people in other occupations will thus have lower salaries. The necessary result is social stratification, or social inequality (Macionis 2000).

Conflict theory considers this view of social institutions both simplistic and idealistic. Since these institutions serve the interests of the powerful in society, they're dysfunctional for many other members of society. Thus the family is a key source of emotional and physical violence against women and children, while religion promotes social conflict and prompts the poor to accept their economic fate instead of blaming society. Contrary to what functional theory says, conflict theory stresses that inequality is quite dysfunctional for those at the bottom of the socioeconomic ladder, and it faults the functional view for ignoring the effects of racism, sexism, and classism on the ability to advance up this ladder.

Conflict theory lies at the heart of the *conflict tradition* in sociology, which goes back to the work of the German social philosopher and political activist Karl Marx (1818–1883), his collaborator Friedrich Engels (1820–1895), and the German sociologist Max Weber (1864–1920) (Collins 1994). Marx and Engels viewed society as composed of classes based on the ownership of the means of production: land, technology, factories, tools, and the like. In capitalist society the two major classes are the bourgeoisie, who own the factories and other modern means of production, and the proletariat, who work for the bourgeoisie. Economic power thus belongs to the bourgeoisie. The proletariat are left with nothing and live in poverty and misery.

Given these facts, the bourgeoisie's primary interest is to keep its advantaged position by exploiting the proletariat and doing everything possible to ensure it stays powerless. The proletariat's primary interest, quite naturally, is to eliminate its oppression by overthrowing the bourgeoisie and seizing the means of production. In this way, the economic interests of these two classes affect their beliefs about the status quo. A revolution can't occur unless the proletariat achieves *class consciousness*, or an awareness of the nature of, and reasons for, its oppression. The ruling class's key task, then, is to prevent this from happening by preventing the proletariat from developing this awareness. To accomplish this task, the ruling class must effectively dictate the *ruling ideas* in society through its control of the *means of mental production*—printing presses, newspapers, and the like—and of social institutions such as the educational system and the law.

Weber joined with Marx and Engels in recognizing economic classes but, unlike them, also recognized *status groups* that have different amounts of power. Some status groups derive from their placement in the economic system, but others are based on religion, ethnicity, urban versus rural residence, and other noneconomic factors. Weber's concept of power and conflict is thus more multidimensional than that of Marx and Engels (Collins 1994).

Conflict Perspectives in Criminology

Since law is one of our most important social institutions, it was inevitable that the debate between consensus and conflict views would eventually enter the field of criminology. As discussed earlier, in the 1960s and 1970s the civil rights, antiwar, and other movements affected a new generation of scholars interested in crime. They saw law used again and again to repress blacks in the South and to harass antiwar protesters, and began to consider whether the criminal law and justice system generally oppress or otherwise harm the powerless.

As this new generation of scholars began to develop conflict perspectives on crime and law, they looked back to Marx, Engels, and Weber for inspiration. Eventually two strands of thought developed. The first, hereafter called *conflict theory*, is more Weberian in orientation: It considers law and crime the result of conflict between various kinds of groups in society, not just economic classes. Austin T. Turk's 1969 book *Criminality and Legal Order* represents perhaps the most important statement of this way of thinking (Turk 1969). Turk's view was heavily influenced by the labeling conception of deviance, as he argued that no behavior is inherently criminal. Instead, crime is a label imposed on the powerless in society as part of the larger struggle for political power. From this vantage point, Turk developed a theory of *criminalization*, which spelled out how criminal labels come to be applied. For example, criminalization is more likely when the subordinate groups are less sophisticated and the dominant groups' beliefs and behavior coincide (as when members of the dominant group say that illegal drug use is wrong and don't use such drugs themselves).

Turk's Weberian orientation on law and crime followed in the footsteps of earlier scholars Thorsten Sellin and George Vold. In 1938 Sellin discussed immigration and crime in his short report, *Culture Conflict and Crime* (Sellin 1938). Sellin stressed that the cultural views of immigrants into the United States differed from those of the larger U.S. society. Some behaviors considered acceptable in immigrant cultures were now illegal in the eyes of the larger society, and thus much crime should be seen as the result of culture conflict. In a famous example, Sellin wrote about a Sicilian father in New Jersey who killed a teenaged boy for having sex with his daughter. Since Sicilian culture approved this way of defending family honor, the man was surprised to be arrested.

In 1958 George Vold presented a group conflict theory of crime in his important book, *Theoretical Criminology* (Vold 1958). Vold said that groups with legislative power also have the power to decide which behaviors will be legal and which will be illegal. He also thought that crime stems from the conflict between various interest groups. The recent efforts of anti-abortion forces illustrate Vold's perspective, as these efforts have included crimes such as the murders of physicians who perform abortions and the vandalism of abortion clinics (Samuels 1999).

In another area, Vold argued that juvenile gangs arise from conflict between young people's values and those of the adult culture. He also thought his theory especially relevant for crimes involving political protest, labor disputes, and racial and ethnic hostility (see Chapter 13). He admitted his theory applies poorly to behaviors not arising from group conflict (e.g., spontaneous violence and thefts done for individual gain).

CRITIQUE OF CONFLICT THEORY

Conflict theory helps to explain the origins of some criminal laws and types of crime. In both areas, it seems especially relevant for crimes committed as part of social movement unrest, including labor strife, and for behaviors such as abortion, drug and alcohol use, and other "public order" crimes on which people have many different views (see Chapter 14). However, conflict theory seems less relevant for conventional street crimes such as murder, assault, robbery, and burglary. Laws prohibiting these behaviors are meant to protect all segments of society, not just the powerful, who suffer less than the poor from these crimes. In another area, conflict theory shares labeling theory's view on disparities in the labeling process. As noted earlier, evidence of these disparities is inconsistent, and scholars continue to disagree on the extent to which they exist.

Some of the best evidence for conflict theory comes from historical studies. In this regard, Chapter 2 traced the development of laws against opium, cocaine, and marijuana to racial and ethnic prejudice. A classic historical example of the conflict position is Joseph R. Gusfield's 1963 book, *Symbolic Crusade*, which discussed the origins and dynamics of the temperance (prohibition) movement of the late 1800s and early 1900s (Gusfield 1963). As his book's title implies, Gusfield saw the temperance movement as a symbolic attack of one group on another group. The movement was composed mostly of devout middle-class, small-town or rural Protestants who considered alcohol use a sin. They looked around them and saw a fair amount of drinking by poor Catholic immigrants in urban areas. To the minds of temperance advocates, these people had several strikes against them: They were poor, they were Catholic, they were immigrants, and they were urban residents. The temperance attack on their drinking is thus best seen as a symbolic attack against their poverty, religion, immigrant status, and urban residence. Since rural Protestants dominated state legislatures and the Congress, they were able to amend the U.S. Constitution to prohibit alcohol.

Radical Theories in Criminology

Conflict theory was the first strand of thought that the new generation of scholars began developing in the 1960s. The second line of thinking is more Marxian than Weberian and views law and crime as the result of conflict between capitalists and workers, or the ruling class and the poor. This perspective has been variously called "critical," "new," "radical," "dialectical," "socialist," and "Marxist" criminology. Although these labels indicate certain differences, all these approaches essentially adopt a Marxian approach to the study of crime and law (Bohm 1982; Lynch 1997). For the sake of simplicity, I'll hereafter refer to them collectively as *radical theory*. Their basic views all stem from the work of Marx and Engels, to whom we now return.

MARX AND ENGELS ON CRIME AND LAW

In contrast to other topics, Marx and Engels actually wrote relatively little about law and even less about crime, and what they did write is scattered throughout their various essays and books (Cain and Hunt 1979). They thought that law in capitalist societies helps the ruling class in at least two ways: (1) It emphasizes and preserves private property, almost all of which belongs to the ruling class; and (2) it gives everyone various legal rights and thus *appears* to provide "equal justice for all." In promoting an appearance of legal equality, the law pacifies the powerless by making them feel good about the status quo and obscuring the true nature and extent of their oppression.

Marx and Engels presented several contrasting views of crime. In some of their writing, they depicted crime as stemming from the misery that accompanies capitalism. Thus Marx (1993 [1887]:47) wrote that the development of capitalism turned the new proletariat into "beggars, robbers, vagabonds, partly from inclination, in most cases from stress of circumstances." In this view, crime, especially theft, is a necessary, logical response by the poor to the conditions in which they live. As Engels (1993 [1845]:48) observed, "The worker is poor; life has nothing to offer him; he is deprived of virtually all pleasures.... What reason has the worker for not stealing?... Distress due to poverty gives the worker only the choice of starving slowly, killing himself quickly, or taking what he needs where he finds it—in plain English—stealing."

At other times Marx and Engels depicted crime as an act of political rebellion by the poor against their exploitation and an expression of their hostility toward the ruling class. As Engels (1993 [1845]:49) put it, "Acts of violence committed by the working classes against the bourgeoisie and their henchmen are merely frank and undisguised retaliation for the thefts and treacheries perpetrated by the middle classes against the workers." Despite this view, Engels thought crime an ineffective act of rebellion, since it's performed individually and not collectively and usually prompts severe legal punishment.

INTERNATIONAL FOCUS

Crime and the Economy in China and Vietnam

Many radical criminologists blame capitalism for much of the crime the United States suffers: Crime results from the economic deprivation caused by capitalism and also from the selfish individualism that inevitably accompanies capitalism. If they're right, then as Communist nations move toward a capitalist economy, crime of many types should increase. The recent experience of China and Vietnam supports this prediction.

In 1984 the Communist party in China initiated economic reforms to reduce government control over business activity, as a move toward a market (capitalist) economy began. During the next few years, China's official crime rate rose sharply, although it still remains much lower than the U.S. rate. Keeping in mind that official crime statistics in China may be even less reliable than those in the United States, China's reported crime rate quadrupled between 1985 and the early 1990s, and its serious crime rate (homicide, rape, aggravated assault, robbery, theft, and fraud) quintupled during that time. To give some examples of actual figures, the number of homicides in China rose from about 10,000 in 1985 to 24,000 in 1992, while the number of assaults rose from 15,000 to 59,000 during that time. Political corruption in China is also thought to have soared during this period of economic change.

This rise in crime occurred even though China continued to treat its offenders quite harshly. In 1993, for example, the government executed 866 people thought to be involved in drug trafficking gangs. As Dai Yisheng, the former director of international law enforcement research for China's Ministry of Public Security, observes, "All of these severe measures have not had the deterrence effect expected; the crime wave has not been curbed" (p. 11). He attributes the rising crime rate to the social changes and growing unemployment accompanying China's move to a market economy.

A rise in crime also followed Vietnam's attempt to move toward a market economy. In the wake of this attempt, theft, drug use and trafficking, delinquency, smuggling, and business-related crime grew into major problems. The growth in delinquency was attributed to a high adolescent unemployment rate, which has prompted many of them to commit theft and other offenses. In response to the growing crime problem, Vietnam instituted punitive and preventative measures alike. It executed a police officer in March 1995 for robbing and murdering a young adult, and also executed two suspected drug traffickers for possessing opium and heroin. At the same time, Vietnam's State Committee of Child Care earmarked funds to implement programs designed to prevent delinquency.

As with the rising crime in former Soviet nations (see the International Focus box in Chapter 6), the growing crime problem in China and Vietnam is doubtless the result of several factors. Their shift to market economies may have prompted greater inequality and selfish individualism, but it also involved other kinds of social changes permeating both nations. Following Durkheim, the resulting anomie, or normlessness, may well be another factor accounting for rising crime in both nations. Still, if both China and Vietnam continue their shift to capitalism, we can expect their crime rates to rise even further.

Sources: Curran and Cook 1993; Faison 1995; Ward 1995; Yisheng 1995.

Taking this negative view a step further, in other work Marx and Engels (1962 [1848]:44) harshly depicted criminals as a lumpenproletariat, or "the social scum, the positively rotting mass" composed of vagabonds, pimps, prostitutes, pickpockets, and the like. Engels wrote (1926:23) that the lumpenproletariat is "an absolutely venal, and absolutely brazen crew." As might be evident from their language, Marx and Engels felt that the lumpenproletariat hindered the chances of a proletarian revolution (Wenger and Bonomo 1993).

WILLEM BONGER: CAPITALISM, EGOISM, AND CRIME

Despite Marx and Engels' occasional concern with crime and law, for a long time Marxists neglected these subjects. Dutch criminologist Willem Bonger (1876–1940) was a major exception. In his 1916 book, *Criminality and Economic Conditions* (Bonger 1916), Bonger argued that a cultural emphasis on altruism characterized precapitalist, agricultural societies. In such societies, everyone was "in the same boat," and people looked out for each other's welfare. The development of capitalism led to a very different situation because as an economic system it promotes competition for profit above all other goals. Competition in turn means that someone wins and someone loses: Your success comes at the expense of someone else's failure.

The competition for profit that characterizes capitalism leads to a cultural emphasis on egoism and greed, to use Bonger's terms. As the familiar saying puts it, "Look out for number one." Given egoism and greed, said Bonger, it's inevitable that people will be quite willing to break the law for economic profit and other advantages, even if their actions hurt others. Bonger thought this was true for all social classes, not just the poor, but also noted that the poor are driven to crime by economic necessity. Although the wealthy commit crimes, he said, they escape legal punishment, since the law in capitalist societies is intended to help dominate the poor: "In every society which is divided into a ruling class and a class ruled, penal law has been principally constituted according to the will of the former" (Bonger 1916:24). Since Bonger attributed crime to capitalism, he thought it would largely disappear under socialism, in which altruism is a much stronger cultural emphasis.

JEROME HALL: THE LAW OF THEFT

Somewhat later, historian Jerome Hall presented a Marxian analysis of the law of theft in his influential book, *Theft, Law, and Society* (Hall 1952), which discussed how the modern concept of theft developed in England some 500 years ago. At that time, England was emerging from a feudal, agricultural society into a budding capitalist economy characterized by merchant trade. When a merchant sold goods to another merchant or landowner, poor people working for the merchant would transport these goods on a horse-drawn cart. No law prohibited these people, who were called "carriers," from keeping these goods for themselves. The idea back then was that the goods technically belonged to the carriers during the time they were transporting the goods. If the carriers decided to keep the goods for themselves, they had the legal right to do so, with no crime committed. Instead the blame was put on merchants for foolishly hiring them.

Fearing being fired or even physically attacked, most carriers simply transported the goods they were delivering. However, some decided to keep the goods for themselves. Naturally the new mercantile, or merchant, class disliked such behavior, since it threatened their business. However, the poor, by far the vast majority of English people, supported it since they were the ones delivering the goods. Eventually this matter reached the courts, and in the landmark 1473 *Carrier's Case* English judges established a new crime by ruling that carriers no longer had the right to keep goods for themselves. Noting that the judges didn't come from the ranks of the poor, Hall argued that their decision protected the interests of the mercantile capitalist class by controlling the behavior of poor carriers. Although today we would all agree that carriers shouldn't keep goods they're delivering (if you buy a refrigerator, you would certainly not want the truck driver to keep it!), the origins of this particular concept of theft do fit a Marxian perspective.

◀ *Sociologist William Chambliss says that vagrancy was outlawed many centuries ago after the plague hit England. The new law against vagrancy helped increase the supply of labor and prevent wages from rising.*

WILLIAM CHAMBLISS: THE LAW OF VAGRANCY

In 1964 William Chambliss authored a similar analysis of the development of vagrancy laws in England. Before the 1340s, no law in England prohibited begging or loitering. Then, the bubonic plague struck England in 1348 and killed about half of the population. With fewer people available to work on the land, landowners faced the prospect of having to pay higher wages. The passage of the first vagrancy law in 1349 aimed to prevent this by making it a crime for people to beg for a living and to move from place to place to find employment. Both provisions in effect increased the size of the labor force, keeping wages lower than they would have been otherwise. Chambliss said this law was "designed for one express purpose: to force laborers … to accept employment at a low wage in order to insure the landowner an adequate supply of labor at a price he could afford to pay" (Chambliss 1964:68). In the following centuries, Chambliss said, vagrancy laws were revived from time to time to benefit the mercantile class. Although Chambliss's analysis has been criticized for overemphasizing the economic motivation for vagrancy law development (Adler 1989), it remains a classic application of radical theory.

CONTEMPORARY RADICAL WORK ON CRIME AND LAW

As radical perspectives on crime and law developed a few decades ago, scholars drew on the work of Marx and Engels, Bonger, Hall, Chambliss, and others. Much of the new work was historical, but a good deal of it also looked at law and crime in the contemporary United States, Canada, England, and elsewhere. Although the major emphasis was on the formation of law and the punishment of criminals, some scholars also focused on the genesis of crime. Reflecting more general Marxist theory (Gold, Lo, and Wright 1975), the new radical work on law and crime is often categorized according to whether it embraces *instrumental*, *structural*, or *dialectical* Marxist views. The first radical scholars in the 1970s took an instrumental view, while more recent radical scholars espouse structural or dialectical views.

INSTRUMENTAL MARXISM Instrumental Marxism considers the ruling class a small, unified group that uses the law to dominate the poor and to advance its own interests. As Richard Quinney (1974:45, 54), the prime proponent of this view, wrote in the 1970s, "It is according to the interests of the ruling class that American society is governed." Law, he wrote, "is an instrument of the state that serves the interests of the developing capitalist ruling class." To the extent that instrumental Marxists explain street crime, they view it as a form of political rebellion by the poor arising from the frustration and hostility caused by inequality. Like Bonger, they believe that crime would greatly diminish and even disappear if the United States and other capitalist nations were to become socialist. In this view, people are more cooperative and altruistic under socialism, and in this sense resemble the precapitalist societies studied by Bonger.

STRUCTURAL MARXISM Structural Marxists consider these views too simplistic. If law were just a means of oppression, they ask, how can we explain civil liberties, health and safety measures, unemployment insurance, and other legally mandated benefits for the working class? The answer to this question, they continue, is that the ruling class is not as unified as instrumental Marxists think. Instead, members of the ruling class often disagree over important issues and compete among themselves for political and economic success. The state and its legal order must thus be *relatively autonomous* in order to ensure the long-term interests of capitalism, in part by providing legal rights and other benefits that help convince the public of the fairness of the existing order. William Chambliss and Robert Seidman (1982:308) summarize this view: "The state and the legal order best fulfill their function as legitimizers when they appear to function as value neutral organs fairly and impartially representing the interests of everyone." According to structural Marxists, legal and political victories by the poor are inevitably a sham, since they help in the long run to legitimate the existing order and to preserve capitalist interests.

In explaining crime, structural Marxists join with their instrumentalist counterparts in stressing the frustration and hostility arising from inequality and exploitation. But they provide a more complex account of the underlying processes. Steven Spitzer's influential 1975 article, "Toward a Marxian Theory of Deviance," presented a major statement of this view (Spitzer 1975). Spitzer thought that crime under capitalism is committed by "problem populations," which have two sources. The first source is capitalism itself, which inevitably creates a "relative surplus population" of the unemployed. Drawing on Marx and Engels, Spitzer considered the unemployed population a double-edged sword for capitalism: On the one hand, it provides a ready mass of workers that helps keep wages low; on the other, this group's unemployment leads to crime and other problems that could threaten social stability.

The second source of problem populations is the institutions making up the *superstructure* of capitalist societies that are meant to preserve capitalist interests. Though they may indeed serve this function, they can also have the opposite effect. Mass education, for example, was introduced a century ago to help give people the necessary skills to become industrial workers, but the knowledge gained in school by the poor may awaken them to their oppression by capitalist institutions. In both these ways, wrote Spitzer, problem populations and thus crime result from the inherent contradictions of capitalism.

Spitzer further divided problem populations into two groups, *social junk* and *social dynamite*. Social junk, as the name applies, are people who live on the fringes of society and pose no threat to society but also don't contribute to economic growth. Examples include the disabled and the mentally ill. Social dynamite are people who are younger and more of a political threat than social junk. Their behavior threatens social order and economic growth and thus is considered crime and controlled by legal sanctions.

DIALECTICAL MARXISM Dialectical Marxists criticize the structural view for ignoring the possibility of real, not just sham, legal victories by the poor. They emphasize that the ruling class in democratic societies does use the law against the powerless, but also note that the law often restricts what the ruling class is able to do. The "rule of law" in democratic societies thus limits the use of "arbitrary extralegal power" (Thompson 1975:264). A study by Isaac Balbus of the legal response to urban protest in the 1960s reached a similar conclusion. Noting that the state followed legal standards of due process in arresting and prosecuting urban rioters, Balbus (1977:vi) emphasized that the rule of law "powerfully conditions—even during periods of extreme 'crisis'—the range of possible responses that emanate from" legal and political authorities.

AN INTEGRATED MARXIST VIEW In 1983 Mark Colvin and John Pauly (1983) presented an interesting "integrated structural-Marxist" theory of delinquency, tracing delinquency to class relations in the workplace. In their view, working-class parents labor in jobs where they are controlled by supervisors so obedience, not autonomy, is the norm they follow. The strain they feel worsens their relationships with their children, who then develop a greater potential for delinquency. In addition, working-class parents "reproduce" the norm of obedience in the workplace by demanding it from their children at home. Their disciplinary style thus takes the punitive form that, as we saw in Chapter 7, increases the potential for delinquency. As should be clear, Colvin and Pauly's theory incorporates parts of Marxist and social control theories. They add that association with delinquent peers is a byproduct of the worsened parental relationships and punitive discipline characteristic of working-class families. Association with delinquent peers is thus one of the mechanisms through which coercive work-place relations ultimately produce greater delinquency. In noting this, Colvin and Pauly incorporate an important concept from learning and differential association theories.

CRITIQUE OF RADICAL CRIMINOLOGY

Nonradical criminologists have vigorously attacked radical criminology. One observer called the "new criminology" the "old baloney" and accused it of sentimentality in glorifying predatory crime by the poor (Toby 1980). Critics challenge radical criminology on several other grounds. Most generally, they charge that radical criminologists unfairly malign the United States and other democracies and overlook the oppressive nature of many socialist and Communist nations. Since crime also exists in these noncapitalist societies, say the critics, it's unfair to blame capitalism for crime, and it's utopian to believe that crime would disappear if socialism replaced capitalism. Critics also charge that radical criminology exaggerates the importance of class relations in the genesis of crime and ignores the many other factors at work (Akers 1997).

In response, radical criminologists fault this criticism for painting an overly simplistic portrait of radical criminology. The radical perspective isn't monolithic and instead includes different strands of thought that share an overall point of view. Radical criminologists say that the criticism of their perspective focuses on instrumental Marxist approaches, which characterized the early work of radical criminologists in the 1970s, but which have been replaced by more structural and dialectical views. In fact, many radical criminologists have also criticized instrumental views. These scholars thus claim that the criticism of traditional criminologists focuses on a particular type of radical criminology that is no longer popular even in radical circles (Greenberg 1993; Lynch 1997).

SOCIAL CLASS AND LEGAL PROCESSING   In another criticism, traditional criminologists challenge radical criminology's (and also conflict theory's) assumption that class and race affect the chances of legal punishment (Chiricos and Waldo 1975; Williams 1980). As we saw earlier, labeling theory has been criticized for the same reason. I said then that empirical support for this assumption is inconsistent, but that class, race, and gender do appear to affect legal punishment, albeit in varied and often subtle ways. We will examine the evidence for this view in more detail later (Chapters 15 and 16). Here I'll just focus on class, the key factor in radical criminology's view of legal punishment.

It seems clear that the poor and the working class suffer by their inability to afford bail, private attorneys, and other legal advantages (Reiman 1998). If this is true, empirical tests of class bias in criminal justice processing may be misguided. The problem is that most criminal defendants in these studies come from the ranks of the poor and near-poor, since people with this economic background commit most street crime. In testing whether, for instance, annual income affects sentencing after conviction, these studies are in effect comparing people with different incomes (e.g., $4,000 versus $12,000) who are all still poor and thus must rely on public defenders or on poorly paid private attorneys. If this is true, we would not expect to find differences in sentence outcomes among people earning different incomes from the ranks of the poor or nonpoor. Studies showing no class difference in sentence outcomes thus find only that minor variations in the extent of poverty do not affect such outcomes, hardly a surprising conclusion.

If this reasoning makes sense, the key disparity in legal treatment must then lie between the poor and near-poor on the one hand and the middle and upper classes on the other. Although the latter group commits relatively few street crimes, when they do their ability to afford legal advantages puts them in a much stronger position legally than the poor and nonpoor. The O. J. Simpson trial in 1994 and 1995 provided a telling example of this basic fact. His legal defense was estimated to cost $50,000 per week. If a poor, unemployed, and unknown defendant had been accused of murdering two people by slashing their throats, he would have been represented by a single, overworked public defender and wouldn't have had the financial access to the experts and expertise that Simpson and his attorneys enjoyed (Barkan 1996).

It's also possible that whether social class affects legal processing depends on how class is measured. We saw in Chapter 3 that social class may be more related to criminality when the measurement of class incorporates William J. Wilson's "underclass" concept than when it involves only status attainment (Farnworth et al. 1994). The same contrast might apply to criminal justice processing. When class is measured following Wilson's concept, it does appear to affect sentences and other legal sanctions, as members of the underclass are treated more punitively than other offenders (Hagan 1989).

If the middle and upper classes commit relatively little street crime, they also commit the majority of white-collar crime, including corporate crime. As we'll see in Chapter 12, despite much evidence that white-collar crime is more harmful than street crime, its legal punishment is usually far more lenient. Some harmful corporate practices are not banned by law and thus not considered criminal. The disparity between the legal treatment of street crime and of white-collar crime provides perhaps the clearest and strongest empirical support for radical criminology (Reiman 1998).

EVALUATION OF RADICAL CRIMINOLOGY

In sum, radical criminology has been harshly attacked and just as staunchly defended. While some early radical views of crime presented an instrumental Marxist view that even other Marxists find too simplistic, more recent formulations present a richer understanding of crime and law formulation under capitalism. Marxist historical work on the development of the police, prisons, and other mechanisms of legal control has been especially useful (Harring 1993). While not usually grounded in Marxism, the studies of inequality and crime discussed in Chapter 6 nonetheless empirically support the basic thrust of radical criminology. Growing evidence of disparity in the legal treatment of street and white-collar crime also supports radical views. However, radical theory has been less successful in presenting a "radical" explanation of street crime that differs substantially from the structural explanations discussed in Chapter 6 (Akers 1997). Like conflict theory, radical theory's view on the origins of laws and operation of the criminal justice system seems less relevant for street crime than for public order offenses and political criminality.

The debate between radical criminologists and their critics has cooled somewhat since the 1970s, but sharp differences of opinion remain. Although one critic concluded in 1979 that radical criminology's "capacity for contribution is exhausted" because of its "theoretical and empirical poverty" (Klockars 1979:478–479), a radical criminologist observed in 1993 that "Marxist criminology is healthier than it has ever been" (Greenberg 1993:21). No doubt radical and traditional criminologists will continue to dispute the validity of radical criminology.

LEFT REALISM CRIMINOLOGY AND PEACEMAKING CRIMINOLOGY

We've seen that traditional criminologists criticized early instrumental Marxist approaches for dismissing the seriousness of street crime. In the 1970s and 1980s, feminist criminologists also took instrumental Marxism to task for neglecting rape and family violence. The advent of the Reagan administration in the 1980s led the United States to regard street crime even more punitively than before. The increasing prominence of victimization surveys in the 1980s in the United States, Canada, and elsewhere made it clear that street crime especially affects the poor and people of color, and that fear of crime was a social fact that could not be ignored.

All these developments led some British criminologists in the 1980s to discuss a new radical approach to crime termed *left realist criminology*, or *left realism* (Lea and Young 1984; Young 1986). This approach was a response to the *left idealism* of instrumental Marxists who viewed street crime as political rebellion and an appropriate result of the hostility and alienation caused by capitalism. The left realists instead insisted that crime causes real distress, not only for the poor and people of color but also for women victimized by rape and family violence. As a key left realist, Jock Young (1992:36), puts it, "Crime, like illness, is a universal problem. It affects men and women of all classes, ages, and races ... [but] affects particular parts of the population to a greater extent than it does others."

Given this reality, left realists say that crime prevention and control are essential. They champion measures similar to those advanced by liberal observers, including improving the socioeconomic conditions underlying crime, community policing, victim compensation, and using imprisonment only for criminals posing a real threat to society. However, some left realists also call for increased police surveillance and more punitive treatment of criminals (Matthews and Young 1992).

Left realism has proved controversial. Some radical criminologists criticize it for being too willing "to inflict punishment as a tool of social justice" and for deflecting blame for crime away from the capitalist system (Menzies 1992:143). Feminist critics also fault it for being blind to gender and for ignoring violence against women (DeKeseredy 1991; Walklate 1992).

Another recent development in radical criminology is *peacemaking criminology*, which combines Gandhiism, Marxism, Buddhism, and other humanistic strains of thought (Pepinsky and Quinney 1991). Peacemaking criminology views crime as just one of the many forms of suffering that characterize human existence. To reduce such suffering, people must find inner peace and develop nonviolent ways of resolving conflict. Since war and crime are similar in many ways and have similar roots, efforts to eliminate both problems must go hand in hand. These efforts must involve a fundamental transformation of our social institutions so that they no longer cause suffering and oppression.

The criminal justice system is a special focus of peacemaking criminology. If crime ultimately stems from the authoritarian, violent nature of society, say peacemaking criminologists, the criminal justice system can do little to reduce crime, since it, too, is both authoritarian and violent. With this view in mind, peacemaking criminologists advocate using alternative types of punishment, such as restitution, community service, and the like.

 ## FEMINIST THEORIES

As we've seen in previous chapters, theories of crime developed before the 1970s were essentially theories of male crime, as scholars either ignored girls and women altogether or else discussed them in stereotypical ways. This combination of neglect and ignorance impoverished criminological theory: "Theories are weak if they do not apply to half of the potential criminal population.... Whether or not a particular theory helps us understand women's crime better is of fundamental, not marginal, importance for criminology" (Gelsthorpe and Morris 1988:103). Thus one of the most exciting developments in criminology is the growth of feminist theory and research on crime and justice that focuses directly on women and girls.

Feminist Perspectives in Criminology

Several feminist perspectives on crime exist: liberal, Marxist, radical, socialist, and women of color (Simpson 1989). All these perspectives emphasize women's subordinate status but differ in their explanations for that status, the solutions they offer to improve it, and the extent to which they consider class and/or race as other dimensions of women's subordination.

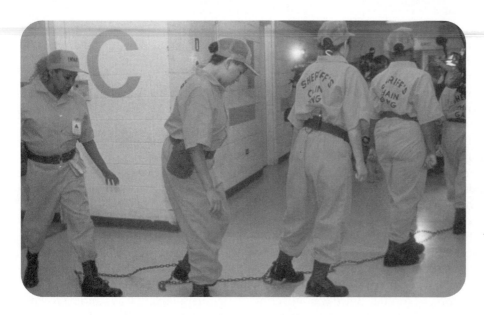

◀ *Feminist perspectives emphasize the importance of gender for understanding criminal behavior, victimization, and legal processing.*

LIBERAL FEMINISM

Liberal feminism traces women's inequality to gender role socialization and the resulting lack of opportunity and discrimination women suffer. Given this emphasis, liberal feminism attributes the gender difference in crime rates to the different ways in which women and men are socialized (Hoffman-Bustamante 1973). A liberal feminist framework led some scholars twenty years ago to argue that greater opportunities in the workplace and changing socialization patterns were causing higher female crime rates in the 1960s and 1970s (Adler 1975; Simon 1975). As Chapter 3 discussed, however, a substantial body of research later disputed this notion.

MARXIST FEMINISM

Marxist feminism sees women's subordination resulting from the capitalist mode of production. In this view, the rise of industrial capitalism led to the development of patriarchy, or the dominance of men over women because production moved from the home to the factory. The predominance of men in factory work forced women to depend on men for economic support. Women's homemaking and childrearing responsibilities allowed their husbands to work outside the home and helped prepare their children to become future workers. Women thus became valued primarily for their contributions to the "reproduction of labor power" necessary for capitalism and were considered little more than the property of men. Today, when women do work outside the home, their jobs are typically low-paying. Their poverty leads "some women to commit crime in order to survive in capitalist society" (Balkan, Berger, and Schmidt 1980:211). The subordinate position of women under capitalism also increases the rape and other violence they suffer (Schwendinger and Schwendinger 1983).

RADICAL FEMINISM

Radical feminism argues that patriarchy precedes capitalism, and that gender relations are more important than class relations. A major reason for patriarchy is biology: Women are smaller and physically weaker than men and must depend on them for help during their childbearing years. Patriarchy thus exists even in pre-capitalist societies. Men try to control women in many ways but especially try to control their sexuality. Instead of viewing rape, battering, incest, and other violence against women as a byproduct of capitalism, then, radical feminists see such violence as a primary means by which men in all societies maintain and extend their dominance over women (Brownmiller 1975; Dworkin 1989; MacKinnon 1982).

SOCIALIST FEMINISM

Socialist feminism combines Marxist and radical perspectives in seeing class and gender, or capitalism and patriarchy, as equally important (Eisenstein 1979; Messerschmidt 1986). The interaction of class and gender relations affects the legitimate and illegitimate opportunities available to people. The class-gender interaction also influences the development of crime and the operation of the criminal justice system. The crimes upper-class men commit, for example, are very different from the ones lower-class women commit. By the same token, we can't understand women's criminality unless we also understand that most women criminals are poor.

WOMEN-OF-COLOR FEMINISM

If socialist feminism highlights the gender-class intersection, a women-of-color perspective stresses the importance of considering race along with gender and class (Simpson 1989). Feminism and the women's movement have often been chided for being oriented toward white middle-class women (Hurtado 1989). Women of color experience subordination not only because of their gender but also because of their race and class. Thus, while it's true that women's crime rates are lower than men's, it's also true that black women's crime rates are higher than white women's (Simpson 1991). As we saw in Chapter 4, black women also have higher victimization rates than white women. Crime by, and victimization of, women of color can thus be understood only if we consider the intersection of gender, race, and class (Simpson and Elis 1995). This intersection is also important for understanding the treatment of women in the criminal justice system and the impact of legal processing on their future criminality (Covington 1986; Myers 1995). Work on the gender-race-class intersection is one of the most important developments in contemporary criminology.

The Scope of Feminist Theory and Research

GENDER, VICTIMIZATION, AND CRIMINOLOGICAL THEORY

The first feminist work on crime in the 1970s focused mostly on the victimization of women by rape and family violence, which previously had received little attention, and feminist research on these and other crimes against women continues (see Chapter 10). Feminists also began in the 1970s to critique criminological theory, and subsequent work has helped us to understand the "gendering" of crime and criminal justice. Much of this work has attempted to explain variation in female criminality. Some scholars have investigated whether the dominant (male) theories of crime apply to females as well; this is the "generalizability" issue in the study of gender and crime (Daly and Chesney-Lind 1988). As we saw in previous chapters, several theories, including strain, learning, and control theories, do help explain variation in female offending and so may indeed be generalizable to women.

Even if this is so, however, none of the dominant theories readily accounts for the fact that women still commit much less crime than men. As noted in Chapter 6, for example, women are much more economically deprived than men. As a result, anomie theory would predict that women should feel more strain than men and thus commit more crime. The same prediction would follow from radical theories of crime and other explanations emphasizing the alienation and hostility resulting from economic deprivation. These predictions notwithstanding, women's criminality is much lower than men's. Although some scholars explain this apparent paradox by saying that women have lower economic aspirations than men (Leonard 1982), others dismiss it as a stereotype (Allison 1987). As this discussion suggests, feminists have been very interested in understanding why girls and women commit so much less crime than boys and men. This is called the "gender ratio" issue in criminology (Daly and Chesney-Lind 1988).

GENDER AND LEGAL PROCESSING

Still other feminist work addresses the impact of gender on arrest and punishment. Three hypotheses on this impact have been developed. The "chivalry" hypothesis predicts that girls and women should be treated more leniently than boys and men. The "evil woman" hypothesis predicts the opposite relationship: Since female criminality is so rare, a woman committing crime looks that much more terrible by comparison. Conflict and labeling theories would also expect more punitive treatment of women given their subordinate status to men (Corley, Cenkovich, and Giordano 1989). A third, "equal treatment" hypothesis predicts that gender should not affect legal processing (see Chapters 15 and 16).

For now it seems fair to say that the empirical evidence is very inconsistent (Daly 1994). Although all three hypotheses receive support, over the years the chivalry hypothesis has received perhaps the most support (Daly 1987). However, studies using pre-1980s data find more chivalrous treatment than studies using more recent data. The most recent and best-designed studies find women treated somewhat more punitively for minor crimes and men somewhat more punitively for serious crimes, but conclude that the effect of gender is weak compared to the effects of legally relevant variables such as prior criminal record and offense severity (Steffensmeier, Kramer, and Streifel 1993). Some evidence exists that any chivalry shown toward women is actually directed toward white women, not black women (Spohn, Gruhl, and Welch 1987). To the extent this is true, it highlights the importance of considering the racial context of gendered justice (Mann 1995). Other documentation indicates that chivalrous treatment of women, to the extent it exists, stems to a large degree from the caretaking of children and other family responsibilities (Daly 1994).

Turning to juvenile justice, many studies find girls treated more punitively than boys for status offenses like truancy, running away from home, and sexual promiscuity, reflecting a traditional sexual double standard (Chesney-Lind 1997). Some studies, however, find gender playing little or no role in juvenile justice processing (Corley, Cenkovich, and Giordano 1989).

Developments in Feminist Criminology

GIRLS' LIVES AND DELINQUENCY

In addition to the work just discussed, several other feminist lines of theorizing and research offer great promise for our understanding of crime and justice. In one area, scholars are devoting increasing attention to the patriarchal aspects of girls' lives that make delinquency and crime more or less likely (Baskin and Sommers 1993). Many studies find that sex-role socialization has changed little since a generation ago. Relative to boys, parents and teachers still encourage girls to be more passive, less independent and competitive, and more interested in the welfare of others. For better or worse, parents continue to monitor their daughters' behavior more than their sons'. As we saw in Chapter 3, these aspects of girls' lives are widely thought to reduce their potential for delinquency (Chesney-Lind 1995).

However, a growing body of research identifies another facet of girls' lives that greatly increases their delinquency: sexual abuse. Although both girls and boys suffer physical abuse, girls are much more likely than boys to be sexually abused (see Chapter 10). Sexual abuse in turn is a prime reason girls run away from home, use drugs, and engage in prostitution. As Chesney-Lind (1995:83) observes, "Many young women, then, are running away from profound sexual victimization at home, and once on the streets they are forced further into crime to survive." The offenses prompted by abuse also differ for the two sexes: While females tend to commit minor property and public order offenses (drugs, prostitution), males tend to commit violence. The heavier involvement of abused girls than abused boys in prostitution reflects patriarchal values defining girls as sexual objects (Chesney-Lind 1995).

MASCULINITY AND CRIME

A second area of research addresses the issue of masculinity and crime. This area complements the new work on the patriarchal aspects of girls' lives inhibiting delinquency: If low criminality is one of the benefits of women's subordination, high criminality is one of the costs of men's domination. As Chapter 3 noted, the crime problem that so concerns us is really the *male* crime problem: If our national crime rates were no higher than women's crime rates, crime would concern us much less. Recognizing this fact, some scholars consider *maleness* and *masculinity* criminogenic conditions. To reduce crime, they argue, male socialization and notions of masculinity must be changed and male dominance reduced (Messerschmidt 1997; Miedzian 1991; Newburn and Stanko 1994). This argument applies not only to rape, family violence, and other crimes that especially target women but also to other crimes and perhaps even to white-collar crime (Levi 1994). Masculinity brings with it attitudes, values, and behavior that underlie a wide range of criminal activities.

As I observed in Chapter 3, we are already doing a good job of raising girls not to become criminals. This is true even if we acknowledge the higher crime rates of poor women of color. Admittedly, some might regard women's low criminality merely as an unintended "silver lining" of their subordinate status, lack of freedom and opportunity, and socialization into feminine values. If so, their low criminality might not be something to praise. But neither is it something to overlook, for it might offer some insight into how we can lower men's criminality.

In this regard, Ngaire Naffine (1987) argues that the nurturing values produced by female socialization should be welcomed as important, positive traits, not as evidence of weakness, passivity, and dependency. Reflecting this view, feminist criminologists Kathleen Daly and Meda Chesney-Lind (1988:527) say they see "some cause for hope" in the gender difference in crime:

> Of whatever age, race, or class and of whatever nation, men are more likely to be involved in crime, and in its most serious forms.... A large price is paid for structures of male domination and for the very qualities that drive men to be successful, to control others, and to wield uncompromising power.... Gender differences in crime suggest that crime may not be so normal after all. Such differences challenge us to see that in the lives of women, men have a great deal more to learn.

One thing men can learn from women, says writer Irene Sege, is that girls' play activities help develop anticrime attitudes. Sege (1994:74) thus recommends that boys replace toy guns with dolls to develop these attitudes themselves: "Playing house teaches important lessons about cooperation and nurturing and responsibility and relationships." It's thus important, she says, that boys learn these lessons as well as girls.

The mass media, elected officials, and criminal justice professionals have ignored the essential link between masculinity and crime. They say little about the need to change masculinity and lessen male dominance if we want to be serious about reducing crime. The new work on masculinity and crime suggests an important but neglected avenue for public policy on the crime problem.

POWER-CONTROL THEORY

A third area of research focuses on the gendered processes of family life that increase or decrease delinquency. The major perspective here is the power-control theory of John Hagan and his associates, which remains one of the few to include both gender and class in explaining delinquency (Hagan, Simpson, and Gillis 1987). Hagan and associates distinguish between *patriarchal* and *egalitarian* households. In patriarchal households, the father works outside the home and the mother stays at home to take care of the children. The mother thus plays a far greater role than the father in children's socialization. Reflecting her own situation, she controls her daughters' behavior much more than her sons' behavior. The daughters' greater passivity and greater supervision lead them to be less delinquent than their brothers.

In egalitarian households, both father and mother work outside the home in positions of authority. As a result, both sons and daughters receive less maternal supervision and, given their mothers' work-place autonomy, are encouraged to be more independent. Mothers thus treat their daughters more like their sons, increasing their daughters' potential for delinquency. The same process holds true for female-headed households. Because daughters in either egalitarian or female-headed households are thus more delinquent, the gender difference in delinquency in these households will be smaller than in patriarchal households where daughters are much more controlled. Since Hagan and associates view working-class families as more patriarchal and middle-class families as more egalitarian, they expect smaller gender differences in delinquency in middle-class families than in their working-class counterparts. Interestingly, they also predict greater delinquency in middle-class families because of the less control these largely egalitarian households exert over their children.

Tests of power-control theory find mixed results (Morash and Lind 1991; O'Brien 1991). Supporting the theory, they generally discover working-class, patriarchal families control their children more than middle-class, egalitarian families. However, contrary to the theory, they often don't find working-class, patriarchal families exhibiting greater gender differences in delinquency, nor higher delinquency rates in middle-class families. Research also indicates that fathers play a greater role in their children's socialization than power-control theory assumes.

In other areas, critics fault the theory for ignoring the criminogenic effects of harsh punishment and negative school experiences (see Chapter 7), for neglecting the racial context of delinquency, and for assuming that mother's employment leads to greater delinquency (Chesney-Lind 1992; Jensen 1993). They say this assumption smacks of the backlash to feminism underlying earlier arguments blaming increased female criminality on the women's movement (see Chapter 3). There's also little evidence linking maternal employment to increased delinquency (Loeber and Stouthamer-Loeber 1986). In a recent article, Hagan and associates (McCarthy, Hagan, and Woodward 1999) conceded some of this criticism and revised their theory to argue that maternal employment decreases male delinquency by exposing sons to less patriarchal attitudes.

A Final Word on Feminism

Feminist work in criminology represents one of the most important advances in the field. Although some scholars question whether it has much to offer for the understanding of crime and criminal justice (Akers 1997), others note that feminist criminology is "still in its infancy" and that it "will undoubtedly play a major role in mapping the future direction of the discipline" (Curran and Renzetti 1994:277). Despite their potential, feminist perspectives have been slow to make their way into criminology and criminal justice curriculums and textbooks (Goodstein 1992; Renzetti 1993; Wright 1992). Without full consideration of gender and its intersection with race and class, the study of crime and criminal justice will remain incomplete.

 ## Summary and Conclusion

We're now leaving the world of theory but will visit it again during the next several chapters on types of criminal behavior, where we'll see that the theories differ in their applicability. I stressed at the beginning of our four-chapter excursion into theory that we must understand the reasons for crime in order to reduce it. The theories we've reviewed in these chapters suggest several avenues for reducing crime. Let's briefly review the theories' implications for crime prevention and crime control.

Biological theories suggest the need to change the biological factors involved in criminality. That, of course, is very difficult and fraught with ethical and political problems. A "softer" biological view is that social factors such as poverty and stress trigger biological predispositions toward crime, for example, those arising from birth complications. It might be possible to change these social factors, many of which are featured in sociological theories of crime.

Psychological explanations focusing on personality do hold some promise for reducing crime, especially if temperament problems are attributable to social factors rather than to genetic or other biological factors. If we can do something about the social factors—poverty, inadequate childrearing, and the like—underlying temperament problems, then we might be able to reduce crime.

Structural theories in sociology point to several conditions underlying many types of crime: economic deprivation and inequality, overcrowding and dilapidated housing, and other aspects of what is sometimes called social disorganization. The physical and economic problems of urban living interact to produce especially high street criminality. While it might not be possible to reduce the emphasis on the American Dream that leads people from many walks of life to commit crime, it might be possible to address the other structural conditions producing street crime. In this regard, if we could indeed reduce poverty and inequality and the neighborhood conditions associated with these problems, we might be able to reduce street crime significantly.

Social process theories highlight the importance of proper parenting, harmonious family relationships, associations with conventional peers, and positive school experiences for reducing the potential for delinquency and later criminality. Public policy efforts designed to address family and school problems thus hold great potential for crime reduction.

In this chapter we discussed critical perspectives on crime and criminal justice. Although these theories' focus on the social reaction to crime represents their most distinctive contribution to criminology, they also have something to say about why crime occurs.

Labeling theory contends that extralegal factors affect legal processing and that legal processing creates increased deviance by inducing deviant self-images and reducing conventional opportunities. The inconsistent empirical evidence for the theory leads many scholars to urge the theory's abandonment. However, recent revisions of labeling theory point to its continued potential for helping us understand deviance, crime, and criminal justice. To the extent that legal processing may sometimes have effects opposite to those we intend, we must be careful that attempts to control juvenile and adult offenders through the law don't increase the likelihood of future offending.

Conflict and radical theories attribute several types of crime and criminal laws to the self-interest of powerful groups in society. As with labeling theory, the empirical evidence for conflict and radical theories is inconsistent. While some scholars thus dismiss the theories, other scholars continue to find them valuable. Conflict and radical theories echo certain structural theories in calling attention to the criminogenic effects of social inequality. Radical theories, of course, suggest the need to eliminate capitalism if we want to reduce crime significantly. Although that's not about to happen, their view underscores the reductions in crime that would occur if social inequality were diminished, even if capitalism itself remained.

Feminist work on crime, delinquency, and justice alerts us to the inadequacy of a criminology that ignores women or discusses them stereotypically. Feminist work stresses that certain features of a patriarchal society help account for both women's criminality and victimization, and highlights the criminogenic effects of masculinity and the price women, men, and society pay for male dominance. In this regard, one of the most effective things we could do to reduce street crime and women's victimization would be to reduce male dominance and to change male socialization and notions of masculinity. Such change, of course, will not come soon and might even be impossible to achieve to any significant degree. However, as feminists are increasingly stressing, masculinity and male dominance can no longer be ignored as major causes of street crime and victimization.

We now turn to several types of criminal behavior, beginning with interpersonal violence. Here we'll see the influence of masculinity and male domination, inequality, and several of the other factors discussed by the theories of crime and delinquency we've reviewed.

KEY TERMS

bourgeoisie	left realism
conflict	Marxism
consensus	peacemaking criminology
criminalization	primary deviation
critical perspectives	proletariat
culture conflict	relativist definition
deviance amplification	ruling class
dramatization of evil	secondary deviation
feminism	shaming
labeling	

STUDY QUESTIONS

1. How does Chambliss's Saints and Roughnecks study provide support for labeling theory?
2. To what extent does labeling have negative consequences for the people who are labeled?
3. How would Bonger explain why the United States has a higher crime rate than Japan?
4. According to recent research on girls' lives and delinquency, what are factors that both inhibit and promote the chances of girls becoming delinquent?

INTERNET EXERCISES

The American Society of Criminology (ASC), a national professional association of criminologists, includes several divisions whose members would probably be quite sympathetic to many of the perspectives discussed in this chapter. To access the ASC's Web site, go to **http://www.asc41.com/**. Scroll down until you see the heading **Divisions**. Under this heading are the ASC's divisions, including those on Critical Criminology, People of Color & Crime, and Women & Crime.

Click on the names of each of these divisions to access their Web sites. Although their sites differ in the amount of information they provide, you should be able to get some idea of the divisions' organizational structure and activities and perhaps the general perspectives of their members. Why do you think the criminologists who founded these divisions felt they needed to be established? What functions should these divisions serve within a national professional organization like the ASC that generally favors "mainstream" criminology rather than the "critical perspectives" discussed in this chapter?

VIOLENT CRIME:
HOMICIDE, ASSAULT,
AND ROBBERY

Crime in the News

It was Christmas in Boston, 1999. Throughout the city, people opened presents and spent time with friends and family. But in one home there was no joy. Here a middle-aged woman, Enzie Bonner, hung her daughter Caryn's favorite ornament on the Christmas tree. Caryn was not there to see it. She had died at the age of 35 earlier that year from multiple stab wounds in her apartment. No one has ever been arrested for her murder. Her mother took little solace from the fact that the number of homicides in 1999 fell in Boston and across the nation, continuing their almost decade-long decline. "There's no celebrating this year, just pain and remembering," she said. "No number could make me feel good."

A few days later, a hotel worker in Tampa, Florida allegedly went on a shooting rampage in a hotel near the airport that was crowded with visitors attending a New Year's Day football bowl game. Firing shots in the lobby and pool area, he killed four coworkers and critically wounded several other people. He then ran to a parking lot and tried to steal a woman's car. When she resisted, he killed her. A witness said, "I came here from New York City to escape the craziness there and wound up in one of the most insane situations I've been in."

Sources: Green 1999:A3; Latour 2000:B7.

*P*eople fear senseless, violent crime more than any other crime. It is the stuff of TV movies and the type of crime the news media favor. It's the reason we lock our doors at night, buy firearms for protection, and build more prisons. Violent crime by strangers makes us afraid and drives public policy.

Much violence occurs between strangers, but much also occurs between acquaintances, friends, and even loved ones. Women and children are especially likely to be victims of nonstranger violence such as rape and other forms of sexual and physical abuse. To emphasize this point, and to underline the seriousness of the crimes suffered, two chapters are devoted to violent crime: Chapter 9 features homicide, assault, and robbery, while Chapter 10 discusses rape, battering, and related crimes against women and children. Continuing my earlier emphasis, the discussion in both chapters highlights the criminogenic effects of inequality and masculinity.

Both chapters focus on *interpersonal* violence, defined as the "threat, attempt, or actual use of physical force by one or more persons that results in physical or nonphysical harm to one or more other persons" (Weiner, Zahn, and Sagi 1990:xiii). "Nonphysical harm" here refers to fear, anxiety, and other emotional states. Thus an armed robbery involving no physical injury would still be considered an act of interpersonal violence because it scares the victim. This definition isn't perfect, of course, as it would apply, for example, to a physician who pulls a dislocated shoulder back into place or to a dentist who extracts a tooth. A better definition might include some mention of whether the person who is hurt is willing to be hurt. But it does convey what is commonly understood to be interpersonal violence, and it certainly covers the crimes featured in this chapter.

The adjective *interpersonal* rules out such things as pollution, unsafe products, and dangerous workplaces, which kill and harm many thousands of people each year. These practices are often called *corporate violence*, because corporations commit them, yet don't involve interpersonal physical force. Another type of violence involving such acts as terrorism, sabotage, and genocide is often called *political violence*. Although most political violence is interpersonal, its special nature places it under the broader category of political crime. Later chapters discuss corporate and political violence.

 ## HOMICIDE AND ASSAULT

The subject of countless mystery novels, TV shows, and films, homicide captures the attention of the public, news media, and criminologists more than any other crime. Partly because of the presence of a corpse, homicides are also far more likely than other crimes to become known to the police. Hence, we have more information about and a greater understanding of homicide than of any other crime.

Defining Homicide and Assault

The FBI's list of Index crimes included in its Uniform Crime Reports (UCR) begins with murder and nonnegligent manslaughter. This category refers to the willful killing of one human being by another and excludes deaths caused by gross negligence, suicide, and justifiable homicide. Justifiable homicide refers to the killing of armed and dangerous felons by police or private citizens.

The criminal law divides murder and nonnegligent manslaughter into four subcategories: (1) first-degree murder, (2) second-degree murder, (3) voluntary manslaughter, and (4) involuntary manslaughter. The placing of a killing into one of these subcategories depends on the offender's intent and the amount and nature of physical force that causes someone to die. Traditionally, first-degree murders were ones committed with "malice aforethought," meaning that the offender planned to kill someone and then did. The popular term for this category, *premeditated murder*, has been extended in the last few decades to include *felony murders*, in which the commission of a felony such as rape, robbery, or arson causes someone's death. Thus if you set fire to a building and someone inside dies even though you didn't intend that to happen, you may be charged with felony murder and hence first-degree murder. Second-degree murders refer to deaths where an offender intended to do serious bodily harm short of killing the victim, but the victim died anyway. Deaths resulting from a "depraved heart" or extremely reckless conduct can also lead to second-degree murder charges.

Manslaughter refers to killings considered less serious or less blameworthy but still not justifiable. Voluntary manslaughter alludes to killings committed out of intense emotion such as anger or fear. Involuntary manslaughter refers to killings committed because offenders have acted recklessly, as when a parent shakes a crying infant and accidentally kills the baby. Traffic fatalities comprise most involuntary manslaughter cases.

In practice, these four subcategories of murder and nonnegligent manslaughter overlap, and it's often difficult to know which one best describes a particular killing. Prosecutors thus have great latitude in deciding which charge to bring against a murder defendant. Their decision depends heavily on whether the evidence will indicate beyond a reasonable doubt the intent, amount, and nature of physical force required for a particular charge. Sometimes other factors such as the race of the offender and the victim also influence, however unwittingly, the prosecutor's decision (see Chapter 16).

The Uniform Crime Reports define *aggravated assault* as "an unlawful attack by one person upon another for the purpose of inflicting severe or aggravated bodily injury." Aggravated assault involves the use of a weapon or other "means likely to produce death or great bodily harm." *Simple assaults* are assaults "where no weapon is used and which do not result in serious or aggravated injury to the victim." Only aggravated assaults are included in the FBI's Index crimes, while both types of assault are included in the National Crime Victimization Survey (NCVS).

The major difference between homicide and aggravated assault is whether the victim dies. Because of the greater reliability of homicide data, most of our discussion focuses on homicide but still pertains to aggravated assault. We'll rely heavily on the UCR for our understanding of homicide, since victimization surveys are obviously irrelevant for this type of crime.

The Patterning and Social Dynamics of Homicide

RACE AND GENDER OF OFFENDERS AND VICTIMS

The race and gender makeup of homicide offenders and victims is very instructive. As you can see in Table 9.1 (on page 240), about half of offenders and victims are black, even though African-Americans comprise only about 12 percent of the U.S. population. As these data suggest, homicide is an *intraracial* crime:

TABLE 9.1

Race and Sex of Murder Offenders and Victims, 1998 (%)

Variable	Offenders	Victims
Race		
White	49	50
Black	49	48
Other	2	2
Sex		
Male	89	76
Female	11	24

Source: Federal Bureau of Investigation 1999.

For single offender-single victim homicides, 94 percent of black murder victims in 1998 were murdered by black offenders, and 87 percent of white murder victims were murdered by white offenders (Federal Bureau of Investigation 1999).

Turning to gender in Table 9.1, men are much more likely than women to both murder and be murdered. As these data suggest, homicide is a "distinctively masculine matter" (Polk 1994:5). Males also commit 90 percent of all murders of female victims. Conversely, females commit only 10–12 percent of all murders of male victims. When women do murder men, the majority kill a current or former husband/boyfriend who had been battering them (Browne 1987). That said, women are still much more likely than men to be murdered by a current or former spouse/partner: In 1998, 32 percent of all female murder victims were killed by male intimates, while only 4 percent of male victims were killed by female intimates. Other nations have a similar, or even larger, gender difference in murder victimization by spouses and partners (Wilson and Daly 1992).

GEOGRAPHIC PATTERNS

As with much other crime, homicide is also patterned geographically. In U. S. metropolitan areas, the homicide rate is 7 per 100,000 residents and 16–18 per 100,000 in some of the largest cities. In rural counties, the rate is only 5 per 100,000 (Federal Bureau of Investigation 1999).

Looking at different regions of the United States, homicide rates are highest in the South (8 per 100,000) and lowest in the Northeast (4 per 100,000), with the Midwest and West in between, with each at 6 per 100,000. Many studies try to explain the South's historically higher rate. Although some scholars say the South has a regional subculture of violence in which disputes that might fade away in other regions become deadly there (Huff-Corzine 1986), other scholars doubt whether such a subculture exists and instead attribute the South's rate to its high level of economic deprivation and inequality (Parker 1989).

Still other researchers question whether the South really does have the highest homicide rate once other factors are taken into account. Some studies find that the existence of regional differences in homicide rates depends on the type of homicide—for example, whether the homicide involves strangers, acquaintances, or family members (Williams and Flewelling 1988). Other research suggests that the issue of regional differences depends on the regions' racial composition. In one study, the West's homicide rate was higher than the South's once regional differences in racial composition were statistically controlled (O'Carroll and Mercy 1989), while in another study the South had a higher homicide rate only for non-Hispanic whites (Nelsen, Corzine, and Huff-Corzine 1994).

Homicide is also patterned geographically across nations. In this regard, the United States has the highest homicide rate, and the highest rate of serious violent crime more generally, of all Western industrial nations (Mayhew and Dijk 1997; Zimring and Hawkins 1997). Its homicide rate has averaged between 6 and 10 per 100,000 during the last three decades, compared to a rate between 1 and 3 per 100,000 in other nations. Here it is useful to compare the homicide rates of U.S. cities with those of other cities of similar size. For example, New York City has 5–6 times as many homicides as London, another city with a huge population. It's interesting to note that the difference between the United States and other nations is much larger for homicide than it is for other types of serious violence (Zimring and Hawkins 1997). We'll return to this issue later.

THE VICTIM-OFFENDER RELATIONSHIP

According to the UCR, 51 percent of all 1998 homicides involved people who knew each other, including 14 percent who were related to their murderers. Another 13 percent were killed by strangers. The relationship between victim and offender was unknown for the remaining 36 percent of homicides (Federal Bureau of Investigation 1999).

An interesting dispute concerns these "unknown" cases. Many scholars believe they primarily involve strangers (Maxfield 1989). However, Scott H. Decker (1993) observes that police often report homicides to the FBI before they're able to make an arrest. In such "unsolved" homicides, the victim-offender relationship is initially recorded as unknown. When arrests are made later, supplemental information, including the victim-offender relationship, is then added to the local police station's case files but often not sent to the FBI and hence not reported by the UCR. The "unknown" category in UCR homicide data is thus artificially high because this information is missing. Tapping into police station files may thus clarify the victim-offender relationship.

Decker and his research assistants did precisely this in a study of all 792 St. Louis homicides reported from 1985 to 1989. Examining original case file and supplemental report information, they determined that the victim-offender relationship was unknown in only 4 percent of the homicides. The total number of homicides included the following relationships: acquaintances, 46 percent; friends, 12 percent; romantic relationships, 12 percent; other relatives, 8 percent; and strangers, 18 percent. Thus more than three fourths of the St. Louis homicides involved people who knew each other, and only about one fifth involved strangers. Decker concluded that the UCR's unknown homicides could be "distributed in a fashion similar to that for most homicides" (Decker 1993:597) and that national victim-offender relationships would then closely resemble those for St. Louis.

Supporting Decker's speculation, a government examination of more than 8,000 murder cases in the nation's 75 largest urban counties in 1988 found that 16 percent involved family members, 64 percent friends or acquaintances, and only 20 percent strangers (Dawson and Langan 1994). Thus four-fifths of murder victims are killed by someone they know, and only one-fifth by a stranger.

TABLE 9.2

MURDER AND TYPE OF WEAPON USED, 1998

WEAPON	PERCENT
Firearms	65
Handguns	52
Shotguns	4
Rifles	4
Other	4
Knives/Cutting Instruments	13
Blunt Objects	5
Personal (Hands, etc.)	7
Other or Unknown	10

Source: Federal Bureau of Investigation 1999.

TYPE OF WEAPON

Another important fact about homicides is the type of weapon used (Table 9.2). In 1998 firearms accounted for more than two-thirds of all homicides, with handguns accounting for 52 percent. We'll return to the issue of handguns and homicides later in this chapter.

CIRCUMSTANCES LEADING TO HOMICIDES

We've seen that most homicides involve the use of handguns and other firearms among people who know each other. With this profile in mind, it's not surprising that the typical murder is a relatively spontaneous event arising from an argument that gets out of hand and escalates into lethal violence, usually involving a handgun. Early research by Marvin Wolfgang (1958) found that the victim precipitates about 25 percent of all homicides by starting the argument or being the first to use physical force. Depending how precipitation is defined, some studies find more than half of all homicides are victim-precipitated (Felson and Steadman 1983). In a typical scenario, the victim insults and angers the eventual offender. The offender responds in kind and may even use physical force. The victim reacts with another verbal or physical attack, and soon is killed. Many homicides are thus the "outcome of a dynamic interchange" between an offender and a victim (Luckenbill 1977:185). Often the offender and/or the victim have been drinking before their encounter, although the exact role alcohol plays in homicides and other violence remains unclear (Collins 1989).

Trends in U.S. Homicide Rates

According to the Uniform Crime Reports, 16,914 people were homicide victims in the United States in 1998. This figure represented a sharp decline in homicides during most of the 1990s. As Figure 9.1 shows, the U.S. homicide rate rose sharply in the 1960s before peaking in 1980. It then declined until 1985, when it again began rising, only to level off and then decline after the early 1990s. The rate by the late 1990s was as low as that in the late 1960s.

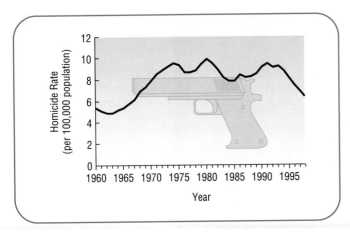

◀ FIGURE 9.1 **U.S. HOMICIDE TRENDS, 1960–1998**
(NUMBER OF HOMICIDES PER 100,000 POPULATION)

Source: Fox and Zawitz 1998; Federal Bureau of Investigation 1999.

The post-1985 homicide rise stemmed from an increase in homicides by young people (Blumstein 1995). During this time, the homicide rate declined for people over 30, remained stable for people 24 to 30, but increased among those under 24. As Figure 9.2 illustrates, this increase was especially great among young African-American males. Homicides *of* teenaged African-American males rose just as sharply during this time (Fox and Zawitz 1998).

This dramatic rise in homicides by and against young black males stemmed from several factors: (1) the growing sense of despair resulting from declining economic opportunities in urban areas during the 1980s; (2) increased drug trafficking in inner cities because of the declining economic opportunities; and (3) the increased possession and use of powerful handguns in urban areas, partly because of drug trafficking battles (Blumstein 1995; Sampson and Wilson 1995).

Together these factors fueled a dramatic rise in urban youth violence that was deadlier than in the past because of guns (Wright, Sheley, and Smith 1995). As David Satcher, director of the U.S. Centers for Disease Prevention and Control, said

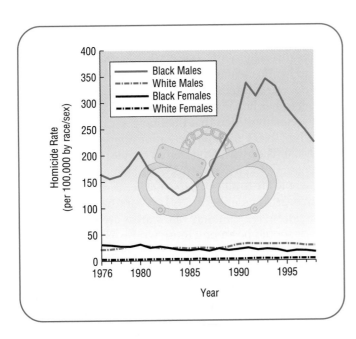

◀ FIGURE 9.2 **RATE OF HOMICIDE COMMITTED BY 18–24 YEAR OLDS**

Source: Fox and Zawitz 1998.

◄ *In 1956, Rosa Parks refused to move to the back of a bus in Montgomery, Alabama. Her action set off a boycott of the Montgomery Bus System by African-Americans and helped ignite the Southern civil rights movement. Almost forty years later, she was assaulted in Detroit by a young African-American male.*

in 1994, "When it comes to violence, in the past what may have led to fistfights now leads to gunfire." Noted criminologist Alfred Blumstein agreed, "We've got to get guns out of the hands of these kids—it's an epidemic. You have kids transforming bloody noses into shootings" (Associated Press 1994:23).

The rise in youth violence also prompted some controversial soul-searching in the African-American community about what is sometimes called "black-on-black" violence (Bruce, Roscigno, and McCall 1998; Shepard 1997). African-American politicians, entertainers, and civil rights leaders held a three-day conference in early 1994 to discuss such crime (Meddis and Cauchon 1994). "More young black people kill each other annually than the sum total of lynchings in our history," civil rights leader Jesse Jackson said shortly before the conference. "We've been conditioned to act against Klan terror, but we've not been conditioned to act against terror no matter what color." Jackson added, "I am rather convinced that the premier civil rights issue of this day's youth is violence in general and black-on-black crime in particular" (Rezendes 1993:1, 4).

Not too long after this conference, a 1994 assault in Detroit brought home the tragedy of violence in urban black neighborhoods. The victim was 81-year-old Rosa Parks, who was credited forty years earlier with starting the Southern civil rights movement by refusing to give up her bus seat in Montgomery, Alabama to a white man. Now living in Detroit, Parks was allegedly punched in the face and chest by a young black man who broke into her house and ran off with $53. According to one reporter, Detroit residents were "mortified that the living symbol of the civil rights movement was attacked by a black man in the nation's largest city with a black majority" (Lessenberry 1994:3). The head of the Detroit chapter of the National Association for the Advancement of Colored People (NAACP) lamented, "To have this woman who has given her whole life to all of us, to have her threatened by one of us is more than I think we can bear" (Lessenberry 1994:3). An African-American columnist similarly noted, "I'm not saying that only black areas are violent. But if Parks should be safe anywhere, it should be among those whose lives her courage so directly touched" (Reynolds 1994:11A).

If the homicide rate rose in the late 1980s and early 1990s, it fell sharply afterwards, as Figures 9.1 and 9.2 show, reflecting the general decline in crime during most of the last decade (see Chapter 3). Scholars attribute the drop in homicide and other crimes during the decade to various reasons, including a strong economy, fewer gang wars over drug trafficking, increased community crime-prevention efforts, more effective gun control, improved policing methods, higher imprisonment rates, and reduced numbers of people in the high-crime 15–25 age group (Fletcher 2000; Steffensmeier and Harer 1999). These reasons remain in dispute, and Chapters 15 and 16 discuss them further.

Explaining Homicide and Aggravated Assault

An adequate explanation of homicide and aggravated assault must answer the following questions arising from the central facts about these crimes: (1) Why is the United States more violent than most other industrial nations? (2) Within the United States, why are homicide and aggravated assault more common in urban areas than elsewhere? (3) Why do men commit almost all homicides and aggravated assaults? and (4) Why do African-Americans have high rates of homicide and aggravated assault, both as offenders and as victims? Sociological explanations are necessary to answer these questions.

WHY IS THE UNITED STATES MORE VIOLENT THAN OTHER INDUSTRIAL NATIONS?

Several studies find that homicide is higher in nations with greater economic inequality, measured as the difference between rich and poor (Avison and Loring 1986; Krahn, Hartnagel, and Gartrell 1986). Because the United States has more inequality than other industrial nations, this may be one reason for its higher violent crime rates (Currie 1985).

As I noted earlier, the difference between the United States and other industrial nations is greater for homicides than for other serious violence. According to Franklin E. Zimring (1997), a major reason for the especially high U.S. homicide rate is its high rate of handgun ownership: 29 percent of U.S. respondents report owning a handgun, compared to rates well under 10 percent for most European nations (Van Dijk, Mayhew, and Killias 1991). The much greater use of handguns by assailants in the United States than elsewhere increases the chance that their intended victims will die. What would have been an aggravated assault in another nation thus becomes a homicide in the United States.

A third reason for the high U.S. violence rate might be historical. Historian Richard Maxwell Brown (1990:4) observes, "Violence has accompanied virtually every stage and aspect of our national existence." He notes that the United States "was conceived and born in violence" (p. 5) by colonists rebelling against England. The Revolutionary experience, says Brown, helped legitimize the use of violence in the new nation in the decades to come: "[T]he meanest and most squalid sort of violence was ... put to the service of revolutionary ideals and objectives.... Thus, given sanctification by the Revolution, Americans have never been loath to employ the most unremitting violence in the interest of any cause deemed a good one" (p. 6).The freeing of slaves by the Civil War further legitimated the use of violence, Brown adds.

At other times, law-abiding citizens often took part in lynch mobs and vigilante actions to preserve law and order and to suppress undesirable individuals and groups. Vigilante justice was especially common during the frontier era in the United States, because of the lack of police and courts in the Wild West (Frantz 1979). This "frontier tradition" reinforced the idea that violence is an acceptable solution for interpersonal disputes.

Why Is Canada Less Violent Than the United States?

Because Canada is just to the north of the United States, its much lower violent crime rate is particularly illuminating. In many ways the two countries are very similar: They share roughly the same tastes in cars, music, and fast food, and they both have a long history of immigration and ethnic conflict. Despite its similarities to the United States, however, Canada remains, as one observer put it, "a remarkably peaceable kingdom planted next to one of the most murder-prone nations on earth" (Nickerson 1994:24). In 1998, for example, Canada's homicide rate was only 1.8 per 100,000 population, compared to the U.S. rate of 6.3. The U.S. rate is thus 3.5 times greater than Canada's rate. This difference is even greater when we look at large cities in both countries. In 1997, for example, 61 homicides occurred in Toronto, a city of just over 4 million people. That same year, a whopping 756 homicides occurred in Chicago, a city of just under 3 million. Toronto's homicide rate was about 1.5 per 100,000, compared to Chicago's rate of about 27. Chicago's rate was thus about eighteen times higher than Toronto's. Rates of other violent crime in Canada are also lower than those in the United States.

Several reasons appear to account for these differences. Canada has much less inequality than the United States and a handgun ownership rate that is only one-seventh that of the United States. An historical reason is Canada's lack of the frontier tradition of lawlessness and vigilante justice, which highlights U.S. history. The settlement of the west in Canada was instead led by the Canadian Northwest Mounted Police, who made sure it proceeded in an orderly and lawful fashion. As one observer summarizes this historical difference between the two nations, "Our [U.S.] heroes ... were grimy, hard-driving, dusty gunmen; theirs were groomed, shaven, disciplined troops with shiny brass buttons. We had people before there was law, while they had law before there were people" (McCaghy and Capron, 1994:141). As one Canadian criminologist argues, "The United States is a society of confrontation, a country born of violent rebellion against authority ... with a wild west tradition of settling differences with guns. Canadians have never seen themselves as a nation of Davy Crocketts. Canada is a country of compromise that evolved peacefully. We have no tradition of revolution or civil war. We do have a tradition of accepting authority and expecting government to look out for the greater good" (Nickerson, 1994:24).

Sources: Federal Bureau of Investigation 1999; McCaghy and Capron 1994; Nickerson 1994; Statistics Canada 1999.

Brown and other historians point to three especially cruel uses of violence in the U.S. past, all committed against subordinate groups: Native Americans, African-Americans, and industrial workers. From 1607, when white settlers killed the first American Indians, to 1890, when U.S. troops massacred some 300 Sioux men, women, and children at Wounded Knee, South Dakota, whites killed tens of thousands of Native Americans. Brown (1990:11–12) feels these killings had a "brutalizing influence on the American character" and did "much to further our proclivity to violence." African-Americans, of course, were the victims of slavery, lynchings, and antiblack race riots. Between 1882 and 1930, Southern whites lynched more than 3,000 African-American men, women, and children, as Southern whites feared that the newly enfranchised ex-slaves would grab economic and political power (Tolnay and Beck 1995).

Industrial workers were another group targeted for violence. Historians Philip Taft and Philip Ross (1990:174) write, "The United States has had the bloodiest and most violent labor history of any industrial nation in the world." During an 1897 coal-mining strike in Pennsylvania, for example, miners who were marching peacefully were ordered by a sheriff and deputies to disperse. Taft and Ross tell what happened next: "When they failed to obey instantly, the sheriff ordered his deputies to fire on the unresisting paraders. Eighteen were killed and 40 seriously wounded, and many of the killed and wounded were shot in the back. The sheriff and several deputies were tried for murder but were acquitted" (p. 177). Shootings and other violence by police and company guards were common during many strikes from the 1870s through the 1930s.

Many historians feel that all these violent episodes help integrate violence into the U.S. character. As Brown (1990:15) observes,

> We have resorted so often to violence that we have long since become a trigger-happy people. Violence is clearly rejected by us as a part of the American value system, but so great has been our involvement with violence over the long sweep of our history that violence has truly become part of our unacknowledged (or underground) value structure.

Although the historians' argument is appealing, other nations such as Japan and Scotland have had very violent pasts but are much less violent today than the United States. In effect, they have succeeded in overcoming their violent pasts, even if the United States has not. Thus, while the violent U.S. past may partially explain why it is more violent today than other nations, other forces must also be at work. The high level of inequality seems to be one such factor. Another might be the U.S. cultural emphasis on strong individualism and distrust of authority, as these values may undermine nonviolent attempts to settle interpersonal disputes.

WHY ARE U.S. HOMICIDES AND AGGRAVATED ASSAULTS MORE COMMON IN URBAN AREAS THAN ELSEWHERE?

Social disorganization and anomie theories help explain why urban areas have higher crime rates, including higher violent crime rates, than other areas: the population density, household overcrowding, dilapidated living conditions, weak social institutions, extreme poverty, and high unemployment of many urban neighborhoods contribute to their high rates of violence (Sampson and Wilson 1995; Stark 1987). As Elliott Currie (1985:160) notes, "[H]arsh inequality is ... enormously destructive of human personality and of social order. Brutal conditions breed brutal behavior." In addition to these problems, urban communities also have high numbers of bars, taverns, and other settings where violence is apt to occur. As routine activities theory would predict, people who frequent these places increase their chances for violent victimization (Roncek and Maier 1991; Sherman, Gartin, and Buerger 1989).

WHY DO MEN COMMIT ALMOST ALL HOMICIDES AND AGGRAVATED ASSAULTS?

We saw earlier that the most typical homicides stem from an argument or other emotionally charged situation that escalates into lethal violence. Kenneth Polk (1994) notes that this scenario almost always involves one man killing another and calls this type "confrontational homicides": essentially "contests of honor" in which men feel the need to respond to an incident or comment that challenges their honor and manhood or insults their female companions. Cross-cultural evidence indicates that this type of male response is common in societies across the world (Daly and Wilson 1988; Gilmore 1990). Polk also says that felony murders and murders committed by men against their female partners further illustrate the violent nature of masculinity. The latter homicides arise out of men's attempts to control the behavior of women with whom they are sexually intimate (see also Kaufman 1998).

Polk's discussion underscores the importance of gender and masculinity for understanding homicide and other violent crime. Males are much more likely than females to get into fights with each other for any number of reasons, and many also assault their female partners. Gender differences in homicide thus stem from gender differences in nonlethal violence. These differences begin in childhood and take on critical importance in adolescence as males become bigger and stronger and more capable of inflicting serious injury (Miedzian 1991). As a 1998 national survey of high school seniors found (see Table 9.3), teenaged males are two to four times more likely than females to commit various acts of violence.

ECONOMIC RESOURCES, MASCULINITY, AND VIOLENCE   Economic deprivation and poverty also interact with masculinity to explain why poor men have higher rates of homicide and assault than wealthier men (Messerschmidt 1997; Newburn and Stanko 1994). Masculinity means many things: academic and economic success; "breadwinning" for one's family; competitiveness, assertiveness, and aggressiveness; lack of emotionality; the willingness to "fight like a man" when necessary (Kimmel and Messner 1998). Thus there are many masculinities and not just one masculinity. In U.S. society, a man's socioeconomic standing affects the way he expresses these ways of "being a man." As James W. Messerschmidt (1993:87–88) puts it, "'Boys will be boys' differently, depending upon their position in social structures and, therefore, upon their access to power and resources." For most U.S. males, economic success is an important part of masculinity. Men at the middle and top of the socioeconomic ladder engage in a masculine behavior pattern involving economic competition and various forms of nonphysical dominating behavior (Connell 1995). This is their way of "doing gender" (West and Zimmerman 1987) and of expressing their masculinity.

Deprived of economic success, men at the bottom of the socioeconomic ladder are more apt to engage in another, "opposition" masculinity involving physical competition, violence, and drinking (Hobbs 1994). They're much more likely than wealthier men (1) to regard insults and other attacks on their honor as major offenses meriting violent responses, and (2) to commit the confrontational homicides described earlier by Polk (1994). Such violence is a prototypical method for these males to demonstrate their masculinity and to gain the respect their low

TABLE 9.3   PROPORTION OF HIGH SCHOOL SENIORS (CLASS OF 1998) REPORTING INVOLVEMENT IN VARIOUS VIOLENT ACTS IN LAST 12 MONTHS (% SAYING AT LEAST ONCE)

ACTIVITY	MALES	FEMALES
Got into serious fight in school or at work	21	11
Fought with group of friends against another group	26	15
Hurt someone badly enough to need bandages or a doctor	23	6
Hit instructor or supervisor	5	1

Source: Maguire and Pastore 1999.

economic standing denies them. As Messerschmidt (1993:85) puts it, violence and other crime by these men can be seen as behaviors "invoked as a resource, when other resources are unavailable, for accomplishing masculinity."

WHY DO AFRICAN-AMERICANS HAVE HIGH RATES OF HOMICIDE AND AGGRAVATED ASSAULT?

Most criminology and criminal justice texts neglect this central question about U.S. crime for fear of being labeled racist (Hawkins 1995; LaFree and Russell 1993; Walker and Brown 1995). A nonracist answer to this question begins by recalling our discussion from this and previous chapters of the structural roots of violent and other street crime: (1) the anger and despair arising from economic deprivation in a society valuing economic success; (2) the stress, social disorganization, and other criminogenic conditions of urban life; (3) the lack of economic resources during adolescence that helps generate a high offending rate during this time; and (4) the violent nature of masculinity.

Along with a U.S. culture that is historically violent and distrustful of authority, each of these explanations by itself helps explain the high U.S. rates of violence. But they all "come together" for African-Americans, and particularly young African-American males, more than for any other group (Gibbs and Merighi 1994; Hawkins 1990; Peterson and Krivo 1999).

To the extent this is true, slavery and other racial mistreatment may have played an important role. As Darnell F. Hawkins (1990:161) observes, "No other ethnic group to whom Blacks as a group are often unfavorably compared was enslaved en masse and brought to this country by force." Some scholars believe this history left African-Americans with "a sense of frustration, hopelessness and powerlessness and a resultant anger that is internalized and long simmering" (Harvey 1986:155). These feelings help turn minor disputes into violent conflicts. Accompanying this anger, some observers say, is a profound sense of despair among urban blacks. "They believe they have nothing to lose," says a social worker who organized a workshop on urban violence. "Even if they should lose their own lives, they feel they will not have lost very much. Besides, why should they be good, they ask. There is no reward for good behavior" (Stengel 1989:114). The anger, despair, and other consequences of economic deprivation and racial mistreatment help explain African-American crime rates. But for young, urban,

◀ *Young African-American males have especially high rates of violent crime. A sociological explanation of this fact focuses on several aspects of their social environment, including economic deprivation, dilapidated neighborhoods, and history of racial discrimination. These and other factors create anger, frustration, and a desire to win the respect denied them by their low socioeconomic status. One result of this is interpersonal violence*

African-American males, these problems interact with notions of masculinity to produce particularly high rates of violence (Gibbs 1992; McCall 1994).

Some scholars of the African-American community see this violence as part of a larger "compulsive masculinity" or "cool pose" behavior pattern adopted by many young, urban, black males (Majors and Billson 1992; Staples 1982). This pattern includes hanging out on street corners, dressing and acting in a "hip" style, and involvement in petty crime and drug use. Such compulsive masculinity helps "compensate for the inability to fulfill the traditional functions of an adult male role due to social and economic exclusion from mainstream society" (Gibbs and Merighi 1994:76).

THE CODE OF THE STREET   Acting out such exaggerated masculinity, young, urban, African-American men have developed what sociologist Elijah Anderson, one of the most sensitive observers of contemporary urban life, calls a "code of the street" (Anderson 1999). This code arises from the despair and alienation of the urban poor and helps explain the interpersonal violence in their neighborhoods. Its most central feature is the need and striving for respect. "People are being told day in and day out that they are not respectable," Anderson says. "This is the message young black people get every day from the system. If you perceive that you're getting those kinds of messages, it may be that you will crave respect—you've got to get it from a *turnip* if you can. So every encounter becomes an opportunity for salvaging respect" (Coughlin 1994).

To help them command respect, Anderson says, young urban men often adopt a certain "look" involving the way they dress, move, and talk. Because it promotes respect, this persona helps deter verbal and physical assaults by other men and is an essential aspect of the conception of manhood in inner cities. Such manhood involves a desire to be in charge of a situation, even if violence is needed to exert one's control. In these respects, manhood and respect go hand in hand. A "real man," says Anderson, knows and follows the code of the street, and if he doesn't, he is less than a man. Displaying nerve by initiating physical and verbal attacks, even at the risk of his life, is another way for a young male to prove his manhood and gain respect. Given urban males' alienation and lack of economic opportunity, says Anderson, these attacks help raise their self-respect. Striving for respect in these ways thus leads masculinity in urban areas to take on an especially violent tone.

Distrust of the police and courts also helps explain urban violence, Anderson adds. Like the frontier settlers of a century ago, young urban males feel they can't count on the legal system for help and deem it necessary to use violence to defend themselves and their families and friends. Gang wars over drugs and the availability of ever more powerful firearms all make an explosive situation even more volatile.

VIOLENCE BY WOMEN

So far we've been looking at African-American males. What about African-American females and other women? Much of the growing body of research on women's deviance concerns prostitution, drug use, and other such offenses. The few studies we have of women's violence suggest it has the same roots—extreme poverty, negative family and school experiences, and disadvantaged neighborhoods—as men's violence (Baskin and Sommers 1998; Kruttschnitt 1994; Simpson and Elis 1995).

Much of the research on women's violence focuses on black women, whose experience represents a striking example of the interaction of race, class, and gender (Simpson 1991). Their violent crime rate is much higher than that for white women and sometimes exceeds that for white men, even though it remains much lower than that for black men (Baskin and Sommers 1998).

In his study of urban communities, Elijah Anderson (1999) notes that young black women seek respect as much as their male counterparts and in the same manner, through displays of bravado, verbal insults, and a willingness to use violence to settle disputes. They're also as sensitive as urban males to verbal assaults on their character. Despite these similarities, young black women's violence lags behind that of their male counterparts because of gender socialization. When young urban women feel the need to retaliate violently, Anderson says, they typically enlist the aid of a brother, uncle, or cousin. When they do fight themselves, they rarely use guns, since, as women, they don't feel a "macho" need to do so.

In a study of street robbery, Jody Miller (1998) found that gender also influences the way that robberies are committed. Whereas male robbers target both male and female victims, female robbers usually target only the latter, as they assume women would be less likely to resist the robbery. Whereas male robbers often use a gun to intimidate their victims, female robbers use either a knife or no weapon at all. But in the relatively few times that female robbers do target men, they almost always use a weapon, usually a gun. Typically they pretend to be sexually interested in the men, either as prostitutes or just as women out to have a good time, and then rob the men when their guard, and sometimes their pants, are down. As one prostitute/robber put it, "If you are sucking a man's dick and you pull a knife on them, they not gonna too much argue with you" (Miller 1998:55).

Earlier I noted that when women commit homicide, their victims are usually men who'd been battering them. This pattern holds true for women of color as well as for white women. Coramae Richey Mann (1990:198) says that black female homicide offenders are part of a "subculture of hopelessness." She adds, "By the time these women reach age 30 or more, they feel the full impact of the hopelessness of their lives. When the last straw is broken, they finally strike back at the closest living representative of their plight."

A recent theory of women's homicide supports Mann's view. Robbin S. Ogle and associates (Ogle, Maier-Katkin, and Bernard 1995:176) argue that women experience significant stress in their lives from the "structural, social, and cultural conditions of contemporary society," with poor women undergoing more stress than wealthier women. The stress women feel is at least as high as men's, with recent research suggesting they suffer more than men from depression, anxiety, and other symptoms of distress (Mirowsky and Ross 1995). Whereas men tend to react to the stress in their lives with anger directed at an external target through violence, women tend to internalize their anger as guilt, hurt, and self-doubt. They thus are much less likely than men to express their stress through violence and aggression. Their ways of coping with stress thus lead to "overcontrolled personalities" that ordinarily commit no violence but occasionally become overwhelmed and "erupt in extreme violence" such as homicide (Ogle, Maier-Katkin, and Bernard 1995:178). The targets of this violence are often the men who abuse women, and sometimes even a woman's own children.

Susan Smith's widely publicized 1994 drowning of her two children exemplifies this theory. Smith, who first claimed on national TV that a black man had kidnapped her children, later confessed to pushing her car into the water while her children slept inside. She had grown up in an unstable family and suffered

Using Violence to Stop Violence

In early 1994, the country of Singapore announced it would cane a U.S. teenager accused of throwing eggs at cars and spray painting buildings. Singapore's action won widespread publicity in the United States, and national polls found members of the U.S. public feeling that similar punishment should be used to reduce violence by adults and violence and other illegal behavior by juveniles. In the wake of Singapore's example, several state legislatures, particularly in the south, began to consider legislation to reinstate the flogging of criminals, a practice that had long ago been banned.

The effort to renew flogging was especially controversial in Mississippi. A state representative who led the effort in that state promoted the new legislation as a way to lower delinquency: "If it works in Singapore, maybe it'll work in Mississippi, too." In response, several Mississippi critics said the new law was racist, especially in their state, where 30 percent of the population is African-American, slavery once flourished, and lynchings and the beatings and murders of civil rights workers were common. One state senator said the legislation "harkens back to the days of sharecropping and, of course, slavery." According to one report, critics thought that renewing flogging "would reopen the wounds of slavery, conjuring up images of white bosses beating black workers." Other critics worried that the new law would hurt economic development in the state. As one state representative put it, "It's embarrassing. It will give us another black-eye. We have this flourishing gaming industry going, and we're trying to attract investment. A lot of people know nothing about the state other than *Mississippi Burning* (a film about murders of civil rights workers), and this will hurt us on the national scene."

Other observers in and outside Mississippi thought the flogging would do nothing to deter violence and could even lead to more violence. As one columnist put it, "We'll have to forget all those silly reports that keep telling us that violence begets violence. Oh, yes, and we'll have to ignore the studies that show that many of the men who beat up women and children probably got smacked around themselves when they were kids." The columnist added, "How simple it would be to think we could really turn a kid's life around with a paddle, a bamboo cane or a leather strap. How much easier than having to wrestle with the nagging problems of drugs, education, poverty, abuse, and hopelessness. But there doesn't seem to be much evidence that beatings are the answer to our crime problems, no matter how desperately some people want to believe it."

Sources: Walsh 1994; Weber 1995; Wilkie 1995; Witt 1994.

---

sexual abuse as an adolescent. Reportedly, her rejection by a wealthy boyfriend who didn't want the burden of her children drove her over the edge (Terry 1994).

SOCIAL PROCESS EXPLANATIONS OF VIOLENCE

So far our explanation of urban violence has emphasized structural conditions. Social process factors help us understand how these conditions lead to violence. Two major sets of factors play an important role: (1) learning, socialization, and differential association from one's peers and immediate social environment; and (2) parental neglect and abuse (Elliott 1994; Sampson and Lauritsen 1994). Children growing up in violent neighborhoods learn norms justifying violence in interpersonal conflicts. Their exposure to these influences depends heavily on the degree to which their parents monitor their activities and encourage their involvement in school, church, and other activities. Elijah Anderson (1999) notes that the vast majority of poor urban residents are self-described "decent," law-abiding individuals who disapprove of "street" residents, as they call them. The "decent" majority are the working poor who value hard work, go to church, and are concerned about their children's education. They teach their children to respect authority and supervise their behavior carefully.

In contrast, "street" parents let their children hang out on the streets where they learn to fight. There, even small children learn to be ready to push, shove, and use other kinds of violence to settle disputes. The kids who are the toughest are the ones who command respect. The code of the street thus begins at an early age, especially for boys. They learn that it dictates they defend themselves and even seek revenge if they're physically or verbally attacked. By the time they become teenagers, then, these urban males have learned to be quite willing to use violence to win respect and achieve other goals.

One final family factor leading to violence is harsh physical punishment and, worse, physical and sexual abuse. Males who were abused as children are more likely than other males to become violent themselves (Smith and Thornberry 1995). This effect holds less true for females who were abused, as they're more apt to develop alcoholism and other psychological problems (Widom 1989). Their abuse thus may lead them to commit various kinds of crimes: Almost 60 percent of adult women prisoners had experienced sexual or physical abuse in the past, and more than one-third had been abused by an intimate (Greenfeld and Snell 1999).

Mass Media and Violence

Another explanation of violence centers on the mass media, particularly television. Many studies have documented the amount of violence in TV shows, Hollywood movies, and other mass media outlets. Scholars and other observers often blame mass media violence for the U.S. violent crime problem, and the issue has received much publicity in recent years, especially after the shootings of more than a dozen people by two students at Columbine High School in Littleton, Colorado in 1999 (Alter 1999). The key question here is whether mass media violence is a *symptom* of a violent culture or a *cause* of our violence. Both possibilities might also be true: The United States might have mass media violence because of its historical emphasis on violence, but mass media violence in turn might promote additional violence in real life.

Going back to Albert Bandura's (1963) work in the early 1960s, much research establishes a strong statistical connection between mass media violence and violent attitudes and/or behavior (Garofalo 1990), but causality is hard to prove. Several lines of research exist. The most common study involves having children, teenagers, or college students watch violent videos; often a control group watches a nonviolent video. Typically, researchers measure the subjects' violent attitudes before and after they watch the videos by, for example, asking them how they'd behave in various scenarios or whether they would approve of violence depicted in certain scenarios. When children are the subjects, researchers often watch them play before and after they view the videos. Regardless of the type of study, researchers typically find that viewing violent videos increases subjects' violent attitudes and/or behavior.

At least two empirical problems limit the value of such studies. First, because the studies are necessarily short-term, they can find only short-term effects on violent attitudes/behavior. Whether viewing violence has long-term effects, especially on criminal violence and not just on aggression, remains unclear. Second, since these are experimental studies, the effects occurring in the "laboratory" may not occur in the real world, where many other influences come into play (Surette 1998).

Another line of research involves surveying children and teenagers and asking them how much TV, or how much violent TV, they watch. Their amount of time watching TV is then compared to their involvement in violent delinquency and other aggression. Researchers often find a statistical correlation between watching TV and committing aggression, and they conclude that watching TV increases aggression (Kruttschnitt, Heath, and Ward 1986). As we know from previous chapters, however, correlation does not necessarily mean causation. In this case, it's possible that the correlation is spurious. Youths might both watch TV and commit violence because they're interested in violence for other reasons. If so, both behaviors stem from this interest, and it can't be said that watching TV *causes* their aggression. Despite this possibility, one longitudinal study found television viewing linked to later aggression regardless of previous interest in violence (Lefkowitz et al. 1977). However, another longitudinal study found no such link (Milavsky et al. 1982).

Another type of study examines the effects of violence reported in the media on later area-wide violence. One of the most interesting investigations of this type found an increase in the nation's homicide rate after heavyweight boxing matches. The increase was particularly large for the boxing matches that received the most publicity (Phillips 1983).

A "natural" field experiment of TV and violence occurred in Canada in 1973. Researchers watched first- and second-grade children play in a town that was about to get TV signals and thus the ability to receive and watch TV programs (the experimental group), and compared them with children in two other similar towns that already had TV (the control groups). Two years later, the researchers watched the same children again. While the control group children's aggression did not rise in the two years, the experimental group children's aggression rose by 160 percent (Joy, Kimball, and Zabrack 1986).

One other study is particularly intriguing. In studying homicide rates in the United States, Canada, and South Africa, Brandon Centerwall (1989) found that in each country they rose dramatically 10 to 15 years after television became widespread in the country. Centerwall reasoned that young children began watching TV and then, 10 to 15 years later, reached their high-crime years (ages 15 to 30). Thanks to the effects of TV, they began committing a higher rate of homicides during these years than previous generations had.

Despite the evidence of mass media effects on aggression and violent crime, the actual strength of these effects, especially compared with the importance of the other influences discussed earlier, remains unclear (Surette 1998). One government report concluded that there's "no clear evidence" of a causal effect of TV violence on criminal violence (Milavsky 1988:3). A conservative conclusion is that mass media violence has a small effect on violence that is eclipsed by other influences. To the extent that an effect has been documented, it appears much more for males than females (Lefkowitz et al. 1977).

Despite the huge volume of research on the issue, the actual effects of mass media violence on real-life violence remain unknown. In view of the possible censorship involved in any legislative attempts to control the mass media, we should remain skeptical of mass media effects until the empirical evidence becomes compelling. Even then, censorship remains an important issue that needs to be addressed.

ROBBERY

When people say they fear crime, they often have robbery (or mugging) in mind. What do we know about this crime?

Defining Robbery

Robbery is "the taking or attempting to take anything of value from the care, custody, or control of a person or persons by force or threat of force or violence and/or by putting the victim in fear" (Federal Bureau of Investigation 1999). As this definition implies, robbery involves both theft and interpersonal violence. The latter component distinguishes robbery from other property crimes and prompts both the UCR and NCVS to classify it as a violent crime.

UCR robbery data include both personal and commercial (e.g., in a convenience store, gas station, etc.) robberies, with personal robberies accounting for about two-thirds of all UCR robberies. The NCVS covers only personal robberies. Because of this difference, the UCR and NCVS give us slightly different pictures of robbery, but together give us a better understanding of robbery than either data source provides alone.

The Extent, Patterning, and Costs of Robbery

As you might expect, the UCR and NCVS differ on the number of robberies, with the NCVS reporting a higher number (Federal Bureau of Investigation 1999; Rennison 1999). The UCR reported some 446,625 robberies of all types in 1998, a 10.4 percent drop from the number reported just a year earlier; like other street crime, robberies declined dramatically after the early 1990s. The NCVS estimated that 886,000 personal robberies occurred in 1998 but agrees with the UCR that robbery declined during much of the 1990s. Of all the UCR robberies, only 28 percent were

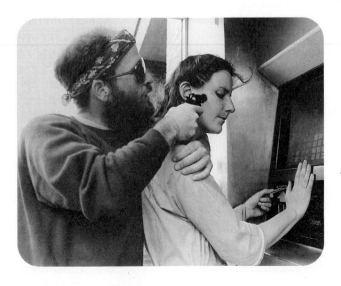

◄ *Robbery is a crime feared by many Americans. It involves far more strangers than other violent crimes and often puts its victims in fear of their safety and even their lives.*

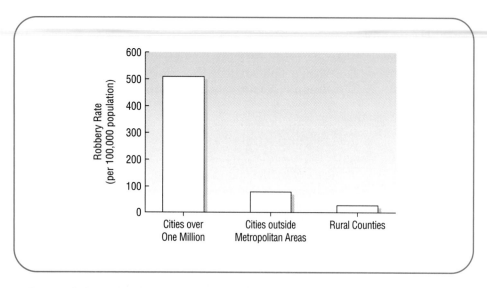

▲ Figure 9.3　UCR Robbery Rates and Population Size, 1998
(Number of crimes per 100,000 population)

Sources: Maguire and Pastore 1999; Federal Bureau of Investigation 1999;
Alan and Zawitz 1998.

cleared by arrest. Combining this figure with the NCVS's estimate of the total number of robberies, including those not reported to the police, yields an arrest clearance rate of only about 14 percent for robbery.

The social patterning for robbery is similar to that for homicide and assault in some ways, but different in others. Two similarities concern robbery's age distribution and location. Robbery is primarily a young person's crime: Persons under the age of 25 account for almost two-thirds of all robbery arrests. It's also much more common in large urban areas than elsewhere (see Figure 9.3). However, the regional distribution of robbery differs from that for other violent crime. UCR robbery rates are highest in the Northeast, with the West and South in a virtual tie for second place, followed by the Midwest.

Like other violent crime, robbery is disproportionately committed by men and by African-Americans. Men comprised 90 percent of all robbery arrests in 1998, and African-Americans 55 percent. Compared to homicide and assault, however, robbery is more interracial, at least where white victims are concerned. Such victims perceive blacks as the offender in about 43 percent of the single-offender robberies they suffer. For black victims, robbery is mostly intraracial, as they perceive blacks as the offender in 88 percent of single-offender robberies (Bastian and De-Berry 1994).

As Table 9.4 indicates, men and blacks are also disproportionately likely to be *victims* of robberies, with black males much more apt to be robbed than people in the other race/gender categories. Turning to ethnicity, Hispanics are robbed more often than non-Hispanics. Reflecting the victimization pattern for violent crime noted in Chapter 4, robbery victimization is also highest among the young and among people from low-income backgrounds.

In one important difference between robbery and other violent crime, robbery is more likely to be committed by a stranger than by someone the victim knows. According to the NCVS, 57 percent of personal robberies in 1998 involved

TABLE 9.4	**ROBBERY VICTIMIZATION RATES BY RACE, ETHNICITY, AND GENDER, 1998** (PER 1,000 PERSONS 12 AND OLDER)

VARIABLE	RATE
Race	
Black	5.9
White	3.7
Other	4.4
Ethnicity	
Hispanic	6.3
Non-Hispanic	3.7
Gender	
Male	4.6
Female	3.5
Race/Gender[a]	
Black males	11.9
Black females	3.6
White males	5.3
White females	2.4
Age	
12–15	7.7
16–19	11.4
20–24	7.9
25–34	4.2
35–49	3.2
50–64	1.7
65 or older	0.5
Annual Household Income	
Less than $7,500	6.5
$7,500–$14,999	5.8
$15,000–$24,999	3.6
$25,000–$34,999	2.4
$35,000–$49,999	0.5
$50,000–$74,999	0.7
$75,000 or more	1.2

[a]1997 data
Sources: Federal Bureau of Investigation 1999; Maguire and Pastore 1999.

an offender and a victim who didn't know each other. Still, 41 percent of robbery victims did know the offender, and 20 percent were even robbed by an intimate or other relative. This figure masks a significant gender difference: About one-third of female victims are robbed by someone they know, compared to about 10 percent of male victims. Female robbery victims are thus three times as likely as male victims to be robbed by someone they know.

According to the NCVS, weapons were involved in 39 percent of all personal robberies. Of these weapons, more than half are guns and about one-fourth are knives. About one third of robbery victims are injured. The UCR estimates that personal and commercial robberies cost $446 million in 1998, or about $1,000 per robbery (higher for commercial robberies, lower for personal ones). The NCVS estimated that personal robberies cost each victim in 1992 an average of $555 in property losses, medical expenses, and time lost from work (Klaus 1994). The UCR's inclusion of commercial robberies undoubtedly accounts for its much higher average loss. Gas stations lost an average of $546 in robberies in 1998, and banks an average of $4,516.

Types of Robbers

Just as there are several types of murderers, there are also several types of robbers. John Conklin (1972) developed the standard classification for robbers. A first type is *professional robbers*. These men carefully plan their robberies, carry guns, and often work in groups. Their targets include "big scores" such as stores, banks, or other commercial targets. A second type is *opportunist robbers*. As their name implies, these men commit robberies when they have the opportunity to do so. They are usually young males who choose vulnerable targets such as people walking alone at night, and they get relatively little money from each robbery. Conklin's third type, *addict robbers*, rob to acquire money to buy illegal drugs. They generally plan their robberies less carefully than professional robbers but more carefully than opportunistic robbers. *Alcoholic robbers* are Conklin's final type and commit robberies when they're drunk and trying to get money to buy more alcohol. Their robberies are rarely planned and usually involve no firearms.

Recall from Chapter 4 the concept of chronic offenders or career criminals, a small group of offenders who commit disproportionate numbers of crimes and whose criminality often lasts well into adulthood. This concept certainly applies to robbery. A study of more than 2,000 inmates in California, Michigan, and Texas found that 10 percent of the robbers had committed about 135 robberies per year each, compared to 90 percent of the robbers who averaged only 10 per year (Chaiken and Chaiken 1982). Still, little evidence of "offense specialization" exists among these inmates, as even those heavily involved in robbery committed other crimes as well.

Explaining Robbery

Robbery is a violent crime committed for economic gain. As such, robbery is a prototypical example of "innovation" in Merton's anomie theory: In a society placing so much value on economic success, the poor often feel pressured to achieve this success through illegitimate means. Robbery is one of the crimes they thus commit.

The explanations we've seen in this chapter for homicide and aggravated assault also apply to robbery. Like these other crimes, robbery stems from the criminogenic features of many urban neighborhoods, including extreme poverty and dilapidated living conditions. Several studies find robbery rates highest in communities with the greatest economic deprivation (Parker and Anderson-Facile 2000).

Routine activities theory also helps explain robbery, as robbery victimization is higher among people who put themselves at risk for robbery. Several studies, for example, find robbery rates higher among people who go out at night for recreation at least once per week (Miethe, Stafford, and Long 1987). Further, certain locations are said to promote robbery because they provide motivated robbers attractive targets who lack guardianship. For example, the advent of automated teller machines

(ATMs) helped increase robbery rates because they provided a location where a lone target could be expected to have a fair amount of money. The recent growth of convenience stores has increased commercial robberies for similar reasons.

So far I've been implying that the motivation for robbery is primarily economic. Other scholars take a different view. Jack Katz (1991) argues that the amount of money persistent robbers gain from their robberies is too small for economic gain to be their primary motivation. If it were, he says, they would engage in more lucrative illegal activities such as drug trafficking or illegal gambling. Instead, Katz continues, persistent robbers' primary motivation lies in their interest in sustaining a "badass" identity involving "the portrayal of a personal character that is committed to violence beyond calculations of legal, material, or even physical costs to oneself" (p. 285). This motivation makes persistent robbers willing to risk arrest and renders them relatively immune to any deterrent effects that the threat of legal punishment might have. Similarly, Bruce A. Jacobs and Richard Wright (1999) say a primary motivation for robbery is the offenders' desire to look "cool" and "hip" through the spending of huge sums of money. To keep up this appearance, they often need money quickly and thus commit robberies with little concern for, or even attention to, the possible consequence.

The arguments of Katz, Jacobs, and Wright suggest that robbery often arises from the emphasis on respect so characteristic of the code of the streets in urban areas, discussed previously. Katz (1991:298) observes that urban adolescents learn the need to exert a "fierceness of will" and "humiliating dominance" by using violence. More than most crimes, robbery embodies these characteristics. Although most urban adolescents don't become robbers, those who do reflect their socialization into the code of the streets. As Elijah Anderson (1999) observed, masculinity is a fundamental part of this code. Although Katz (1991) doesn't stress the point, masculinity is thus fundamental to his own argument on the nature of robbery and helps explain why robbers are almost always men.

Carjackings

Carjackings are a type of robbery that has won major headlines in recent years. They differ from other motor vehicle theft because "the victim is present and the offender uses or threatens to use force" (Klaus 1999:1). The NCVS estimates that about 49,000 attempted or completed carjackings occurred each year from 1992 to 1996. About half were completed, meaning the victim's car (or to be more accurate, motor vehicle) was taken, and half were unsuccessful. About 70 percent of completed carjackings involved firearms, compared to only 20 percent of attempted carjackings.

Although carjackings concern us and get a lot of publicity when they occur, they are actually rare events. Between 1992 and 1996, the rate of carjackings was about 2.5 per 10,000 persons age 12 or older. Although in the media the most popular image of a carjacking victim is probably that of a woman, in real life men are more likely to be carjacking victims. Carjacking victims are also disproportionately likely to be black, Hispanic, divorced or never married, and living in urban areas. In all these respects the social backgrounds of carjacking victims resemble those of victims of violent crime in general (Klaus 1999). Carjacking victims reported that 97 percent of their offenders were males and perceived 58 percent of their offenders to be black. They also reported that 72 percent of their offenders were strangers and 15 percent were intimates or relatives.

WORKPLACE VIOLENCE

"Going postal" entered the U.S. lexicon a decade or more ago as disgruntled workers, some of them U.S. Post Office employees, entered their workplaces with handguns or other firearms and took a deadly toll on their current or former bosses and coworkers. One such worker was Mark Barton, who on July 29, 1999 allegedly entered two Atlanta office buildings where he had worked as a day trader and began shooting. He killed nine people and wounded 12 others (Giradet 1999). Although Barton was evidently a disgruntled worker, other violence occurs in the workplace when strangers enter to commit a robbery or other crime or when estranged lovers come to confront their partners, sometimes with deadly force. Sometimes workplace violence is random. An example of this occurred on March 1, 2000, when Ronald Taylor, angry over a broken door in his apartment building, shot and killed his apartment's maintenance man and then went to a nearby McDonald's and Burger King where he resumed his shooting and killed two more people, both strangers (Spangler 2000). Still other workplace violence is committed against people, such as police, performing their jobs but not technically in a workplace.

Whatever its source, workplace violence is quite common, and UCR and NCVS data paint a disturbing picture (Warchol 1998). From 1992 to 1996, about 2 million violent victimizations (equal to 18.5 percent of all violent victimizations) occurred in workplaces each year, including more than 1,000 homicides, 400,000 aggravated assaults, 1.5 million simple assaults, 84,000 robberies, and 51,000 rapes and sexual assaults. These figures have since declined along with the rest of U.S. crime but remain very high. About 83 percent of the people committing workplace violence are men, 58 percent are white, and almost half are 30 or older. About 12 percent of all victims of workplace violence say they were physically injured, with half of these victims needing medical treatment. Although 60 percent of all workplace violence is committed by a stranger to the victim, this figure differs by gender: 66 percent of men are victimized by a stranger, compared to only 47 percent of women. Women are thus more likely to be victimized in the workplace by someone they know than by a stranger.

One reason so much workplace violence occurs is that many people are angry at work. In a recent Gallup poll, almost 25 percent of adults who were employed full or part time said they were usually at least "somewhat angry" at work. The most common reason for their anger was the way they had been treated by their supervisor. Other causes of their anger included the actions of coworkers and pressure from deadlines and heavy workloads. Such anger can build up until a worker explodes. As one business professor puts it, "In an environment where you think people are satisfied with their jobs, there is a sort of undercurrent of anger and resentment aimed at the workplace that could potentially lead to the kinds of explosions and rage we have seen" (Giradet 1999:D6).

GUNS AND GUN CONTROL

The issue of guns and gun control is one of the most controversial topics in criminal justice today. It has been the subject of countless stories and debates in the mass media, including TV and radio talk shows. About one-third of the public favors a complete ban on handgun possession, and 70 percent or more support less restrictive measures, including permits, registration, and waiting periods (Kleck 1997;

Teret et al. 1998). Some of my students' strongest feelings concern gun control. I don't try to force them to adopt any particular view, and I certainly won't be doing that here. But I do want to acquaint you with scholarly research on the topic to help you draw your own conclusions. As we'll be seeing, even scholars disagree on what this evidence is telling us.

Research on guns and gun control focuses on five questions: (1) How many handguns and other firearms exist, and what is the social patterning of firearm ownership? (2) How involved are handguns in violent crime? (3) Do handguns deter crime or do they make firearm violence more likely? (4) How much would gun control reduce the availability of handguns and their use in violent crime? (5) How successful would stiffer penalties for handgun crimes be in deterring such crimes? Notice I didn't mention the question of whether the Second Amendment to the U.S. Constitution prohibits gun control laws. That question is for legal scholars, many of whom dispute the National Rifle Association's (NRA) view that the Second Amendment does prohibit gun control laws (Savage 1994). We'll focus here instead on the research of sociologists and other criminologists on guns and gun control.

The Extent and Distribution of Guns

Let's first get an idea of how many guns exist in the United States. Though estimates are imprecise, the best evidence indicates that 25–30 percent of all U.S. households own handguns and 25 percent own a rifle or shotgun. In all, about 35 percent of U.S. households have a firearm of some type, with more than two-thirds of handgun owners also owning at least one rifle or shotgun. The primary motive for almost 75 percent of handgun owners is self-protection. Of the almost 200 million firearms in the United States, about one-third, or 65 million, are handguns, with almost 2 million more added annually. About 340,000 handguns are stolen each year. Gun ownership differs by region of the country: The South has the highest ownership rate, and the Northeast the least. More whites (27 percent) than blacks (16 percent) and more men (42 percent) than women (9 percent) own one or more guns. In many inner-city neighborhoods, more than 20 percent of male high school students report owning a handgun, mostly for self-protection. More than 200,000 handguns and 380,000 other firearms are stolen from gun-owing households each year (Cook and Ludwig 1997; Kleck 1997; Wright and Vail 2000).

The Use of Handguns in Violent Crime

In 1998, according to the NCVS, firearms, most of them handguns, were involved in 670,500 violent crimes in the United States, including some 9,000 homicides, 29,000 rapes and sexual assaults, 343,000 robberies, and 475,000 assaults (Rennison 1999). In any year, males are about twice as likely as females to be handgun crime victims, and blacks three times as likely as whites. Young black males have the highest annual handgun victimization rate, and white females the lowest (Rand 1994).

Although handguns are involved in many violent crimes in the United States, the actual contribution they make to violent crime remains unclear. Studies generally find no relationship at the ecological level (i.e., city-by-city comparisons) between gun availability and nonfatal violent crime rates, but do find a small

▲ *Gun control opponents believe that gun ownership deters violent crime.*

▲ *Gun control advocates believe that effective gun control would reduce the number of deaths from firearms.*

relationship between gun availability and homicides. Because correlation doesn't mean causation, however, it remains unclear whether this relationship means that gun availability increases homicides, or simply that more people own guns in high-crime areas (Cook 1991). This issue notwithstanding, the increase in handgun crime, especially drive-by shootings and gang violence, in the late 1980s and early 1990s led to a flurry of efforts in several states to control guns. Although violent crime had declined by the late 1990s, several notorious school shootings during this time, including the ones at Columbine High School in Colorado in 1999, again highlighted the issue of gun control (Fortgang 1999; Sitton 1994).

Do Handguns Deter or Promote Violent Crime?

One of the most important questions in the gun control debate is whether handgun ownership by law-abiding citizens raises or lowers their risk of becoming violent crime victims (Witkin 1994). As noted earlier, self-protection is a primary motive for handgun ownership. Citizens feel that possessing a handgun will keep someone from assaulting them or burglarizing their house or at least help them if they're attacked. A popular slogan says, "If guns are outlawed, then only outlaws will have guns." Gun control opponents feel that reduction of handgun ownership by law-abiding citizens will make them more vulnerable to crime, not less.

One major problem with this argument lies in the understanding we gained earlier on the nature of homicide. Recall that most homicides occur between people who know each other, often after an argument arising out of a minor dispute or as part of ongoing family violence. In many ways we thus have more to fear from someone we know than from someone we don't know. The ready presence of a handgun in law-abiding households greatly increases the chances that a gun will be used against a victim by someone he or she knows (Bailey et al. 1997).

It's often said that "guns don't kill people; people kill people." While that's true, it's also true that handguns are far more lethal than knives, baseball bats, and other weapons. Many experts believe that if (and this is a big "if") handguns were effectively controlled, fewer homicides would take place. In the typical scenario involving a relatively spontaneous incident where emotions run rampant, the offender would have to use a less lethal weapon if no handgun were available. Although he (assuming a man) might still use this weapon on his intended victim and sometimes the victim will die, death will be less likely than if a handgun were used (Roth 1994).

Supporting this viewpoint, a 1993 study compared households with guns with ones without guns in the same neighborhoods and matched by age, sex, and race of household members (Kellerman et al. 1993). The researchers found that the households with guns were 2.7 times more likely than the others to have someone in the house murdered, usually by a family member or close friend. This was true even when the researchers controlled for the household use of alcohol or illegal drugs and a history of domestic violence. The results led one scholar to note, "This study confirms that guns are more likely to be used when you're drinking and you have a fight with someone you know. It indicates that people tend to use guns not for the reason they brought them into the house, but in fights with family members and friends." Another scholar concluded, "The fact is that people buy guns so they won't be killed, but as this study shows, they are 2.7 times more likely to be killed if they have a gun in the house" (Bass 1993:3). Although these scholars applauded this study, others disputed its methodology and conclusions (Kleck 1997), reflecting the sensitivity and complexity of the gun control issue.

Additional studies suggest that although gun ownership may deter violent crime in theory, this can't easily happen in reality. In most burglaries, residences or businesses are unoccupied, and in most robberies the offender surprises the victim, leaving little time to pull out a gun to defend oneself. Moreover, most criminals can't know in advance whether a potential target is armed. A potential burglar can't know whether a handgun is inside the home he's targeting, nor can a potential robber know whether a possible victim has a concealed weapon (Green 1987; McDowall, Lizotte, and Wiersema 1991).

If handgun ownership does deter crime, as gun control opponents argue, then in communities that ban handguns, crime should go up, and in communities that require handgun ownership, crime should go down. Some interesting "real-life" tests of these possibilities occurred in the 1980s (McDowall, Lizotte, and Wiersema 1991). In June 1981, Morton Grove, Illinois banned the possession or sale of handguns, and in September 1982 so did Evanston, Illinois. The bans received heavy publicity in the press. Despite the bans, burglaries in the two cities didn't rise after the bans took effect. Meanwhile, in March 1982 the town of Kennesaw, Georgia required every household to own a firearm. Despite press reports that the new requirement lowered the burglary rate there, later analysis found no evidence for such a reduction. The authors of the study concluded that "there is currently no solid empirical support" for a deterrent effect of civilian firearm ownership on crime (McDowall, Lizotte, and Wiersema 1991:556).

Although it doesn't seem that gun ownership deters crime, it's possible that once a crime has begun, a gun may help the intended victim resist his or her offender. According to the NCVS, citizens use firearms about 65,000–85,000 times per year to defend themselves or their property, or in less than 1 percent of all violent crime, suggesting to some scholars that gun ownership provides little help to an intended victim (McDowall and Wiersema 1994). Disputing the NCVS figure as a gross underestimate, Gary Kleck and Marc Gertz (1995) estimate from a survey they conducted that defensive firearm use occurs about 2.5 million times per year. This figure gained wide press attention and has been often cited by gun control opponents. However, other scholars have criticized Kleck and Gertz's methodology for grossly overestimating the amount of defensive gun use (Duncan 2000; Hemenway 1997). Still other scholars say the amount of defensive gun use is probably between about 300,000 and 1.2 million times per year (Smith 1997). Regardless of whose figures are correct, such use can prevent the intended victimization from succeeding but may also increase the chance of victim injury or death (Cook 1986). As this brief discussion indicates, the issue of defensive gun use to resist an ongoing crime remains very controversial in scholarly circles.

The Effectiveness of Gun Control

We saw earlier that if effective gun control were feasible, it would probably reduce homicides and other gun crimes. But what might be feasible in theory might be less possible in the real world. Here scholars reach very different conclusions: Some think gun control efforts reduce gun crimes (Roth, 1994), while others think they don't (Kleck 1997). Their disagreement stems from the complexity of the empirical evidence. For example, in 1975, Washington, D.C. banned the sale and possession of handguns. Gun crimes went down in Washington after the ban, especially for homicides resulting from family and acquaintance disputes. More generally, gun homicides and gun suicides decreased, but homicides and suicides committed without guns didn't decrease (Loftin et al. 1991). However, gun crimes also declined in other cities that had not banned handguns, suggesting that the reduction in Washington may have arisen from reasons other than the ban (Walker 1998). The results of the Morton Grove and Evanston gun bans discussed previously were less ambiguous: Although burglaries didn't go up in those towns, as gun control opponents would have expected, neither did gun crimes go down, as proponents would have predicted (Kleck 1997).

These and other studies lead several scholars to conclude that gun control would do little to reduce gun crimes or gun availability (Kleck 1997; Wright and Vail 2000). Even if Congress passed a federal ban on handguns, they say, much of the country would resist this law, and it would probably do little to reduce the already existing 75 million handguns. As Samuel Walker (1998:198) puts it, "Banning guns is an empty gesture, given the number of handguns already in circulation." After the ban in Evanston, for example, the town's estimated 5,000 handgun owners turned in only 116 handguns, and police did little to enforce the ban (Kleck 1991).

Even if law-abiding citizens turned in their guns, criminals would not, say these scholars. The major problem is that handguns are easy to acquire through illegal channels. A study of criminals and handguns even found that only one-sixth of all felons who use guns had acquired them via a legal purchase (Wright and Rossi 1986). As Walker (1998:189) notes, "All of the evidence indicates that active criminals either have weapons or can readily obtain them if they want to."

Recognizing this problem, some scholars feel that even if gun control could be effective for law-abiding citizens, it would drive up crime rates by turning them into more vulnerable targets for criminals (Polsby 1994). Emphasizing the number of gun crimes involving people who know each other, other scholars sharply dispute this view (McDowall, Lizotte, and Wiersema 1991). They also note that since many criminals steal their handguns from law-abiding households, reducing the availability of handguns in these households would lessen their availability to the criminal community. Experts disagree on whether criminals in this case would simply turn to even more lethal weapons if denied access to handguns (Reiss and Roth 1993; Wright and Rossi 1986).

The Effectiveness of Tougher Penalties for Handgun Crimes

If handgun control might not reduce gun crimes, what about more certain and severe legal punishment for offenders who use guns to commit crimes? Several jurisdictions have instituted mandatory sentencing (e.g., a minimum one-year prison term) for such offenders. Have these laws reduced gun crime? Scholars once more disagree on what the complex evidence is saying. In 1975 Massachusetts implemented the Bartley-Fox law, which required a one-year prison term for people carrying firearms outside their homes without a permit. Gun crimes in the state went down substantially in the next two years, but they also went down in other cities that had no such law (Pierce and Bowers 1981). Michigan passed a law in 1977 requiring a two-year prison term for gun-related crimes. A later analysis found that although murder, robbery, and assault in Detroit declined after the law took effect, this decrease began five months before the law became operative. The researchers thus concluded that the law had little effect on violent crime in Detroit (Loftin and McDowall 1981).

About a decade later, Detroit passed a similar law that took effect in 1987. This law required a jail sentence for anyone carrying a gun illegally in public and was aimed at reducing homicides occurring on the streets, in stores, or other places outside the home. A team of researchers found that such "outside homicides" increased 10 percent in the year after the law took effect, while homicides occurring inside the home increased 22 percent. The increase in gun homicides was lower than the increase in nonfirearm homicides. Although this evidence indicates the law may have prevented outside gun homicides from increasing even more than they did, the researchers concluded that no definite conclusion could be drawn from their findings. They also noted that the law was not enforced because of lack of space in the local jail system (O'Carroll et al. 1991).

Despite the complexity of these studies' results, many scholars conclude that tougher penalties for gun crime have reduced such crimes (Roth 1994). Others are not so optimistic. James D. Wright and Teri E. Vail (2000:579) conclude, "None of the 20,000 firearms regulations so far enacted has reduced the incidence of criminal violence by any appreciable amount...." Although he shares this view, Gary Kleck (1997) nonetheless favors efforts that target people with criminal records or histories of violence or mental illness. He would use background checks and permit laws to deny such people the right to own firearms.

In sum, the scholarly evidence leaves us uncertain that stricter gun control or stiffer penalties for gun crimes will reduce these crimes. A recent government report on violence concluded that gun control efforts "may reduce firearm homicides" if they're enforced well enough (Reiss and Roth 1993:279), and this view remains popular among many experts. Other scholars are more pessimistic. The U.S. gun culture is simply too strong, they say, and the number of handguns and other firearms too large, for these measures to be effective. Kleck (1995:34) argues that gun control efforts by liberals and "get tough" proposals by conservatives both ignore the far more important causes of violence in the United States, including inequality and "the all-pervasive economic and social consequences of a history of slavery and racism." Wright and Vail (2000:578) concur, "[S]olutions to the problems of crime and violence in this nation will probably have to be found elsewhere." Additional research and evaluation of gun control efforts are clearly needed.

What can we do to reduce violent crime? Recall the explanations of crime stressed in this chapter: economic deprivation, criminogenic urban conditions, masculinity, racial discrimination, and inadequate and abusive parenting. A sociological approach to reducing violent crime focuses on all these causes. Programs that would reduce poverty and joblessness, lessen urban blight, and improve the quality of parenting all hold the potential for significant reductions in violent crime. It's beyond the scope of this book to discuss which specific programs would best accomplish these goals. Although they certainly haven't been in fashion as federal spending on social issues has been severely cut back during the last two decades, such programs are essential if we want to make a dent in violent crime (Currie 1985).

To the extent that racial discrimination against African-Americans and other people of color heightens their angry aggression and use of violence, successful efforts to reduce such discrimination would also help reduce violent crime. More than thirty years ago the Kerner Commission (1968), appointed by President Lyndon Johnson to consider the urban riots of the late 1960s, warned that the United States was becoming two societies—one black, one white—separate and unequal. Unless steps were taken to reduce racial discrimination in employment, housing, and other areas, the Commission said, we could expect more riots. A generation later, whites and blacks are even more separate and more unequal (Hacker 1992; Massey and Denton 1993). Unless this situation is reversed, we may well be setting the stage for a surge in urban violence, especially if and when the strong economy that marked much of the 1990s begins to slow down.

A final focus for reducing violent crime must be masculinity. We must begin to raise our sons differently from how we have been raising them. If we continue to accept the notions that "boys will be boys" and that they need to learn to "fight like a man," we're ensuring that interpersonal violence will continue.

What History Tells Us

None of these roots of violent crime will be easy to eliminate, but if we don't begin to address them, our nation will continue to be beset with violent crime. Lest we despair too much over our situation, history tells us that reductions in violent crime *are* possible. Homicide rates in Europe were much higher in the Middle Ages than now, historians say (Butterfield 1994; Gurr 1989a). Amsterdam's rate in the mid-1400s was about 47 per 100,000, compared to about 1.5 per 100,000 in the early 1800s. Medieval England's rate was about ten times higher than it is now, and about twice as high as the current U.S. rate.

Most homicides in medieval England took place among farmers in their fields who literally fought over scarce resources (e.g., land) and over insults to honor they took quite seriously. Because the courts were seen as slow and expensive, violence was a preferred way to resolve disputes. More generally, medieval people in England and other nations lived in a culture that "accepted, even glorified, many forms of brutality and aggressive behavior" (Gurr 1989a:21). Knives and quarterstaffs, the heavy wooden stick used by Little John in the Robin Hood movies, were their weapons of choice (Butterfield 1994).

The major reason for the drop in high homicide rates in England and other European nations in the 1500s and 1600s was the development of a "civilizing process" marked by the rise of "courtly manners" and an increase in the use of courts to resolve private disputes (Elias 1978 [1939]). The increase in such state power first occurred in cities, whose homicide rates, surprisingly, were lower than those in rural areas.

A similar process later occurred in the United States, where the homicide rate peaked in the mid-1800s and then fell after the Civil War through the early 1900s, even though cities were growing rapidly (Monkkonen 1981). The same trend occurred in Canada (Boritch and Hagan 1990). Scholars attribute this homicide decrease in the face of urban growth to the greater control that factories exerted over people's behavior, to the spread of public schools, and to the growth of the YMCA and other institutions that stressed moral behavior (Butterfield 1994; Lane 1980). U.S. homicide rates rose during the Great Depression of the 1930s and then generally fell until the 1960s.

Looking at the historical decrease in homicides until the 1960s, historian Eric Monkkonen sees some hope: "What we are finding is that violence is not an immutable human problem.... The good news is violence can go down. The bad news is, we need to learn how to make it happen" (Butterfield 1994:16).

If history tells us that violence can go down, it also tells us that this won't happen if we don't provide economic opportunity for the poor and people of color. For example, despite the general decrease in U.S. homicide rates between the post-Civil War period and the 1960s, the African-American homicide rate did not decrease during this time, as African-Americans continued to experience racial discrimination and declining economic opportunity (Lane 1986). Their rates finally did drop in the late 1940s and early 1950s, when increasing employment opportunities in factories and offices lowered black unemployment rates. Later in the 1950s, however, these unemployment rates rose as factories closed or moved from northern cities, and the urban decay that we see today accelerated. Not surprisingly, African-American homicide rates rose as a result (Lane 1989).

The increase in African-American rates after the 1950s reflected a more general, sharp increase in homicide rates in the United States and many other Western nations (Skogan 1989). Much of this rise stemmed from the great increase in the number of young men in the 1960s from the post-World War II baby boom and the decreased influence of conventional institutions in that turbulent decade. The Vietnam War may also have had an effect, since the historical record in the United States and elsewhere indicates that war contributes to increased violent crime. A possible reason for this connection is that wars legitimize violence (Gurr 1989b).

Underscoring this chapter's focus on economic inequality, a final reason for the post-1950s homicide increase is that the United States and other Western nations had become "post-industrial" societies providing fewer jobs for people at the bottom of the socioeconomic ladder (Gurr 1989b). The growing black unemployment rate in the late 1950s thus reflected a larger structural problem. Urban working-class youths in particular could no longer count on factory jobs and faced increasing unemployment or, at most, *underemployment* in fast-food and other low-paying jobs. As political scientist Ted Robert Gurr (1989b:48) observes,

> The result is a high level of structural unemployment among the least well-educated young people in virtually every European and North American city. Many are intensely resentful of their status at the lower margins of affluent societies. Because of their class background and social experiences they also are the people who are least likely to feel inhibited against interpersonal violence.

SUMMARY AND CONCLUSION

Violent crime remains one of the most serious problems in the United States. The fact that some groups—the poor, people of color, women—are more vulnerable to violent crime than others underscores the consequences of economic, racial, and gender inequality in U.S. society.

Throughout this chapter, I emphasized the structural and cultural sources of homicide, assault, and robbery. This sociological perspective reminds us that the ultimate causes of violent crime lie in the social environment. That means that even if we could somehow eliminate the violent individuals among us, others will soon take their place unless we also do something about the structural problems that make violence so common. A sociological understanding of violent crime thus underscores the need to reduce economic and racial inequality and to reshape masculinity if we want to reduce violent crime significantly.

One important theme of this chapter was that people we know, and in some cases know very well, account for much of the violence against us: Nonstrangers commit about 80 percent of all homicides and at least half of all assaults. In the next chapter we examine several kinds of violence that women and children are especially likely to suffer from family members and other intimates.

KEY TERMS

assault	manslaughter
handgun control	masculinity
homicide	mass media
interpersonal violence	robbery
interracial	victim-offender relationship
intraracial	

STUDY QUESTIONS

1. How does an understanding of the type of weapon involved in homicides help us understand why homicides occur?
2. Why is the United States more violent than many other industrial nations?
3. Why do men commit almost all serious violent crime? To what extent do you think the gender difference in crime is biologically caused?
4. Do you think various gun control policies would help reduce the homicide rate? Why or why not?

The National Consortium on Violence Research (NCOVR) is an organization of scholars from many universities and other organizations whose focus is, quite naturally, on violence research. According to NCOVR, "Its members come from different disciplinary backgrounds including the social, biological, medical, legal and political sciences. The Consortium is comprised of 57 members who are eminent scholars in the field of violence research and who are affiliated with 32 institutions, across 19 states and in 3 countries.

Access the NCOVR Web site at **http://www.ncovr.heinz.cmu.edu**. Click on **Research** in the left window. Under **The Research Program** heading that appears, you'll see that NCOVR "works to increase knowledge about the dynamics of violence at three related levels: individual development, situational dynamics, and community influences." What are the differences among these three levels of analysis? How, if at all, do they conform to the several explanations of crime chapters included in our textbook?

Now click on **Publications** in the left window. A series of NCOVR published research reports will now appear. Click on any one of these reports to access its abstract. Read through the abstract. What hypothesis is this report exploring? At what level of analysis is its investigation addressed? Judging from the abstract, how does the report's research extend our knowledge of origins, dynamics, and/or outcomes of violence and of ways to reduce violence?

VIOLENCE AGAINST
WOMEN AND CHILDREN

Crime in the News

"*Boyfriend Charged in Grisly Slaying,*" the headline said. *According to the article under it, a 25-year-old man allegedly killed his former girlfriend and tried to kill their two-week-old baby daughter and his former girlfriend's sister and mother. When the police arrived at the crime scene, they found that the girlfriend and her mother had been beaten with a shovel, tied up with duct tape, and their heads wrapped with plastic. The baby had also been covered with plastic but was found barely alive. Before fleeing the house, the suspect forced the mother to give him her ATM pin number and then stole her car.*

Source: Hunter 2000.

271

The murder of more than 1,300 women each year by their husbands, ex-husbands, boyfriends, or ex-boyfriends has been called a "silent epidemic" (Stone, Einhorn, and Litvin 1994:3). It received extra attention when football star and television celebrity O. J. Simpson was arrested in June 1994 after his ex-wife, Nicole Brown Simpson, and one of her friends, Ron Goldman, were found viciously murdered. It soon became known that O. J. Simpson had previously beaten Nicole Brown Simpson, a revelation that shocked the defendant's friends and much of the public. Scholars and other observers pointed out that the beatings were symptomatic of the violence women routinely experience from their current and former husbands and boyfriends and from other men in their lives (Ehrenreich 1994; Gardner 1994).

A few months after O. J. Simpson's arrest, a young mother, Susan Smith, was arrested for allegedly murdering her children by pushing her car into a lake while they slept inside. As noted in the last chapter, Smith initially claimed that a black man had abducted her children. Her later confession to the murders angered people throughout the nation and led several observers to reflect on the much larger problem of violence against children that her crime reflected. Most of this violence, they noted, is committed by parents and other people the children know (Kastor 1994).

Although the old saying "Women and children first!" was meant to protect women and children on the Titanic and other capsized ships, too often this saying also applies to violent victimization by family members and other nonstrangers. This violence takes on several related forms: rape and battering of women and physical and sexual abuse of children.

Just thirty years ago, rape and battering were hardly ever discussed in or outside the classroom, even though they'd been occurring for centuries. Then these crimes began to capture the attention of the modern women's movement, which was still in its early stages. Because of the feminist movement, there are now probably thousands of scholarly studies and mass media reports of rape and battering. Many college courses now deal with these crimes, and many campuses have Rape Awareness Weeks and other events calling attention to their nature and extent. This chapter discusses the major findings from the burgeoning research on these crimes and continues the book's emphasis on the structural sources of criminality.

 ## VIOLENCE AGAINST WOMEN

Most criminology texts place rape and spousal violence as separate sections in a violent crime chapter. This separation obscures the gendered nature of these two crimes: Although most victims of homicide, assault, and robbery are men, almost all victims of rape, and most victims of violence between spouses and other intimates, are women.

Sociologically speaking, this isn't surprising. Socially, economically, and physically, women have much less power than men. As the previous chapter's discussion of violence against Native Americans and African-Americans indicates, powerless groups are often the victims of violence by those with power. Rape and battering are no different. We can't understand violence against women unless we recognize men's social, economic, political, and physical dominance and women's lack of the same. It's no accident that men are almost always the ones who rape and batter, nor that women are their targets. Given this context, rape and battering may even be regarded as the equivalent of hate crimes against women. To emphasize these points and to develop some common themes, I examine rape and battering here in a single section.

An International Problem

As we look around the globe, violence against women appears to be a worldwide phenomenon. Summarizing the results of hundreds of studies, a recent report estimated that one-third of women across the world have been raped, beaten, or otherwise abused (Associated Press 2000). Amnesty International and other human rights groups have documented such violence (Curtius 1994). In Pakistan, for example, women in police custody are sexually and physically abused. In Kuwait, male employers routinely rape their foreign maids. In other countries, female genital mutilation is a routine practice, affecting some 114 million women worldwide. In India and Pakistan, "dowry deaths" claim the lives of many women (see the International Focus box). Other forms of domestic violence are also common in India and elsewhere. In a recent survey of married men in Northern India, about half said they had physically or sexually abused their wives (Martin et al. 1999).

INTERNATIONAL FOCUS

Dowry Deaths in India and Pakistan

In India and Pakistan, a bride's parents are supposed to pay the groom money or goods. If they fail to come up with the dowry they've promised, the groom often beats his wife, and he and his relatives may even murder her. To hide the murder, they often burn the woman with kerosene and claim she caught fire accidentally in the kitchen. Police then accept bribes from the husband and/or his relatives to certify the murder as an accident.

Estimates of the number of annual dowry deaths in India range from 6,000 to 15,000. Human rights workers and physicians in Pakistan estimate that about thirty women are burned alive there each month by their husbands and in-laws. The mother of one such victim murdered by her husband recalled what happened. "She was burned to death; my beautiful daughter was burned to death," she said. "In the hospital, she just kept saying, 'They burned me.... They burned me.' She was our darling, our oldest daughter, and she was so beautiful and young." A Pakistani human rights attorney noted, "These cases are some of the most horrifying and gruesome human rights abuses in the world." Although they are common in Pakistan, she added, they reflect a larger international problem. "It is really, at bottom, simply about violence and cruelty to women. That is not a story unique to Pakistan."

To make matters worse for the burned Pakistani women, there are only two hospital burn units in the entire nation. The two units have few beds and are plagued by filthy conditions causing many burn victims to suffer fatal infections even if they survive the burns. A U.S. reporter who visited one of the burn units wrote of four victims begging a doctor to help them: "The women were writhing in pain, and needed pain killers and fresh bandages, all of which he [the doctor] said he did not have." In one bed was a 17-year-old woman whose burns had left her without her nose and lips. She managed to whisper to the doctor, "I was very beautiful before this happened.... Please pray for me. Please help me."

Sources: Fischbach and Herbert 1997; Gargan 1993; Mandelbaum 1999; Sennott 1995.

Some of the worst abuses of women occur in wartime. This is not a new phenomenon. In one of the first books on rape, Susan Brownmiller (1975) wrote that the wartime rape of women has been occurring for centuries. In the 1990s, some 80 percent of the victims of ethnic conflicts and wars in various nations were civilians, and most of these civilians have been women and children. In nations as dissimilar geographically and culturally as Mexico and Bosnia, women have been routinely raped and genitally mutilated during ethnic and other conflicts (Curtius 1994).

Rape and battering in the United States are thus part of a larger, international pattern of violence against women that also includes murder, torture, sexual slavery, incest, genital mutilation, and involuntary sterilization. Jane Caputi and Diana E. H. Russell (1992:15) term these acts *sexist terrorism*. They're directed against women *because* they are women and are motivated by "hatred, contempt, pleasure, or a sense of ownership of women."

In its most severe form, such violence involves what Caputi and Russell call *femicide*, or the murder of women. They liken femicide and other anti-women violence to the lynchings of blacks that were designed to reinforce white dominance over African-Americans. In a similar fashion, they say, men's violence against women helps maintain their dominance over them. Femicide goes back at least to the witch hunting in medieval Europe that killed some 300,000 people, most of them poor women. The gendered nature of these witch killings leads one scholar, Marianne Hester, to see them as "part of the ongoing attempt by men ... to ensure the continuance of male supremacy" (1992:36). In the modern era, women in the United States and elsewhere are murdered by men who have been battering them. In other countries they are also killed during ethnic and political conflicts or because they violate rigid cultural codes of sexuality (Caputi and Russell 1992). Whatever the reason and the context, women are murdered or assaulted because they are women. Men are not killed or assaulted for the same reasons.

Defining Rape and Battering

Put most simply, rape may be defined as forced sexual intercourse. The National Crime Victimization Survey (NCVS) defines rape as "carnal knowledge through the use of force or threat of force, including attempts; attempted rape may consist of verbal threats of rape." The NCVS interviewer's manual is more specific: "Rape is forced sexual intercourse and includes both psychological coercion as well as physical force. Forced sexual intercourse means vaginal, anal, or oral penetration by the offender(s). The category also includes incidents where the penetration is from a foreign object such as a bottle." A related crime, sexual assault, involves unwanted sexual contact that does not involve sexual intercourse. The NCVS says that sexual assaults "include attacks or attempted attacks generally involving (unwanted) sexual contact between victim and offender. Sexual assaults may or may not involve force and include such things as grabbing or fondling. Sexual assault also includes verbal threats" (Bachman and Saltzman 1995:6–7).

Battering or domestic violence may be defined as physical attacks committed by intimates: spouses or ex-spouses, boyfriends or girlfriends, and ex-boyfriends or ex-girlfriends. These attacks include both aggravated assaults, where a weapon is used or a serious injury occurs, and simple assaults, where no weapon is used and only a minor injury occurs. Although this definition of battering allows for men to be battered, we'll see later that almost all battering is done against women. One problem with defining battering as physical attacks is that doing so excludes psychological abuse, which is often as harmful or even more harmful than physical abuse (Johan 1994). Because there's much more research on physical rather than psychological abuse by intimates, we'll limit our discussion to the physical dimension.

The Extent of Rape and Battering

RAPE

When the women's movement turned its attention to rape in the early 1970s, it documented the role rape played in women's daily lives. Thus, Susan Griffin began her now-classic essay, "Rape: The All-American Crime" (1971), by saying, "I have never been free of the fear of rape. From a very early age I, like most women, have thought of rape as a part of my natural environment—something to be feared and prayed against like fire or lightning. I never asked why men raped; I simply thought it one of the many mysteries of human nature."

Research since the early 1970s confirms the magnitude of the rape problem. The NCVS estimates that 333,000 rapes and sexual assaults occurred in 1998 against people age 12 or older, for a rate of 2.7 per 1,000 females and only 0.2 per 1,000 males. Most of these rapes/sexual assaults, 74 percent, were committed by nonstrangers, and only 25 percent were committed by strangers (Rennison 1999). Although these data were listed in Chapter 4, they bear repeating here (Table 10.1).

While the NCVS focuses on crimes in the past year, other studies estimate how many women have been raped at some point in their lifetime. The National Violence against Women Survey (NVAW), also mentioned in Chapter 4, found that 18 percent of women had been raped at least once in their lifetime, with 83 percent of the rapes committed by men they knew (Tjaden and Thoennes 1999). Other studies find that about 20–25 percent of women have experienced a rape or an attempted rape, with 75 percent or more of the rapes committed by men they know (Koss, Gidycz, and Wisniewski 1987; Russell 1984). Reporting a higher rate of victimization, a study of San Francisco women estimated that 46 percent of them suffered a completed or attempted rape at least once in their lives (Russell and Howell 1983).

A study of a random sample of 420 women in Toronto, located in a country not normally known for its violence, found even more alarming figures. Melanie

TABLE 10.1 VICTIM-OFFENDER RELATIONSHIP FOR RAPE AND SEXUAL ASSAULT (% OF ALL OFFENSES)

OFFENDER	PERCENT
Nonstranger	74
Intimate	18
Other relative	8
Friend/acquaintance	48
Stranger	25
Relationship Unknown	2

Source: Rennison 1999.

Randall and Lori Haskell (1995) supervised face-to-face interviews with the subjects that lasted about two hours each. Of the 420 women, 56 percent reported at least one experience of forced or attempted forced sexual intercourse, with 83 percent of these rapes committed by someone they knew. When Randall and Haskell included other forms of sexual assault, including unwanted sexual touching to the breasts or genitals, two-thirds of the subjects reported at least one completed or attempted sexual assault, including rape. The researchers concluded that "it is more common than not for a woman to have an experience of sexual assault during her lifetime" (p. 22).

Many rapes are "marital rapes" committed by intimates (husbands/ex-husbands or boyfriends/ex-boyfriends). These rapes are often more traumatic for women than stranger rapes for at least two reasons: First, they cause a woman to question whether she can trust any man. Second, women raped by husbands or boyfriends they live with often have to continue living with them (Bergen 1996; Russell 1990).

In Table 10.1 we saw from NCVS figures that intimates account for almost one-fifth of all rapes and sexual assaults. The National Women's Survey, a federally sponsored survey of a random sample of 4,000 women, found similarly that intimates had committed about one-fifth of the rapes reported by its respondents (Skorneck 1992). The San Francisco study noted earlier found 14 percent of ever-married women reporting they'd been raped by a husband/ex-husband (Russell 1990). The NVAW survey found that intimates, including dates, committed 62 percent of the rapes its respondents reported. The Toronto study discussed previously found that 30 percent of all sexual assaults occurring after a woman reached the age of 16 were committed by current and former husbands and boyfriends. Taking all these studies together, a fair estimate is that intimates commit at least one-fifth of all rapes. Such rapes are especially likely to occur in marriages or relationships that also include battering (Fagan and Browne 1994). In the Toronto study, half of the women reporting a physical assault by an intimate had also been sexually assaulted by the same man.

BATTERING

What about battering? The best evidence indicates that battering is even more common than rape. The NCVS estimates that about 800,000 assaults (including 174,000 aggravated assaults) by intimates occurred in 1998, for a rate of close to 4 assaults per 1,000 persons. Although done several years earlier, the National Family Violence Survey (NFVS), a widely cited national survey of married couples, yields an even higher estimate. In 1975 the NFVS asked its respondents whether several violent acts, ranging from using a weapon or beating to slapping, shoving, or pushing, had taken place in the past year or at any time during the marriage. It found that 12 percent of the husbands had committed at least one of these acts against their wives during the past year, and 27 percent had committed at least one of the acts during the entire marriage (Straus, Gelles, and Steinmetz 1980). A 1985 follow-up survey by the NFVS found an 11 percent figure for husband-to-wife violence taking place in the past year, yielding an estimated 6,250,000 assaults against wives in 1985 among the entire population (Straus and Gelles 1986). As almost one-third of these incidents involved serious assaults such as punching, beating up, and using a knife or gun, the estimated number of serious assaults against wives in 1985 was 1,800,000.

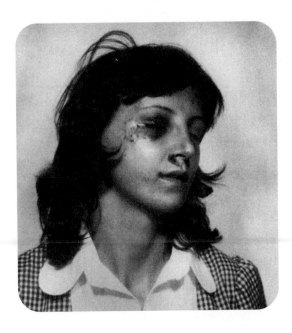

◄ *Hundreds of thousands of U.S. women are physically attacked each year by male intimates.*

Allowing for underreporting and other methodological problems, the researchers estimated that the *true* amount of violence against wives may be twice as high as the figures just mentioned, with (using the 1975 data) about 24 percent of wives suffering at least one of these acts of violence in a given year, and about 54 percent at any time in the marriage. Thus as many as 12 million wives may have been assaulted by their husbands in 1985, with about 3.6 million suffering serious assaults.

The NVAW survey found that physical assault by intimate partners occurred at a rate between those reported in the two surveys just discussed. Just over 22 percent of the women in the NVAW survey said they had been assaulted (defined by acts in a list similar to that used by the NFVS) in their lifetime by a partner, and 1.3 percent reported being assaulted in the last year, for an estimate of 1.3 million such assaults annually (Tjaden and Thoennes 1998).

Research in Canada also reveals a high prevalence of battering, even though Canada, as noted earlier, isn't normally considered as violent as the United States. In the study of 420 Toronto women mentioned earlier, 115 women, or 27 percent, reported having been physically assaulted by a husband or other male intimate. In about one-fourth of the cases of physical assault, or about 6.5 percent of the whole sample, the male partner had threatened to kill the woman (Randall and Haskell 1995). A 1993 government survey of a national, random sample of some 12,300 Canadian women found a similar prevalence of battering, with 25 percent of the women in the survey reporting at least one physical assault by a husband or common-law (i.e., living together) partner, a figure that rose to 29 percent among women who had ever been married or lived with someone (Randall and Haskell 1995).

Figures like the ones just mentioned lead family violence expert Angela Browne to conclude that women "are more likely to be attacked and injured by a male partner than any other category of person. They are also more likely to be killed by a male partner than any other category of person" (Reynolds 1987:A18). The American Psychological Association reports that about one-third of all U.S. women will be assaulted by a male partner during their lifetime (Elias 1994).

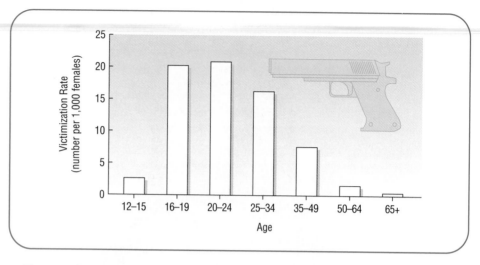

▲ Figure 10.1 Age and Intimate Violence Committed against Women, 1997
(Number of victimizations per 1,000 women in each age group)
Source: Greenfeld et al. 1998.

The Social Patterning of Rape and Battering

Like many other crimes, rape and battering are more common among some demographic subgroups than others. One of the biggest risk factors is age: Young women are much more likely than older women to experience intimate violence (see Figure 10.1).

The Question of Social Class

The question of social class differences in rape and battering is a bit more complicated. Many treatments of these crimes emphasize that they transcend class boundaries. Although that's true, the NCVS does find that the poorest women have rates of intimate violence almost eight times as high as women in the highest income bracket (Figure 10.2). Supporting the NCVS's finding of a poverty-intimate violence link, the NFVS survey of married couples found family violence rates five times higher among the poorest families in its sample than among the richest (Straus, Gelles, and Steinmetz 1980). Such social class differences underscore an important consequence of economic inequality in society.

That said, it remains true that rape and battering aren't rare in the middle and upper classes. As O. J. Simpson's case illustrates, men in all walks of life commit these crimes (Johnson and Hermelin 1995). In 1989, police responding to a "domestic dispute" saw Nicole Brown Simpson, "her lip bloodied, face swollen and eye blackened," running across the lawn and collapsing. At that point she screamed, "He's going to kill me, he's going to kill me!" When the police asked her who, she said, "O. J." (McGrory 1994:12).

Studies of college students provide strong evidence that rape transcends social class boundaries. About 20 to 30 percent of college women report having experienced completed or attempted rapes, and about the same proportion of male students report they have forced, or attempted to force, women to have sex with them (Kanin 1970; Koss, Gidycz, and Wisniewski 1987). These students include campus

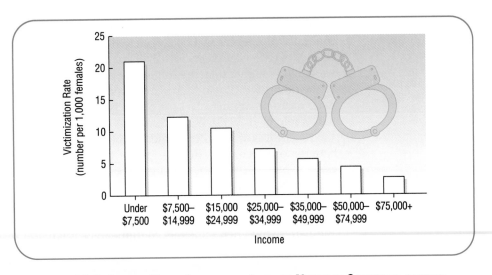

▲ FIGURE 10.2 ANNUAL FAMILY INCOME AND INTIMATE VIOLENCE COMMITTED AGAINST WOMEN, 1997
(NUMBER OF VICTIMIZATIONS PER 1,000 WOMEN IN EACH INCOME GROUP)
Sources: Greenfeld et al. 1998; Gelles 1978; Rennison 1999.

leaders, athletes, and fraternity members (Martin and Hummer 1995; Schwartz 1995). Other studies ask male students to say whether they would commit a rape if they knew they wouldn't be caught. In these studies, 25 to 40 percent of male students indicate they would be at least somewhat likely to rape (Briere and Malamuth 1983; Tieger 1981). The college student evidence leads Diana Scully (1995:207) to conclude that "sexual aggression is commonplace in college dating relationships."

INTIMATE VIOLENCE AGAINST WOMEN OF COLOR

Although there do appear to be social class differences in rape and battering despite their distribution throughout the population, the evidence on race and ethnicity is less clear. Although several studies find that black and white women and Hispanic and non-Hispanic women are equally likely to experience these crimes (Lockhart 1987), the NCVS finds that black women experience an intimate violence rate of 11.7 per 1,000, while white women experience a lower rate of 8.2 per 1,000. However, the NCVS also finds that non-Hispanic women experience a slightly higher rate of intimate violence than Hispanic women (Greenfeld et al. 1998).

The 1975 NFVS found the battering rate higher for black women than for white women, but also found black women's rate lower than that of their white counterparts of similar incomes (Straus, Gelles, and Steinmetz 1980). The 1985 follow-up also found the battering rate slightly higher among Hispanic women than among non-Hispanic white women (Straus and Smith 1990). Several methodological problems, including underreporting by women of color which may be even greater than that for white women, probably account for these contradictory findings (Rasche 1988). At this point it must remain unclear whether African-American, Hispanic, and other women of color are indeed more likely than non-Hispanic white women to be battered and victims of other intimate violence (Fagan and Browne 1994). If women of color do have higher victimization rates, their lower incomes and disproportionately urban residence probably help explain these rates.

For homicide, there may be a clearer race/ethnicity difference. A study of intrafamily homicides in Los Angeles in the 1970s found the following rates per 100,000 of each group: Anglo, 2.3; Hispanic, 3.1; Black, 17.9. Thus the Hispanic rate was slightly higher than the Anglo rate, and the Black rate much higher than either of the other two (Loya, Mercy, and Associates 1985). Nationally, the rate of intimate murders among blacks is about four times higher than that among whites (Greenfeld et al. 1998).

Regardless of whether women of color are more likely than white women to be battered or raped, they do face greater problems in seeking help from rape-crisis centers, battered women's shelters, social service agencies, the police, and other sources (Matthews 1989; Rasche 1988). A major problem is that the anti-rape and battered women's movements were begun by white feminists, and over the years have not included women of color in great numbers. As a result, rape-crisis centers and battered women's shelters continue to be relatively absent in inner cities and other areas, such as Native American reservations, where women of color live.

For women in the United States who do not speak English, another problem is the language barrier, says Christine E. Rasche (1988). Even when rape-crisis centers and battered women's shelters do exist, they do not always have interpreters to whom these women could talk. The same problem applies when a non-English-speaking woman calls the police for help. Many times her husband or partner may speak English better than she, and thus be able to convince the police there is no real problem. Sometimes the husband or partner even has to translate the woman's words to the police; as you might expect, they can't be trusted to tell the police exactly what the woman is saying.

For immigrant women and undocumented workers, the problem is even worse, notes Rasche. In addition to the language barrier, these women also face possible legal problems, including deportation or arrest, should they seek help from the police or social service agencies.

Certain racial or ethnic groups may also contain cultural traditions that make battered or raped women especially reluctant to seek help. As Rasche points out, a strong norm on Native American reservations is that one doesn't seek help outside one's own community. Reservations are usually in isolated rural areas, and it may be difficult for a woman to get off the reservation even if she wants to get help. If she decides to seek help on the reservation, it's likely that law enforcement officers and social service agency workers know her and/or her abuser.

In Asian-American communities, Rasche notes, hostility toward the larger, white society may inhibit women from reporting their victimization. The particularly high respect in Asian-American families for men leads to the same inhibition.

Another problem affecting many women of color is fear of, and hostility toward, the police. A good deal of evidence suggests that people of color of either sex are more likely than whites to distrust the police (Huang and Vaughn 1996). This feeling may lead women of color to be less likely than white women to call the police in cases of battering or rape (Rasche 1988). One additional problem facing battered African-American women is that the police may have more trouble noticing bruises on their bodies than they would on white women's bodies (Rasche 1988).

Explaining Rape and Battering

A basic issue in explaining rape and battering is whether the crimes are more psychological or sociological in origin. A psychological perspective assumes that many and even most rapists and batterers are psychologically abnormal. A noted proponent of this view is A. Nicholas Groth (1979:5), who says, "Rape is always a symptom of some psychological dysfunction, either temporary and transient or chronic and repetitive." Although Groth wrote this more than twenty years ago, many psychologists continue to believe that psychopathological disorders account for most rape and battering (O'Leary 1993). In contrast, a sociological approach emphasizes the structural and cultural roots of rape and battering. Adopting this view, Diana Scully (1995:199) says it's wrong to assume that "individual psychopathology is the predisposing factor that best explains the majority of sexual violence against women." This assumption, she says, overlooks the social sources of this violence and implies it's "unusual or strange" (p. 204) rather than a common phenomenon of everyday life.

In evaluating this debate, recall Chapter 5's point that psychologically normal people are quite capable of committing antisocial and even violent behavior. Although it might be difficult to understand how psychologically normal men could rape and batter, there's ample evidence that normal men commit these and other crimes. While no one will deny that some rapists, batterers, and other criminals have mental disorders, these individuals comprise only a very small proportion of all criminals. The remainder are as psychologically normal as you or I.

Support for this view comes from the evidence, discussed previously, on the prevalence of rape and battering. If these crimes are so common, it becomes very difficult to argue that they stem from psychological abnormality, unless we want to assume that 20 to 50 percent of all men are psychologically abnormal. That, of course, would be silly. Instead, these figures indicate that structural and cultural forces must be at work.

GENDER AND ECONOMIC INEQUALITY

A key force here is gender inequality. Feminist scholars see rape and battering as inevitable consequences of patriarchy, or male dominance. These crimes reflect women's social and economic inequality but also allow men to exert and maintain their power over women (Bart and Moran 1993; Dobash and Dobash 1992; Scully 1995). This doesn't mean that all men rape or batter women but that a gender-based analysis of violence against women is necessary.

Anthropological evidence supports this view. Peggy Reaves Sanday (1981) studied 95 tribal societies on which a wide variety of information had been gathered. In 47 of these societies, rape was unknown or rare, and in 18 rape was common. She then compared the rape-absent societies with the rape-prone societies and found that women in the rape-prone tribes had less decision-making and other power than women in the rape-absent tribes. A similar study by Rae Lesser Blumberg (1979) focused on women's economic power in 61 preindustrial societies. Beatings of women by male partners were more common in societies where women had less economic power.

Evidence from the United States complements this anthropological evidence. Larry Baron and Murray A. Straus (1987) compiled a "gender equality index" for each of the fifty states. The index measured women's economic, political, and legal equality with men and was based on such things as women's median income compared to men and the proportion of women in state legislatures. They obtained rape rates for each state from the UCR. In a complex analysis holding many other variables constant, they then found that states with greater gender inequality had higher rape rates. The authors concluded, "This finding is consistent with feminist theory and suggests that gender inequality contributes to a social climate that is conducive to violence against women (p. 481)." In a related study, Straus (1994b) found that states with greater gender inequality also had higher rates of assaults against wives by their husbands.

If gender inequality contributes to rape, so does economic inequality. In her classic essay, Susan Griffin (1971) observed that women become convenient scapegoats for the anger some men feel over their low socioeconomic status: "For every man there is always someone lower on the social scale on whom he can take out his aggressions. And that is any woman alive." In this regard, recall Chapter 9's discussion of masculinity and violence. We saw then that men with low socioeconomic status use violent, "opposition" masculine behavior against each other to gain the respect their low status deprives them. A similar argument may be made for their interaction with women, as rape and battering allow them to take out on women their frustration over their economic inequality and to prove their masculinity (Petrik, Olson, and Subotnik 1994).

Supporting this view, several ecological studies find economic deprivation linked to higher rates of rape (Peterson and Bailey 1992). In their study of the fifty states, Baron and Straus (1987:483) also found that states with higher economic inequality had higher rape rates. The authors concluded that "rape may be a way for some men to assert their masculinity in the absence of viable avenues of economic success." Making this same point, a study of rape and battering by African-American men against their spouses and other female partners traced these crimes to the men's anger over their poverty and perceptions of racial mistreatment (Marsh 1993).

CULTURAL MYTHS SUPPORTING RAPE AND BATTERING

If economic and gender inequality make rape and battering inevitable, so do cultural beliefs that either minimize the harm these crimes cause or somehow blame women for their victimization (Dobash and Dobash 1979; Karmen 1995; Yllo 1993). Because these beliefs distort reality, they're often called *cultural myths*. The myths about the two crimes are similar in many ways, but for clarity's sake I'll discuss them separately.

RAPE MYTHS   Two of the most common rape myths are that women like to be raped and ask to be raped by their dress and/or behavior (Warshaw and Parrot 1995). Regarding the first myth, one of the most famous scenes in U.S. cinema occurs in *Gone with the Wind*, when Rhett Butler carries a struggling, resisting Scarlett O'Hara upstairs to have sex with her—in short, to rape her. The next scene we see takes place the following morning, when Scarlett awakens with a satisfied, loving smile on her face.

Unfortunately, traditional psychoanalytic views of women support the idea that they want to be raped. Well-known psychoanalyst Karen Horney (1973) once wrote, "The specific satisfactions sought and found in female sex life and motherhood are of a masochistic nature.... What the woman secretly desires in intercourse is rape and violence, or in the mental sphere, humiliation." Another psychoanalyst, Ner Littner (1973), distinguished between "professional victims" of rape and "true victims." The former unconsciously want to be raped and thus act unknowingly in a way that invites rape, while the former do not unconsciously want to be raped. While psychoanalysts have begun to abandon such notions in the last twenty years, they remain common in both psychoanalytic circles and popular culture (Scully 1995).

Decades after *Gone with the Wind*, many men still believe that women enjoy being forced to have sex and thus don't take her "no" for an answer. A popular saying of the anti-rape movement is that "no means no," but the opposing cultural myth is still very much with us. The traditional dating ritual demanding men "make the first move" feeds into this myth. So does the traditional component of masculinity that says men are more masculine, or "studs," if they have a lot of sex. As we saw from the studies of approval by male college students of hypothetical rapes, many men, even those who do not rape, find the idea of forcing a woman to submit to them to be sexually stimulating. This notion combines with the cultural myth that women enjoy being forced to have sex to produce tragic consequences for women and their loved ones.

The other myth is that women "ask" or "deserve" to be raped by the way they dress and/or behave and thus precipitate their own victimization. In this view, if a woman dresses attractively, drinks, walks into a bar by herself, or hitchhikes, she wants to have sex. If a rape then occurs in these circumstances, it's thought that she really wanted it to happen anyway or at least was "asking" for it to happen. Either way, she bears some blame for the rape. As writer Tim Beneke (1995) puts it, "A woman who assumes freedoms normally restricted to a man (like going out alone at night) and is raped is doing the same thing as a woman who goes out in the rain without an umbrella and catches a cold. Both are considered responsible for what happens to them." In turn, the man who rapes her is held only partly responsible, or perhaps not even held responsible at all.

This reaction is especially common if the women has been sexually active in the past. Unless a woman in any of these circumstances suffers physical injuries in addition to the rape, it's often assumed that she consented to have sex and thus was not raped. Many people don't believe a "real rape" has occurred unless all of the following are true: (1) an injury or other evidence indicates forced intercourse; (2) the woman has not been sexually active; and (3) the woman didn't dress or act in any way that might suggest she wanted to have sex (Estrich 1987; LaFree 1989). This way of thinking ignores the fact that women are often raped without visible injuries. Often they don't physically resist the rape out of fear of even worse consequences, or out of paralysis induced by the sheer terror of the situation.

These rape myths start early in life. A study of Rhode Island students in sixth through ninth grades found more than half saying it's okay for a man to force a woman to have sex if they'd been dating at least six months. About a fifth said it was acceptable for him to force her to have sex if he'd spent money on her on a date. Responding to another item, about half of the students said a woman who dresses "seductively" and walks alone at night is asking to be raped. More than 80 percent said rape is okay when a couple is married, and almost a third said it "would not be wrong" for a man to rape a sexually active woman (Hood 1995; White and Humphrey 1995).

BATTERING MYTHS   Myths about battering also abound. One myth blames battered women for being hit and says that they must have done something to anger their male partners. This myth is akin to the victim-precipitation myth that women "ask" to be raped. Feeding into this myth, a batterer will often say he hit his wife or partner only because she did something to provoke him (Smith 1990). As Andrew Karmen (1995) points out, such statements "are just rationalizations designed to justify and excuse his behavior."

Another, more common myth is that, since many women don't leave their batterers or call the police, the battering can't be that bad. If it were bad, the reasoning goes, then they would leave or call for help. This myth distorts reality in at

Here a woman at a New Jersey shelter for battered women receives counseling. Although shelters for battered women have been an invaluable resource for women trying to leave men who have been beating them, they are only a short-term solution.

least two ways. First, most battered women *do* try to leave their batterers or at least call the police. Second, when women don't leave, they typically have many practical reasons for being hesitant to leave or to otherwise seek help. Perhaps you even know a woman who has been beaten but who has not tried to end the relationship or call the police. Did you ever wonder why she didn't do either of these things? Let's examine her possible reasons (Barnett and LaViolette 1993; Browne 1995).

First, there is often nowhere to go, especially if a woman has children. Battered women's shelters are only a short-term solution and are often filled to capacity. Relatives or friends may be able to house a battered woman and her children for a while. However, this again is only a short-term solution, and many women cannot find a relative or friend to stay with. Second, the question of money applies particularly to wives and other women living with their batterers: Since many battered women have no income independent from their husband or partner's, economically they simply can't afford to leave.

Next, women may fear that if they do try to leave their batterer, he'll track them down and batter them even more than before. They may fear the same consequence if they call the police. Unfortunately, this fear is often warranted. Studies indicate that at least 50 percent of women who do try to leave their batterers are harassed or further assaulted, and that more battered women are killed while trying to leave their abusers than at any other time (Browne 1987). As family violence researcher Angela Browne observes, "If a woman attempts to end or ends the relationship, there's often an escalation in violence just at that point because the man believes he's losing the woman" (Elias 1994:10). Alana Bowman, supervisor of the domestic violence unit in the Los Angeles City Attorney's office, agrees, "The one constant we see is an expectation of traditional roles between men and women—that she'll always do what he says. And very often the violence starts when she won't do what he says anymore, when she threatens to walk out" (Elias 1994:10). Echoing these views, one batterer said about beating his wife, "Every time, Karen would have ugly bruises on her face and neck. She would cry and beg me for a divorce, and I would tell her, '… If I can't have you for my wife, you will die. No one else will have you if you ever try to leave me'" (Browne 1995:232).

In this context, the O. J. Simpson case again serves as a reminder. As sociologist Saundra Gardner (1994:A9) wrote at the time, "Nicole Simpson left. Not only did she leave, she took legal action and divorced her husband. And, she is dead. Unfortunately, this scenario is ... not unusual."

Another reason battered women don't leave is that many continue to love their batterers despite their victimization at his hands. Most relationships and marriages begin in love, and battered women often continue to love their batterers and to hope things will soon improve. Feeding this hope, many batterers are very apologetic after hitting their wives, partners, or girlfriends, and say it won't happen again. It's also true that women often blame themselves for being battered, just as rape survivors often blame themselves for being raped, feeling they shouldn't have "dressed that way," led the guy on, and the like. In short, battered women often accept the myth, noted earlier, that the battering is their fault. Helping this to happen, a man might tell a woman he's battering her for any number of reasons: The kids are noisy; the dinner was cold; she allegedly looked at another man. He thus tries to get her to think it was her fault she had to be hit, and she often believes him. If she does blame herself for being battered, she's less apt to try to leave or call the police.

Finally, experts on women's violence talk about a sense of "learned helplessness" that some women develop from repeated battering (Walker 1984). This self-defense mechanism helps a woman cope with the battering by giving up any hope of improvement and becoming very passive. Social scientists have identified a similar personality syndrome in victims of natural disasters and wars (Walker and Browne 1985).

With all these reasons in mind, the surprising thing might be that so many battered women *do* try to leave or call the police. Certainly if a woman takes neither action, it shouldn't be assumed that the battering "can't be that bad."

The Issue of Husband Battering

The issue of husband battering is the source of a heated debate in the criminology literature. Murray A. Straus, Richard J. Gelles, and associates, the researchers behind the 1975 and 1985 National Family Violence Surveys, have repeatedly stressed that the prevalence of violence by wives against husbands is the same as or even greater than that by husbands against wives, with about 12 percent of each sex committing at least one act of violence (contained in a "Conflict Tactics Scales" [CTS] list ranging from slapping to using a knife or gun) against a spouse in a given year (Straus 1993; Straus and Gelles 1986). Studies using the CTS to examine dating relationships also report gender equivalence in battering (Marshall and Rose 1990).

In their early work, Straus and his colleagues noted this gender similarity obscures some important differences that make battering a far more serious problem for women (Straus 1980). One difference is that a wife's violence is usually in self-defense or the result of a history of battering, while a husband's violence is intended simply to injure and dominate his wife. Another difference is that women tend to commit the more minor acts of violence (e.g., slapping or pushing), while men tend to perpetrate the more severe acts (e.g., beating or using a weapon). Men are also much more likely to repeat their violence. In another difference, even when women and men both slap or punch, the man's greater strength allows him to inflict a far more severe injury. A final difference is that batterers tend to be especially likely to hit a pregnant partner.

In their more recent work based on their 1985 survey, the original CTS researchers have abandoned their earlier argument that women's violence tends to be in self-defense. Instead, they conclude from their 1985 data that women often initiate violence against their husbands and are not acting in self-defense or in response to a history of battering (Stets and Straus 1990; Straus 1993). Their assertion of "sexual symmetry in marital violence," as it's often called, has received considerable attention in the popular media and has often been cited as evidence that the attention given to the battering of women is misdirected because it ignores the battering of men (Pagelow 1994; Young 1994). As the title of one newspaper column critical of the attention given to battered women put it, "Yes, There's Spouse Abuse, But ..." (Urschel 1994).

As you might expect, the assertion of gender equivalence in battering has been very heavily criticized (Browne 1993; Dobash et al. 1992; Schwartz 1987). Some of the most common criticisms invoke the important qualifications that Straus and colleagues noted in their early work, namely that women's "violence" against their husbands and partners is best considered self-defense or the result of repeated battering, and that men injure women far more than women injure men. Among other things, critics also charge that CTS measures ignore the context of violence and don't include rapes and other acts that husbands and male partners inflict.

Another problem is that some CTS measures are too broad to discriminate among various kinds of violence. For example, one of the CTS items is "bit, kicked, or hit with fist." As Demie Kurz (1993:94) points out, "a woman who bites is equated with a man who kicks or hits with a fist." Kurz also argues that even a woman who "initiates" violence is often still acting in self-defense from fear that her husband/partner is about to beat or rape her.

Some of the most important evidence against gender equivalence in battering comes from the NCVS and victimization surveys in Canada and Great Britain, which don't find the equivalence that CTS studies find (Sacco and Johnson 1990; Schwartz 1987; Worrall and Pease 1986). As noted earlier, about 85 percent of the intimate violence uncovered by the NCVS is experienced by women. About 7.5 of every 1,000 women experience intimate violent victimization annually, compared to only 1.0 of every 1,000 men. Women's rate of intimate violent victimization is thus more than seven times greater than men's (Greenfeld et al. 1998). In the NVAW survey discussed earlier, women were similarly "7 to 14 times more likely to report that an intimate partner beat them up, choked or tried to drown them, threatened them with a gun, or actually used a gun on them" (Tjaden and Thoennes 1998:7). This body of evidence leads critics to label the assertion of sexual symmetry in marital violence as yet another myth that obscures the true nature of such violence (Dobash et al. 1992).

Scholars on either side of the issue will no doubt continue to debate the validity of CTS measures and other methodological issues. Until this debate is resolved, a recent review concluded, "conclusions about the absence of gender differences [in marital violence] are unwarranted. The weight of current empirical evidence ... suggests that such conclusions are premature and incomplete" (Fagan and Browne 1994:171). For now, then, it seems fair to say that assertions of gender equivalence in battering are not justified and do an injustice to the tens of thousands of women each year who fear for their lives from men they once loved, and from men they sometimes continue to love despite the battering they experience.

Reducing Violence against Women

If violence against women is a consequence of gender inequality, then to reduce it we must first reduce male dominance. As Melanie Randall and Lori Haskell (1995:27) put it, "Understanding the causes and context of sexual [and physical] violence in women's lives, and examining how and why it continues to happen on a massive scale, means calling into question the organization of sexual inequality in our society."

Similarly, if economic inequality precipitates violence against women, then efforts to reduce poverty should also reduce violence against women. Reducing male dominance and economic inequality are, of course, easier said than done. But unless these underlying causes are addressed, rape and battering will surely continue.

A related solution focuses on the nature of masculinity. As the last chapter stressed, the violent nature of masculinity underlies much violent crime. If men in the United States and elsewhere learn to be violent, then it's no surprise they commit violence against women as well as against men. To reduce violence against women, we must begin to change the way we raise our boys.

In another area, one of the major accomplishments of the women's movement has been the establishment of rape-crisis centers and battered women's shelters. These have been an invaluable aid to women who have been raped and/or battered. There is a need for even more crisis centers and shelters, especially in urban areas where many women of color live. To this end, more money needs to be spent to expand the network of existing rape-crisis centers and battered women's shelters.

One final possible solution to violence against women lies in the criminal justice system. Compared to thirty years ago, police, prosecutors, and judges are more likely to view rape and battering as real crimes, not just as private matters where the woman was to blame. That said, many of these legal professionals still subscribe to the myths discussed previously. A recent study of police reactions to male-on-female spousal violence illustrates this problem (Fyfe, Klinger, and Flavin 1997). The study found that police were only half as likely to make an arrest in such assaults as they were in other types of serious assaults. As this study indicates, efforts to educate criminal justice officials on the true nature of intimate violence continue to be needed. In other problems, women who are raped and battered often face a difficult time if they choose to bring charges. If they testify on the witness stand, defense attorneys often question their character and try to vigorously suggest that they share the blame for their own victimization. More women might bring charges if this line of questioning were limited or prohibited. Whether the defendant would then be able to receive a fair trial remains a hotly debated issue (see the Crime and Controversy box on page 288).

ARRESTING BATTERERS: DETERRENCE OR ESCALATION?

Does arresting batterers make it more or less likely that they'll batter again? Because batterers traditionally have often not been arrested, the answer to this question is important for both theoretical and practical reasons. Theoretically, it addresses the more general issue of the degree to which arrest, prosecution, and punishment deter criminal behavior. Practically, it holds important implications for how we can best protect battered women. If arresting batterers does indeed help keep them from battering again, as deterrence theory would predict, then batterers should be routinely arrested. On the other hand, if arrest increases the chances for future battering, as labeling theory would predict, then arresting batterers may put battered women even more at risk. What does the research say?

In a widely cited investigation of this issue in Minneapolis in the early 1980s, the government sponsored a study in which police randomly did one of the following when called to the scene of a battering: (1) arrested the batterer; (2) separated him from his wife/partner for eight hours; or (3) advised the batterer as the officer saw fit but did not arrest or separate him. Researchers then compared the battering recidivism (repeat offending) rate for batterers in the three groups, and found that arrest produced the lowest recidivism rate in the six months after the police were

Is a Woman's Sexual Past Relevant in a Rape Case?

As the woman's movement began to address rape in the early 1970s, one of its focuses was the treatment of women in the criminal justice system after they had been raped. Many critics noted that a woman would routinely be asked by the defense attorney whether she had been sexually active before she was raped. This line of questioning, they charged, implied that a woman was to blame for her rape if she had been sexually active. In effect, the woman was put on trial.

In response to this criticism, the various states passed "rape shield" laws restricting the use of a woman's sexual history in rape cases. "Rape shield laws were historically one of the unsung triumphs of the women's legal movement," says one law professor. "It was a massive reform to rework the evidence laws in almost every state, so that the system no longer put the victim on trial."

However, the degree to which rape shield laws restrict evidence of a woman's past sexual conduct varies from state to state. Some states prohibit any such evidence unless it concerns a prior sexual relationship between the defendant and his accuser, while other states allow this evidence if the judge decides it's relevant to the case. Many states allow evidence of a woman's past sexual conduct if it might show that sexual activity with a third person accounted for any semen that was found. All states permit evidence concerning a previous sexual history with the defendant.

Rape shield laws continue to be controversial. Some rape law reformers feel the laws are not restrictive enough and still permit inappropriate evidence into the legal record. In contrast, many defense attorneys and civil libertarians feel the rape shield laws prevent some defendants from getting a fair trial by excluding evidence that might support a not guilty verdict.

One interesting question concerns the extent to which rape shield laws have indeed precluded evidence of a woman's past sexual conduct. In an interesting investigation of this issue, Cassia Spohn and Julie Horney wrote descriptions of six hypothetical rape cases. In each case, the defendant wanted to introduce evidence of certain aspects of his accuser's sexual past into the record. Spohn and Horney presented these descriptions to 162 judges, prosecutors, and defense attorneys in six cities: Atlanta, Chicago, Detroit, Houston, Philadelphia, and Washington, D. C. The researchers asked their respondents to indicate how likely it would be that the evidence would be admitted into the record in their jurisdiction. Generally their responses depended on the kind of evidence involved and on the jurisdiction in which they worked. But the researchers also found that some legal officials thought the evidence would be admitted even though their jurisdiction's rape shield law prohibited such evidence.

This last finding suggested to Spohn and Horney that "the letter of the law will not always be followed in cases involving sexual history evidence." One reason for noncompliance with rape shield laws, they suggest, is that judges and prosecutors sometimes feel that sexual history is relevant even if a rape shield law prohibits it from the trial record. Despite this problem, the general compliance they found with rape shield law restrictions led the authors to conclude that "the attitudes expressed by officials today toward rape cases and rape victims appear to have shifted considerably from the attitudes cited in the early calls for reform."

Sources: Lewin 1993; Samborn 1994; Spohn and Horney 1991.

---

called. Specifically, the proportion of batterers committing repeat violence against their wives/partners was lowest in the arrest group, and the average length of time until repeat violence was longest in the arrest group (Sherman and Berk 1984). The finding that arrest "worked" in these two ways prompted many jurisdictions across the country to begin arresting battering suspects routinely, even when battering victims didn't want an arrest to occur (Sherman and Cohn 1989).

However, the Minneapolis experiment suffered from several methodological problems that cast doubt on its conclusions (Binder and Meeker 1988; Sherman 1992). For example, its measurement of recidivism didn't examine the frequency of repeat battering or the average number of battering offenses per offender, and it

◀ *Some jurisdictions have begun mandatory arrest policies for men suspected of battering their wives and girlfriends. Scholars disagree on whether such policies help battered women more than they hurt them.*

also didn't consider the seriousness of repeat offending in terms of injury and hospitalization. In another problem, it only examined recidivism for the six-month follow-up period. It's possible that arrest may reduce recidivism during this period but increase it beyond this period. Further, since Minneapolis differs from other cities in its racial composition, climate, and other factors, its results were not necessarily generalizable to other locations.

These concerns led the government to sponsor several replication experiments in other cities, including Charlotte, North Carolina; Colorado Springs; Miami; Milwaukee; and Omaha. Although the results are complex, in Colorado Springs and Miami, arrest generally reduced future battering, but in Charlotte, Milwaukee, and Omaha arrest often increased recidivism after first decreasing it. The effects of arrest depended to a large extent on certain offender characteristics. In three of the cities, arrest reduced recidivism by employed offenders but increased it by unemployed offenders. In one city, arrest increased recidivism by unmarried offenders but did not increase it among married offenders.

Lawrence W. Sherman (1992), the primary architect of the Minneapolis study, notes that the equivocal results of the replication studies leave police and other officials with some major policy dilemmas. Although arrest apparently increases battering in some cities but reduces it in others, we cannot tell whether a city will experience an increase or a decrease. As Sherman observes, "Cities that do not adopt an arrest policy may pass up an opportunity to help the victims of domestic violence. But cities that do adopt arrest policies—or have them imposed by state law—may catalyze more domestic violence than would otherwise occur" (p. 19).

Further, because arrest may increase battering by unemployed men but reduce it among employed men, mandatory arrest policies may protect women whose husbands/partners work but harm those whose husbands/partners do not work. As Sherman notes, "Even in cities where arrest reduces domestic violence overall, as an unintended side effect it may increase violence against the poorest victims" (p. 19).

Another dilemma arises from the finding in some cities that arrest reduces battering in the short-term but increases it in the long run. With such evidence in mind, it becomes difficult to know whether arrest would do more harm than good.

The advisability of arrest for battering remains a controversial issue. Richard A. Berk (1993:336), one of the Minneapolis researchers, feels that arrest is not the perfect solution to battering but that "on the average, we can do no better than arrest." Citing the Minneapolis results, attorney Jessica L. Goldman (1994:100) similarly feels that arrest deters battering, and she further argues that mandatory arrest would "send a valuable message" that battering is a crime and would increase the potential for successful lawsuits against the police if they do not arrest.

In contrast, two criminologists, Eve S. Buzawa and Carl G. Buzawa (1993:345), worry about arrest's possible effects and feel that "long-term counseling and other rehabilitation measures may ultimately prove more effective than arrest in deterring future violence." They also argue that a battered woman's preferences regarding arrest should be respected, as she may have very good reasons for feeling that arrest would only make things worse: It might put her more at risk for future battering, for example, or affect her family's financial stability. For his part, Sherman (1992) concludes from all the evidence that mandatory arrest laws should be repealed where they now exist, especially in locations with high unemployment rates, but he's much more pessimistic than Buzawa and Buzawa about being able to reduce battering through treatment and other nonpolice programs.

Kathleen J. Ferraro (1995) agrees with attorney Goldman that arrest helps redefine battering as a real crime and not just as a family dispute, but feels that police will ignore mandatory arrest policies or else enforce them more against poor people and people of color than against wealthy whites. She also fears that these policies will lead battered women themselves to get arrested if the police view battering as "mutual combat" and feel that both parties are at fault. This view, she says, ignores the fact, noted previously, that women's violence against male partners is usually minor and almost always in self-defense. These many problems, continues Ferraro, "continue to limit the effectiveness" of the police and the rest of the criminal justice system "as a resource for battered women" (p. 266). She concludes,

> This pessimistic overview is not intended as a plea to abandon the criminal justice system as a locus of work against male violence. As stated above, it is often the only option available to women in immediate danger. But it is important to recognize the inherent limitations of the police and courts and the failures of previous efforts (p. 270).

Ferraro believes that battering and other violence against women will be reduced only to the extent that the patriarchy underlying these crimes is also reduced: "It is vital that battering not be viewed only as a crime but also as a manifestation of structured gender inequality" (p. 270). While the criminal justice system may remove individual batterers from the scene, more will take their place as long as patriarchy continues to exist.

 ## VIOLENCE AGAINST CHILDREN: PHYSICAL AND SEXUAL ABUSE

One of the most tragic forms of violence in the United States and elsewhere is committed against children. This violence takes two forms: physical abuse and sexual abuse. Children can also suffer from neglect and other problems, and these are often included in discussions of child abuse. For the sake of simplicity, we'll limit our examination to physical and sexual abuse, and look at each problem in turn.

Defining Child Physical and Sexual Abuse

Of the two, child physical abuse is somewhat more difficult to define, because any definition must distinguish between physical abuse and spanking, which is legal and socially approved in the United States. Child physical abuse might thus be said to refer to the excessive and unjustified use of physical force against a child. As we'll see later, however, what's considered "excessive" and "unjustified" is subject to many different interpretations. Child sexual abuse is defined more simply as any physical contact or interaction of a sexual nature between a child and an adult. This definition excludes behavior, such as a parent washing a child's genital region, that isn't done for sexual reasons.

The Extent of Physical and Sexual Abuse

PHYSICAL ABUSE

We'll never know how many children are beaten or otherwise abused each year. A major reason is that children are usually unlikely to report their victimization. The youngest ones, infants, obviously can't even talk, and toddlers are little better. But even older children, around age 7, don't report their abuse for several reasons: They don't typically define their abuse as abuse; they may feel their parents have the right to hit them; they may feel they deserved to be hit and thus blame themselves; they may fear parental retaliation; they may not know how or where to report the abuse. As a result, most child abuse remains hidden, and children can only hope that a teacher, nurse, physician, or other adult will notice their bruises and injuries.

We do have some idea of how many abused children receive medical care in hospitals and other settings, but these represent only the tip of the iceberg. That said, much of our knowledge of abused children comes from two surveys of social service agencies, schools, hospitals, and other institutions (Garbarino 1989). The first, the National Incidence Study (NIS), was conducted in 1980 and 1986 by the National Center on Child Abuse and Neglect. The NIS gathered information from the types of agencies and institutions just listed. It estimated that some 208,000 children, for a rate of 3.4 cases of abuse for every 1,000 children, were physically abused in 1980, and that the rate for physical, sexual, and/or emotional abuse combined was 5.7 for every 1,000. The second survey was conducted by the American Humane Association (AHA), which gathers and analyzes information from child protective service agencies only. The AHA reported a 1985 annual victimization rate of 22 per 1000 for major physical injuries and 154 per 1000 for minor physical injuries. The different rates indicated by these two studies reflects their different definitions of abuse and different data collection procedures. Although these studies find the average age of abused children to be about 5 or 6, adolescents aged 12 to 18 also suffer much abuse (Libbey and Bybee 1979).

Surveys of children might help uncover some child abuse, but such surveys are usually impractical. A major reason is that the youngest children obviously cannot respond to questions from interviewers. Another is that parental permission is almost always required for any study involving children, and parents who abuse their youngsters will be apt to deny permission for a study of child abuse. For these and other reasons, the NCVS doesn't interview anyone in a household under 12 years of age.

One way to study child abuse is to ask parents whether they've committed any one of several acts of violence against their children. Even here the data are unreliable, since the most violent parents may not tell interviewers about their violence. That said, some of the best data we have come from the 1975 and 1985 National Family Violence Surveys conducted by Straus and his colleagues. In addition to asking spouses which acts they had committed against each other, they also asked parents which they had committed against their children. In the 1975 survey, parents reported committing the acts listed in Table 10.2 at least once against a child. Focusing on only the last four acts as those most nearly fitting most people's conceptions of child abuse, the researchers estimated that between 1.4 million and 1.9 million children were abused in 1975 (Gelles 1978). Because of underreporting and the exclusion from their sample of single-parent families and families with all their children under 3 years of age, Straus and his colleagues speculated that this estimate is probably lower than the true prevalence of child abuse. Their 1985 follow-up survey found that serious abuse had declined only slightly (Straus and Gelles 1986).

In a recent methodological development, the Gallup Corporation queried a 1994 sample of adult respondents about any physical abuse they had suffered as children. Twelve percent of the respondents said they'd been punched, kicked, or choked during childhood (Moore 1994). Extrapolating this figure to the roughly 204 million U.S. adults in the 2000 population yields an estimated 24.5 million adults who had been physically abused as children.

Sexual Abuse

If data on physical abuse of children are unreliable, data on sexual abuse of children are even more unreliable. Whereas physical abuse sometimes results in visible injuries that an outsider might notice, sexual abuse does not. Estimates of the amount of sexual abuse vary widely. The NIS estimated that some 45,000 children were sexually abused in a single year, for a rate of .7 per 1000. In contrast, the AHA estimates a much higher annual rate of 117 per 1000 (Garbarino 1989).

Perhaps the best studies we have on child sexual abuse come from surveys where adolescents and adults are asked to recall whether they had ever been sexually abused as a child. Yet even these studies have several major faults. First, some sexual abuse is so terrible that it's repressed and forgotten. Second, infants and

TABLE 10.2   Percentages of Parents Reporting at Least One Act of Violence against Their Children in Past Year

Act of Violence	Percentage
Slapped or spanked	58.2
Pushed, grabbed, shoved	40.5
Hit with something	13.4
Threw something	5.4
Kicked, bit, or hit with fist	3.2
Beat up	1.3
Threatened with knife or gun	0.1
Used knife or gun	0.1

Source: Richard J. Gelles, "Violence toward Children in the United States," *American Journal of Orthopsychiatry* 48 (1978). Copyright © 1978 by American Orthopsychiatry Association, Inc. Reprinted by permission of *American Journal of Orthopsychiatry*.

toddlers who suffer sexual abuse are too young to remember these acts years later. Third, many subjects in these studies are college students, whose age, income, and other characteristics don't represent the entire population.

That said, studies of sexual abuse tell us several things about it. One finding is that while most physical abuse of children is committed by parents, sexual abuse is committed both by parents (almost always the father—or step-father, male partner to the mother, etc.) and by other relatives. Another finding is that sexual abuse of children under 18 seems more common than many people think. A study of 530 women at New England colleges and universities found 11 percent reporting they had sexual experiences before the age of 13 with adults 18 and older. The same study found 4 percent of 266 male students reporting such experiences (Finkelhor 1979). As this gender difference suggests, most research indicates that girls are much more likely than boys to experience sexual abuse. According to one review, about 25 percent of girls are sexually abused at least once, compared to 10 percent of boys (Peters, Wyatt, and Finkelhor 1986). The AHA reports that 78 percent of all sexually abused children each year are girls (Garbarino 1989).

The Toronto study discussed earlier found an especially high level of sexual abuse among the 420 women it interviewed (Randall and Haskell 1995). Researchers asked the subjects whether they had experienced any form of completed or attempted sexual contact, including intercourse, from a relative before turning 16 years old. Excluded from this definition was consensual sexual contact with someone no more than three years older. In effect, the researchers were asking about incestuous sexual abuse. About 17 percent of their sample reported at least one incestuous contact. The researchers also asked the subjects whether they had experienced unwanted sexual contact from a nonrelative before turning 16. About one-third of the sample reported such sexual abuse.

Combining these two figures, 42 percent of the sample reported at least one experience of incestuous or nonrelative sexual abuse before turning 16. Almost 18 percent had been raped (attempted or forced sexual intercourse) by a relative or nonrelative before turning 16. Including other sexual experiences, such as unwanted kisses or having someone expose his genitals, raised the proportion reporting sexual abuse to 54 percent. Almost one-third of the abuse was committed by a family member or other relative, and another 50 percent was committed by someone else the subject knew at the time. Only 20 percent was committed by strangers.

The Patterning of Physical and Sexual Abuse

Because data on physical abuse are unreliable, it's difficult to know whether its commission and victimization vary by gender, race, or class. Any discussions of such variation must be treated cautiously. That said, the best evidence from several studies is that there is some variation.

Let's look first at gender. Early research suggested that mothers were more likely than fathers to commit physical abuse against their children because of psychological disorders and other personal problems (Helfer and Kempe 1979). However, more recent evidence indicates that fathers commit more physical abuse than previously thought and are especially responsible for serious abuse requiring hospitalization. Much of mothers' abuse is now attributed to their battering by their husbands (Bergman, Larsen, and Mueller 1986; Hegar, Zuravin, and Orme 1994). Whether there are gender differences in victimization is less certain. Although many studies find boys more likely than girls to suffer serious injuries (Rosenthal

1988), other studies don't find this difference, and the differences that are found are often small (Hegar, Zuravin, and Orme 1994).

Turning to race and class, several studies find African-American children more likely than white children to suffer serious injuries or death (Hampton 1987). However, these findings must be interpreted cautiously for at least two reasons. First, several of these studies fail to control for social class, and the differences found for African-Americans may be a result of their greater poverty. Second, racial bias may tinge assessments of whether abuse has occurred. The Gallup poll discussed earlier underscores the need for caution in assuming a higher African-American rate of child physical abuse. Twelve percent of whites, but only 9 percent of blacks, said they were "punched or kicked or choked" by a parent or other adult guardian when they were children (Maguire and Pastore 1995:278).

Despite data unreliability and possible class bias in determining abuse, it does seem clear that physical abuse is more common in poor families than in nonpoor families (Kruttschnitt, McLeod, and Dornfeld 1994). In the Gallup poll, 17 percent of respondents with annual incomes under $20,000 said they'd been punched, choked, or beaten by a parent or adult guardian, versus only 6 percent of respondents with incomes $50,000 and higher (Maguire and Pastore 1995:278).

Less research exists on race and class differences in child sexual abuse, and the unreliability of sexual abuse data again demands caution in discussing such differences. Still, the best evidence indicates that the men who sexually abuse children are relatively poor, and that child sexual abuse does not vary by race (Alexander and Lupfer 1987).

Explaining Child Abuse

While many theories of child physical abuse stress psychological disorders in the adults who batter their children, sociological approaches instead emphasize the structural and cultural conditions that make child violence inevitable. Following the theme of this book, I focus here on these conditions.

Earlier in this chapter, I underscored inequality as a major contributor to violence against women. Because of their smaller size, intellectual immaturity, and lack of economic resources, children are yet another powerless group, perhaps the most powerless of all. Sociologically speaking, it's no accident, and maybe even inevitable, that children will suffer violence at the hands of adults (Gil 1979).

I've also emphasized in this and earlier chapters that people are more likely to commit violence when they're economically deprived. As we saw earlier, child physical abuse appears to be more common in poorer families than in wealthier families. If so, this income patterning underlines yet another alarming consequence of economic deprivation. A key mechanism here is stress (Gil 1979; Wauchope and Straus 1990). Many studies document that poverty can be a source of enormous stress as parents cope with paying bills, crowded housing conditions, and other problems that the poor face much more than the nonpoor. Given such stress, tempers often flare, with children a convenient target. Even in the best of circumstances, children often annoy parents; in worse circumstances, parents are annoyed more easily and can go over the edge.

Another important factor in child physical abuse is whether parents were physically abused themselves as children. Several studies document that parents who were so abused are more likely to abuse their own children in a vicious cycle of violence (Egeland 1993; Widom 1996). Having learned from their parents that it's acceptable to beat children, they discipline their own children in the same way.

◄ *The high approval of spanking as a method of discipline in the United States helps to account for the nation's high level of child physical abuse.*

Another explanation for child physical abuse derives from the high approval in the United States of spanking as an appropriate method for disciplining children. The General Social Survey, given to a national sample of U.S. residents, indicates that close to 75 percent of the public strongly agrees or agrees that "it is sometimes necessary to discipline a child with a good, hard spanking." Reflecting the old saying, "spare the rod and spoil the child," most parents spank their children regularly, with some national surveys indicating that 90 percent of the parents of toddlers spank them at least three times a week (Meltz 1995).

Although spanking is quite common, it still fits the previous chapter's definition of interpersonal violence as the use of force to cause physical injury, even if the injury is typically very slight. Spanking is thus a violent act, even though parents intend it for good purposes (Straus 1994a). Unfortunately, there's a very thin line between a "good, hard spanking" and physical abuse. Once parents are accustomed to using any force against a child, undue force, or abuse, is inevitable. As Barbara A. Wauchope and Murray A. Straus (1990:147) point out, "Although most physical punishment does not turn into physical abuse, most physical abuse begins as ordinary physical punishment." Moreover, not everyone defines a "good, hard spanking" the same way. While most of us might say that anything beyond a few slaps on a child's rear end goes beyond spanking and becomes abuse, some might feel that a slap on the face or even worse is still acceptable. Coupled with the vulnerability of children, cultural approval of violence against them in the form of spanking makes child physical abuse inevitable.

Turning to child sexual abuse, psychological explanations center on such factors as men's craving for love and affection, extreme jealousy and authoritarianism, and various personality disorders (Holmes 1991). A sociological explanation of child sexual abuse would emphasize power and gender inequality. Since the typical episode of sexual abuse involves an adult man and young girl, the power and gender inequality dimensions are apparent. These dimensions becomes especially important in incest, where fathers and stepfathers assume their daughters are their sexual property (Russell 1984). Beyond this structural explanation, we can't forget that girls and women in our society are still regarded as sex objects existing for men's pleasure. This belief contributes to our high levels of child sexual abuse and adult rape.

Reducing Child Abuse

There is so much child physical and sexual abuse remaining behind closed doors that any effort to reduce child abuse faces huge obstacles. Still, certain measures should help. To the extent that child abuse is more common in low-income families, public policy efforts that reduce poverty should also eventually reduce child abuse. Beyond this approach, it's also critical that we design and implement prevention programs, including those intended to help parents deal with the stress of parenting (Plummer 1993). Although many social service agencies now work with families with children at risk for abuse and neglect, it remains true that these agencies are underfunded and understaffed. At a minimum, these agencies need to be provided the funds required to help keep children safe from their parents and other adults with whom they live.

 ## SUMMARY AND CONCLUSION

This chapter continued the previous chapter's emphases on the huge amount of violence by nonstrangers and on the inequality lying at the heart of much of this violence. If most homicides and rapes, about half of all assaults, and almost all child abuse occur between nonstrangers, it becomes difficult to attribute this violence to a few psychologically abnormal strangers in our midst. Instead larger structural and cultural forces must be at work. The structural forces include inequalities based on race, class, and gender: As long as these inequalities continue to exist, the crimes resulting from them will continue as well.

Violence against women is an international problem that manifests itself in the United States through rape, battering, and other behaviors. While it's true that most men don't rape and batter, it's also true that rape and battering are two of the most dire consequences of patriarchy and gender inequality. It might not be too much of an exaggeration to say that men who do rape and batter are fulfilling—in an extreme and terrible way—common, masculine notions of virility. While we certainly must hold individual men responsible for their violence against women, we must also seek to reduce gender inequality and change the norms of masculinity if we want to reduce this violence. Because women have much more to fear from men they know than from men who are strangers, it's not enough to focus on making the streets safer for women. The problem goes far beyond popular conceptions of strangers lurking in alleyways.

Violence against children is another tragic problem with multiple roots. While I stressed a sociological explanation centering on power and inequality, individual-level explanations of child abuse are also valuable. Even in child abuse we see an instructive gender patterning, as men commit the majority of serious physical injuries against children and commit almost all of the sexual abuse.

It's time now to consider property crime. We'll return to the issue of violence in later chapters on white-collar crime, where we'll discuss corporate violence, and on political crime, where we'll examine political violence. These chapters will show that violence takes many forms and is even more common than this and the previous chapter indicated.

KEY TERMS

battering   genital mutilation

child abuse   male dominance

cultural myths   patriarchy

dowry deaths   rape

femicide   sexual assault

STUDY QUESTIONS

1. How does an understanding of the victim-offender relationship help us understand why rapes occur?

2. What special problems do women of color face in regard to intimate violence?

3. What are three cultural myths that underlie the amount of rape and battering in the United States today?

4. Do you think men who abuse their female partners should always be arrested? Why or why not?

5. To what extent are factors such as gender, race, and class related to the commission of the physical and sexual abuse of children?

INTERNET EXERCISES

The federal Centers for Disease Control and Prevention sponsors the National Violence Against Women Prevention Research Center (NVAWPRC). Go to its Web site at **http://www.nvaw.org/home.html**. Enter its main menu, where you'll see a list of headings that you can access. Click on **Overview and mission** to find out more about NVAWPRC. Then go back to the main menu and click on **Overviews and Statistics**. Several topics will now appear; click on **Intimate Partner and Domestic Violence**. Scroll through the page that appears to get some basic information on this topic. How many U.S. women are abused by their partners each year? What percent of all rapes are committed by husbands or boyfriends?

Now go back to the main menu and click on **Center's Philosophy and Approach**. Scroll down until you find **Theoretical Approach Guiding the Center's Research Activities**. What are the five theoretical concepts that guide the Center's research? How does a sociological understanding of violence against women help us understand how to prevent such violence?

PROPERTY
CRIME

Crime in the News

*T*he state of Maine has one of the lowest crime rates in the nation, but in March 2000 a rash of thefts won big headlines in daily newspapers. In one case, the police apprehended two suspects, one 18 and one 17, for allegedly committing a series of car burglaries. When they searched the apartment of one of the youths, they found several items that had been reported stolen, including compact disks. Meanwhile, police in five Maine towns got together to share evidence on a series of thefts of musical instruments from high school band rooms around the state. Among the stolen items were alto, baritone, and tenor saxophones, French horns, trombones, and a guitar. One school band director said, "They were very selective in what they took. They took the newest and best instruments and the most expensive. They left the stuff that is forty years old and held together with duct tape."

Meanwhile, on the other side of the country the Academy of Motion Picture Arts and Sciences reported the same month that 55 of its Academy Awards statues, the Oscars, were stolen en route to the site of the award ceremony. All but three of the Oscars were later found in a trash bin. The police arrested two men who worked for the trucking company in charge of shipping the Oscars. A police detective said, "They did it for profit. They thought they could make money."

Sources: Germain 2000; Harrison 2000; Kessell 2000.

The thefts described in the "Crime in the News" vignette might seem minor and even a bit quaint to many readers, but they remind us that property crime can happen anywhere and to anyone. Legendary folk singer Woody Guthrie used to sing that some people rob you with a gun, while others rob you with a fountain pen. As his words imply, many crimes are committed for economic gain. The next two chapters discuss these crimes. We look at property crime in this chapter and then discuss white-collar crime in the next chapter. Although these two types of crime differ greatly, they both aim to improve the offender's financial status. Most property criminals aren't as desperate as the proverbial parent who steals bread to feed a starving family, but they're still pretty poor to begin with. In contrast, white-collar criminals are often quite wealthy, with their crimes smacking more of greed. To the extent this is true, the motivation of white-collar criminals is perhaps more shameful than that of property criminals. As we'll be seeing, white-collar criminals also cause more financial loss, injury, and death than do property criminals.

Still, as Chapter 2 pointed out, the public fears property crime far more than white-collar crime. There's no doubt that property crime is very costly. The FBI estimates that about $15 billion in property is stolen annually, including cash, jewelry, clothing and furs, motor vehicles, office equipment, televisions and stereos, firearms, household goods, and livestock. The NCVS estimates property crime costs the nation some $17 billion annually in total economic loss (property loss, medical expenses, time lost from work). By any measure, property crime is a serious problem. We thus need to understand the causes and dynamics of the many types of property crime that exist.

 ## DEFINING PROPERTY CRIME

Before we move on, let's review UCR definitions of the various property crimes to make sure we understand the differences among them (Federal Bureau of Investigation 1999). The first four crimes discussed in the following sections are Part I, or Index offenses, while the remainder are Part II offenses. Most of this chapter's discussion focuses on the Index offenses.

Burglary is attempted or completed "unlawful entry of a structure to commit a felony or a theft." Most burglarized structures are homes and businesses.

Larceny-theft (hereafter *larceny*) is attempted or completed "unlawful taking, carrying, leading, or riding away of property from the possession or constructive possession of another." Larceny's key feature is that it involves stealth but doesn't involve force, the threat of force, or deception. It's a miscellaneous, catch-all category that includes such things as shoplifting, pickpocketing, purse snatching, the theft from autos of their contents, and bicycle theft, but excludes property crimes involving deception, including embezzlement, fraud, and forgery.

My students are sometimes puzzled whether a given act is best considered burglary, larceny, or robbery, so let me illustrate the differences. If someone stops you at gunpoint on a street and demands your purse, wallet, or any jewelry you might be wearing, that's a robbery because it involves the use or threat of physical force. The involvement of physical force in robbery classifies it as a violent crime even though it's committed for economic gain. If someone runs down the street and grabs your purse or snatches your gold chain before you realize what's happening and then runs away, that's larceny. If he pickpockets your wallet, that's also larceny.

If someone steals an object from a store while the store is open for business, that's larceny (shoplifting), because the person had the right to be in the store. If he breaks into the store at night and steals the same object, that's a burglary. If someone breaks into your house and steals an object, that's also a burglary. If you invite someone into your house and he steals the same object, that's larceny. If you answer the doorbell and someone holds you up at gunpoint, that's a robbery. In one other area of confusion, if someone steals your car's hubcaps, CD player, or cell phone, that's larceny. But if he takes the whole car, that's motor vehicle theft.

To return to our definitions, *motor vehicle theft* is, as the name implies, the attempted or completed theft of a motor vehicle. Such vehicles include cars, trucks, buses, snowmobiles, and motorcycles, but exclude boats, farming equipment, airplanes, and construction equipment. About 80 percent of all motor vehicle thefts involve cars.

Arson, the final Index property crime, is "any willful or malicious burning or attempt to burn, with or without intent to defraud, a dwelling house, public building, motor vehicle or aircraft, personal property of another, etc." To be counted by the UCR, arson must be definitely proven. Fires of unknown or suspicious origins aren't counted. The FBI didn't classify arson as an Index crime until 1979. The reporting system is still not fully in place, as about one-third of law enforcement agencies didn't submit arson reports for all twelve months in 1998. Patrick G. Jackson (1988) found the number of arson fires reported by a national survey of fire departments more than twice as high as the UCR's estimate. His findings suggest caution in drawing conclusions from UCR arson data.

The UCR's Part II offenses include several other property crimes, all of which involve deception of some kind. *Forgery and counterfeiting* involve "making, altering, uttering, or possessing, with intent to defraud, anything false in the semblance of that which is true." *Fraud* involves "obtaining money or property by false pretenses." *Buying, receiving, and possessing stolen property* is another Part II property offense and is just what its name implies. We'll take a further look at forgery, fraud, and stolen property offenses in the text that follows. A final Part II property offense is *embezzlement*, defined as the "misappropriation or misapplication of money or property entrusted to one's care, custody, or control." We'll save our discussion of embezzlement until the next chapter.

 ## The Extent of Property Crime

Although the Uniform Crime Reports (UCR) and National Crime Victimization Survey (NCVS) provide different estimates of the amount of property crime, they both indicate how common it is. Table 11.1 (on page 302) reports UCR and NCVS estimates for burglary, larceny, and motor vehicle theft. Because of incomplete reporting of arson, the UCR's arson estimate isn't included in the total figures. With so much property crime, it's not surprising that the risk of becoming a property crime victim adds up over time: The NCVS estimates that 72 percent of U.S. households will suffer at least one burglary over a twenty-year period (Koppel 1987). Unfortunately, only about 15 to 20 percent of all reported property crime is cleared by arrest. Because the actual number of property crimes is more than twice as great as the reported number, the actual clearance rate for property crime may well be as low as 7 to 10 percent.

TABLE 11.1

NUMBER OF PROPERTY CRIMES, UCR AND NCVS DATA, 1998

TYPE OF CRIME	UCR	NCVS
Burglary	2,329,950	4,054,000
Larceny-theft	7,373,886	17,999,000
Motor vehicle theft	1,240,754	1,138,000
Total crimes	10,944,590	23,191,000
Arson	*78,094*	

Source: adapted from Table 3.3, Chapter 3.

The UCR and NCVS also report different pictures of trends in property crime. The UCR show that property crime rose sharply from 1960 until the mid-1970s, when it leveled off, only to rise again in the late 1970s before peaking about 1980. It then dropped before rising in the late 1980s, before declining once again in the 1990s. In contrast, the NCVS shows that property crime victimization has declined fairly steadily since 1973, the first year of the NCVS. These different pictures stem from the different definitions and coverage of property crime in the data sets. The exclusion of commercial crime from the NCVS makes comparisons especially difficult. But because both data sets tell us that property crime declined in the 1990s, we can be pretty sure that this is in fact what happened.

Why has property crime declined? No one is sure, but experts offer several possible reasons: *target hardening*, involving the greater use of alarm systems and other measures; less cash being carried because of the greater use of credit and checking cards; and the fact that people probably stay at home more to watch cable TV and videos (Chaiken 2000).

THE PATTERNING OF PROPERTY CRIME

Like violent crime, property crime is patterned both geographically and demographically. Let's look first at geographical differences, and then at demographic (gender, race, class, age) differences.

Figure 11.1 displays regional differences in UCR property crime for the United States in 1998. (Because of incomplete reporting, arson is excluded from the figure.) Property crime is highest in the South and lowest in the Northeast. The West follows the South, with the Midwest a close third. However, the NCVS reports that the West has the highest rate of property crime victimization, with the South and Midwest tied for second (Rennison 1999). Both data sets agree that the Northeast has the lowest rate.

Figure 11.2 displays UCR urban-rural differences in property crime. (Again because of incomplete reporting, arson data are excluded from this figure.) Like violent crime, property crime is lowest in rural areas, a finding the NCVS confirms. This urban-rural difference has also been found in several other nations (Shover 1991).

Turning to demographic differences, property crime tends to be a young person's offense, as people under 25 years of age account for about two-thirds of all property crime arrests. Self-report data indicate that various kinds of theft and property damage are quite common during adolescence (see Table 11.2 on page 304).

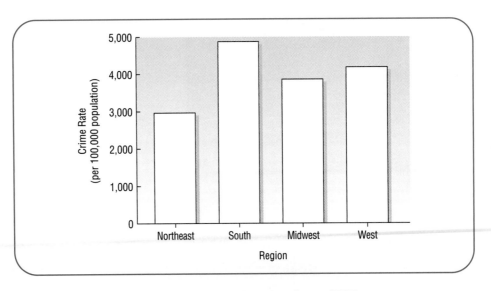

▲ Figure 11.1 Regional Differences in Property Crime, 1998
(Number per 100,000 population)

Source: Federal Bureau of Investigation 1999.

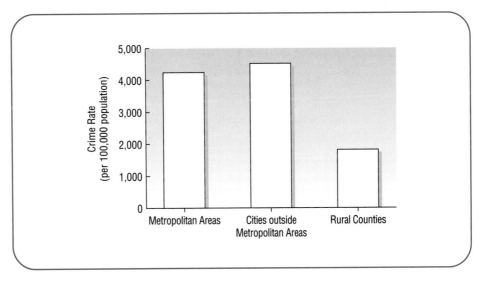

▲ Figure 11.2 Urban-Rural Differences in Property Crime, 1998
(Number per 100,000 population)

Source: Federal Bureau of Investigation 1999.

Property crime also exhibits a significant gender pattern, as males account for about 88 percent of all burglary arrests, 84 percent of all motor vehicle theft arrests, 85 percent of all arson arrests, and 65 percent of all larceny arrests. The male proportion of larceny arrests is lower than for the other crimes because females are more involved in one type of larceny, shoplifting, than they are in other crimes. As the high school survey reported in Table 11.2 indicates, however, more males than females shoplift. Male shoplifters steal more items, and also more expensive items, than do female shoplifters and are also more likely to be professional shoplifters

◀ *Women and girls account for a greater proportion of shoplifting than for other property crimes. Although store personnel monitor female shoppers especially closely, more males than females shoplift.*

| TABLE 11.2 | PROPORTION OF HIGH SCHOOL SENIORS (CLASS OF 1998) REPORTING INVOLVEMENT IN VARIOUS PROPERTY CRIMES IN PAST 12 MONTHS (% SAYING AT LEAST ONCE) |

ACTIVITY	MALE	FEMALE
Taken something from a store without paying for it	34	26
Taken something not belonging to you worth under $50	38	24
Taken something not belonging to you worth over $50	17	7
Taken a car without owner's (nonrelative) permission	6	3
Taken part of a car without owner's permission	8	2
Gone into house/building when not supposed to be there	31	19
Set fire to someone's property on purpose	4	1
Damaged school property on purpose	22	8
Damaged property at work on purpose	13	2

Source: Maguire and Pastore 1999.

instead of amateurs. Despite these gender differences, store personnel monitor female customers' behavior more closely because they believe women are more likely than men to shoplift (Horowitz and Pottieger 1991).

According to arrest data, the typical property offender is white, although African-Americans are disproportionately represented (see Table 11.3). Although the UCR and NCVS don't report social class backgrounds of property offenders, it's safe to say that the typical property offender comes from the ranks of the poor or near-poor.

THE SOCIAL ORGANIZATION OF PROPERTY CRIME

A rich literature describes the social organization of property crime. By social organization I mean the roles that different property criminals play and the social networks that support their illegal enterprise. Much of this literature follows the useful distinction between *amateur* and *professional* criminals (Hepburn 1984) introduced in the last chapter's discussion of robbery. Amateur criminals (also called opportunistic or occasional criminals) comprise the vast majority of property offenders. Most are in their teens or early twenties; they are unskilled and commit their crimes when the opportunity arises rather than plan them far in advance. In another defining feature, their illegal profit from any one property crime is relatively small.

In contrast, professional property criminals, first studied in 1937 by Edwin Sutherland (1937), are older and much more skilled at what they do. They plan their offenses carefully, and the illegal profit from each crime can be high. Often they "learn the ropes" from other professional criminals, who serve as tutors into the world of professional crime. Professional property criminals excite our imagination. Cat burglars and other professional thieves have been the subject of many movies and books over the years. We treat them somewhat like Robin Hood: While we intellectually condemn their crimes, we secretly admire their brave daring, perhaps because of our own longing for economic success.

The amateur-professional distinction helps us understand the different types of offenders committing the different property crimes. In a classic study of shoplifting, Mary Owen Cameron (1964) categorized shoplifters as *snitches* and *boosters*. Most shoplifters are snitches, or amateurs, who steal merchandise of little value that they keep for themselves. Boosters, some 10 percent of all shoplifters, are skilled professionals who sell their stolen goods to fences or pawnshops.

TABLE 11.3	RACE AND PROPERTY CRIME ARRESTS, 1998 (% OF ALL ARRESTS)		
	CRIME	WHITE	BLACK
	Burglary	68	29
	Larceny-theft	65	32
	Motor vehicle theft	58	39
	Arson	74	24

Source: Federal Bureau of Investigation 1999.

Motor vehicle theft exhibits a similar distinction between amateur and professional offenders. Most analysts divide motor vehicle theft into two kinds, *joy riding* or *professional* theft. Joy riding is committed primarily by teenaged boys working in groups as amateur motor vehicle thieves. As their name implies, these joy riders steal cars for a lark, take them for a short ride, then dump them, often before the owner even knows the car is gone. They target unlocked cars with the key in the ignition or else crudely break into locked cars and hot wire them. Because they abandon their stolen vehicles so soon, it's difficult to arrest them.

Professional car thieves are older and more highly skilled. They can get into very secure vehicles, drive them away, and quickly dismantle them for parts in "chop shops" or otherwise deposit them into a very sophisticated auto "resale market" where they'll be sold for a tidy profit. These professionals are so good at what they do that they're rarely discovered and arrested (Clarke and Harris 1992).

Burglary

The literature on the social organization of burglary is especially extensive. Although the image of the solitary, professional cat burglar crawling up buildings and breaking into heavily guarded structures has been the stuff of several movies and books, most burglars aren't nearly so skillful or specialized. They enter buildings through unlocked doors or windows or break into them in crude, unskilled ways. Most burglars don't specialize in burglary and instead commit other crimes over the long haul, but some do specialize in burglary for short periods (Shover 1991; Wright and Decker 1994). Many burglars prefer burglary to, say, armed robbery, but even for them burglary is part of a larger criminal lifestyle. Unlike the legendary cat burglar, many burglars work in groups of two or more, evidently feeling there's safety in numbers.

Beyond these generalizations, burglars differ in other ways. Mike Maguire (1982) identifies three categories of burglars: low-level, middle-range, and high-level. *Low-level* burglars are adolescents and young adults who get together to commit spontaneous, unskilled burglaries as a lark. They typically spend only a few minutes in the residence they enter and steal only small amounts of money and video and other items popular in their age group. They don't think of themselves as criminals and lack access to fences and other members of what might be called the "burglary support system."

Middle-range burglars tend to be older than low-level ones and more apt to spend time searching for attractive targets. They tend to act alone and often choose suburban areas featuring wealthy, isolated homes. They're more skilled than their low-level counterparts and more able to defeat home security systems. Middle-range burglars spend a fair amount of time in the residences they enter in order to find the most valuable items.

High-level burglars are the most skilled of all and tend to act in groups of two or more. They spend a lot of time planning their burglaries and are ready and willing to travel long distances to their targets. They also plan how to dispose of the items they steal through fences and other parts of the burglary support network. Neal Shover (1991) likens their burglary method to "military commando operations."

Does gender influence the experiences of female and male burglars? Unfortunately, we have few studies of female burglars and other property criminals. To remedy this research deficit, Scott Decker and associates (Decker et al. 1993) interviewed 105 urban residential burglars, 18 women and 87 men. Although the small sample size for the women makes for only rough comparisons, the researchers found some interesting similarities and differences. Female and male burglars were similar in their extent of drug and alcohol use and in their degree of specialization in burglary. Compared with the male burglars, however, female burglars began their crimes at a later age, were more likely to commit burglaries with other burglars, and were less likely to have been convicted of burglary. Additional studies of women burglars are needed to determine how they compare to male burglars. Such information will yield a more complete understanding of the genesis and dynamics of burglary.

TIPSTERS AND FENCES

The burglary literature also describes what might be called a "burglary support system" (Shover 1973). *Tipsters* provides burglars with information about potential targets, and *fences* help them dispose of their illegal booty. Burglars also rely on bail bond people and attorneys to help them when they get arrested. Let's take a brief look at tipsters and fences.

Tipsters let burglars know of safe, attractive targets. Tipsters come not only from the criminal world but also from legitimate occupations: Unscrupulous attorneys, repairpeople, police, bartenders, and the like all tip off burglars about residences and businesses ripe for the taking. No one really knows how many tipsters exist or how much of a role they play in burglary, but it's safe to say they often help middle-range and high-level burglars.

If you were to enter a home and steal an expensive stereo system and valuable jewels and silver, what would you do with these items? You might keep the stereo but want to get rid of the jewels and silver in return for money. How would you dispose of the latter items? You can't just walk into a jewelry store and say you found the items. It might also sound suspicious if you say they were in your family and you need money to pay your bills. As these problems suggest, burglars often need fences to dispose of their stolen goods and give them money in return (Cromwell and McElrath 1994). Fences sell the stolen goods to customers, many of whom are in legitimate occupations (and some of whom are even police and public officials) and realize the shady nature of their transaction. Since they can buy the stolen goods for much less than they'd otherwise cost, they're willing to overlook the fact that they're aiding and abetting burglary. The world of professional burglars thus cannot exist without the help of otherwise law-abiding citizens.

The most famous fence in history was probably Jonathan Wild, who controlled the London criminal world from 1714 until his death by hanging in 1725 (Steffensmeier 1986). He advertised in newspapers that he could capture thieves and return stolen property to its rightful owner. In reality, burglars and robbers gave Wild their stolen goods willingly, and he would sell it back to their original owners for a tidy sum. His "take," and therefore the amount he could give back to the thieves, was greater than that of most other fences. To ensure his credibility, he occasionally turned a thief over to law enforcement officials.

Darrell J. Steffensmeier (1986) sees fences as working "in the shadow of two worlds," to quote the subtitle of his book on fencing. One world is that of any legitimate businessperson, whose activities a fence's functions resemble. Financial success in both fencing and legitimate business depends on marketing and management skills and on the ability to be reliable and punctual. As noted a moment ago, fences also deal with law-abiding customers, further placing them in the world of legitimate business. The other world is the criminal world. The fence not only engages in illegal activity but interacts with many types of criminals.

Another topic in burglary research concerns burglars' decision-making processes (Bursik 2000). Research on this issue tries to get into the minds of burglars to see how and why they decide to commit a crime and how they carry out the crime once they've decided to commit it. Most studies of these decision-making processes draw on in-depth interviews of small samples of burglars, some of whom are in prison at the time they're interviewed (Cromwell 1994; Tunnell 1996; Wright and Decker 1994).

As Chapter 5 noted, these studies disagree on whether burglars pay much attention to their risk of arrest, prosecution, and imprisonment. On other points there is some consensus. In choosing a geographic area in which to commit a crime, burglars and other property criminals rely on their knowledge of the area from their noncriminal activities (Bursik 2000). Once they're chosen an area, burglars tend to select homes less visible to possible scrutiny by neighbors and homes believed to be unoccupied. As the police and news media remind us, burglars look for signs, including accumulating mail and newspapers, that people are away on vacation. Some burglars even scan newspaper obituaries to determine when homes will be empty while families attend funeral services. Other homes at risk include those whose residents are away for long periods at work or school.

PROPERTY CRIME VICTIMIZATION: COSTS AND CIRCUMSTANCES

To understand property crime further, let's examine its costs and the circumstances under which it occurs. The costs of property crime are both economic and psychological, and are especially high for burglary. Homeowners and businesses spend millions of dollars annually on elaborate security systems, firearms, and other items to prevent burglaries and protect themselves from intruders. Although burglary rates have been declining, this spending continues apace, and burglary remains very costly. The UCR estimate that burglary victims lost $3.1 billion in 1998, with the average loss per burglary of $1,343. About two-thirds of all reported burglaries are residential, the remainder commercial. About 60 percent of residential burglaries occur during the day, compared to only 37 percent of nonresidential burglaries. The NCVS estimates that the total economic loss (including medical expenses and time lost from work) averages $834 per burglary, or almost $4 billion overall per year.

Although burglary typically doesn't threaten its victims with injury, it still violates their privacy and sense of "personal space." Accordingly, about one-third of burglary victims become depressed, lose sleep, or suffer other similar problems. Women burglary victims are more likely than male victims to report being afraid and upset, while male victims are more apt to report being angry or annoyed. Women burglary victims who live alone are the most likely to feel afraid, evidently reflecting their concern over their physical vulnerability and possibility of rape (Burt and Katz 1984; Shover 1991).

The NCVS has compiled some interesting figures on residential burglaries (Bastian and DeBerry 1994). In about 13 percent of all burglaries reported to the NCVS, a household member was at home and saw the intruder(s). A surprisingly high proportion of these intruders, about 40 percent, were known to the household member: Twenty-five percent were acquaintances; 11 percent were relatives, including ex-spouses; and 6 percent were known only by sight.

Property Crime in Eighteenth-Century England

Looking at the amount of property crime in the United States today, we're tempted to yearn for a time long ago when crime presumably was much rarer.

In this regard, a comparative and historical perspective is illuminating. More than 200 years ago, eighteenth-century England was plagued by property and violent crime. In the early 1700s, according to historian J. M. Beattie (p. 218), "public alarm and panic about London offenses moved in distinctive waves." After 1750, things got worse, as a combination of rising food prices and waves of unemployment sent robbery and property crime soaring. Newspapers and magazines were filled with stories about burglary, shoplifting, and robbery. "What seemed particularly frightening," says Beattie (p. 219), "was the number of gangs and the apparent inability of the authorities to do much about them." By the 1780s, he adds (p. 224), the widespread belief was that "criminals were more desperate and more violent than ever before." One London magazine lamented that "not only pickpockets but street-robbers and highwaymen, are grown to a great pitch of insolence at this time, robbing in gangs, defying authority, and often rescuing their companions and carrying them off in triumph."

The concern over crime in eighteenth-century England prompted an increase in the number of offenses, almost all of them property crimes, punishable by death. By the end of the century, an estimated 200 crimes could result in execution; these included burglary, horse theft, poaching, shoplifting, sheep stealing, forgery, and the taking of shipwrecked goods. Property offenses, including robbery, accounted for 92 percent of one jurisdiction's more than 1,000 hangings that century. Historian V. A. C. Gatrell estimates that some 35,000 people were sentenced to death in England and Wales between 1770 and 1830, almost all of them for property offenses, with about 7,000 executed, usually by hanging.

Several historians liken this widespread use of capital punishment against property crimes to a rule by terror. Beattie (pp. 223–224) says that executions in the 1780s reached an "astonishing level ... in what was to be in effect the last large-scale effort of terror to prevent men from robbing and stealing."

If Gatrell's figures are correct, although 7,000 people were executed, 28,000 sentenced to death were not executed. As these figures suggest, legal pardons were surprisingly common. One interesting question is why this was so. Douglas Hay argues that England's use of capital punishment against property offenders, almost all of them poor, involved both terror and mercy. On the one hand, Hay says, propertied interests in England established the death penalty for numerous property offenses in order to strengthen their rule. On the other hand, the great number of pardons of property offenders sentenced to death, with many of them coming at the request of wealthy landowners, helped convince the poor that the legal system was fair and merciful after all: "Here was the peculiar genius of the law. It allowed the rulers of England to make the courts a selective instrument of class justice, yet simultaneously to proclaim the law's incorruptible impartiality.... Discretion allowed a prosecutor to terrorize the petty thief and then command his gratitude, or at least the approval of his neighbourhood as a man of compassion. It allowed the class that passed one of the bloodiest penal codes in Europe to congratulate itself on its humanity" (pp. 48–49).

As this example from England indicates, property crime flourished long ago, and its widespread commission in the United States today is certainly not unprecedented. Just as the poor and near-poor committed most of the property crime in England 200 years ago, so it is in the United States today. In both periods, social class and economic problems in the larger society seem to account for the high prevalence of burglary, larceny, and other property crime.

Sources: Beattie 1986; Gatrell 1994; Hay 1975.

Several aspects of a burglary influence a victim's decision to call the police. Victims are far more likely to call the police when forcible entry was involved (77 percent call the police) than when unlawful entry (e.g., entering an open window) was involved (43 percent). The reason for this difference is probably that forcible entry involves more damage to the residence. They're also far more likely to call the police when larger amounts of loss are involved. When losses total $1,000 or more, 89 percent of victims call the police, versus only 14 percent when losses total less than $10. Middle- and upper-income households are also more likely to report burglaries than poor households.

Other property crimes are also costly. The UCR estimate that 1998 larcenies cost each victim an average of $650 in property loss, for a total property loss from reported larcenies of close to $5 billion. Since so many larcenies are not reported, the true property loss may be $12 billion or more. As Table 11.4 indicates, the amount per larceny varies widely by the type of larceny.

Motor vehicle theft also adds up to billions of dollars annually. The FBI reports that about 1.24 million motor vehicles were stolen in 1998. Most of these vehicles, 76 percent, were cars, with another 19 percent trucks or buses. The estimated value of all motor vehicles stolen was about $7.5 billion, or $6,030 per vehicle. According to the NCVS, most motor vehicle theft occurs at night. The most common location for such theft is a parking lot or parking garage, with about one-third of thefts occurring there. About one-fifth of all motor vehicle thefts occur at the victim's driveway or garage, and another fifth occur on the street outside the victim's home.

The average arson in 1998 cost $12,561 in property loss, for a total loss of more than $800 million. Slightly less than half, or 47 percent, of all arson involved buildings. Motor vehicles, trailers, and other mobile property comprised almost 30 percent of all arson, with other property, such as crops or woods, accounting for the remainder.

 ## FORGERY AND FRAUD

Forgery and fraud are common property crimes we haven't yet discussed. I've saved them for last because they're Part II offenses and serve as a bridge between the property crime already discussed and the white-collar crime examined in the next chapter. Many fraud cases could easily be considered white-collar crime, as they're committed by businesses and wealthy professionals. We'll keep most of our discussion of these types of fraud until the next chapter, and instead focus here on forgery and fraud by less wealthy individuals. According to the UCR, about 114,600 people were arrested in 1998 for forgery and counterfeiting, and another

---

TABLE 11.4

AVERAGE PROPERTY LOSS BY TYPE OF LARCENY, UCR, 1998

TYPE OF LARCENY	AMOUNT LOST
Thefts from buildings	$1,028
Motor vehicle contents	675
Pocket-picking	407
Purse-snatching	362
Coin machines	328
Bicycles	262
Shoplifting	142

Source: Federal Bureau of Investigation 1999.

394,600 were arrested for fraud. Some of the fraud arrests were for the kinds of crimes discussed later in this chapter, and others were for the crimes covered in the next chapter.

Check Forgery and Credit Card Fraud

Check forgery, or the writing of "bad" checks, is the most common type of forgery. Edwin M. Lemert's (1953) classic study of check forgers several decades ago remains one of the few studies we have. Adopting the familiar distinction between amateur and professional property criminals, Lemert divided check forgers into two types: *naive* and *systematic*. Naive check forgers are the vast majority of check forgers. These occasional criminals commit their crime because of economic problems and don't generally commit other crimes. They also tend to be older and more educated than other property criminals. Systematic check forgers are more akin to professional criminals and use some sophisticated techniques to commit their crimes, including stealing checks and impersonating the people whose names are on the checks. Like naive check forgers, however, most systematic check forgers work alone, Lemert said. However, a more recent study found professional check forgers working in groups: One person would steal checks, while another would use them to make purchases in stores and get cash from banks. Often they would use fences to sell any merchandise bought with the checks (Tremblay 1986).

The modern equivalent of check forgery is credit card fraud, which amounts to at least $1 billion a year and usually involves lost or stolen cards. As with cars, the abundance of credit cards provides tempting targets for motivated criminals. Some robbers or burglars acquire credit cards along with money and then use the cards until the victim informs the credit card company of the theft. Others steal credit cards from the mail (Wells 2000).

Coupon Fraud

Coupon fraud is also very common. Manufacturers print several billion coupons each year to induce shoppers to buy their products. But many stores redeem coupons they've collected without anyone having bought the product. Although each coupon is usually $1 or less, so many coupons are redeemed fraudulently that coupon fraud is estimated to be at least $500 million annually. Some store owners gather their own coupons, while others rely on coupon "rings" to collect and give them the coupons (Halverson 1991). Perhaps unwittingly, many charities participate in coupon fraud by collecting coupons and turning them over for money to other groups that send them to manufacturers (Alaimo 1990). Because of the involvement of store owners in coupon fraud, it could easily be considered a white-collar crime.

Welfare and Tax Fraud

Before welfare reform in the middle 1990s, welfare fraud received much attention. Some people receiving welfare or food stamps would claim extra children who didn't exist or underreport their income. The amount of welfare fraud committed was about $1 billion annually. Despite the attention given this crime, it involved only about 2 to 4 percent of all people receiving welfare or food stamps (Associated Press 1994).

A far more serious problem is tax fraud, or tax evasion, which steals some $150 billion per year from the federal government (The Wall Street Journal 1994). This amount is far more than the total value of all property losses from the other property crimes described in this chapter. Because of who's involved, tax fraud could easily also be considered white-collar crime, but it's worth describing here to reinforce that economic crime is found in all walks of life.

It's difficult for the average person whose taxes are withheld from paychecks to cheat the IRS. Much tax fraud thus arises from the failure to report self-employment income and also from the claiming of false deductions. A common example of the former practice is the failure of restaurant employees to report their tips. But much more self-employment income is hidden from the IRS by small businesses and self-employed individuals, both blue-collar (such as a plumber) and white-collar (such as a physician). Much, and perhaps most, of such income belongs to middle- and upper-class professionals. However, the IRS has little way of knowing their income and thus must rely on them to report their incomes honestly. Many don't. Because of their occupations, investments, and other aspects of their status, many are also in a position to claim phony deductions that might sound plausible for them but implausible for less-wealthy people (Duke 1991).

As we'll discuss further in the next chapter, corporations also commit much tax fraud. The U.S. General Accounting Office estimates that two-thirds of all U.S. corporations fail to report some of their income. Corporate tax cheating accounts for about one-third of all revenue lost to tax fraud, or about $50 billion (The New York Times 1991).

Despite the enormity of tax fraud, our society doesn't condemn it. Everyone "hates" the IRS, and "ripping it off" is considered acceptable. As a technique of neutralization, we reason that since our taxes are so high, it's okay to lower the tax bite through fraudulent means. The IRS gets so much money each year, it won't miss the relatively small sum of money we individually keep from it. We criticize, as we should, crimes such as burglary and larceny but readily minimize the harm of tax fraud that costs many times more than these crimes combined.

Insurance Fraud

A final type of fraud is insurance fraud, which accounts for some 10 percent of all U.S. insurance claims. Estimates of yearly insurance fraud run as high as $70 billion in the United States and $13 billion in Canada (Daniele 1993; Slattery 1994). The U.S. amount is several times greater than the economic loss from the property "street" crimes that worry us much more. The billions of dollars lost to insurance fraud don't come from us at gunpoint but are costly nonetheless, as they raise our auto, health, and other insurance premiums. The FBI estimates that auto insurance fraud adds $200 annually to an average household's car insurance premiums (Associated Press 1995).

As with tax evasion, many otherwise law-abiding citizens think insurance fraud is acceptable. A national survey of 2,000 U.S. residents found over 25 percent approving of at least one or two types of insurance fraud, even though they thought of such fraud as generally a serious problem (Sprinkel 1993).

Several subtypes of insurance fraud exist, and I can mention only a few here. As we saw previously, many fires are set to collect fire insurance, and one-third of all arson could be considered insurance fraud. Another common type of insurance fraud involves cars. Of the $60 billion or more paid in auto insurance

◀ *Some auto insurance fraud involves car owners who deliberately commit minor accidents or feign injuries. About $6 billion per year is paid out in fraudulent insurance claims.*

claims annually for stolen or wrecked cars, about 10 percent, or $6 billion, is paid for fraudulent claims (Consumer Reports 1993).

In 1995 the FBI conducted "arrest and search" raids in 31 states of groups of people who staged car accidents to get insurance money. The FBI's effort was the culmination of its so-called Operation Sudden Impact investigation, which ultimately arrested or indicted more than 400 people. The arrests occurred in cities across the United States, including Atlanta, Baltimore, Boston, Chicago, Cleveland, Miami, Los Angeles, New Orleans, San Antonio, San Francisco, and Seattle. The cases targeted by the FBI fell into three categories: (1) "paper" accidents where no accident actually occurred but false reports were filed to collect insurance money; (2) minor accidents (e.g., the sideswiping of an innocent driver's car) deliberately committed to collect insurance; (3) staged accidents in which cars already damaged are driven to the same location so that the drivers can pretend an accident occurred (Associated Press 1995).

Other types of auto insurance fraud involve automobile owners who abandon or hide their car and pretend it was stolen. Some cases involve people in real accidents who then pretend to have whiplash or other injuries in order to collect medical insurance. There are also reports of drivers arriving at the scene of an accident and pretending they were injured in order to collect medical insurance. The state of New Jersey has documented many examples of "ghost riders," people arriving at bus accidents and claiming they were injured (Kerr 1993).

 ## EXPLAINING PROPERTY CRIME

To help us understand property crime further, let's examine several general explanations of property crime, and then turn to explanations of specific crimes.

Cultural Emphasis on Economic Success

An important reason for property crime lies in the U.S. culture, which emphasizes economic success above other goals. As Chapter 6's discussion of anomie and the American Dream indicated, the high emphasis on economic success underlies economic crime, which aims to achieve such success through illegal means

(Merton 1938; Messner and Rosenfeld 1997). The poor want more because they haven't fulfilled the American Dream, while the rich want more because one can never have enough in a society stressing economic success and "conspicuous consumption" (Veblen 1953 [1899]). Coupled with our other cultural emphases on competition and individualism, U.S. residents from all walks of life are thus quite ready to break the law for economic gain.

To explore this argument further, consider auto theft. Both as a status symbol and as a vehicle for transportation, cars are so important in U.S. society that most families own one or two of them. Auto manufacturers spend billions of dollars annually on advertising to persuade consumers to buy their cars. Many of their ads target young men and stress the excitement and even the sex appeal of owning a car.

Against this backdrop, if you're a young man who can't afford a car, you might well be tempted to steal one. With so many cars around, it's very easy to find one to steal. Given their advertisement-induced fascination with cars, many young men "borrow" them for a quick thrill. Other auto thieves are more economically motivated. Because cars are so expensive and need to be repaired so often, these thieves realize they can make a lot of money by stealing cars and either reselling them or dismantling them to sell their parts for repairs. For several reasons, then, auto theft is an inevitable property crime in our society.

Although many criminologists consider the emphasis on economic success an important source of property crime, it's also true that our class position affects the way we break the law for economic gain. An important principle of criminology is that people have differential access to illegitimate means, or, to put it another way, different opportunities for illegal gain (Cloward and Ohlin 1960). Poor people commit property crimes because they're not in a position to engage in complex financial schemes or to market unsafe products. Wealthier people wouldn't dream of breaking into a house or robbing someone on a street, but think nothing of defrauding the government, private citizens, and other parties in any number of ways.

Techniques of Neutralization

Chapter 7 noted that offenders engage in techniques of neutralization, or rationalizations, to justify their illegal behavior (Sykes and Matza 1957). Another cultural underpinning of property crime is thus the rationalizations property offenders use. A store or other business is ripping us off or charging us too much, so we'll rip it off. Everyone else does it, so why not me? The business is so big and rich, it won't miss what I take. While most of us have not stolen a car or burglarized a home, many of us have done other things. Hotels and motels estimate that about one-third of their guests steal something from their room (Shaw 1994). We justify these thefts by saying the lodging establishments charge too much for their rooms and won't miss what we take.

FENCING

Let's further explore the role of rationalizations in property crime by looking at fences. Techniques of neutralization are central to Darrel J. Steffensmeier's (1986) analysis of the experiences of one fence, Sam Goodman (an alias). Goodman, a white man, was close to 60 years old when Steffensmeier met him in January 1980 while Sam was serving a three-year prison term for receiving stolen property. Sam recognized his activities were illegal but denied he was a thief: "A thief is out there stealing, breaking into people's places.… A fence would not do that. A fence is just buying what the thief brings, he is not the one crawling in windows.… The fence is no angel, but he's no devil either. Think about it. He's not mugging old ladies, he's not pushing drugs on kids, he's not burning down buildings" (Steffensmeier 1986:238–240).

Sam thought that his fencing did burglary victims little harm, as most of them, homeowners or businesses, were wealthy and could get insurance to pay for their losses. He even occasionally returned "keepsake" items to their owners. In another rationalization, Sam argued that fencing is similar to legitimate businesses. As Steffensmeier (p. 243) puts it, "Sam is in his store every day of the week. He buys and sells things, waits on customers, transports merchandise, and advertises in the yellow pages."

Sam also emphasized that his work benefited many people. The Red Cross would send him victims of fires to pick out home furnishings, and he would bill the Red Cross for what they chose. At Christmas he would give church groups household goods for poor families. Sam was especially proud of how many toys he would give to children and of how many youngsters he paid to do odd jobs around his store.

In another rationalization, Sam also reasoned that many legitimate businesses deceive and manipulate their customers. Two of his favorite examples were funeral directors who persuade the bereaved to buy expensive caskets, and building contractors who mislead customers about the effectiveness of security systems. As Sam put it, "Your fence really isn't much more crooked than your average businessman, who are many times very shady. It's very hard to do well in business unless you chisel or clip in one way or other" (p. 243).

In evaluating Sam's reasoning, Steffensmeier observes that Sam "adheres to deeply ingrained 'American' values—competition, material success, individual action, freedom, hard work, acquisitiveness, and loyalty." These, of course, are the primary values of the American Dream that, as noted earlier, underlie much economic crime. As Steffensmeier notes of Sam, "There is a good bit of the American Dream in his fencing" (p. 251). The values leading you and your friends to go to college and to strive to be economically successful through legitimate means thus propel others into criminal activity. Perhaps property criminals aren't that different from many of us after all.

Economic Deprivation and Unemployment

So far I've presented a cultural explanation for property crime. Structural factors also matter, as several studies link economic deprivation and urban living conditions to such crime (Bennett and Basiotis 1991; Patterson 1991). Some research finds that deprivation increases property crime because it promotes social disorganization and the weakening of community social control. To the extent this is true, the effect of deprivation on property crime is said to be *indirect*. Other research finds a deprivation-property crime link even when social disorganization factors are held constant, suggesting that property crime provides the poor "an alternative means of gaining economic" resources (Bursik and Grasmick 1993:266). To the extent this is true, economic deprivation has a *direct* effect on property crime. This theoretical debate notwithstanding, either set of findings underscores the importance of economic deprivation for property crime.

A related body of research examines the effects of unemployment on property crime. Some ecological studies assess the effects of changing unemployment levels on property crime rates, while others examine the property crime rates of communities with different unemployment levels. Several individual-level studies also assess whether the unemployed and their families commit higher rates of property crime. Despite many reasons to expect a strong unemployment-property crime link (Hagan 1993), research findings are inconsistent. Some find the expected link, others do not, and some studies have even found higher unemployment related to less property crime (Bursik 2000).

Methodological differences appear to account for these inconsistent findings. In particular, ecological studies analyzing data for Census tracts or other small geographical areas more often find an unemployment-property crime link than studies analyzing national-level data (Chiricos 1987). Individual-level studies also find a link more often than ecological studies. Whether the presumed relationship is found may also depend on which age group is studied, how unemployment is measured, and which property crime is studied (Allan and Steffensmeier 1989). It may also be important to examine the unemployment-property crime relationship separately for different races. When Gary LaFree and his associates did so, they found changes in unemployment related to white property crime rates, but not to black rates (LaFree, Drass, and O'Day 1992).

One final explanation for the inconsistent findings comes from the routine activities/lifestyles literature. Although unemployment may increase the motivation to commit property crime, it may also reduce the opportunities for property crime (Cantor and Land 1985). For example, in areas and times of high unemployment, fewer people will be working or—because of their reduced incomes—vacationing, eating out, or engaging in other leisure activities. For all these reasons, they'll be more likely to be at home, ironically making their homes safer from would-be burglars and themselves safer from would-be robbers. Citing all these possibilities, a recent review concluded that "many criminologists may have rejected prematurely the unemployment-crime hypothesis" (Bursik 2000:222).

Routine Activities and Social Process Factors

As this discussion implies, the routine activities/lifestyles literature provides another explanation for property crime. Simply put, certain activities and lifestyles put people more at risk for burglary, larceny, and motor vehicle theft (Lynch and Cantor 1992). For example, people whose homes are vacant for long periods of time because of work or vacationing are more apt to suffer burglaries, while those who often walk on crowded streets are more likely to become the victims of pickpockets or purse snatchers.

Social process factors such as learning and negative family and school influences also contribute to property crime. As Chapter 7 indicated, a large body of literature documents the effects of criminal peer influences, dysfunctional family environments, and negative school experiences on criminality, including property crime.

Property Crime for Thrills

In a novel formulation, Jack Katz (1988) argued that much violent and property crime is done for excitement and thrills. Crime, he wrote, is seductive and is committed because it is "sensually compelling" (p. 3). He described property offenses as "sneaky thrill" crimes that offenders commit because they're excited by the idea of stealing and by the prospect of obtaining objects they desire. Since its presentation, Katz's view has attracted much attention, some favorable and some critical (Hagan 1990; Turk 1991). A major criticism is that Katz overstated the importance of thrills and emotion for understanding why crime occurs. Still, his theory provides a nice "intervening" mechanism for understanding some of the patterning of property crime we've already discussed.

Recent evidence for this conclusion comes from an analysis by Bill McCarthy (1995) of data from a survey of almost 2,000 respondents from New Jersey, Iowa, and Oregon. Among other questions, the respondents were asked (1) whether they had ever been so attracted to an object that they had considered stealing it, and (2) how likely they would be in the future to steal an object they desired. McCarthy found that males and adolescents were more likely than females and adults to report being so "seduced" by an object that they considered stealing it. To the extent such seduction differs by gender and age, it's not surprising that so much property crime is considered by young males: Once again, masculinity is an important underlying cause. Here auto theft would be a most appropriate example.

Importantly, Katz also found that although socioeconomic status didn't affect whether someone was attracted to an object he or she didn't own, it did affect the likelihood of considering stealing the object. Whether people act illegally on their material seductions, then, may well depend on their social class. As McCarthy (1995:533) puts it, "People desire goods regardless of their structural conditions, whereas only those lacking [economic] opportunities are more willing to consider future theft if seduced."

A Look at Shoplifting and Arson

The several kinds of explanations just discussed—cultural emphasis on economic success, techniques of neutralization, routine activities, and sneaky thrills—all help explain why property crime is so common. To emphasize this point, let's focus on two otherwise dissimilar crimes, shoplifting and arson.

We saw earlier that shoplifting is very common. The high school survey reported in Table 11.2 indicated that about one-fourth of female seniors and one-third of male seniors had shoplifted in the previous year. Other studies suggest that 8 to 10 percent of all shoppers shoplift, with some $8 billion in merchandise stolen annually (Ray 1987).

Most shoplifters, even boosters, would condemn anyone robbing a store cashier at gunpoint of $10 or $20, yet they rationalize their own behavior. If you have friends who have shoplifted, you might have heard some of these justifications: The store charges them too much, makes them wait in line too long, treats them impersonally, or is so big it won't miss the shoplifted items. Like Sam the fence, shoplifters see crime and deviance as something other people do, even though the estimated annual loss from shoplifting runs into the billions of dollars.

Why else is shoplifting so common? For one reason, it's exciting, especially for the many adolescent shoplifters who act in groups of two or more to see what they can get away with. But cultural, gender, and class forces also explain adolescent shoplifting. Young people are part of an expensive "teen consumer subculture" that pressures them to steal items they can't afford (Chesney-Lind and

Sheldon 1992:43). This consumer subculture is a natural outcome of a larger cultural emphasis on possessions and appearance. This emphasis leads girls to be especially interested in shoplifting cosmetics and clothes. For female and male adolescents, shoplifting stems from "the bombarding of young people with images of looks and goods attainable only with money many of them do not have" (Chesney-Lind and Sheldon 1992:44).

Routine activities theory also helps explain why shoplifting is so common. One reason shoplifting rose in the 1960s was the rapid development of large department and discount stores and especially of shopping malls, which didn't exist before the late 1950s and early 1960s. For obvious reasons, it's easier to shoplift in large stores and malls than in smaller establishments. Large stores and malls thus presented the combination of motivated offenders, attractive targets, and lack of guardianship that, as routine activities theory stresses, results in crime and victimization. The rise in shoplifting was both predictable and inevitable.

Arson, thankfully, is far less common than shoplifting but still exhibits a mixture of motivations. Some fires are set for thrills or for revenge: Adolescents set fires to their school after getting detention; estranged lovers burn the residences of the person who rejected them; employees torch a business after being fired; evicted tenants burn their apartment building. Some cases of arson are hate crimes (Chapter 13) directed against people of color or other unpopular groups. In the early 1990s, three teenagers were convicted and imprisoned for setting fires to several African-American churches in Missouri (The New York Times 1993).

Other fires are economically motivated and set by owners of failing businesses or apartment buildings or by homeowners facing high mortgages and mounting bills. The aim here is to collect fire insurance. Experts estimate that this "arson for profit" accounts for up to one-third of all arson fires (Brady 1993). Not surprisingly, evidence from the United States and Canada indicates that arson rises as the economy worsens (McMullan and Swan 1989; Nordheimer 1992). James Brady (1993) notes that much arson occurs in the most devastated neighborhoods of central cities and blames this arson on declining property values caused by banks' refusal to loan money to improve homes and other property in these neighborhoods. Some banks, he says, even sell foreclosed properties in these areas to "racketeers" at an inflated price and thus an inflated mortgage. The racketeers then obtain artificially high insurance and hire a "professional torch" to burn the building. Both racketeer and bank keep the insurance proceeds.

One other type of arson for profit occurs in the nation's forests. Michael Francis, an official with the Wilderness Society in Washington, D.C., says most Americans underestimate the proportion of forest fires caused by arson. "They think most fires are accidental, or caused by lightning. They'd be shocked" (Cole 1995:1). According to one estimate, 90 percent of forest fires on federal land in the Southeast are caused by arson. In California, only 13 percent of fires on state land are caused by arson, but they account for almost 75 percent of all monetary costs from forest fires. Although some arson forest fires are set for thrills, many are done for profit. Because forest fires generate large contracts for things like bulldozers, food, and toilet paper, individuals who would benefit financially from a forest fire are thus tempted to set one. As one example, several fires in Northern California in 1992 and 1993 were set by someone who owned a water tender truck that he leased to the U.S. Forest Service to fight the fires he had started. Other forest fires are set by volunteer firefighters, who are paid only if they fight a fire. Against this backdrop, they're sometimes tempted to start a fire to earn a little extra income.

Popular efforts today to reduce property crime focus on the criminal justice system, on making it more difficult for property criminals to gain access to their targets, and on neighborhood watch groups.

Regarding the criminal justice system, the federal government and state legislatures have provided more money for additional police and mandated longer prison terms for persons convicted of serious property crime. As indicated earlier, however, many and perhaps most property criminals don't weigh their chances of arrest and imprisonment as they decide whether to commit a crime. We've also seen that as little as 5 percent of all property crime is cleared by arrest. Against the backdrop of these two points, efforts to reduce property crime by adding more police or increasing prison terms promise little hope in reducing such crime (Tunnell 1996).

Another popular response to property crime, especially burglary, in the last two decades has been *target hardening*: efforts to make residences and businesses more difficult to burglarize (see the Crime and Controversy box on page 320). These efforts include stronger locks, better lighting, burglar alarms, and other home-security measures, all of which can reduce burglaries. Unfortunately, the most effective security measures, including burglar alarms connected to police stations, are also the most expensive, putting them beyond the means of average citizens. Moreover, while alarms and other security measures deter some burglars, they don't deter others. The most effective burglary deterrent still seems to be the presence of someone at home (Rosenbaum 1988). A review concluded "there is no reason to dispute" the view that target hardening can have only a limited effect on burglary (Shover 1991:99).

Ironically, one of the most effective security measures may also be one of the cheapest: a dog. As Paul Cromwell (1994:43) observes, "Large dogs represent a physical threat to the burglar, and small ones are often noisy, attracting attention to his or her activities." When Cromwell interviewed thirty active burglars, they

◄ *One of the most effective deterrents to burglary is a dog. Even small dogs can cause burglars to avoid a home.*

Target Hardening: Is Increased Security Worth the Price?

For better or worse, one of the consequences of concern over property crime has been target hardening, or making residences and businesses more secure against burglary, robbery, and other property and violent crime. Many observers lament that the United States has been turned into a "fortress state," with people locking their doors and installing sophisticated burglary alarm systems, and whole neighborhoods walling themselves in and euphemistically calling themselves "gated communities." While all these measures bring some sense of security and perhaps do make people safer, they come at a high economic and social price.

The many issues involved in target hardening are illustrated in the story of Green Acres, a two-floor, 200-store shopping mall on Long Island, not too far from New York City. By the early 1990s, Green Acres had acquired a reputation as an unsafe place to shop, as in the preceding years there had been reports of many car thefts, two kidnappings, and gunfire at a nearby cinema complex. In 1984 alone, 532 cars were reported stolen from the mall's parking lot, for an average of more than 10 per week. Finally, in August 1994 a fight ended with the stabbing of a college student in a lingerie store. The fight resulted from a year-long dispute over a stolen bicycle, and ended with the stabbing after the assailant chased the victim from the mall's food court into the store.

In response, Green Acres management put security guards on the roof of the mall to watch the parking lot. It beefed up its fleet of patrol cars, which circle the mall constantly. It began a valet parking service and increased its number of electronic cameras, watched constantly by security officials. By early 1996 it appeared that the measures had paid off with a decline in reported car thefts, purse snatchings, and other crimes. A Chamber of Commerce official noted the change with approval: "You can see the security personnel, but they're not obtrusive that you're worried about walking around there. They've been able to strike that balance." The Green Acres experience echoed that of other malls around the country in the last decade, as public concern over mall safety led other malls to beef up their security.

Ironically, most malls are actually safer than most city streets and other locations. For example, 12 million people shop at Green Acres each year. With so many people, some crime is bound to happen. Even at Green Acres, it turned out that many of the reported car thefts were filed by people who had actually abandoned or destroyed their cars and then filed the reports to obtain insurance money. Between 1987 and 1991, authorities charged 386 people with filing such false reports. Although the mall was the scene of the lingerie store stabbing, the mall's security director noted that "the two men knew each other prior to coming to the mall. There was bad blood stemming from over the years. That incident could have occurred in a schoolyard or train station."

With the added surveillance by additional security guards and police, some on horseback, and by increased numbers of security cameras, people at the Long Island mall are now being watched constantly. The good news is that crime at the mall evidently went down, although, statistically speaking, it was probably not that bad to begin with. The bad news is that Green Acres adopted more of a fortress mentality than it had before and sacrificed public freedom of movement for the sake of public feelings of security.

Sources: Barry 1996; Keen 1994; Skogan 1990.

named dogs as the second-most effective burglary deterrent, or "no go" factor, topped only by the presence of someone at home. One burglar said, "I don't mess with no dogs. If they got dogs, I go someplace else" (p. 44). Supporting this point, a study of college students at nine campuses found that theft victimization was lower for those who owned dogs than for those without a dog (Mustaine and Tewksbury 1998).

Target hardening has also been tried with automobiles. To combat auto theft, auto manufacturers now use sophisticated security devices. Many cars now come with standard alarm systems, and some come with electronic transmitters enabling police to track the car if it's stolen. Unfortunately, transmitters and other sophisticated devices can be quite expensive, putting them beyond the reach of the average car owner. For better or worse, the increased security measures have apparently helped make auto theft more of a professional crime than it used to be, as the new measures often frustrate the efforts of would-be joy riders to steal cars (Incantalupo 1993).

In addition to target hardening, neighborhood watch groups have also been established. However, Shover (1991:100) concludes the effectiveness of these groups is "scarcely more encouraging" than that for target hardening. The neighborhoods with the worst burglary problems are the least likely to start neighborhood watch groups, and when such groups are started, the households most likely to be burglarized are the least likely to join the groups. When groups do begin, people are enthusiastic and "gung-ho" at the outset but, as with many voluntary enterprises, quickly lose their interest (Garofalo and McLeod 1989). Research on the effectiveness of neighborhood watch groups and other community crime prevention programs has been plagued by serious methodological problems. The best-designed studies find these programs have only limited success. An additional problem is that even if the programs do succeed, the crime they prevent is often displaced to other locations (Sherman et al. 1998).

If efforts involving the criminal justice system, target hardening, and neighborhood watch groups offer only limited hope in reducing property crime, what can we do? A sociological prescription for crime reduction would involve the cultural emphasis on economic success, economic deprivation, and social process factors. Perhaps it's too much to hope that the United States will soon decrease its emphasis on economic success and conspicuous consumption, but it's possible that public policy can do something about the economic deprivation, urban conditions, family dysfunction, and other by-now familiar factors that set the stage for much property and other crime.

 ## SUMMARY AND CONCLUSION

Several theories and factors introduced in previous chapters help explain property crime, especially by the poor. Anomie, economic deprivation, and social process and routine activities factors all contribute to the higher involvement of the poor in robbery, burglary, and related crimes. We also cannot underestimate the role of gender, as males account for 85 to 90 percent or more of most property crimes. In the previous chapter we explained this basic gender difference in terms of what masculinity means in modern U.S. society. Involvement in most of the property crimes in this chapter also demands the various traits that we associate with masculinity. The role that race plays is a bit more complex. African-Americans comprise only a minority of property criminals. Still, African-American involvement in property crime exceeds the African-American proportion of the population, underscoring once again the criminogenic conditions in which many blacks live.

The criminals in many property crimes can be divided into two basic types. Amateurs are the vast majority of all property criminals, but professionals steal more on the average because of their higher skills, greater willingness to take risks, and more frequent criminal involvement. Although I didn't make the point, people and organizations committing tax and insurance fraud could also be divided along these lines, with many white-collar criminals sounding and behaving very much like fences and other professional property criminals. We'll come back to this point in the next chapter.

If this chapter did nothing else, I hope it showed that economic crime in the United States is rampant. Many people have doubtless stolen or damaged property at some time in their lives. That is especially true if we include employee theft and other crimes to be discussed in the next chapter. The poor commit the economic crimes we fear the most, but the middle class and the wealthy also commit many economic crimes.

As I emphasized at the outset, the kind of economic crime we commit depends on our opportunities. As Charles H. McCaghy and Timothy A. Capron (1994:200) remind us, "Criminals must break into buildings or point guns because they may have few other alternatives. Good citizens, however, have a wider range of alternatives: Their respectability permits them a form of violence-free theft inaccessible to the poor and the unemployed." This is a crucial distinction because, as McCaghy and Capron (p. 200) also point out, "Theft is most tolerable to American sensibilities if it is genteel and unassuming, without threats and the waving of guns."

This is true even though "genteel" theft costs us much more than the "street" variety that concerns us so much. Robbery and Index property crime (burglary, larceny, auto theft, and arson) costs us less than $20 billion annually, still an astronomical figure, but insurance fraud costs $70 billion and tax evasion $150 billion. The combined annual cost of these two crimes, $220 billion, is 12 to 14 times greater than the cost of Index property crime. Thus, although this chapter looked for the most part at economic crimes by the poor, it's also important to understand economic crimes by the nonpoor and especially the wealthy. We began to discuss some of these crimes when we examined fraud, and we will continue to do so in the next chapter, where we'll study the many forms of white-collar crime committed by the wealthy and respectable elements, individuals and businesses alike, of our society.

KEY TERMS

amateur theft	rationalization
booster	sneaky thrill crimes
decision-making processes	snitch
fencing	social organization
joy riding	support system
professional theft	target hardening

STUDY QUESTIONS

1. How does the distinction between amateur and professional criminals help us understand the nature and dynamics of property crime?
2. Do coupon, welfare, and tax fraud occur for the same reasons as burglary and larceny? Why or why not?
3. How does an understanding of techniques of neutralization help us in turn to understand the behavior and motivation of fences and other people involved in property crime?
4. Evaluate the desirability and effectiveness of target hardening as a means of reducing property crime.

INTERNET EXERCISES

As this chapter indicates, property crime is very common in the United States, and many people and households have been or one day will become victims of property crime. Go to **http://www.apbnews.com** to access the APBnews.com Web site. Click **Safety Center** at the top right. At the bottom right you should see a list of safety tips to keep your home and property safe from crime. Explore some of these tips. What does this Web site advise people to do to reduce their chances of becoming property crime victims? Have your or members of your family followed this advice?

To discover the chances of being arrested for property crime, go to the FBI UCR site at **http://www.fbi.gov/ucr.htm**. Access the 1999 UCR. Click **Crime Index Offenses Cleared**. Scroll down until you find the clearance rates for larceny-theft, burglary, and motor vehicle theft. Why do you think these clearance rates are so low? Why do you think they're much lower than those for violent crime?

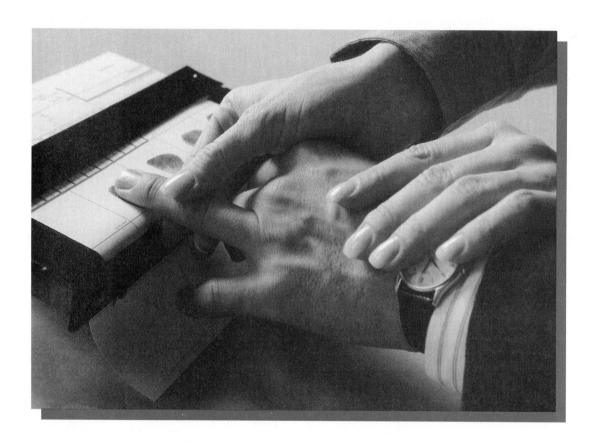

WHITE-COLLAR
CRIME

Crime in the News

As the 1990s ended, white-collar crime stories could readily be found in the nation's newspapers, even if the number of these stories was just a minute fraction of those appearing on street crime. In one case, the Odwalla food company, which sells nutritional juice and shakes in much of the country, pleaded guilty in July 1998 to violating federal food safety laws and paid a $1.5 million fine for selling bacteria-laden apple juice that killed a toddler and made dozens of other people sick. Fourteen of these were children who became seriously ill. Also that summer, the Honda and Ford auto companies agreed to pay millions of dollars in fines for selling cars that would pollute too much on the road even though they were certified to pass emissions tests. The government said Honda had programmed many of its cars' pollution-control computers to ignore spark-plug failures. When such failures, which cause emissions of hydrocarbons to double, occurred, the cars' "check engine" idiot light would not go on, and drivers would not know they needed to have their cars repaired. The government also said that 60,000 Ford Econoline vans were designed to emit more pollutants on the highway than they did on treadmill tests. Neither company admitted any wrongdoing. Honda's fine was $12.6 million, while Ford's was $2.5 million. Although Honda's fine was substantial, its profits for 1997 were $1.96 billion. Honda's fine was thus less than 1 percent of its profits. After paying its fine the company would be left with a profit of $1.947 billion.

The beginning of the new millennium did not mark the end of alarming stories of corporate behavior. In February 2000, the Boston Globe reported that the W. R. Grace company, the subject of the book and movie A Civil Action involving chemical pollution of groundwater, sold millions of bags of attic insulation containing asbestos in the 1960s and 1970s without warning the public. The company knew about the asbestos but was worried that a warning label would make the public reluctant to buy the insulation. Since there was no warning label requirement back then, the company did not break the law. During this time it repeatedly told the government that its insulation was safe. Two weeks after the Globe's report, two state agencies said they would conduct soil tests at two former W. R. Grace plants where asbestos products were made.

Sources: Appel 2000; Appel and Swidey 2000; Belluck 1998; Wald 1998.

The incidents described in the "Crime in the News" vignette were hardly the first times that corporations endangered public health and welfare. Consider the case of Buffalo Creek, a mining community in West Virginia. After days of torrential rain in February 1972, a 20-foot-high flood surged into this peaceful valley of several thousand homes, destroying everything in its path, killing 125 people, and leaving 2,500 others homeless. The water had built up behind an artificial dam composed of the mine waste, or slag, which remains after coal has been mined and washed. When the flood struck, this dam weighed one million tons and had reached enormous proportions: 465 feet wide, 480 feet front-to-back, and as high as 60 feet. The coal mining company was adding one thousand tons of slag to it daily. Behind the dam lay 132 million gallons of "black water" used to wash the coal—the size of a 20-acre, 40-foot-deep lake.

At 7:59 A.M. on February 26, the dam finally burst. The 132 million gallons of black water gathered up one million tons of solid waste, rocks, and debris along the way and destroyed the nearest town in seconds. As sociologist Kai T. Erikson (1976:29) recounts, "It did not crush the village into mounds of rubble, but carried everything away with it—houses, cars, trailers, a church whose white spire had pointed to the slag pile for years—and scraped the grounds as cleanly as if a thousand bulldozers had been at work." Years later, the flood's survivors still suffered from anxiety, depression, and nightmares.

This tragedy could have been prevented. Despite the rain and flood, this was entirely a human disaster, not an act of God. The danger the dam posed to the people of Buffalo Creek was no secret, as they had worried about the dam's safety. Although the company's behavior was directly responsible for the 125 deaths and other devastation, no one from the company was indicted or prosecuted for murder or manslaughter. Nor were the 125 deaths it caused added to the list of homicides known to the police in 1972, the year in which the flood occurred. The company did pay $13.5 million to the flood survivors to settle a lawsuit, but this was an amount the company could easily afford to lose, as it was owned by a large corporation.

Thirty years later, the Buffalo Creek disaster remains a poignant example of corporate wrongdoing. Many aspects of the disaster are common to other corporate misconduct: reckless behavior by corporate officials in the name of profit; their denial of any wrongdoing; death, injury or illness, and property loss; little or no legal punishment (Shover and Hochstetler 2000). Despite growing awareness of these problems, the public, elected officials, and the news media remain much more concerned about street crime. Although criminologists are increasingly studying white-collar crime, the field was late to "discover" this crime, and most criminological research continues to focus on street crime (Cullen and Benson 1993).

In this chapter we'll examine the many dimensions of white-collar crime. We'll see that white-collar crime is a loose term that covers many different behaviors. We'll then discuss specific examples of white-collar crime and attempt to document its profound social and economic cost. The chapter will end with a look at explanations of white-collar crime and its treatment by the legal system.

Defining White-Collar Crime

For most of its history, criminology neglected white-collar crime as it focused almost entirely on crimes by the poor, or street crime. Classical thinkers Cesare Beccaria and Jeremy Bentham addressed the punishment of common criminals, while Cesare Lombroso and other scientists examined their biological traits. The sociologists who developed social disorganization, anomie, learning, control, and other theories also focused on street crime and delinquency.

In retrospect, this focus was not surprising. As cities grew rapidly in nineteenth-century Europe and the United States because of industrialization, public and official concern over the "dangerous classes" of the poor in these cities also grew (Cullen and Benson 1993). Although much of this concern arose from ethnic, religious, and class prejudice, it was also true that the violence, disorderly conduct, and other crime of the urban poor was often quite visible and quite frightening.

While industrialization fueled concern over the dangerous classes, it also led ironically to a new form of crime that was much less visible and thus pretty much ignored. This was the crime of a new form of business organization, the industrial corporation, that changed the face and economy of the United States after the Civil War. In this period, the oil, steel, railroad, and other industries brought the United States squarely into the Industrial Revolution. Men like Andrew Carnegie (steel), J. P. Morgan (banking), John D. Rockefeller (oil), and Jay Gould, Leland Stanford, and Cornelius Vanderbilt (railroads) acquired massive fortunes as they developed and headed the major industrial corporations of the day. They were honored in their time, and are still honored today, as the pioneers of the Industrial Revolution and as philanthropists who donated hundreds of millions of dollars to worthy causes.

Yet most of them repeatedly broke the law or at a minimum engaged in questionable business practices. While some call these men "captains of industry," others call them "robber barons" (Josephson 1962). Their crimes included bribery, kickbacks, and other complex financial schemes, and their industries established factories and other work settings with inhumane working conditions.

By the end of the nineteenth century, their crimes and workplace conditions began to raise concern. Congress passed the Sherman Antitrust Act in 1890 to prohibit restraint of trade that raised consumer prices. In the early 1900s, "muckrakers" bitterly criticized business and political corruption and condemned the cruel ways workers were treated. Two leading muckrakers were Ida M. Tarbell, who wrote a scathing history of Rockefeller's Standard Oil Company, and Upton Sinclair, whose 1906 novel, *The Jungle*, addressed the horrible sanitary and work conditions in the U.S. meatpacking industry and helped lead to federal food laws. Another was Lincoln Steffens, whose 1904 book on political corruption, *The Shame of the Cities*, remains a classic (Sinclair 1990 [1906]; Steffens 1904; Tarbell 1904).

About the same time, sociologist Edward A. Ross (1965 [1907]) also wrote about the corrupt and dangerous practices of corporate leaders, whom he called "criminaloids." Like the muckrakers, he noted that the actions of industrial leaders and their corporations often caused great financial and physical harm, even if they didn't violate any criminal laws. Ross blamed corporate wrongdoing on the intense pursuit of profit he saw as the hallmark of industrialization and capitalism.

Edwin Sutherland and White-Collar Crime

Given the work of the muckrakers and sociologist Ross, the stage was now set for the burgeoning fields of criminology and sociology to study white-collar crime. Unfortunately, that stage remained empty for another forty years or so, as scholars continued to focus on street crime. In the 1940s, however, Edwin Sutherland wrote some important works about *white-collar crime*, a term he coined, and his views remain influential today. Sutherland (1949) studied the 70 largest U.S. manufacturing, mining, and retail corporations and found they had violated antitrust, false advertising, and other laws 980 times, or 14 each on the average. Their crimes included bribery of public officials and were not just accidental violations but deliberate, repeated, extensive, and harmful.

Because Sutherland was forced to rely on official determinations of these violations, he noted that the true extent of corporate lawbreaking was undoubtedly much higher. He added that any common criminal committing even his low estimate of an average 14 offenses would be considered an habitual or chronic offender worthy of public and legal condemnation. The widespread corporate lawbreaking Sutherland found caused him to challenge the assumption of "conventional theories that crime is due to poverty or to the personal and social pathologies connected with poverty" (p. 25).

Many of the corporations Sutherland studied had been charged with engaging in crimes during World Wars I and II. These crimes included illegal profiteering; the manufacture of defective military parts and the sale of rancid food to the Army; tax evasion; the sale of munitions and other war materials to Germany and other nations with which the United States was at war; and even the revealing of military secrets to these nations. From these crimes, Sutherland concluded that "many corporations have used the national emergency as an opportunity for extraordinary enrichment of themselves" (p. 175). This led him to observe that "profits are more important to large corporations than patriotism, even in the midst of an international struggle which endangered Western civilization" (p. 174).

Despite Sutherland's pathbreaking work, sociologists and criminologists ignored his call for increased scholarship on white-collar crime for at least another twenty years. Let's begin our own examination of white-collar crime by looking at Sutherland's definition of the term and later attempts to improve his definition.

Conceptual Problems in Defining White-Collar Crime

In one of the most famous definitions in criminology, Sutherland (1949:9) defined white-collar crime as "a crime committed by a person of respectability and high social status in the course of his occupation." Sutherland's definition has two major components. First, the crime must be committed by someone of "respectability and high social status." Sutherland's definition thus excluded crime by blue-collar workers. Second, the crime must be committed "in the course of" one's occupation. Thus, a wealthy corporate executive who murders a lover would not, according to Sutherland, be committing white-collar crime. Like Ross and the muckrakers, Sutherland stressed that behavior of respectable persons can be quite harmful even if it doesn't violate any criminal laws.

Over the years, Sutherland's definition of white-collar crime led to much criticism and many attempts to revise it. Some early critics argued that behavior that doesn't violate any criminal laws should not be considered a crime, no matter how harmful it may be (Tappan 1947). Others noted that Sutherland's definition rules out lawbreaking behavior by the wealthy, such as tax evasion, that is not committed in the course of their occupation but does involve many elements of other forms of white-collar crime (Edelhertz 1970). Still other critics noted that his definition excluded crimes by blue-collar workers and blue-collar businesses that, notwithstanding the color of the "collar," share many features of crimes committed by persons of high social status (Shaprio 1990).

One other conceptual problem arose from Sutherland's own "operationalization" of his definition. Although he defined white-collar crime as crime committed by people of high social status as part of their occupations, his 1949 book, *White-Collar Crime*, focused almost entirely on crime by corporations, or corporate crime. This inconsistency led to some confusion over whether white-collar crime is something individuals do or something corporations and other businesses do (Geis 1992).

Contemporary Views

Given white-collar crime's complexity, many substitute terms have been proposed over the years and many topologies of white-collar crime developed. Some of the substitute terms include *elite deviance, respectable crime,* and *upperworld crime* (Simon 1999). Given the popularity of Sutherland's coinage, most scholars continue to favor *white-collar crime,* although some call for the term to include crime by blue-collar workers in the course of their occupation and crime by blue-collar businesses. Others fear that including these sorts of crimes would dilute the message that Sutherland, and, before him, Ross and the muckrakers, sought to send.

Of the many topologies of white-collar crime, one of the most influential was advanced in 1973 by Marshall Clinard and Richard Quinney (1973). They divided white-collar crime into two types, *occupational* and *corporate.* Occupational crime is committed by individuals in the course of their occupation for personal gain. Common examples of occupational crime are employee theft, which is committed against one's employer, and corruption by physicians and other professional workers, which is committed against these professionals' clients or the government.

As the name implies, corporate crime is committed by corporations. Although the crime is obviously planned and carried out by executives in the corporation, the crime is committed for the corporations' financial gain. Although corporate executives may well benefit from any corporate success generated by their illegal activity, their primary intention is to benefit the corporation (Vaughan 1983). While liking Clinard and Quinney's typology, some scholars suggest that their corporate crime category be relabeled *organizational crime* (Ermann and Lundman 1978). This term emphasizes that crime can be done by and on behalf of organizations, many of them corporations, but some of them small businesses, including blue-collar businesses such as auto repair shops.

The revised typology of occupational and organizational crime has proven quite popular and will be used here even though, as health-care fraud will illustrate, it's often difficult to know whether to classify a given crime as occupational or organizational. With this typology in mind, sociologist James W. Coleman (1998:7) proposes the following definition of white-collar crime first advanced by the National White Collar Crime Center: "illegal or unethical acts that violate fiduciary responsibility of public trust committed by an individual or organization, usually during the course of legitimate occupational activity, by persons of high or respectable social status for personal or organizational gain." One advantage of this definition is that it includes harmful but legal corporate behavior. Nancy K. Frank and Michael J. Lynch (1992) refer to such behavior as "corporate crime," defined as "socially injurious and blameworthy acts, legal or illegal, that cause financial, physical or environmental harm, committed by corporations and businesses against their workers, the general public, the environment, other corporations and businesses, the government, or other countries. The benefactor of such crimes is the corporation."

Now that we've examined the elements of white-collar crime, let's take a look at specific examples. Using the categories outlined earlier, we'll start with occupational crime and then turn to corporate and other organizational crime.

OCCUPATIONAL CRIME: LAWBREAKING FOR PERSONAL GAIN

Employee Theft: Pilferage and Embezzling

If you are or ever have been employed, write down everything you've taken from your workplace without paying for it: pens and pencils, dishes or glassware, store merchandise, tools, and so forth. Next to each item, note its approximate value. Now write down how much cash you might have taken. Finally, if you ever got paid for more hours than you worked because you misreported your time, write down the amount you were overpaid. Now add up the value of all the items on your list.

No doubt many readers will report taking at least a few small items adding up to $10 to $20, with a few reporting taking more expensive items amounting to several hundred dollars or more. Several have probably been overpaid because they misrepresented their time. Even if the average employee theft per student was only, say, $20, that would still mean that students at a 10,000-person campus would have stolen $200,000 from their workplaces.

As this exercise might indicate, employee theft is quite common. A survey of more than 9,000 employees in the U.S. retail, hospital, and manufacturing industries found one-third reporting stealing something in the previous year (Clark and Hollinger 1983). In a survey of U.S. supermarket employees, 90 percent said they'd stolen something from their store, damaged its property, or come to work hung over (Moreland 1994). Employee theft is also common in Canada. A survey of Canadian residents found 80 percent saying they steal from their workplace sometimes (60 percent) or often (20 percent) (Holt 1993).

◀ *Although the public is routinely warned about shoplifting, employee theft is another crime that costs the United States about $40 billion to $50 billion each year. Employees who are the most dissatisfied with their wages or otherwise antagonistic toward their employers are the most likely to engage in this form of theft.*

Estimates of annual employee theft in the United States vary widely but number in the billions of dollars. A few estimates put the figure at $5 billion to $10 billion, while others run as high as $75 billion to $120 billion a year, including $1 billion worth of paper clips, pens and pencils, postage, and stationery (Guthrie 1993; Wells 1994). The U.S. Department of Commerce estimates that employee theft amounts to $40 billion to $50 billion annually, or at least $110 million per day, and accounts for 20 percent of all business failures. Any of these estimates far exceeds the total amount stolen by all the robbery and burglary combined (Delaney 1993). In Canada, employee theft is estimated at $20 billion annually and thought to account for 30 percent of all business failures and to raise the price of goods and services by 15 percent (Holt 1993).

Employee theft may be divided into *pilferage* and *embezzling*. Pilferage involves the theft of merchandise, tools, stationery, and other items, and embezzling involves the theft of cash and the misappropriation or misuse of funds.

The most common reason for pilferage is employee dissatisfaction with their pay, working conditions, and treatment by supervisors and the company itself. Employees who are more dissatisfied for one or more of these reasons are more likely to steal than those who are more satisfied. One study found that manufacturing workers whose pay had been reduced 15 percent in a cost-cutting measure reported "significantly higher" rates of workplace theft *after* the pay cut than *before* it. Their rates of theft were also much higher after the pay cut than a control group of employees whose pay had not been cut (Greenberg 1990).

Another reason for pilferage is what might be called the "workplace culture." In many workplaces, the employees develop informal norms of what is acceptable and not acceptable to steal. These norms generally dictate that expensive, important company property should not be stolen, but that inexpensive, less important property is "up for grabs." As the research on dissatisfaction and employee theft indicates, the workplace culture also includes the by-now familiar techniques of neutralization that help employees rationalize their theft: They don't pay us enough; they treat us too harshly; the business won't miss the property we take.

Compared to pilferage, embezzling is more a solo activity (Green 1993). In a classic study, Donald R. Cressey observed that embezzlers are employees with access to company funds who face financial problems they want to keep secret because of their embarrassment or shame (Cressey 1971 [1953]). To use Cressey's term, their financial problems are *nonshareable*. They typically rationalize that they're only borrowing the money or that their company won't miss the funds.

An individual act of embezzlement ranges from the tens of dollars to the millions. A recent example of multimillion-dollar embezzling involved the treasurer of the Episcopal Church, who admitted to embezzling $2.2 million from the Church from 1990 to 1995. She used the money to buy a house in New Jersey and a farm in Virginia and to pay for jewelry, travel, and school tuition for her children (Franklin 1995). In other examples, the controller of a perfume company pleaded guilty to embezzling $2.3 million from his employer (Women's Wear Daily 1989); the managing partner of a major Chicago law firm was sentenced to 24 to 30 months in prison after pleading guilty to embezzling $750,000 from his firm by overbilling it for hours he and his wife hadn't worked (Samborn 1995); and the postmaster of a New Jersey post office pleaded guilty to embezzling $870,000 from the postal service (Levy 1994).

Although embezzling involves both sexes, it includes an interesting gender difference that reflects gender differences in employment. Female embezzlers tend to be store cashiers and bank tellers who take relatively small amounts of money. In contrast, male embezzlers tend to be in positions with access to much higher sums of money and often embezzle sums in the thousands and million (Daly 1989).

Collective Embezzlement in the Savings and Loan Industry

As just noted, embezzlement is usually a solo activity. Henry N. Pontell and Kitty Calavita (1993) argue that a new form of embezzlement emerged in the 1980s in the savings and loan, insurance, stock brokerage, and other financial industries that "handle people's money." Pontell and Calavita call this new type of crime *collective embezzlement*, where top management steals company funds. Often such embezzlement involves groups of two or more financial executives who carefully plot their crimes and sometimes use their institution's own resources to loot it. Other examples of financial industry crime, some of which we'll explore later, include insider trading and securities fraud (Rosoff, Pontell, and Tillman 1998).

Collective embezzlement and other financial fraud was rampant in the 1980s. By late 1992, the U.S. Department of Justice had indicted 2,942 defendants in major financial fraud cases and convicted some 2,300. More than 1,100 of these defendants came from the savings and loan scandal that caused more than 650 savings and loans institutions to fail. This scandal will cost U.S. taxpayers as much as $500 billion by the year 2030, and perhaps more than $1 trillion (Pontell, Calavita, and Tillman 1994).

Deregulation in the early 1980s allowed savings and loans to make riskier loans than they had previously made. Many of these loans failed, costing their institutions billions of dollars, and violated various regulations still on the books. More important for our discussion, savings and loan executives engaged in outright collective embezzlement and fraud that accounted for three-fourths of savings and loan failures. Many times, "outsiders," including real estate developers and appraisers and accounting, law, and stock brokerage firms, joined the savings and loan executives in these illegal actions (Calavita and Pontell 1990).

Some savings and loan executives spent hundreds of thousands or even millions of dollars on expensive parties, worldwide travel, or artwork and other high-value household goods. Others took salaries, fees, and commissions that exceeded federal limits on such compensation (Mayer 1990). The most common form of collective embezzlement was the use of "special deals" to siphon funds from the executives' loan institutions. In a common scheme, executives would practice "land flips" by selling each other land back and forth, with each transaction involving a higher price, which artificially inflated the land's value. In one example, a loan broker bought a piece of land in California for $874,000 and subjected it to several land flips. He then bought a savings and loan in Salt Lake City and had his thrift buy his land for $26.5 million. His savings and loan went under the next year and left more than $400 million in federally insured deposits for the government to repay.

Fraud in the Professions

Physicians, lawyers, and other professionals are in a tempting position to defraud their patients, clients, and the government (Arnold and Hagan 1992; Rosoff, Pontell, and Tillman 1998). Their work is private and complex, and it is difficult for investigators to know when fraud occurs. They are also more autonomous than most other workers and able to work without someone looking over their shoulder. Their patients and clients thus are in no position to know whether their bills are truthful and accurate. As one example, lawyers sometimes bill their clients for more time than they actually put in or even charge them for work never done. These clients, of course, have no way of knowing they were overbilled. As an example of this autonomy problem, a Philadelphia cardiologist was convicted in the early 1980s of billing government and private health insurers in three states for $1.5 million in medical services he never performed. Explaining how he initially got away with his crime, he explained, "The problem is that nobody is watching. Because of the nature of the system, I was able to do what I did. The system is extremely easy to evade. The forms I sent in were absolutely outrageous. I was astounded when some of those payments were made" (Cohen 1994:6). Thirteen years later he was arrested for committing the same crime again.

Most professions engage in *self-regulation*: Professional societies develop the rules guiding the behavior of members of that profession and take charge of investigating and sanctioning professional misconduct. Unfortunately, this is often like the proverbial fox guarding the chicken coop. Regulations often allow professionals great latitude in their behavior, often with lax and weak enforcement and punishment. Professionals also tend to look out for one another. As one expert on medical fraud observed, "There's a great reluctance on the part of doctors to interfere with another doctor's reputation and means of livelihood. The philosophy apparently is that a man's reputation is more important than the welfare of his patients" (Coleman 1998:124).

In another problem, professionals typically subscribe to informal norms that rationalize their wrongdoing. As with fences and other property criminals and employees who steal from their workplaces, professionals develop techniques of neutralization through which they view their crimes as justifiable and even necessary, however illegal they may be. The particular rationalizations depend on the profession and the type of crime involved, but all of them help ease any guilt professionals might feel from breaking the law.

Health-Care Fraud

Health-care fraud by physicians and other health-care providers such as dentists and pharmacists has received perhaps the most attention of any professional fraud, and we'll concentrate on it here. The General Accounting Office estimates that health-care fraud costs $70 billion annually, or almost 10 percent of the total health-care budget (Andrews 1994). A report by the minority staff of the U.S. Senate Special Committee on Aging estimated that health-care fraud costs $100 billion yearly (Cohen 1994). Whatever the amount, health-care fraud involves tens of billions of dollars a year.

Such fraud is committed by physicians, both general practitioners and specialists, including psychiatrists; other medical practitioners such as dentists; pharmacists; medical equipment companies; nursing homes; medical testing laboratories; home health-care providers; medical billing services; and ambulance services. As this list indicates, some health-care fraud is committed by individuals and thus falls into the occupational crime category, while other fraud is best characterized as organizational criminality. But often it's difficult to classify a particular example of health-care fraud as occupational or organizational. For example, pharmacies, medical laboratories, nursing homes, and medical equipment companies commit much Medicare fraud. Some pharmacies bill the government for larger numbers of pills than they actually dispense, while laboratories put in claims for phony tests. Medical equipment companies are also a "major source of fraudulent and abusive practices in the health care system" because they sell inferior products to patients and health-care institutions and bill for items never provided

(Cohen 1994:11). But often the people committing the fraud are the owners of these various businesses. Does this fact make their crimes occupational or organizational? This question again underscores the complexity of the white-collar crime concept.

This classification issue aside, the Senate Special Committee report, commissioned by Senator William S. Cohen (R-Maine), listed several kinds of health-care fraud, including (1) overbilling; (2) billing for services not rendered; (3) *unbundling* (where a medical procedure or piece of equipment is billed as many separate procedures or equipment parts); (4) *upcoding* services to obtain higher reimbursements from the government and insurance companies; (5) providing inferior products to patients; (6) paying kickbacks and *inducements* (i.e., bribes) for referrals of patients; (7) falsifying medical records to make an individual eligible for benefits; (8) billing for "ghost" patients or for services never rendered; (9) billing for inferior products or for items never provided; (10) falsifying prescriptions; and (11) inflating charges for ambulance services.

The report provided fifty examples of *scams*, as it called them, to "illustrate how our health care system is rife with abuse, and how Medicare, Medicaid and private insurers have left their doors wide open to fraud" (Cohen 1994:1). In one example, a group of New York physicians stole over $1.3 million by billing the state Medicaid program for more than 50,000 "phantom" psychotherapy sessions that were never held. In another, nursing home operators billed Medicaid for personal expenses such as swimming pools and jewelry and even one family's nanny. In a third example, the owner of a heart pacemaker distribution company sold $6 million worth of used, expired, or contaminated pacemakers to doctors' offices. According to the report, he "also provided a variety of kickbacks to attending physicians, cardiologists and surgeons to induce them to implant" these pacemakers into their patients (p. 17). These bribes included entertainment tickets, vacation trips, office medical equipment, cash, and the services of prostitutes. In a final example, Michigan pharmacists dispensed expired medication to nursing home patients. When one pharmacist heard of complaints that their medications were not working, the pharmacist said, "Those people are old, they'll never know the difference and they'll be dead soon anyway" (p. 27).

The Senate Special Committee report found that fraud is "particularly rampant" in Medicaid and Medicare (p. 3). A recent example involved one of the largest medical testing laboratories in the United States, which agreed in 1995 to pay $8.6 million to settle federal charges that it billed Medicaid and Medicare for bogus tests (Associated Press 1995). Physicians also perform unnecessary surgery and practice self-referral involving conflicts of interest in medical testing. Given that the need for medical care is often subjective, it's difficult to demonstrate that unnecessary surgery and self-referral are fraudulent, but they still cost the public and medical insurers billions of dollars and cause death and injury. Let's look at each of these practices in turn.

IMPROPER BILLING AND MEDICAID FRAUD

The introduction of the U.S. government's Medicaid program in the 1960s prompted physicians to engage in several kinds of illegal behavior that continue into the present (Jesilow, Pontell, and Geis 1993). The government estimates that 10 to 25 percent, or about $7 billion to $18 billion, of all Medicaid billing is fraudulent, with individual Medicaid fraud offenders guilty of bilking the government of thousands or hundreds of thousands of dollars. Medicaid and Medicare fraud combined is estimated to cost $31 billion annually (Cohen 1994). In justifying their fraud, physicians reason that the government reimburses them too little money for Medicaid patients to cover their expenses. In contrast, Blue Cross and other private insurers provide higher reimbursement rates, in part accounting for the lower physician fraud they suffer (Jesilow, Pontell, and Geis 1993).

Medicaid's structure helps explain how and why so much fraud occurs. As Paul Jesilow and associates (1991:3318) observe, "The fee-for-service reimbursement of Medicaid provides the essential basis for physicians to increase their income illegally with little risk of apprehension." When they treat Medicaid patients, physicians are reimbursed with set fees for medical procedures. This process prompts them to engage in several forms of improper billing. One common method exaggerates the services rendered to patients. For example, providers may give a patient a limited exam but submit a Medicaid claim for a full physical exam, or they may pretend they gave a patient various blood, heart, and other tests that were not given. In an example provided by the Senate Special Committee report, a Maryland physician stitched up a cut in a young boy's chin but billed Medicaid for a throat culture, a nasal culture, and three hearing tests that weren't needed and were never performed.

Another method involves billing the government for fictitious patients or for patients who were dead at the time they were supposedly treated. Physicians such as psychiatrists who charge by the hour may submit bills listing more time than they actually spent with the patient. Some psychiatrists have even submitted Medicaid bills totaling more than twenty-four hours in a single day (Geis et al. 1985). Another fraudulent practice involves Medicaid coupons. Although California and other states give Medicaid-eligible people coupons to give to health-care providers, some providers obtain these coupons illegally. Other practices include *pingponging* (sending patients to other doctors for unnecessary visits); *family ganging* (examining all members of a family when only one is sick); and *churning* (asking patients to come in for unnecessary office visits).

Unnecessary Surgery

Another common medical practice is unnecessary surgery. What's considered *unnecessary*, of course, is often a matter of interpretation. Physicians and patients alike naturally want to err on the side of caution and often decide on surgery as the safest course of action to treat a disease or injury, even though the surgery itself may pose some risks. Such prudence notwithstanding, several investigations have determined that a surprising amount of surgery exceeds any reasonable exercise of caution and is thus clearly unnecessary (Consumer Reports 1992). For example, an estimated 350,000 unnecessary Caesarean sections are performed on pregnant women each year, amounting to about half of all Caesareans (The New York Times 1993). Studies also find that about 27 percent of hysterectomies, 16 percent of tonsillectomies, 14 percent of heart bypass operations, and 14 percent of laminectomies, the most common type of back surgery, are unnecessary. In all, there are probably 2 million to 4 million unnecessary surgical operations each year that cost $16 billion to $20 billion and cause 12,000 to 16,000 deaths from medical complications (Consumer Reports 1992; Reiman 1998).

The profit unnecessary surgery provides for physicians is a major reason why it occurs. Several studies find that more operations are performed on patients with private insurance (thus giving physicians a high fee for each operation) than on those belonging to prepaid health plans where doctors receive a set salary regardless of the operations they perform (Coleman 1998).

Suppose you were a physician who owned or had invested in a medical testing laboratory. Do you think you might, consciously or unconsciously, end up referring more patients to that laboratory than you would if you had no financial stake in it? Such self-referral often occurs and leads to "lavish profits" for the physicians involved (Waldholz 1989:A1).

Several studies find that physicians are more likely to refer patients for tests and other procedures when they have a financial interest in the laboratory or other facility to which the patients are referred (Morreim 1989). One study found that physician-owned labs in Florida performed twice as many tests per patient as independent labs. In another kind of self-referral, physicians who own expensive equipment are more likely to order expensive tests using that equipment. One study found that physicians with diagnostic imaging equipment in their offices were four times more likely to order imaging exams than doctors who had no such equipment (Consumer Reports 1992). Other evidence indicates that physicians who own laboratories prescribe almost one-and-a-half times as many tests for Medicare patients as physicians with no such financial stake (Bacon 1989). Although self-referral may not satisfy the legal requirements of fraud, at a minimum it falls into a gray area of medical and business ethics.

Financial Fraud

Earlier we examined collective embezzlement in the savings and loan industry. This was just one example of a growing number of crimes in the many financial industries becoming a dominant part of the U.S. economic landscape. Some of these crimes, like the savings and loan embezzlement, are committed for personal gain and thus should be considered occupational crimes. Others are committed for the benefit of brokerage houses and other financial enterprises and thus are organizational crimes. We'll look here just at the financial crimes committed for personal gain, and hold our discussion of crime by financial companies for the next section.

One common financial crime is *insider trading*. Here a company executive, stockbroker, or investment banker with special knowledge of a company's economic fortunes (such as a proposed merger) buys or sells stock in that company before this information is shared with the public. The most notorious insider trading scandal of the 1980s involved three men: Dennis Levine, Ivan F. Boesky, and Michael Milken (Stewart 1991). Levine was an executive with the Wall Street firm Drexel Burnham Lambert. Although he was already quite wealthy, he sold inside merger information to Boesky, a multimillionaire stock trader. Levine's alleged take from this criminal behavior was $12.6 million. He eventually pleaded guilty to insider trading, received a two-year prison term, and was fined $11.6 million. As part of his plea bargain, Levine agreed to "spill the beans" on Boesky and some sixty other people. Boesky eventually received a three-year prison term for trading on insider information received from Levine and others and was fined $100 million, only part of his total wealth. Boesky in turn implicated Michael Milken, another Drexel Burnham Lambert executive whose control of junk bond trading worth $120 billion involved many violations of federal law. After pleading guilty to mail fraud, tax evasion, and security law violations, Milken received a ten-year prison term, later reduced to three years for cooperating with federal prosecutors and for good behavior in prison, and was fined $600 million (Lambert 1992). To settle lawsuits against him, he also agreed to pay $500 million into a compensation fund (Cowan 1992). Although his monetary losses from his crimes thus amounted to $1.1 billion, his remaining wealth still totaled some $600 million.

Police and Political Corruption: Violations of Public Trust

Another form of occupational crime is corruption by police and politicians, who violate the public trust by accepting bribes and kickbacks and by occasionally engaging in extortion and blackmail. Such public corruption in the United States goes back at least to the nineteenth century, and, as noted earlier, was the subject of Lincoln Steffens's renowned *The Shame of the Cities*. In the twentieth century, it reached into the upper echelons of mayors' and governors' offices, police administration, the Congress, and the White House. We'll explore political corruption further in the next chapter and police corruption in Chapter 15.

Computer Crime

A relatively new category of crime involves the use of computers and is labeled *computer crime* or *cyber crime*. A decade or so ago, this type of crime hardly existed, as personal computers were still rare before the 1990s. But now they and the Internet are ubiquitous, providing many types of opportunities for many types of offenses. With so many types of offenses, computer crime does not fit neatly into any crime category. For example, a man who makes a woman's acquaintance in a chat room and then rapes or robs her when he finally meets her is not a white-collar criminal. Instead, his computer-related act is a violent crime. Much computer crime involves fraud and could easily fall into the *forgery and fraud* category included in the previous chapter's discussion of property crime. But because cyber crime is associated in the public consciousness with highly educated people and white-collar workers and often involves embezzling, it's often thought of as white-collar crime for personal gain (Coleman 1998), and we'll discuss it here as such.

Most computer crime involves *hacking*, in which, as you know, someone breaks into a restricted site or acquires information illegally from someone's computer files. In February 2000, an individual hacked into the sites of Amazon.com, Yahoo, eBay, and several other well-known Internet companies and tied them up for hours with so-called denial of service messages (Levy and Stone 2000). A few years earlier, a 33-year-old hacker was charged with 25 felony counts after he allegedly broke into several companies' computer systems, damaged their computers, and stole their software. He pleaded guilty and was sentenced to almost four years in prison (Harrison 1999).

Other computer crime involves possible infringement of copyright laws and even plagiarism. For example, it's now easy to download songs and entire CDs illegally from the Internet. Many people, including college students, routinely upload their music to their computers and send it to their friends or allow their friends to access their computers to obtain the music. Term paper "mills," which a generation ago consisted of stacks of old papers in an offender's room that he or she made known were for sale, now exist at any number of sites on the Internet (Schneider 1999). A click of a mouse button can access these sites, and a quick (and expensive) credit card purchase allows a user to download some very well-written—and some not so well-written—term papers. Students can also use the

Internet to access electronic journal indexes. Many of these print the abstracts and entire contents of journal articles, and a quick "click and drag" can copy parts of these articles into a student's term paper. Some instructors are becoming more reluctant to assign the traditional term paper since such plagiarism is now so easy to do.

Critics say the U.S. government has been slow to react to computer crime. One study found that although federal agencies referred 417 cases of possible computer fraud to federal prosecutors, only 20 percent were prosecuted. This figure was much lower than the 50 percent of referrals for all federal crimes that get prosecuted (Kaplan 1999). A few reasons probably account for the lower prosecution rate of computer fraud. First, it's often difficult to determine the identity of the person committing the fraud. Second, despite well-publicized cases, much computer fraud involves only minimal damage and is thus not worth prosecuting. Third, some companies that are victims of computer fraud might be reluctant to cooperate with federal prosecutors because of the bad publicity that they might suffer. As cyber crime likely increases and becomes more worrisome, prosecutions of this crime will likely increase as well.

ORGANIZATIONAL CRIMINALITY AND CORPORATE CRIME

As discussed earlier, much white-collar crime is committed for the sake of corporations and other business enterprises. The primary intent of the persons committing the crime is to benefit the organization for which they work. They know, of course, that if they help the corporation or other business, the business will help them. But their primary goal of helping the business classifies their crime as organizational, not occupational. As we've seen, this classification becomes problematic when the owner of a business is involved. That said, let's look at some common forms of organizational crime.

Because of its seriousness, we'll focus mostly on corporate crime, but let's first consider the many blue-collar or small businesses that cheat their customers and otherwise commit fraud. Auto repair shops are notorious in this regard. Federal estimates put the amount of auto repair fraud (overcharging, unnecessary repairs, etc.) at more than $20 billion per year, or about half of all repairs done at small repair shops and the repair divisions of automobile dealerships and national department and discount chain stores (Coleman 1998).

A notable auto repair scandal in 1992 involved Sears, Roebuck department stores in California. Sears was accused by California officials of overcharging its customers by telling them unnecessary repairs were needed on their cars. Sears management had pressured its auto repair divisions to increase profits. To do this, auto repair personnel were paid a commission for the repairs they did. With this incentive, they recommended repairs that were clearly not needed. Sears agreed to pay almost $50 million to compensate some 900,000 customers $50 each and to pay California legal expenses (Fisher 1992). In another example of auto repair fraud, an investigation by the California Bureau of Automotive Repair found that auto body repair shops cheat on 30 percent of repairs (Gellene 1994).

Sometimes investigators use field experiments to uncover auto repair fraud. In one investigation, Paul Jesilow and associates brought cars with supposedly dead batteries to 313 auto repair shops. The batteries were actually still working. Over one-tenth of the shops said the batteries could not be recharged and that a new battery would be needed (Jesilow, Geis, and O'Brien 1985). A smaller experiment

◀ *One common example of organizational criminality is auto repair fraud. Several investigations have found some auto repair specialists all too ready to cheat the public by performing unnecessary repairs.*

conducted by a Chicago TV station involved cars in fine condition taken to thirteen repair shops, six of which said the cars needed repairs up to $600 (Molla 1994).

In another field experiment, Paul E. Tracy and James Alan Fox (1989) arranged for a team of drivers to take four collision-damaged cars—two Buick Skylarks, one Ford Tempo, and one Volvo—to a random sample of ninety-six Massachusetts body shops. Sometimes the drivers said that the car was insured; sometimes that it was not. The repair estimates for the "insured" cars were 32.5 percent higher than for the "uninsured" cars, leading the researchers to conclude that the higher estimates were fraudulent.

The auto repair fraud just described is conducted by legitimate businesses that defraud the public as part of their business practice. Other organizational criminality involves illegitimate businesses that are fraudulent from the outset and have the sole purpose of defrauding the public. Examples include phony home improvement businesses, contests, and charities; land frauds; and various financial, medical, and other enterprises. Some of the health-care and savings and loan fraud discussed previously was committed by illegitimate enterprises formed to specifically defraud the public and/or government.

We now come to crime by corporations, which, because of their size, scope, and influence, are perhaps the worst offenders of all (Reiman 1998). According to one study, the federal government in 1975 and 1976 accused almost two-thirds of the 500 largest U.S. corporations with violating the law (Clinard and Yeager 1980). *U.S. News & World Report* (1982) reported that 23 percent of these corporations were convicted of (or did not contest) at least one criminal or civil offense during the 1970s. Some 2,300 corporations overall were convicted in the 1970s of federal offenses.

Corporate crime takes two general forms: financial and violent (the distinction being whether people are hurt financially or physically by corporate misconduct). We'll look first at financial crime by corporations and then at the violence they commit.

Corporate Financial Crime

The economic cost of corporate crime is enormous. The *U.S. News & World Report* article just cited estimated that financial crime by corporations, including price fixing, false advertising, bribery, and tax evasion, costs the public $200 billion per year. Let's consider some common types of corporate financial crime.

Even if you've never taken an Introduction to Economics course, you probably know that in a free-market economic system like our own, sellers of goods and services compete with each other for profit. To maximize profit, they sometimes lower their prices to maximize consumer demand. This competition ensures that consumer prices will be as low as possible so that consumers save money.

This is the way capitalism should ideally work. But in the real world, what should happen often does not happen. If corporations get together and set high prices for goods and services rather than allowing the free market to determine prices, consumers pay more than they should. Such price fixing thus constitutes a costly form of theft from the public. In the ideal world of capitalism, there should also be many sellers of goods and services to produce as much competition for consumer demand as possible, and thus prices that are as low as possible. If one company buys out all the others, it doesn't have to worry about competition and can raise its prices without fear of losing sales to another company. This action, too, constitutes a theft from the public, even though we're not really aware of it and don't worry about it.

As noted earlier, Congress passed the 1890 Sherman Antitrust Act because the major corporations were engaging in so much restraint of trade. Standard Oil and the other corporations bought up competitors or used questionable practices to prevent others from forming or to drive them out of business. The Sherman Antitrust Act was intended to prohibit these practices. Other legislation over the years has also sought to prevent and punish corporate restraint of trade. One additional type of restraint of trade now prohibited by antitrust laws involves *anticompetitive agreements*, in which a manufacturer sells its products only to retailers who agree not to sell rival manufacturers' products.

Despite antitrust laws, corporations continue to practice much illegal restraint of trade. Price fixing costs U.S. consumers some $60 billion every year, or about $1,000 for a family of four, and involves virtually every industry (Simon 1999). Just a few years ago, several of the world's largest vitamin manufacturers agreed in 1999 to pay $1.17 billion to settle a lawsuit that charged them with fixing prices over a nine-year period. Despite the large payment, it amounted to only 20 percent of the companies' sales from their price fixing (Moore 1999). In other recent cases, three oil companies—Chevron, Mobil, and Shell—agreed in 1993 to pay $77 million to settle federal price-fixing charges (The Oil Daily 1993); four airlines—American, Delta, United, and USAir—agreed to send their customers millions of dollars in coupons to settle federal price-fixing charges (Schwartz 1993); and the Nintendo video game company agreed to distribute millions of dollars of coupons to settle a suit charging it with dictating the retail prices of its video games (Television Digest 1991). Although some of the fines and legal settlements for price fixing in these and other cases range in the millions of dollars, the corporations involved are usually so wealthy that these financial penalties scarcely worry them.

Perhaps the most celebrated price-fixing scandal was uncovered in 1959–1960 and involved General Electric, Westinghouse, and 27 other heavy electrical equipment manufacturers that controlled 95 percent of the electrical industry (Geis 1987). Executives from these companies conspired over several years to fix prices on $7 billion of electrical equipment, costing the public about $1.7 billion in illegal profit. After pleading guilty in 1961, seven of the electrical executives received thirty-day jail terms for their conspiracy, later reduced to twenty-five days because of good behavior, while twenty-one others got suspended sentences. These were obviously light sentences compared to what a typical property criminal might get for stealing only a few dollars. In somewhat stiffer punishment, the corporations were fined a total of $1.8 million. This might sound like a lot of money but still amounted to only $1 of every $1,000 the corporations stole from the public and left them holding about $1.698 billion in illegal profit. Worse yet, they were able to deduct their fines and legal expenses from their corporate taxable income.

To be accurate, I should note that the electrical corporations eventually had to pay out huge sums of money to settle lawsuits by municipalities and other purchasers of their equipment during the years of the conspiracy. GE, for example, had to pay some $160 million to settle 1,800 claims. Yet even these legal costs still left the companies with the bulk of the $1.7 billion they had acquired illegally. And, again, they were tax-deductible (Simon 1999).

After pointing out that the corporations' fines amounted to only $1 of every $1,000 they got through price fixing, I ask my students whether they would consider robbing a bank of $1,000 if they knew their only penalty would be to pay a $1 fine. Many usually raise their hands to signify yes. Would you? GE's fine was $437,000. This might be a lot of money for you or me to pay, but for GE it was the equivalent of someone with an annual income of $175,000 paying a $3 fine. To bring this down to more meaningful figures, if you had an income of $17,000 and knew that your punishment for robbing a bank would be only 30 cents, would you rob the bank?

A practice related to price fixing is price gouging, where companies take advantage of market conditions to raise prices and "gouge" the consumer. Sometimes these companies artificially create these market conditions themselves. A prime example here was the 1973–1974 oil "crisis" begun when oil nations announced they would suspend oil exports to the United States. Claiming a shortage, oil companies raised prices and their profits dramatically, even though it was later discovered that oil deliveries had not been suspended. In fact, U.S. oil companies had so much oil that they sent some to European nations (Cook 1982). A similar "crisis" occurred in 1979 when Iran announced it would suspend oil deliveries to the United States. Even though Iran accounted for only 5 percent of U.S. oil imports and the United States, as was discovered only later, still had plenty of oil, oil prices again rose sharply, with oil company profits rising some 200 percent. In several states, gasoline was rationed, with huge lines of cars waiting at gas stations (Wildavsky 1981).

FALSE ADVERTISING

Another common corporate financial crime is false advertising. We all know that advertisers do their best to convince us to buy products we may not really need and that they engage legally in exaggerated claims or puffery. A particular product, for example, may claim it's the best of its kind or, as in the case of cigarettes and beer, imply that using it will make you popular. But much advertising goes beyond puffery and makes patently false and illegal claims. Such deceptive advertising is quite common, with the cosmetic, food, pharmaceutical, and many other industries accused of it (Preston 1994). There have also been many examples of *bait-and-switch* advertising, in which a store advertises a low-priced item that isn't actually available, or available only in small quantities. When customers come in to buy the item, it's not there, and the sales clerk switches them to a more expensive product in the same line.

A final category of corporate financial crime involves fraud, cheating, and corruption not falling into the antitrust or false advertising categories. Much of this fraud and corruption parallels what individuals do for personal gain as occupational crime. The difference here is that the fraud and corruption are performed primarily for the corporation's benefit, not for the corporate executives engaging in these crimes.

Since there are too many examples of corporate fraud and corruption to describe here, I'll just discuss corruption in the defense industry, which, as Sutherland found, features some of the most costly and notorious corporate fraud and is now estimated at $15 billion annually. More than half of the Pentagon's biggest 100 defense contractors have allegedly broken the law through such means as overbilling, bribery, kickbacks, and the deliberate provision of defective weapons components and other military equipment (Simon 1999). You might have heard jokes about $200 hammers and $1,000 toilet seats bought by the military, but these astronomically high prices are part of the fraud and waste that ultimately costs taxpayers billions.

One of the most publicized scandals in the military-industrial complex occurred in the late 1980s, when an investigation called "Operation Ill Wind" found that the undersecretary of the U.S. Navy and many other Navy and Air Force officials had sold classified information to fifteen defense contractors in return for bribes. Several of these officials and the corporate executives with whom they dealt pleaded guilty to fraud and other crimes, and the companies paid up to $5.8 million each in fines (Howe 1989). Many other scandals have occurred in the last few decades, with some defense corporations being seriously *chronic* offenders. Bribery of officials in other nations is a favorite crime. In the 1970s, Lockheed allegedly paid some $200 million in commissions and bribes to officials and lobbyists in countries as diverse as Indonesia, Iran, the Philippines, Italy, Venezuela, Japan, and the Netherlands (Clinard and Yeager 1980).

Some defense corruption goes beyond the mere financial and also endangers lives. Although we'll explore such corporate violence much more in the next section, one example is worth noting here. In the late 1960s, B. F. Goodrich won a contract to build brakes for the Air Force. To submit as low a bid as possible, Goodrich proposed a brake much smaller and lighter than normal. However, Goodrich's own testing later revealed its brakes were not up to the job and could lead to crashes. Instead of improving the brakes or telling the Air Force about the problem, Goodrich engineers falsified test data. After the brakes were installed in some planes, several near crashes occurred. When all this came to light, Goodrich agreed to design a better brake system. Neither it nor its several middle-level managers and executives involved in the scandal were charged with any wrongdoing. Two of the officials who were most involved even got promoted (Vandivier 1987).

Corporate Violence: Threats to Health and Safety

When I tell my students that corporations kill many more people each year than all the murders combined, they don't believe me. Even if corporations are corrupt, my students reply, they don't murder. It's difficult for any of us to believe that corporations maim and kill. We equate violence with *interpersonal violence*, which dominates public discussion, fills us with fear, and even controls our lives. *Corporate violence*, in contrast, is less visible, and has been called "quiet violence" (Frank and

Lynch 1992). By corporate violence, I mean actions by corporations that cause injury, illness, and even death. These lives are lost in the name of profit, as corporations pursue profits with reckless disregard for the health, safety, and lives of their workers, consumers, and the general public (Mokhiber 1988). Let's look at each of these three groups of victims in turn and discuss some of the more grievous examples of corporate violence that victimize each group.

WORKERS AND UNSAFE WORKPLACES

Each year many workers die or become injured or ill because of hazardous occupational conditions, while others suffer long-lasting psychological effects (Rosoff, Pontell, and Tillman 1998). Some hazardous workplace conditions violate federal and state laws, while others are technically not illegal but still pose dangers to workers. Most hazardous conditions involve worker exposure to toxic substances such as vinyl chloride, cotton and coal dust, asbestos, and a host of other chemicals and materials that cause several types of cancer and respiratory illness such as asthma, bronchitis, and emphysema. One study, for example, found that workers exposed to vinyl chloride had abnormally high levels of liver, lung, and brain cancer (Wu et al. 1989). Another found one-fourth of all bladder cancer to be work-related (Raloff 1989). Working with dangerous equipment and in dangerous circumstances causes injury and death.

The sad thing is that it doesn't have to be this way. Although some jobs and workplaces are inevitably hazardous, the prime reason for the high rate of occupational injury, illness, and death in the United States is that corporations disregard their workers' health and safety in the name of profit. To compound the problem, the government has lax rules on workplace health and safety and does relatively little to enforce the ones that do exist. Lest any of this sound too critical, consider the experience of Japan, which has far fewer occupational health and safety problems because of its safer workplaces. Japanese management places greater emphasis on worker safety than does its U.S. counterpart and, in fact, considers worker safety a greater priority than production quantity. For U.S. management, the priorities are reversed (Engelman 1993b).

Exact data on workplace illness, injury, and death are hard to come by for several reasons (Reiman 1998). First, it's often difficult to establish that illness and death are work-related. Second, the Bureau of Labor Statistics, a major source of workplace death estimates, gathers data only from workplaces with at least eleven employees. Third, corporations and smaller businesses often hide injuries and illnesses their workers suffer.

Not surprisingly, then, estimates of workplace illness, injury, and death vary widely (Reiman 1998; Simon 1999). It's generally thought that at least 150,000 workers each year come down with serious workplace-induced illnesses and that at least 50,000 eventually die each year from these illnesses. More than 9,000 deaths and 1.7 million serious injuries also result from workplace accidents annually. Some workplaces and industries, such as construction, are inevitably dangerous, and accidents will happen no matter how careful workers and their employers are. But several investigations reveal that about half of all workplace accidents result from regulatory violations or unsafe working conditions. Thus, close to 5,000 workers die and 850,000 are injured each year because of corporate misconduct.

If we add up all these admittedly rough figures, we end up with about 55,000 workers dying annually and another 1,000,000 suffering serious illness or injury from corporate misconduct. Because of underreporting and other measurement problems, the true numbers of work-related death, illness, and injury may well be much higher.

◀ *For four decades the asbestos industry suppressed evidence of asbestos health hazards. Thousands of asbestos workers have reportedly contracted asbestos-related diseases, and many of them have died.*

Sometimes the harm done to workers is immediate and visible. In the mining industry, for example, accidents kill about 150 people per year and injure another 50,000. Mining companies' failure to observe safety codes accounts for most of these accidents. In one example, a 1981 explosion in a Colorado mine killed 15 miners. The mine had been cited more than 1,000 times in the preceding three years for safety violations. In another example, a 1984 underground fire in Utah killed 27 miners. The mine had previously been cited for 34 safety violations, 9 of which led to the fire (Simon 1999).

Fatal accidents also occur in other industries. A particularly tragic example was a September 1991 fire that killed 25 workers and injured 56 more at a poultry plant in Hamlet, North Carolina (Aulette and Michalowski 1993). At the time of the fire, the plant's doors were locked and it had no fire alarms or sprinklers. Because smoke inhalation killed all but one of the 25 people who died, they likely would have survived had the doors not been locked. Compounding the problem, federal and state authorities had not inspected the plant in eleven years. It's not too much an exaggeration to say that the plant's owners and managers were at least partly responsible for the 25 deaths, even if they didn't set the fire.

Usually, however, the harm done to workers occurs over the long haul and is much less obvious. Two prime examples here are the coal and asbestos industries. Long-term breathing of coal dust leads to several respiratory problems, including *black lung disease*, which has killed some 100,000 coal miners in this century and still kills about 4,000 annually. In 1991, the federal government fined 500 mining companies for submitting false air tests for coal dust (Wokutch and McLaughlin 1992). If anything, the asbestos industry is guilty of even worse crimes. Beginning in the late 1960s, medical researchers began to discover that asbestos, long used as a fire retardant in schools, homes, and other buildings and as an insulator in high-temperature equipment, is an extremely hazardous substance that can cause asbestosis, a virulent lung disease. Since this disease takes a long time to develop, it's estimated that more than 200,000 people, mostly asbestos workers but also consumers, will eventually die from asbestos-related cancer and lung disease by the first third of the new century (Brodeur 1985).

"Where's the crime?" you might be asking. "What if no one happened to know that asbestos was dangerous?" If this were the case, then asbestos deaths would be considered a tragic problem for which the industry perhaps should not be blamed. Unfortunately there is plenty of blame, and even murderous criminal neglect, to go around. It turns out that the asbestos industry began to suspect at least as early as the 1930s that asbestos was dangerous, as it saw its workers coming down with serious lung disease. Responsible corporations would have dutifully reported their suspicions to the appropriate federal and state authorities, and taken every safety measure possible to limit or prevent their workers' exposure to asbestos fibers.

But the asbestos companies did not do this. Instead, they deliberately suppressed evidence of lung disease in their workers and settled workers' claims out of court to avoid publicity (Lilienfeld 1991). For more than thirty years, they continued to manufacture a product they knew was dangerous before medical researchers discovered this danger. During that time, more than 21 million U.S. residents worked with asbestos, and asbestos was put into many schools and newly built structures. It's not an exaggeration to say that the companies' concern for profit was and will be responsible for more than 200,000 deaths by the early part of the new century, or that the asbestos industry was guilty of "corporate malfeasance and inhumanity … that is unparalleled in the annals of the private-enterprise system" (Brodeur 1985:7).

Even if you work in a safe workplace, you're not necessarily safe from corporate violence. Every year corporations market dangerous products that injure us, make us sick, and even kill us. The National Commission on Product Safety estimates that 30,000 people are killed each year by unsafe products, with another 110,000 permanently disabled and millions more injured (Abrams 1989). Three industries posing the greatest danger to consumers are the automobile, pharmaceutical, and food industries.

THE AUTOMOBILE INDUSTRY   We all know that cars often have many defects, some of them safety hazards. Given cars' complexity, some defects are inevitable and perhaps not that blameworthy. But there have been many tragic cases where automobile manufacturers *knew* of safety defects that killed and injured many people, but decided not to do anything—in order to save money.

The most infamous case is probably that of the Ford Pinto, first put on the market in 1971, even though Ford already knew that the Pinto had a defective gas tank that in rear-end collisions could easily burst into flames and explode. Ford did a cost-benefit analysis to determine whether it would cost more money to fix each Pinto, at $11 per car, or instead to pay settlements in lawsuits after people died or burned in Pinto accidents. Specifically, Ford calculated that it would cost $49.5 million to settle lawsuits from the 180 burn deaths, 180 serious burn injuries, and 2,100 burned cars it anticipated would occur, versus $137 million to fix the 12.5 million Pintos and other Fords with the problem. Because not fixing the problem would save Ford about $87 million, Ford executives decided to do nothing, even though they knew people would die and be seriously burned. About 500 people eventually did die (although one estimate puts the number at "only" some two dozen) when Pintos were hit from behind, often by cars traveling at relatively low speeds. The Pinto was finally recalled in 1978 to make the gas tank safe (Cullen, Maakestad, and Cavender 1987; Dowie 1977).

Ford was responsible for more deaths and injuries beginning in 1966 because of faulty automatic transmissions that slipped from "park" to "reverse." This defect has received much less attention than the Pinto's but was almost as deadly (Consumer Reports 1985; Kahn 1986). Drivers would put their car in park while they got out to get groceries from the trunk, open up their garage door, or get the mail from a streetside mailbox. The transmission would shift unexpectedly into reverse, causing the car to roll backward and hit or run over the driver.

By 1971, Ford was receiving six letters per month on this problem but chose to do nothing. In fact, for years it denied its vehicles had any reversal problem at all. Ford's inaction led to at least 207 deaths and 4,597 injuries by 1985 from Ford vehicles rolling backward onto people.

The federal government did little to prevent these deaths and injuries. Instead of ordering a recall, the U.S. Department of Transportation allowed Ford in 1980 to send warning stickers to owners of all Ford vehicles manufactured between 1966 and 1979. Since many original owners had sold their cars, about 2.7 million owners of used Fords never received the stickers. At least 80 people died in Ford reversal accidents between 1980, when the stickers were mailed, and 1985.

Ford claimed its vehicles were no worse than any other manufacturer's and blamed the problem on drivers' failure to actually put their cars in park in the first place. Unfortunately for Ford, compared to the 80 recorded deaths from Ford cars between 1980 and 1985, the National Highway Traffic Safety Administration (NHTSA) recorded only 31 similar fatalities for General Motors, Chrysler, and

American Motors combined. Unless we're to assume that Ford drivers were somehow more inept than others at putting their vehicles into park, the Ford transmission had to be at fault. Ford eventually corrected the problem beginning in its 1980 models.

Earlier I recounted B. F. Goodrich's manufacture of defective brake systems for the Air Force. In the early 1970s, another tire company, Firestone, knew that its new Firestone 500 tires could separate and blow out, posing a serious danger to drivers. Instead of fixing the tire and recalling the ones already sold, as requested by the government, Firestone continued to tout the tire's prowess and eventually sold almost 24 million. When NHTSA publicized the tire's dangers, Firestone sold its remaining Firestone 500 tires at steep discounts to get rid of them. At least 34 people are known to have died after their Firestone 500 tires blew out, and several thousand more were involved in accidents, with many being injured. In 1980, Firestone paid a $50,000 fine for selling its unsafe tire (Mokhiber 1988). Like Ford and other companies, then, Firestone knew full well that its unsafe product would cost lives and cause much injury but decided that profits were more important than people. Although Firestone's decision was responsible for 34 deaths and many injuries, no one in the company was criminally prosecuted.

THE PHARMACEUTICAL INDUSTRY   The pharmaceutical industry has also put profits above people by knowingly marketing dangerous drugs. As one scholar says, "Time after time, respected pharmaceutical firms have shown a cavalier disregard for the lives and safety of the people who use their products" (Coleman 1998:74). Many of these people live in poor nations, as pharmaceutical companies haven't been reluctant to market unsafe products in their quest for profit (see the International Focus box on page 348).

One well-known example of pharmaceutical misconduct involved Eli Lilly and Company, which in the 1980s put a new arthritis drug, Oraflex, on the market overseas. Shortly after taking the drug, at least 26 people died. These patients' doctors reported the deaths to Lilly. Since the patients were usually elderly, any individual physician couldn't assume that Oraflex was the cause of death. After getting several reports of such deaths, however, a responsible company would have told the government, conducted more tests, and perhaps taken the drug off the market. Lilly did none of these things and kept the deaths a secret. As a result, the Food and Drug Administration allowed Lilly to market the drug in the United States in April 1982. More deaths took place, and Lilly pleaded guilty in August 1985 to deceiving the government. By this time, Oraflex had killed at least 62 people and made almost 1,000 more seriously ill. Lilly's legal punishment was a $25,000 fine for the company and a $15,000 fine for one of its executives (Coleman 1998).

A similar case involved the Richardson-Merrell Company, which developed a cholesterol drug in the 1950s called MER/29. When the company tested MER/29 on rats, many of the rats died or came down with serious eye problems. In response, Richardson-Merrell falsified its test data to pretend the drug was safe. Before the drug was finally removed from the market, some 400,000 people had taken it, and at least 5,000 developed serious skin and eye problems and suffered hair loss. The company made $7 million in gross income from MER/29 but was eventually fined only $80,000, meaning the drug made it a tidy profit (Mokhiber 1988).

A more publicized example of pharmaceutical corporate violence involved the A. H. Robins Company and its Dalkon Shield IUD, or intrauterine device (Hicks 1994). Robins, the maker of Robitussin, Chap Stick, and other products you've probably used, distributed over 4 million Dalkon Shield IUDs between 1971 and 1975 in 80 nations, including 2.2 million in the United States, *after* falsifying safety

Pharmaceutical "Dumping" in the Third World

The United States has stricter standards for new drug products than many other nations. Testing of a new drug and gaining its approval by the U.S. Food and Drug Administration can take some time. Sometimes the FDA rejects a new drug as potentially too dangerous. In the meantime, the pharmaceutical company has spent much money to develop it. Faced with these circumstances, pharmaceutical companies often decide to market unsafe or expired drugs overseas, especially in the Third World, where safety standards are much weaker and there's a ready market of millions of people. This practice is called "corporate dumping," and involves pesticides, unsafe baby pacifiers, and other dangerous products in addition to unsafe drugs. Often the companies fail to tell overseas consumers about the problems with their products. Pharmaceuticals, for example, fail to list side effects of the drugs that must be listed in the United States.

To gain approval to market their drugs in these nations, companies have sometimes bribed public officials and other individuals. In a major study of the pharmaceutical industry, John Braithwaite found a decade ago that 19 of the 20 largest U.S. pharmaceutical companies had been accused of committing bribery during the 1970s and early 1980s in an effort to market unsafe drugs or drugs that had not yet been thoroughly tested. The recipients of their bribes lived in many countries and included customs officers, health inspectors, hospital administrators, physicians, and police. Falsifying drug testing results was commonplace. When some companies tested their drugs on rats and monkeys and saw these animals developing tumors, blindness, and other problems, they replaced them with other animals and didn't report the problems.

The effects of corporate dumping in the Third World and other nations have been devastating. A. H. Robins (see text) sold its deadly Dalkon Shield IUD overseas even after the device's dangerous side effects had become known in the United States. Two companies sold birth control pills with dangerously high levels of estrogen to Third World women. Another company, Upjohn, sold an antibiotic overseas even when it was banned in the United States after it had been linked to twelve deaths.

Sources: Braithwaite 1984; Braithwaite 1995a; Muller 1982; Silverman, Lee, and Lydecker 1982.

tests. The IUD turned out to be a time bomb ticking inside women because its "tail string" carried bacteria from the vagina into the uterus where it caused pelvic inflammatory disease for thousands of women, leading to sterility, miscarriage, or, for at least 18 U.S. women, death.

Five percent, or 110,000, of the U.S. women became pregnant despite using the IUD, even though Robins had falsely claimed only a 1 percent pregnancy rate. Sixty percent of these women miscarried. Hundreds of those who did not miscarry gave birth to babies with severe defects including blindness, cerebral palsy, and mental retardation, and others had stillborn babies. The Shield IUD probably killed hundreds or thousands of women outside the United States. In 1974 the FDA asked Robins to stop selling the Shield in the United States. Robins recalled the IUD, and then continued to sell it in other nations for up to nine months. Several thousand women eventually filed lawsuits against A. H. Robins, which eventually paid more than $400 million to settle the suits.

Like other corporations, says Morton Mintz (1985:247), a former investigative reporter for the *Washington Post*, A. H. Robins "put corporate greed before welfare, suppressed scientific studies that would ascertain safety and effectiveness, [and] concealed hazards from consumers." He adds that "almost every other major drug company" has done similar things, often repeatedly.

THE FOOD INDUSTRY   A third industry that has put profit over people is the food industry, cited even decades ago as a menace to public health (Kallet 1933). The more than 1,500 chemical additives in our food may cause cancer, gallbladder symptoms, allergies, and other health problems. Historically, one of the worse food offenders is the meatpacking industry, which has supplied spoiled meat to U.S. soldiers in more than one war. Earlier I mentioned Upton Sinclair's muckraking novel, *The Jungle*, on the meat industry. Among other things, Sinclair wrote that rats routinely would get into meat in meatpacking plants. Workers used poisoned bread to try to kill the rats. The meat sold to the public thus included dead rats, rat feces, and poisoned bread. Sinclair's novel led to the Federal Meat Inspection Act in 1906 (Frank and Lynch 1992).

Despite this Act and other regulations, meatpacking companies still act in a way that endangers our health, thanks in large part to lax federal monitoring of the meat industry. In 1984, for example, the government accused a Colorado meatpacking company of hiding evidence of disease in slaughtered animals, putting rancid meat into its hamburgers, and placing false dates on old meat. The company was the largest ground meat provider for school lunch programs and an important supplier to supermarkets, fast-food stores, and the military (Simon 1999).

Sometimes companies sell meat so contaminated that it makes us ill and even kills us. A recent example occurred in early 1993, when three children died and almost 500 adults and children became seriously ill after eating hamburgers at Jack in the Box restaurants in Washington State. Improper handling by a California meat plant had allowed the beef in the hamburgers to become contaminated with deadly bacteria. The tragedy led to widespread criticism of federal meat inspection laws and procedures and prompted calls for tougher laws and enforcement (Kushner 1993). A few months after the tragedy, the USDA shut down thirty slaughterhouses after surprise inspections. Still, more than a year later seven other people became ill in July 1994 after eating contaminated meat in New Jersey. The Secretary of Agriculture then called contaminated meat a serious problem that demanded increased federal attention. Not surprisingly, meatpacking companies criticized the calls for tougher meat inspection (Skrzycki 1994).

THE PUBLIC AND ENVIRONMENTAL POLLUTION

No doubt some pollution of our air, land, and water is inevitable in an industrial society. If people become ill or die from it, that's unfortunate, but unavoidable. But much of our pollution *is* preventable. Federal environmental laws are weak or nonexistent; corporations often violate the laws that do exist; federal monitoring and enforcement of these laws are lax; and the penalties for environmental violations are minimal (Coleman 1998). According to one report, this fact creates "a system where major polluters can operate with little fear of being caught or punished." As a result, an estimated 20 percent of U.S. landfills and incinerators, 25 percent of drinking water systems, and 50 percent of wastewater treatment facilities violate health regulations (Armstrong 1999:A1).

The consequences of all these problems are illness, disease, and death. We're only beginning to understand the health effects of environmental pollution. For many reasons, it's very difficult to determine how many people die or become ill each year from pollution, or whether pollution even harms health at all (Engelman 1993a). That said, a growing body of epidemiological and other research strongly suggests that pollution does hurt our health, and an increasing number of medical journal articles warn physicians to be on the alert for pollution-related health problems in their patients (Dockery 1994). Some studies estimate that air pollution kills between 10,000 and 60,000 each year in the United States from cancer, respiratory diseases, and other problems (Reiman 1998), but these figures remain rough at best.

If it's impossible to know how many people die or become sick each year from pollution, it is also impossible to determine how many of these deaths and illnesses could be prevented if corporations acted responsibly and put people above profit. A conservative figure of annual pollution deaths due to corporate crime and neglect would be 20,000.

In this regard, a recent report deplored several major corporations, including General Motors, Standard Oil, and Du Pont, for engaging in a "sad and sordid commercial venture" by conspiring from the beginning of the automobile age to manufacture and market gasoline containing lead, a deadly poison, even though the companies knew there were safe alternatives. Along the way they suppressed evidence of the health dangers of lead. More than 60 years after it was first used, lead was finally banned as a gasoline additive in 1986. A 1985 study by the U.S. Environmental Protection Agency estimated that some 5,000 Americans had been dying each year from lead-related heart disease. The author of the report noted that most of the 7 million tons of lead burned in gasoline during the last century still remains in our land, air, and water, and that leaded gasoline is still used overseas, especially in poor nations (Kitman 2000).

One form of pollution attracting recent attention is the dumping of toxic waste. The United States produces close to 300 million tons of toxic waste each year, and as much as 90 percent of this is disposed of improperly into some 600,000 contaminated sites across the nation (Simon 1999). Perhaps the most infamous toxic waste dumping crime occurred in an area known as Love Canal, near Niagara Falls, New York. For years a chemical company had dumped toxic wastes at Love Canal and then donated the land to the Niagara Falls School Board in 1953. The school board sold the land to a developer, and houses were eventually built on top of the toxic waste. Eventually the waste leaked into the surrounding land and water, causing birth defects, miscarriages, and other health problems. By the 1980s, more than 500 families had to leave their homes, which were later destroyed. The company had also dumped toxic wastes in several other communities (Levine 1982).

In an example of corporate misconduct with immediate consequences, a Union Carbide chemical plant in Bhopal, India, leaked deadly gas in December 1984, killing at least 3,500 and leaving tens of thousands ill and injured. The leak occurred after Union Carbide had ignored several warnings by U.S. and Indian engineers of such a possibility. No Union Carbide official was ever prosecuted for homicide or manslaughter (Friedrichs 1996).

U.S. corporations also sell and use overseas (typically in the Third World) some 75,000 tons of pesticides, which are banned in this country. For example, the notorious pesticide DDT was sold in Central and South America after being banned in the United States. These pesticides are estimated to poison about 400,000 people each year and kill at least 10,000 (Mokhiber 1988).

THE ECONOMIC AND HUMAN COSTS OF WHITE-COLLAR CRIME

In this and earlier chapters, I've said that white-collar crime costs us more in lives and money than street crime. Many criminologists share this view (Coleman 1998; Meier and Short 1995). Before moving on, let's collect the various figures I've presented on the costs of both types of crime to see why they feel this way.

We'll first start with the value of property and money stolen annually from the public, government, and/or private sector by street crime versus white-collar crime. For street crime, let's use $15 billion, the FBI's estimate of total property loss from all property crime (see Chapter 11). For white-collar crime, we'll use several estimates presented earlier in this chapter: $200 billion, the *U.S. News & World Report* estimate for the cost of all corporate crime, including price fixing, false advertising, tax evasion, and various types of fraud; $70 billion in health-care fraud as estimated by the General Accounting Office; and $45 billion in employee theft as estimated by the U.S. Department of Commerce. These figures add up to $315 billion annually. Add to that, $100 billion in noncorporate tax evasion (see Chapter 11), and the total cost of white-collar crime, broadly defined, reaches $415 billion. As you can see in Figure 12.1, this figure towers over the annual loss from street crime.

Now let's do a similar calculation for the number of people killed each year by street crime (murder and nonnegligent manslaughter) versus white-collar crime and misconduct. The UCR's estimate for 1998 homicides was 16,914 (see Chapter 9). For white-collar crime (and misconduct), we'll use the estimates presented earlier in this chapter: 55,000 work-related deaths from illness or injury; 30,000 deaths from unsafe products; 20,000 deaths from environmental pollution; and 12,000 deaths from unnecessary surgery. Adding these figures together, about 117,000 people a year die from corporate and professional crime and misconduct. As Figure 12.2 (on page 352) illustrates, this number far exceeds the number of people murdered each year.

EXPLAINING WHITE-COLLAR CRIME

In many ways, white-collar criminals aren't that different from street criminals. Both groups steal and commit violence, even if their methods differ in ways already discussed. In addition, certain explanations of street crime also apply to white-collar crime. Like street criminals, white-collar criminals don't usually break the law unless they have both the opportunity and the motivation to do so (Shover and Hochstetler 2000). But the opportunity for corruption and other white-collar

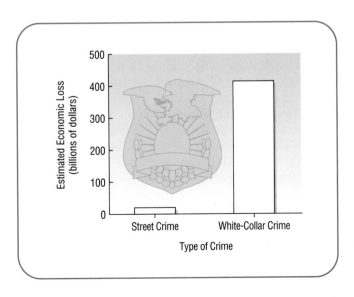

◀ FIGURE 12.1 ESTIMATED ANNUAL ECONOMIC LOSS FROM STREET CRIME AND WHITE-COLLAR CRIME

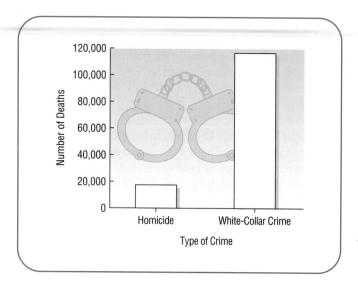

◀ FIGURE 12.2 ESTIMATED NUMBER OF ANNUAL DEATHS FROM HOMICIDE AND WHITE-COLLAR CRIME

crime differs across occupations and industries. This helps us understand why some occupations and industries have more crime than others. For example, financial corruption is, to the best of our knowledge, much less common among professors than among businesspeople, physicians, and politicians. Are professors that much more virtuous than these other professionals? I would certainly like to think so! But as a sociologist I have to concede that the reason might simply be that professors have much less opportunity than the other professionals to make a buck through illegal means (Heeren and Shichor 1993).

In another similarity with street crime, white-collar criminals develop many techniques of neutralization to justify their crimes and other misconduct (Coleman 1987). At the corporate level, executives and middle managers see their behavior as necessary to compete in very competitive markets: The whole industry does _____ (fill in the blank), why shouldn't we? The government overregulates us and makes it impossible to do our jobs, so it's okay to violate the regulations. Despite massive evidence to the contrary, corporate executives deny again and again that their workplaces harm their workers, that their products harm consumers, and that their pollutants harm the public. We'll never know if they actually believe what they're saying, or if they're lying to protect themselves and their companies. Probably some do believe what they say, while others know full well the harm they've caused.

In a further possible similarity that's been debated, both white-collar criminals and street criminals may lack self-control. Michael Gottfredson and Travis Hirschi (1990) put lack of self-control at the root of all criminality (see Chapter 7). In a study of UCR fraud and embezzlement data, the two authors said that white-collar criminals have the same motivation—greed—as property criminals and act on this greed because they, too, lack self-control (Hirschi and Gottfredson 1987). This fact, they continued, explains why white-collar crime is relatively rare, since few people with low self-control are able to achieve high-status jobs. It also challenges, they added, the popular scholarly view that white-collar crime results from values and techniques of neutralization justifying such behavior: If this view were correct, then white-collar crime would be much more common.

Hirschi and Gottfredson's argument has been sharply challenged. Darrell Steffensmeier (1989:347) noted that the UCR fraud and embezzlement data they used "have little or nothing to do with white-collar crime." Most people arrested for fraud haven't committed occupational crime, and most people arrested for embezzlement aren't in high-status occupations. He also argued that white-collar crime is much more common than Hirschi and Gottfredson assumed. In another critique, Michael Benson and Elizabeth Moore (1992) found white-collar criminals much less likely than street criminals to have done poorly in school when younger or to have drinking or drug problems. From this evidence, the authors concluded that white-collar criminals have much more self-control than Hirschi and Gottfredson assume. Agreeing with these critics, Gilbert Geis (1995:218) comments, "For most scholars who study white-collar crime, the idea that low self-control holds the key to such offenses as antitrust conspiracies seems exceedingly farfetched."

So far I've discussed a few possible explanations of street crime that may also apply to white-collar crime. Other conceivable reasons for street crime certainly don't apply. Consider, for example, the view, rejected by most sociologists, that violent and other street criminals suffer from biological or psychological abnormalities. Although corporate executives are responsible for more deaths each year than all the murderers in our midst, it would probably sound silly to say they have some biological or psychological abnormality that causes them to allow people to die.

Turning to popular sociological explanations of conventional crime, it would also sound silly to say they fleece the public because as children they suffered negative family and school experiences and consorted with delinquent friends. Corporate executives and many other white-collar criminals are, after all, successful. They've achieved the American Dream, and one reason for this is that they were raised in the best of surroundings and went to the best schools. To explain their criminal behavior, then, we must look beyond explanations stressing individual failings and instead consider a combination of structural and cultural forces (Coleman 1987).

When we do this, we immediately find that one of the most important structural forces for street crime, economic deprivation, is irrelevant. As Sutherland (1949) noted years ago, we can't attribute the crimes of corporate executives and other wealthy white-collar criminals to the distress of poverty because most white-collar criminals are by definition wealthy to begin with. Sutherland instead stressed that white-collar crime stems from a process of differential association in which business offenders learn shared views on the desirability of their criminal conduct. Most contemporary scholars of white-collar crime agree with his view, especially where corporate crime is concerned, as many corporations develop subcultures of resistance that encourage corporate lawbreaking to enhance corporate profits (Braithwaite 1989).

Many scholars also blame white-collar crime on an insatiable thirst for money and the power accompanying it. This greed in turn arises from the stress placed in our society on economic success (Passas 1990). Even if we're already wealthy, we can never have enough. As discussed in Chapter 6, the pursuit of profit in a capitalist society can be ruthless at times, and individuals and organizations will often do whatever necessary to acquire even more money, wealth, and power.

Another reason corporate crime occurs is that enforcement of its penalties is so lax. James W. Coleman (Coleman 1995:266) says that "white-collar crime continues to take such an economic and social toll because the government often does little or nothing to punish white-collar criminals, especially those involved in the most serious organizational crimes." Regulations forbidding corporate misconduct are either weak or nonexistent. Part of the reason for this is that corporations, whether you like them or not, are very powerful and influential, and are often able to prevent or water down regulatory legislation. Also, since federal and state regulatory agencies are woefully underfunded and understaffed, much corporate misconduct goes undetected.

Even when corporate crime is suspected, it's difficult to prove and punish. A major reason for this is again corporate power. Simply put, corporations have more resources, including sheer wealth and highly paid, skilled attorneys, than do enforcement agencies and district attorney offices. A regulatory agency or district attorney bringing charges against a major corporation is like David fighting Goliath. In the Bible, David won, but in the contemporary world of corporate crime, Goliath usually wins. Regulatory agencies and district attorneys often have to settle for promises by corporations that they will stop their misconduct, which they often don't even admit they were doing (Coleman 1998).

The complexity of corporate crime compounds the problems facing regulatory agencies and prosecuting attorneys. It's often difficult to determine when and how a law or regulation was violated, and who made the decision to violate it. A famous passage at the beginning of John Steinbeck's classic novel, *The Grapes of Wrath*, illustrates the difficulty in pinpointing individual responsibility in corporate behavior. A poor Oklahoma farmer during the Great Depression is about to have his house run over by a bulldozer because he's behind in his mortgage. Armed with a rifle, he stands in front of his house ready to shoot the bulldozer driver. The driver says he's not at fault, since the local town's bank is the one that told him to bulldoze the house. The farmer asks who at the bank made this decision so that he can go shoot this person. The driver replies that the bank was acting under the direction of its parent corporation back East. Frustrated, the farmer asks sadly, "Then who can I shoot?" puts down his rifle, and allows the bulldozer to do its dirty work.

Even when guilt is determined, corporate executives and high-status occupational offenders usually receive lenient treatment (Coleman 1998; Rosoff, Pontell, and Tillman 1998). Part of the reason for this is the high-powered attorneys and other resources they can bring to the fore and the unwillingness of judges to regard them as real criminals deserving actual punishment. Many studies find corporate executives and other professional and wealthy occupational criminals less likely than street criminals stealing far less money to receive long prison terms, or even to be sentenced to prison at all (Tillman and Pontell 1992).

It's also true that the mass media gloss over the damage caused by corporate and other white-collar crime (Randall 1995). This is unfortunate, because the threat of publicity can deter such crime (Scott 1989). Morton Mintz (1992), the former *Washington Post* investigative reporter cited earlier, attributes the media's neglect to cowardice, friendships, libel risks, and its pro-business orientation. Although Mintz concedes the press now covers corporate crime more than in the past, he says it's still guilty of a "pro-corporate tilt" that leads to a lack of adequate coverage of corporate crime and other misconduct. In making the same point, Sutherland (1949:247) much earlier noted that corporations own the major newspapers and other segments of the news media. Because the media's income comes largely from advertisements by other corporations, he observed, they "would be likely to lose a considerable part of this income if they were critical of business practices in general or those of particular corporations."

 # REDUCING WHITE-COLLAR CRIME

To reduce corporate and other white-collar crime, several measures are necessary. To list but a few, federal and state regulatory agencies must be provided much larger budgets so they will become at least somewhat stronger Davids against corporate Goliaths. The media would have to focus as much or more attention on corporate and other white-collar crime as they now do on street crime. More severe punishment might also work. Because the major corporations can easily afford to pay even millions of dollars in fines, these would have to be increased substantially to have a noticeable deterrent effect. Since so few corporate executives and other high-status offenders are threatened with imprisonment, many scholars think the increased use of even short prison terms may induce these offenders to obey the law (Cullen, Maakestad, and Cavender 1987).

Others say that stiffer fines and greater use of imprisonment won't work and will lead only to other problems, including overburdening a legal system already stretched beyond its means. These observers feel that self-regulation and compliance strategies emphasizing informal sanctions such as negative publicity campaigns threatening corporate reputations would ultimately reduce corporate crime more effectively (Braithwaite 1995b). However, Pontell and Calavita (1993) think this approach would not have prevented the 1980s savings and loan fraud, partly because savings and loan executives looted their own institutions and would thus not have cared about their institutions' reputations.

 ## Summary and Conclusion

I once saw an editorial cartoon depicting two men. One was a middle-aged man dressed in a slick business suit and listed as a corporate executive; the other was young and shabbily dressed with unkempt hair and a day-old beard. Under the cartoon was the question, "Who's the criminal?" This chapter has explored this question.

By any objective standard, white-collar crime causes more financial loss, injury, illness, and death than street crime. Publicity given to the worst white-collar offenses has increased public awareness of white-collar crime, and in public opinion surveys some white-collar crimes are considered more serious than street crime (Cullen, Link, and Polanzi 1982). Although some observers take such evidence as equivalent to public concern over white-collar crime (Meier and Short 1995), the two do not necessarily go hand-in-hand. As Weisburd and Schlegel (1992:361) point out, "White-collar crimes may be perceived as serious crimes by the public, but they are not the crimes that make us feel unsafe in our homes and neighborhoods."

Street crimes remain the ones we worry about. We lock our doors, arm ourselves with guns, and take many other precautions to protect ourselves from muggers, rapists, burglars, and other criminals. These are all dangerous people, and we should be concerned about them. Because white-collar crime is more indirect and invisible than street crime, it worries us far less, no matter how much harm it causes. White-collar crime is less visible partly because of its nature, and partly because of press inattention. One consequence of its invisibility is that white-collar crime victims "are often unaware of their victimization" (Weisburd and Schlegel 1992:359).

As a result, most white-collar crime remains hidden from regulatory agencies and law enforcement personnel. If someone poisoned a bottle of aspirin or other consumer product, the press would publicize this crime heavily. We would all be alarmed and refuse to buy the product, and its manufacturer would probably take it off retail shelves. Meanwhile, we use dangerous products that kill thousands each year because we don't know they're dangerous.

Even when we are aware of two other kinds of corporate violence, unsafe workplaces and environmental pollution, there's often little we can do. Workers have to go to work each day to pay their bills. Locked doors will not keep out air, water, or land pollution. The same is true for economic white-collar crime that steals from the public: Locked doors, guns, and mace will not protect the average family of four from losing $1,000 to price fixing each year.

One other consequence of white-collar crime merits some comment. Several observers have noted that white-collar crime undermines public trust in business, government, and other social institutions (Weisburd and Schlegel 1992). By breeding cynicism about the legal and moral orders, white-collar crime may promote other types of criminality.

White-collar crime remains an elusive concept. As used here, it encompasses petty workplace theft by blue-collar workers as well as complex financial schemes by wealthy professionals and major corporations. The inclusion of crime by blue-collar workers and businesses takes us far from Sutherland's original focus on corporate and other crime by high-status offenders. But it does remind us that crime takes on a variety of forms and involves many otherwise law-abiding people who would denounce robbers and burglars but see nothing wrong with occasionally helping themselves to a few items from their workplaces or to cheating a customer now and then.

However, given the power and influence of corporations, wealthy professionals, and other high-status offenders, we'd be remiss if we didn't keep their behavior at the forefront of the study of white-collar crime. As Sutherland reminded us, crime is not just something that poor nonwhite people do. And as he also reminded us, the harm caused by corporate and other high-status crime greatly exceeds harm caused by the street crime of the poor. Sutherland and other scholars are not saying we should minimize the problem of street crime. That would not be fair to its many victims, most of them poor, and many of them people of color. But they are saying that perhaps it's time to give white-collar crime the concern and attention it so richly deserves.

If white-collar crime has still received relatively little scholarly and other attention, political crime has received even less. This crime again challenges traditional views of criminality and forces us to question the nature and legitimacy of law when lawbreaking is committed by the government itself or by members of the public acting not for personal gain but for a higher end. We'll examine this fascinating topic in the next chapter.

KEY TERMS

collective embezzlement	pilferage
corporate violence	price fixing
embezzlement	professional fraud
muckrakers	restraint of trade
occupational crime	self-referral
organizational crime	

1. What are some of the conceptual problems in defining white-collar crime? What do you think is the best definition of such crime?
2. Why is it so difficult to detect and reduce professional fraud?
3. What are three types of health-care fraud? Why does such fraud occur? To what degree do techniques of neutralization help us understand the origins of such fraud?
4. What are any three examples of corporate violence discussed in the text?
5. Why, generally, does white-collar crime occur?

One of the best Web sites for white-collar crime is the one maintained by the National White Collar Crime Center (NW3C). Go to this site at **http://www.nw3c.org/**. If necessary, click on **welcome** to access the NW3C's home page. Here you should see a link to **Initiatives**. Click on this link to find out more about the activities of the NW3C.

Now go back to its home page and scroll down until you see a link to the **latest research** on white-collar crime. Click on this link to read about the organization's research initiatives. Click on National Public Survey on White Collar Crime to read some of the results of a national survey the Center conducted a few years ago. After reading these results, answer the following questions: How concerned is the public about white-collar crime? How much of the public has been victimized by white-collar crime? What factors increase the chances of being victimized?

A provocative Web page on corporate crime is **www.corporatepredators.org**. This site includes a summary of a book on white-collar crime by Russell Mokhiber and Robert Weissman and links to many columns they've written on various types of white-collar crime. It also includes a link to the **top 100 criminals of the 1990s**. Click on this link. According to Mokhiber and Weissman, what was the top corporate criminal?

Chapter

13

POLITICAL
CRIME

Crime in the News

*I*n late November 1999, up to 50,000 protesters converged on Seattle during a conference of the World Trade Organization (WTO). They came to the city to demonstrate against WTO policies that, they said, exploited poor nations and took jobs away from U.S. workers. They marched in the streets, held rallies, and engaged in illegal sit-ins. Almost all the protesters were peaceful, but a small minority trashed some Seattle streets and stores, causing several millions of dollars in damage. The National Guard was brought in, and a curfew was established. Over several days the police arrested hundreds, sprayed many with tear gas and pepper spray, and shot some with rubber bullets. Many of those sprayed were not doing anything illegal at the time. The police were charged both with underreacting by letting the protests get out of hand and then with overreacting after the protests began, and a week later the Seattle police chief resigned.

Sources: Greenhouse 1999; Verhovek 1999.

On the first day of my Criminology class, I ask whether anyone in the room has ever been arrested. Usually a few hands go up. When the culprits confess to offenses like shoplifting, vandalism, and drunk or reckless driving, other students usually chuckle or smile knowingly. At this point I reveal that I was arrested and spent several hours in jail when I was 20 years old. Most students are startled to hear this and ask what I was arrested for. I then explain I was one of a dozen protesters who chained themselves to a Federal Building in 1972 in a nonviolent protest against the Vietnam War.

Our crime was very different from the crimes covered in earlier chapters. These offenses are committed either for economic gain, if we're talking about property crime or white-collar crime, or out of strong emotion or impulsiveness, if we're talking about violent crime. My fellow protesters and I broke the law for none of these reasons. Instead, our motivation was ideological. We aimed to call attention to what we considered an unjust war and, in this small way, to increase public pressure to end the war.

The crime for which we were arrested was a *political crime*. Although political crime has existed for centuries, criminology, sociology, and the other social sciences have given it relatively little attention. This chapter discusses the many types of political crime that exist. As we'll see, political crime often plays a key role in the struggle between government and dissenters.

DEFINING POLITICAL CRIME

Part of the reason for the neglect of political crime by the scholarly world is the ambiguity of the political crime concept. As one example of this ambiguity, we could say that all crimes are political crimes, since all crimes by definition violate criminal laws passed by legislative bodies. However, this conceptualization would render the term "political crime" meaningless. As another example, political officials, as we'll be seeing, often take various actions that are legal but still violate various standards of human decency and democracy. Should we consider their actions political crimes? Should social problems such as hunger, poverty, corporate violence, and institutionalized sexism and racism be considered political crimes, as some scholars argue (Bohm 1993)? In a related issue that rose in the 1960s, should African-Americans and other poor people of color languishing in our prisons for street crime be considered political criminals and political prisoners (Lefcourt 1971)? Were the urban uprisings of the 1960s and other periods political revolts or just common violence? What about politicians who take bribes and are otherwise corrupt for personal gain? Are their crimes political crimes?

None of these questions is easy to answer. A major part of the struggle between any government and its dissenters is to influence public views of the legitimacy and necessity of actions taken by both sides (Diani and Porta 1999). The state does its best to frame its own actions, however harmful, as legal and as necessary to protect the social order from violent and even irrational individuals. To further this goal, it may try to conceal certain activities sure to provoke public and media outrage. For their part, dissenters call attention to the evils of state policies and frame their own activities, even if illegal, as necessary to bring about a more just society. Public officials thus call an urban uprising a riot, while others call it a revolt (Balbus 1977). Public officials refer to protesters as "long-haired, animal-type, junkie hippies," as the head of my draft board during the Vietnam War once called a group of people picketing peacefully outside the board, while protesters liken officials to common criminals or worse. "Hey, hey, LBJ! How many more did you kill today?" was a common chant at antiwar rallies during Lyndon Johnson's presidency, as he and his successor, Richard Nixon, were often compared with the worst war criminals of World War II.

Against this backdrop, any attempt to define and categorize *political crime* is itself a political act fraught with ideological consequences (Tunnell 1993b). Omitting injurious, unethical, and even illegal actions by the state risks obscuring behaviors that are often far worse than what any common criminal does. On the other hand, calling any state policy or social condition that oppresses some deprived group (the poor, women, people of color) a political crime might dilute the concept's analytic power.

As with white-collar crime, it thus seems best to take an eclectic view of political crime, one broad enough to encompass what many people mean by political crime—including political corruption and injurious but legal governmental actions—but one not so broad that the concept becomes unclear and useless. A reasonable definition of political crime might then be *any illegal or socially injurious act aimed at preserving or changing the existing political and social order*. This is not a perfect definition, as it leaves open, for example, the question of who defines whether a given act is "socially injurious," but it does get at what most scholars mean by political crime (Tunnell 1993a). Although the actual behavior involved (e.g., murder) in political crime may be very similar to that involved in conventional crimes, the key difference is that political crime is performed for *ideological* reasons. Thus tax evasion intended for personal gain is best considered fraud, while nonpayment of taxes to protest U.S. military or taxation policy is best regarded as a political crime.

Let's further divide political crime into two major categories: crime by government and crime against government. *Crime by government*, also called *state-organized crime* or *state criminality* (Barak 1991; Chambliss 1989), aims to preserve the existing order and includes: (1) political repression and human rights violations (genocide, torture, assassination, and other violence; surveillance and disruption; and arrest, prosecution, and imprisonment); (2) unethical or illegal experimentation; and (3) the aiding and abetting of corporate crime. Many governments, including the United States and other democracies, commit some or all of these crimes, which occur inside or outside their national borders.

A fourth type of crime by government is political corruption. As the previous chapter noted, many scholars place such corruption in the occupational crime category. Others, myself included, regard political corruption as a special case of occupational crime that violates the public trust by illegally enhancing the wealth and influence of specific individuals in the political structure. Because political corruption in this sense thus helps preserve the existing political order, it does fit under the definition of political crime outlined earlier. This is especially true for corruption involving broad conspiracies of people at the highest levels of government, such as in the Watergate and Iran-Contra scandals.

Hate crime is an additional crime intended to preserve the existing order. This intent is clearest when hate crime results from organized efforts by groups such as the Ku Klux Klan to terrorize certain classes of citizens. Although hate crime offenders are not usually government officials, the similarity of its intent to that of crime by government leads some scholars to classify it as an additional type of political crime. Other scholars treat hate crime as one form of interpersonal violence. I prefer the former classification and will examine hate crime here as a "crime by government," which might more accurately be called "crime by government and other established interests."

Crime against government aims to change the existing order and includes: (1) terrorism, assassination, and other political violence; (2) nonviolent civil disobedience; and (3) espionage and treason. Although I, like other observers, call this category "crime against government," it might be more accurate to call it "crime against government and other established interests." For example, although much illegal protest is directed against government, as during the Vietnam War, much is also directed against corporations and other targets. Illegal protest by organized labor, nuclear power opponents, and animal rights activists are just a few that fall into this category.

With these broad categories of political crime in mind, let's explore its nature and extent by turning to specific examples.

CRIME BY GOVERNMENT

Political Repression and Human Rights Violations

In the ideal world of political theory, all societies would be democratic and egalitarian and would treat their citizens and those of other nations with dignity and respect. This ideal world has never existed. History is replete with governments that have used both violent and legal means to repress dissent and to preserve inequality. The worst offenders are typically totalitarian regimes, but even democratic governments, including the United States, have engaged in various types of repression (Goldstein 1978). To do justice to all victims of repression would take much more space than we have here, but several examples should give you an idea of its use by officials in both totalitarian and democratic societies.

GENOCIDE

The ultimate act of repression is *genocide*. Genocide, a term coined during World War II, refers to the deliberate extermination of a group because of its race, religion, ethnicity, or nationality (Kuper 1985). The term comes from the Greek word *genos*, or race, and the Latin root *-cide*, or killing. By definition, genocide is the worst crime of all by government and is often called a "crime against humanity." The most infamous example of genocide, of course, is the Nazi slaughter during World War II of 6 million Jews, more than two-thirds of all the Jews in Europe, and of 5 to 6 million other people, including Poles, Slavs, Catholics, homosexuals, and gypsies (Gilbert 1987). In the late 1800s, Russia also committed Jewish genocide by murdering hundreds of Jews in massacres called *pogroms*. More than 2 million Russian Jews fled their homeland for the safety of the United States, Palestine, and other areas (Klier and Lambroza 1992). In yet another act of genocide, about 1 million Armenians died from thirst, starvation, or attacks by roving tribes after Turkey forced them into the surrounding desert in 1915 (Nazian 1990).

Unfortunately, genocide did not end with the Nazis. Just a few years ago, ethnic conflict in two regions of the world led to tens of thousands of deaths and repeated charges of genocide. One region was Bosnia-Herzegovina, a former republic of Yugoslavia that declared its independence in a referendum in early 1992. At the time of the declaration, Bosnia consisted of three nationalities: Muslims, Serbs, and Croats. The Muslims and Croats voted overwhelmingly for independence, while the Serbs mostly boycotted the referendum. The move to independence led to a

◀ *During World War II, the Nazis imprisoned Jews and other groups in concentration camps such as this one, and eventually slaughtered some 6 million Jews and 5 to 6 million other people.*

civil war pitting the Serbs against the other two groups. By the end of 1992, Serbs controlled about 70 percent of Bosnian land and had begun forced expulsions, called "ethnic cleansing," of Muslims from the land they captured. They also began to massacre thousands of unarmed Muslim and Croat men, women, and children (Darnton 1993). In addition, Serb troops raped an estimated 20,000 Muslim women in an act termed "gynocide" by some observers (Lewis 1993; Quindlen 1993).

In 1994 a civil war also tore apart the African nation of Rwanda, which consisted of two major ethnic groups, the Hutu, who controlled the country, and the Tutsi. In April 1994, a plane carrying the Rwandan President, a Hutu, crashed after reportedly being shot, and the government blamed a Tutsi rebel group. Government troops and Hutu civilians responded by massacring some 200,000 Tutsis in the next three weeks and 500,000 to 1 million by the end of June. Tutsi forces fought back, scored some significant victories, and captured the Rwandan capital in July. Some 1 million Hutus fled the nation in response (Lynch 1995).

Some 15 years earlier in the late 1970s, more genocide had taken place in Cambodia, where the Khmer Rouge regime of dictator Pol Pot forced city residents to move to rural areas and slaughtered hundreds of thousands of Cambodians (Martin 1994). In 1979, Vietnamese troops helped Cambodian opponents of the regime overthrow it.

Genocide is typically linked to totalitarian governments, but democracies can also commit it. Here the U.S. treatment of Native Americans is widely cited. When Europeans first came to this continent, about 1 million Native Americans lived here. Over many decades, tens of thousands were killed by white settlers and then U.S. troops, while many others died from disease introduced by the Europeans. Deaths from these two sources reduced the Indian population to less than 240,000 by 1900. Many historians and other scholars say the killings constituted genocide against American Indians (Wilson 1999).

The term "genocide" was used again during the Vietnam War years. The Vietnam War cost the United States more than $150 billion and killed some 58,000 U.S. soldiers and other personnel and almost 2 million Vietnamese. Ten million South

Vietnamese became refugees. The United States dropped four times as many tons of bombs as the Allies had dropped over Germany in World War II. Many of these bombs targeted civilian populations. Some were strictly antipersonnel in nature, sending out small nails able to shred muscles and body organs but not able to dent military equipment, or steel pellets able to penetrate flesh but not trucks (Branfman 1972). Many bombs contained napalm, a jellied gasoline that would ignite when the bomb dropped from the plane, splatter across a wide area, and burn anything it touched. Often the *anything* was children and other civilians. In 1968, U.S. troops massacred up to 200 civilians at My Lai village (Hersh 1970). Although this massacre received wide attention after it was publicized, Vietnam veterans later revealed many other civilian massacres that never came to light (Meyrowitz and Campbell 1992).

Passions still flame over the Vietnam War. Its supporters felt, and still feel, that the war was necessary to contain Communism and that it was lost because the United States fought it "with one hand tied behind its back." Opponents charged the United States with waging an immoral war and with committing war crimes by violating the Nuremberg Principles established after World War II in response to Nazi atrocities (DeBenedetti and Chatfield 1990). In 1995, Robert S. McNamara, Secretary of Defense under Lyndon Johnson, published a book in which he apologized for the war, which he called an immoral mistake (McNamara and VanDeMark 1995). McNamara's apology did little to douse the emotions the war still arouses.

Torture, Assassination, and Related Violence

Governments often resort to political violence that stops short of genocide. This violence includes torture and beatings; assassination, execution, and mass murder; and related actions including forced expulsion. This is government rule by terror, and has been termed "state terrorism" (Bushnell 1991; Chomsky 1988). One of the most notorious examples of state terrorism in this century occurred under Soviet Union dictator Joseph Stalin in the 1930s and 1940s. In that period, a purge of Communist Party leaders who might have threatened Stalin's reign executed thousands as Stalin's secret police terrorized the Soviet citizenry (Conquest 1990).

State terrorism did not end with Stalin. International human rights groups have documented thousands of government-sponsored murders, beatings, and related violence across the world. In Latin America, the Middle East, and elsewhere, dissenters are kidnapped, tortured, and murdered. In Bosnia and elsewhere, government troops rape women routinely. These human rights violations are once again much more common under totalitarian regimes than in democratic societies, but, as we'll see later, the United States has seen its share of government violence over the years.

Perhaps the most widely publicized government violence of recent years was the June 1989 massacre at Tiananmen Square in China. A democracy movement of thousands had shaken China to the core. On June 4, 1989, several thousand unarmed demonstrators, many of them students, gathered at Tiananmen Square in Beijing, China's capital, to demand democratic reforms. The military's response was to open fire and slaughter several hundred demonstrators. Many others were arrested and imprisoned, with some later executed (Black 1993).

Governments also assassinate selected dissenters whom they perceive as special threats. As just one example, in the late 1970s, peasants and other poor citizens in El Salvador began demanding that the government provide land, jobs, and other help to the poor. Many Roman Catholic priests and nuns supported the protesters. One of the most vocal clergy was Archbishop Oscar Arnulfo Romero, who was assassinated by government troops in March 1980. His death sparked riots

Human Rights Abuses in Nigeria

Human rights violations occur in many nations around the world, and Nigeria, on Africa's west coast, is no exception. Nigeria was a British colony from 1861 until 1960, when it finally won its independence. After a military junta took over the country in 1966, the military ruled Nigeria until 1979, when a civilian government was elected. The military overthrew this government in 1983, and different military officers headed the government for the next decade. A week after Moshood Abiola was democratically elected the next Nigerian president in June 1993, the military government voided the election. A new military dictator, Sani Abacha, took control of the country five months later. In June 1994 he had Abiola arrested and charged him with treason. Abiola remained behind bars into 1996. In September 1994 Abacha proclaimed that he was immune from judicial review of his activities.

The backdrop was thus set for a series of events involving human rights abuses. Many of them revolved around oil, which had emerged since the 1960s as Nigeria's most profitable export at 1.8 billion barrels a day, 41 percent of this going to the United States. A two-month oil worker strike led to beatings, arbitrary arrests, and other repressive acts. In March 1995 the Nigerian government arrested several people for plotting to overthrow Abacha and sentenced fourteen to death while later commuting the sentences. Scores of other government critics were arrested on bogus charges and sentenced to prison without fair trials. Some just disappeared.

Meanwhile, environmental activists in Ogoniland, in southern Nigeria, had begun to protest the oilfields of the Royal Dutch/Shell oil company. They charged that Shell, which pumps half of Nigeria's oil, was ruining their land and was not paying them enough money for the oil. A January 1993 demonstration attracted some 300,000 Ogoni residents. The demonstration, other protests, and apparent sabotage against Shell's equipment finally prompted Shell to ask the military government in 1994 to send in its so-called mobile police.

The government complied, as Shell paid for the transportation of some of the police and gave them salary bonuses. Beginning a ruthless campaign to quell Ogoni dissent, the police reportedly destroyed about 30 Ogoni villages and killed 2,000 people. Finally, in November 1995, the government executed Ken Saro-Wiwa and eight other Ogoni activists for allegedly inciting a riot that led to the murder of four pro-government chiefs. Two of the government witnesses against Saro-Wiwa later said the government bribed them to testify against him. Not surprisingly, the charges against the activists were widely viewed as trumped-up and prompted worldwide outrage and calls for boycotts of the Shell oil company. Many critics charged Shell with complicity in the deaths of the activists by failing to call on the government to stop the executions.

In the wake of the executions, Wole Soyinka, a Nigerian activist and winner of the 1986 Nobel Prize in Literature, wrote that Abacha "has gone beyond any other dictator in Nigeria in degrading the quality or expectations of human life in the nation and committed crimes against humanity that deserve public trial."

Sources: Boyd 1995; Lewis 1995; Lewis 1996; Soyinka 1995.

throughout the country and remained a rallying cry for dissident forces for several years (Goldston 1990).

The United States has also seen its share of political violence committed against dissenters. Much of this was committed against the labor movement. In Chapter 9 we saw that, during an 1897 coalmining strike, law enforcement officials fatally shot 18 strikers, many of them in the back, and wounded 40 more. Another well-known labor massacre occurred in Ludlow, Colorado in April 1914 at a tent city of striking miners and their families evicted from their company-owned homes. On Easter night, April 20, company guards and National Guard troops poured oil on the tents, set them afire, and machine-gunned the families as they fled from the tents. Thirteen children, one woman, and five men died from bullet wounds or smoke inhalation (McGovern and Guttridge 1972).

During the Southern civil rights movement of the 1960s, violence against demonstrators and activists was common (Blumberg 1991). The instigators were local police and deputies, state troopers, and white civilians. Several dozen civil rights workers were murdered, and hundreds more were beaten. The murdered included Southern blacks as well as Northerners who had come to help the movement. Among the most publicized murders were those of Medgar Evers, 1963, Mississippi; James Chaney, Andrew Goodman, and Michael Schwerner, 1964, Mississippi; and Viola Liuzzo, 1965, Alabama. Other violence greeted civil rights demonstrators engaging in protest campaigns. The two most publicized episodes of this sort of violence occurred in Selma, Alabama in April-May 1963, and in Birmingham, Alabama in March 1965, in response to civil rights protest campaigns in both cities. In Birmingham, police clubbed nonviolent demonstrators, attacked them with police dogs, and swept them away with powerful fire hoses. In Selma, state troopers again clubbed the demonstrators with nightsticks, attacked them with police horses, and used tear gas. Both episodes shocked the nation and helped win federal civil rights legislation (Button 1989).

On the heels of the civil rights movement came the founding of the Black Panther Party in Oakland, California, and later in other cities. The Panthers initially organized free breakfast programs for poor children and criticized police brutality against blacks. Police and other law enforcement agencies responded with a multifaceted effort to harass and discredit the Panthers (Churchill and Wall 1990). This effort included official violence that became lethal. In December 1969, Chicago police knocked down the door of Panther leader Fred Hampton one night and shot him fatally as he lay in his bed. They also shot another Panther leader, Mark Clark, who died later from his wounds. The police claimed that Hampton had fired at them when they burst into his room, but later investigation revealed that all the bullets in the room, except perhaps one, came from the police, suggesting Hampton and Clark were murdered in cold blood (Balkan, Berger, and Schmidt 1980).

The kind of official violence used against Southern civil rights activists and the Black Panthers was much less common during the Vietnam antiwar movement, but some still occurred. On May 4, 1970, National Guard troops fired into an antiwar rally at Kent State University in Ohio and killed four students and wounded nine others. Several of the students were just watching the rally or were walking to classes (Davies 1973). Ten days later, campus protests not related to the Vietnam War brought police and state troopers onto the campus of Jackson State College, an historically black college in Mississippi. At one point they fired rifles, shotguns, and submachine guns into a dormitory and killed two students and wounded 12 others (Spofford 1988).

At the federal level, the U.S. government has conspired in or otherwise supported the torture and murder of dissidents and the assassination of political leaders in other nations in the last half-century. During the Vietnam War, for example, the Central Intelligence Agency (CIA) established the notorious "Operation Phoenix" program that arrested, tortured, and murdered some 40,000 Vietnamese civilians (Chomsky and Herman 1979). Following orders of the White House and State Department, the CIA has supported coups that deposed and often killed national leaders in countries such as Chile, the Dominican Republic, Guatemala, Iran, and South Vietnam. Each of these assassinations and coups made these politically unstable nations only more chaotic and often plunged them further into civil war or led to despotic governments that terrorized their citizenry (Moyers 1988). When CIA involvement later came to light, the U.S. government called such efforts necessary to advance U.S. interests, while critics charged the United States with wanton interference in other nations' affairs.

◄ *On May 4, 1970, the National Guard killed four students and wounded nine others at Kent State University in Ohio.*

◄ *Also in 1970, ten days after the Kent State incident, police at Jackson State College in Mississippi fired at a dormitory, killing two students and wounding twelve others.*

The assassination of the Chilean premier, Salvador Allende, is instructive. Allende was democratically elected the head of Chile in 1970 but was a Marxist opposed to U.S. corporate involvement in the Chilean economy. In response, the CIA helped undermine the economy and aided right-wing terrorist and other groups opposed to Allende. In this context, the resulting coup in 1973 that killed Allende was perhaps inevitable. It replaced a democratic government, even if socialist, with a military junta that murdered, tortured, and imprisoned thousands of citizens over the next several years (Davis 1985).

SURVEILLANCE, INFILTRATION, AND DISRUPTION

In George Orwell's classic novel *1984*, Big Brother was always watching, and citizens had no freedom of movement. The aim here, of course, was to make sure that no one could do anything unobserved that might threaten the existing order. *1984* remains a frightening indictment of totalitarian societies that even today have police and other law enforcement agents spy on the citizenry, infiltrate dissident groups, and harass and disrupt their activities.

One of the cornerstones of democracy is freedom of movement and lawful dissent. Government surveillance, infiltration, and disruption of its critics' activities violates this freedom. Given this context, congressional disclosures in the 1970s of massive violations of these principles were particularly disturbing. In the previous three decades, the FBI, CIA, and other federal, state, and local law enforcement agencies had systematically and illegally spied on hundreds of thousands of U.S. citizens (Davis 1992; Halperin 1977). These citizens had exercised their First Amendment rights of freedom of speech and assembly through lawful involvement in civil rights, antiwar, and other protest. The FBI and the other agencies considered them threats to the nation and compiled dossier after dossier after dossier. These agencies also infiltrated many civil rights, antiwar, and other dissident groups and did their best to disrupt their activities. Perhaps the most famous target of FBI harassment was the great civil rights leader, Martin Luther King, Jr. The head of the FBI, J. Edgar Hoover, believed that the civil rights movement was Communist-inspired and that King was at best a dupe of Communists or at worst a Communist himself. To gather evidence of alleged extramarital affairs, the FBI bugged motel rooms in which King stayed, and at one point wrote him an anonymous letter urging him to commit suicide before this evidence became public (Garrow 1981).

The bugging and harassment of King was part of the FBI's counterintelligence program called COINTELPRO, begun in 1941 (Swearington 1995). For its first 20 years, COINTELPRO targeted members of the Communist and Socialist Workers parties in the United States. With the advent of the 1960s, the FBI turned its attention to the civil rights, antiwar, and other social movements that began during that decade. Using informants who infiltrated these groups, it monitored the activities of tens of thousands of citizens, some of them leaders of these movements but most of them unknown except to their families and friends.

I was one of the unknowns upon whom the FBI spied. After the Kent State shootings in May 1970, many campuses across the country, including mine, went "on strike." Instead of going to classes, students and faculty held educational workshops on the Vietnam War and related issues and went into the community to collect signatures on antiwar petitions. In a letter to parents, my college's president commended the behavior of students at my college as responsible and constructive. Despite his praise, someone reported my attendance at some of the workshops on my campus to the FBI, as I later found out when I obtained my FBI file under the Freedom of Information Act. Because I was a quiet, unknown freshman at the time, the FBI informant was probably one of a small group of people involved in our campus effort who knew me. Someone, probably the same person, also told the FBI that in September 1970 I attended three meetings of "an ad hoc group formed … to protest the war in Vietnam"—a group that soon ceased to exist. The informant even mentioned the name of the dormitory lounge in which we met. Because only 10 to 15 people attended each meeting, the informant had to have been someone I knew, trusted, and even cherished.

Some FBI and other informants further acted as "agents provocateurs" who tried to disrupt dissident groups by fostering internal ideological debates and by urging them to violence (Churchill and Wall 1990; Marx 1974). The chief aide to Fred Hampton, the Black Panther leader killed by Chicago police, was in fact an FBI informant who tried to get Hampton's group to be more militant and told authorities the layout of Hampton's apartment so that they knew where he would be sleeping when they raided it (Cockburn 1990).

In addition to surveillance and infiltration, the FBI also burglarized offices of activist groups and stole their files (Davis 1992). Perhaps that is why my FBI file contained a photocopy of my subscription label from a pacifist, antiwar magazine to which I subscribed during the early 1970s. Evidently, either the FBI burglarized the magazine's office and stole its subscription list or planted an informant who photocopied or otherwise obtained the list and gave it to the FBI.

The CIA also monitored the activities of U.S. citizens, even though by law it was prohibited from domestic surveillance. For about 20 years beginning in the 1950s, the CIA opened and photographed some 250,000 first-class letters and kept files on more than 10,000 U.S. citizens. These illegal activities fell under the CIA's Operation Chaos, its counterpart to COINTELPRO that was begun in 1967 under orders from the White House (Halperin 1977).

All these surveillance tactics come together in the story of Scott Camil, a Marine decorated with nine medals for his service in Vietnam who later became a leader of Vietnam Veterans Against the War (VVAW) in the early 1970s. Because VVAW represented a powerful voice in the antiwar movement, the FBI and local and state police infiltrated it extensively, with several agents becoming VVAW leaders and others doing their best to get VVAW to be violent (Schultz and Schultz 1989). The FBI began monitoring Camil's activities in 1971, when he began speaking publicly about atrocities he and other U.S. troops had committed in Vietnam. An August 1971 entry in his FBI file noted, "Subject continues to be very active in his capacity as Southeastern Regional Director of the Vietnam Veterans Against the War and has maintained his non-violent approach in his antiwar activities. Subject has shown no propensity for violence" (Camil 1989:323–324).

By December the FBI had changed its mind about Camil. A December 11th memo mentions an investigation aimed at "neutralizing Camil at earliest logical date" (Camil 1989:325). A month later he was arrested on kidnapping charges that were eventually dropped. He was also arrested but later acquitted for marijuana possession. His house was burglarized and his files taken; his lawyer's office was burglarized, with only Camil's file taken.

Several months later, Camil and seven other VVAW members were arrested for allegedly conspiring to disrupt the 1972 Republication National Convention; the defendants became known as the Gainseville Eight. One of the prosecution's witnesses was Emerson Poe, one of Camil's best friends and his chief aide in VVAW. Camil and his girlfriend used to babysit for Poe's child, and Poe attended meetings the Gainesville Eight held with their attorneys. It turned out that Poe was an FBI informant planted in VVAW to monitor its activities. Camil later learned that more than half the people at some of his VVAW meetings were undercover agents from the FBI, Miami Police Department, and other agencies. There were so many agents that, according to one police informant, "The spies were spying on the spies that were spying on the spies" (Camil 1989:328). According to Camil, "Since they didn't know each other as agents, they lied about each other as well as about us" (Camil 1989:330).

Some time later, according to Camil, two undercover Drug Enforcement Agents beat him without identifying themselves and then shot him as he was trying to escape. Camil was prosecuted for assaulting them. The jury found him not guilty and recommended that the DEA agents be indicted for attempted murder.

The Congressional investigations' disclosure in the 1970s of all these surveillance activities prompted much public and news media outrage. Congress enacted legislation to limit such surveillance. Despite this legislation, the FBI continued its surveillance efforts (monitoring, informants, burglaries, etc.) in the 1980s when it spied on some 2,400 individuals and many organizations in the United States opposed to the White House's policies in Central America (Gelbspan 1991). As part of its efforts, the FBI photographed rallies on college campuses and elsewhere and investigated individuals who attended films on U.S.

Central American policy (Ermann and Lundman 1992). More recently, FBI documents revealed similar surveillance of gay rights groups in the early 1990s (Hamilton 1995:3).

LEGAL REPRESSION

A favorite repression strategy in totalitarian nations is to arrest and imprison dissidents. The aim here is to use the guise of law to legitimate political repression, even though the arrests, prosecutions, and imprisonment are all based on trumped-up, fraudulent charges. Stalin's reign of terror involved many *show trials* in which his opponents were depicted as dangerous threats to law and order (Conquest 1990). In the classic work on the subject, Otto Kirchheimer (1961) called this repressive use of legal procedure "political justice." Its goal is to put dissidents behind bars, to discredit their movement by labeling their conduct as criminal, and to intimidate supporters and potential sympathizers. Dissidents imprisoned under these circumstances are commonly called "political prisoners." When trials do occur, they are sham *political trials* lacking the due process found in democratic legal systems (Christenson 1986).

Human rights organizations like Amnesty International have identified thousands of political prisoners throughout the world over the years. In just one of many recent examples, China arrested and detained several dissidents in the weeks before the sixth anniversary of the Tiananmen Square massacre in 1995 in order to intimidate the dissident movement from holding protest rallies to mark the occasion (Reuters 1995).

Kirchheimer (1961) noted that political trials and other repressive uses of the law also occur in democratic societies, even if the outcome is not nearly so certain. A free, sympathetic press may criticize the government's repressive use of the law, and juries may acquit political defendants. Even with these risks, democratic governments often choose the law as a primary means of repression. Officials hope that arrests and prosecutions will prompt the press and the public to view dissidents as common criminals. They also hope to intimidate the dissidents and their movement and to force them to spend large amounts of time, money, and energy in their defense (Barkan, Cohn, and Whitaker 1995). Even if the defendants ultimately win a jury acquittal, they may find the whole process so expensive and draining that the government's use of legal repression succeeds politically even when it fails legally. For these reasons, democratic governments often prefer legal repression to violent repression, which risks looking "too repressive," antidemocratic, and even illegal.

U.S. history has been filled with legal repression (Goldstein 1978). Early in this century, federal law prohibited virtually all criticism of World War I. Arrests and prosecutions of some 2,000 labor radicals and socialists during the war muffled dissent and destroyed the Industrial Workers of the World, a radical labor union. Perhaps the most well-known defendant was Socialist Party leader Eugene V. Debs, who was arrested for criticizing the war in a Canton, Ohio speech. Representing himself, Debs, 63, addressed the jury with some words that became famous: "While there is a lower class, I am in it; while there is a criminal element, I am of it; while there is a soul in prison, I am not free." His eloquence notwithstanding, Debs was convicted, sentenced to ten years in prison, and pardoned three years later by President William Harding. While in prison, he ran for U.S. president on the Socialist Party ticket in 1920 and won 1 million votes (Ginger 1949).

The legal repression of anarchists, socialists, Communists, and other radicals continued after World War I ended. Federal agents infiltrated various radical groups and became informants and agents provocateurs. Then, on January 2, 1920, federal agents and local police acting under the orders of U.S. Attorney General A. Mitchell Palmer raided homes, bowling alleys, restaurants, and other places in 33 cities across the country and arrested some 10,000 radicals. A key figure behind these Palmer Raids, as they came to be called, was 26-year-old J. Edgar Hoover, who in 1924 became director of the Bureau of Investigation (renamed the Federal Bureau of Investigation in 1935) and later originated COINTELPRO (O'Reilly 1983).

As this brief history suggests, COINTELPRO-like policy existed long before Hoover began the program, as the First Amendment was all but abandoned from 1917 through the early 1920s. As former U.S. Senator Charles Goodell (1973:86) wrote of this period of legal repression, "One by one, the right to freedom of speech, the right of assembly, the right to petition, the right to protection against unreasonable searches and seizures, the right to a fair trial … all were sacrificed in attempts to preserve political orthodoxy and to protect the status quo."

This sacrifice of First Amendment rights continued during the Communist-witchhunting era of the late 1940s and early 1950s, commonly called the "McCarthy era" after U.S. Senator Joseph McCarthy (R-WI), who held congressional hearings on alleged Communist involvement in labor unions, Hollywood, and elsewhere. Witness after witness was called by McCarthy's committee and its counterpart in the House of Representatives to "name names" by revealing the identity of other Communists. Hundreds of suspected Communists were fired from their jobs, writers and actors in Hollywood were blacklisted, and lives were ruined (Navasky 1980). The legendary folksinger Pete Seeger refused in 1955 to testify before the House Un-American Activities Committee and was eventually convicted for contempt of Congress. He was blacklisted from radio, TV, and concert halls for more than a decade (Seeger 1989).

As part of the government's legal effort during this time, the Justice Department prosecuted more than 120 Communists under the 1940 Smith Act that prohibited advocating the use of violence to overthrow the government and belonging to any organization with this goal (Belknap 1978). The major Smith Act prosecution occurred in 1949 and involved 11 Communist Party leaders who were convicted and sentenced to long prison terms. The eleven were charged with conspiring to overthrow the government, not with committing any actual criminal acts, and the primary evidence of this "conspiracy" were publications in their possession containing the works of Karl Marx and V. I. Lenin. The defendants believed in Marx's famous prediction that the proletariat would one day rise up and overthrow capitalist government but had not themselves urged anyone to use violence to make this happen.

During the Southern civil rights movement of the 1960s, legal repression proved a very effective strategy (Barkan 1985). Thousands of civil rights activists were arrested and jailed for no good reason, forcing them to spend large sums of money on their defense and subjecting them to beatings and the very real possibility of death in Southern jails. Few attorneys were willing to defend the activists, and those who did were harassed by authorities and saw their normal law practice suffer. Convictions by white judges and juries were a foregone conclusion. Although some of these convictions were later overturned by the U.S. Supreme Court and other federal courts in landmark rulings, that was of small comfort to the activists whose energy and commitment had been sapped by the legal repression they'd experienced. Several Southern cities used a systematic policy of mass arrests and prosecutions to thwart civil rights protest campaigns. By avoiding the violence in Birmingham, Selma, and other communities that attracted so much national publicity and prompted federal intervention, these cities' efforts seemed reasonable in comparison and even won plaudits from the press and federal officials.

This repressive use of the law was less common during the Vietnam War, when antiwar activists usually ended up in court because they committed civil disobedience. However, the government did not abandon its legal repression entirely. In 1968 it prosecuted the renowned "baby doctor," Benjamin Spock, and four others for conspiracy to violate Selective Service laws by advocating draft resistance, even though some of the defendants had never even met each other (Mitford 1969). Four of the five defendants, including Spock, were convicted and sentenced to two years in prison. A year later a federal appeals court overturned the convictions.

Shortly after Spock and four others were convicted, a series of antiwar rallies and marches at the Democratic National Convention in Chicago prompted repeated police brutality. The Justice Department later prosecuted eight activists for conspiracy to come to Chicago to incite a riot. The resulting trial of the Chicago Eight, as the defendants were called, became one of the most publicized in U.S. history, as the defendants, provoked by a hostile, belligerent judge, often disrupted the courtroom (Dorsen and Friedman 1973).

As part of their campaign against the Black Panthers, federal, state, and local authorities used legal repression as well as violence and surveillance (Churchill and Wall 1990). More than 760 Black Panthers were arrested across the nation in the late 1960s, with their bail reaching almost $5 million. One of the most celebrated Black Panther trials took place in New York City in 1970–1971 and involved thirteen defendants arrested in 1969 for twelve counts each of conspiracy to bomb department stores and police stations and to murder police (Zimroth 1974). The prosecution's major witnesses were four undercover agents who had infiltrated the local Panther chapter and become some of its leaders. Despite an eight-month trial, the jury deliberated only three hours and found the defendants innocent of all 156 counts. Despite the acquittal, most of the defendants had been in jail for over two years. The government's multifaceted repression effectively ended the Black Panther Party by 1972 (Wolfe 1973).

Native American activists have also been subject to legal repression. In 1975 two federal agents entered the Pine Ridge Indian Reservation in South Dakota to arrest a Native American suspected of stealing a pair of boots. A violent confrontation resulted in the deaths of the two agents and of one member of the American Indian Movement (AIM), an Indian activist organization. The killing of the AIM member was never investigated. Of four Native Americans arrested for killing the two agents, one, Leonard Peltier, an AIM member, was convicted despite a lack of evidence and apparent improper conduct by the prosecution and judge at his trial. Peltier was sentenced to life in prison and has been cited as a political prisoner by Amnesty International (Peltier 1989)

Unethical or Illegal Experimentation

In the concentration camps of World War II, Nazi scientists performed some hideous experiments in the name of science (Gilbert 1987). In one typical experiment, they would strip camp prisoners naked and leave them outside in subfreezing temperatures in order to see how long it would take them to freeze to death. When experiments like this came to light at the end of the war, they outraged the world community.

This outrage did not prevent similar, government-sponsored experiments from occurring in the United States during the next few decades. That is a strong charge, to be sure, but the evidence supports the accusation. Perhaps the most notorious experiment began before the Holocaust and lasted 40 years. In 1932 the U.S.

Public Health Service identified some 400 poor, illiterate African-American men in Tuskegee, Alabama, who had syphilis, a deadly venereal disease that was incurable at the time. In order to gather information on the disease's progression, the government decided to monitor these men for many years. When a cure for syphilis, penicillin, was discovered in the 1940s, the government decided not to give it to the men because the study would be ruined if they were cured. They remained untreated for three more decades, until the press finally revealed the Tuskegee experiment in 1972. During that time, their wives who caught syphilis from them also remained untreated, as did any of their children born with syphilis. After the experiment was disclosed in 1972, commentators compared it to the worst Nazi experiments and charged it would not have occurred if the subjects had been white and wealthy (Jones 1981).

The Tuskegee experiment was not the only one in which the U.S. government treated U.S. citizens as human guinea pigs. Congressional and other investigations since the 1970s have revealed many secret experiments conducted by the military and the CIA over the years. Many of these involved radiation. From 1946 to 1963, for example, the military subjected up to 300,000 soldiers and civilians to radiation during atomic bomb tests (Fradkin 1989; Gallagher 1993). In many cases, soldiers were made to stand near the sites of the bomb tests; in others, nuclear fallout was spread in the air over civilian populations in the Southwest (Schneider 1993a; 1993b). The groups exposed ended up with abnormally high levels of leukemia and cancer, and medical records of their exposure either disappeared or were destroyed.

During that period, federal agencies also injected people with plutonium, uranium, and radium or gave them high doses of x-rays (Lee 1995; Simon 1999). These government guinea pigs included prisoners, mentally retarded individuals, and others who were not fully informed of the nature of the experiments. In Idaho, radioactive iodine was added to land and drinking water. The U.S. Army also released deadly bacteria into the air 239 times between 1949 and 1969 in order to learn about biological warfare. One of these tests occurred over San Francisco and was linked to twelve cases of pneumonia, including one that was fatal. The CIA conducted its own medical experiments, one of them involving spiking Army scientists' drinks with LSD. Two days later one of the scientists jumped from a hotel window and died. The CIA hid the true circumstances of his death from his family for more than two decades (Thomas 1989).

While all this was going on, the federal government remained quiet about the radiation experiments and about what it knew about the dangers of nuclear fallout. These dangers include thyroid cancer caused when fallout eventually enters cow's milk and then human bodies. Although the government did not inform the public about these dangers, it did decide to let the Eastman Kodak company know about any nuclear tests after the company noticed that fallout was fogging its film. When this history was disclosed a few years ago, a member of Congress remarked, "It really is odd that the government would warn Kodak about its film but it wouldn't warn the general public about the milk it was drinking" (Wald 1997:A16).

State-Corporate Crime

In the previous chapter I noted that much corporate crime occurs because of the government's inability or unwillingness to have stronger regulations and more effective law enforcement. Picking up on this theme, some scholars have discussed episodes in which government agencies and corporations cooperate to commit illegal or socially injurious activities. Such *state-corporate crime* represents the intersection of corporate crime and crime by government. An example is the North Carolina poultry plant fire discussed in the previous chapter that killed or injured many workers trapped in the burning building. North Carolina had long sought industrial development by limiting government safety regulation of its industries and by vigorously moving to stem the growth and power of labor unions. Such a climate allowed and even encouraged North Carolina industries to have unsafe workplaces. The poultry plant fire was thus a tragic but almost inevitable result of North Carolina's failure to have stronger safety regulations and of its active efforts over the years to block unionization (Aulette and Michalowski 1993).

An even more notable example of state-corporate criminality was the January 1986 explosion of the *Challenger* space shuttle that killed six astronauts and schoolteacher Christa McAuliffe. When people around the nation watched in horror as the *Challenger* exploded, little did we know that the explosion was, as Ronald C. Kramer notes (1992:214), the "collective product of the interaction between" the National Aeronautics and Space Administration (NASA) and Morton Thiokol, Inc., the corporation that built the flawed O-ring seals that caused the explosion. After the United States finally reached the moon in the late 1960s, support for NASA began to dry up. The space shuttle program became its salvation. However, NASA was under orders to implement the program at relatively low cost. As a result, says Kramer (p. 220), "NASA began to promise the impossible in order to build the shuttle and save the agency."

This pressure mounted in the 1980s as the Reagan administration became eager to use the shuttle system for commercial and military purposes. Its interest in using the shuttle as part of its planned Star Wars missile defense system placed particularly strong "demands on an already overburdened and underfunded space agency" (Kramer 1992:223). In July 1982, President Ronald Reagan declared the

◀ *The explosion of the Challenger space shuttle resulted from the failure of NASA and Morton Thiokol officials to heed warnings about problems with the O-ring seals.*

shuttle system "fully operational," meaning all bugs had been eliminated from the system and that it was ready to deploy. As it turned out, however, the president's declaration was premature, since NASA had not yet finished developing the shuttle. Despite this problem, the president's declaration led to "relentless pressure on NASA to launch shuttle missions on an accelerated schedule" (p. 221). This pressure in turn led NASA officials to overlook evidence of problems in the O-ring design.

Morton Thiokol was also to blame for the *Challenger* disaster. Thiokol tests in the 1970s indicated problems with the O-ring seal design. The company reported these problems to NASA but said they were no cause for concern. Engineers at NASA's Marshall Space Flight Center reported similar problems in the late 1970s, more than six years before the disaster. One 1978 memo warned the O-ring seal design could produce "hot gas leaks and resulting catastrophic failure" (p. 225). Marshall mangers didn't transmit these concerns to higher NASA officials. However, in 1982, Marshall managers finally did classify the O-ring seals as a hazard but called them an "acceptable risk." In 1985, Marshall and Thiokol engineers repeatedly warned that the O-ring design could cause a catastrophe. High-level officials at both NASA and Thiokol ignored these warnings and certified the O-ring seals as safe. To do otherwise would have scuttled the shuttle and reduced Thiokol's profits (Boisjoly, Curtis, and Mellican 1992).

The launch of the *Challenger* was set for January 28, 1986. With very cold weather predicted, Thiokol engineers became concerned that the O-rings would become brittle and even more risky. On the 27th they aired their concerns to Marshall officials, who reacted hostilely and pressured Thiokol officials into overriding their engineers' concerns and into recommending that the launch proceed. The *Challenger* went up the next day and seconds later exploded in a ball of flame, killing everyone on board.

Political Corruption

There are two major forms of political corruption. In the first, public officials misuse their office for personal economic gain. These officials are at the local, state, and national levels of government. Most commonly they accept bribes and kickbacks for favors they give businesses and individuals. These favors include approving the purchase of goods and services from certain companies and handing construction contracts to other companies. This form of graft goes back at least to the last century, when public officials in the major U.S. cities were notorious for corruption, documented by muckraker Lincoln Steffens in his famous book, *The Shame of the Cities*, in which he detailed corruption in many cities, including Chicago, Minneapolis, New York, Philadelphia, Pittsburgh, and St. Louis. Perhaps the worst offender was William March "Boss" Tweed, the head of New York City's Democratic party organization after the Civil War. Tweed and his associates robbed New York of up to $200 million in a ten-year span, as more than two-thirds of every municipal contract went into their pockets (Hershkowitz 1977).

Many politicians might be corrupt or otherwise unethical, but only a few are prosecuted. Much political corruption remains hidden, while other corruption might be suspected but tolerated as something "they all do." Interestingly, some evidence emerged in the mid-1990s that the race and ethnicity of politicians might also affect whether they're prosecuted for corruption.

The cabinet appointed by President Bill Clinton in 1993 included 14 members, six of them African-American or Hispanic. By 1996, four of the six minority cabinet members had been investigated for possible ethics violations, compared to none of the white members. In one case, Secretary of Agriculture Michael Espy, an African-American, resigned in 1995 after he'd been accused of accepting illegal contributions from the Tyson Foods corporation. In another, the secretary of Housing and Urban Development, a Hispanic, was investigated for lying to the FBI about money he had reportedly given to a woman with whom he was having an affair.

Through 1995, 70 members of Congress had been prosecuted for alleged corruption since 1970. Of these, 15 percent were minorities, even though minorities comprised only about 4 percent of all members of Congress during this time. In one case, Mel Reynolds, an African-American representative from Illinois was sentenced to five years in prison for having sex with a minor. Yet at least three other representatives, all white, were accused of similar charges since 1980 and either were not prosecuted or were else treated much more leniently than Reynolds. Another investigation involved California Representative Walter R. Tucker III, also an African-American, who was convicted in December 1995 for accepting and seeking bribes while he was mayor of Compton, California.

An attorney from Illinois commented, "They went after Mel Reynolds because he was uppity. I know this is a crime that is often reported to the police, often reported to the state's attorney, and seldom prosecuted." Abner Mikva, an attorney who served as White House counsel for President Clinton, noted that African-American officials accused of corruption "aren't doing anything that everybody else isn't doing. But they get caught because they're black." The U.S. attorney for Washington, D.C. disagreed, saying that minority politicians had not been singled out for prosecution during his 15 years working as a U.S. prosecutor.

One of the most famous national scandals, Teapot Dome, occurred under the administration of President Warren G. Harding in the early 1920s. The secretary of the interior, Albert B. Fall, took bribes in 1922 of more than $400,000 for leasing government-owned oil fields to private oil companies. Fall then resigned in 1923 to join one of the companies. He was convicted in 1929 of accepting a bribe, fined $100,000, and sentenced to one year in prison. Harding's attorney general was tried but not convicted in 1926 for other corruption. In yet another scandal, the director and legal adviser of Harding's Veterans Bureau were accused of embezzling bureau funds. The director was convicted and imprisoned, while the legal adviser committed suicide (Noggle 1965).

In this century, former Vice President Spiro Agnew undoubtedly holds the dubious honor for the most celebrated political corruption for personal economic gain. During the 1960s, Agnew was a Baltimore County executive and then Maryland's governor. Baltimore County grew rapidly during that time, with many roads, highways, bridges, and sewers built. Contractors and engineering and architectural firms kicked back as much as 5 percent of their contracts to Agnew and other officials who approved the contracts. Agnew continued to receive these kickbacks when he was governor and later vice president. He eventually resigned in 1971, pleaded no contest to one charge of income tax evasion. His punishment was a fine of $10,000 (far less than the $80,000 in kickbacks he took just as vice president) and three years' probation (Cohen and Witcover 1974). His bust now sits in the Capitol in Washington, D.C.

In the second form of political corruption, political officials misuse their office for political power and influence. There are too many examples of such corruption, including campaign fraud, to recount here, but the most celebrated examples of the last quarter-century, the Watergate and Iran-Contra scandals, do deserve some mention.

The Watergate scandal, of course, is well known. It began with a mysterious burglary in June 1972 at Democratic party headquarters in the Watergate office complex and hotel in Washington, D.C. and two years later toppled President Nixon and many of his chief aides and Cabinet members, including former U.S. Attorney General John Mitchell. It involved illegal campaign contributions in the millions from corporations and wealthy individuals, dirty tricks against potential Democratic nominees for president, lie after lie to the Congress and the public, obstruction of justice, and the secret wiretapping of people critical of the Nixon presidency (Bernstein and Woodward 1974).

A decade later the Iran-Contra scandal occurred and had the potential for toppling the Reagan presidency. The scandal involved key figures in the upper levels of the U.S. government, including CIA Director William Casey, National Security Council advisers John Poindexter and Robert McFarlane, and their aide, Colonel Oliver North. They and others had helped supply weapons to Iran in exchange for the release of hostages held in Lebanon. The money gained from the Iranian arms sales was then used illegally to supply weapons and other materials to the Contras in Nicaragua, a group of right-wing rebels trying to overthrow the left-wing, democratically elected Nicaraguan government. The arming of the Contras in this manner violated congressional prohibitions on Contra funding. Some of the illegal funds for the Contras also came from drug smuggling in Latin America that was aided and abetted by military and CIA officials. There is strong evidence that President Reagan knew of and approved the arms sale to Iran, even though at times he denied any such knowledge. North and other officials later lied to Congress (Arnson 1989; Cohen and Mitchell 1988).

HATE CRIME

Hate crimes are crimes of violence or property committed against individuals or groups because of their race, ethnicity, religion, national origin, disability, or sexual orientation. The key factor that distinguishes hate crime from "normal" violent or property crime is the motive of the offender(s). If the offender's motivation includes prejudice or hostility based on the victim's race, religion, and the like, then it is a hate crime (Hamm 1994; Jenness and Broad 1997).

Defined this way, hate crimes have always been with us. In this country, they go back at least until the 1600s, when Puritans in Massachusetts Bay Colony hanged Quakers (Brinton 1952). These hangings were official government actions motivated by religious hostility against people of a different faith. Although the term "hate crime" had not yet been coined in the days of slave holding, lynchings of African-Americans, and killings of Native Americans, the racial hostility underlying these acts classifies them as hate crimes.

Although whites are sometimes themselves the victims of racially motivated hate crime, most hate crime is committed by dominant or established groups against people perceived as different, many of them without power or at least statistically in the minority (Brown 1990). Thus, whites have committed hate crimes against people of color, long-time citizens against immigrants, Protestants against Catholics, non-Jews against Jews, and heterosexuals against homosexuals. Sometimes hate crime takes the form of mob violence. Between 1830 and 1860, the major U.S. cities were racked by dozens of riots, many of them begun by native white Protestants who attacked blacks, immigrants, Mormons, Catholics, and other non-WASP groups (Feldberg 1980).

Most hate crimes, however, are committed by organized groups or by individuals, not by mobs. The most notorious hate group in U.S. history is the Ku Klux

Klan (KKK), which over the years lynched many blacks and also terrorized Catholics, Jews, and other groups (Tolnay and Beck 1995). Although the KKK is commonly associated with the South, it has also had a strong presence elsewhere in the United States. For example, in the 1920s the KKK numbered some 550,000 members in New England. During that time, notes historian C. Stewart Doty (1994), KKK rallies with thousands of members occurred across the region. Franco-Americans were a major target of these rallies, as their immigrant status and Catholic religion angered the Protestants who made up the KKK. According to Doty, during these rallies Franco-Americans would darken their houses and hide under beds and in closets to avoid Klan violence.

A relatively new hate group with roots in the terrible experience of the Nazi Holocaust is the neo-Nazis, including Skinheads (Hamm 1995). Skinhead gangs, typically composed of working-class young men and also some women, first formed in England in the 1970s but had spread to the United States, Germany, and other European nations by the 1980s.

Individuals can also commit hate crimes. One particularly repulsive such crime occurred at a suburban Tampa, Florida, shopping plaza in January 1993. Two young white men attacked Christopher Wilson, an African-American tourist from New York City and forced him to drive to a nearby field. They then poured gasoline on him and laughed as they ignited him. Almost 40 percent of Wilson's body was burned. The judge who sentenced the men to life in prison called their crime one of the most horrible he'd ever seen. Wilson told the judge that he still had pain and nightmares from the crime and that he was no longer able to work or go outside in the sun (Martinez 1993).

As this example suggests, hate crimes are not just a thing of the past. The KKK, though much smaller than 70 years ago, is still with us. In January 1994 it held eight rallies in southern and other state capitals to protest Martin Luther King Day

◄ Skinhead gangs promote hatred of Jews, African-Americans, gays, and other groups.

(Southern Poverty Law Center 1994c). Other far-right, paramilitary hate groups have appeared in the last few decades (Mullins 1993). One specific type of hate crime, violence against lesbians and gay men, has attracted particular attention in recent years. In response to this violence, gay and lesbian communities throughout the United States have established anti-violence projects that provide evidence of assaults on gays and lesbians to law enforcement authorities and sponsor crisis intervention and victim-assistance programs to help lesbians and gays who have been assaulted (Jenness and Broad 1997).

Because hate crime is vastly underreported, the true number of hate crimes remains unknown. In 1990, Congress passed the Hate Crime Statistics Act to improve the gathering of hate crime data, but law enforcement agencies remain slow to report these data to the FBI. Thus it is difficult to know whether hate crime is rising. According to the FBI, 7,755 hate crime incidents occurred in the United States in 1998 (Federal Bureau of Investigation 1999). This is undoubtedly a serious underestimate. The Southern Poverty Law Center (SPLC) considers hate crimes against Native Americans so underreported that it calls these citizens "hidden victims." There is evidence that crimes against Native Americans grew rapidly in the late 1980s and early 1990s (Southern Poverty Law Center 1994b). The SPLC also estimates that crimes against immigrants in the United States in the early 1990s were the highest in 70 years, or since the KKK was at its height. Three examples of such violence included the fatal beating in August 1992 of a Vietnamese-American premed student in Florida by white youths who called him "chink" and "Vietcong"; the beating in October 1992 of a Hispanic migrant worker in California by six white men wielding baseball bats; and the fatal beating in August 1993 of a Cambodian immigrant in Massachusetts by twelve men (Southern Poverty Law Center 1994a).

 CRIME AGAINST GOVERNMENT

The repression, experimentation, and other crimes just discussed form only one side of the political crime picture. The other part consists of crimes by individuals and organizations opposed to government and other established interests. The motivation for their criminality is largely ideological: They want to change the existing order (Turk 1982). The strong political convictions underlying their illegal behavior leads some scholars to call them "convictional criminals" (Schafer 1974). These political criminals can be on the left side of the political spectrum, or on the right. They can be violent or nonviolent. They usually act as members of organized protest groups, but they can also act alone.

Whatever form it takes, crime against government is an important part of the dissent occurring in most societies. Some of the most important people in world history—Socrates, Jesus, Joan of Arc, Sir Thomas More, Mahatma Gandhi, and Martin Luther King, Jr., to name just a few—were political criminals who were arrested, tried, imprisoned, and, in some cases, executed for opposing the state. Though condemned at the time, their illegality contributed to the freedom of thought many societies enjoy today, and history now honors them for opposing oppression and arbitrary power (for a similar view, see Durkheim 1962 [1895]).

Of course, not all crime against government is so admirable. History is also filled with terrorism and other political violence where innocent victims die. Other illegal dissent has evoked sharply different reactions at the time it occurred. In the civil rights movement, for example, many white Southerners condemned civil rights protest as anarchy and Communism, while most Northerners saw southern governments and police as the real criminals. Vietnam antiwar protest aroused similar passions pro and con. When David Miller burned his draft card in October 1965 and became the first person prosecuted for doing so, many authorities and editorial writers condemned his action as unpatriotic and even traitorous. In a quite different response, critics of the Vietnam War considered Miller's action "the highest expression of loyalty," as one antiwar leader put it, and an attempt "to illustrate the urgency of the situation and his own personal refusal to collaborate with government policy" (Gray 1970:99).

Whether we favor or oppose a particular crime against government obviously depends on our own ideological views. Some of us may liken political criminals to common lawbreakers, while others may consider them heroes. With that in mind, let's turn to some of the many crimes against government that have highlighted social change efforts.

Mass Political Violence: Rebellion, Riots, Terrorism

Individuals and groups often commit terrorism and other political violence to change the status quo. While it is tempting to think of this violence as irrational acts of demented minds, its motivation and purpose are quite rational: to force established interests to grant social and political reforms or even to give up power altogether. In this sense, mass political violence is no less rational, and its users no more deranged, than is true for the government violence discussed earlier. The people ordering and committing government violence know exactly what they are doing, and so do the people committing violence against government. As sociologist Charles Tilly (1989:62) observes,

> As comforting as it is for civilized people to think of barbarians as violent and of violence as barbarian, western civilization and various forms of collective violence have always clung to each other.... People seeking to seize, hold, or realign the levers of power have continually engaged in collective violence as part of their struggles. The oppressed have struck in the name of justice, the privileged in the name of order, those between in the name of fear. Great shifts in the arrangements of power have ordinarily produced—and have often depended on—exceptional moments of collective violence.

As Tilly notes, violence can be effective. Just as governments and other established interests can cement their power through violence, so can opposition groups gain power and force reforms through violence (Gamson 1990). This is said not to justify either kind of political violence, but rather to grant the method to the madness that many of us may see in either kind.

Not surprisingly, mass political violence has deep historical roots. "Long before our own time," Tilly (1989:65) notes, "Europeans were airing and settling their grievances in violent ways." Peasant revolts were quite common in preindustrial Europe, with labor riots replacing them after industrialization (Berce 1990). Agrarian revolts also marked early U.S. history. Perhaps the first was led by Nathaniel Bacon in Virginia in the late 1600s (which burned Jamestown); this was followed by such revolts as Shays' Rebellion in Massachusetts in 1786–1787 and the Whiskey Rebellion in Pennsylvania in 1794. There was also a spurt of farmer revolts after the Civil War and in the early 1900s. Historian Richard Maxwell Brown (1989:45) writes that these agrarian revolts "formed one of the longest and most enduring chronicles in the history of American reform—one that was often violent."

Often the targets of violence, Native Americans and the labor movement were violent themselves, usually in self-defense, as they fought back when assaulted. The famous massacre of General George Armstrong Custer and more than 200 soldiers at Little Bighorn in Montana is a famous example, as it came after Custer entered Indian territory to capture Sioux and Cheyenne and forcibly move them to reservations. He encountered the largest gathering of Native Americans in Western history and attacked them. After one hour of fierce fighting, the Indian warriors prevailed, and Custer and his men lay dead (Connell 1988).

Violent labor strife was common in the many strikes in the United States after the Civil War. The strikes themselves, writes historian Brown (1989:46), resulted from "the unyielding attitude of capitalists in regard to wages, hours, and working conditions." Workers often turned to violence to protect themselves when police and company guards used violence to suppress strikes, but they also rioted and used other violence as a more "proactive" tactic to force concessions. One of the most violent labor groups was the Molly Maguires, a secret organization of Irish miners in 1870s Pennsylvania who murdered company officials and committed terrorism. They took their name from an Irish folk hero said to have led a peasant revolt in the 1600s (Broehl 1964).

Over the years, African-Americans have also used violence to improve their lot. The first slave uprising occurred in New York City in 1712, and several more slave uprisings occurred before slavery ended with the Civil War. The most famous took place in Virginia in 1831 and was led by Nat Turner, later memorialized in William Styron's acclaimed 1967 novel, *The Confessions of Nat Turner* (Styron 1967). Turner's rebellion involved more than 60 slaves who killed some 60 whites, including the family of Turner's owner. Twenty of the slaves, including Turner, were later hanged, and some 100 other slaves who had not participated in the revolt were also murdered by vengeful whites (Oates 1983).

African-Americans have also rioted in major U.S. cities in this century. This was a change from the past, when many cities in the 1800s and early 1900s were the scenes of race riots begun by whites, who typically encountered no resistance as they beat and slaughtered blacks (Feldberg 1980). The celebrated report of the federal Kerner Commission (1968:21) on the 1960s riots recalled one such race riot in St. Louis in 1917. "[S]treetcars were stopped, and Negroes, without regard to age or sex, were pulled off and stoned, clubbed and kicked, and mob leaders calmly shot and killed Negroes who were lying in blood in the street. As the victims were placed in an ambulance, the crowds cheered and applauded."

Beginning in the early 1900s, blacks began to fight back when attacked by white mobs, and antiblack riots were met by a violent black response in cities such as Chicago and Washington, D.C. in 1919 and, later, Detroit in 1943. In the 1960s, African-American urban violence assumed a new character as blacks struck out against white-owned businesses and white police and National Guard in cities such as Chicago, Cleveland, Los Angeles, Philadelphia, and Newark. These riots were met with lethal force and a massive legal response but led to increased federal funding to urban areas and other gains for African-Americans (Button 1989).

Despite depictions in the news media of the rioters as alienated, unemployed "riffraff," numerous studies found them strongly rooted in, and largely representative of, the black urban community as a whole (Fogelson 1971). Many scholars viewed these riots as small-scale political revolts stemming from blacks' anger over their poverty and other aspects of racial oppression by a white society (Balbus 1977). Reflecting this view, the Kerner Commission (1968:1) blamed the 1960s riots on economic inequality and institutionalized racism and observed in a now-famous statement, "Our nation is moving toward two societies, one black, one white—separate and unequal." Little has changed since the 1960s to alter the Kerner Commission's fundamental conclusion (Massey, Gross, and Shibuya 1994).

Political scientist Richard E. Rubenstein (1970) notes that the United States has long been characterized by a "myth of peaceful progress." According to this myth, deprived groups in U.S. history make social and economic gains by working within the electoral system. This myth has at least two consequences: (1) blacks and other deprived groups who use violence are seen as historically abnormal; and (2) the reasons for their violence are seen to lie in their personal inadequacies rather than in social and economic inequality. Looking at the expanse of U.S. history, Rubenstein counters that the myth of peaceful progress is just that—a myth: "For more than two hundred years, from the Indian wars and farmer uprisings of the eighteenth century to the labor-management and racial disturbances of the twentieth, the United States has experienced regular episodes of serious mass violence related to the social, political and economic objectives of insurgent groups" (p. 7). Against this historical backdrop, he says, the 1960s' urban riots and other episodes of insurgent violence over the years are hardly atypical, and instead are quite understandable as normal, if extreme, responses to racial and economic deprivation.

TERRORISM

If revolts and riots are often hard for us to understand, terrorism is even more baffling, since it usually involves the killing and maiming of innocent bystanders. Wartime violence is understandable, if tragic, since the soldiers being killed and wounded are socially sanctioned as legitimate targets. But the innocent lives lost through terrorism are seen as *senseless* killings that fill us with rage. This was the common reaction in the United States after the two most vicious terrorist acts against U.S. citizens in the late 1980s and early 1990s, both of which were carried out by Middle Eastern forces: the December 1988 bombing of Pan Am flight 103 over Scotland that killed 270 passengers, crew, and people on the ground (Schmidt 1993); and the February 1993 bombing of the World Trade Center in New York City that killed 6 people and injured more than 1,000 (Dwyer 1994).

Our fury over these acts, however, paled in comparison to what we felt after the April 1995 bombing of the Federal Building in Oklahoma City that killed 169 people, including many children in a day care center. Despite widespread speculation in the bombing's aftermath that Middle Eastern terrorists were again at fault, it turned out that the alleged bombers were "homegrown" U.S. citizens linked to right-wing militia groups who hated the federal government (Grunwald and Kranish 1995). This bombing, occurring as it did in the heart of the United States and involving so much destruction and loss of life, including children, was perhaps the most senseless terrorist act of all.

It's easy to view terrorism as the act of irrational, demented minds, but such a view would obscure the rational, political purposes of terrorism, which is best seen as a strategy, however horrible and desperate, for achieving political goals (Barkan and Snowden 2001). This understanding of terrorism is reflected in its definition: "the use of unexpected violence to intimidate or coerce people in the pursuit of political or social objectives" (Gurr 1989:201). The motivation here is to frighten or demoralize one's political targets or the public at large. Such terrorism, political scientist Ted Robert Gurr (1989) points out, has played an important role in U.S. history. In this regard, we have already discussed one type of terrorism, *state terrorism*, in which governments use the police and other agents to repress their citizenry through violent means. As we saw, state terrorism is common in totalitarian nations but has also occurred in the United States. Gurr (1989) identifies a second type of

◄ *In April 1995 a bomb at the Federal Building in Oklahoma City killed 168 people. Two men with ties to right-wing militia groups were arrested and prosecuted for their role in the bombing.*

terrorism, *vigilante terrorism*, that is initiated by private groups against other private groups to preserve the status quo. Much vigilante terrorism takes the form of hate crime as discussed previously. The systematic use of violence by the Ku Klux Klan and other right-wing hate groups is thus a prime example of vigilante terrorism, as were the shootings and bombings of 1960s Southern civil rights workers. More recent examples of vigilante terrorism include the bombings of abortion and family planning clinics and the murders of physicians performing abortions (Clemetson and Gegax 1998). Many feminists also consider rape and battering to be a form of vigilante terrorism against women (Chapter 10).

A third type of political terrorism, and the one falling under the "crime against government" rubric now being discussed, is *insurgent terrorism*, which is "directed against public authorities for the purpose of bringing about radical political change" (Gurr 1989:209). The violence involved includes bombings, shootings, kidnapping, and hijacking, and its targets include public figures, the general public, public buildings, and public transportation.

Insurgent terrorism from the left side of the political spectrum has characterized many periods of protest in U.S. history. Indeed, much of the colonists' violence in the Revolutionary War period is best regarded as terrorism (Brown 1989). A major goal of the colonists was to intimidate the Tories living in the colonies who supported England. Tarring and feathering of Tories was a common tactic. This was, of course, far less lethal than bombing them, but should still be considered a terrorist act. The colonists also engaged in "savage guerrilla warfare, desperate hit-and-run forays, and the thrust and counterthrust of pillage and mayhem" against the British forces occupying colonial cities (Brown 1989:25). As historian Richard Maxwell Brown (1989:25) observes, during this period "the meanest and most squalid sort of violence was put to the service of revolutionary ideals and objectives." No doubt the British regarded the colonial terrorists as the basest of criminals, while the colonists opposing Britain considered them freedom fighters.

Insurgent terrorism has distinguished other periods of protest since the colonial days. Some of the labor violence discussed earlier can be considered insurgent terrorism; the Molly Maguires in particular were a terrorist organization. More recently, insurgent terrorism marked the U.S. landscape in the late 1960s and early 1970s. In northern cities, the Black Liberation Army and other African-American militants ambushed and murdered 26 police officers between 1970 and 1973 (Gurr 1989). Out of the Vietnam antiwar and "New Left" movements of the 1960s grew a group called the Weathermen, later called the Weather Underground. It first organized the "Days of Rage" in Chicago in October 1969, during which a few hundred antiwar militants committed vandalism and fought with police. The Weather Underground soon turned to terrorism and bombed the New York police headquarters in June 1970, the Capitol in March 1971, and the Pentagon in May 1972. Although the Weather Underground faded by the mid-1970s, some former members bombed other public buildings in the 1980s and took part in an October 1981 armed robbery of a Brink's truck in which a guard was killed (Gurr 1989).

The Weather Underground inspired other, smaller terrorist groups, most of them in California, including the New World Liberation Front, which committed some 30 bombings in 1974 and 1975 against International Telephone and Telegraph and Pacific Gas and Electric. Another terrorist group that arose was the Symbionese Liberation Army, which murdered Oakland's superintendent of schools in 1973 and, in its most celebrated act, kidnapped newspaper heiress Patty Hearst in 1974 (Gurr 1989).

Puerto Rican nationalists have also engaged in terrorism over the years to press their call for independence for Puerto Rico. Two nationalists tried to assassinate President Truman in 1950, and four others shot and wounded five U.S. representatives in the Capitol in 1954. Nationalists committed almost 300 terrorist acts in the United States and Puerto Rico from 1970 to 1988. One nationalist group exploded several bombs in New York City in the mid-1970s and a few dozen more in New York and other cities in the late 1970s and early 1980s (Gurr 1989).

Although, historically, much insurgent terrorism has been committed by left-wing groups and individuals, the Oklahoma City bombing was reportedly an instance of insurgent terrorism by people with right-wing views and reflected an increase in anti-government violence by far-right groups since the 1980s (Mullins 1993). These right-wing groups, says Bruce Hoffman (1993:222), a terrorism expert with the RAND Corporation, are "extremist, white supremacist paramilitary groups oriented toward 'survivalism,' outdoor skills, guerrilla training, and outright sedition." They are "extremely violent," Hoffman (p. 220) notes, and "have no reservations about killing." They call Jews and people of color the "children of Satan" and consider the United States the Promised Land for white Anglo-Saxons. Unlike past U.S. terrorist groups, they're very skilled in the use of weapons and explosives.

Despite the history of left-wing terrorism in the United States, Hoffman (p. 224) says that right-wing supremacist groups now pose "the most serious threat.... Although one might be inclined to dismiss the members of these groups as intemperate hot-heads, country bumpkins, or mentally unstable alarmists, they have demonstrated that they are serious in their beliefs and dedicated to their causes—and that they are willing to use violence in pursuit of their goals" (p. 224). The Oklahoma City bombing, occurring several years after Hoffman made this observation, indicates his warning was no mere exaggeration.

Outside the United States, some of the most violent and widespread insurgent terrorism has occurred in Israel and Northern Ireland. In Israel, Palestinian nationalists have bombed busses, public buildings, and other targets to protest Israeli annexation of Palestinian land (Cobban 1985), while in Northern Ireland and England the Provisional Irish Republican Army has used similar terrorist tactics in its continuing campaign for Irish independence (Cullen 1996).

POLITICAL ASSASSINATION

A related form of political violence is political assassination, or the murder of public figures for political reasons. Political assassinations are often part of a larger campaign of political terrorism, but they also are sometimes committed by lone individuals bearing a political grudge. Murders of public figures are considered *political* assassinations only if they are politically motivated. If someone assassinates a public figure out of jealousy or because of mental illness, the act is not a political assassination and therefore not a political crime as conceived here.

Political assassination has a long history. One of its most famous victims was Roman dictator Julius Caesar, killed by a group including his friend Brutus and memorialized in Shakespeare's famous play. Moving much forward in European history, the assassination of Archduke Ferdinand of Austria in 1914 helped start World War I.

The list of public figures assassinated just in my lifetime is dismaying. It includes Medgar Evers, southern civil rights leader; Indira Ghandi, prime minister of India; John F. Kennedy; Robert Kennedy; Martin Luther King, Jr.; Malcolm X; Yitzhak Rabin, prime minister of Israel; Anwar Sadat, president of Egypt; and Joseph Yablonski, United Mine Workers activist. Two lesser known figures, San Francisco Mayor George Moscone and Supervisor Harvey Milk, were assassinated in late November 1978 by a former supervisor with personal and political grudges. I was living near San Francisco at the time and will never forget how the whole Bay Area seemed to stop in mourning, as department stores even saw a sharp drop in Christmas shopping. In addition to this list of assassination victims, several other figures in the United States were the targets of would-be assassins in the last three decades. Former Georgia Governor George Wallace was paralyzed by an assassin's bullet in 1972; President Gerald Ford suffered two assassination attempts only weeks apart in 1975; and President Ronald Reagan almost died from an assassination attempt in 1981.

When political assassinations occur, a common reaction is that the assassins must have been mentally ill individuals suffering from delusions of persecution and grandeur and other psychiatric problems. This view goes back at least to the 1843 assassination by Daniel M'Naughton of Edward Drummond, private secretary to England's Prime Minister Sir Robert Peel. M'Naughton had intended to murder Peel but mistook the secretary for the prime minister. He was later found not guilty by reason of insanity and institutionalized until he died a natural death. The insanity verdict, writes sociologist Richard Moran (1981), obscured the political nature of M'Naughton's crime. M'Naughton was in fact involved in working-class activism and blamed Peel for the miserable conditions confronting the English poor. He had seen Drummond entering and leaving Peel's office and quite reasonably assumed, there being no TV at the time, that Drummond was Peel. Given this political context, the insanity verdict "served to discredit Daniel M'Naughton and the political ideas he represented by interpreting his act as the product of a diseased mind. The widespread political problems that the Tory government was experiencing throughout Britain were reduced to a personal problem plaguing Daniel M'Naughton" (Moran 1977:22–23).

Political scientist James W. Clarke (1982) calls the view that political assassins are mentally ill the "pathological theory of assassination" and says it is largely a myth. He adds that "probably no group of political actors is more poorly understood than American assassins" (p. 4). In a study of 15 attempted or completed assassinations of U.S. Presidents and other national figures involving 16 assassins, Clarke concluded that only three were insane. Of the remainder, five, including John Wilkes Booth, assassin of President Abraham Lincoln, and Sirhan Sirhan, assassin of Robert Kennedy, were very rational and very politically motivated. The rest suffered from various personal problems they thought their assassinations would ease, but they were by no means insane.

Civil Disobedience

Civil disobedience is the violation of law for reasons of conscience. It is usually nonviolent and public. In the classic act of civil disobedience, protesters violate a law they consider morally unjust and then wait to be arrested. Political and legal philosophers have long debated the definition and justification of civil disobedience in a democratic society, but that debate lies beyond our scope (Cohen 1971; Hall 1971). Instead I'd like to sketch the history of civil disobedience in the United States to give some idea of its use to bring about social change.

Here I should first distinguish between direct and indirect civil disobedience. *Direct* civil disobedience is the "violation of a law which is itself considered morally unjust" (Hall 1971:31). This is how civil disobedience is usually conceived, and many scholars consider it the only "proper" kind of civil disobedience in a democratic society. The famous refusal in 1955 of Rosa Parks to move to the back of a bus in Montgomery, Alabama, was a striking example of direct civil disobedience that helped spark the Southern civil rights movement. *Indirect* civil disobedience is the "violation of a law for reasons of conscience where the law violated is not itself considered immoral" (Hall 1971:31). The people involved typically want to publicize their political and moral grievances and to arouse public opinion in their favor. When South Africa still had apartheid, students at campuses across the country were arrested at sit-ins to protest their universities' investments in corporations operating in that nation (Rodden 1977). These sit-ins were acts of indirect civil disobedience.

The idea of civil disobedience goes back at least to ancient Greece. After the death of King Oedipus, according to Greek mythology, his two sons, Eteocles and Polynices, killed each other in a battle for the throne. The new king, Creon, considered Polynices a traitor and ordered that he not be given a proper burial. His sister, Antigone, thought this order violated divine law and defiantly buried Polynices. In response, Creon sentenced her to death. She soon disappeared, and Greek mythology differs on whether she was executed, committed suicide, or fled (Bushnell 1988). The ancient Greek philosopher Socrates was also sentenced to death for conscientiously defying the state: His "crime" was teaching unorthodox religious views. After his sentence, he declined several opportunities to escape from prison, and eventually drank a cup of hemlock and died (Stone 1989). Both Antigone and Socrates remain symbols of courageous, conscientious resistance to unjust state authority.

Civil disobedience also appears in the Bible. In the New Testament, Jesus' disciples disobeyed government orders to stop their teachings, as they felt their loyalty was to God rather than to the state. Jesus himself can also be regarded as a civil disobedient who died for refusing state orders to stop his religious teaching. The conflict between religious belief and state decrees continued to be addressed in the medieval period, when Christian theologian Saint Thomas Aquinas wrote in the 1200s that people are obligated to disobey the laws of the state when they conflict with the law and will of God (Kenny 1983).

A few centuries later, Sir Thomas More was executed for practicing this obligation. More was lord chancellor, the highest judicial authority in England, from 1529 to 1532. During that time, King Henry VIII wanted a divorce so that he could marry Anne Boleyn. The Pope refused to grant permission. More resigned his post to protest the King's actions. Two years later he was imprisoned for refusing to take an oath that the King ranked higher than other rulers, including the Pope, and was beheaded in July 1535 (Kenny 1983). Like Antigone and Socrates, More remains a symbol of conscientious resistance to state authority, and his courageous defiance became the subject of the award-winning play and film, *A Man for All Seasons* (Bolt 1962).

Disobedience to the law for religious reasons continued during colonial America, as pacifist Quakers refused to pay taxes to support the colonial effort in the war against England (Brock 1968). Depending on how civil disobedience is defined, many of the colonists' acts of resistance to British rule can also be considered civil disobedience. One of the earliest and most famous nonviolent instances of this resistance occurred in the 1730s, when John Peter Zenger's newspaper criticized the New York royal governor and Zenger was prosecuted for seditious libel. Even though the law clearly stated that it was illegal to publish any statement, however true, that criticized the British government, the colonial jury found Zenger not guilty, and their verdict helped establish freedom of the press in the colonies and later in the new nation (Finkelman 1981).

A major event in the history of civil disobedience occurred in 1849 with the publication of Henry David Thoreau's famous essay on the subject (Thoreau 1969). Thoreau had spent a night in jail in 1846 for refusing to pay taxes to protest slavery and the Mexican War, and the essay arose from a public lecture he gave in 1848 to justify his tax resistance.

Thoreau's essay is one of the most famous in U.S. history and had a profound influence on such important literary and political figures as Leo Tolstoy, Mahatma Gandhi, and Martin Luther King, Jr. Thoreau began his essay by saying, "I heartily accept the motto—'That government is best which governs least'" (p. 27), and went on to ask, "Unjust laws exist: Shall we be content to obey them, or shall we endeavor to amend them, and obey them until we have succeeded, or shall we transgress them at once" (p. 34)? Answering his own question, Thoreau continued that if a law "is of such a nature that it requires you to be the agent of injustice to another, then, I say, break the law. Let your life be a counter friction to stop the machine" of government (p. 35). He added, "Under a government which imprisons any unjustly, the true place for a just man [and woman] is also a prison" (p. 37).

The abolitionist period during which Thoreau wrote was marked by the systematic use of nonviolent civil disobedience against the 1850 Fugitive Slave Law that required citizens to help capture and return runaway slaves and prohibited interfering with their capture. In response, abolitionists were arrested for helping slaves escape in the South and for obstructing their capture or freeing them once imprisoned in the North. Northern juries often acquitted abolitionists in the trials that resulted (Friedman 1971).

One of the most celebrated acts of civil disobedience in the nineteenth century occurred in November 1872 when suffragist Susan B. Anthony voted in violation of a federal law prohibiting people from voting when they had no right to vote. As a woman, Anthony was not allowed to vote, and thus her 1872 vote violated the law. During the next few months, Anthony gave more than 50 speeches in upstate New York criticizing the lack of women's suffrage. At her June 1873 trial in Canandaigua, New York, the judge, Supreme Court Justice Ward Hunt, refused to let her say a single word in her defense and ordered the jury to find her guilty. Before sentencing, he did permit Anthony to say a now-famous statement that attracted wide attention and ended with the stirring words, "I shall earnestly and persistently continue to urge all women to the practical recognition of the old revolutionary maxim, 'Resistance to tyranny is obedience to God.'" Anthony's civil disobedience and subsequent trial are widely credited with helping to advance the right of women to vote (Barry 1988).

Moving forward almost a century, nonviolent civil disobedience was the key strategy of the southern civil rights movement. Rosa Parks's heroic refusal to move to the back of the bus was only the beginning of civil disobedience aimed at protesting and ending segregation. Southern blacks were arrested for sitting-in at segregated lunch counters, libraries, and movie theaters and for "kneeling-in" at segregated churches. They were also arrested countless times for peacefully marching after being unfairly denied parade permits (Chong 1991).

One such arrest landed Martin Luther King, Jr. in jail in Birmingham, Alabama, where he wrote an essay, "Letter from Birmingham City Jail," that rivals Thoreau's essay in its fame and influence. King began his "Letter" by detailing Birmingham's notorious segregation and reviewing the civil rights movement's legal efforts to end it. Justifying his decision to violate a city injunction prohibiting peaceful marches, King distinguished between just and unjust laws and said, "Any law that degrades human personality is unjust. All segregation statutes are unjust because segregation distorts the soul and damages the personality" (King

▲ *Acts of civil disobedience by Rosa Parks and Martin Luther King, Jr. helped start and propel the southern civil rights movement.*

1969:77). He continued, "Now there is nothing wrong with an ordinance which requires a permit for a parade, but when the ordinance is used to preserve segregation and to deny citizens the First Amendment privilege of peaceful assembly and peaceful protest, then it becomes unjust" (p. 78).

Commenting further on civil disobedience, King wrote, "One who breaks an unjust law must do it *openly*, *lovingly* … and with a willingness to accept the penalty. I submit that an individual who breaks a law that conscience tells him is unjust, and willingly accepts the penalty by staying in jail to arouse the conscience of the community over its injustice, is in reality expressing the very highest respect for law" (pp. 78–79; emphasis his). He then noted, "We can never forget that everything Hitler did in Germany was 'legal'.… It was 'illegal' to aid and comfort a Jew in Hitler's Germany. But I am sure that if I had lived in Germany during that time I would have aided and comforted my Jewish brothers even though it was illegal" (p. 79).

The civil rights movement's use of nonviolent civil disobedience inspired similar protest by other social movements of the 1960s and decades since. There are too many instances to detail here, but some of the most dramatic, moving, and controversial occurred during the Vietnam War when Catholic clergy and laity burned draft files. Wearing Roman Catholic clerical clothing or otherwise dressed neatly, groups of such protesters went into several draft board offices, seized their files, took them outside and then poured blood on them or burned them and waited to be arrested while they prayed. About 30 such draft board raids occurred between 1967 and 1971 in cites such as Chicago, Minneapolis, New York, Philadelphia, and Rochester. The raids involved more than 150 Catholic priests, nuns, and lay Catholics and destroyed more than 400,000 draft files (Bannan and Bannan 1974).

The most celebrated such action occurred in May 1968 when seven men and two women burned 378 draft files with homemade napalm and awaited arrest while they joined hands and said the Lord's Prayer. A statement to the press said in part, "We confront the Catholic Church, other Christian bodies and the synagogues of America with their silence and cowardice in the face of our country's crimes.… May God have mercy on our nation" (Gray 1970:47). A meditation written by one of the participants, Father Daniel Berrigan, said in part, "Our apologies, good friends, for the fracture of good order, the burning of paper instead of children.… We have chosen to say with the gift of our liberty, if necessary our lives: The violence stops here; the death stops here; the suppression of the truth stops here; this war stops here" (Berrigan 1970:93–95). The police who arrested the Catonsville Nine, as the participants came to be called, were "shaken and courteous, awed by the sight of Roman collars" (Gray 1970:47). Although the defendants were all convicted at their subsequent trial, they were allowed to talk at great length about the Vietnam War and their reasons for opposing it. At one point, the judge told the defendants, "I would be a very funny sort of man if I had not been moved by your sincerity on the [witness] stand and by your views" (Gray 1970:218). He later allowed them to recite the Lord's Prayer in court while the jury deliberated.

The civil disobedience and criminal trials of the "ultra-resistance," as the draft board raids came to be called, received heavy media attention and helped galvanize the antiwar movement. One observer wrote, "It is a conservative estimate to say that tens of thousands were reached by the action and many of these were undoubtedly moved to more direct opposition to the war" (Zahn 1970:126). However, some members of the antiwar movement condemned the property destruction that accompanied the draft board raids (DeBenedetti and Chatfield 1990).

Blood and Hammers against Nuclear Weapons

Since the early 1980s several Catholic clergy and laity have engaged in an unusual form of civil disobedience. Members of the so-called Plowshares movement, they typically trespass onto the sites of manufacturers of nuclear weapons systems, pour their own blood on the weapons, strike at them with hammers, and then wait to be arrested. The blood symbolizes the suffering that Plowshares activists say nuclear weapons cause, while the hammering symbolizes the "beating of swords into plowshares"— from the famous Biblical passage (Isaiah 2:4) that calls for changing weapons into tools of peace.

One of the Plowshares activists is Philip Berrigan, one of the participants in the Catonsville 9 draft file burning case (see text on page 389). Berrigan has spent close to nine years in prison for his various acts of civil disobedience, including a two-year term in the late 1990s. In a recent essay, Berrigan wrote how he and other Plowshares activists were inspired by the Isaiah passage: "This prophecy, complemented by the injunction to 'love thy enemies' in Matthew and Luke, offered us inspiration and authority for resisting first strike nuclear terror. In biblical texts like these, it becomes clear that a people faithful to God is a disarmed people. You can't love your enemies at the point of a gun. Just as clearly, we cannot be disarmed as long as such weapons exist."

Another Plowshares activist is Stephen Kelley, S. J. In October 1997 he was given a two-year prison term for joining Berrigan and other Plowshares members in an act of civil disobedience at Bath Iron Works in Bath, Maine, where the group defaced a Navy destroyer capable of carrying nuclear missiles. Interviewed in prison, Father Kelley was asked how other prisoners reacted when they heard about why he was arrested. He responded, "In local jails, you overwhelmingly meet poor people and minorities from the margins of society who immediately understand why we did what we did—that it was partly in protest against the disproportionate amounts of money available for weapons of destruction, like nuclear missiles, when adequate funds for the simple basics of food, social programs, clinics and education are underfunded. They see these unmet needs in their own neighborhoods." When asked how it felt to realize that Plowshares movement activities receive little attention in the press, Father Kelley also said, "We'd all be in a mess if that were the criterion for whether we acted or not. Even if no one is listening, at least I'm not changed by a culture that focuses on the use of arms. We may not be able to change the culture, but it isn't going to dictate to me how I live out my faith."

Many people might sympathize with the concern of Plowshares activists over nuclear weapons but still criticize their means of expressing their concern. Whether we agree with their actions or not, they remind us that the nuclear age is still a threat to people across the world.

Sources: Anderson 1987; Berrigan 1998.

Espionage and Treason

A final category of crime against government is espionage and treason. Espionage, or spying, has been called the world's "second oldest profession" and has probably been with us for thousands of years (Volkman 1994). In the Old Testament, Moses sent spies into Canaan. During the Revolutionary War, George Washington used many spies to obtain information on British forces. One of them, Nathan Hale, was captured in September 1776 and executed the next day. According to legend, as you undoubtedly already know, Hale said as he was about to be hanged, "I only regret that I have but one life to lose for my country" (Johnston 1914). Schoolchildren today still learn about Hale's heroism, and espionage remains the stuff of James Bond movies and countless spy thrillers.

Today many governments employ spies, and spying by the United States and the Soviet Union was a virtual industry during the Cold War (Kessler 1988). Spies' activities, of course, are not considered crimes by the government that employs them, only by the government upon which they're spying. Today when such spies are detected and captured, they're often deported to their home country, but sometimes they're arrested, tried, and in some nations, executed.

Treason involves the aiding and abetting of a country's enemy by, for example, providing the enemy military secrets or other important information that puts the country at risk (Pincher 1987). Historically, the terms "treason" and "traitor" have been used rather loosely to condemn legitimate dissent falling far short of treacherous conduct. During much of the Vietnam War, for example, much of the country considered antiwar protest unpatriotic at best and traitorous at worst (DeBenedetti and Chatfield 1990).

Occasionally treason charges have been lodged against individuals because of their race, religion, or the like. The most famous case here, and one involving anti-Semitism, is undoubtedly the so-called Dreyfus Affair, in which Alfred Dreyfus, a Jewish French army officer, was charged in October 1894 with spying for Germany. His conviction two months later and sentence to a life term on Devil's Island aroused protests around the world. Two years later a French officer found strong evidence of Dreyfus's innocence but was ordered to do nothing about it. Dreyfus finally won a second trial in 1899, but the biased proceedings again resulted in his conviction, prompting renewed worldwide protest. France's highest court finally overturned the verdict in 1906 (Griffiths 1991).

The most famous actual traitor in U.S. history is undoubtedly Benedict Arnold, a decorated Revolutionary War general who resented what he perceived as ingratitude from the colonial government and conspired in 1780 to surrender the West Point military base he commanded to the British. When his plot was discovered, he escaped and joined the British army and led troops that burned Richmond, Virginia and New London, Connecticut (Randall 1990). Today his name in the United States is synonymous with treason.

When citizens spy on their own country, espionage and treason become the same. Some do so for ideological reasons, and some do so for money and other personal reasons (Hagan 1989). One of the most famous and controversial cases of espionage for ideological reasons resulted in the 1953 execution of Ethel and Julius Rosenberg for allegedly conspiring to supply the Soviet Union with U.S. atomic bomb secrets. The Rosenbergs were U.S. citizens and members of the Communist Party. Ethel Rosenberg's brother, a machinist helping to make an atomic bomb at Los Alamos, New Mexico, was arrested in 1950 for allegedly supplying the Soviet Union with critical information and implicated his brother-in-law, Julius. The Rosenbergs were convicted in 1951 after an emotionally charged trial and sentenced to death. Their sentence aroused protests around the world, and their innocence and the fairness of their trial are still debated today (Sharlitt 1989).

In a recent case of espionage for money, CIA operative Aldrich Ames spied for the Soviet Union as a "mole" from 1985 to 1994 and was paid or promised more than $4 million for his efforts. He gave the KGB, the Soviet CIA counterpart, the names of dozens of Soviet citizens whom the CIA had recruited. The Soviets executed ten of these people and imprisoned others. Aldrich also supplied the KGB with information about hundreds of CIA operations. Arrested in February 1994, Ames was sentenced to life in prison in April of that year (Adams 1995).

EXPLAINING AND REDUCING POLITICAL CRIME

Political crime is perhaps best seen as a consequence of power. Crime by government and other established interests is crime by those with power. Crime against government and other established interests is crime by those without power. The history of nations around the world indicates that governments are quite ready to use violence, the law, and other means to intimidate dissenters and the masses at the bottom of society. Powerful individuals within government are similarly quite ready to use their offices for personal economic gain and political influence.

If the experience of nations indicates that power promotes these sorts of crimes, it also indicates that the lack of power motivates crime and other dissent against government. Explanations of why people dissent fall into the sociological subfield of social movements. Some of these explanations emphasize social-psychological factors, while others emphasize structural ones (Diani and Porta 1999).

Social-psychological explanations emphasize emotions and other psychological states that motivate people to engage in protest. Thus people are considered more apt to protest when conditions worsen and they become more upset, or when they compare themselves to more successful groups and feel relatively deprived. Structural explanations focus on "microstructural" factors such as preexisting friendship and organizational ties: People having friends or belonging to organizations already involved in social movements are considered more likely to join themselves. Another type of structural explanation, usually called "political opportunity" theory, stresses that movements are more likely to arise when changes in the national government promise it will prove receptive or vulnerable to movement challenges.

The Social Patterning of Political Crime

So far we've said little about the race, class, and gender of the people who commit either crime by government or crime against government. Understanding political crime as a function of power helps us in turn to understand the sociodemographic makeup of the people who commit this crime. Simply put, their race, class, and gender often mirror those of the powerful and powerless in any particular society.

Thus in the United States and other Western nations, crime by government is almost always committed by white men of middle- or upper-class status, if only because privileged white men occupy almost all positions of political power in Western societies. It's true that working-class soldiers, police, and other individuals, often nonwhite and occasionally female, often carry out repression and other government crimes, but they do so in Western nations under orders from privileged white men. In non-Western nations, men are in positions of power, and race is sometimes less of a factor depending on the nation involved. However, in such nations ethnicity and/or religion often become more important, and the privileged men with political power usually belong to the dominant ethnicity or religion in the nation. Such men are thus responsible for the government crime that occurs.

The targets of government crime are typically those without power. In non-Western and Western nations alike, that often means the poor and people belonging to subordinate races, ethnicities, and religions. Which sociodemographic factor becomes most important in determining government crime targets depends on the particular society. For the Nazis, religion, nationality, and ethnicity were what mattered. They saw people not belonging to the Aryan "race" as less than human and thus suitable targets for genocide. Jews had the same skin color as Nazis but not the "correct" religion. In the United States, however, skin color has often mattered, as a similar *dehumanization* process made it possible for white Europeans to target Native Americans for slaughter. When Europeans began to take Africans to the New World as slaves, it was no accident that their skins were much darker than those of their captors. Race has also played an important role in determining the targets of vigilante terrorism and other hate crimes.

Whether race, class, or gender affects the targets of government repression in the United States has depended on the specific social movement that the government wishes to repress. The targets of repression during the labor movement were obviously working-class people, men and women, usually white but sometimes black or of other races. In the South, the victims of government crime during the civil rights movement were obviously black, though whites who supported the movement were also arrested, attacked, and sometimes murdered. During the Vietnam antiwar movement, however, the targets of surveillance and other government crime were often middle- and upper middle-class whites, since many of them were involved in the movement (Turk 1982). People from the same backgrounds were the targets of government surveillance of Central American protest groups in the 1980s and gay rights groups in early 1990s.

The targets of U.S. government experimentation often come from the ranks of the poor and nonwhite, but not always. It's difficult to imagine the government deciding to conduct the equivalent of the Tuskegee syphilis experiment on the children of corporate executives. Likewise, since most soldiers are working-class, the soldiers upon whom the government conducted its radiation and other tests did not come from the ranks of the wealthy. Yet when the government spread nuclear fallout into the air and ground water, everyone was vulnerable, white or black, male or female, rich or poor.

We've seen that most crime against government is committed by members of various social movements. Not surprisingly, the kinds of people who are the *targets* of government crime are usually the kinds of people who commit crimes *against* government. What we've said about the racial, class, and gender makeup of the targets of government crime thus applies to the makeup of the perpetrators of crime against government. In non-Western nations, they are usually the poor or members of subjugated ethnicities and religions. In Western nations, including the United States, their specific makeup depends on the particular social movement. Thus the abolitionists and women's suffragists who broke the law were white and middle-class, while labor movement activists who broke the law were working-class and mostly white but sometimes of color.

Reducing Political Crime

Compared to the literature on reducing the kinds of crimes discussed in earlier chapters, the political crime literature devotes little attention to reducing crime by or against government. Part of the reason for this inattention is that the political crime literature is relatively scant to begin with. Another reason is that political crime is so universal, both historically and cross-nationally, that it almost seems natural and inevitable. If, as I've argued, political crime is best understood as a function of power, then to reduce political crime we must reduce the disparities of power that characterize many societies. At a minimum, this means moving from authoritarian to democratic rule.

As we've seen, however, even democracies have their share of political crime, and the historical record in the United States doesn't yield much hope that crime by government and by political officials will soon end. The historical record also indicates that dissenters will turn to civil disobedience and other illegal activities as long as they perceive flawed governmental policies. One way to reduce some political crime, then, would be to reduce poverty, racial discrimination, military adventurism, and other conditions and policies that promote humanitarian dissent. It would be more difficult, however, and even anti-democratic, to change governmental policies in such as way as to placate violent militias and other groups and individuals committed to terrorism and hate crime. At a minimum, responsible political officials from all sides of the political spectrum must state in no uncertain terms their opposition to these inhumane forms of dissent.

SUMMARY AND CONCLUSION

Political crime is part of the perpetual struggle between established interests, especially the state, and forces for social change. Because of the ideological issues and goals so often at stake, political crime differs in many ways from the other kinds of crime to which criminology devotes far more attention.

Crime by government takes on many forms, including political repression involving surveillance, arrest, imprisonment, torture, and other violence. Political repression is almost a given in totalitarian societies, but occurs surprisingly often in and by democratic nations such as the United States. It's tempting to dismiss U.S. repression as historically abnormal, but there has been so much of it over the years—the examples discussed in this chapter being just the tip of the iceberg—that it would be wrong to succumb to such a temptation. To say that the United States is not as repressive as totalitarian nations is of small comfort. Our own Declaration of Independence, after all, speaks eloquently of God's gift to humanity of "certain unalienable rights" including "life, liberty, and the pursuit of happiness." The Pledge of Allegiance we've cited throughout our lives speaks of "one nation, under God, indivisible, with liberty and justice for all." U.S. government repression takes us far from these democratic ideals, as our country has too often denied its own citizens, and those living elsewhere, their liberty, their happiness, and even their lives. Surely we should aspire to a higher standard than that.

If much of the crime *by* government deprives its opponents of liberty and justice, the goal of much of the crime *against* government is to secure these elusive states. There is a long history in the United States and other nations of mass political violence and nonviolent civil disobedience aimed at producing fundamental social change. Whether or not we agree with the means and/or the goals of such lawbreaking, history would be very different if people had not engaged in it. The "myth of peaceful progress" notwithstanding, change often does not come unless and until aggrieved populations resist their government. Often their protest is legal, but sometimes it is illegal and even deadly. While it is easy to dismiss terrorism, assassination, and other political violence as the desperate acts of fanatical minds, it would be neither correct nor wise to obscure the political motivation and goals of politically violent actors.

Political crime raises some fascinating questions about the nature of law, order, and social change in democratic and nondemocratic societies. Unless some utopian state is finally reached, governments and their opponents will continue to struggle for political power. If history is any guide to the future, that struggle will inevitably include repression by the government and lawbreaking by its opponents. Whatever form it takes, political crime reminds us that what is *legally* right or wrong sometimes differs from what is *morally* right or wrong. For these and other reasons, political crime deserves far more attention that it has received from criminologists and other social scientists.

KEY TERMS

agents provocateurs

civil disobedience

COINTELPRO

espionage

genocide

hate crime

Iran-Contra scandal

political violence

political trial

repression

state terrorism

state-corporate crime

terrorism

treason

Watergate scandal

STUDY QUESTIONS

1. The text mentions that some critics claimed the United States was committing genocide during the Vietnam War. How valid is this charge?

2. For a government, what are the advantages of using the law to repress social movements instead of using violence?

3. Is hate crime a recent phenomenon in the United States, or does its occurrence go back further into U.S. history? Explain your answer.

4. What were Thoreau's and Martin Luther King, Jr.'s arguments for justifying civil disobedience?

INTERNET EXERCISES

Nonviolent civil disobedience is a common form of political crime. The United States includes several social movement organizations whose members practice civil disobedience. Some of these organizations are included in the **www.nonviolence.org** Web site. Go to this site and read its issue pages on **peace and taxes, conscience and the state**, and **direct action**. Then go to **www.nonviolence.org/wrl** to access the Web site of the War Resisters League, an organization founded in 1923 that, in its words, "advocates Gandhian nonviolence as the method for creating a democratic society free of war, racism, sexism, and human exploitation." Read through this site.

Once you've become a bit more familiar with nonviolent civil disobedience, answer these questions. Why do these social movement organizations engage in this form of protest? Is civil disobedience ever justified in a democracy? Were Martin Luther King, Jr. and other members of the Southern civil right movement justified in breaking the law? Why or why not? Must civil disobedience always be nonviolent? Should people committing civil disobedience wait to be arrested? Would you have a different reaction to civil disobedience committed by groups on the right side of the political spectrum than to civil disobedience committed by groups on the left side of the political spectrum?

PUBLIC ORDER
CRIME AND
ORGANIZED CRIME

Crime in the News

In August 1999, Gary E. Johnson, then the Repub-lican governor of New Mexico, said he had smoked marijuana in college and also used cocaine a couple of times. About the same time, reports were cir-culating that the men who later became the two major candidates in the 2000 presidential elec-tion had used illegal drugs when they were much younger. Reports alleged that Vice President Al Gore had often used marijua-na in the early 1970s after returning from service in Vietnam. While not acknowledg-ing illegal drug use, Republican candidate George W. Bush, governor of Texas, con-ceded that he had committed "youthful in-discretions" and strongly implied he had used illegal drugs in his 20s; several unsubstantiat-ed reports alleged he had used cocaine.

These reports highlighted important questions raised at least since President Bill Clinton acknowl-edged during his first presidential campaign that he had tried marijuana but not inhaled: Is it okay if politi-cians used illegal drugs when they were much younger, long before they entered the political arena? Should they be forgiven for experimenting with drugs that were so commonly used by their baby-boom genera-tion? Is it hypocritical for the nation to forgive candi-dates for "youthful indiscretions" involving illegal drug use even as it annually arrests and imprisons hundreds of thousands of people (most of them young and a disproportionate number black or Latino) for using illegal drugs?

Sources: Apple 1999; Hertzberg 1999; Huffington 1999; Janof-sky 1999; Scheer 1999.

What should be done about illegal drugs? What should be done about other illegal behaviors, such as prostitution and illegal gambling, in which people engage voluntarily? As the "Crime in the News" vignette indicated, there are no easy answers to these questions. They reflect a larger conflict in U.S. society over using the law to enforce notions of how morally proper people should behave. Because of differing standards of morality, reasonable people hold quite different views on certain behaviors, especially those involving drugs, sex, or gambling. Not surprisingly, individuals and groups morally opposed to these behaviors often try to use the law to prohibit them and to punish their participants. Sometimes once-legal behavior becomes a crime against morality and the public order.

OVERVIEW OF THE PUBLIC ORDER CRIME DEBATE

Unlike most of the crimes we've studied so far, where unwilling victims are threatened or hurt physically or financially, *public order crimes* (also called *vice crimes* or *victimless crimes*) usually hurt no one except perhaps the offenders themselves. Because these offenders are willing participants, some scholars say they should be free in a democratic society to engage in these behaviors, however unwise such conduct may be. The state should stay out of the business of enforcing morality and of "coercing virtue" (Geis 1979; Skolnick 1968). Other scholars say that participants in these crimes don't just hurt themselves. Illegal drug use and gambling, for example, may also hurt the offenders' families and even lead to other crimes where there are unwilling victims. If so, public order crimes are less a matter of morality than one of protecting society.

In response, critics of laws against public order crimes point out that families are often hurt by all kinds of things a family member may do, including investing unwisely in the stock market, starting a business that fails, clogging one's arteries with high-fat food, and other normal, legal practices. Just as the law can't begin to prohibit these practices, so should it not prohibit other practices that seem less socially acceptable.

The critics also argue that public order crime laws reflect the moral beliefs of legislators, powerful interest groups, and other actors with the ability to make laws or to influence lawmaking. Such people in U.S. history have tended to be white, middle- and upper-class Protestants with strict moral views on drugs, sex, gambling, and the like. A common focus of their concern has been the behavior of the poor, people of color, immigrants, and other subordinate groups (Lesieur and Welch 2000). A prominent example here is the temperance movement of the late 1800s and early 1900s, led by white, rural Protestants who considered alcohol use a sin and disliked Catholics, immigrants, and urban residents who used alcohol (Gusfield 1963). When prostitution laws are enforced, poor streetwalkers are much more at risk than call girls who cater to a richer clientele, and female prostitutes in general are more at risk than their male customers, many of whom are respectable businesspeople. Gambling by the poor, such as "playing the numbers," has long been illegal, but gambling on the stock market or on land speculation is legal. As these examples indicate, the enactment and enforcement of public order crime laws often reflect and reinforce the social inequality already in society.

Complicating matters further, moral standards can change dramatically over time. For much of U.S. history, premarital sex was considered highly immoral, and people of the opposite sex who lived together unmarried were "living in sin." An earlier generation thought that "proper" high school girls should look "ladylike" by wearing dresses or skirts, but by the 1960s many students had begun to reject this standard as hopelessly old-fashioned and even sexist, not to mention impractical in cold weather. As we'll see later, a century or more ago, opiate, cocaine, and marijuana use was common in the United States and even socially acceptable. Prostitution was legal in many places and tolerated as a normal if undesirable behavior.

One final problem with the laws prohibiting public order crimes is that they might do more harm than good. Among other things, they may (1) increase police and other official corruption; (2) lead public order offenders to commit other types of crime that they would not commit if their public order crime behaviors were legal; (3) generate public disrespect for the law; (4) divert much time, money, and energy from fighting more serious crime to futile efforts to stop what so many people want to do; (5) prompt law enforcement agencies to engage in wiretapping and other possible violations of civil liberties; and (6) provide much of the revenue for organized crime, which is all too willing to supply the goods and services prohibited by public order crime laws but still sought by large segments of the population (Meier and Geis 1997).

With this overview in mind, let's turn to the major public order crimes of illegal drug use; prostitution and pornography; and gambling. One theme we'll explore is that public order crime laws are often arbitrary and even illogical. For example, some gambling is legal while other gambling is illegal, and some of the most harmful drugs are the legal ones. We'll also explore the negative consequences of the laws against public order crimes, with drugs as our prime example. The chapter ends with a look at organized crime, which provides many of the goods and services banned by public order crime laws and acquires money and influence by giving the public what it wants.

ILLEGAL DRUG USE

Illegal drug use and trafficking continue to be the most publicized public order crimes in the United States. We hear much from public officials and the news media about a drug crisis, and many statistics about the drug problem exist (Dorsey and Zawitz 1999). The federal and state governments spend $30 to $35 billion yearly on the illegal drug problem. More than two-thirds of this sum is spent on law enforcement's "war against drugs," with the remainder spent on treatment and prevention programs and on research. About 5.1 percent, or 780, of all homicides in 1997 were committed during drug felonies such as drug trafficking or manufacturing. Almost one-fifth of state prisoners say they committed their offense to get money for drugs, and one-third say they committed their offense while under the influence of drugs. More than half who had committed violence against an intimate said they'd been drinking or using drugs at the time of the offense. Meanwhile, about two-thirds of adult arrestees in our large cities test positive for an illegal drug. In many of our cities, drug dealers operate openly at street corners and drug gangs control entire neighborhoods.

Reflecting the focus of the mass media and public officials on the drug problem, public concern over illegal drugs accelerated dramatically in the late 1980s even though illegal drug use was actually declining (Chapter 2). In January 1985, only 2 percent of Gallup Poll respondents named drug abuse as the most important problem facing the United States. This proportion rose the rest of the decade and peaked at 38 percent in November 1989, then dropped to 6 percent by January 1993 as the Middle East crisis (Gulf War) and then a slow economy captured our attention. It then rose to 17 percent by 1997 before falling back to 5 percent in 1999 (Dorsey and Zawitz 1999).

Despite this drop, the public continued to be concerned about illegal drugs as the 1990s ended (Maguire and Pastore 1999). In a 1998 Gallup Poll, 52 percent of adults said drugs were a "very serious" problem in their public schools, ranking it ahead of any other problem in the list, including discipline, smoking, and fighting. In another 1998 survey, 68 percent of Americans said we are spending "too little" to deal with drug addiction. Teenagers themselves also expressed concern: In a 1998 national survey, they named drugs as the second most important problem in their schools. A few years earlier, a 1993 Gallup Poll asked people to indicate how important various factors were in causing crime. Almost two-thirds, or 64 percent, named the "influence of drugs" as a "critical" factor in causing crime. This proportion was higher than for any other factor in the poll, including gun availability, lack of moral training in the home, and few job opportunities for young people (Maguire and Pastore 1995).

Amid such concern over illegal drugs, it's easy to get caught up in a frenzy of mythology and misinformation and lose sight of carefully gathered, scientific evidence. Perhaps nowhere is this more true than the drug problem. As Samuel Walker (1994:253) observes, "Public hysteria over drugs and drug-related crime inhibits sensible discussion of policy. There is enormous misunderstanding about the extent of drug use, the trends in usage, the harmful effects of different drugs, and the connection between drugs and crime." While even the experts disagree on these issues, let's take a look at the evidence.

Drug Use in History

As with many of the behaviors discussed in earlier chapters, drug use has occurred throughout human history. As sociologist Erich Goode (1984:3) observes, "Humans have ingested drugs for at least ten thousand years." Primitive people during the Stone Age drank alcohol; South American Indians have chewed coca leaves containing cocaine since before the time of the Incas; people in ancient China, Greece, and India smoked marijuana; Mexican Indians have chewed hallucinogenic mushrooms since before the time of the Aztecs. Anthropologists continue to find widespread use of psychoactive drugs in folk societies around the world (Edgerton 1976).

Drug use was quite common in the United States in the late nineteenth century (Musto 1999). Dozens of over-the-counter products containing opium and its derivatives (such as morphine) were used across the country by people with headaches, toothaches, menstrual cramps, sleeplessness, depression, and other problems. About 500,000 Americans, many of them middle-aged, middle-class women, were addicted to opium at the turn of the century. These addicts weren't considered criminals, as their drugs were legal and readily available. Instead they were considered unfortunate individuals in need of help. Only slightly less popular was cocaine, which was used in many over-the-counter products and as an anesthetic for some surgeries. As you might have heard, it was also a major ingredient in Coca-Cola, which was first marketed in 1894 and, not surprisingly, became quite popular. Marijuana was another common drug and was used as a painkiller by people with menstrual cramps, migraine headaches, and other aches and pains.

As this brief historical review suggests, drug use in contemporary life is hardly a new phenomenon. In fact, a society with little or no drug use is rare in human history. As Goode (1984:3) again observes, "In the thousands of tribes, cultures, societies, and nations around the world and throughout history, only a tiny handful of peoples have not routinely taken drugs to experience their effects. Drug-taking comes close to being a cultural universal."

Contemporary U.S. Drug Use

Drug use remains quite common in the United States today. To illustrate this, let's first define a psychoactive "drug" as any substance that physiologically changes our mood, emotion, perception, or other mental states. Defined this way, each of the following substances is a psychoactive drug or contains such drugs: beer, wine, and other alcohol; Coca-Cola, Pepsi, and other colas; coffee and tea; chocolate; cigarettes and other tobacco products; cocaine and crack; heroin; No-Doz and other over-the-counter products that help us stay awake; various weight-control products; and Valium, Librium, and other anti-anxiety drugs.

As this list makes clear, most of us use drugs at one time or another, and many of us use at least some of these drugs daily. Some drugs, like caffeine (found, of course, in coffee, colas, chocolate, and many other products) are "good drugs": Their use is socially acceptable, celebrated in advertising, and very much a part of our culture. Alcohol, too, would fall into this category, despite growing recognition of its contribution to drunk driving, domestic violence, rape, and other crimes. Cigarettes (tobacco) were another good drug not too long ago and are still the subject of much advertising but have become much less socially acceptable in the last two decades. Other drugs are "bad drugs": Their use is not only socially unacceptable but also illegal, and we view users of these drugs much more negatively than someone who drinks coffee or beer every day. Both good and bad drugs can cause physiological and/or psychological dependence, as anyone smoking a pack of cigarettes or drinking several cups of coffee daily can attest to (Goode 1999).

◀ *The United States is a nation of drug users, even if many of the drugs we use, such as caffeine in coffee, are legal.*

In fact, it's not an exaggeration to say that the United States is a nation of drug users, even if we disregard such common products as aspirin, Tylenol, and cold and allergy medications. A few figures from self-report surveys and other studies help illustrate this point (Goode 1999; Maguire and Pastore 1999). Let's start with legal drugs. About 90 percent of U.S. residents use coffee and other caffeine products regularly, with the average U.S. resident consuming about 16 pounds of caffeine yearly from all sources. Physicians write about 250 million prescriptions annually for psychoactive drugs such as Valium. About two-thirds of the adult population, or more than 100 million people, drink alcohol occasionally or regularly, while a little less than one-third of the adult population, or about 50 million people, smoke cigarettes. About 42 percent of students in grades 6 through 8 report drinking alcohol at least once in the past year, with almost 15 percent reporting drinking in the past month; these figures rise among high school seniors to 76 percent in the past year and 47 percent in the past month. Reflecting the adult population, more than one-third of high school seniors have smoked cigarettes within the past month.

Turning to college students, almost 85 percent have drunk alcohol in the past year and about 68 percent in the past month, while 44 percent have smoked cigarettes in the past year and 30 percent in the past month. Almost 43 percent of college students report having five or more drinks in a row—binge drinking—in the last two weeks. Binge drinking is especially common among college freshmen and at campuses in the northeastern and north central states (Kong and Brelis 1995). College students who don't drink report being treated as social outcasts by those who do. A substance abuse counselor at one New England campus said that the alcohol-free dorm there "is described by students giving campus tours as 'the place where the geeks live'" (Milne 1995:1).

Turning to illegal drugs, U.S. residents spent an estimated $57 billion on these drugs in 1995, the last year for which figures were available at the time of this writing. This amount included $38 billion on cocaine and crack, $10 billion on heroin, $7 billion on marijuana, and $3 billion on other drugs (Rhodes et al. 1997). The proportion of the U.S. population using selected illegal drugs in 1998 appears in Table 14.1, with the data taken from the annual National Household Survey on Drug Abuse of people age 12 and older. To look at just a few numbers in the table, about one-third of this population, or 72 million people, have used marijuana, with 9.0 percent, or almost 19 million people, using it in the last year.

TABLE 14.1 PREVALENCE (%) OF ILLEGAL DRUG USE, 1998
(NATIONAL HOUSEHOLD SURVEY ON DRUG ABUSE)

	AGE 12 AND OLDER			18–25		
	Ever Used	Past Year	Past Month	Ever Used	Past Year	Past Month
Marijuana	33	9	5	45	24	14
Cocaine	11	2	1	10	5	2
Hallucinogens	10	2	1	17	7	3
LSD	8	1	—	14	3	—
Heroin	1	<1	—	1	<1	—

Source: Gustin 1999.

Eleven percent of the population, or 23 million people, have used cocaine, with 2 percent, or almost 4 million people, using it in the last year.

The "age 12 and older" population obviously includes people in early adolescence and in their middle ages and older years who are unlikely to use illegal drugs. Because a fairer picture of illegal drug use involves only young adults, Table 14.1 includes data on the 18–25 age bracket. As expected, these young adults are especially likely to be using illegal drugs. However, their illegal drug use in the past year is still relatively low. Although marijuana remains their illegal drug of choice, less than 8 percent used any one of the other illegal drugs in the last year. Apart from marijuana, recent illegal drug use is thus uncommon among young adults.

This conclusion is even more evident when we examine their illegal drug use in just the past month, a common indicator of more serious drug use. For example, although 14 percent of the 18–25 age group used marijuana in the past month, fewer than 4 percent used the other illegal drugs. These figures are much lower than the 52 percent of the 18–25 group who used alcohol in the past month, and the 42 percent who smoked cigarettes. Their alcohol rate, in fact, is about 26 times higher than their corresponding cocaine rate. For this and the other age groups, alcohol and tobacco use is thus more common—and, statistically speaking, much more of a problem—than use of illegal drugs.

In general, and this might surprise you, illegal drug use in the United States in the 1990s was much lower than in the late 1970s and early 1980s. For example, the 24 percent of the 18–25 age bracket reporting last-year marijuana use in the 1998 survey (Table 14.1) was down considerably from its peak of 47 percent in the 1979 survey. Similarly, the 5 percent of this bracket reporting last-year cocaine use in the 1993 survey was also down considerably from its peak of almost 20 percent in 1979.

Since the 1970s the federal government has sponsored annual surveys of high school students called Monitoring the Future. The survey's findings on illegal drug use by high school seniors, reported in Table 14.2, mirror the portrait just drawn of low and even declining illegal drug use among young adults. Almost all the 1998 last-year rates for the seniors are lower than the 1981 rates. Although marijuana use remained rather common in 1998, less than 11 percent had used the

TABLE 14.2

REPORTED DRUG USE BY HIGH SCHOOL SENIORS, 1981 AND 1998
(% USING DRUG IN PAST YEAR)

DRUG	1981	1998
Marijuana	46	38
Cocaine	12	6
Heroin	<1	1
Other opiates	6	6
Hallucinogens	10	9
Stimulants*	20	10
Alcohol	87	74

*1982 figure used instead of 1981
Sources: Maguire and Pastore 1995; Maguire and Pastore 1999.

other illegal drugs in the last year. In contrast, 74 percent had used alcohol in the last year, and more than 40 percent had smoked cigarettes. The Monitoring the Future survey also asks the seniors whether they had used any of the drugs in the past month, an indication, once again, of more serious use for this young age group. Although 23 percent of the 1998 sample had used marijuana in the last month, the rates for the other illegal drugs were all under 5 percent, with cocaine used only by 2.4 percent. In contrast, as noted previously, about half had used alcohol in the last month (with about one-third binge drinking in the last two weeks), and 35 percent had smoked cigarettes in the last month.

Taken together, these data on high school seniors and young adults do *not* yield a portrait of a nation in a drug crisis, say some observers, at least not one involving illegal drugs (Stephens 1992). In terms of sheer numbers, if there is a nationwide drug crisis, it is a crisis of alcohol and tobacco, not of illegal drugs. Apart from marijuana, illegal drug use is uncommon and has declined since the late 1970s and early 1980s. This decline was unrelated to the law enforcement war against drugs, since it preceded the mid-1980s' intensifying of the drug war. Instead the decline most likely resulted from increasing recognition of the dangers of illegal drugs and a greater interest in healthy lifestyles (Lehigh 1995).

ANOTHER VIEW

Despite the national self-report data, the portrait just drawn of low illegal drug use nationwide is misleading in three important ways (Currie 1994). First, the low proportions of illegal drug use still translate into millions of people. For example, the 5 percent of the 18–25 age group reporting cocaine use in the last year (Table 14.1) is equivalent to some 1.4 million people, and the 1 percent of the 12 and older population using cocaine in the past month translates into about 1.2 million monthly users. Thus, although illegal drug use is low in percentage terms, it is high in absolute numbers. Whether you think illegal drug use is "low" or "high" thus depends on whether you think percentages or actual numbers are better measures of such use.

Second, there were signs from the national self-report data in the 1990s that the decline in illegal drug use had stopped and even reversed, with illegal drug use increasing somewhat among high school students in the Monitoring the Future surveys. For example, last-year marijuana use by high school seniors rose from 21.9 percent in 1992 to 37.5 percent in 1998, while last-month use rose from 11.9 percent to 22.8 percent in the same period. The increase was accompanied by a decrease in the proportion of high school students viewing illegal drug use as dangerous (Maguire and Pastore 1999). Although illegal drug use by students in the surveys remains below its peak in the early 1980s, the new figures represented a disturbing trend.

Third, and most important, the national self-report surveys exclude people whose illegal drug use is especially high, including prisoners, youths in juvenile detention centers, the homeless, runaway teenagers, and high school dropouts, who are concentrated in our largest cities (Mieczkowski 1996). The national surveys also obviously include many people living in smaller cities and towns and rural areas, where at least some illegal drug use is less common. For these and other reasons, the portrait of low illegal drug use at the national level overlooks the illegal drug problem in poor, urban neighborhoods. Simply put, though national level percentages are low, the cocaine/crack, heroin, and other illegal drug use that exists is concentrated in these neighborhoods. The small national rates thus translate into much higher rates in our largest cities, where cocaine/crack and heroin use are much more common and much more of a crisis. For example, a study of chronic delinquents in Miami found 87 percent reporting regular use of crack (Inciardi, Horowitz, and Pittieger 1993). Another study of young residents of Harlem found some 15 percent reporting heroin use and 21 percent reporting cocaine use in the past month, much higher figures than the national data in Table 14.1

Thus, although there might not be a drug crisis for the population as a whole, there *is* one for "America's have-nots," as sociologist Elliott Currie (1994:3) calls them: the residents, all of them poor and most of them people of color, of the nation's inner-city neighborhoods. As Currie observes, "Serious drug abuse is not evenly distributed: It runs 'along the fault lines of our society.' It is concentrated among some groups and not others, and has been for at least half a century" (pp. 4–5).

Explaining Illegal Drug Use

As Currie's comment indicates, much of the illegal drug problem is an urban phenomenon reflecting the many problems that also prompt high rates of other crimes in urban areas. The urban drug problem grew after World War II, when heroin entered the poorest neighborhoods of the largest U.S. cities, most of them populated by African-Americans or Puerto Ricans (Currie 1994). Researchers at the time emphasized the economic deprivation responsible for this geographical patterning of heroin use, as inner-city residents were left out of the postwar spurt in the U.S. economy. Heroin use increased in the 1960s, as economic opportunities in inner cities continued to decline even as the U.S. economy continued to grow. By the end of the 1960s, inner-city youths had come to view heroin addiction and its associated activities—stealing to support their habit, buying from drug dealers, and so forth—as a romantic, exciting alternative to the despair of their existence (Preble and Casey 1969). Ironically, the legal and medical risks of using heroin helped attract these youths to it (Currie 1994).

Previous chapters discussed the worsening economic conditions in U.S. cities in the 1970s and especially the 1980s, which expanded the urban underclass and aggravated street crime in inner cities. As a reminder, unemployment soared in the 1970s and 1980s for urban youths, federal cutbacks in the 1980s reduced federal aid to the poor, and poverty rates increased, even as federal tax cuts in the 1980s favored the wealthy. As a result, inequality—the gap between the rich and the poor—also increased. Amid such growing economic despair, it's not surprising that drug abuse also worsened in inner cities during these two decades. As Currie (1994:123–124) observes, the "drug crisis of the 1980s flourished in the context of an unparalleled social and economic disaster that swept low-income communities in America in ways that virtually ensured that the drug problem would worsen." The introduction of crack in the mid-1980s especially devastated large U.S. cities and "struck hardest at the poorest of the poor" (Currie 1994:80), as the most blighted urban neighborhoods saw the highest levels of crack sales and use, with crack becoming more popular than heroin.

ECONOMIC DEPRIVATION AND DRUG ABUSE

Why does economic deprivation often lead to illegal drug use? This connection involves both structural and social process factors. As several theorists have argued (Chapter 6), severe deprivation fills your life with despair. Given this basic fact, illegal drug use may provide a temporary way to forget about your poverty and related problems and to feel high and euphoric (Harrell and Peterson 1992). Given the medical and legal risks associated with illegal drugs, they come to be viewed as exciting pursuits that appeal to young people's desire for thrills and adventure.

Social process factors also matter. When, as is often the case, drug use is common among one's peers in poor, urban neighborhoods, their influence is difficult to ignore (Kandel and Davies 1991). If you refuse to use drugs, they may regard you as an uncool wimp. Conversely, your willingness to use illegal drugs is instant evidence of your daring and "coolness." Not surprisingly, many studies confirm peers' drug use as an important influence on one's own use. The quality of a youth's family life also makes a difference, as stable, functional families can help youths resist the lure of the streets. But it's also true that neighborhoods with chronic joblessness and poverty create dysfunctional families whose children are at greater risk for delinquency and crime. Not surprisingly, many studies find they're also much more at risk for illegal drug use.

If all these factors prompt especially heavy illegal drug use in the poorest urban neighborhoods, the drug use and associated drug dealing make neighborhoods even more blighted, increasing the likelihood of even greater drug use (Currie 1994). In a related problem, addicted parents are especially unable to keep their own kids from using drugs. Since their families are likely to be poor and jobless, their children may well turn to drug dealing as a source of income. Even when families have a little money, the high incomes promised by drug dealing often lure adolescents into the drug trafficking community, especially when they have few other prospects for income-producing jobs. One result of all these factors is a drug spiral from which there is little escape as long as economic deprivation continues.

If this sociological view makes sense, then it's shortsighted to view the urban poor's drug abuse mainly as an individual problem with biochemical and psychological roots. Such a view ignores the systematic social inequality lying at the heart of the problem. Urban drug abuse occurs, says Currie (1994:122), because it helps in many ways "to meet human needs that are systematically thwarted by the social and economic structures of the world the users live in." If this is true, then urban drug abuse is best regarded not as a decadent, aberrant act but rather as "a predictable response to social conditions that destroy self-esteem, hope, solidarity, stability, and a sense of purpose" (Currie 1994:123).

This structural perspective has important implications for social policy on the drug problem. Simply put, efforts to reduce urban drug abuse will succeed only to the degree they help reduce the economic deprivation, joblessness, and related problems underlying such abuse. As Currie (pp. 77–78) continues:

> The link between drug abuse and [economic] deprivation is one of the strongest in forty years of careful research.... We will not begin to comprehend America's drug problem, much less resolve it, until we understand that drugs and inequality are closely and multiply linked. And our national willingness to tolerate unusually severe levels of social deprivation and marginality goes a long way toward explaining why we lead the world in drug abuse.

GENDER AND ILLEGAL DRUG USE

Research on women's illegal drug use lags far behind men's. For a long time most studies examined heroin or other illegal drug use only by males. In the last decade or so, scholars have begun to pay more attention to women's illegal drug use. What have they found?

The best evidence of one area of research is that women tend to use illegal drugs less than men, but that this gender difference isn't very large. According to the National Household Survey on Drug Abuse, 30 percent of women have ever used an illegal drug, compared to almost 42 percent of men. About 4.5 percent of women report illegal drug use in the past month, compared to 8.1 percent of men (Gustin 1999). However, other evidence suggests that crack dependence is higher among women than men in some communities (Inciardi, Lockwood, and Pottieger 1993).

Women's illegal drug use appears to arise from the same structural and social process factors underlying male use (Taylor 1993). Women users in urban areas resemble male users in their poverty, family backgrounds, and other factors discussed earlier. In one study, more than half of 164 women arrestees in New York City tested positive for cocaine and/or heroin use. Like the males studied in previous research, they tended to be high school dropouts from poor, dysfunctional families (Graham and Wish 1994).

In other areas, certain gender differences, all reflecting women's subordinate status, emerge in the new research. Some studies find that females are more likely than males to use illegal drugs to cope with depression and other psychological distress, often stemming from sexual abuse, whereas men are more likely to use illegal drugs for excitement (Chesney-Lind 1997; Inciardi 1993). To the extent this gender difference exists, it reflects women's greater sense of powerlessness and the greater psychological distress they suffer in a sexist society and internalize instead of expressing through anger (Mirowsky and Ross 1995). It also reflects the fact that in many urban communities, male illegal drug use is approved while female use is more disapproved. Whereas males who use illegal drugs are seen as daring and manly, females who do so are viewed as deviant "junkies" (Inciardi, Lockwood, and Pottieger 1993).

One other gender difference in motivation for illegal drug use is economic. Because they have fewer job opportunities than men and much more often have children to support, young women face economic crisis more often than young men. In a study of female crack users in New York City, Lisa Maher and Richard Curtis (1995) argue that the 1980s' economic decay in U.S. cities thus affected women more than men and contributed especially heavily to their increase in crack and other illegal drug use in that decade. These women, Maher and Curtis note, were largely shut out of the male-dominated drug-trafficking industry and had to turn to prostitution for their income. Other studies also stress that women turn to prostitution to get money for illegal drugs and daily living expenses (Hunt 1990).

One final gender difference concerns the reaction to women who use illegal drugs during pregnancy. In the 1980s and early 1990s, the news media and public officials sounded an alarm about illegal drug use during pregnancy. Prosecutors charged dozens of drug-using pregnant women with child abuse or drug trafficking, and the term *crack babies* became a household word. In response, several scholars noted: (1) The much more common use of alcohol, tobacco, and even caffeine during pregnancy was at least as dangerous to the fetus as illegal drug use; (2) prosecuting pregnant women for using illegal drugs would harm the fetus more by discouraging the women from seeking prenatal medical care or drug treatment; and (3) prosecutions of *crack mothers* obscured the many other problems these women faced (Humphries et al. 1995; Paltrow 1990). Finally, although the number of crack babies was estimated in 1988 to be 375,000, or about 11 percent of all births, later research revealed that this number was greatly exaggerated (Walker 1998).

The Drugs–Crime Connection

One question that comes up again and again is whether drugs *cause* crime. As I mentioned at the beginning of this section, respondents in a national poll named drugs as a major cause of crime more than any other factor. As we've seen in previous chapters, however, popular beliefs do not always square with scientific evidence. Keeping that in mind, what does the evidence say about the drugs–crime connection?

Before we can answer this question, we must first be clear on what we mean when we say that drugs *cause* crime. We could mean that drugs cause crime because of their physiological and psychological effects on drug users. Or we could mean that they cause crime because people deciding to use illegal drugs inevitably begin to associate with other illegal users, many of whom are involved in other types of crime. Finally, we could mean that people using illegal drugs commit other crimes, such as robbery, burglary, and prostitution, to get money to pay for their drug habit.

One thing is clear: A very strong *correlation* exists between illegal drug use and other types of crime (Chaiken and Chaiken 1990; Zawitz 1992). People who regularly use illegal drugs commit a lot of crime, and people who commit a lot of crime regularly use illegal drugs. More to the point, people using illegal drugs regularly—heroin is most often considered in the research—commit much more crime than people using illegal drugs less often or not at all.

Does this mean that illegal drug use causes crime? Not necessarily. There are at least two reasons for doubting a simple drug-crime causal relationship. First, most illegal drug use is experimental or recreational, and very few of the millions of illegal drug users each year go on to commit other kinds of crime. Second, although illegal drug use and crime are strongly correlated, remember that correlation does not necessarily mean causation. The correlation *might* mean that illegal drug use leads to other crime, but it might also mean that committing other crime leads to illegal drug use, because, for example, you get involved with other offenders who already use illegal drugs. It's also possible that the correlation is spurious: Perhaps the same factors, such as economic deprivation and inadequate parenting, that lead to illegal drug use also lead to other criminality.

Scholars have examined these possibilities with juvenile offenders and young adults. Although the evidence is complex, a rough consensus is that much of the illegal drugs–crime connection is indeed spurious, with both kinds of illegal behavior the result of the various structural and social process factors we've examined in this and previous chapters (Dembo and Williams 1993). When a causal relationship *is* uncovered among adolescents, it's more often true that delinquency precedes drug use than the reverse: Adolescents begin to commit delinquency and then start using illegal drugs, perhaps because of the influence of delinquent friends or because their delinquency worsens their relationship with their parents (Huizinga, Menard, and Elliott 1989). Once that process has started, illegal drug use does seem to increase the likelihood of future offending. That said, the strong drugs–crime connection is best explained partly as a spurious correlation and partly as one indicating that crime causes drug use, rather than one showing that drug use causes crime. The "illegal drug use causes crime" belief thus turns out to be largely a myth (Kappeler, Blumberg, and Potter 2000).

What about drugs leading to crime because of their physiological and psychological effects? Research on this issue, says criminologist Jeffrey A. Roth (1994:2), challenges "several common assumptions about connections between

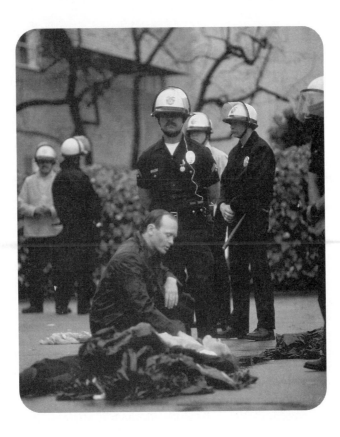

◄ *Many scholars consider the violence associated with drug trafficking a result of the laws forbidding the drugs involved.*

drugs and violence." While there is anecdotal evidence that people using certain illegal drugs, including crack, hallucinogens, amphetamines, and PCP, can become violent, there is no evidence of a systematic, cause-and-effect relationship. Any such violence tends to occur only rarely and is committed primarily by individuals with histories of emotional problems or antisocial behavior. Some drugs, notably marijuana and opiates, reduce violent behavior.

Ironically, the one psychoactive drug linked to interpersonal violence is a legal drug, alcohol: "Alcohol is the only psychoactive drug that in many individuals tends to increase aggressive behavior temporarily while it is taking effect" (Roth 1994:4). It's tempting to attribute this aggression to the way alcohol affects the central nervous system, but such a connection would ignore the many societies studied by anthropologists in which alcohol use doesn't lead to violence (Edgerton 1976). Alcohol does affect behavior, but its effects depend on cultural expectations. In the United States, one cultural expectation is that alcohol leads to violence. In a self-fulfilling prophecy, this often happens. Alcohol use by the offender, victim, or both, immediately precedes at least half of all violent crimes, including homicides and rapes. While some of these crimes would occur even if no one had been drinking, most experts feel that alcohol use in the United States greatly increases the chances that someone will become aggressive and commit an assault, rape, or even a murder (Giancola 1999; Parker 1995).

What about the many times illegal drug users commit crimes to get money to pay for their drug habit? Here a clear "illegal drug use causes crime" connection is not due to the illegal drug use itself but rather to the fact that the drugs being used are illegal. When drugs are illegal, simple *supply and demand* economics dictate that their prices will be much higher than if they were legal. Because they're so expensive, their users, most of them quite poor, cannot afford to pay for them unless they steal the necessary funds. Ironically, the more the government's war against drugs reduces the supply of illegal drugs, the higher their prices become, and the more theft by illegal drug users occurs. Such theft thus results from the laws against the drugs, not from the drugs themselves (MacCoun and Reuter 1998).

This also applies to the illegal drug users who commit crime because they start associating with other illegal drug users and traffickers and, in general, become more involved in the criminal community. Although this might sound a bit simplistic, if the drugs they were using weren't illegal, they wouldn't start associating with other criminals. To the extent they then wouldn't become involved in the criminal community, they wouldn't commit other crimes. Even here, then, the drugs–crime connection is the result of the laws against drugs rather than the drugs themselves.

When people talk about drugs causing crime, they often are talking about the drive-by shootings and other violence taking place between drug gangs in our largest cities that often kill or injure innocent bystanders. Once again, such violence, as horrible as it is, results from the laws against the drugs, not from the drugs themselves. When sellers of legal products compete for profit, they use advertising, lower prices, friendly service, and other such means to succeed in the market. Drug traffickers don't have these alternatives. Moreover, their potential profits are enormous because illegal drugs command high prices. As a result, controlling drug trafficking in as many neighborhoods as possible becomes critical (Hagedorn 1994). Because so much is at stake, drug gangs and other drug traffickers are quite willing to use violence to control the local market. However, their violence is the direct result of the laws against the drugs they are selling, not of the drugs themselves: We don't see such violence from the traffickers (large supermarkets, small "Mom-and-Pop" stores, etc.) of legal drug products such as coffee and cigarettes.

To summarize, the answer to the question "Do drugs cause crime?" is yes if we're talking about alcohol, and generally no if we're talking about illegal drugs. To the extent that illegal drugs are connected to crime, the connection results from laws against these drugs rather than their physiological or social effects. Ironically, the war against drugs aggravates one of the very problems it is intended to stop.

The Legalization Debate

Earlier I sketched two criticisms some scholars have about laws against public order crimes. The first criticism is philosophical: In a democratic society, people should be free to engage in self-destructive behavior, and it is arbitrary and even hypocritical for a society to decide which such behaviors it will allow and prohibit. This philosophical, *libertarian* view goes back at least to the writing of the famous philosopher John Stuart Mill (1892 [1859]) and remains an important contemporary view (Lesieur and Welch 2000; Meier and Geis 1997). The second criticism is more social scientific: Public order crime laws do more harm than good, or so some scholars think. Perhaps nowhere is the debate over public order crime laws more important—and also more controversial—than on the issue of illegal drugs.

THE PHILOSOPHICAL ARGUMENT

Let's first explore the philosophical grounds for legalization. For the sake of argument, let's assume that no drug use is truly *victimless*: Any drug will be harmful if taken in large enough doses, and some drugs are harmful even in small doses (Goode 1999). Let's further assume that the victimization caused by drug use often involves people other than the drug users themselves. If drug use causes someone to lose a job, that person's family suffers. If it affects the person's ability to do other everyday activities, the person's family also suffers. If enough people hurt themselves with legal or illegal drugs, society also suffers from lost economic productivity and increased health-care costs. If any drug use is potentially harmful, then the philosophical question becomes one of whether the state should prohibit all drug use, some drug use, or no drug use.

Obviously the state can't prohibit all drug use. Someone downing a bottle of aspirin causes more personal, familial, and social harm than another smoking a marijuana joint or even snorting a typical amount of cocaine, but the state is not about to prohibit aspirin use. The question thus becomes which drugs will the state prohibit, if any, and which will it allow.

Any answer to this question has to be arbitrary. If society permits behaviors it likes or at least tolerates and prohibits behaviors it doesn't like, the door opens for some moral views to have more sway than other moral views. This is as true for drug use as it is for any other behavior. Moreover, sometimes decisions on which behaviors should be prohibited rest on beliefs about how dangerous or harmful a given behavior is. Yet the harm a behavior causes often has little to do with whether it's permitted or prohibited. For example, eating the all-too-typical U.S. diet of red meat, butter, ice cream, and other fat-laden food causes far more death and illness—with incalculable social harm from increased health-care costs, lost economic productivity, and the tears of bereaved spouses and children—than does marijuana smoking, which is not known to have ever killed anyone.

Surely, however, we can distinguish more harmful drugs from less harmful drugs and prohibit the former while allowing, however grudgingly, the latter. Yet even here our decisions have less to do with the harm of the drugs than with various political and social factors, including how many people use the drug, the extent to which it's ingrained in our culture, and the influence of the organizations manufacturing and selling the drug.

To illustrate this, let's consider two groups of drugs. Our first group consists of alcohol, caffeine, and tobacco (nicotine), all legal drugs; our second group: cocaine, heroin, and marijuana, all illegal drugs. How many people die in the United States each year from taking these drugs? Death is not the only harm drugs cause, of course, but is their *ultimate* harm and can be counted. Take a moment and write down your best estimate of the number of annual deaths from the physiological effects of each drug in our two groups, and add up the total number of deaths caused by each drug group. Did you get more deaths in the legal or the illegal drug list?

Now compare your estimates to the best estimates we have from federal agencies (National Center for Health Statistics 1999). The most deadly drug on the list is tobacco, with about 430,000 people dying each year from lung cancer, emphysema, heart disease, and other illnesses caused by tobacco ingredients. Next on the list is alcohol, with an estimated 100,000 people dying each year from alcohol-induced liver disease and other illness, alcohol-related motor vehicle accidents, and homicides committed under the influence of alcohol. Caffeine is a pretty safe drug as long as you don't overdo it, so let's assume no annual deaths from its effects.

What about the illegal drugs? The physiological effects of all illegal drugs kill about 9,000 to 10,000 people each year (Dorsey and Zawitz 1999), often because the drugs have been adulterated with other toxic substances, with cocaine/crack and heroin the major culprits. No deaths occur from marijuana use. Although constant use of high doses of marijuana might in the long run have health effects similar to tobacco's, very few people use this much marijuana for that long. This doesn't mean marijuana is a safe drug, only that it is not a lethal one (Goode 1999).

Now let's add up these deaths. The group of legal drugs kills about 530,000 each year, while the group of illegal drugs kills about 10,000. This difference is graphically displayed in Figure 14.1. Are the illegal drugs more harmful than the legal ones?

Of course, it might be argued that the illegal drugs would kill more people if they were legal, since more people would then use them (Inciardi 1999). If this is so, the disparity in the graphs might indicate the success of the laws prohibiting cocaine, heroin, and other illegal drugs. I discuss this argument later, but for now simply ask: If the legal drugs kill far more than the illegal ones, then where is the logic behind our drug laws?

The answer to this question might be that there is little logic here. Tobacco is legal not because it's safe—far from it—but because so many people for so long have smoked cigarettes and because tobacco companies provide thousands of jobs to people in the South and millions of dollars in campaign contributions to members of Congress. Although tobacco doesn't distort perception and motor ability as many other psychoactive drugs do, it is nonetheless a slow, deadly poison: If cigarettes were just now invented by a small, entrepreneurial company, the Food and Drug Administration would never approve their sale and use. Alcohol is legal not because it's safe—again, far from it—but because so many people for so long have drunk alcohol that it's an integral part of our culture, and because the alcohol industry spends millions of dollars each year advertising its drug's supposed ability to help people have a good time and become popular.

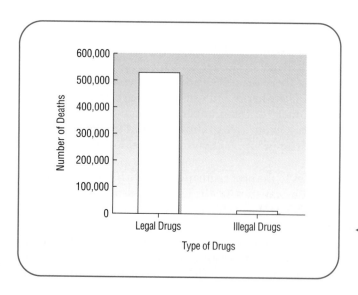

◄ FIGURE 14.1 ESTIMATED ANNUAL U.S. DEATHS
FROM LEGAL AND ILLEGAL DRUGS

Sources: Gustin et al. 1999;
Maguire and Pastore 1995, 1999.

THE SOCIAL SCIENCE ARGUMENT

If the philosophical dimension to the drug legalization debate is complex, the social science dimension—do drug laws do more harm than good?—is even more so. When U.S. Surgeon General Jocelyn Elders in December 1993 proposed considering drug legalization, a firestorm of protest greeted her remarks (Labaton 1993). Yet several prominent people, including noted conservatives William F. Buckley, Milton Friedman, and George Schultz, as well as the then-mayors of Baltimore and San Francisco and the former police chiefs of Minneapolis, New York City, and San Jose, had already made the same proposal or have made it since (Kappeler, Blumberg, and Potter 2000). In October 1999 the governor of New Mexico, Gary Johnson, also endorsed legalization: "I hate to say it, but the majority of people who use drugs use them responsibly. They choose when to do it. They do them at home. It's not a financial burden. For the amount of money we're putting into the war on drugs, I suggest it's an absolute failure. Make drugs a controlled substance like alcohol. Legalize it, control it, regulate it, tax it. If you legalize it, we might actually have a healthier society" (Jackson 1999:A19). Several drug scholars also advocate some form of legalization. Their belief rests on the harms they now see in drug laws and the benefits they say would result if the laws were abolished (Bertram and Sharpe 1997; Nadelmann 1992).

In making their case, legalization proponents often point to the experience of Prohibition. In 1920 a constitutional amendment banned alcohol manufacture and sale and began the Prohibition era. Scholars disagree on whether Prohibition decreased alcohol use: Some cite evidence that it did, while others cite evidence that alcohol use actually went up, with drinks more potent (Dibacco 1993; Moore 1989). Regardless of whether alcohol use went up or down, bootlegging was clearly widespread and otherwise law-abiding people obtained alcohol illegally in "speakeasies" and elsewhere.

Worse yet, Prohibition had other unintended negative effects. The illegal profits to be had from bootlegging were so enormous that organized crime decided to provide this service and in a few short years became much more wealthy and powerful, with Al Capone, the famous organized crime leader, making $200 million a year (Rorabaugh 1995). In attempts to control bootlegging turf, different organized crime groups fought each other with powerful weapons—machine guns—and committed many drive-by shootings. To stop the bootlegging, police and other parts of the criminal justice system devoted much time, energy, and money. Many police were wounded or killed by organized crime members; other police, including at least 400 in Chicago, took bribes to look the other way, as did politicians and other officials (Rorabaugh 1995). Prohibition, in short, was a disaster, and the nation repealed the Prohibition amendment in 1933.

In drawing on the Prohibition experience, legalization proponents make the following points. First, as we've already seen, drug laws create the very crime they're intended to stop. Addicts commit robberies and other crimes to obtain money to support their habit; drug gangs and other traffickers terrorize whole neighborhoods with deadly violence to control trafficking turf; people taking illegal drugs are much more apt than those taking legal ones to become involved in the criminal community and to commit other crimes themselves. Drug laws are also responsible for most of the 9,000 to 10,000 annual deaths from using illegal drugs. Most of these deaths result from the adulteration of the drugs with various toxic substances and from their users' willingness—because of the drugs' expense—to take the drugs in an unsafe manner (e.g., smoking crack instead of snorting cocaine) to get the most intense high for their money. If the drugs were legalized with some government regulation, many of these deaths would be prevented. The drugs would not be adulterated, and their lower expense would allow users to take them in a safer manner. In reducing all these problems, legalization, says one of its proponents, "may well be the only way to reverse the destructive impact of drugs and current drug policies in the ghettos" (Nadelmann 1992:317).

Second, drug laws cost billions of dollars to enforce even though millions of people still use illegal drugs. The illegal drug problem continues to be worst in the inner cities, where the drug war has been fought the hardest (Currie 1994). The billions of dollars spent on the drug war could be better spent on truly violent criminals and on prevention and treatment programs that ultimately would be more effective in lowering drug abuse (Rasmussen and Benson 1994). Third, in a related point, the drug war fills our prisons and jails with hundreds of thousands of people who would otherwise not be there (Zimring and Hawkins 1995). In 1998, for example, there were more than 1.5 million drug abuse arrests (including about 600,000 for marijuana possession) in the United States, a figure about 40 percent greater than the total number of arrests for homicide, rape, robbery, aggravated assault, burglary, motor vehicle theft, and arson combined (Federal Bureau of Investigation 1999). The flood of drug defendants and prisoners has forced the criminal justice system to release violent criminals who pose much more of a threat to society.

Fourth, drug laws create disrespect and even contempt for the law because of the illogic in allowing legal use of the two most deadly drugs, tobacco and alcohol. This disrespect may carry over into other laws and create a more general climate of disobedience to the law.

Fifth, drug laws are good for organized crime. As happened during Prohibition, they are a major source of organized crime's money and influence.

Sixth, drug laws create official corruption throughout the criminal justice system. Bribery of police and thefts by police of confiscated drugs are common. In 1995 several attorneys, including a former top U.S. Department of Justice official and a former assistant U.S. attorney, were among a group of fifty-nine people indicted for corruption involving the Colombian drug cartel supplying most of the world's cocaine (Lester 1995). Most of this corruption would disappear if drugs were legalized.

Seventh, if illegal drugs were legalized and sold like any other product, they could be taxed like any other product. The taxes on the drugs would add billions of dollars annually to federal and state revenues. Much or all of this money could, if we wished, be used for drug treatment and prevention programs.

Eighth and last, enforcement of drug laws often involves the use of informants, wiretapping, and other legally distasteful procedures. Drug testing in the workplace and in the schools has become commonplace. Like many other public order crime laws, drug laws, say their critics, thus threaten the nation's civil liberties by turning us all into "a society of suspects" (Wisotsky 1995).

Opponents of legalization concede some of these points but argue that drug laws have indeed reduced the use of illegal drugs, even if many people still use them. They predict that many more people would use illegal drugs if they were made legal, leading to more drug addicts and much more death, illness, and other problems than we now see with tobacco and alcohol. While they concede these two drugs would be illegal in an ideal world, they say we should not compound the problem by legalizing other drugs. As Erich Goode (1994:197) observes, "Current policies have worked, in their clumsy, limited, even damaging way.... Any major change on the scale of outright legalization is likely to be a disaster."

This disaster, say legalization's opponents, would be greatest in the nation's inner cities, where the increase in drug abuse after legalization would be especially great. As Currie (1994:188) observes, "If consumption increased, it would almost certainly increase most among the strata already most vulnerable to hard-drug use—thus exacerbating the social stratification of the drug crisis."

Opponents also ask whether drugs would become legal for adolescents as well as for adults (Inciardi 1992). While adults, perhaps, could be expected to control their drug use to at least some degree, adolescents could well get carried away. If drugs remained illegal for adolescents, opponents charge, the same problems that proponents now cite as reasons for legalization would continue.

In response to the opponents' assertions, legalization proponents counter that we simply can't know whether drug laws have reduced drug use, and they point to times, such as in New York City in the 1970s, when drug use increased after the imposition of new, very harsh penalties for drug trafficking. It's uncertain, they add, whether more people would use illegal drugs if they were made legal. Illegal drugs are so easy to get now, they say, that anyone who wants to use them already does. If people aren't using them now, it's because they don't like using drugs or are afraid of their effects, not because the drugs are illegal.

Support for this argument comes from the high school senior surveys discussed earlier. In these surveys, the proportion of seniors using illegal drugs is far smaller than the proportion feeling they could obtain the drugs "fairly easily" or "easily." For example, although 90 percent of seniors in 1998 reported they could easily obtain marijuana, only 37.5 percent of the seniors reported using it in the last year. Similarly, although 45.7 percent of the seniors said they could easily obtain cocaine, only 5.7 percent had used it in the last year (Maguire and Pastore 1999). To legalization proponents these data indicate that people, including the urban poor, who don't use illegal drugs now also wouldn't use them if they were legalized.

In fact, the proponents say, in what is sometimes called the "forbidden fruit" argument, many youths now use illegal drugs precisely *because* they are illegal, as the drugs' illegality contributes to the excitement of using them. Responding to one further charge, proponents say that a major reason education and treatment programs have not worked well among the urban poor is that they haven't been well-funded and in many ways hardly exist. Legalization, they argue, would free up billions of dollars that could go toward devising and implementing effective programs.

To support their views, legalization proponents point to the recent history of marijuana use. When marijuana was decriminalized in many states in the 1970s, marijuana use did not go up in those states as compared to other states that did not decriminalize it. In fact, despite generally less punitive laws regarding marijuana use in the last two decades in the United States, marijuana use has declined during that time. Marijuana use also declined after it was decriminalized in the Netherlands in the 1970s (Nadelmann 1992). Legalization opponents counter that what might be true for marijuana might not hold true for other illegal drugs, which are much more enticing and addictive (Currie 1994).

Both sides to the debate make valid points. Unfortunately, we can't test their views unless we first legalize drugs, which isn't about to happen soon. Thus, as Samuel Walker (1998:266) notes, "The full impact of legalization remains entirely a matter of speculation." The key questions are whether more people would use illegal drugs if they were made legal and, if so, how many and at what social cost. Even some legalization proponents concede that it may promote more drug use. Ethan A. Nadelmann (1992:317), a notable proponent, admits that legalization "is a risky policy, one that may indeed lead to an increase in the number of people who abuse drugs." However, he adds, "That risk is by no means a certainty."

Assuming for the sake of argument that there would be some increased use, the question then becomes whether this risk is worth taking to obtain the benefits of legalization that even its opponents sometimes concede. Nadelmann (1992:317) thinks the risk is well worth it: "Current drug control policies are showing little progress and new proposals promise only to be more costly, and more repressive. We know that repealing the drug prohibition laws would eliminate or greatly reduce many of the ills that people commonly identify as part and parcel of the 'drug problem.'" New Mexico's governor Gary Johnson agrees: "There are going to be new problems under legalization. But I submit to you they are going to be about half of what they are today under the prohibition model" (Kelley 1999:A7). Goode (1994:196–197) summarizes our dilemma when he notes that legalization "will eliminate some drug-related problems, as its proponents suggest—the murders, much of the crime, many of the medical maladies of junkies. It is society's choice as to which we want: a relatively small number of sick, violent, criminal addicts or [after legalization] a much larger number of healthier, less violent, and less criminal addicts. Most Americans would choose the former." Perhaps the final word should go to criminologist Walker (1998:266), who concludes, "Legalization is a high-risk gamble that needs further discussion."

Harm Reduction and Drug Courts

Many drug experts who think legalization goes too far, and even those who favor some form of it, think our nation would be better off if it adopted a *harm reduction* policy regarding illegal drug use and drug offenders (Schmidt and Williams 1999; Tucker 1999). In such a policy, drug use is treated as a public health problem and not as a crime problem. Drug users are treated not as criminals but as persons in need of medical, psychological, and other help. To deal with the drug problem, much more money would be spent on drug prevention and treatment programs and much less on criminal justice approaches. Sterile needles would be made available to known drug users to reduce the spread of AIDS and other diseases. Several European nations have adopted harm reduction policies along these lines.

In the United States, talk of harm reduction is almost as anathema as talk of legalization, but a few years ago Baltimore began to adopt some harm reduction measures in what has been called "an unusual social experiment" (Gammage 1997:A1; Grunwald 1997). An estimated one-ninth of Baltimore's adult population was said to be using illegal drugs. Against this backdrop, a $25 million pledge from a Baltimore philanthropist was welcomed as a way to try to deal with the city's drug problem. Baltimore estimated that every nonviolent drug offender who was imprisoned was costing taxpayers about $20,000 a year but would cost only about $3,000 to $4,000 if he or she entered a treatment program.

While the Baltimore mayor was firmly behind the city's move toward harm reduction, its police commissioner was just as firmly opposed. One measure upon which the city's opposing forces agreed was its use of a *drug court* to deal with nonviolent drug addicts. Such courts typically sentence drug users to intensive supervision and drug treatment rather than to jail. This saves money and is thought to hold much more potential for weaning them from drugs. Drug courts have become more popular in recent years. In the middle 1990s there were only 12 in the nation, and now there are more than 400. Preliminary evidence indicates they provide a promising alternative for dealing with nonviolent drug offenders. Critics feel they still treat drug users as criminals and rob offenders of their rights to due process and privacy since they often require a defendant to plead guilty to be allowed to enter a drug treatment program (Cole 1999).

 ## Sexual Offenses: Prostitution and Pornography

Prostitution

Prostitution is often called the world's oldest profession, and it might well be. It existed in ancient Mesopotamia, where priests had sex with women whose religious duty was to help procreate the species. In ancient Greece, legal brothels (houses of prostitution) were common. One class of prostitutes served the needs of Greek political officials, and another class served the common citizenry. Prostitution also flourished in ancient Rome. In the Old Testament, prostitution "was accepted as a more or less necessary fact of life and it was more or less expected that many men would turn to prostitutes" (Bullough and Bullough 1977:137–138). Licensed brothels providing much tax revenue existed throughout Europe during the Middle Ages, as the Church disapproved but still tolerated the practice as one that prevented more wanton lust. In the 1500s, however, brothels were shut down across Europe as the Church and political officials became alarmed by the possibility that prostitutes were spreading syphilis. Brothels and certainly prostitution didn't disappear, and in the 1700s and 1800s many European cities permitted licensed brothels and required regular medical exams of their employees (Bullough and Bullough 1987).

Prostitution was also common in the United States in the 1800s, as poor young women chose it as one of the few jobs available to them (Bullough 1980). Individual prostitutes solicited business at street corners and respectable hotels and businesses throughout many cities, and camps of prostitutes would travel to railroad construction sites and other locations where men lacking wives or other female partners would be found. Railroad workers visiting a prostitute would hang their red signal lamps outside her tent so that they could be found in case they were needed suddenly for railroad work. The term *red-light district* comes from the red glow that would emanate from the prostitutes' encampment on busy nights. Earlier, during the Civil War, men from either side's army were potential customers for prostitutes. The modern term *hooker* comes from the prostitutes who had sex with soldiers under the command of Union General Joseph Hooker.

Through the early 1900s many U.S. cities had legal brothels, which were often segregated in certain parts of the cities. Brothels were especially common in New Orleans and San Francisco, but other cities had them, too. A "moral crusade" against brothels, carried out by the same white, middle-class Protestants behind the temperance movement, began in the United States about 1910 and sounded the alarm about prostitution's influence on middle-class girls lured into sexual depravation by the promise of lots of money for little time and effort. The crusade was especially strong in Chicago, and its brothels ceased business by late 1912. Dozens of other cities shut down their brothels during the next six years (Hobson 1987).

Despite the bans on brothels, some have continued their business over the years. In Nevada, of course, brothels are legal outside the counties containing

Las Vegas and Reno, and these "ranches," as they're called, are a favorite tourist attraction among men. Some illegal brothels in other states have also received their share of publicity. During World War II, a madam named Sally Stanford ran a fancy brothel in San Francisco, where the customers included many of the city's leading politicians, law enforcement officers, and businessmen. Stanford required regular health exams of her employees to guard against venereal disease, and her rather luxurious enterprise ensured that the employees would not suffer the various problems that streetwalkers often experience. Stanford later became mayor of a town across the bay from San Francisco and published her autobiography with a major publishing house (Stanford 1966).

Another elegant brothel was run in the 1980s by Sydney Biddle Barrows in a posh New York City neighborhood. Barrows, a descendant of the Mayflower settlers, quickly became known as the *Mayflower* Madam after her brothel was uncovered and eventually she also published her autobiography (Barrows and Novak 1986). A high-class prostitution service in the news a decade later was run in Hollywood by Heidi Fleiss, whose customers included notable actors, producers, and other Hollywood folks. Fleiss eventually received a three-year prison term in 1994 for pandering, which was criticized by feminists and even some of the jurors in her trial for being too long. Feminists also criticized the fact that none of her male customers were prosecuted (Smolowe 1994).

EXPLAINING PROSTITUTION

Most prostitutes are women, and the majority of the 94,000 arrests in 1998 for prostitution and commercialized vice were women (Federal Bureau of Investigation 1999). The men arrested are usually male prostitutes serving a male clientele. Pimps are only occasionally arrested, and male customers of female prostitutes hardly at all, notwithstanding the widely publicized 1995 arrest of British actor Hugh Grant for "lewd conduct" in a car with a California prostitute. The estimated number of U.S. prostitutes is 500,000 (Clinard and Meier 1995). Assuming a conservative five acts of prostitution per week per prostitute, at least 2.5 million acts occur weekly, or more than 120 million acts per year. According to a national survey on sexual attitudes and behavior, about 5 million U.S. women have engaged in acts fitting the definition of prostitution (Janus and Janus 1993). The survey also estimated that 20 percent of U.S. adult males have had sex with a prostitute.

Prostitution is widely disliked and even detested because it involves sex in exchange for money or other economic gain. Not surprisingly, our negative attitudes toward prostitution apply much more to (female) prostitutes than to their (male) customers, many of whom are middle-class businessmen and other so-called respectable individuals. Over the years, critics have condemned prostitutes as immoral women with uncontrolled sexual desire, but they've said little about their customers. Scholars have studied why women become prostitutes, yet few, if any, studies exist of why men become their customers. The message is that it's "normal" for men, often in a sort of rite of passage, to have sex with a prostitute, but abnormal for women to take money for sex with these men.

Many scholars say that prostitution symbolizes the many ways in which society victimizes women (James 1982). It's no accident, they say, that most prostitutes are poor. Poor women turn to prostitution because they lack the income alternatives available to men, even poor men. As we saw earlier, prostitution is a particularly tempting option if money is needed to support an illegal drug habit. Women also commit prostitution because in a society that continues to regard women as sex objects that exist for the pleasure of men, female prostitution is inevitable and perhaps even a logical extension of "normal" female-male relationships where men continue to be dominant (Millet 1973). Further, many young women turn to prostitution as a tragic, complex psychological response to long histories of incest and other childhood and adolescent sexual abuse and family disorder. In prostitution, then, we see a striking manifestation of the many ways in which women suffer in a sexist society.

Some scholars also note that prostitution, however disagreeable to many people, still provides several important functions for prostitutes and their customers (McCaghy and Capron 2000). For prostitutes, their behavior is a source of income. For their customers, prostitution is a sexual outlet for men who have no other sexual alternatives. Some of these men lack female partners because they are at locations, such as military bases, where few women live; others lack partners because of a physical disability or other problem; still others lack partners because they have unusual sexual desires. In 1937 sociologist Kingsley Davis (1937) proposed that prostitution even helps preserve marriages, and thus lowers the divorce rate, by providing married men unhappy with their marital sex with a love-free sexual outlet. Otherwise a married man might have to have an affair and could more easily fall in love with another woman. To determine whether Davis's view reflects antiquated sexism or practical reality, we would have to legalize prostitution and see what happened to the divorce rate.

Prostitutes themselves readily mention some or all of these functions as justifications for their behavior (Davis 1981). In 1995 these supposed benefits were at the center of a controversy in Bangor, Maine, concerning "relaxation spas," in which female employees give genital massages to male customers until they ejaculate. Since Maine law at the time didn't forbid such contact for money, the centers were legal. The owner of one of the centers, named The Classic Touch, justified her business, which employed fourteen women, as one that provided safe "stress release" for various kinds of men and even offered a senior citizen discount. "We have many senior citizens and handicapped people," she said. "We have some men who are impotent and others who are divorced or in bad marriages. This is a safe, AIDS-free environment ... [and] helps marriages. Husbands come in here and get a stress release and then they are able to go home and take on more. These are men who aren't in bars picking up strange women" (Ordway 1995:1).

Contemporary debate over prostitution extends into the question of legalization. Proponents say that legalizing prostitution would reduce some of the problems now associated with it, while opponents fear that legalization would increase prostitution and victimize women even further. The Crime and Controversy box on page 420 examines this debate in more detail.

Pornography

Like prostitution, pornography has been around since ancient times. The term comes from the Greek word *pornographos* and literally means writings about prostitutes. As the history of the term suggests, pornography, which for now we'll define as sexually explicit materials, was common in ancient Greece and Rome and especially popular in ancient India and Japan. It persisted through the Middle Ages but lost popularity in the West because of rigid Judeo-Christian views on sexuality. Like prostitution, the Church tolerated pornography but didn't approve it. Pornography remained uncommon in the United States until the late

Should Prostitution Be Legalized?

As with drugs, various observers debate whether prostitution should be legalized. Legalization proponents offer both philosophical and social scientific arguments. Philosophically, prostitution is an act involving two individuals consenting to the behavior. Although many people do not like the idea of exchanging sex for money, that is ultimately a moral view on which the state should not legislate. Other people, including athletes and models, "sell their bodies." Some women and men go out on dates where, even today, the man still expects sex in return for showing the woman a good time and spending lavishly on their evening together. Any sex that then occurs is thus not too different from what the law bans.

Perhaps more important, say legalization proponents, the problems we associate with prostitution stem from the laws against it and would be reduced greatly, and perhaps eliminated, if we decriminalized. Right now, prostitutes are sometimes beaten and robbed by their customers, and sometimes customers are robbed by prostitutes or their pimps. Prostitution provides some money, though a dwindling amount, for organized crime. Prostitutes help spread venereal disease, a particular concern during the AIDS era, even if most such disease is spread by people engaging in sex not involving prostitution. To reduce these problems, say some scholars, we should legalize prostitution and regulate it like any other business. In short, we should adopt and improve on the licensed brothel model common in the United States for much of its history.

This model is now used in many parts of Nevada, where prostitution ranches largely lack the problems just noted. If prostitution were legalized, then, the crime we now see associated with prostitution would diminish and perhaps even disappear. Organized crime would be less in the picture. Regular health exams could be required to check for venereal disease, and the use of condoms could be enforced. In addition, hundreds of millions of dollars of tax money would be added to federal, state, and local government revenues. Moreover, the time, energy, and money the criminal justice system now spends on the almost 100,000 prostitute arrests each year would be more wisely used against the truly violent criminals who are real threats to public safety.

Some scholars and feminists say we should make prostitution legal but not regulate it. In Nevada and other areas, such as France and Germany, where prostitution is regulated, prostitutes face severe restrictions on their freedom to go where they want and on other aspects of their lives. Since prostitutes might be responsible at most for only a very small proportion of all venereal disease, required medical checks are seen as unfair. In these and other respects, regulation itself thus punishes women unnecessarily for the choices they've made with their behavior.

As this brief discussion suggests, legalization of prostitution is not about to happen soon. Perhaps the most difficult issue to deal with in legalization is that of adolescent prostitution. Few legalization proponents advocate legalizing prostitution for adolescents under 18, who are thought not mature enough to be able to decide to commit prostitution. Thus some problems now associated with prostitution may continue if it remained illegal for those under 18 even if it were legalized for adults. As with drug use, adolescent involvement in prostitution thus remains a problem that neither side to the legalization debate can adequately address. As several scholars stress, teenaged prostitutes, both male and female, typically come from homes filled with incest and other sexual and physical abuse. The most effective way to reduce teenaged prostitution is thus by reducing childhood abuse and the structural conditions promoting it.

Sources: Hepburn 1993; Jenness 1993; McCaghy and Capron 2000; Quindlen 1994.

1800s, when it became more popular amid the great social and economic upheaval after the Civil War (Kendrick 1987; Richlin 1992).

The years since have seen various federal, state, and local efforts to ban or control the distribution of pornography. These efforts were filled with controversy over the definition of pornography and over questions of censorship in a democratic society. Finally in 1973 the U.S. Supreme Court said that pornography could be considered obscene and therefore banned: (1) If an average person applying current community views would conclude that the work appealed to the "prurient" interest; (2) if the work depicts sexual conduct in a "patently offensive way"; and (3) if the work taken as a whole lacks "serious literary, artistic, political, or scientific value" (*Miller v. California*, 413 U.S. 15). As critics pointed out, even this definition raised more questions than it answered. For example, who is an "average person"? Who is to decide whether the way a work depicts sexual conduct is "patently offensive" or, alternatively, just unpleasant or even appealing? Who is to decide whether a work lacks serious literary or other value? What if a few people think it has such value and most do not? How much value constitutes *serious* value?

In 1987 the Court modified its 1973 ruling when it noted that a work could be judged obscene and thus banned if a "reasonable person" applying a national standard would conclude that the work lacked any social value (*Pope v. Illinois*, 107 S.Ct. 1918). This ruling still left unanswered several questions, including who is a "reasonable person" and how do we know what the national standard would be (Albanese 1996).

CONTEMPORARY VIEWS ON PORNOGRAPHY

Not surprisingly, the public holds many different views about pornography. In the 1994 General Social Survey (GSS), 67 percent of the sample felt that pornography provides "an outlet for bottled-up impulses." At the same time, 54 percent felt that

◀ *People have long been interested in viewing sexually explicit materials and activities. Controversy continues over what, if anything, society should do about pornography.*

"sexual materials lead people to commit rape" and 61 percent thought pornography "leads to a breakdown of morals." Reflecting these divergent views, more than half of the 1998 GSS, or 59 percent, opposed laws against the distribution of pornography for people 18 and older. Almost everyone (94 percent), however, supported laws banning the distribution of pornography to people under 18.

As the questions about the Supreme Court rulings suggest, one of the most important issues regarding pornography is how to define it. Related to this issue is the question of censorship. Just as beauty is in the eyes of the beholder, so may be pornography. Some of the greatest works in art history depict nudes in paintings or sculpture: Many of these were considered pornographic by various secular or religious authorities at the time of their creation. Some books now hailed as literary masterpieces, such as James Joyce's *Ulysses*, were considered obscene and even banned when they were first published. If pornography is defined as sexually explicit or sexually arousing material, then even the most benign works have the potential to be considered pornographic. In the 1950s, for example, adolescent boys would look at pictures of semi-nude women in *National Geographic* to become sexually aroused. Not surprisingly, some religious groups considered the pictures pornographic and urged the magazine to omit them. More recently, a classic episode in the 1990s TV comedy *Seinfeld* began with one of the characters, George, telling his friends that he'd been caught by his mother in the act of masturbating while reading *Glamour* magazine. As these examples indicate, any effort to ban pornography, no matter how disgusting the vast majority of the public finds certain kinds of pornography, inevitably raises the ugly specter of censorship (Strossen 1995).

Those in favor of banning pornography say that censorship is not an issue. Even in a democratic society, they note, some speech is prohibited without it being considered censorship. People may not shout fire in a crowded theater, nor may they libel or slander other individuals. Given these exceptions to the First Amendment, they think that banning pornography isn't a question of censorship but rather one of protecting society.

The kind of protection urged depends on why one opposes pornography in the first place. In the last two decades, two otherwise very different groups, religious moralists and antipornography feminists, have been especially vocal in criticizing pornography and calling for its banning. Religious moralists condemn the sexual aspect of pornography. Representing traditional Judeo-Christian views, they feel that sexual pleasure should be a means to an end—reproduction of the species—and not an end in itself. Depictions of nudity and sexual behavior thus violate their religious views, which prompt them to feel that pornography both offends and threatens society's moral order (Berke 1995).

Many feminists also call for the banning of pornography but for very different reasons. To them pornography, like rape, is not about sex but rather about male domination and violence against women (Dworkin 1989; Russell 1993). It's no accident, say feminists, that virtually all pornography depicts women rather than men, and that when men are present, they usually dominate women sexually and/or violently. Whether or not it involves violence, pornography expresses contempt for women and degrades them as sexual objects existing solely for men's pleasure. As such, pornography is "one of the mechanisms that has sustained the systemic domination of women by men throughout history" (Diamond 1982:339). Perhaps the worst aspect of pornography, say many feminists, is that it contributes to rape by reinforcing men's beliefs that women like or need to be raped. As Robin Morgan (1977:169) asserted more than twenty years ago in a now-famous phrase, "Pornography is the theory, and rape the practice."

In criticizing pornography, some feminists distinguish between *violent pornography*, which depicts sexual violence against women, and *erotica*, which depicts "respectful" nudity and consensual, loving sexual interaction between adults (Berger, Searles, and Cottle 1991). They also distinguish violent pornography from nonviolent pornography, which falls short of the respect and loving nature of erotica but does not include violence against women. Other feminists make no such distinctions, as they consider nudity like that appearing in *Playboy* or *Penthouse* little better than violent pornography. They would thus ban virtually any pornography. Other feminists feel this goes too far and would ban only the most violent pornography.

Still other feminists criticize pornography but don't feel it should be banned, as they worry about the censorship issue. They and other free-speech advocates fear that any bans on pornography would inevitably extend to erotica and even to feminist depictions of the nature of rape, prostitution, and crimes involving women (Itzin 1992; Kaminer 1992). The disagreement among feminists over the censorship issue has led to some heated debates. In a controversial 1992 incident, antipornography feminists forced the closing of an art exhibit at the University of Michigan featuring films and videos by women about prostitutes (Vance 1993).

PORNOGRAPHY AND RAPE

Does pornography cause rape or other violence against women, as many feminists charge? Like many questions in criminology, this one has no clear answers (Lesieur and Welch 2000). Anecdotal evidence indicates the homes of convicted rapists often contain a good deal of violent pornography. Some people interpret such evidence as proof of a pornography-rape causal connection, but it may simply mean that men with violent sexual attitudes are likely both to read and view violent pornography and to rape women. The 1970 National Commission on Obscenity and Pornography concluded that pornography didn't cause rape and other violence against women, but it was later criticized for relying on studies that examined only the effects of nonviolent pornography and erotica, not of violent pornography (Bart and Jozsa 1982). The growth in the 1970s of violent pornography fueled feminist concerns over its potential effect on rape and other anti-women violence (Scott and Cuvelier 1987).

Several studies since that time have shown that men, usually male college students, shown violent pornography in laboratory experiments often, but not always, exhibit short-term increases in aggressive attitudes toward women and in acceptance of rape myths (Donnerstein, Linz, and Penrod 1987). However, these laboratory studies don't necessarily mean that pornography actually causes men to go out and rape in real life.

Another kind of study has examined the geographical, statistical correlation between circulation of *Playboy*, *Penthouse*, *Hustler*, and other "men's magazines" and official rape rates. One study found a positive correlation at the state level but concluded that the correlation may well be spurious, indicating simply that states with more violent, rape-prone cultures are likely to have both higher rates of men's magazine circulation and of rape (Baron and Straus 1989). A later study found no correlation at all at the metropolitan level and concluded that any conclusions of a causal connection between pornography and rape were premature (Gentry 1991). The authors of both studies concluded that efforts to limit or ban pornography would do little if anything to reduce the number of rapes.

At this stage of our knowledge, the fairest conclusion is that violent pornography may prompt a short-term increase among men in aggressive attitudes toward women, but that any clearer pornography-rape cause-and-effect relationship in the real world is far from being proven. As Chapter 10 indicated, there are many structural and cultural sources of rape, and pornography is probably more a symptom of these structural and cultural conditions than an independent cause of rape. Of course, we can't completely rule out the possibility that pornography does increase the number of rapes, but any such effect is likely very small compared to the effects of the other sources of rape in our society.

Even if pornography doesn't cause rape, much of it, depending on how it is defined, degrades women by portraying them as men's sexual playthings. No matter what pornographers try to tell us, women are far more than collections of attractive body parts. Unfortunately, many men, subscribing to antiquated notions of masculinity and femininity, can't see beyond these limits. As a result, they also don't recognize that pornography harms men as well as women. As Harry Brod (1995:396) notes, pornography depicts women not as a man's equal but rather as "already presented to him for the 'taking.' The female is primarily there as sex object, not sexual subject." By reinforcing the myth of perpetual male sexual readiness, says Brod, pornography actually reduces the sexual pleasure men experience, since they end up overly worried about their sexual performance. And by regarding women as "trophies awarded to the victor" (p. 396), pornography reinforces an artificial standard of female beauty that restricts men's ability to form loving relationships with the vast majority of women who fall short of this unreal ideal.

Certainly, religious moralists and antipornography feminists are not about to stop their efforts to ban offensive sexual material. Yet the very fact that these two radically different groups both want to ban pornography suggests the danger of taking such an action in a free society. However repugnant many of us find much pornography, the civil liberties issues raised by calls for its prohibition demand that we proceed with the greatest caution in this area. Judging from the other public order crimes already discussed, any outright ban on pornography may well prove futile. For better or worse, there is simply too much interest in pornography, however it's defined, for such a ban to work well, and too many individuals willing to provide it. The abundance and popularity of pornography on the Internet underscores the difficulty of having such a ban succeed.

 GAMBLING

Like the other behaviors discussed in this chapter, gambling has a very long history punctuated by laws designed to regulate the conduct of society's poor (Lesieur and Welch 2000; Wykes 1964). In ancient Egypt, authorities prohibited gambling because they worried it would distract workers from mining and other labor. A similar concern prompted the kings of England and France in the late twelfth century to prohibit gambling for the poor while allowing it for the nobility. Several centuries later, vagrancy laws expanded in England in 1743 to forbid certain types of gambling. Additional legislation in 1853 further outlawed most of the types of betting in which the English poor were involved, although they flouted the law and continued to bet anyway.

In the American colonies, Massachusetts Bay Puritans considered gambling a sin and banned it in 1638 (Fenster 1994). Despite this early prohibition, gambling eventually became quite popular in the colonies. Lotteries were the game of choice, as lottery revenue helped finance the construction of public buildings and early universities such as Harvard and Yale. Lotteries eventually fell prey to corruption and were abolished during the 1800s. In their place grew illegal betting, most commonly in the form of bookmaking and "numbers running," in which people bet on the last few numbers of stock exchange and other numerical indicators. Over the years, illegal gambling has provided much of the revenue for organized crime and fueled corruption by police, politicians, and other public officials.

Of all the behaviors discussed in this chapter, gambling is the most common and by far the most accepted. Most U.S. residents gamble at one time or another, and many gamble repeatedly. Recent studies estimated that more than 20 million Americans either have gambling problems or are at risk for developing them and put the number of addicted gamblers between 1.8 million and 5 million. One study estimated that gambling addiction costs the nation $5 billion each year in lost wages, bankruptcy, and legal fees for divorce and other problems (Arnold 1999). There are many "how to" books about winning at gambling. In fact, it's not an exaggeration to say we are a "nation of gamblers" suffering from "gambling fever," as the titles of recent articles put it (Fenster 1994; Welles 1989). We spend more than $300 billion per year on legal gambling at casinos, horse- and dog-racing tracks, state lotteries, and church bingo, and probably tens of billions on illegal gambling, much of it sports-related, with numbers rackets concentrated in large cities.

For better or worse, gambling is becoming increasingly legal. As Walker (1998:235) notes, "The legal status of gambling in the United States has undergone a massive change in recent years. The old moralistic objections have collapsed as many states have created lotteries and authorized casino gambling." After more than a century of no legal lotteries, about two-thirds of the states now have them, and various communities, especially those along the Mississippi River, have established or are considering establishing water- and land-based casinos. Reflecting the growth in legal gambling and police decisions to de-emphasize control of illegal gambling, gambling arrests have dropped dramatically in the last few decades, from some 123,000 in 1960 to only 12,800 (90 percent male and 30 percent white) in 1998 (Federal Bureau of Investigation 1999).

At least three reasons explain the growth of legal gambling (Rosecrance 1988). First, the United States in general has become more tolerant in the last few decades of the various public order or vice crimes. Given such a relaxation of attitudes, legalization of gambling was probably inevitable. Second, and perhaps more important, states and cities have turned to lotteries and casinos as sources of much-needed revenue (McDowell 1992). While the lotteries are very profitable for the states, with the odds against winning several million to one, casinos have been a different story. The introduction of casinos into Atlantic City, New Jersey, two decades ago largely failed to live up to its promise of economic growth for the city, and the financial returns from new casinos at Mississippi River towns in the 1990s were often disappointing (Francis 1994). A third reason for casino growth lies in decisions by various Native American tribes to start casinos on their reservations, again as a source of much-needed revenue. The casinos have stirred much controversy in certain tribes, as some Native Americans fear that the casinos will destroy the tribes' traditional way of life and cause other problems (Judson 1994).

Despite the growing acceptance and legalization of gambling, religious groups warn against it. In addition to worrying about the amount of money people will lose from legal gambling and the resulting harm done to their families, they view gambling as an immoral attempt to get something for nothing, which destroys personal character (Zipperer 1994). Religious critics of lotteries and other legalized gambling condemn them as acts of moral degeneration that prey on human weakness. Interestingly, despite the religious condemnation of gambling, various churches have long held regular bingo or beano games to raise funds, and these games appear to be increasing (Sudetic 1995).

The churches' inconsistency aside, their concern over legal gambling's economic harm is worth restating. There is little question that the growth of lotteries and casinos has increased the number of gamblers and the amount of money spent on gambling. Noting that the poor and near-poor are the major players of state lotteries, several secular observers charge that the lotteries exploit the poor and worsen their financial condition (Luke 1990). Amid evidence of growing teenaged gambling, other observers warn that legal gambling will only aggravate the problem (Scherer 1995). Still others point to compulsive gambling that ravages hundreds of thousands of families, even if compulsive gamblers comprise only a minuscule fraction of all gamblers (Estes and Brubaker 1994).

As these warnings attest, gambling, like the other behaviors in this chapter, can't be truly victimless. But it's a choice that people make, and critics of gambling laws and other public crime laws question whether we should stop people from making unwise choices. So much gambling occurs anyway, they add, that there's little hope of banning it effectively. Despite the problems it may cause, the growing legalization of gambling may be keeping some gambling revenue from organized crime, and the great decrease in gambling arrests has freed up scarce criminal justice resources for more important crime fighting. As with the other behaviors discussed in this chapter, gambling remains an activity that provides thrills and excitement for millions of people even as it causes some of them to suffer. For better or worse, gambling is here to stay, and its legalization, however distasteful to some, may lead to more good than harm.

 ORGANIZED CRIME

I noted earlier that when the public demands goods or services, organized crime is all too ready to provide them. Sometimes this is true even if the products and services are legal. For example, organized crime is thought to be involved in several legitimate businesses, including trash-hauling operations and the vending and amusement machine industries (Abadinsky 2000). It's also believed to be involved in the toxic-waste dumping industry, often working hand-in-hand with the legitimate businesses that produce toxic waste and want to dispose of it quickly and quietly (Block and Scarpitti 1985).

Despite its involvement in these kinds of businesses, however, organized crime's primary source of income remains the activities and products discussed earlier—drugs, prostitution, pornography, and gambling—along with loan sharking (loaning money at extraordinarily high interest rates) and extortion (obtaining money through threats). Throughout its history, organized crime has flourished because it has catered to the public's desires and has had the active or passive cooperation of political, legal, and business officials. The rest of this section explores these themes.

History of Organized Crime

If by organized crime we mean coordinated efforts to acquire illegal profits, then organized crime has existed for centuries. The earliest example of organized crime is piracy, in which pirates roamed the high seas and plundered ships. Piracy was common among ancient Phoenicians on the Mediterranean Sea and, many centuries later, among Vikings in what is now Western Europe. In the 1600s, buccaneers—Dutch, English, and French pirates—began plundering ships carrying goods to and from the Spanish colonies in the New World and then branched out to colonies farther north. By the end of the 1600s, pirates openly traded their plunder with merchants in Boston, New York, Philadelphia, and other port cities in what is called the "golden age of piracy." The merchants bought the pirated booty at low cost and sold the pirates food and other provisions. Royal governors and other public officials took bribes to look the other way, with corruption especially rampant in the New York colony.

Piracy eventually faded by the late 1720s after honest officials exposed their brethren's corruption and several pirate leaders were killed. But perhaps the major reason piracy ended was that merchants began to realize they could get greater profits by trading with England than with pirates. "At that point," say criminologists Dennis J. Kenney and James O. Finckenauer (1995:70), "the markets for pirate goods dried up, and the public demand for their services and support for their existence disappeared." The merchants who once traded with pirates now called them a public menace. One lesson of the golden age of piracy is that "colonial piracy flourished only because the colonists wanted it to" (Kenney and Finckenauer 1995:70). Piracy's success depended on the willingness of merchants to trade with pirates, the public's willingness to buy the pirates' plunder from the merchants, and the readiness of political officials to take bribes. The situation today with organized crime is not much different.

Organized crime began anew in New York City in the early 1800s, where almost 1 million people—most of them poor, half of them immigrants, and many of them unemployed—lived crammed into two square miles. Amid such conditions, stealing and other crime were inevitable. Young women were forced to turn to prostitution, while young men formed gangs, enabling them to commit crime more effectively and protecting them from the police. These gangs were the forerunners of today's organized crime groups and, like the pirates before them, had a cozy relationship with public officials, as crooked city politicians used them at polling places to stuff ballot boxes and intimidate voters (Kenney and Finckenauer 1995).

By the end of the century, the gangs had developed in New York and elsewhere into extensive operations, many of them involving vice crime such as prostitution and gambling. The ethnic makeup of these organized crime groups reflected the great waves of immigration into the United States during the nineteenth century. As in New York, most immigrants settled in the major cities and faced abject poverty and horrible living conditions. As cities grew and the vice trade developed, it was inevitable that many immigrants would turn to organized crime to make ends meet. Irish-Americans were the first to take up organized crime, and eventually became very dominant in many cities. Later in the century Italians and Jews immigrated into the country in enormous numbers and soon got their share of the vice trade, working closely, as the Irish had before them, with politicians, police, and various legitimate businesses. In this century, African-Americans, Asian-Americans, and Hispanics have become more involved in organized crime. Although many scholars question whether the United States has been, as popularly thought, one big "melting pot" of various ethnic and racial groups, organized crime ironically is one area where diverse groups have pursued economic opportunity and the American dream (O'Kane 1992).

If New York and other city gangs were the forerunners of organized crime, the nineteenth-century robber barons were the role models, says criminologist

Howard Abadinsky (2000) (see Chapter 12). Railroad baron Leland Stanford, for example, who later established Stanford University, bribed members of Congress and other officials to gain land grants and federal loans for his Central Pacific Railroad. John D. Rockefeller's Standard Oil Company forced competitors out of business with price wars and occasionally dynamite. The Du Pont family, which made its fortune on gunpowder, cornered its market after the Civil War with bribery and explosions of competing firms. Abadinsky cites these and other examples as evidence of the corruption and violence long characterizing the U.S. scene. Twentieth-century organized crime is merely its latest manifestation.

Abadinsky's robber baron examples indicate that organized crime and corporate crime might be more similar than we think. Taking up this theme, many scholars have argued that there is little difference between the two (Calavita and Pontell 1990). Both kinds of crime involve careful planning and coordinated effort to acquire illegal profits. Both rely on active or passive collusion of public officials and on public willingness to buy the goods and services they provide. Although organized crime is more willing to use interpersonal violence to acquire its profits, corporate crime, as we saw in Chapter 12, can also be very violent.

Organized crime's power and wealth increased enormously during Prohibition (Fox 1989). Before this time, organized crime was primarily a local phenomenon with little coordination across cities. Bootlegging demanded much more coordination, as it involved the manufacture, distribution, and sale of alcohol. Organized crime groups in different cities now had to coordinate their activities, and organized crime became more organized to maximize bootlegging's enormous profits. At the same time, rival gangs fought each other to control bootlegging turf. Politicians and federal and local law enforcement officials were all too willing to take bribes. For all these reasons, Prohibition fueled the rise and power of organized crime. Bribery of politicians and police was common in cities like Chicago, where organized crime acquired enormous influence.

After Prohibition ended, organized crime's primary source of income for several decades was gambling. Starting in the 1960s, it moved more into the illegal drug trade, which now provides the most important source of organized crime's annual income, estimated between $50 billion and $150 billion in the United States, with gambling a fairly distant second. Due in large part to drug trafficking, organized crime in recent years has taken on an international focus, with cocaine smuggled into the United States from Colombia and elsewhere (McGee 1995). There is evidence of CIA involvement with international drug smuggling during the Iran-Contra scandal and since (Cockburn and Clair 1998).

The Alien Conspiracy Model and Myth

One of the most controversial political and scholarly issues in U.S. organized crime today is whether it is controlled by a highly organized, hierarchical group of some twenty-four Italian "families." This view, often called the "alien conspiracy model" or the "Mafia mystique," was popularized in important congressional hearings beginning in the 1950s (Albanese 2000). It was later dramatized in the various *Godfather* films and other movies and books, and was the central theme of sociologist Donald Cressey's (1969) classic book, *Theft of the Nation*. In addition to specifying a hierarchical, Italian-dominated structure of organized crime, the model argues that organized crime was largely unknown before Italians immigrated to the United States in the late 1800s. It also assumes

The Globalization of Public Order Crime and Organized Crime

Despite all law enforcement efforts, public order crime and organized crime continue to flourish in the United States. One reason for their success is that they transcend national boundaries.

The issue of pornography on the Internet illustrates this problem. When the U.S. Congress banned indecent material on the Internet in early 1996, several observers noted that pornographers could easily evade the ban by putting their materials on computer servers in other nations with more lenient laws. This action would put them beyond the reach of U.S. law. Given that people with access to the Internet can immediately obtain information from anywhere in the world, there's simply no way a single U.S. law can hope to eliminate pornography on the Internet. Moreover, there are far too many countries in the world to hope that they would all adopt stringent bans against such pornography.

Illegal drug use and trafficking in the United States are also part of a larger international problem equivalent to a multibillion-dollar industry. As of a few years ago, some 80 percent of our cocaine came from the Colombian Cali drug cartel, which processes coca leaf crops grown in Peru, Bolivia, and Colombia and channels much of the cocaine through Mexico. A few years ago the Cali cartel expanded its cocaine trade to countries in Europe and the former Soviet Union and began collaborating with organized crime groups in these nations. Colombia also accounts for almost one-third of the heroin sold in the United States. While arrests of key Cali cartel officials in 1995 were thought to have weakened the cartel, smaller traffickers have filled in the gap to maintain the distribution level of cocaine and other drugs.

Many political and other officials in the countries in which drug traffickers operate have been accused of taking bribes from them. In Mexico, for example, a former deputy attorney general, who was his nation's chief drug "czar," was investigated in 1995 for allegedly cooperating with drug traffickers thought to have given him and other Mexican officials tens of millions of dollars to allow the traffickers to operate. Concerned with protecting the North American Free Trade Agreement, both the Bush and Clinton administrations reportedly ignored strong evidence of this drug corruption and exaggerated the success of the Mexican government's war against drug trafficking. Meanwhile, the Colombian president was accused of taking almost $5.9 million from the Cali drug cartel when he ran for office in 1994. Documents taken from a founder of the Cali cartel indicated that it had paid off thousands of people, including politicians, police, and journalists.

Linked to international drug trafficking, organized crime also transcends national boundaries. After the Soviet Union collapsed, many Russians, attracted by the profits promised by new markets, began organizing for illegal gain. Organized crime groups reportedly took control of several Russian banks and import-export businesses and began to trade in weapons and nuclear materials. In October 1994 an investigative journalist in Russia, who reportedly was about to expose a secret military base that trained hired assassins for organized crime, was killed by a suitcase bomb. In March 1995 just a few months later, the director of Russia's largest TV station was murdered in what was widely considered an organized crime assassination.

Later that year the U.S. government indicted 15 Russians now living in the United States for allegedly cheating the government of $140 million in fuel taxes. The defendants had reportedly bought tax-free home heating oil, transferred it through several dummy companies, finally sold it as diesel fuel, which is taxable, and then hid the tax proceeds. The defendants were thought to be part of a Russian organized crime group operating on the East Coast with ties to organized crime in Moscow.

Sources: Bray 1996; Filipov 1995; Levy 1995; Rohter 1999.

that organized crime exists because immigrants, first Italians and later Asians and others, corrupt righteous U.S. citizens and prey on their weaknesses.

As with certain other criminological theories, the alien conspiracy model is best regarded as a myth (Kappeler, Blumberg, and Potter 2000). In emphasizing

Italian domination, this particular myth ignores the long history of organized crime before Italian immigration and overlooks the involvement of many other ethnic and racial groups. It also diverts attention from organized crime's roots in poverty, in the readiness of citizens to pay for the goods and services it provides, and in the willingness of politicians, law enforcement agents, and legitimate businesses to take bribes and otherwise cooperate with organized crime.

As the history of organized crime indicates, the public, politicians, and other officials aren't very righteous after all. That is still true today. As criminologist Gary W. Potter (1994:147) observes, "It is a fallacy that organized crime produces the desire for vice. Organized crime doesn't force people to gamble, snort cocaine, or read pornography. It merely fills an already existing social gap. The law has made organized crime inevitable because it denies people legal sources for those desired goods and services."

Nor does organized crime seduce honest politicians, police, and other officials and owners of legitimate businesses. Instead, these keepers of the public trust are often very willing to take bribes and otherwise cooperate with organized crime. In a Seattle study, William Chambliss (1988) found organized crime, business leaders, politicians, and police working hand-in-hand. In a more recent study of organized crime in "Morrisburg," a pseudonym for an East Coast city of 98,000, Potter (1994:101–102) concluded, "It is quite clear to anyone walking the streets of 'Morrisburg' that the political fix is in and extends from the cop on the beat to the most senior political officials." Such corruption, he noted, "is critical to the survival of organized crime. In fact, organized crime could not operate at all without the direct complicity and connivance of the political machinery in its area of operation" (p. 149).

Like Chambliss and other organized crime researchers, Potter also found legitimate businesses cooperating with organized crime in Morrisburg and noted, "The close interrelationships between legitimate and illicit businesses have been documented time and again in every local study of organized crime groups" (p. 135).

Chambliss, Potter, and other scholars also argue that the alien conspiracy model exaggerates the hierarchical nature of organized crime and the degree to which it is Italian-dominated. Instead, they say, organized crime today is best seen as a loose confederation of local groups consisting of people from many different ethnic backgrounds. Organized crime's decentralized, fluid structure permits it to adapt quickly to the ebb and flow of the vice trade and government's efforts to control it.

 ## REDUCING PUBLIC ORDER CRIME AND ORGANIZED CRIME

We've seen that public order crime laws generally don't work and may well do more harm than good. Because drug use, prostitution, pornography, and gambling have been around for centuries, they're not about to disappear, and the historical record provides little hope that we can do much about them. That said, economic deprivation does seem to underlie some illegal drug use and much prostitution. To the extent this is true, efforts to reduce poverty hold much potential for reducing these two crimes. Unfortunately, because current approaches to these two crimes, including the legal "war against drugs" and education and treatment programs for drug users, ignore their structural roots in economic inequality, they ultimately offer little promise for reducing these crimes.

Because organized crime helps provide the goods and services associated with public order crime, it also will not soon go away. Here the debate over the alien conspiracy model has important implications for how we should try to control organized crime, and for how effective any approach will be. If the alien conspiracy model is correct, arrests and prosecutions of selected organized crime bosses should eliminate its leadership and thus weaken its ability to entice the public to use its goods and services and various officials to take bribes. The government has used this strategy at least since the days of Al Capone.

If, however, organized crime has a more fluid, decentralized structure whose success depends on public and official readiness to cooperate with its illegal activities, this strategy will not work. As long as public demand for illicit goods and services remains, the financial incentives for organized crime will also remain. And as long as politicians, police, and the business community are eager to cooperate, organized crime will be able to operate with impunity. Organized crime, in short, is too much a part of our economic, political, and social systems for the current law enforcement strategy to work well (Albanese 2000).

To reduce organized crime's influence, then, we first must reduce public demand for its illicit goods and services. For better or worse, as we've seen, that's probably a futile goal. If so, a more effective way to fight organized crime might be to admit defeat and to legalize public order crimes, since the laws against these crimes have ironically generated opportunities for organized crime for huge financial gains (Kappeler, Blumberg, and Potter 2000). Legalizing public order crimes wouldn't reduce the behaviors that laws now ban, but would at least lessen organized crime's power and reduce the other problems now caused by the laws against pubic order crimes. Whether legalization would do more harm than good, of course, remains hotly debated.

Legalization might weaken organized crime in an additional way, as current enforcement of the laws in fact strengthens organized crime. The reason is that organized crime figures who get arrested tend to be the smallest, weakest, and most inefficient operators. Their removal from the world of organized crime allows the stronger and more efficient organized crime figures to gain even more control over illicit goods and services. They can also charge more for these goods and services they provide, increasing their profits even further (Kappeler, Blumberg, and Potter 2000).

Of course, legalization isn't about to happen soon. Given that fact, another promising way to fight organized crime would be to concentrate on the cooperation given it by politicians, police, and legitimate businesses. Unfortunately, this would entail a law enforcement focus that hasn't really been tried before. It's unlikely the government would want to take this approach, given that in some ways it would be investigating itself.

One final way to reduce organized crime would be to provide alternative economic opportunities for the young people who become involved in it each year. That means that if we could effectively reduce poverty and provide decent-paying, meaningful jobs, we could reduce the attraction of organized crime to the new recruits it needs to perpetuate itself. Unfortunately, there are no signs that our nation is eager to launch a new "war on poverty" with the same fervor that has guided our war against drugs and other illicit goods and services that now make so much money for organized crime.

SUMMARY AND CONCLUSION

The behaviors we call public order crimes or vice crimes have existed since ancient times and will doubtless continue far into the distant future. Illegal drug use, prostitution, pornography, and gambling occur because many people desire them. This is a fact. The question is what, if anything, society should do about this fact.

One problem with public order crime laws is that the distinction between legal and illegal behavior can be blurry and artificial. We prohibit some drugs but allow use of legal drugs like alcohol and tobacco, which kill hundreds of thousands annually and cost tens of billions of dollars in health-care costs, lost economic productivity, and other expenses. We prohibit prostitutes from selling their bodies for sex but pay athletes, models, and other people large sums of money to sell their bodies. We allow some forms of gambling but prohibit others, with no logical reason for why some are allowed but others banned. We try to ban pornography even as reasonable people disagree on what is pornographic and what is merely erotic.

Vice behavior raises some fascinating philosophical and social scientific questions on the role of the state and the nature of individual freedom. The major philosophical question is how far the state should go in prohibiting people from engaging in consensual behavior that may harm themselves or indirectly harm others. The major social scientific question is whether laws against consensual behaviors do more harm than good. There are many things wrong and even counterproductive about our current approach to illegal drugs, prostitution, pornography, and gambling. Unfortunately, it's easier to note these problems than to come up with workable solutions. Should we pour even more time, money, and energy into fighting public order crimes? Or should we instead consider a radically different approach like legalization? Reasonable people will debate these questions for many years to come.

KEY TERMS

alien conspiracy model

bribery

brothel

casino

erotica

forbidden fruit

goods

legalization

moral crusade

morality

more harm than good

nonviolent pornography

piracy

services

sin

violent pornography

STUDY QUESTIONS

1. Briefly summarize the philosophical debate over illegal drug use and other public order crime. Also summarize the sociological debate over public order crime.

2. It is often said that the United States has a "drug culture." What evidence does the text give that such a culture exists?

3. What are the arguments for and against legalizing some of the drugs that are now illegal? Do you think any illegal drugs should be made legal? Why or why not?

4. Do you think pornography helps cause rape? Why or why not?

5. The text says that organized crime has often "had the active or passive co-operation of political, legal, and business officials." What evidence does the text provide for this allegation?

INTERNET EXERCISES

A leading organization in the debate on the legalization of drugs is The Lindesmith Center, a drug policy research institute named after Alfred R. Lindesmith, a drug policy researcher of the last century. The Lindesmith Center advocates the "harm reduction" approach to drug use that is discussed in the chapter. Go to its Web site at **http://www.lindesmith.org**.

Once there, click on **Focal points** in the left window. Click on the various marijuana links you'll find on the page that appears, including **medicinal marijuana** and **marijuana regulation**. After exploring these other sites, answer the following questions. How popular was marijuana in the United States a century or more ago? When and why was it made illegal? What, if any, are the medicinal effects of marijuana use? Do you think marijuana should be made legal for people undergoing chemotherapy or for those who might need marijuana for other medical reasons? Do you think marijuana should be made legal for all adults? Why or why not? What are the advantages and disadvantages of keeping marijuana an illegal drug? What are the advantages and disadvantages of making marijuana legal for certain medical patients or for adults in general?

Chapter 15

POLICING: DILEMMAS
OF CRIME CONTROL
IN A DEMOCRATIC SOCIETY

Crime in the News

In February 1999, Amadou Diallo, an unarmed African immigrant, was in the doorway of his apartment building in New York City shortly after midnight when he was approached by four white men. The men were plainclothes police officers. One of the officers later said he held out his badge and told Diallo he wanted to talk with him. Diallo turned away and reached into his pocket and pulled out a black object. One officer yelled, "Gun!" and they all opened fire on Diallo, shooting him with 41 bullets, 19 of which struck him. The black object Diallo pulled out turned out to have been his wallet. The officers were arrested and charged with second-degree murder, but their trial a year later ended with an acquittal. Although the jury evidently concluded that the police sincerely but mistakenly thought Diallo in fact was pulling out a gun, critics said the police would have been less quick to jump to that conclusion if Diallo had been white. As one observer put it, "A wallet has a way of looking like nothing more than a wallet when held by a white man but somehow morphs into a gun in the hands of a black man."

Source: Haberman 2000:section 4, p. 3.

*T*he Amadou Diallo tragedy described in the "Crime in the News" vignette reminds us that the police have great powers over us and are authorized to exercise deadly force when necessary. Sometimes, as in this case, they make mistakes, and sometimes, if the critics of this case were correct, they act consciously or unconsciously out of racial and other biases. The role of police in a democratic society remains one of the most important issues in the study of crime. Suppose the police set up roadblocks in urban neighborhoods that would stop every car driving into and out of the neighborhood. Do these roadblocks make sense? Would they help lower the crime rate? Even if they helped lower the crime rate, would they be too expensive? Since cars would be stopped without reasonable grounds for suspicion, does that violate our civil liberties? Would the police single out people of color in these roadblocks? If so, does that violate their civil rights? How far should the police go in a democracy in their efforts to control crime? What do you think?

Questions like these lie at the heart of contemporary debate over police and crime. Law professor Herbert L. Packer has outlined two competing "models of the criminal process" (Packer 1964). These Crime Control and Due Process models, as Packer labeled them, reflect the tensions of crime control in a democratic society. As its name implies, the Crime Control model's key concerns are the apprehension and punishment of criminals. In this model, said Packer (1993:17), "The repression of criminal conduct is by far the most important function to be performed by the criminal process." Assuming that most suspects are indeed guilty, this model stresses the criminal justice system's need to capture and process criminals in the most efficient manner possible. It raises the image of an assembly-line conveyor belt quickly sending cases from one station to the next until the final outcome, punishment, is reached.

In contrast, said Packer, the Due Process model's image is more like an obstacle course that presents "formidable impediments to carrying the accused any further along in the process" (p. 20). This image results from the model's assumption that the detection and prosecution of suspects are unreliable and fraught with error. Some of these errors are honest mistakes; others stem from deliberate deception and bias. In any event, according to the Due Process model, the criminal justice system needs to protect suspects from these errors and, more generally, to limit the government's ability to use the legal system arbitrarily and abusively. As Packer (pp. 21–22) put it, "The Due Process model insists on the prevention and elimination of mistakes to the extent possible; the Crime Control model accepts the probability of mistakes up to the level at which they interfere with the goal of repressing crime." The Due Process model, in short, emphasizes *procedural justice* above all else and is reflected in the old saying that it's better to let ten guilty individuals go free than to find one innocent suspect guilty.

In many ways, the Due Process model derives from the U.S. Constitution and Bill of Rights, which provide several legal protections, including the rights to have counsel and jury trials, to confront witnesses, and to be free from unreasonable searches and seizures and cruel and unusual punishment. This interest in procedural justice stemmed from the colonial experience, when England often denied colonists jury trials and, in other respects, used the law and courts arbitrarily. These legal abuses were included in the grievances listed in the Declaration of Independence (Burns and Burns 1992).

Despite the Due Process model's roots in colonial history, over the years it has competed with the Crime Control model for public and political sentiment. It had its heyday during the so-called Warren Era of the 1960s, during which the U.S. Supreme Court under the direction of Chief Justice Earl Warren expanded the rights of criminal suspects and defendants in a series of famous decisions. Critics charged these decisions would let too many criminals go free on technicalities. Although later research suggested these fears were groundless, the Due Process model continued to come under attack by conservative observers. In the late 1980s and especially the 1990s, a more conservative Court began to limit some of the rights conferred by the Warren Court.

CRIME CONTROL IN A DEMOCRATIC SOCIETY

The tension between the Crime Control and Due Process models goes to the heart of fundamental questions in criminology, the sociology of law, and political theory. Simply put, the more crime control we want, the less due process we can have; the more due process we want, the less crime control we can expect. In a classic book about police first published in 1966 and later reissued with added material, Jerome H. Skolnick (1994:1) referred to this problem as a "dilemma of democratic society." Law, Skolnick wrote, "is not merely an instrument of order, but may frequently be its adversary" (p. 7). Skolnick asked whether the basic commitment of police should be to crime control above all else or instead to the "rule of law, even if this obligation may result in a reduction of social order" (p. 1). In a democratic society, he continued, the rule of law, or legality, demands that order be achieved only by following standards of procedural justice designed to protect individual freedom from arbitrary state power. The phrase "order under law" reflects this demand: "Order under law, therefore, subordinates the ideal of conformity to the ideal of legality" (p. 9).

The dilemma of enforcing law in a democratic society is perhaps best illustrated by using an exaggerated example of the Crime Control model. Consider a society with no due process, which is to say no procedural justice. In such a society, the police can arrest suspects without probable cause, torture them to extract confessions, and throw them in jail and even execute them without benefit of a fair trial. Suppose further that this system of "justice" applies not just to political dissidents but also to the most minor criminals: Pickpockets, for example, could have their arms amputated. Crime in such a society would likely be quite low, as people would live in terror of doing anything wrong, however minor. Such effective and efficient crime control, however, is achievable only at the expense of individual freedom.

Of course, no reasonable crime control advocate in the United States proposes such an exaggerated model. The question then becomes one of what balance to strike between the polar opposites of the Crime Control and Due Process models. Do we err on the side of Crime Control, and sacrifice individual freedom, or do we err on the side of Due Process, and perhaps sacrifice public safety?

Certainly, most of the public feels we should have even more crime control than we do now. In the 1998 General Social Survey, 79 percent of respondents said the courts don't deal harshly enough with criminals. Much of the U.S. public—almost 40 percent in some polls—applauded the 1994 caning of a U.S. teenager in Singapore for egging and spray-painting cars (Witt 1994). The youth, Michael P. Fay, received several lashes with a rattan cane that tore into his flesh and were expected to leave permanent scars. Defending their action, Singapore officials attributed their low crime rate to such harsh punishment, and several U.S. observers urged that flogging and similar measures could reduce urban vandalism and other crime in the United States (Buckley 1994).

Lost in all the discussion were serious questions about whether Michael Fay had even committed the vandalism he was accused of, as he said he was innocent and confessed to the vandalism only because the police beat and psychologically abused him (Shenon 1994). Supporting Fay's claims, human rights observers said police torture was common in Singapore.

At the time of the caning, then, Singapore was best regarded as a repressive society that, as one news report later put it, "limits freedom of speech and the press, arrests citizens without warrants, and restricts and intimidates political opponents" (Dembner 1995:22). A year after Fay's caning, Singapore aroused an international furor for hanging a maid from the Philippines after what critics charged was a murder confession coerced by torture (Shenon 1995). About the same time, Singapore's highest court violated U.S. standards of press freedom when it found a U.S. professor and the International Herald Tribune guilty of contempt for publishing an article criticizing the nation's judiciary (*New York Times* 1995).

It might be true that if we became more like Singapore we could lower our crime rates drastically. But is this the kind of society we want? Emile Durkheim (1962 [1895]) noted long ago that a society (like the United States) valuing freedom of thought will also have high levels of deviance, as both presuppose a weak *collective conscience* that permits people both to think individually and to violate social norms: One does not occur without the other. As Carl Klockars (in Rosen 1995:109) observes, "Crime may be one of the prices we pay for the individualism that we have in this society." The dilemma of crime control in a democratic society thus becomes one of deciding what kind of society we want to have.

Reflecting this view, some of the most crime-free nations in the world are, like Singapore, some of the least free societies politically and intellectually. At the same time, however, several relatively crime-free nations, including Britain, Canada, Sweden, and Switzerland, are also democratic. These examples indicate it's possible to have a society that is free politically and intellectually but also relatively free of crime (Adler 1983; Clinard 1978). As we've seen in previous chapters, these societies have less crime than the United States because they have lower inequality and because they have different, less criminogenic cultures. In the long run, they point to directions the United States should pursue to lower its crime rate. Currently, however, the United States is pursuing a *crime control* strategy instead. Thus the dilemma posed by Durkheim, Packer, Skolnick, and others remains relevant: How far are we willing to sacrifice our legal freedoms in the name of public safety?

The Ideal of Blind Justice

So far I've been talking about the problem of civil liberty. But if one of the cornerstones of democracy is freedom, another is equality. In the legal system, this means justice should be "blind" to personal differences: People should be treated the same regardless of their race, ethnicity, social class, gender, or other extralegal characteristics. Crime control in a democratic society thus also raises the problem of civil rights. As we try to control crime, we have to be careful that citizens are not singled out because of *who* they are instead of *what* they did and *how* they did it. If one dilemma of crime control in a democratic society involves striking the right balance between public safety and individual freedom, another dilemma concerns striking the right balance between public safety and equality of treatment. Civil rights advocates and "law and order" champions often have different views on where this balance should be struck.

A Preview of the Discussion

This and the next chapter explore some aspects of these two basic dilemmas of crime control in democratic society. In the limited space available, we'll discuss the major issues facing the police, courts, and prisons as they try to control crime and the issues our society faces as it uses the criminal justice system as its primary means of dealing with crime. We'll also examine the complex evidence on inequality in crime control and explore how aspects of the social structure affect how the criminal justice system operates. Anticipating the book's final chapter on reducing crime, we'll also critically examine our criminal justice system's effectiveness. Our view will stress what Packer (1968) called "the limits of the criminal sanction." Simply put, the amount of crime control tolerable in a democratic society can ultimately do little to prevent criminality. Given this reality, "get tough" approaches to crime will do little to reduce crime, and efforts to address the roots of crime hold more promise.

This chapter begins our discussion with a look at police. Most of us have had contact with the police at one time or another and, indeed, have had more contact with the police than with any other government representatives. Perhaps you called the police because you, a family member, or a friend was the victim of a crime. Perhaps you even committed a crime yourself, or were at least suspected of a crime, and were questioned by the police. More likely, you were driving a car and were stopped by an officer for an alleged speeding or other traffic violation. Besides my antiwar protest arrest (Chapter 13) and some speeding tickets, I was once detained by the police after I jaywalked in front of a police station and forced an unmarked police car to stop suddenly only to be hit from behind by another car. The officers in the unmarked car took me into the station house, where I sweated for more than an hour, but eventually they let me go with only a warning against further jaywalking.

That incident is laughable now, but police work is usually quite serious and, as Skolnick noted, raises important questions in a democratic society. Let's review the history of police and then discuss sociological research on police behavior and the impact of policing. For the most part, research on police didn't exist before the 1960s, as criminological work focused on the etiology, or causation, of criminal and delinquent behavior. The social and political upheaval of the 1960s that stimulated critical approaches to the study of law and crime also awakened interest in the social reaction to crime. In particular, the possibility of police racial bias in arrest practices motivated government-sponsored, observational studies of police behavior that we'll examine in the following sections.

The Development of the Modern Police Force

The concept of police goes back to ancient times, as ancient Egypt, Mesopotamia, and Rome all had organized police forces to maintain public order (Mosse 1975). Although this sounds like a benign function, the police forces in effect were private bodyguards whose primary purpose was to protect the societies' rulers from uprisings and other threatening conduct by the masses.

During the Middle Ages, policing became decentralized. In England, a system of community policing called the *frankpledge* developed in the eleventh century as groups of ten families, called *tithings*, strived to maintain order within each tithing. Ten tithings living on a particular noble's estate were called a *hundred*. The noble appointed an unpaid constable to monitor their behavior; one of the constable's main duties was to control poaching on the noble's land. Several hundreds eventually constituted a *shire*, or county, which were put under the charge of a *shire reeve*, the root of the modern term *sheriff*. Eventually English units of government called *parishes* developed and appointed unpaid constables to watch out for disorderly conduct and perform various services such as trash collection. The constables in turn appointed watchmen as assistants (Critchley 1972).

By the early 1800s the constable system was no longer working, as London was the scene of repeated riots and increased crime by the poor. There were too few constables who were too poorly trained to handle these problems. Many people, especially political and business leaders, began calling for a larger, more organized police force to quell the social chaos. Others worried that such a police force would endanger individual freedom. Finally, Prime Minister Sir Robert Peel persuaded Parliament in 1829 to establish the first paid, specialized police force in London, whose police soon became called *bobbies* because of Peel's influence. London was divided into small districts called *beats*, and police were given jurisdiction over specific beats.

The development of police forces in the United States followed the English model. In the colonial era, the constable and watch system was typical. As in England, by the early 1800s this system had outlived its usefulness. Cities were growing rapidly and were the scenes of repeated mob violence in the decades preceding the Civil War, most of it instigated by bands of white youths who preyed on immigrants and African-Americans. This violence prompted calls by established interests for organized police forces similar to London's. In 1838, Boston created a daytime police force to complement the night watchmen, and then in 1844, New York City established the first full-time force. Within a decade most big U.S. cities had gone the same route. Although northern cities developed police forces because they feared mob violence, southern cities developed them because they feared slave revolts. In these cities, police forces evolved from "slave patrols" that tracked down runaway slaves (Walker 1980).

These early U.S. police forces were notoriously corrupt and brutal and were of little help against crime. The problem, says Samuel Walker (1980), arose from how police were recruited: "Officers were primarily tools of local politicians; they were not impartial and professional public servants" (p. 61). In most cities, local political leaders appointed the police to patrol the leaders' neighborhoods. These recruits were thus hired more on the basis of whom they knew and would be loyal to than on their skills and qualifications, and received little training after being hired. Many drank heavily while they patrolled and used their nightsticks freely on suspects, most of them poor immigrants. As Walker (1980:63) notes, "Police brutality was a form of 'delegated vigilantism' by which the middle class tolerated and even approved violence against the outcasts of society."

As Walker's comment suggests, a major function of U.S. police in the nineteenth century was to control the behavior of immigrants, who were widely considered by "respectable society" to be "dangerous classes" in need of careful monitoring (Adler 1994). In a recent study of this function, M. Craig Brown and Barbara D. Warner (1995) examined arrest rates for drunkenness in 1900 for the nation's fifty largest cities. These rates were higher in cities with higher proportions of immigrants, even after controlling for alcohol consumption. The authors concluded that "social control is not entirely driven by levels of crime, but is in part a response to potentially threatening groups" (p. 94).

Another theme of nineteenth-century policing is corruption, which was so rampant that Walker (1980) calls it probably their "main business." He continues,

> The police systematically ignored laws related to drinking, gambling, and prostitution in return for regular payoffs; they entered into relationships with professional criminals, especially pickpockets, tolerating illicit activity in return for goods or information; they actively supported a system of electoral fraud; and they sold promotions to higher rank within the department (p. 64).

This corruption reflected a more general pattern of municipal corruption in most U.S. cities during the 1800s. Beginning in the early 1900s, cities began to reform their police departments by developing a professional model of policing in which police were hired on their qualifications and properly trained to carry out their job efficiently and honestly. As we'll see later, police brutality and corruption may be less common than a century ago but are still a problem.

Sidney L. Harring (1993) argues that important changes in police forces began in the 1870s as workers began striking in cities and towns across the country against their pitiful wages and wretched living and working conditions. For example, New York City from 1880 to 1900 had 5,090 strikes involving almost 1 million workers, while Chicago had 1,737 strikes involving almost 600,000 workers. In response, police forces doubled or tripled in size during this period and developed the patrol wagon and signal system consisting of alarm stations (to which only "respectable" citizens were given keys) placed throughout a city. This system enabled police to respond quickly to calls for help. In this time of major labor unrest, says Harring (1993:558), "the local police were most often the major antistrike institution, did effective antistrike work, and almost always took an aggressive stand against the workers and in favor of the corporations." Police helped guard company property, beat workers while violently breaking up strikes, prevented workers from meeting to plan strikes, and arrested strike leaders arbitrarily on bogus disorderly conduct charges.

WORKING PERSONALITY AND POLICE BEHAVIOR

Police spend a surprisingly low amount of their time responding to 911 calls, questioning witnesses, arresting suspects, and other aspects of crime control. Only about 20 percent of police time is spent on these activities, with most police time spent on activities like directing traffic, responding to traffic accidents, and other much more mundane matters. It's also true that policing is less dangerous in terms of fatality rates than several other occupations, including construction and mining (Kappeler, Blumberg, and Potter 2000).

These facts notwithstanding, police remain afraid for their safety, especially in urban areas. They realize that anyone they confront, even in a routine traffic stop, poses a potential threat of injury and even death. As a result, says Jonathan Rubinstein (1980:71), police bring "some degree of suspicion and uncertainty" to almost all their encounters with citizens and are constantly on the alert for any signs that their safety is in danger. The fact that these citizens aren't exactly happy, and often become downright hostile, only heightens an officer's concern. The importance of this basic feature of policing cannot be underestimated, as it has important implications for all other aspects of police behavior.

In his classic book on policing, Jerome Skolnick (1994) developed the very influential concept of the police officer's *working personality*. Skolnick noted that the work people do affects the way they view the world and even their personalities. The working personality of the police, wrote Skolnick, stems from the danger of their job. This inevitably makes police suspicious of, and even hostile toward, the public and strengthens police solidarity, or mutual loyalty. The public's hostility toward the police further reinforces police solidarity and creates among police an "us against them" mentality (Herbert 1998). These and other aspects of policing prompt police officers to develop a working personality that is authoritarian, cynical, and suspicious, which prompts them to be quite ready and willing to use violence when they feel it's necessary.

This structural basis for police behavior is dramatically illustrated in a classic article by George L. Kirkham (1984), a criminology professor who became a police officer. As a professor, Kirkham often criticized police behavior. Many of his students were police, and they told him that he "could not possibly understand what a police officer has to endure in modern society until I had been one myself" (p. 78). At the age of 31, Kirkham took up their challenge and, after completing police academy training, joined the Jacksonville, Florida, police force and quickly began to learn his "street lessons."

As a professor, Kirkham had always thought that police exaggerated the disrespect they encountered from the public. On his first day on the beat in Jacksonville, Kirkham learned how wrong he'd been. He writes,

> As a college professor, I had grown accustomed to being treated with uniform respect and deference by those I encountered. I somehow naively assumed that this same quality of respect would carry over into my new role as a policeman ... [but] quickly found that my badge and uniform ... only acted as a magnet which drew me toward many individuals who hated what I represented (p. 81).

In one of his first encounters, Kirkham asked a drunk to leave a bar. Smiling pleasantly at the man, Kirkham asked him, "Excuse me, sir, but I wonder if I could ask you to step outside and talk with me for just a minute?" Kirkham describes what happened next: "Without warning ... he swung at me, luckily missing my face and striking me on the right shoulder. I couldn't believe it. What on earth had I done to provoke such a reaction?" (p. 81). Kirkham recalls how startled he was that his "gentle, rapport-building approach," which had worked so well in other settings, had failed him here.

In the weeks that followed, fear "became something which I regularly experienced" (p. 82). In one incident where he and his partner tried to arrest a young male in a dilapidated neighborhood, an ugly crowd gathered and threatened their safety. Kirkham felt a "sickening sensation of cold terror" as he put out a distress call on his police car radio and grabbed a shotgun to protect himself and his partner. He writes, "How readily as a criminology professor I would have condemned the officer who was now myself, trembling with fear and anxiety and menacing an 'unarmed' assembly" with a shotgun (p. 83). Circumstances, he notes, "had dramatically changed my perspective, for now it was my life and safety that were in danger, my wife and child who might be mourning" (p. 84). Kirkham writes later in the article that as a criminology professor he could always take his time to make decisions, but as a police officer he was "forced to make the most critical choices in a time frame of seconds, rather than days: to shoot or not to shoot, to arrest or not to arrest, to give chase or let go" (p. 85).

Police Misconduct: Brutality

The picture Kirkham and other observers present of policing helps explain why police brutality and corruption occur. Let's look first at brutality, more neutrally called the unjustified or undue use of force.

A defining feature of the police is that they are authorized to use physical force when necessary to subdue suspects (Westley 1970). As we've seen, the police are often in tense situations where their safety and lives might be on the line. They confront suspects who are often hostile and who often insult them. Tempers flare. Inevitably, police will use force when none was needed or will use more force than was needed to subdue a suspect. The result is police brutality.

Perhaps the most notorious recent example of police brutality was the March 1991 beating in Los Angeles of Rodney King, an unemployed, 25-year-old African-American, after police stopped him for alleged traffic violations. King suffered several serious injuries, including skull fractures, a broken leg, and a broken cheekbone, after he was beaten by several white officers as others watched. Captured on home video, the beating was later broadcast across the nation and aroused public and official outrage. The jury acquittal a year later of King's alleged police assailants on almost all the charges against them touched off a five-day riot in Los Angeles that killed more than 50 people and caused some $1 billion in property damage. A government commission found that the King beating was not an "aberration," as the L.A. police chief had termed it. Instead, brutality was a repeated behavior of a "significant number" of LAPD officers. The commission also found that police often talked eagerly about the prospect of beating suspects, with many of their discussions filled with racial slurs against African-Americans, Asian-Americans, and Latinos (Christopher Commission 1991).

No one really knows how many cases of police brutality occur each year (Adams et al. 1999). Usually its only witnesses are the police and their victims. Their solidarity usually leads the police to keep quiet about these incidents. The victims are often reluctant to lodge a complaint, since they feel they won't be believed or it won't do any good. After the Rodney King beating, the number of police brutality complaints reportedly increased around the nation. A recent Gallup Poll shed some light on the national prevalence of police brutality. Five percent of the respondents in the poll answered yes when asked whether they had "ever been physically mistreated or abused by the police" (Blumberg 1994:111). That figure translates to more than 8 million U.S. adults. One problem with this measure is that it doesn't distinguish the *unjustified* use of police force. It's possible that some of the respondents were resisting arrest or otherwise behaving in a way that *justified* the police behavior in question.

One of the best studies of police behavior occurred in the summer of 1966, when 36 trained observers funded by the federal government accompanied police officers in Boston, Chicago, and Washington, D.C., on their patrols for seven weeks. The observers recorded several kinds of information on the 3,826 encounters that officers had with suspects and other citizens. Some of this information concerned brutality. In the seven-week study, the observers found 37 cases of brutality involving 44 citizens. Because the police knew they were being observed, it's possible that even more brutality would have occurred had they been unobserved. Typically, the police committing brutality falsely claimed they were acting in self-defense, and some even carried guns and knives to plant on suspects to support these bogus claims (Reiss 1980b).

Albert J. Reiss (1980b), the study's director, later discussed whether these 37 cases represented a high or low level of brutality. Since there were 3,826 encounters in the study, "only" 1 percent (37 of 3,826) involved brutality. Of the 10,564 citizens in these encounters, "only" .4 percent (44 of 10,564), or 4 out of 1,000, were beaten. However, said Reiss, since many of these encounters were with victims or witnesses, who are not the logical targets of police violence, a better denominator is the number of *suspects*, 1,394, whom the police encountered. Using this figure, the brutality rate rises to 44 of 1,394, or 3.16 percent. Whether 3.16 percent is a lot or a little is up to you to determine; Reiss concluded from this figure that police brutality in large cities is "far from rare" (p. 288). This is especially true if we keep in mind that Reiss's police knew they were being observed and thus might have been on their best behavior. Moreover, even a small 3.16 percent still translates to large numbers of cases. Although some disputed evidence indicates police brutality has declined since Reiss's study (Armstrong 1991), if we venture to apply this rate to the roughly 14.5 million people arrested in 1998 for all offenses, then about 458,000 people (3.16 percent of 14.5 million) were victims of police brutality in that year. In California alone, about 1.6 million people were arrested. Our estimate of police brutality in California would thus be some 50,600, or 139 per day.

One important factor affecting the amount of brutality across police forces is their "operating philosophy" (Blumberg 1994). In cities where police administrators make it very clear that brutality won't be tolerated, brutality rates appear lower than in cities where administrators make no such proclamations. Police killings of civilians are also less common in police departments where administrators set clear limits on police use of force (Fyfe 1993). The organizational philosophies and policies of individual police departments thus seem to have an important effect on how much police violence occurs. This effect parallels one found in studies of corporate crime, as the amount of such crime also appears to depend on the organizational culture and operating philosophy of each corporation (Friedrichs 1996).

RACISM AND POLICE BRUTALITY

The issue of racism in police brutality remains highly controversial. Many consider the Rodney King beating typical: King was African-American, and the police who beat him were white. Blacks have long listed brutality as one of their major grievances against the police, and beatings of African-American suspects were widely blamed for igniting many of the 1960s urban riots (Kerner Commission 1968). After King's beating, many observers deplored the racial pattern in this brutality as all too common. As an official of the National Association for the Advancement of Colored People (NAACP) testified to Congress, "The problem of police brutality is pervasive, deep-rooted and alarming.... For too long, African-Americans and other racial minorities have been among the special targets of police abuse.... [T]oo often innocent black people—including many of our youngsters—find themselves the victims of the abuse of authority and law" (Henderson 1991:23, 28). A New York newspaper columnist similarly wrote, "White traffic violators are handled differently.... Police brutality against blacks is as American as the Ku Klux Klan" (Payne 1991:36).

Comments by one of the police officers involved in the 1994–1995 O. J. Simpson case confirmed the worst fears of African-Americans. During Simpson's trial, it was revealed that former Los Angeles detective Mark Fuhrman, who had found a key piece of evidence in the Simpson case, had uttered dozens of racial slurs and profanities aimed at blacks, Hispanics, and women during a series of interviews with a college professor doing research for a screenplay. In the taped interviews he also boasted of having beaten blacks and arrested them on bogus charges. When the tapes of his comments were played in court, they were broadcast across the country and outraged people in all walks of life (Pertman 1995).

Fuhrman's words and professed actions were revolting, and the beatings he said he committed were just a few of the thousands that African-Americans and other people of color suffer every year. Certainly some of these beatings are as racially motivated as Fuhrman's. But is that true of most beatings? Or, as some scholars argue, do the many beatings each year of African-Americans simply reflect the heavily African-American composition of large U.S. cities? African-Americans there may suffer beatings not because of police racism, but because they are the suspects that police encounter, and suspects in general, black or white, are at risk for brutality.

If so, police brutality may in fact be color-blind, and African-Americans may be victims of brutality not because of their race but because of where they live. Although most of the people beaten by L.A. police are probably African-American, that may simply be because most L.A. suspects are African-American. They might be suspects because a racist society denies them full equality (Chapters 6 and 9), but that doesn't necessarily mean that racism motivates the police brutality they suffer.

Evidence for this view comes from the 1966 Reiss study noted earlier. Although Reiss's observers recorded brutality for 31.6 of every 1,000 suspects, this rate broke down to 41.9 for every 1,000 white suspects and 22.6 for every 1,000 black suspects (Reiss 1980b). The risk of white suspects for brutality was thus twice as great as that for black suspects. Reiss's observers also found no evidence that white police were more likely to beat black suspects than white suspects. (Keep in mind, however, that Reiss's police knew they were being watched and thus might not have beaten suspects they normally would have beaten.) While Reiss readily acknowledged that white officers are racially prejudiced, he couldn't conclude that their prejudice motivated the brutality they did commit against blacks. Instead, he noted (using the acceptable term for African-Americans at the time), "[T]he facts just given suggest that white policemen, even though they are prejudiced toward Negroes, do not discriminate against Negroes in the excessive use of force. The use of force by the police is more readily explained by police culture than it is by the policeman's race" (Reiss 1980b: 289).

Examining his data further, Reiss concluded instead that social class prejudice helps explain police brutality, as all the brutality victims in his study, black or white, were poor, even though a "sizable minority" of middle- and upper-class citizens were involved in the police encounters observed. In his words, "it appears that the lower class bears the brunt of victimization by police" (p. 290).

While Reiss's view is certainly not the final word on the subject of police brutality and racism, it does reinforce the complexity of determining their nature and extent, especially when we keep in mind that police do not have to be white to commit brutality. At a minimum, however, there is ample evidence, as Reiss himself acknowledged, of racist attitudes among white police (Skolnick 1994), and 72 percent of the officers in his study uttered racially prejudiced remarks (Skolnick and Bayley 1986). The key question is whether these attitudes lead white police to treat blacks and whites differently.

Even if most police don't commit brutality because of racism, there are undoubtedly individual officers like Fuhrman whose racism does generate brutality. In the Gallup Poll mentioned previously, 9 percent of people of color said the police had "physically mistreated or abused" them, versus less than 5 percent of whites (Blumberg 1994). Yet even this difference is difficult to interpret: Does it

◀ *In 1999 New York City police killed Amadou Diallo, an African immigrant, when he pulled a black object from his pocket. The object was his wallet. Critics said that the police would have been less likely to think the wallet was a gun if Diallo had been white.*

mean that police commit brutality out of racism, or does it mean that a greater proportion of blacks live in urban areas and are more likely to be suspects and hence beaten? Whether racial prejudice systematically motivates brutality by white police against African-Americans and other people of color remains an important empirical question.

RACISM AND POLICE USE OF DEADLY FORCE

Scholars have also considered whether racism affects the police use of deadly force. As with brutality, a disproportionate number of the civilians killed by police, more than 50 percent in many studies, are people of color, especially African-American. Espousing a "community violence hypothesis," many scholars think this fact simply reflects the disproportionate number of felons and other suspects who are people of color (Fyfe 1988). Espousing a "conflict hypothesis," other scholars think it reflects police racism and a desire to bolster systematic inequality, with one scholar asserting that police have "one trigger finger for whites and another for blacks" (Takagi 1974:30).

Which view is correct? Here again the evidence is complex. Supporting the community violence view, several studies find that police killings of civilians are highest in areas with high violent crime rates and that white officers tend to kill white suspects and black officers tend to kill black suspects. Such findings suggest that "the application of deadly force by officers is not racially motivated" (Sorensen, Marquart, and Brock 1993:429). Supporting the conflict view, however, other studies find that police killings of civilians are highest in areas with the greatest racial inequality and with higher proportions of African-Americans (Jacobs and O'Brien 1998). These results suggest that the "police response in these areas is higher than is warranted by the levels of violent crime" (Sorensen, Marquart, and Brock 1993:437).

In view of these mixed findings, the issue of systematic racism in police shootings of civilians requires continued investigation. The evidence that does exist of racial and economic disparity in such shootings indicates that street-level justice might not be as "blind" as it should be in a democracy.

POLICE VIOLENCE AGAINST WOMEN

The available evidence indicates that women are rarely the victims of police brutality as it's usually defined. Of the 44 citizens beaten by police in Reiss's study, only two, both African-Americans, were women. Several reasons probably account for women's low incidence of brutality victimization. Compared to men, few women are suspects (and thus less at risk than men for brutality) because their crime rates are far lower than men's. Because of socialization differences in aggressiveness, when women do become suspects they are probably less likely than male suspects to act belligerently, and thus less likely to arouse police ire. It's also possible that police may be reluctant to hit female suspects because of notions of chivalry.

Although women's gender may protect them from police beatings, it subjects them to police sexual violence (PSV). Such violence includes rape and other sexual assaults and unnecessary strip searches and body cavity searches by male officers. Peter B. Kraska and Victor E. Kappeler (1995) note that while human rights groups have documented PSV against women in other nations, criminologists have ignored it in the United States. Kraska and Kappeler examined newspaper accounts of PSV between 1991 and 1993 and federal lawsuits between 1978 and 1992 alleging PSV. Their research revealed 124 cases of PSV, with many more, they assume, not reaching press or judicial attention. About 30 percent of the cases involved rape and other sexual assaults; 56 percent, strip and body cavity searches; and 15 percent, violations of privacy such as voyeurism.

The authors blame PSV on at least three factors. The first is male officers' sexist ideology, which, as Chapter 10 noted, helps explain sexual violence against women in general. The remaining factors are more structural. The first of these concerns the "extreme power differential between policemen and female citizens" (Kraska and Kappeler 1995:106), which is even greater than the normal power differential underlying sexual violence in our society. The second structural factor concerns the "situational opportunity of the police to commit acts of PSV" (p. 107). Just as police are corrupt because they have many opportunities to be corrupt, so do they commit PSV because they have opportunities to do so. As Kraska and Kappeler (p. 107) put it, "The police possess exceptional access to women, often in situations with little or no direct accountability."

Police Misconduct: Corruption

As they accompanied officers on their patrols, the observers in Reiss's 1966 government study also noticed police corruption. More than one-fifth of the officers engaged in at least one act of corruption, including taking bribes and stealing objects from stores they were checking (Reiss 1980a). As this figure suggests, the police corruption that existed a century ago remains common despite periodic investigations and exposés by the press and government commissions. The police in Reiss's study may even have been less corrupt than normal because they knew they were being observed.

Perhaps the most famous investigation was conducted in 1972 by the so-called Knapp Commission (1973). The Commission was established after New York City police officer Frank Serpico disclosed corruption by his fellow officers and then was set up by some of them and almost murdered. The Commission found corruption throughout New York's police force that stemmed primarily from illegal drug trafficking and gambling. It divided corrupt officers into *meat-eaters* and *grass-eaters*. The former were a small percentage of all corrupt officers who pursued corruption aggressively and made the most money. Grass-eaters were more passive in their corruption and made less money but lay at the heart of the problem by making corruption respectable, keeping quiet about the corruption, and threatening with physical injury or worse any officer who disobeyed this code of silence. One such officer was Serpico.

Police corruption arises from structural roots similar to those motivating brutality. The nature of police work fuels police perceptions that the public not only dislikes the police but also doesn't appreciate the hard job they do. Combine these perceptions with the many opportunities for police to obtain money through bribes and other forms of corruption, and you inevitably end up with much corruption. This sort of explanation suggests that the problem of such *blue-coat crime* extends far beyond a "few rotten apples" and instead reflects a "rotten barrel" that will remain even if the bad apples are removed from the force. As a former Philadelphia police officer put it, "[P]olice corruption results from a system where honest police recruits are placed into a dishonest police subculture" (Birch 1984:120). As the last chapter discussed and as the Knapp Commission documented, illegal drug trafficking, gambling, and other public order crimes are responsible for most of this corruption. This was true more than a century ago and remains true now. Legalizing these behaviors should reduce the corruption by drying up the opportunities police have for acquiring money illegally.

Police Scandals

Sometimes police brutality, corruption, and other misbehavior become so rampant that, when discovered, they take on a new life as a full-fledged *scandal* that reminds us of the dangers of having out-of-control police in a democratic society. In early 2000 a large and frightening scandal in Los Angeles made major headlines. Months earlier, an L.A. police officer, Rafael Perez, had been arrested for stealing drugs. In return for a plea bargain, he told authorities that dozens of L.A. anti-gang police and supervisors in the city's Rampart Division and elsewhere had engaged in massive corruption, brutality, and other wrongdoing. Their acts included many beatings, several unjustified police shootings, the planting of weapons on their victims, the planting of illegal drugs on other citizens to justify false arrests, false testimony at trials, and the stealing of drugs and money. More than 70 officers eventually were investigated for either engaging in these acts or for covering them up.

In one case, Perez said he saw an officer plant a gun on a dying suspect and he witnessed a supervisor delay an ambulance so that the officers involved in the unjustified shooting would have time to make up a story. In another act, police allegedly shot an unarmed man in handcuffs. In still another act, police allegedly used a suspect as a battering ram by banging his head on a wall when he wouldn't tell the police about a gun they were trying to find. Sometimes police even reportedly had "shooting parties" in which they got awards for wounding or killing people. Because of the scandal, dozens of criminal convictions were overturned (Glover and Lait 2000a; Glover and Lait 2000b).

A similar scandal came to light a few years earlier in Philadelphia. There a group of police engaged in practices similar to those in Los Angeles, including false testimony, beatings, and planted evidence. About 300 convictions were overturned because of the scandal (Fazlollah 1997).

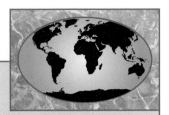
Police and Policing in Japan

In the United States, there are as many police forces as there are cities and towns, and they all have many different styles and sets of procedures. As a result, there is little standardization among U.S. police of training, equipment, or procedures. The situation is quite different in Japan, as the Japanese police force is a branch of the national government called the National Police Agency (NPA). This allows the Japanese police to be more standardized than their U.S. counterparts, as they all receive the same type of training and are expected to conform to the same sets of rules. At the same time, Japanese police are much more oriented toward *community policing* than most U.S. police, as they operate at the level of the immediate neighborhood.

A key feature of the Japanese model of policing is a type of mini-police station located in neighborhoods across the country. The mini-station in urban neighborhoods is called the *koban*, while the mini-station in rural areas is called the *chuzaisho*. Both sets of police stations are small operations: The koban usually has fewer than fifteen officers per shift, while the chuzaisho is staffed by one officer.

The police at either kind of station integrate law enforcement with community service functions, and they typically solicit community input on crime and other problems. To do this, they often make house calls, and use these calls to allow them and citizens to get to know one another better. They keep petty cash funds to help the homeless and other people in need of money, and their mini-stations often include counseling rooms in which specially trained officers sit down to talk with families or individuals in need of help.

Another difference between U.S. and Japanese police lies in police decision making. In the United States, police management style follows a top-down model in which police supervisors command the officers under them and make almost all policy decisions. In Japan, police decision making is more consensual. Police officials still make decisions but are expected to be aware of what the average officer thinks and to take the rank and file's views into account.

Compared to their U.S. counterparts, the Japanese police enjoy two significant advantages. One is the respect and gratitude of the public. In the United States, a cultural value of autonomy and distrust of authority underlies the hostility with which much of the public views police. In Japan, a cultural value of respect for authority and of harmonious relations prompts the Japanese citizenry to respect the police and to regard them as important public servants. The Japanese community policing orientation reinforces the positive view with which the public views the police.

The other advantage enjoyed by the Japanese police is their nation's low crime rate. The high U.S. crime rate puts pressure on police to see themselves as law enforcement officers first and foremost and to view the public with suspicion. It also leads the U.S. public to see the police as inefficient and as harassing. In contrast, the low Japanese crime rate allows the police to act more as public servants than as law enforcers and reinforces the public's positive view of police and policing in that nation.

Sources: Ames 1981; Bayley 1991; Bayley 1994; Westermann and Burfeind 1991.

 ## POLICE DISCRETION: TO ARREST OR NOT TO ARREST?

At every stage of the criminal justice system, officials make decisions. Police decide whether to arrest someone once they've identified a probable suspect. Once a person's arrested, a prosecutor decides whether to prosecute the case and which charges to bring against the defendant. The judge determines whether to require bail and how much bail should be required. A judge or jury decides whether to find the defendant guilty, and the judge determines how severe the sentence for a convicted offender will be. Such discretionary justice helps the criminal justice system remain flexible and individualized, but it also opens the system to the possibility of disparate treatment of suspects and defendants based on their race, social class, gender, and other extralegal variables.

The first stage of discretionary justice is the police officer's decision to arrest or cite someone for an alleged offense. As Shakespeare might have put it, to arrest or not to arrest, that is the discretion. You probably know many people, yourself included, who've been stopped by the police for speeding or some other possible traffic violation. Sometimes the driver gets a ticket, and sometimes not, even if the driver and officer both know that a traffic violation was committed. What determines whether the driver is lucky or unlucky in this situation? Does the driver's chance of getting a ticket (or does a suspect's chance of getting arrested) depend more on legal factors such as the evidence and severity of an offense, or more on extralegal factors such as the person's race, gender, and behavior toward the officer?

Most studies find that the police arrest only a small percent of all suspects they encounter (Mastrofski 2000). In the 1966 police observation study discussed earlier, for example, police arrested only 15 percent of all juvenile suspects. The chances of arrest depended heavily on the seriousness of the alleged offense, as almost 75 percent of juveniles suspected of *felonies* were arrested, compared to only about 33 percent of *juvenile misdemeanor* suspects and 10 percent of *rowdiness* suspects.

What factors influence arrest probability beyond offense seriousness? One of the most important factors is the *strength of the evidence*. As one of the study's researchers, Donald Black (1980:155), says, "The stronger the evidence in the field situation, the more likely is an arrest." Another factor is what Black (p. 157) calls *intimacy*: Arrest is more likely if the alleged offender and victim are strangers than if they know each other. Yet another factor is the *complainant's preference*: Arrest is more likely when victims or complainants prefer arrest than when they do not.

Black also found that suspects who were hostile toward the police were more likely to get arrested than respectful suspects. This is often called the *demeanor dimension* and has long been thought to affect the chances of arrest. However, David A. Klinger (1994) argues that studies finding demeanor effects err in including as "poor demeanor" conduct that is itself a crime, such as hitting an officer, instead of restricting their measure of poor demeanor to legally permissible conduct such as verbal criticism. In a study using Florida data that corrected for this problem, Klinger found that demeanor did not affect arrest. Hostile suspects were more likely to be arrested but only because "they are more likely to commit crimes against and in the presence of the police, not because their demeanor connotes a lack of respect for police authority" (p. 489). Klinger concluded that his study "challenges the conventional wisdom that hostility, by itself, increases the odds of arrest" (p. 490). Other scholars have challenged his conclusion and continue to think that demeanor affects the chances of arrest (Lundman 1996). No doubt this issue will occupy researchers' attention for some years to come.

Race, Ethnicity, and Arrest

Perhaps the most controversial issue in police discretion is whether arrest practices are racially discriminatory. In 1998, 30 percent of all persons arrested were black, a figure that rose to 34 percent for Index crimes, 40 percent for violent Index crimes, and 53 and 55 percent for homicides and robberies respectively (Federal Bureau of Investigation 1999). Since blacks comprise only about 12 percent of the total population, there is ready evidence of disproportionate arrest of African-Americans.

◀ *African-Americans are arrested far out of proportion to their numbers in the U.S. population. Whether their arrest rate indicates high levels of criminality or, instead, police bias, remains one of the most controversial issues in the criminal justice system.*

Indeed, about one-third of all young African-American men are arrested in any given year (Duster 1995). Arrest and imprisonment of Hispanics also exceed their proportion in the population, but not by as much as the difference for blacks. Hispanics comprise about 18 percent of all prisoners, even though they represent only about 10 percent of the U.S. population (Beck and Mumola 1999).

The major debate is whether the disproportionate arrests of African-Americans and Hispanics reflect police racial prejudice or, instead, simply the disproportionate involvement of these groups in street crime. Here *consensus* and *conflict* theories disagree (Bridges and Crutchfield 1988). Consensus theories assume that justice is administered fairly. Although there may be a few individual police and other criminal justice officials who discriminate against blacks, Hispanics, and other groups, race and ethnicity are assumed to have no overall systematic effect on one's chances of being arrested, prosecuted, and imprisoned. Consensus theories attribute the disproportionate arrest rates of blacks, Hispanics, and other groups to their greater criminal involvement, not to police racial and ethnic prejudice.

Conflict theories take the opposite position. In their view, justice is administered unfairly against the poor and against blacks, Hispanics, and other minorities. Compared to whites committing similar crimes, people of color are assumed to be more likely to be arrested, prosecuted, and imprisoned, and more likely to receive longer prison terms once imprisoned. Conflict theories thus attribute the high arrest rates of blacks, Hispanics, and other groups more to racial and ethnic prejudice than to their greater criminal involvement.

The disproportionate arrest of African-Americans has more than theoretical significance, as a major source of dissatisfaction by African-Americans with police is their belief that arrests are racially motivated (Hagan and Peterson 1995). This belief underlies much of their cynicism about the entire criminal justice system and is thought to increase their reluctance to report crimes and to otherwise cooperate with police investigations.

Not surprisingly, the issue of racial and ethnic discrimination in arrest has been the subject of much research. Does the evidence show that police arrest practices are motivated by racial prejudice or instead simply reflect the disproportionate involvement of African-Americans in street crime? Unfortunately, the evidence is ambiguous, as arrest discrimination is very difficult to study. Let's look at some of this research.

Reiss's 1966 police observational study found no discrimination. Although a greater proportion of black suspects than white suspects were arrested, the study attributed this disparity not to police racism but to at least three other reasons: (1) Blacks tended to be suspected of more serious crimes than whites; (2) black suspects were more hostile than white suspects toward police; and (3) complainants (who, given the intraracial nature of interpersonal crime, were usually black) in cases involving black suspects preferred arrest more often than did the (mostly white) complainants in cases involving white suspects (Black 1980). Other studies report similar conclusions (Riksheim and Chermak 1993). Whether police might again be "on their best behavior" because they know they're being observed is an important question in interpreting these studies' results.

Further support for a conclusion of nonracism comes from the similarity of racial disparity in arrest data to that found in self-report and victimization studies. As Chapter 3 noted, self-report surveys and the National Crime Victimization Survey (NCVS) also indicate disproportionate involvement in crime by people of color, including African-Americans. To the extent these crime measures are more valid measures of crime than the UCR, they bolster the conclusion that racial disparities in arrest don't reflect police racism (Hindelang 1981). These studies lead William Wilbanks (1987) to conclude that white officers do not take suspects' race into account when they decide whether to arrest them.

Other evidence disputes this conclusion. For one thing, the proportion of people arrested who are African-American exceeds the proportion of offenders identified by victims in the NCVS as being African-American (Figure 15.1). This difference suggests to some observers that African-Americans are disproportionately likely to

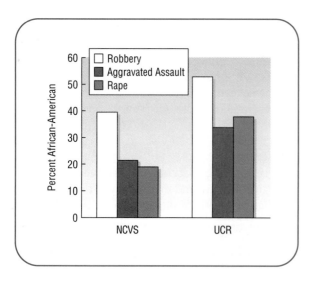

◄ FIGURE 15.1 PERCEIVED RACE OF OFFENDER (NCVS) AND RACE OF PERSONS ARRESTED (UCR), 1997
(% AFRICAN-AMERICAN)
Source: Maguire and Pastore 1999.

be arrested (Reiman 1998). However, whether this is due to police racism or to some other factors (e.g., the nature of the crimes or even the possibility that victims are more likely to report crimes to the police when their offenders are black), remains unclear.

Better evidence for actual racial bias in arrest would come from observational studies. Although the observational studies cited previously found no racial bias in arrest, other observational studies have found such evidence (Walker, Spohn, and DeLone 2000). Further, despite the correlation in some work between black suspects' disrespectful demeanor and their likelihood of arrest, it's possible that blacks' poor demeanor stems from hostile treatment by police and even from the arrest itself. Thus "arrest may cause disrespect as much as disrespect causes arrest" (Sherman 1980:80).

In a more subtle form of police discrimination, a few studies have found that police are more likely to investigate crimes and make an arrest when *victims* are white than when they're black, suggesting that police put more emphasis on crimes with white victims (Bynum, Cordner, and Greene 1982; Smith, Visher, and Davidson 1984). These findings "appear to contradict norms of equity on which the American criminal justice system is based" (Smith 1986:340).

Some studies also find that race and ethnicity affect the strength of the evidence needed for arrest. Police tend not to arrest whites unless the evidence against them is fairly strong. In contrast, they often arrest African-Americans and Latinos even when the evidence is fairly weak (Petersilia 1983). In one study of arrest in small cities, police repeatedly arrested, and then quickly released, the same Chicanos and blacks over a three-year period. When the police did not release the suspects, the prosecutors often dropped the charges because the evidence was too weak. The authors of the study interpreted this pattern as racial harassment (Hagan and Zatz 1985).

Once again, then, we have mixed, complex findings on police racism. Many white police, like many white civilians, are racially prejudiced, and there is ample if somewhat anecdotal evidence that police routinely harass African-Americans, Latinos, and other people of color by, for example, stopping and questioning them for no apparent reason and by verbally abusing them (Conley 1994). In the late 1990s this practice became known as *racial profiling*, and the "suspect behavior" became known as *DWB (Driving While Black)*. Investigations in Maryland and New Jersey found strong evidence of racial profiling. In Maryland, for example, African-Americans were 17 percent of the drivers on a major highway but 77 percent of all the drivers stopped by state troopers. The governor and attorney general of New Jersey acknowledged that state troopers had targeted black and Latino drivers for alleged traffic violations and were three times more likely to search their cars than those of white drivers they stopped (Cole 1999).

Although the police may harass people of color and pull their cars over, does that mean they are also more likely to arrest them for non-traffic offenses? Here the evidence is unclear; people can be racially prejudiced but still act in a nondiscriminatory way (Skolnick 1994). That said, the weight of the evidence is that police arrest practices are racially biased to a degree, but that racial disparities in arrest reflect disproportionate racial involvement in crime more than police racial bias (Walker, Spohn, and DeLone 2000). As with brutality, some arrests are undoubtedly racially motivated, but overall the higher arrest rates for blacks and other people of color "are not substantially the result of bias" (Tonry 1994:71). This conclusion notwithstanding, the evidence that does exist of *any* racial bias in arrest, and also in the use of brutal and deadly force, is troubling in a society whose Pledge of Allegiance professes "liberty and justice for all."

RACE, ARREST, AND THE WAR ON DRUGS

So far we've explored racial discrimination in arrest by focusing on the proportion of black and white suspects arrested. Racial discrimination in arrest occurs in at least one other, less direct way. If a law targets a behavior in which African-Americans or other people of color tend to engage while neglecting an equally harmful behavior in which whites tend to engage, the effect of the law (and arrests resulting from it) is racially discriminatory. One obvious example here is the huge number of arrests for street crimes, committed disproportionately by poor people of color, and the few arrests for white-collar crime and especially corporate crime, committed disproportionately by wealthy whites (Reiman 1998).

An objection to this example might be that street crime threatens, harms, and frightens us much more directly than white-collar crime and thus merits more police attention. The strongest evidence of racial discrimination motivates the *differential enforcement* of two behaviors that are essentially similar except for the fact that people of color tend to do one and whites the other.

We've had such a situation since the mid-1980s, when the government intensified its legal war on drugs. This was mainly a war against crack cocaine, which African-American drug users tend to use and sell. In contrast, white drug users prefer to use and sell powder cocaine. Taking their cue from the congressional, media, and public concern over crack, police departments focused their efforts in poor African-American neighborhoods and ignored powder cocaine and other drug use and sales in wealthier, white neighborhoods and other settings.

Once they made this decision, it was inevitable—as many observers at the time predicted—that blacks would be arrested far out of proportion to their actual involvement with drugs, even if individual officers did not practice racial discrimination in arresting (Tonry 1994). The *enemy* in the war against drugs thus became young black males involved in street sales of less than $75 worth of cocaine in major U.S. cities. Drug sales in other, less visible settings (such as powder cocaine sales inside middle-class homes) went undetected (Duster 1995). Reflecting the focus on crack, the penalties for selling it became far more severe than those for selling powder cocaine. For example, selling only 5 grams of crack yielded the same federal sentence as selling 500 grams of powder cocaine.

Not surprisingly, the war on crack led to huge racial disparities in arrest. Although only about 15 percent of all illegal drug users in the United States are African-Americans, some 40 percent of all people arrested for drug offenses since the mid-1980s have been African-Americans, most of them young males. This figure was only 22 percent in the mid-1970s. While the annual white arrest rate for drug offenses stayed at about 300 per 100,000 whites during the 1980s, the non-white arrest rate soared from 450 per 100,000 nonwhites in 1980 to a peak of 1,500 in 1989, before falling to just under 1,100 by 1991. People of color are thus about four times as likely as whites to be arrested for drugs, even though about 80 percent of all illegal drug users are white (Blumstein 1993).

The racial discrimination suggested by these figures concerns many observers and reminds us of the racial/ethnic bias underlying efforts to thwart drug use in earlier periods of U.S. history (Chapter 2). As Alfred Blumstein (1993:4–5), a former president of the American Society of Criminology, observes, "What is particularly troublesome … is the degree to which the impact [of the drug war] has been so disproportionately imposed on nonwhites. There is no clear indication that the racial differences in arrest truly reflect different levels of activity or of harm imposed." Calling the war on drugs "a major assault on the black community," Blumstein comments, "One can be reasonably confident that if a similar assault was affecting the white community, there would be a strong and effective effort to change either the laws or the enforcement policy" (p. 5). Despite some concern over this issue and calls to make the penalties for selling powder cocaine and crack more equal, the drug war continues to be, as one former criminal justice official put it, a "search and destroy" mission in the black community (Miller 1996). Largely because of it, one in three young black men is now under correctional supervision by being behind bars or on probation or parole (Mauer 1999).

ECOLOGICAL EVIDENCE FOR RACIAL DISCRIMINATION IN POLICING

The example of the war on drugs shows that racial/ethnic discrimination in policing occurs if the police target a behavior popular in one subordinate racial or ethnic group while ignoring similar behavior popular among wealthier whites. Similar discrimination occurs if police resources are focused more on communities with high proportions of blacks or other minorities than on those with lower proportions but similar crime rates. Drawing on Hubert Blalock's (1967) famous *power-threat* theory, the idea here is that dominant groups (whites) feel more threatened as the size of minority groups grows and respond with legal control and other measures designed to protect their dominant status.

Supporting this view, several studies find police force size and police expenditures higher in cities with higher proportions of African-Americans, even after controlling for crime rates. Their findings indicate that "police expenditures are a resource that is mobilized when minority groups appear to threaten the political and economic position of more dominant groups" (Sheley 2000:41). Supporting this view, increases in the 1960s and 1970s in spending on police resources were highest in cities with the greatest increases in black population, even with crime rates held constant (Jackson 1989).

As we saw earlier, a major theme of nineteenth-century policing was the use of police to control the behavior of immigrants and workers, perceived as the major "dangerous classes" of the time. These latest studies suggest that the police still serve a similar function for African-Americans and other groups perceived as today's "dangerous classes," with the war on drugs perhaps the prime example (Brown and Warner 1995; Miller 1996).

Gender and Arrest

The issue of gender discrimination in arrest is perhaps less controversial but no less interesting. In 1998, 78 percent of all people arrested were men, and 83 percent of the people arrested just for violent Index crimes (including 90 percent of those arrested for homicide and robbery) were men (Federal Bureau of Investigation 1999). Although almost all scholars agree these high percentages reflect heavier male involvement in crime (Steffensmeier and Allan 2000), it's possible they also reflect more lenient treatment of women by police. This is the view of the *chivalry hypothesis*, which says that male police don't arrest female suspects because of notions of chivalry: They feel that women need to be protected, not punished; that arrest would harm them and their families; and that women do not pose a threat to society. Police may also be reluctant to arrest women because they don't want to have to use physical force on a woman who resists arrest. A contrasting *evil woman hypothesis* predicts the opposite: Since women are normally regarded as more virtuous than men, a woman suspected of a crime might seem that much worse by

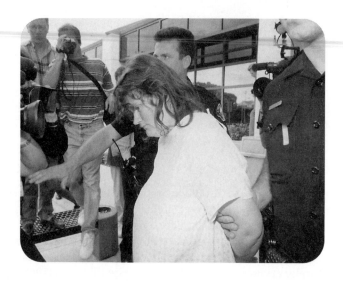

◀ *Women are arrested much less often than are men. While most scholars think women's low arrest rate reflects their low level of criminality, some also believe it reflects the reluctance of police to arrest women who have committed crimes.*

comparison, prompting police to be particularly likely to arrest her. What does the evidence say?

Here we have to consider juvenile and adult arrests separately. The evidence for juvenile arrests is fairly clear that girls are disproportionately arrested or otherwise brought to the attention of juvenile authorities for status offenses such as running away from home, parental curfew violations, and premarital sexual intercourse (Chesney-Lind 1997). This discrimination arises from the traditional *double standard* view that girls need protection more than boys do.

The evidence for adults is less clear. Female prostitutes, of course, are far more likely than their male customers to be arrested, representing significant gender discrimination against women. For other crimes, the evidence for either harsh or lenient treatment of women in arrest appears to depend on the race and age of the suspects and the degree to which female suspects act "femininely" (Mann 1995). Supporting the chivalry argument, one study of the elderly found that arrest is less likely for older women suspects than for older male suspects (Shichor 1985). Another study found that police were more lenient with young women than young men only if the women cried or otherwise conformed to traditional female stereotypes (DeFleur 1975). Women who were hostile toward the police were not treated leniently.

In one of the best studies of chivalry and arrest, Christy A. Visher (1983) analyzed data from 785 police–suspect encounters in Rochester, St. Louis, and Tampa–St. Petersburg in 1977. Visher initially found that police arrested 16 percent of female suspects and 20 percent of male suspects, a statistically insignificant difference. But when she held other variables such as offense seriousness constant, some interesting gender differences emerged. Replicating the findings of earlier studies, police in her study were less likely to arrest older women and women who acted femininely. Police also treated white women more leniently than black women. To be more specific, black women were arrested as often as black men, but white women were arrested only half as often as white men. Visher concluded that women receive more lenient police treatment only when they conform to traditional gender roles:

> Female suspects who violate typical middle-class standards of traditional female characteristics and behaviors (i.e., white, older, and submissive) are not afforded

any chivalrous treatment during arrest decisions. In these data, young, black, or hostile women receive no preferential treatment, whereas older, white women who are calm and deferential toward the police are granted leniency (pp. 22–23).

While cautioning that her study needed to be replicated, Visher added that gender stereotypes will continue to influence the treatment of women offenders as long as men continue to dominate the criminal justice system as police officers, prosecutors, and judges.

In considering whether chivalrous treatment exists, it's important to look at the context of arrests. In a study of marijuana arrests, Weldon T. Johnson and associates (1977) found women marijuana users less likely to be arrested than male users. In considering the circumstances under which the arrests occurred, the authors found that this gender difference did not reflect chivalry. Instead, it simply reflected the fact that the women were less likely than men to use marijuana in public places. Because women users were less visible than male users to police, they were less at risk for arrest.

 # THE IMPACT OF POLICING ON CRIME

Do police make a difference in crime? On the face of it, this is an absurd question. Of course police make a difference in crime. If we had no police, we would probably have chaos, as happened in Montreal in 1968 when the police went on a one-day strike. Looting was common, and bank robberies and other crimes also increased during the day (Clark 1971).

But when we ask whether police make a difference in crime, we're not posing an all-or-nothing alternative. Instead we're asking whether more police make a difference than fewer police (once some minimal threshold is reached), and whether more arrests make a difference than fewer arrests (again assuming some threshold is reached). Answers to these questions have important social policy implications. If more police and more arrests do make a difference, it would make sense to hire a lot more police. This was one of the rationales for a major federal crime bill in 1994 that, in part, provided $9 billion for hiring 100,000 new police officers around the country. But if more police and more arrests don't make a difference, it would not make sense to spend our money this way. What does the evidence say?

Do Additional Police Deter Crime?

If the hypothesis is that more police result in lower crime rates, support for this hypothesis is mixed. Although most studies don't support this hypothesis, recent research does suggest that the number of police can make a difference under some circumstances (Sherman et al. 1998). Let's review the evidence.

Even with police strikes, the evidence is inconsistent. Contrary to the Montreal experience noted previously, a study of U.S. police strikes in the 1970s found that crime didn't always increase when the police went on strike (Pfuhl 1983). However, this study was later criticized for methodological weaknesses and its conclusions challenged (Sherman et al. 1998). In any event, police strikes are rare and beg the question of whether more police and more arrests make a difference in a normal, non-strike context.

In another type of research, scholars have analyzed U.S. cities and other geographical areas in terms of how their ratio of police to city/area population size (e.g., the number of police for every 1,000 residents) compared to their UCR crime rates. If the number of police does make a difference, areas with higher police ratios should have lower crime rates. Most studies don't find this effect (Moran 1995; Walker 1998). However, a recent, well-designed study found that additional police do reduce the crime rate, and even estimated that each additional officer in a big city prevents 24 crimes a year (Marvell and Moody 1996). This study led a major review of crime prevention research to conclude that adding police is a promising if not proven policy for lowering crime (Sherman et al. 1998).

Another line of research involves experiments in which a city adds police in certain areas but not in others. The most famous experiment took place in Kansas City in the early 1970s. One large district of Kansas City was divided into three groups of five patrol beats each. In one group, the number of patrol cars doubled or tripled. In another group, patrol cars were eliminated and entered the area only when a citizen called for help. In a third, control group, the number of patrol cars remained the same as before. Using victimization surveys and official data, the researchers found that the number of patrol cars didn't affect the crime rate. Compared to the control group, crime did not go down in the beats where patrol cars increased, nor did it go up in the beats where patrol cars disappeared (Kelling et al. 1974). The Kansas City experiment was later criticized for several methodological problems, including allowing patrol cars, in the two groups of beats where they were present, to be seen (as they responded to calls) from the beats where they were eliminated (Larson 1975). Some scholars have called for better-designed experiments of this type (Sherman 1986).

These methodological issues aside for the moment, Walker (1998) says that several reasons account for the lack of an effect in this experiment. Even when police patrol is doubled or tripled, the actual presence of police at a given place and point of time hardly increases. Further, many violent crimes involve people who know each other and occur indoors, where the police can't see them and can't prevent them. Even when more police are added, the risk of detection and arrest for public crimes such as robbery still remains low. Finally, as noted in Chapter 5, many criminals give little thought to their chances of arrest, and those that do so assume they can get away with it.

These comments suggest that *how* additional police are used is at least as important as whether they're used in the first place. As Walker (1998:76) notes, "Simply hiring more police officers does not necessarily mean that more patrol officers will be on the street or that they will be more effective in fighting crime." Far more important, he says, is how efficiently the officers operate regarding such things as how many patrol at night (when the most crime occurs), where they patrol, and how active they are on patrol.

Evidence that the police can reduce crime if they're used properly arises from several kinds of research. One line of research explores whether police can deter crime in closed environments such as subway stations. Even a few additional officers in a subway station will be very visible, suggesting that a deterrent effect will occur. This seems to be the case. When New York City added police to subway stations and trains in the 1970s, crime went down. However, this decrease was not cost-effective, as it cost New York some $35,000 (equal to more than $100,000 in today's dollars) for each reduced felony (Chaiken, Lawless, and Stevenson 1975).

Other research examines the effects of *directed* police patrol, in which the police focus their attention on *hot spots* of crime. As Chapter 4 pointed out, cities have a few hot spots where most of their crime occurs. It makes sense to think that a greater police presence in these hot spots might reduce their amount of crime. This again seems to be the case. In an experiment in Minneapolis, additional police cars were added to a group of 55 hot spots, while a control group of 55 other hot spots received no additional patrol. The additional police patrol led to modest declines in the crime rates in the hot spots where the patrol cars were added (Sherman 1995). This and other studies suggest that directed patrol in high-crime locations can help reduce the crime rate (Sherman et al. 1998).

A related approach involves directed patrols in hot spots for *gun crime*. Here another experiment in Kansas City was telling. The experiment involved intensive efforts to take handguns from people who had them illegally. In a high crime area of Kansas City, police officers trained in detecting concealed firearms stopped cars and pedestrians for legitimate reasons. They found many illegal handguns on the people they stopped, as gun seizures rose by 60 percent. At the same time, gun crimes dropped by 49 percent (Sherman and Rogan 1995). This and other studies suggest that efforts targeted at reducing gun carrying, especially that by urban youths, can reduce gun crimes (Hagan and Foster 2000; Sherman et al. 1998). However, these efforts are likely to be expensive and raise civil liberties questions (Walker 1998).

CRACKDOWNS AND AGGRESSIVE POLICING

If directed patrol in hot spots can reduce crime, what about an even more intense police presence in the form of a police *crackdown*? Here, police saturate a small area and arrest drug pushers, prostitutes, gang members, and others committing visible crime. For better or worse, research on crackdowns suggests they don't offer much hope for reducing crime. Some studies find that crackdowns reduce drug trafficking and other crime in the target areas, but other research finds that crackdowns have no such effect (Sherman 1990). Even when a deterrent effect is found, it tends to be a short-term one only, as crime rates generally rise back to their initial levels. Often the drug trafficking and other crime are simply displaced to other neighborhoods. In another problem, crackdowns raise serious civil liberties questions for drug dealers and law-abiding citizens alike and flood the courts and jails with new defendants and inmates. Crackdowns thus appear to be at best a "quick fix" to the crime problem with no long-term effects and have had little success in the war against drugs. As Elliott Currie (1994:206) puts it, "On balance, it is not that crackdowns make no difference, but that, especially where drug dealing is heaviest and most widespread, any effects they have are likely to be short-lived."

If crackdowns do have short-term effects, these results probably stem from the heightened visibility of police. Assuming this connection, several police departments, especially in New York City, began in the 1990s to use an ongoing, aggressive style of *zero-tolerance* policing that falls short of a crackdown but is more intense than directed policing. It involves frequent traffic stops and questioning of suspicious persons and frequent arrests for disorderly conduct, vagrancy, and other minor offenses. It's possible that such visible, aggressive policing may lower crime rates by increasing the chances that criminals do get arrested and by deterring potential criminals from breaking the law. Aggressive policing may also reduce incivilities such as disorderly youth and public drunkenness, which prompt potential offenders to think that residents don't care what happens in their neighborhoods—in short, that "anything goes." This may be another reason such aggressive policing can lower crime rates (Kelling and Coles 1998).

To assess the effectiveness of aggressive policing, several studies compared crime rates in cities that differ in police style. In a study of 35 U.S. cities with population over 250,000, James Q. Wilson and Barbara Boland (1978) found that cities with higher numbers of traffic tickets per officer had lower crime rates. In a study of all 171 U.S. cities with a population of 100,000 or more, Robert J. Sampson and Jacqueline Cohen (1988) found that cities with higher arrest rates for disorderly conduct and drunk driving had lower robbery and burglary rates. However, the authors cautioned they were not suggesting "that the police should start being more aggressive. Obviously any crime control policy entails certain trade-offs, and it is quite conceivable that the costs of … [more aggressive policing] are too high relative to expected gains" (p. 186). One of these costs, they say, is that aggressive policing, even if it doesn't involve brutality, may anger urban residents, harm police–community relations, and contribute to rioting. The Diallo tragedy recounted at the beginning of this chapter represents a perhaps inevitable consequence of aggressive policing.

Another cost is that aggressive policing raises important civil rights and civil liberties questions. Even before the Diallo killing occurred, complaints of racial harassment against New York City police had increased in the wake of their new, zero-tolerance approach, leading one observer to condemn, after the Diallo not-guilty verdict, "the humiliation and brutalization of thousands of innocent New Yorkers, most of them black and brown, by police officers who are arrogant, tyrannical, poorly trained, often frightened and not infrequently racist" (Herbert 2000:A23; Reibstein 1997). All these potential costs of aggressive policing once again underscore the dilemma of law enforcement in a democratic society. As one former New York City police sergeant said, "New York City has paid a huge price. What the NYPD did was throw people at the problem, putting cops on every corner, but who wants to live in a society like that?" (Butterfield 2000:A1).

Did the turn to aggressive policing in the 1990s explain the drop in the crime rate during that decade? There's no easy answer to this question. Although crime rates lowered in cities where such policing was used, they also lowered where it wasn't used. Also, the crime rate began declining in New York City and other areas *before* they started using aggressive policing. Although aggressive policing sounds like a plausible crime control policy, and many scholars tout it, others conclude it probably played little or no role in the 1990s' drop in the crime rate. (See the Crime and Controversy box).

Does Arrest Make a Difference?

We've seen that the evidence on additional police is complex. What about arrest? Here again we're not talking about some arrests versus no arrests; instead we're considering more arrests versus fewer arrests. A common line of investigation is to determine an arrest or "certainty" ratio for states or cities by dividing the number of annual arrests in a given location by the official number of crimes for that location. The resulting ratio provides a rough measure of the chances that a crime will lead to an arrest.

A *police deterrence* hypothesis would predict that locations with higher certainty ratios should have lower crime rates than locations with lower ratios (Tittle 1980). This correlation is usually found but difficult to interpret because of the familiar "chicken-and-egg" question: Which comes first, the certainty of arrest or the crime rate? Although a deterrence view would interpret this correlation as support for its perspective, it's also possible that crime rates affect certainty rates. In this view,

The 1990s' Drop in Urban Crime: A Result of "Zero-Tolerance" Policing?

As noted back in Chapter 3, homicide and other crime in the United States began declining sharply in the early 1990s and continued to decline for the rest of the decade. Perhaps nowhere did this decrease get more attention than in New York City, where the murder rate fell 70.6 percent from 1991 to 1998, and where the robbery rate fell 60.1 percent. The drop in crime prompted news media stories on why the decline was occurring. Not surprisingly, police and criminologists came up with very different explanations.

Police attributed the drop in crime to their own intensified efforts to fight it. In the mid-1990s, several cities adopted a new style of aggressive or "zero-tolerance" policing involving frequent arrests for disorderly conduct, public urination, graffiti, and other minor offenses. New York City's police also established a Street Crime Unit that stopped thousands of people in high-crime areas and frisked them for guns. New York's zero-tolerance policing was given wide credit for the crime decline in that city. Houston was another area using this method. In just one month, December 1995, its police arrested hundreds of people in a high-crime area for minor infractions such as jaywalking. They also stopped thousands of others to either question them or search them for illegal weapons.

Disagreeing with the police assessment, some criminologists noted that crime declined even in cites that had not adopted zero-tolerance policing. For example, the murder rate fell 76.4 percent (a sharper drop than in New York City) from 1991 to 1998 in San Diego and 69.3 percent in Boston, barely under New York's decrease. The robbery rate fell 62.6 percent in San Diego (also a sharper drop than in New York City) and 50.2 percent in Boston. But neither of these cities had adopted New York's zero-tolerance policy. Instead, San Diego used a community policing strategy involving frequent meetings with citizens and the use of citizen volunteers to patrol neighborhoods, and Boston used a multi-faceted strategy involving police

and black ministers meeting with the most notorious drug dealers and gang members and federal prosecution of offenders who did not heed their warnings to desist from violence.

Moreover, crime also fell in cities that didn't use any of the strategies that New York, San Diego, or Boston used. For example, the murder rate fell almost 63 percent from 1991 to 1998 in San Antonio, 59.3 percent in Los Angeles, and 52.4 percent in Dallas. The decrease in Los Angeles was especially surprising in view of the fact that its police department was beset by scandals involving corruption and brutality and by low morale. The fact that crime dropped so much in so many cities suggested to some criminologists that it might well have dropped in New York City even had it not adopted zero-tolerance policing and in San Diego and Boston even if they had not used their other approaches. The nationwide drop in crime, these criminologists said, instead reflected other factors.

What were these factors? One was demographic, as criminologists cited the decline in the number of people in the crime-prone 15–25 age group along with the aging of the large baby-boom generation. A second was a stabilizing of the crack market in our largest cities. The onset of crack trafficking in the mid-1980s fueled a large increase in violent crime in our urban centers for the next five or six years. Inevitably, the crack market began to stabilize as drug gangs established their turf and began to realize the self-destructiveness of their violence against each other. Because drug trafficking thus became less violent, crime in our large cities declined. A third factor, criminologists said, was the thriving economy that began about 1994 and continued through the rest of the decade. Despite the attention that zero-tolerance policing has gained, then, its effectiveness in reducing crime remains far from proven.

Sources: Butterfield 2000; Fletcher 2000; Lacayo 1996; Mc-Grory 1996; Steffensmeier and Harer 1999.

police in areas with low crime rates will be able to devote more resources to solving the few crimes they do have and thus be able to solve more crimes through arrest, creating high certainty ratios. Conversely, police in areas with high crime rates will simply not have the time or resources to investigate many crimes, resulting in low certainty ratios. These possibilities support a "system capacity" argument and are at least as compelling as deterrence views (Decker and Kohfeld 1985; Pontell 1984). If so, the evidence on certainty ratios and crime rates can't be interpreted as supporting the deterrence hypothesis. It's also possible that the certainty rate–crime rate correlation is spurious, with both rates due to other factors such as poverty or urbanization.

To investigate these possibilities, longitudinal studies looking at certainty ratios and crime rates over time are necessary. Several such studies find little or no impact of arrest certainty, or, to be more precise, *changes* in arrest certainty, on crime rates. A review concluded that these studies "provide little, if any, evidence consistent with the general deterrence perspective" (Chamlin 1991:188). It's possible, however, that no deterrence evidence was found because the certainty ratios in these studies never reached a minimal threshold, after which deterrence may start to occur. A study of this possibility by Mitchell B. Chamlin (1991) found that such a "tipping effect" for ratios exceeding 40 percent may exist for cities under 10,000 population. However, he also found that most cities of this size don't reach this certainty threshold, and larger cities almost never do. Even if a tipping effect does occur in the few small towns reaching the threshold, these towns have relatively low crime rates to begin with and aren't the ones with the crime problem that worries us. Chamlin concluded that his findings reinforce the conclusion of other studies that arrest rates have little to do with crime rates.

However, a recent study indicated that arrest does make a difference. Stewart J. D'Alessio and Lisa Stolzenberg (1998) studied arrests and the number of crimes in Orlando, Florida, and its surrounding county over a 184-day period. The daily number of arrests ranged from 8 to 104, with an average of almost 54 per day. The authors concluded that "as the number of arrests made by police increases, criminal activity decreases substantially the following day," (p. 748), probably because word gets around after an arrest and deters would-be offenders from committing a crime. Although their findings are important and should guide future research, the best conclusion from the arrest/deterrence literature is that arrests in general do not reduce crime, but that arrests from directed patrol may lower crime.

PERCEPTIONS OF ARREST RISK AND PROBABILITY OF OFFENDING

One reason arrest rates might not affect crime rates is that potential criminals have little idea of what the arrest rates are (Erickson and Gibbs 1978). Imagine two cities, City A and City B, where City A has a higher certainty ratio (40 percent) than City B (25 percent). Now let's pretend there are two male criminals, one in each city. Even if these criminals do sit down and calculate their chances of arrest, can we really expect that the one in City A will know that his chances, judging from its certainty ratio, are much higher than his counterpart's in City B? If we can't expect the criminals to know their cities' arrest rates, then we should not expect the arrest rates to affect the crime rates.

This problem emphasizes the importance of would-be criminals' *perceptions* of their risk for arrest. Because of this importance, scholars began some years ago to study *perceived deterrence*. The typical study asks adolescents or college students to estimate their risk for arrest for a given offense and to report how often they've committed the offense in the past and how likely they'd be to commit it in the future. Such studies often find that adolescents who perceive greater risks of arrest for a given crime are less likely to have committed that offense in the past and less likely to say they would commit it in the future (Krohn 2000). In one specific finding, girls in these studies generally perceive greater arrest risk than boys, and this might be one reason they commit fewer offenses than boys (Miller and Iovanni 1994).

Although some scholars interpret the perceived risk–offending correlation as evidence of a perceived deterrent effect, others scholars raise the familiar chicken-and-egg question. In their view, the correlation could just as well mean that delinquency affects perceptions of arrest risk. In this way of thinking, adolescents who have committed many offenses have probably been arrested for very few or even none of them. Because of this, they will perceive low risks of arrest. Most longitudinal studies investigating this possibility conclude that perceived arrest has little or no effect on delinquency, although some studies do find the presumed deterrent effect (Nagin 1998). Overall, the perceived deterrence literature does not provide strong reasons for expecting a substantial deterrence effect from perceived risks of arrest, at least for the typical street criminal. A greater effect might exist for some individuals, such as middle-class tax evaders, who have a high stake in conventional behavior and thus would find arrest to be a very stigmatizing event (Nagin 1998).

Community Policing: Real Promise or False Hope?

Community policing has been growing in popularity as communities attempt to address their crime problems. In this style of policing, police work closely with neighborhood residents on various activities designed to reduce crime, including youth programs and cleanup projects. Perhaps most important, community policing replaces car patrol with foot patrol. Theoretically, foot patrol allows police officers and citizens to get to know each other better and *humanizes* the police to the citizenry. In return, citizens are more likely to trust the police, to report crimes to them, and to work with them on community projects. Foot patrol also allows officers to notice trash and other neighborhood incivilities that contribute to fear of crime and actual crime itself and to bring these incivilities to the attention of local officials (Kratcoski and Dukes 1995).

How successful is community policing? Studies indicate that foot patrol and other aspects of community policing make residents feel better about their neighborhoods and reduce their fear of crime (Skolnick and Bayley 1986). However, there is less evidence that community policing actually reduces crime rates: Some studies find community policing successful in this regard, while other studies do not (Greene and Mastrofski 1988). A recent study found that community policing in Oakland helped lower drug trafficking and other crime in certain hot spots (Green 1995), and early evidence from Chicago suggests that community policing has helped lower crime rates there (Skogan and Hartnett 1999). As the Crime and Controversy box noted, community policing in San Diego has also been credited with the crime decline there, but crime has declined in cities where such policing has not been used. The evidence on community policing is thus complex, but the studies that do find some success in community policing suggest that this approach should be given more consideration.

Legal Technicalities and Police Effectiveness

Many critics charge that the Warren Court's rulings in the 1960s have forced the police to fight crime with one hand tied behind their backs. Suspects and defendants now have too many rights, the critics say, forcing the police not to arrest them or prosecutors to release them. In either case, public safety suffers as the law shackles police and prevents them from carrying out their job. Reduce the controls on police, and they'll be able to arrest more criminals and otherwise do a better job of keeping the public safe (Walker 1998).

The two Court rulings most under attack are the ones that developed the *exclusionary rule* and the *Miranda* warning. In the first case, the Court ruled in *Mapp v. Ohio* (367 U.S. 643 [1961]) that evidence obtained by police in violation of the Fourth Amendment of the Constitution cannot be used in court. In the second case, the Court ruled in *Miranda v. Arizona* (384 U.S. 436 [1966]) that police must advise suspects that they may remain silent, that anything they say could be used against them, and that they have the right to have an attorney present during questioning.

How valid is the argument that these rules restrict arrests, let criminals go free, and raise our crime rates? Our preceding discussion suggests at least one problem with this view: Even if the police could arrest more people if legal technicalities were reduced, these extra arrests would probably have little effect on the crime rate, although they would at least incapacitate the people arrested. But how many more would be arrested and prosecuted? To put this question another way, how many people are currently not arrested or, if arrested, not prosecuted because of legal technicalities? Satisfactory answers to this question go to the heart of the legal technicalities debate.

The best evidence suggests that technicalities do little to hinder police and court effectiveness, and that the belief to the contrary is yet another of the many myths about crime and criminal justice. Let's look first at the exclusionary rule. The clear conclusion from many studies is that very few suspects are freed because of the exclusionary rule. Of more than 500,000 felony arrests in California between 1976 and 1979, for example, prosecutors dismissed only 4,130 cases, or less than 1 percent, because of illegally obtained evidence (Fyfe 1983). The cases dismissed tend to be not violent crimes but drug cases, where police sometimes conduct improper searches to find the drugs. Walker (1998) concludes, "The exclusionary rule does not let 'thousands' of dangerous criminals loose on the streets and it has almost no effect on violent crime.... Yes, some convictions are overturned and some of those defendants are factually guilty. But these are fairly rare events." In fact, he adds, the exclusionary rule has improved police work by forcing them to do a better job of gathering evidence.

The *Miranda* warning also hasn't impeded the police. Walker (1998) points out that up to half of all suspects confess anyway, since the evidence against them is often substantial and they want to plea bargain to reduce their sentence. Police also have various ways of getting around the *Miranda* warning (Hoffman 1998b). They're required to give suspects the warning only when they are about to ask them questions. If a suspect confesses or provides other information before questioning has begun, this evidence is admissible. Some officers also continue questioning suspects even after they give the *Miranda* warning and eventually wear them down. Sometimes this practice has led to confessions by innocent people (Hoffman 1998a). As political scientist Herbert Jacob (1978:70) observes, "The requirement that counsel be made available almost immediately after arrest is more frequently honored in Supreme Court cases than in lower court practice." Walker (1998:92) concludes from the evidence that "repeal or modification of the *Miranda* warning will not result in more convictions."

The Impact of Policing on Crime, Revisited

Overall, the literature on police, arrest, and crime rates suggests that adding more police to high-crime areas or otherwise increasing the arrests of serious offenders in those areas can reduce the rates of some crimes, but it also suggests that this reduction will be modest at best (Mastrofski 2000). As criminologist Carl Klockars observes, "The police at best are a small and marginal influence on the level of crime, and no criminologist I know has much faith that the institution of police is going to be able to change things" (Rosen 1995:108). If additional police do help, they help only when used in confined areas such as subway stations or in directed patrol in high-crime areas. Additional police and directed patrol would probably have little effect on the many crimes of violence, including homicide, assault, rape, battering, and child abuse, that typically occur behind closed doors among people who know each other. And they certainly would leave untouched corporate crime, which should not be forgotten in this discussion. Another problem is money. Even if additional police and directed patrol could reduce subway crime and some robberies and burglaries, the economic cost of each deterred crime is large and perhaps prohibitive. Finally, intensified police efforts at crime control also raise serious civil liberties questions for a democratic society.

These questions arose repeatedly in New York City in the last decade when it adopted its aggressive, zero-tolerance approach to policing. At its best, this policy may have helped lower New York's crime rate, although, as we've seen, the evidence for this is far from clear. At its worst, it helped lead to tragedies like the death of Amadou Diallo and reduced civil liberties, as critics said the police were going too far in stopping and frisking tens of thousands of city residents and in arresting many for minor infractions. In one case, a subway rider named Zachary Schlee was sitting in an empty subway car on his way home from college classes, reading an anthropology book. Because he had his feet up on the seat next to him, a police officer ordered him off the car and gave him a $50 summons for occupying more than one seat. The officer gave him another $50 summons for not having proper identification. Schlee's father responded angrily, "Do you destroy all the protections of civil society in the hopes of finding a few criminals? Should the police just be able to stop anyone and ask for identification? Whose quality and whose life are we protecting?" Schlee's summons was one of 30,000 the New York police issued in 1996; three years earlier they had issued fewer than 2,000. A month before Schlee got his summons, another subway rider was ordered off a train and given a $50 summons for having his books on the seat next to him (Goldman 1997).

The jury is still out, then, on aggressive, zero-tolerance style of policing adopted in the last decade. It's far from clear that this style of policing has lowered crime. It *is* clear that such policing is expensive, further overcrowds our courts and jails, and may anger urban residents and endanger civil liberties. If labeling theory is correct, it's even possible that in the long run aggressive policing will increase crime because of the effects of an arrest record on a person's attitudes and employment chances (Sherman et al. 1998).

Our discussion underscores the difficulty of fighting crime in a democratic society that values freedom. If we became a police state with tens of thousands of police flooding each of our cities and exercising powers now prohibited by our Constitution, we might be able to lower the crime rate substantially, but only at great cost to the freedoms we now cherish. The fact that much of the public and many politicians are apparently willing to sacrifice some of these freedoms in order to try to lower crime rates suggests how desperate we have become.

The alternative, and one in line with a sociological perspective on crime, is to address the *causes* of U.S. criminal behavior, including economic deprivation, criminogenic living conditions, inadequate parenting, violent masculinity, and a culture that values individualism over community. This approach would reduce crime without diminishing the individual freedoms we now enjoy and add the United States to the list of other democratic nations "not obsessed with crime" (Adler 1983).

WOMEN AND PEOPLE OF COLOR IN POLICE FORCES

In a democratic society where everyone is held equal under the law, everyone should also be equal *in* the law. All citizens, regardless of gender, race, or ethnicity, should have the same opportunity to become police officers and should be treated equally if and when they do join the police. Since police are our first line of defense in creating order under law, anything less than equitable recruitment and treatment is unacceptable. Thus another dilemma of crime control in a democratic society is ensuring that equality prevails in the recruitment of police and in their treatment once on the job.

With these ideals in mind, how equitable is our law enforcement institution? As you might expect, not too long ago few people of color and hardly any women at all were on our police forces. In the last three decades more women and people of color have joined police forces, and conditions for them on the job have improved. As the old saying goes, however, the more things change, the more they stay the same. People of color and women still face obstacles in joining police forces, in their treatment by other officers, and in opportunities for advancement once they're on the job.

Let's look first at race and ethnicity issues in police work. On the eve of World War II, more than a half century ago, only 1 percent of all U.S. police officers were people of color. That figure rose to 2 percent in 1950, almost 4 percent in 1960, and about 6 percent by 1970. One result of the urban riots of the 1960s was increased pressure for the recruitment of more people of color. Coupled with new affirmative action hiring regulations, recruitment of people of color into police forces accelerated in the 1980s. Today about 20 percent, or one fifth, of all sworn officers in the United States are people of color. African-Americans comprise more than 12 percent of all police and Hispanics about 8 percent (Walker, Spohn, and DeLone 2000). These proportions reflect their representation in the general population but vary

◀ *Women and people of color have joined police forces in increasing numbers but still face many obstacles.*

greatly across cities. In New York City and Los Angeles, for example, African-Americans comprise about 11 percent and 14 percent respectively of all officers, while in Chicago and Philadelphia they comprise about 25 percent. They also account for more than half of all officers in Atlanta and Detroit and two-thirds of all officers in Washington, D.C. (Maguire and Pastore 1999). This intercity variation reflects differences not only in city racial composition but also in the cities' police recruitment policies and efforts.

Once they're on the police force, people of color face obstacles that their white counterparts do not (Sullivan 1989). They tend to be denied prestigious positions on special anticrime units and undercover patrols, and are far less likely than their white peers to be promoted. Their chances for promotion are greatest in cities with the largest populations of people of color. Not surprisingly, the racial prejudice of many white officers often contaminates their relationship with officers who aren't white. Black officers in Los Angeles and elsewhere commonly report bigoted comments and discriminatory treatment by white officers (Noble 1995).

Women police officers also face discrimination but of a different sort. Women now comprise about 10 percent of all police officers, and black women comprise 31 percent of all female officers. In most police departments, however, policing is still seen as "men's work," and "sexist attitudes and behaviors remain widespread" (Martin 1994:386). Women officers thus confront many of the same problems that women entering other male-dominated occupations have faced, including sexual harassment. But because police work sometimes involves dangerous confrontations with suspects, women officers face the additional burden of overcoming widespread doubts of their ability to handle themselves during such incidents. Studies of this issue find women officers at least as capable as male officers in persuading or subduing suspects to submit to arrest (Martin 1990).

Research on African-American and other women officers of color indicate they face a double burden of both racism and sexism (Martin 1994). In 1982 one African-American officer, Cheryl Gomez-Preston, was transferred to the largest precinct in Detroit, only to receive from fellow officers written racial slurs such as "nigger bitch," "die, bitch," and "go back to Africa." When she went to her commanding officer to tell him about these notes, he responded by showing her pictures of nude women in pornographic magazines. Once, when she and six other officers were chasing an armed robbery suspect, the other officers failed to back her up when she confronted the suspect as he tried to pull out his gun. Gomez-Preston eventually sued the Detroit Police Department for sexual harassment and won a jury award of $675,000 (Gomez-Preston 1995).

Susan E. Martin (1994) notes that, historically, white women have been "put on a pedestal" by being considered frail and in need of male protection. In contrast, black women have been considered very capable of performing "heavy physical labor in fields, factories, and the homes of white women" (p. 390). These stereotypes, Martin says, contribute to differences in the tasks assigned to African-American and white female officers. In particular, white women are more likely than black women to be given station house duties, instead of more dangerous street patrol assignments. On patrol, white male officers typically back up white female officers but often fail to back up black female officers, as Gomez-Preston's experience illustrates. In the station house, women of both races "face a hostile working environment filled with sexual propositions, pornographic material, and cursing" (p. 391), but the treatment of black women is harsher than that of white women. Black women, Martin found, resent the preferential treatment that white women receive, and white women accept many of the racially stereotyped views that white male officers espouse. All these differences contribute to deep divisions between black and white women in police forces and prevent them from acting together to fight sexism in policing.

 ## SUMMARY AND CONCLUSION

Policing in a democratic society is filled with dilemmas. First and foremost, the police must enforce the law while staying within it. Where the balance should be established between police powers and democratic rights remains a hotly debated topic. The evidence is clear, however, that judicial restrictions on police powers don't hamper police officers' ability to fight crime and protect public safety. It also appears that "get tough" crime-reduction efforts focusing on increasing police resources and more aggressive patrolling will have only a modest effect, if any, on crime rates. Short of developing a police state, then, the police in our democratic society are already doing about as good a crime control job as can be expected. Efforts to reduce street crime substantially will have to look elsewhere.

In a democratic society, police also need to exercise their discretion without regard to race, gender, or other extralegal variables. Experts continue to disagree on whether police practices in arrest and brutality differ by suspects' race/ethnicity and gender. Certainly there is evidence to support very different conclusions. A reasonable conclusion—though one with which partisans on either side of the discretion debate will disagree—is that race/ethnicity and gender play a small but significant role in police behavior.

Regardless of this issue, it's clear that, for better or worse, the police pay more attention to crimes by the poor than by the wealthy. Historically, the police arrested and beat up workers who were protesting horrible wages and working conditions, but didn't arrest company officials for their mistreatment of their workers. In contemporary times, the police arrest poor street criminals but largely ignore wealthy white-collar criminals. This class difference in today's policing reflects larger social and institutional priorities, including the public's concern over the immediacy of street crime and lack of concern over its white-collar counterpart.

We now turn to the remaining stages of the criminal justice system and continue focusing on the two major themes introduced in this chapter: the extent to which race/ethnicity, gender, and class bias affect the exercise of legal discretion, and the ability of the criminal justice system to control crime.

KEY TERMS

brutality	discretion
community policing	discrimination
constable	double burden
corruption	due process
crackdown	encounter
crime control	exclusionary rule
democratic society	extralegal
deterrence	grass-eaters

meat-eaters

police sexual violence (PSV)

technicalities

working personality

zero-tolerance policing

 ## STUDY QUESTIONS

1. What do we mean by the "dilemmas" of crime control in a democratic society?

2. How and why did the modern police force develop? Does the operation and behavior of today's police forces resemble their historical roots? Why or why not?

3. What explains the working personality of police? How does the working personality of police help us understand their behavior?

4. To what degree does racial prejudice affect police decisions to arrest suspects and other aspects of police work? Explain your answer.

5. Would a change in policing strategy help to reduce the crime rate? Why or why not?

 ## INTERNET EXERCISES

As the text notes, community policing is gaining both attention and popularity in the United States. The Community Policing Consortium is composed of five leading U.S. policing organizations: the International Association of Chiefs of Police, the National Organization of Black Law Enforcement Executives, the National Sheriffs' Association, the Police Executive Research Forum, and the Police Foundation. Go to its Web site at **www.communitypolicing.org**.

Now click on its link to **about community policing**, and read the text that appears. Go back to the previous page and click on other links that appear there to gain an even better understanding of community policing. Once you've finished your investigation, answer these questions. What is community policing? What evidence does this Web site present about the effectiveness of community policing? Do you think community policing represents a reasonable approach to helping deal with the crime problem in the United States? Why or why not? If you were an adviser to the mayor and police chief of a major city, what recommendations would you give them about policing strategies?

Chapter

16

PROSECUTION
AND PUNISHMENT

Crime in the News

*R*olando Cruz is lucky to be alive. In 1985 he was convicted of murder, rape, and kidnapping in the death of Jeanine Nicarico, a 10-year-old girl who was taken from her home in a Chicago suburb by a man who kicked in her front door. Her body was found two days later not too far from her house. Cruz was sentenced to die by lethal injection even though no physical evidence implicating him in the rape and murder was introduced at his trial. Later, DNA evidence virtually cleared Cruz of the rape of the child and implicated another man, who confessed to her rape and murder. When Illinois prosecutors refused to reopen Cruz's case, a detective and an assistant attorney general resigned in protest. Finally, a police officer who had testified against Cruz admitted he had lied under oath. This revelation led a judge to free Cruz from prison in 1995. He had spent more than ten years on death row for a crime he didn't commit. A special prosecutor later indicted four police officers and three former prosecutors for perjury and obstruction of justice in Cruz's case.

Source: Berlow 1999.

*P*olicing is only the first stage of the criminal justice process. After an arrest, the prosecutor determines whether to prosecute the case or to drop it, and the judge decides how much bail to require. If the decision is to prosecute, the prosecutor then determines what charges to bring against the defendant. The defendant must decide whether to plead guilty, which most do, or to plead not guilty and have a trial. At the end of the trial a jury or judge decides on the verdict. If the defendant pleads guilty or is found guilty after a trial, the judge next determines the punishment. Here the judge's major decision is whether to incarcerate the defendant by putting him or her behind bars. If the decision is to incarcerate, the judge must also determine the length of the sentence.

No doubt you're already familiar with these basic stages of the legal process after arrest. But notice that decisions are made at every stage, with each creating the possibility of mistakes and/or of bias for or against defendants because of their race/ethnicity, gender, social class, or other extralegal variable. The Rolando Cruz case described in the "Crime in the News" vignette is just one example of the injustice that can result. Much of this chapter examines whether mistakes and bias exist. As with arrest, we'll see that the evidence is quite complex.

Another major issue in criminal justice today is whether a "get tough" approach can reduce crime. The previous chapter questioned whether extra policing and additional arrests can lower the crime rate. This chapter returns to this issue by asking whether the greater use of imprisonment can reduce crime. Most criminologists think it cannot, even as most politicians and members of the public call for tougher treatment of criminals involving longer prison terms and the building of more prisons.

This chapter, then, continues the themes of the previous chapter on policing: the extent to which social inequality affects the exercise of legal discretion, and the extent to which reliance on the criminal justice system can reduce crime. These are arguably the two most important issues for a sociological understanding of criminal justice and thus deserve our full attention.

 CRIMINAL COURTS AND THE ADVERSARY SYSTEM

Sociologists have long noted that the actual behavior of people in organizations often differs from the formal procedures required by the organizations. The reason for this is simple: Organizational rules are often too rigid and bureaucratic, and, if followed, reduce efficiency and productivity. Organizational rules can also be incomplete, meaning they can't hope to cover all possible situations that might arise. To address these unanticipated circumstances, organizational actors sometimes have to bend the rules (Perrow 1986).

This also happens in the criminal courts. For example, the United States has long been said to have an *adversary system* of criminal justice. The adversary model is one of combat. Like the knights of old, prosecutor and defense attorney fight each other with all the weapons at their disposal. Their weapons are not lances or swords but rather their legal skills and powers of oratory. With these weapons they vigorously contest the evidence as the judge referees their fight. The fate of the defendant lies in the balance, just as the fate of the proverbial "fair maiden" lay in the balance in the old, and probably sexist, knightly tales of mortal combat.

This exciting image of the courtroom process is the setting for many novels, films, and TV shows, most notably the "Perry Mason" books and TV series. Unfortunately, the adversary system is largely a myth. Although the most serious and publicized cases, such as the O. J. Simpson case of 1994–1995, do follow the adversary model, most cases involve unknown defendants accused of less heinous crimes. Few of these "run-of-the-mill" defendants can afford the "dream team" of attorneys O. J. Simpson hired for his double-murder case and the estimated $10 million his legal expenses cost. Instead they're forced to go with overworked and underpaid public defenders or court-appointed attorneys, who provide them only perfunctory representation. Not surprisingly, most of these defendants plead guilty.

This was the central finding of work by sociologists and other scholars that began in the 1960s. As with the police research that also accelerated in the 1960s, this body of work was motivated by events of that decade that questioned the fairness and justness of U.S. institutions. These events stimulated the development of the labeling and conflict theories that suggested the decks of the legal system were stacked against poor and nonwhite defendants (see Chapter 8).

To test these theoretical claims, researchers began to study how the criminal courts really worked, not how they claimed to work. In this sense they took up where earlier *sociological jurisprudence* and *legal realism* movements, popular in the first few decades of the twentieth century, had left off. These movements, led by such legal scholars as Roscoe Pound, dean of Harvard Law School, argued that "law in action" was very different from "law in the books" and decried the fate of poor defendants in the criminal courts. However, the social science community generally ignored their claims for some forty years. Starting in the early and mid-1960s and continuing into the 1970s, however, scholarly articles and books documenting the lack of equal, adversarial justice came out in rapid succession.

In one of the most influential studies, David Sudnow (1965) developed the concept of the "normal crime" and applied it to cases involving poor defendants. He argued that prosecutors and public defenders all develop the same idea of what constitutes a typical or "normal" crime—based on such things as the strength of the evidence, the seriousness of the charges, and the defendant's prior record. These assumptions allow them to classify particular crimes as either serious or minor cases and to quickly dispose of them through guilty pleas by agreeing on appropriate punishment for the defendant.

Sudnow concluded that the courts feature much more cooperation than combat between prosecutors and public defenders. Other work extended his view to private counsel assigned by judges to represent poor defendants, and even to private defense attorneys paid by defendants. Abraham S. Blumberg (1967) charged the latter sell out their clients in a "confidence game" in which they do little for their clients but pretend to do a lot. Their object is to collect their fees while minimizing the time spent on any one case. Blumberg further termed defense attorneys "double agents" for cooperating with prosecutors to obtain guilty pleas instead of vigorously defending their clients.

In short, this early body of work charged that poor but innocent defendants were being railroaded into pleading guilty by lawyers who cared more for courts' administrative needs and their own professional needs than for their clients' wellbeing. It was quickly followed by additional scholarly and journalistic accounts (with titles like "The Tipped Scales of American Justice," *Injustice for All*, and *Justice Denied*) of the ways in which urban criminal courts violate due process standards and the hallowed adversary model of criminal justice. Urban courts were depicted as "assembly lines" in which the typical defendant, accused of a misdemeanor or minor felony, spends at most a few moments with a public defender or assigned counsel before pleading guilty. Public defenders and assigned counsel were depicted as undertrained and overworked, and urban courtrooms as dismal, dirty, and crowded settings (Downie 1972; Mather 1973). Many early studies charged that the poorest defendants received the harshest treatment (Clarke and Koch 1976).

In a typical critique, Leonard Downie, Jr. (1972:7), an award-winning court reporter for the *Washington Post*, wrote that "chaos, injustice, and cynical indifference" run throughout the legal system. Urban courthouses, he continued, are settings for "vagrants sleeping in the corridors, incompetent lawyers and bail bondsmen swarming like vultures, and hack political appointees clothed in the robes of justice destroying lives through prejudice, whim, and limited legal ability" (p. 16). The lives most often destroyed are those of "the poor, including a large proportion of urban blacks, [who] find that they are treated as second-class citizens in court" (pp. 15–16).

Like other observers of the time, Downie was especially critical of rampant plea bargaining, which, he said, denies defendants due process: "A lawyer who knows next to nothing about his client or the facts of the crime with which he is charged barters away a man's right to a trial, and, along with it, the presumption that a defendant is innocent until proved guilty" (p. 23). Often, he said, it also permits serious offenders to receive light sentences. The result is that plea bargaining does everyone a disservice: "In fact, nobody can be certain that innocent persons are not being convicted or, more frequently, that habitual criminals are not being let off lightly" (p. 30).

A second wave of research since the 1970s refined our understanding of the criminal courts. Although it supported many of the earlier critiques, it also suggested they were somewhat overstated. Perhaps most important, it found that the race and class of defendants do not generally affect their chances of conviction and the sentences they receive (Zatz 1987). These findings deserve additional attention, and I discuss them further in the following sections.

Prosecutors, the Courtroom Work Group, and Plea Bargaining

In another area, the new scholarship yielded better understanding of the flow of criminal cases after arrest. It stressed that heavy caseloads burden prosecutors, public defenders and other defense attorneys, and judges alike. Recognizing this, the courtroom work group (consisting of all three parties) realizes the best thing for everyone is to resolve the case as quickly as possible through a guilty plea. Plea bargaining thus accounts for up to 90 percent of all guilty verdicts in many jurisdictions, and judge or jury trials are relatively rare (Eisenstein and Jacob 1977).

For prosecutors, plea bargaining ensures convictions and helps process huge caseloads as quickly as possible, as they realize they simply can't afford to prosecute all the cases the police hand them. Because defendants have the right to jury trials, prosecutors usually don't proceed with a case unless they're fairly confident that a jury would find the defendant guilty. They thus drop up to half of all felony arrests because of weak evidence or lack of cooperation from victims and other witnesses. To decide which cases to drop or plea bargain, prosecutors determine whether the case is a strong, ideal one from their perspective.

Several elements make up such a case: (1) a serious offense (e.g., murder compared to simple assault); (2) an injured victim; (3) strong evidence, including eyewitnesses or recovered weapons or stolen property; (4) the defendant's use of a weapon; (5) defendants with serious prior records; and (6) a "stand-up" victim whom "the jury would believe and consider undeserving of victimization" (Myers 2000:452). Ideally, these are victims who are articulate, who have no criminal background, who didn't know their offender, and who did nothing to cause

◄ *Like other members of the courtroom workgroup, judges recognize that plea bargaining expedites the processing of huge caseloads.*

their victimization. If victims don't fit this profile or are unwilling to cooperate, prosecutors are apt to drop the charges altogether or to reduce them as part of a plea bargain. Thus, in rape cases, prosecutors are less likely to prosecute if, among other things, the woman knew her rapist, had been sexually active in the past, or, especially, was on a date with the offender. Because prosecutors worry, rightly or wrongly, that many jurors believe some women precipitate their rapes, they're less likely to proceed when the evidence might lead jurors to reach this conclusion (Frohmann 1997; Spears and Spohn 1997).

The cases remaining after this initial screening are the "best" ones from the prosecutor's standpoint, cases where the evidence is strongest and the charges the most serious. Most of these defendants are thus probably guilty of the crime for which they were arrested. Given this likelihood, the new scholarship said, plea bargaining does not constitute the miscarriage of justice that earlier critics had cited. If anything, it helps defendants since it gives them some sense of what sentence they would likely receive if they insisted on their right to a jury trial and were then found guilty. Recognizing this, most defendants in fact favor guilty pleas. Many defendants, moreover, can't afford bail and would have to wait weeks or months in jail until their trial began: Guilty pleas resolve their cases much sooner and shorten the time until defendants can resume their normal lives. Because defense attorneys realize all this, they're usually very willing to plea bargain instead of taking the case to trial. Along with the rest of the courtroom work group, they realize they could quickly shut down the court system if they demanded even a few extra jury trials for their clients. Such demands would cause their other clients to languish in jail even longer and also antagonize the prosecutors and judges with whom they have to work every day (Eisenstein and Jacob 1977).

The new scholarship further challenged critics' charges that plea bargaining lets serious offenders off too lightly. When the courtroom work group determines the sentence for serious offenses and chronic offenders, little actual bargaining over the sentence occurs, as the courtroom work group already knows what the sentence will be. Suspects guilty of serious crimes thus receive stiff sentences even if they plead guilty (Feeley 1979). These sentences are at least as harsh as those for similar crimes in other Western nations, and often harsher (Kappeler, Blumberg, and Potter 2000).

Although the new scholarship took a more benign view of plea bargaining than did the earlier critiques, it still supported their view that courtroom work groups usually fail to vigorously contest the guilt of defendants. For better or worse, the adversary model is largely a myth for most criminal cases.

PUNISHMENT, SOCIAL STRUCTURE, AND INEQUALITY

Since the time of Emile Durkheim, punishment has been central to sociological theories of law and society. Durkheim (1933 [1893]) thought that punishment reinforced social stability by clarifying social norms and uniting conventional society against the deviants who are punished. He further argued that the social structure of a society helps determine the type of punishment it adopts. Here he distinguished societies according to their role specialization, or division of labor. In the small folk societies studied by anthropologists, there is little role specialization. The *collective conscience* (see Chapter 6) is extremely strong, and there's also little individualism. Durkheim said that *mechanical solidarity* characterizes such societies. When deviance occurs, Durkheim added, such societies engage in *repressive* law marked by harsh physical punishment of deviants.

More advanced societies, in contrast, are larger and more individualized, with a weaker collective conscience and much greater role specialization. Their basis of social solidarity is *organic*, said Durkheim, meaning that their solidarity derives from the *interdependence* of the many roles. When deviance occurs in these societies, they engage in *restitutive* law marked by an interest in restoring relationships to their previous state. Restitution, such as payments to aggrieved parties, becomes a primary punishment. Such societies also develop prisons as a substitute for physical punishment (Durkheim 1983 [1901]).

Although some scholars question Durkheim's view of social evolution and punishment, his basic theme that a society's social structure influences its type of punishment remains compelling (Garland 1990). It is a basic theme, of course, of the work inspired by Karl Marx and Friedrich Engels, which falls under the broad rubric of conflict and radical theories. These theories see the inequality in society as a central influence on the type and severity of punishment and view legal punishment as a way for the ruling class to preserve its power by controlling the poor, people of color, and other subordinate groups.

Tests of these theories concentrate both on policing and on imprisonment. The previous chapter reviewed the evidence on policing and noted some support for conflict theory's predictions. In imprisonment, the classic statement is that of George Rusche and Otto Kirchheimer (1939), who contended in their book *Punishment and Social Structure* that imprisonment increases when unemployment increases. When more people are unemployed, Rusche and Kirchheimer argued, they're more angry and prone to rebellion. To prevent mass uprisings, the ruling class puts more of the poor behind bars. This action helps intimidate the poor from rebelling and also reduces their labor supply, leaving fewer of them to compete for scarce jobs. The greater job prospects that result reduce the poor's anger and thus their potential for revolt.

Several scholars have since tested Rusche and Kirchheimer's view. Some study samples of defendants to see whether unemployed defendants are more likely than employed ones to be sentenced to prison. Others analyze macrolevel data (for the entire United States, for example) to see whether higher aggregate levels of unemployment are linked with higher rates of imprisonment. The evidence is very complex and inconsistent. Some studies do find that unemployed defendants are more likely than their employed counterparts to be imprisoned, and that incarceration is higher in locations with higher employment (Chiricos and Delone 1992). However, other studies don't find the presumed relationship or find it in some locations but not in others (Nobiling, Spohn, and DeLone 1998). Reflecting on these inconsistent findings, some scholars say that Rusche and Kirchheimer overestimated the "role of economic forces in shaping penal practice" (Garland 1990:108) and ignored the caseload and other bureaucratic pressures that limit the criminal justice system's ability to respond to social and economic changes (Pontell 1984). However, Raymond J. Michalowski and Susan M. Carlson (1999) recently found that the unemployment–imprisonment relationship is stronger for some periods of U.S. history than for others and speculated that the inconsistent findings reflect the fact that various studies have used data from various periods of U.S. history. Because unemployment is linked to imprisonment in some of these periods but not in others, it's no surprise that the research has yielded inconsistent results. Certainly Rusche and Kirchheimer's view will stimulate research for some time to come.

Another line of research on inequality and punishment focuses on the African-American experience in the postbellum (post–Civil War) South. Much of this research is inspired by Hubert Blalock's (1967) *power-threat theory*, which attributes racial prejudice and discrimination to competition for economic and political power. The postbellum period was a time of great competition between whites and newly freed slaves. Supporting Blalock's theory, imprisonment of blacks, and especially of young black males, for minor property offenses and other crimes increased steadily during this time as Southern whites feared that the freed slaves would gain political and economic power in the South. Lynchings, which targeted young black males, increased for the same reason. As Martha A. Myers (1990:627) notes, "As the position of whites and blacks became more similar, racial antagonisms intensified and found expression in efforts to suppress and intimidate blacks through lynchings and executions." Imprisonment was another, more common method of intimidation and control. Myers (p. 628) says it "symbolically affirmed" white power and, more practically, removed young black males from direct competition with whites for scarce jobs in the cotton fields and elsewhere.

Patterns of lynchings and imprisonment of blacks across time and place further support Blalock's thesis (Tolnay and Beck 1995). Lynchings tended to accelerate in periods where black economic gains relative to whites were greatest and when the price of cotton was falling and threatening employment. They were also higher in Southern counties where the number of blacks posed the greatest competition threat to white labor, although they were lower in counties where blacks outnumbered whites. The evidence for imprisonment is more complex, but imprisonment rates and sentence lengths of young black males accused of rape in Georgia also increased when cotton prices fell. Ironically, the increased imprisonment of black males for rape appears to have reduced their lynchings for the same accusation (Myers 1995).

Most contemporary work on punishment, social structure, and inequality focuses on class, racial/ethnic, and gender differences in prosecution and sentencing. Most studies analyze data on samples of individual defendants, but some analyze macrolevel data from states, cities, and other aggregates. This body of work is both important and complex, and we explore it here in some detail.

Social Class and Legal Outcomes

To test whether social class influences legal outcomes, researchers have examined the conviction and imprisonment rate and the average sentence length of criminal defendants. Although most of these defendants are poor, this research finds that the poorest defendants do not fare worse than less poor defendants after offense seriousness, prior record, and other factors are held constant. Some observers view this lack of class differences in sentencing as contradicting conflict theory views (Chiricos and Waldo 1975).

Other scholars challenge this conclusion. Since most defendants are from lower- and working-class backgrounds, these scholars argue, there is too little income variation among them to allow class differences in outcomes to emerge, and there are too few middle- and upper-income defendants accused of street crimes with whom to compare them. Wealthy people, after all, rarely commit robbery, burglary, auto theft, or the like. Tests of class differences in sentencing and other outcomes are therefore meaningless (Shelden 1982).

Further, although it may be true that most (poor) defendants who plead guilty probably did commit the crime(s) of which they were accused, the fact remains that wealthier defendants accused of the same crime would be far more able to contest the evidence and to receive more lenient sentences even if found guilty. Factual guilt is not the same as legal guilt: "Although most defendants may have committed illegal acts, their conviction depends on the prosecutor's ability to prove it beyond a reasonable doubt while abiding by the procedural strictures of the law" (Eisenstein and Jacob 1977:302–303). Guilt, in short, must be proven beyond a reasonable doubt, and even in strong cases it's often difficult for a prosecutor to do this. However, because of their lack of resources and perfunctory representation by public defenders, assigned counsel, or unskilled private attorneys, poor defendants cannot and do not contest the evidence.

Were a wealthy person accused of a street crime, he (or she) would be able to afford bail, hire a skilled, private attorney, pay for investigators, and the like. In short, such a defendant would be able to contest the evidence vigorously in the manner envisioned by the adversary model. Herbert Jacob (1978:185–186) observes the following:

> Those few defendants who are not poor can often escape the worst consequences of their involvement.... They can afford bail and thus avoid pretrial detention. They can obtain a private attorney who specializes in criminal work. They can usually obtain delays that help weaken the prosecution case.... They can enroll in diversion programs by seeking private psychiatric treatment or other medical assistance. They can keep their jobs and maintain their family relationships and, therefore, qualify as good probation risks. They can appeal their conviction (if, indeed, they are convicted) and delay serving their sentence.

Here again the 1994–1995 O. J. Simpson case is instructive. A poor defendant accused of two ghastly murders and facing strong DNA evidence would most likely have pleaded guilty or had a much shorter and more perfunctory trial handled by a lone public defender. Simpson's "dream team" defense cost $10 million, hundreds of thousands of dollars of which helped pay for expert forensic and DNA witnesses who effectively challenged the credibility of the evidence against the wealthy, celebrated defendant (Barkan 1996).

Perhaps the clearest class disparity in legal outcomes is seen by comparing poor defendants accused of street crime with much wealthier defendants accused

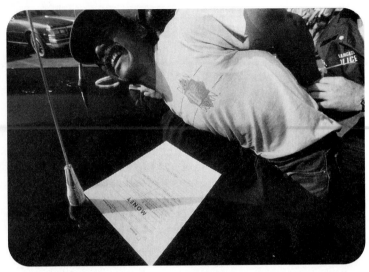

▲ *Criminal defendants who are wealthy tend to receive more lenient treatment from the criminal justice system, in part because they can afford skilled, private attorneys and other legal resources.*

of white-collar crime. In an illuminating documentation of this disparity, Robert Tillman and Henry N. Pontell (1992) compared sentences received in California by Medicaid fraud defendants (physicians and other health-care professionals) and grand theft defendants. Only 38 percent of the former were incarcerated, compared to 79 percent of the latter, even though the median economic loss from Medicaid fraud was ten times greater than the loss from grand theft.

Some may argue, of course, that street crimes should be treated more harshly than white-collar crimes because the public is so much more concerned about them. Notwithstanding this argument, the fact remains that criminal courts are "fundamentally courts against the poor" (Jacob 1978:185). The reason for this, say James Eisenstein and Herbert Jacob (1977:289), is that "the behaviors most severely punished by governmental power are those in which persons on the fringes of American society most readily engage.... Crimes (especially white-collar crimes) committed by other segments of the population attract less public attention, less scrutiny from the police, and less vigorous prosecution."

Other scholars share this assessment. Jeffrey Reiman (1998:102) says that the "criminal justice system effectively weeds out the well-to-do" at every stage of the process so that the poor and not the rich are the ones who go to prison. In pointed language, Randall G. Shelden (1982) asserts that "sentencing practices in America's courts reflect a consistent bias that favors the rich and influential and discriminates against the poor and the powerless." Assessments of class differences in the punishment of poor street-crime defendants thus miss this basic fact of U.S. society, law, and criminal justice.

◀ *Some studies find that defendants accused of killing whites are more likely to be indicted for first-degree murder than those accused of killing members of other races.*

The Impact of Race and Ethnicity

Much research examines whether race and ethnicity influence the decisions of prosecutors, judges, and juries. We'll look first at research on prosecutorial decisions and then at studies of conviction and sentencing.

PROSECUTORIAL DECISIONS

Several studies explore whether race and ethnicity affect prosecutorial decisions to dismiss charges against defendants or to bring serious charges against defendants whose cases they don't dismiss. Here the evidence is mixed: Although some studies find no racial or ethnic differences in these decisions, others do find them after controlling for relevant variables. After studying 33,000 felony cases from Los Angeles, Cassia Spohn and two colleagues (Spohn, Gruhl, and Welch 1987) found prosecutors much more likely to dismiss charges against white defendants than against African-American or Hispanic defendants. In a study of 745 shoplifting cases in Washington, D.C., Kenneth Adams and Charles R. Cutshall (1987) found prosecutors more likely to dismiss charges against white defendants than black defendants who had similar prior records and who had allegedly stolen similar amounts.

In another type of racial discrimination paralleling some findings for police arrest decisions, some studies also find prosecutors bringing more serious charges in homicide and rape cases when whites are victims than when blacks are victims (Myers 2000). Thus, in homicide cases, people accused of killing whites are more likely to be indicted for first-degree murder, and thus more likely to receive the death penalty if convicted, than people accused of killing blacks. Reflecting a sort of "double racism" involving the race of both the defendant and the victim, the charges in homicide and rape cases tend to be the most severe when blacks are accused of victimizing whites. For example, in a study of rape cases in a large Midwestern city, Gary D. LaFree (1980) found prosecutors more likely to lodge felony charges against blacks accused of raping white women than against blacks accused of raping black women or whites accused of raping white women. Although incomplete data often make it difficult to control adequately for the strength of the evidence, these findings "raise the disturbing possibility that some prosecutors define the victimization of whites, especially when African-Americans are perpetrators, as more serious criminal events than the comparable victimization of African-Americans" (Myers 2000:451).

CONVICTION AND SENTENCING

African-Americans and Hispanics in the United States are far more likely than whites (non-Hispanic) to be in prison. A few figures will illustrate the huge racial and ethnic disparities in imprisonment (Beck and Mumola 1999). In 1997, about 49 percent of all state and federal prisoners in the United States were African-Americans, and about 18 percent were Hispanics. These figures far exceed the African-American proportion, 12 percent, and the Hispanic proportion, 8 percent, of the entire U.S. population. In fact, about 8 percent of black men in their twenties are now in prison. Imprisonment rates (the number of prisoners per 100,000 residents of each race) present an even more vivid picture of racial disparity (see Figure 16.1). The rate for African-Americans of both sexes is much higher than that for the other groups, and the rate for whites of both sexes is much lower. All these rates reflect our chances of going to prison sometime in our lifetime: Almost 29 percent of black males are expected to go to prison, compared to less than 5 percent of white males; just under 4 percent of black females are expected to go to prison, compared to less than 1 percent of white females (see Figure 16.2 on page 482). Clearly race and ethnicity affect our chances of landing in prison.

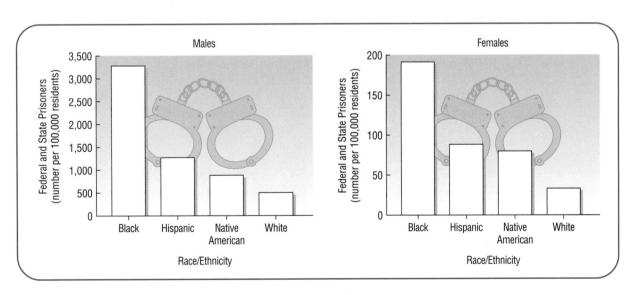

▲ FIGURE 16.1 RACE, ETHNICITY, GENDER, AND IMPRISONMENT RATES, 1997
(NUMBER OF FEDERAL AND STATE PRISONERS PER 100,000 U.S. RESIDENTS OF EACH GROUP)
Source: Beck and Mumola 1999.

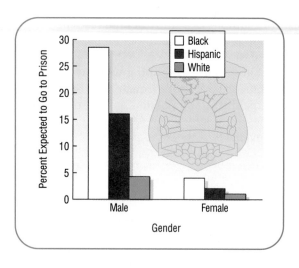

◀ FIGURE 16.2 RACE, ETHNICITY, GENDER, AND LIFETIME
LIKELIHOOD OF GOING TO PRISON
Source: Bonczar and Beck 1997.

Do these large racial and ethnic disparities reflect systematic racial and ethnic discrimination in the criminal justice system, or do they simply reflect disproportionate involvement of blacks and Hispanics in street crime? Once again consensus and conflict theories offer different explanations. Consensus theories attribute the much higher imprisonment rates of African-Americans and Hispanics to their greater involvement in the serious street crime that is most likely to lead to imprisonment. Conflict theories, on the other hand, attribute the imprisonment rates to systematic discrimination against these groups after arrest occurs. According to this argument, defendants of color are more likely than white defendants accused of similar offenses to be convicted, sentenced to prison, and sentenced to prison for longer terms (Bridges and Crutchfield 1988).

Not surprisingly, racial and ethnic discrimination in conviction and sentencing is perhaps the most hotly debated topic in criminal justice today (Mann 1993; Walker, Spohn, and DeLone 2000; Wilbanks 1987). Although we have too little class variation among criminal defendants for adequate tests of class differences in legal outcomes, we do have enough racial/ethnic variation for testing racial and ethnic differences. Once they are arrested, do African-Americans and other people of color receive harsher treatment than whites? Are they more likely to be convicted, sent to prison, and incarcerated for longer durations? The findings generally parallel those for arrest that we reviewed in the previous chapter. But there are many more studies of race and sentencing than of race and arrest, and, if anything, the evidence on sentencing is even more complex than it is for arrest.

Scholars continue to dispute what the evidence on race and conviction and sentencing is saying. On the one hand, William Wilbanks (1987:5–6) charges that "the perception of the criminal justice system as racist is a myth." While acknowledging that some individuals in the system engage in racially biased behavior, Wilbanks says that "conceding individual cases of bias is far different from conceding pervasive racial discrimination" and adds that there is no *systematic bias* against blacks in sentencing (his emphasis). However, Coramae Richey Mann (1993:191) reaches a very different conclusion and says the data "continue to suggest racial discrimination in sentencing" that is both systematic and pervasive. Let's take a look at the evidence and draw some conclusions of our own. Most studies have compared African-Americans and whites, but we will also discuss evidence on other racial and ethnic groups.

Pre-1970 studies of race and sentencing focused on simple black–white differences in sentencing and usually found that blacks received harsher sentences. They were more likely than whites to be sent to prison once convicted and also more likely to receive longer prison terms. This was true in both noncapital (i.e., non-death penalty) cases and capital cases. By the end of the 1960s, then, the general conclusion in the sociological community was that serious racial discrimination did exist in sentencing (Zatz 1987).

In the late 1960s and early 1970s, however, that conclusion began to shift, as scholars began to point out methodological deficiencies in the earlier work. They also said that any racial discrimination found was generally located more in southern jurisdictions than in northern areas, and that racial changes in the South were reducing and even eliminating sentencing bias.

The most influential critique was undoubtedly that of John Hagan, whose 1974 article in a leading journal criticized earlier research for ignoring the effects of offense seriousness and prior record (Hagan 1974). Hagan argued that sentences will naturally be harsher, regardless of the defendant's race, for more serious offenses and for defendants with greater numbers of prior convictions. Blacks' harsher sentences may thus derive from the fact that they tend to be convicted of more serious offenses than whites and the fact that they tend to have greater prior records of offenses than whites. If so, blacks' harsher sentencing is the result of legally permissible influences and not of actual racial prejudice against them.

Hagan reviewed the existing studies of race and sentencing and found that most of them didn't hold offense seriousness and prior record constant, casting doubt on their findings' validity. He was able to reanalyze the data in several studies and control for these variables. When he did so, the racial difference found in the original studies disappeared. Hagan's article indicated that blacks do receive harsher treatment than whites in sentencing because of their more serious offenses and greater prior records, not because of racial prejudice at the sentencing stage. A later review of the sentencing literature by Gary Kleck (1981) generally supported Hagan's view. The work of Hagan and Kleck helped lead to a new conclusion in the social science community of nondiscrimination in sentencing (Zatz 1987).

Other scholars challenged this new conclusion. In one type of critique, some researchers said the use of prior record to determine sentences discriminates against blacks, since they are more likely than whites to have a prior record. In turn, they're more likely to have this criminal involvement because of race-based social inequality. In this sense, prior record is a self-fulfilling prophecy that worsens the legal treatment of blacks in a type of vicious circle (Farrell and Swigert 1978). To the extent this is true, the use of prior record in sentencing may manifest larger institutionalized racism, if not actual racism in criminal justice processing (Kleck 1981). Other scholars charged that Hagan and Kleck glossed over evidence in their own reviews of studies that found racial discrimination in sentencing even when offense seriousness and prior record were held constant (Kempf and Austin 1986).

Studies of race/ethnicity and sentencing have increased since Hagan's review, and the evidence is very complex. A major study by Joan Petersilia (1983) for the Rand Corporation examined sentencing and other legal outcomes for several thousand white, black, and Hispanic offenders in California, Michigan, and Texas. Generally, whites were less likely than blacks and Hispanics to be incarcerated, and whites who were sent to prison received shorter sentences than their black and Hispanic counterparts. Other studies have found racial/ethnic discrimination in some jurisdictions but not in others, for some types of offenses but not for others, and at some stages of the courtroom process more than at others (Myers 2000; Zatz 1987). Let's review selected findings from this large body of research.

The Race of the Victim One very interesting type of investigation focuses on the victim's race. Several studies, especially of rape and capital (death sentence) offenses, find that sentencing is more punitive when whites are victims than when African-Americans are victims (LaFree 1989; Paternoster 1991). These findings parallel those sometimes found for arrest decisions and prosecutorial decisions and suggest that judges, prosecutors, and police all place more importance on white victims than on black victims (Hawkins 1987). Several studies also find that when whites are victims of homicides and rapes, black offenders receive longer sentences than white offenders. Because earlier studies didn't control for the victim's race, they didn't uncover this sort of racial discrimination in sentencing. Underscoring the complexity of the evidence, however, a recent study of sexual assault cases did not always find harsher treatment for those involving black men assaulting white women. Rather, the victim–offender relationship and victim's behavior in such cases heavily influenced the way they were treated. The authors concluded that previous research both overstated and simplified the degree of racial discrimination in sexual assault cases (Spohn and Spears 1996).

The Liberation Hypothesis and Less Serious Crimes A second line of research finds racial discrimination in less serious crimes but not in more serious crimes (Smith and Damphousse 1998). The idea here is that in the most serious cases, there is little room for prosecutorial or judicial discretion to affect the sentence. As Cassia Spohn and Jerry Cederblom (1991:306) put it, "In these types of cases a severe sentence is clearly called for; judges therefore have relatively little discretion and thus few opportunities to consider legally irrelevant factors such as race." In less serious cases, however, more discretion is possible, and thus greater opportunity exists for racial bias. Less serious cases thus "liberate" judges to use their discretion and also, perhaps, to base sentencing decisions on racial prejudice.

In a test of this so-called liberation hypothesis, Spohn and Cederblom (1991) studied Detroit felony cases involving 4,655 defendants. They first found that black defendants were more likely than whites to be sentenced to prison with other relevant variables held constant. This finding, they said, "is clearly important; it indicates overt discrimination against black defendants in a nonrural, nonsouthern context. It is yet another piece of evidence that racial bias in sentencing has not disappeared" (p. 315). In contrast, they also found no racial effect on *sentence length* among defendants that judges decided to incarcerate.

However, further investigation uncovered *indirect* effects of race on both the decision to incarcerate and on sentence length. In particular, race affected whether defendants were released on bail before trial, with blacks more likely than whites to be detained. Detention in turn increased the probability both of incarceration and of greater sentence length. These two findings replicated those of previous studies (Patterson and Lynch 1991). Defendants detained before trial can't help gather evidence for their case, making it more likely they'll be convicted, and often lose their jobs and family support, making it more likely that judges will view them unsympathetically at sentencing. Thus blacks in Spohn and Cederblom's study were at greater risk for incarceration and longer prison terms in part because they were more likely than whites to be detained in jail pending trial.

Spohn and Cederblom then divided their cases into more and less serious offenses on each of the following five dimensions: (1) the seriousness of the charge for which the defendant was convicted; (2) the magnitude of the defendant's prior record; (3) whether the victim was a stranger; (4) whether the victim was injured; and (5) whether the defendant used a gun. On each of these dimensions, they found that "black defendants face a greater risk of incarceration only in less serious cases"

(p. 318), supporting the liberation hypothesis, but found no racial differences in sentence length. They then repeated this type of analysis for each of the four felonies in their study: murder, rape, robbery, and assault. After they did this, they found support for the liberation hypothesis (with regard to incarceration) only among assault cases. Evidently, they concluded, judges regard murder, rape, and robbery as so severe that they feel most of these defendants deserve imprisonment regardless of race and regardless of the five dimensions on which these crimes can still differ.

As in most studies of sentencing discrimination, Spohn and Cederblom studied only felonies. According to the liberation hypothesis, sentencing discrimination would be more likely to be found in misdemeanor cases than in felony cases. In one of the few studies of misdemeanors in the sentencing discrimination literature, James F. Nelson (1994) analyzed data for some 105,000 persons arrested for misdemeanors in New York State in 1985 and 1986. Nelson found that black and Hispanic defendants with prior records were more likely than their white counterparts to be sentenced to jail in each of New York's many counties. For the state as a whole, they were 20 percent more likely to be sentenced to jail. Among those sentenced to jail, Nelson found no racial/ethnic differences in sentence length, and he also found little discrimination among defendants with no prior record. His findings for the incarceration decision among those *with* prior records led him to conclude that "disparities in sentencing decisions in criminal court substantially contribute to the concentration of minorities in New York State's jails" (p. 198).

HISPANICS AND NATIVE AMERICANS   Although most studies of discrimination compare African-Americans and whites, a few focus on Hispanics and Native Americans. The Hispanic research is inconsistent: Some studies find Hispanics treated more punitively than non-Hispanic whites; others find them treated less punitively than whites; while still other studies find no Hispanic–white differences. Some studies also find Hispanic defendants treated more harshly than black defendants, while others find the reverse or no Hispanic–black differences (Farnworth, Teske, and Thurman 1991; LaFree 1985; Unnever and Hembroff 1988).

The few studies we have of Native American defendants suggest they "are treated more harshly in some stages of criminal justice decision making compared to non-Indians" (Zatz, Lujan, and Snyder-Joy 1991:105). One early study found American Indian defendants more likely than non-Indians to be incarcerated (Hall and Simkus 1975). However, other studies find that Native Americans receive shorter sentences than non-Indians among those who are incarcerated (Feimer, Pommersheim, and Wise 1990). In some studies, prior record played a more important role in the sentencing of American Indians than of non-Indians (Bynum and Paternoster 1984; Feimer, Pommersheim, and Wise 1990). Looking at a different type of dependent variable, a study of parole decisions found that Native American defendants received shorter prison terms than whites but later won parole only after serving a higher proportion of their sentences than was true of whites (Bynum 1981).

Marjorie S. Zatz (1987; Zatz, Lujan, and Snyder-Joy 1991) notes that Hispanics, Native Americans, and other defendants whose primary language is not English may experience language and cultural difficulties in the court system. Plea bargaining, for example, is a complex process, and defendants who don't speak English well may have trouble understanding and evaluating the advantages and disadvantages of pleading guilty. The behaviors and practices of some Indian cultures may also lead to difficulties in court. In some, direct eye contact is seen as disrespectful. Defendants from these cultures may thus avoid direct eye contact with the judge, who in turn might assume these defendants are disrespectful to the court. In another type of problem, Plains tribes such as the Sioux tend to be very assertive in their interpersonal interaction. As a result, they may appear menacing to police, prosecutors, and judges.

THE COMMUNITY CONTEXT OF RACIAL/ETHNIC DISCRIMINATION   Some of the most interesting work on sentencing bias addresses its structural and social context. States and local communities differ in many ways, including poverty rates, the degree of white–black inequality, the proportion of the population that is urban or black, and so forth. Some of these community differences may have important implications for how African-Americans and other minorities are treated once they're arrested.

Here three studies are particularly illuminating. In the first study, George S. Bridges and Robert D. Crutchfield (1988) compared black and white imprisonment rates for each of the fifty states. Controlling for crime rates and other relevant variables, black imprisonment rates were higher in states with larger proportions of African-Americans among the states' urban residents. The difference between black and white imprisonment rates was also higher in states with greater black–white inequality. The authors concluded that "social characteristics of states contribute significantly to racial disparity in imprisonment" (p. 718).

In the second study, Bridges and associates (1987) examined nonwhite (blacks, Hispanics, and Native Americans) and white imprisonment rates in all the counties of the state of Washington. Controlling for crime rates and other relevant factors, nonwhite imprisonment rates were higher in counties with higher proportions of nonwhite residents. They were also higher in counties that were more urbanized.

In the third study, Theodore G. Chiricos and Charles Crawford (1995) reviewed all the studies of race (almost always comparing African-Americans and whites) and sentencing in the United States published between 1975 and 1991. Some of these studies focused on the decision to incarcerate (the "in/out" decision), while the others focused on sentence length for those incarcerated. Of the findings where offense and prior record had been held constant, 41 percent showed statistically significant discrimination against blacks in the in/out decision, and 15 percent in sentence length. From this the authors concluded that "race is a consistent and frequently significant disadvantage for blacks when in/out decisions are considered ... [but] much less of a disadvantage when it comes to sentence length" (p. 297).

Focusing on the in/out decision, Chiricos and Crawford then found more evidence of greater racial discrimination in the South than outside the South, in areas with high proportions of black residents than in those with lower proportions, and in areas with higher unemployment than in those with lower unemployment. Overall, the authors concluded, "there remains frequently significant evidence of a *direct* impact of race on imprisonment" (p. 300; emphasis theirs), if not on sentence length, that was shaped by the structural context of the communities examined. These structural differences indicated that "criminal punishment not only responds to crime, but responds as well to specific community conditions" (p. 301). The authors concluded that previous assertions by Wilbanks (1987) and other scholars of no sentencing discrimination were premature because "there is much yet to be learned about the issue of race and imprisonment" (p. 301).

In trying to account for the complex evidence on sentencing discrimination, Robert D. Crutchfield and colleagues (1994) cite several methodological problems. First, many studies of sentencing discrimination examine a single jurisdiction only. Such studies are less likely to find discrimination than those that examine two or more jurisdictions. Second, too many studies have looked only at "single points of decision making in criminal justice" (p. 169). Within any one jurisdiction, racial discrimination may be present at one stage and not at others. If a researcher fails to examine the appropriate stage of decision making, she or he will fail to find the discrimination present in that stage. To compound the problem, in some jurisdictions discrimination might appear at earlier stages, while in others it might appear at later stages. To uncover discrimination, it's necessary to examine as many decision points as possible within single jurisdictions and across many jurisdictions.

Reinforcing the argument of Crutchfield and colleagues, a recent study of juvenile justice processing using data from multiple decision points and jurisdictions in one state found significant racial and ethnic discrimination (Wordes, Bynum, and Corley 1994). Compared to white youths accused of similar offenses and having similar prior records and family backgrounds, African-American and Latino youths were more likely to be "securely detained" at the several juvenile processing stages examined in the study. The authors concluded that "race was a significant factor in locking up youth, whether at the police or court level" (p. 164). They called for political and legal officials to address this problem, since "the devastating repercussions of a justice system in which a young person's physical liberty is in part determined by his or her race are intolerable" (p. 165).

In another methodological point, Crutchfield and colleagues (1994) further argued that studies using national data mask possible differences in discrimination among jurisdictions. If some states, for example, are discriminatory, and others are not, the two kinds of states may "cancel each other out" if only national data are examined, resulting in a false conclusion of no or only small discrimination. To illustrate their argument, Crutchfield and colleagues collected black and white imprisonment rates and violent crime arrest rates for all fifty states. When they examined their results for all the states combined, they found that the states' differences in black–white arrest rates accounted for 89.5 percent of their differences in black–white imprisonment rates. However, when they examined the states separately, they found considerable variation in the extent to which racial differences in arrest rates accounted for racial differences in imprisonment rates. In Massachusetts, for example, racial differences in arrest accounted for only 40 percent of its racial differences in imprisonment; the corresponding figure in Alabama was only 54 percent.

The authors concluded, "Our analyses show that there is great variation within the United States in racial patterns of imprisonment, and that these variations probably account for the diversity of results that have been reported" in the literature (p. 179). A major goal of research, they said, should be to "identify social and demographic conditions in which inequality in punishment is most likely to emerge" (p. 181).

Not all studies find that structural context makes a difference. In an analysis of more than 62,000 cases in Pennsylvania from 1985 to 1987, Darrell Steffensmeier and colleagues (1993) found that county-level measures of urbanization, the black proportion of the population, and the proportion of registered voters who were Republican (as a measure of county conservatism) all had no effects on sentencing. Supporting a conclusion of no racial discrimination in sentencing, they also found that defendants' race (black versus white) had little or no effect on incarceration or on sentence length. A study of sentencing in counties throughout Georgia similarly found "little system-wide discrimination against blacks in criminal sentencing" (Myers and Talarico 1987:170). Contradicting some of the structural evidence cited earlier, this study also found that sentencing was not generally harsher in counties with greater proportions of African-Americans. The negative findings of these two studies underscore the need for additional research in this area.

A Cautious Conclusion on Racial and Ethnic Discrimination in Sentencing

Looking at all the evidence, how much of a difference do race and ethnicity make? Evidence on race/ethnic discrimination in the juvenile justice system seems more consistent than the evidence for the adult criminal justice system. A review found that about two-thirds of 46 studies of juvenile justice discrimination uncovered such discrimination (Pope and Feyerherm 1992). Citing this review, Carl Pope and Todd Clear (1994:132–133) observe that "the preponderance of evidence within the juvenile justice system suggests that race does make a difference and that underclass poverty and racial inequality have a major impact on the administration of juvenile justice." Supporting this conclusion, a recent study found that minority youths in California were twice as likely as white youths to have their cases transferred from juvenile court and tried as adults, even when their offenses were the same. An author of the study remarked, "The imbalances this study reveals are stark, vast and deeply disturbing. Discrimination against kids of color accumulates at every stage of the justice system and skyrockets when juveniles are tried as adults. California has a double standard: Throw kids of color behind bars, but rehabilitate white kids who commit comparable crimes" (Lewin 2000:A14).

The evidence on the adult criminal justice system is less clear. Several studies, including the well-designed study by Steffensmeier and colleagues just noted, find little or no racial/ethnic discrimination in sentencing. Moreover, national data indicate that racial differences in arrest account for about 80 percent of racial differences in imprisonment (Blumstein 1993). Although the remaining 20 percent could stem from discrimination, many scholars feel that disproportionate involvement in street crimes thus accounts for most of the disproportionate number of African-Americans and other people of color in the nation's prisons and jails. They further support Hagan's (1974) conclusion that legal variables play a far more important role than race/ethnicity and other extralegal ones in sentencing. Representing these views, sentencing expert Michael Tonry (1994:68) concludes that "comparatively little systematic difference in contemporary sentencing outcomes appears to be attributable to race." In sharper language, Wilbanks (1987), as noted earlier, terms perceptions of sentencing discrimination a "myth."

Other scholars reach a different conclusion even while conceding, as Marjorie S. Zatz (1987:86) does, that "findings over the years have been contradictory" as a "plethora of research has been published without arriving at any definitive answers." Despite this problem, Zatz says, "Overall ... research has consistently unearthed subtle, if not overt, bias" (p. 86).

The studies discussed earlier support this assessment. Discrimination is found relatively often for the in/out decision and for earlier stages of the post-arrest process and is sometimes found for sentence length decisions, and it also tends to be found for less serious offenses. It is found more often in studies looking at several jurisdictions rather than just one jurisdiction or the whole nation, and it is found more often in studies taking into account the race/ethnicity of the victim. Discrimination also sometimes appears in the way judges determine sentences, as some studies find that judges place more emphasis on prior record, and/or on offense seriousness, when defendants are black or Hispanic than when they are white (Walker, Spohn, and DeLone 2000). In another example of subtle bias, one study found no racial differences when offenders knew their victims but did find racial differences, with blacks incarcerated more often than whites, when offenders didn't know their victims (Miethe 1987).

To complicate matters further, Steffensmeier and colleagues (1998) found in a reanalysis of their data that young black males were sentenced more harshly than other defendants in Pennsylvania even when offense severity, prior record, and other factors were taken into account; their sentences averaged 2.74 months longer than those for young white males. The authors speculated that judges share the stereotypes in the larger community against young black males and base their sentencing decisions partly on these stereotypes.

So what should we conclude about race/ethnicity and sentencing from all this evidence? As Samuel Walker and colleagues (2000:218) concede, "a definitive answer to the question, 'Are racial minorities sentenced more harshly than whites?' remains elusive." A fair conclusion from all the studies is that the perception of racial/ethnic bias in sentencing is not quite the myth that Wilbanks (1987) claims it to be, and that—as they do in arrest decisions—race and ethnicity sometimes play a small but significant role in sentencing and other court outcomes. Walker and colleagues (2000:218) say that "discrimination against racial minorities is not universal, but is confined to certain types of cases, settings, and defendants." As Chiricos and Crawford (1995) note, then, the key question is not *whether* race and ethnicity affect imprisonment but *when* and *where* race and ethnicity make a difference.

THE DRUG WAR REVISITED

This cautious conclusion would be much stronger were it focusing on two specific types of sentencing. The first is the death penalty, for which the evidence consistently indicates pervasive racial discrimination. I discuss this evidence later in this chapter. The other type of sentencing derives from the war on drugs, which, as we saw in Chapter 15, has targeted African-Americans, and especially young black males, far out of proportion to their actual illegal drug use. That chapter noted the disproportionate arrests of African-Americans for illegal drug use and sale. Not surprisingly, they have also been disproportionately imprisoned. Nationally, about one-third of young black males (ages 20–29) are under "correctional supervision," meaning that they're either in prison, in jail, or on probation or parole. In some cities, more than half of young black males are under correctional supervision (Duster 1995; Mauer 1999).

The drug war's focus on crack cocaine, and its much higher penalties for crack than for similar amounts of powder cocaine, account for much of these proportions. As noted in the previous chapter, when the drug war began in the mid-1980s, Congress and several states passed laws setting higher penalties for crack than for the powder version, even though the two drugs are identical pharmacologically. For example, for sentencing purposes federal law treats one gram of crack the same as 100 grams of powder. This means that, gram-for-gram, crack possession yields far stiffer sentences than powder possession. In the last decade, someone convicted of possessing five grams of crack with intent to distribute would receive a mandatory, minimum sixty-month prison term, while someone convicted of possessing five grams of powder would receive a minimum term only about half as long. In Minnesota, the maximum sentence for possessing three grams of crack was twenty years, versus a maximum term of only five years for possessing the same amount of powder (Duster 1995; Tonry 1994). Given racial differences in the use of crack and powder, it was inevitable that blacks would be imprisoned in greater numbers and for longer periods than whites.

This is exactly what happened. As Michael Tonry (1994:49) observes, "Blacks are arrested and confined in numbers grossly out of line with their use or sale of drugs." In 1997, African-Americans accounted for 56 percent of all state prisoners who were convicted of drug offenses, and in any one year account for about three-fourths of persons sentenced to state prison for drug possession (Beck and Mumola 1999; Mauer 1999). Other kinds of data underscore the racial effect of the drug war. In North Carolina, the white prison admission rate (number of whites imprisoned per 100,000 whites in the population) stayed the same during the 1980s and 1990s, at just under 200 per 100,000. The black admission rate rose from about 500 per 100,000 in 1980 to about 550 by 1985 before accelerating more sharply because of the war on crack to about 960 in 1990. The black admissions rate thus doubled in the 1980s, and rose by a huge 75 percent in the 1985–1990 period alone, even as the white rate stayed the same (Tonry 1994).

Other states replicated the North Carolina experience. In Pennsylvania, prison admissions for drug offenses rose by 1,613 percent in the 1980s for nonwhite males, but by only 477 percent for white males. In Virginia, 65 percent of drug offenders admitted to prison were people of color in 1989, compared to only 38 percent in 1983. Nationally, the black proportion of all people admitted to state and federal prisons rose throughout the 1980s and 1990s, even though the black proportion of arrests for violent and property crime stayed the same during that time. Tonry (1994:115) concludes from these data that "the recent blackening of America's prison population is the product of malign neglect of the [drug] war's effects on black Americans."

Gender and Sentencing

There is ready evidence of gender disparity in imprisonment, as about 94 percent of all state and federal prisoners in the United States are men (Beck and Mumola 1999). Earlier chapters noted that men are much more likely than women to commit serious offenses, and this fundamental gender difference in criminality undoubtedly accounts for much of the gender differences in imprisonment. However, as criminologists turned increasing attention to gender in the last two decades, they began to ask whether gender affects sentencing. Perhaps women would be more likely to be imprisoned were it not for the chivalry of prosecutors and judges. Perhaps there are crimes for which women are more likely than men to be imprisoned. What does the evidence say?

The data on gender and sentencing parallel those for gender and arrest (see Chapter 15). In the juvenile justice system, girls are treated more harshly than boys for status offenses but a bit less harshly for more serious offenses. Nonwhite girls are less likely than their white counterparts to benefit from chivalrous treatment (Chesney-Lind 1992).

In the adult criminal justice system, the evidence is more complex, partly because of methodological problems. In particular, early studies failed to control for offense seriousness and/or prior record. Because few women are criminal defendants, several studies examine only small numbers of cases. Many studies also disregard the race of defendants. Some of those that do control for race find more lenient treatment extended to white women than to black or Hispanic women (Spohn, Gruhl, and Welch 1987).

These problems notwithstanding, the best-designed studies generally find that women are 10 to 25 percent less likely than men with similar offenses and prior records to be incarcerated (Daly 1994; Steffensmeier, Kramer, and Streifel 1993). This difference stems from prosecutors' and judges' beliefs that women are less of

Punishing Criminals in Denmark and the Netherlands

As we see in this chapter, the U.S. response to crime has focused on harsher and more certain imprisonment for criminals. Although this policy is politically popular, it arguably has done very little, if anything, to reduce crime. In Europe, various nations have confronted rising crime with quite different measures and have rates of imprisonment (number of inmates per 100,000 population) up to ten times lower than the U.S. rate. Let's take a look at the European experience and focus on Denmark and the Netherlands.

Europe in general is far more pessimistic than the United States about the effectiveness of imprisonment. As Matti Joutsen and Norman Bishop, two officials at the Helsinki Institute for Crime Prevention and Control, observe, "Skepticism concerning the prison as a place of treatment has now become a part of formal criminal policy in virtually every European country." Almost all European criminal justice officials surveyed by the Helsinki Institute felt that prison often makes offenders worse and that alternative sanctions should be used whenever possible. They also acknowledged that prisons are very expensive and that prison overcrowding increases the chances that prisoners will come out of prison worse than when they went in.

These views lead Europe to favor "noncustodial sanctions" such as probation and community service as prison alternatives. Although these are not a cure-all for crime, say Joutsen and Bishop, they "are at least as successful as sentences of imprisonment on several important counts, and … lack many of the drawbacks of imprisonment." The experience of Denmark and the Netherlands illustrates the European approach.

Denmark began to face a growing crime problem in the 1960s, which continued into the next decade. According to H. H. Brydensholt of Denmark's Prison and Probation Administration, the increase in crime stemmed from several reasons, including growing industrialization, rising youth drug use, and increasing unemployment. In response, Denmark devised a multifaceted response in 1973 that in many ways was the opposite of U.S. crime policy. It replaced longer indeterminate sentences (e.g., three to seven years) with shorter fixed ones; reduced the length of prison terms and the number of offenses (especially nonviolent property offenses) leading to imprisonment; and reallocated funds from prisons to community-based corrections. These measures amounted to a policy of "using incarceration more carefully, and for shorter periods," and reduced the number of Danish prisoners in the next several years.

Denmark had several reasons for wanting to reduce imprisonment. First, it considered imprisonment a harsh measure in a democratic society in that it stigmatized inmates and hurt their families. Second, it feared that imprisonment would lessen inmates' self-respect and increase their aggressiveness and other problems. Third, it considered imprisonment too harsh a penalty for many nonviolent property offenses. Finally, Denmark realized that increasing imprisonment would be too expensive.

The Netherlands' view of and experience with imprisonment is similar to Denmark's. Like Denmark, it considers imprisonment a costly, ineffective alternative to be avoided whenever possible, and it favors relatively short prison terms for offenders it thinks need to be imprisoned. Much of the Dutch distaste for imprisonment can be traced to its culture. As Elmer H. Johnson and Alfred Heijder point out, "the Dutch prefer to see themselves as good people, willing to experiment, … committed to softening socioeconomic distinctions adverse to the underprivileged, holding basic trust in one another, and prepared to bargain with one another when there are disagreements." An important reason for its low crime rate is the government's "distribution of personal wealth through heavy inheritance taxes, progressive income taxes, and a substantial program to provide resources for meeting socioeconomic crises." Although the number of Dutch prisoners has risen since the 1960s because of growing crime rates, the Dutch policy of short prison terms has kept this number from rising as high as it would have otherwise.

Although the United States is very different from Denmark, the Netherlands, and other European nations, their strikingly different view of punishment and imprisonment is worth considering. Their experience reminds us that not only is our ready use of prisons not reducing the crime problem, it may even be making it worse. At the minimum, it is costing us billions of dollars that could be spent on crime prevention and custodial alternatives.

Sources: Brydensholt 1992; Downes 1996; Joutsen and Bishop 1994; Tak 1994.

a threat than men to society, that their families and children would suffer if they were incarcerated, that they are less blameworthy than men for the crimes they committed, and that they have more community ties. Some noted scholars view these reasons as evidence of "warranted disparity in judicial decision making" involving women and men (Daly 1994:268).

As with race/ethnicity, some evidence exists that the type and location of a study affects whether sentencing differences are found. Gender differences in sentencing appear more often when single jurisdictions are studied than when multiple jurisdictions are studied; and they appear more often in urban areas than in rural areas, in the Northeast or South than in other regions, and in felony cases than in misdemeanor cases (Daly and Bordt 1995). More lenient treatment of women is also found more often in incarceration (in/out) than in conviction or sentence length among those incarcerated.

In a study hailed as "the most rigorous and sophisticated statistical study of gender and sentencing to date" (Daly 1994:267–268), Steffensmeier and colleagues (1993) examined gender differences in sentencing with data from more than 62,000 cases in Pennsylvania from 1985 to 1987; I cited this study in the earlier discussion on race/ethnicity. The authors found that gender did not affect sentence length but did affect the in/out decision, with female defendants 12 percent less likely overall than male defendants to be incarcerated. At the same time, the most important determinants of judges' imprisonment decisions were offense seriousness and defendants' prior record. The researchers speculated that sentencing practices have become more uniform in the last two decades and therefore more gender neutral, and noted that most studies of gender and sentencing use older data from the 1970s.

 ## THE IMPACT OF PUNISHMENT ON CRIME

During the past few decades a "get tough" approach has guided the U.S. approach to crime. The federal government and states and cities across the country have established longer prison terms and mandatory minimum prison terms for many crimes. As noted earlier, the war on drugs that began in the mid-1980s involved drastic crime control efforts in our large cities targeted largely at African-Americans. In 1994 many states and then the federal government enacted "three strikes and you're out" legislation requiring that defendants convicted of a third felony receive life imprisonment. The death penalty has increasingly been used, with the number of offenders on death row rising from 134 in 1973 to 3,565 in 1999 (Maguire and Pastore 1999).

The result of all these efforts, and especially of the drug war, has been an enormous increase in the number of people incarcerated in our jails and prisons (Mauer 1999). These new prison admissions have swelled already overcrowded prisons far beyond capacity and forced states to spend billions of dollars on new prisons. As Figure 16.3 illustrates, the number of federal and state prisoners quadrupled from 1980 through 1998, rising from just over 300,000 in 1980 to about 1.3 million in 1998. The number of people in jail more than tripled during this period from about 180,000 to more than 600,000. Meanwhile, the number of people on probation or parole also more than tripled, rising from 1.3 million in 1980 to more than 4 million in 1998. Adding up all these figures, the number of adults under correctional supervision (in prison or jail, or on probation or parole) rose from 1.84 million to about 6 million in just 18 years. By any standard, this is a very high number. In fact, the United States has the highest imprisonment rate of any Western nation.

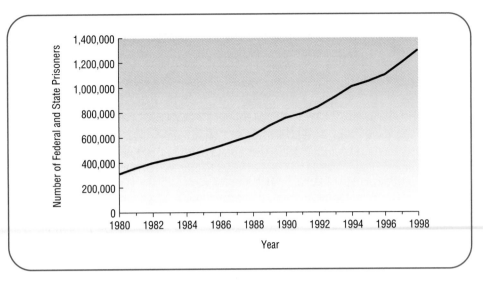

▲ Figure 16.3 Number of Adults in Federal and State Prison, 1980–1998
Sources: Beck and Mumola 1999; Maguire and Pastore 1999.

Despite this fact, the United States also has, as we know, higher crime rates than those of many other industrial nations.

The recent "get tough" approach reflects the widespread belief among the public and politicians alike that harsher and more certain punishment has a general deterrent effect on crime (Skolnick 1995). As we've seen earlier in this book, however, what people believe about crime and criminal justice sometimes turns out to be a myth. What, then, does the evidence say about the effect of harsher punishment on crime rates?

The conclusion here is similar to the one reached in the previous chapter on arrest: More certain and harsher punishment does not deter crime. This conclusion is probably shared by most criminologists and is supported by many kinds of evidence (Skolnick 1995; Walker 1998). Let's examine this evidence.

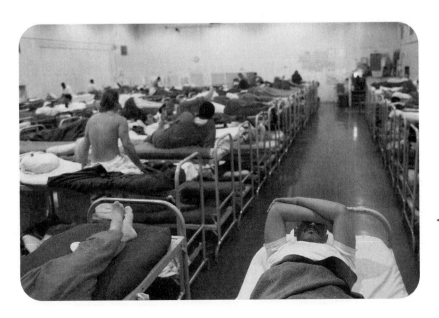

◀ The new prison admissions resulting from the "war on drugs" have swelled already overcrowded prisons far beyond capacity and forced states to spend billions of dollars on new prisons.

"Three Strikes and You're Out" Legislation

In the mid-1990s the federal government and at least 23 states established "three strikes and you're out" legislation mandating prison terms of 25 years to life for anyone convicted of a certain number of felonies, usually three. Responding to public concern about crime, legislators said these "three strikes" laws would send a message to potential criminals and also keep society safe from the convicted offenders who now would be staying in prison for life.

As three strikes laws were being debated by Congress and state legislatures, criminologists and even many prosecutors immediately pointed out that these laws would do little good and, even worse, would cost billions of dollars. A common criticism focused on the fact that only a small proportion of all chronic offenders are apprehended and convicted. Because any defendants sentenced under three strikes guidelines would be only a small fraction of all criminals, the proportion of crime prevented by their imprisonment would thus be minuscule at best.

To compound this problem, said many criminologists, criminality declines as people move out of their twenties and almost always halts by the time they reach their middle-aged and elderly years. As a result, almost all three strikes offenders would end up staying in prison long after they would have stopped being a public threat anyway.

Another criticism focused on the laws in several states that apply three strikes policies to offenders regardless of the seriousness of their third felony. While some states restricted their laws to violent felonies, others, most notably California, did not. Critics predicted that many California defendants would receive a life sentence for nonviolent property felonies such as shoplifting and auto theft. Because prisons are overcrowded, other offenders would have to be released from prison to make room for these new prisoners.

Criminologists and prosecutors also pointed out that three strikes laws would make defendants accused of a third felony reluctant to plead guilty. Jury trials, they predicted, would increase, clogging an already slow criminal court system and costing much money.

A final criticism focused on the prison costs to be generated by the new three strikes laws. The many more defendants being sentenced to prison for long prison terms and even life would each cost some $25,000 annually in prison maintenance costs. Since prisons are already bulging beyond capacity, three strikes laws would intensify the pressure for new prison construction, which would cost billions. Further, as three strikes defendants entered their elderly years in prison, many would require increasing amounts of very expensive health care. Some wings of prisons would have to be turned into virtual geriatric wards.

Ironically, after the wave of new three strikes laws, only California and Georgia used them to any large extent. For better or worse, the dire predictions of their impact came true in California. In 1995 a California state agency reported that only about one-third of three strikes convictions in that state were for violent felonies, with the remainder largely for burglary and drug possession. Some California defendants were sentenced to life for shoplifting, auto theft, or even for stealing a pizza or cigarettes. Many judges reportedly erased previous felony convictions from defendants' records to avoid having to sentence them to life. There were also reports of victims refusing to prosecute, and juries refusing to convict, defendants facing a life sentence for a nonviolent third felony. The predictions of clogged courts also became true, as more than half of all accused felons were now refusing to plead guilty. Because of the increased number of jury trials they were demanding, California was even running out of potential jurors.

California's prison costs also soared. Just a few months after its three strikes law took effect, California's prison population was growing by 300 to 400 inmates weekly, compared to less than half that number before the law began. California's State Department of Corrections estimated that 20 more prisons would have to be built because of that state's three strikes law, and that in the next 30 years California would have to house almost 276,000 more prisoners at an annual cost of almost $6 billion by the year 2027. By 1998 California had sentenced more than 40,000 offenders under the three strikes legislation, accounting for almost one-fourth of California's prison population.

Sources: Butterfield 1995; Dickey and Stiebs 1998; Jacobius 1995; Skolnick 1995.

The Evidence against a Deterrent Effect

First, the huge increases in incarceration over the last two decades have not prompted comparable decreases in crime rates. As Chapter 3 noted, the crime rate either stayed level throughout the 1980s or dropped and then rose, depending on whether UCR or NCVS data are used. Neither of these trends corresponds to the large increases in incarceration. These increases occurred even though the crime rate wasn't rising, and, once they happened, they didn't lower the crime rate.

Second, at the state level only a weak and inconsistent relationship exists between severity of punishment (e.g., length of prison terms) and crime rates (Chiricos and Waldo 1970). States with longer prison terms have only slightly smaller crime rates than states with shorter terms. As with similar research on arrest rates (see Chapter 15), even this small relationship doesn't necessarily mean that harsh sentences deter crime. Using a *system capacity* argument, it's just as likely that states with lower crime rates and presumably less crowded prisons can afford to keep their prisoners behind bars for longer periods (Pontell 1984).

Third, studies of perceptual deterrence find virtually no relationship between respondents' perceptions of the severity of punishment and their likelihood of committing various offenses (Paternoster 1987). Thus neither perceived severity of punishment nor perceived certainty (see Chapter 15) appear to deter criminality.

Fourth, and perhaps most tellingly, decreases in crime rates don't generally occur after the establishment of harsher penalties for various crimes. For example, laws mandating minimum or harsher sentences for gun crimes don't generally lower the rates of these crimes (see Chapter 9). In a recent, comprehensive investigation of this topic, Thomas B. Marvell and Carlisle E. Moody (1995) studied the effects of firearm sentence enhancement (FSE) laws in all forty-four states that established them since the 1960s. In a few states, FSE laws apparently decreased crime rates, but in some other states they had the opposite effect. The authors concluded that "on balance the FSE laws do little nationwide to reduce crime or gun use" (p. 274).

Fifth, the dramatic increase in prisoners during the last two decades has forced the early release of convicted offenders already there. If harsher punishment makes a difference, these offenders should have higher rates of repeat offending (recidivism) than offenders convicted of similar crimes who aren't released early. However, studies of this issue find that released offenders do not generally have higher recidivism rates than their counterparts who stay in prison and sometimes even have lower recidivism rates (Austin 1986). These studies thus suggest that longer sentences do not reduce recidivism and may even increase it. Other research on sentence length and recidivism reaches the same conclusion (Petersilia, Greenwood, and Levin 1978). As labeling theory predicts, longer stays in prison may embitter offenders and increase their exposure to the prison's criminal subculture. These and other problems make some offenders more crime-prone when they leave prison than when they went in.

In many respects, it's not that surprising that harsher punishment doesn't deter crime. When people commit violent offenses, they usually do so fairly spontaneously. At the time they lash out, they're not carefully weighing the possible penalties for their actions. Property offenses are more planned, allowing time for potential offenders to consider the prison term they may receive. Yet many property offenders either pay little attention to their chances of arrest or punishment or, at a minimum, assume they simply won't get caught (see Chapter 11). Given this basic understanding of violent and property crimes, it would be surprising if harsher or more certain punishment did deter criminal behavior.

If harsher punishment doesn't work, perhaps we could at least keep society safer by imprisoning larger numbers of criminals, especially chronic, hard-core offenders, and keeping them off the streets for longer amounts of time. This is called the *incapacitation* argument. Unfortunately, this argument is faulty for several reasons (Visher 2000; Zimring and Hawkins 1995). It assumes we don't have enough people already in prison and that there's room for even more. As this chapter has shown, however, our prisons are already stretched to the limit with little impact on the crime rate. It also assumes we can easily identify the chronic offenders who need to be incapacitated. However, it's not clear whether we can accurately identify such offenders and predict their future behavior (Auerhahn 1999; Gottfredson and Gottfredson 1994). The incapacitation argument also ignores the fact that any extra people we put in prison are only a small percentage of all offenders and will quickly be replaced on the streets by other offenders, a point the next chapter will consider further. The billions of dollars we would have to spend to house them will thus be largely wasted. Finally, the incapacitation argument overlooks the fact that the chronic offenders it addresses must be caught in the first place, which is unlikely to happen given the low arrest rates for crimes of all types (Currie 1985).

Putting all these factors together, if somehow we could imprison large numbers of chronic offenders, the crime rate might go down, but only by a very small amount. Currie (1985:88) offers this pessimistic appraisal of the incapacitation argument: "No one seriously doubts that a modicum of crime can be prevented by incapacitating offenders.... [But] the potential reduction in serious crime is disturbingly small, especially when balanced against the social and economic costs of pursuing this strategy strenuously enough to make much difference to public safety." The next chapter will give some idea of the economic costs.

Ironically, the massive increase in incarceration of the last few decades may eventually make the crime problem worse for at least two reasons. First, the hundreds of thousands of extra offenders now behind bars or with arrest records include many minor offenders. If labeling theory is correct, their experiences in the criminal justice system may embitter them and reduce their employment chances and thus make it more likely that they'll commit additional and more serious crime (Abramsky 1999; Sherman et al. 1998). Second, the increase in incarceration may also be damaging our urban communities, as the imprisonment of so many of their young men weakens the communities' families and other social institutions. When these men return to their communities after being released from prison, their stronger "deviant orientation" may be a bad influence on some community residents. By intensifying the communities' social disorganization in these ways, massive incarceration may ironically raise their crime rates and worsen the very problem it has been trying to stop (Rose and Clear 1998).

Ultimately, then, "get tough" measures involving harsher or more certain punishment will do little, if anything, to reduce our crime rate, no matter how much common sense and popular opinion tell us otherwise. The drastic increase in incarceration has cost the nation tens of billions of dollars in the last three decades with no real payoff. As Currie (1985:100) observes, "After years of investigation, we are not sure that the prisons deter crime to any significant extent, and we *are* sure that they do not deter it effectively." To reduce crime, another approach is required. The next chapter sketches what such an approach might look like.

THE DEATH PENALTY DEBATE

The themes of this chapter—discrimination in sentencing and the deterrent effect of punishment—come together in the heated, ongoing debate over the death penalty, which produces passions pro and con as perhaps no other issue in criminal justice (Bedau 1998; Smith 2000) Certainly, as noted earlier, the United States is relying increasingly on the death penalty for persons convicted of murder (Figure 16.4). Let's look at the death penalty debate in detail.

Death penalty proponents make at least three arguments: (1) People convicted of heinous murders deserve to be executed; (2) the death penalty saves the money that would be spent on years of confinement were the offender to serve a life sentence; and (3) the death penalty sends a message to potential murderers and thus has a general deterrent effect on homicide.

Death penalty opponents, probably including most criminologists, attack all these arguments. The first argument, that vicious murderers deserve to be executed, raises philosophical and religious issues lying beyond the scope of this book. Whether it is moral for the state to take a life, even that of a vicious murderer, is a philosophical or religious question, not a sociological one. But criminologists do point out that the United States is the only remaining Western nation to use the death penalty, the rest having decided long ago that civilized nations should not commit what opponents call "legal murders" against those who have murdered. As a slogan of death penalty opponents asks, "Why do we kill people to show that killing people is wrong?"

The Cost of the Death Penalty

The second argument, that the death penalty saves money, is an appropriate one for social scientists to address. Here the evidence is clear: The death penalty actually costs more than life imprisonment in constant dollars. Keeping someone in

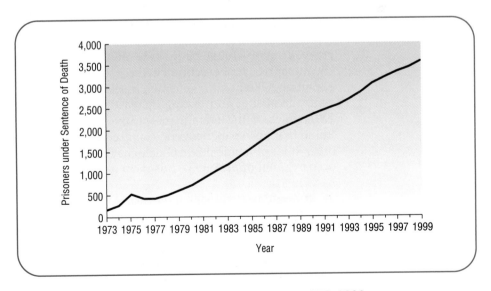

▲ FIGURE 16.4 PERSONS UNDER SENTENCE OF DEATH, 1973–1999

Sources: Bonczar and Beck 1997; Maguire and Pastore 1999; Beck and Mumola 1999.

prison for life would cost about $25,000 per year in constant dollars: $1 million for 40 years, for example. Because someone' life is at stake, death penalty cases are especially complicated from pretrial motions through sentencing and appeals, with the state usually having to pay for all costs at least through appeals to state courts. The cost of each death penalty case is roughly $2 million to $3 million (Keve 1992). Thus it actually costs taxpayers less to keep someone in prison for life than to execute him or her (almost always him).

General Deterrence and the Death Penalty

The third argument, that the death penalty has a general deterrent effect, is one that social scientists have tested for several decades. Almost all studies show that the death penalty does not have this effect (Bailey and Peterson 1999) This conclusion comes from several kinds of studies. Some of the earliest research compared the homicide rates of states with and without the death penalty. Contrary to the general deterrence argument, states with the death penalty don't have lower homicide rates than those without it. States that eliminated the death penalty earlier in the twentieth century did not see their homicide rates rise compared with states that retained the death penalty. Conversely, states that established the death penalty did not see their homicide rates decrease compared with states that did not have the death penalty.

More recently, scholars have examined the consequences of well-publicized executions. If the death penalty does deter homicide, homicide should go down in the month or so after stories about these executions appear in the press. Although a few studies find this effect (Stack 1987), most find no effect (Peterson and Bailey 1991). Some studies even show that homicide actually increases after executions occur. This is called the "brutalization effect." The argument here is that executions desensitize the public to the immorality of killing and thus increase the likelihood that some people will decide to kill. Executions may also increase homicide in a sort of imitation effect (Bowers and Pierce 1980).

In a recent demonstration of the brutalization effect, John K. Cochran and two colleagues (1994) studied the aftermath of a September 1990 execution in Oklahoma, the first execution in the state in 25 years. In the three years after the execution, Oklahoma's general homicide rate did not change. There was, however, "an abrupt and lasting increase in the level of stranger homicides" (p. 129), which on the average rose by one per month. A replication of their study found that newspaper coverage of executions *outside* Oklahoma also increased other kinds of homicides in Oklahoma (Bailey 1998). If brutalization does indeed occur, capital punishment thus increases the number of homicides rather than reducing them.

It would be surprising if the death penalty did deter homicide. As noted previously, most people who commit violence don't weigh the punishment they might receive before they strike. Most homicides are fairly spontaneous events, and offenders certainly don't pause to mull over their chances of being executed before they kill their victims. Offenders who commit felony murders—murders in the course of another felony like robbery—also don't have time to consider the consequences. Given the nature of homicide, it's simply very unlikely that the death penalty can deter it.

Arbitrariness and Racial Discrimination in the Death Penalty's Application

In addition to challenging the arguments of death penalty proponents, opponents of the death penalty cite other problems with capital punishment. Many of these have to do with the way the death penalty is applied. In 1972 the U.S. Supreme Court ruled 5–4 in *Furman v. Georgia* (408 U.S. 238) that capital punishment as it was then practiced violated the Eighth Amendment's prohibition of cruel and unusual punishment. The Court found that jurors in capital cases had few standards to guide their decision to impose the death penalty, leading them to impose death sentences in some murder cases but not in others that were equally appalling. Far from logical and rational, the capital punishment process was, the Court declared, both capricious and arbitrary and held the potential for racial discrimination.

In the wake of *Furman*, states revised their death penalty laws and procedures in an attempt to reduce the arbitrary application of the death penalty. Some mandated death sentences for any convictions of first-degree murder, while others devised a system of "bifurcated" juries that would first decide on the guilt of the defendant and then decide whether to impose the death penalty. In this second phase, juries would have to consider both *aggravating factors* (e.g., the murder was committed while the defendant was committing another felony) and *mitigating factors* (e.g., the defendant had no prior history of criminality) as they determined whether a death sentence was appropriate.

In a series of decisions in 1976, the Supreme Court struck down the mandatory death penalty statutes but upheld, in *Gregg v. Georgia* (428 U.S. 153), the statutes establishing bifurcated juries and aggravating and mitigating factors. Social scientists since that time have studied whether the new, post-*Furman* system of capital punishment has continued to exhibit the same arbitrariness, capriciousness, and racial discrimination that motivated the *Furman* decision (Smith 2000).

Continuing Arbitrariness

On the issue of arbitrariness the evidence is clear: Throughout the country, defendants accused of similar murders are treated differently for no logical reasons (Berk, Weiss, and Boger 1993). Some are charged with capital murders, while others are not. Some receive the death penalty after conviction, while others do not. Even within the same state, murder defendants are more likely to receive the death penalty in some jurisdictions than in others. While such disparities inevitably exist in the criminal justice system for all kinds of crimes, they have even more ominous implications when a defendant's life is at stake. Researchers in this area conclude that the capital punishment process is akin to a lottery system and that "being sentenced to death is the result of a process that may be no more rational than being struck by lightning" (Paternoster 1991:183).

Here again the 1994–1995 O. J. Simpson case is illustrative. Simpson was accused of the extremely vicious murders of two people. Many aspects of the alleged murders fit the circumstances that ordinarily allow, and persuade, California prosecutors to ask for the death penalty when they charge defendants. Simpson's prosecutors chose not to ask for the death penalty in his case. Legal observers attributed their decision to Simpson's celebrity, and assumed the prosecutors were afraid that a jury would never convict such a famous, well-liked defendant, even if he had committed the two murders, if they knew he could be executed. Thus O. J. Simpson didn't face the death penalty, even though many poor, unknown defendants accused of far less vicious murders have faced it and continue to face it.

RACIAL DISCRIMINATION

Another line of research has focused on racial discrimination. As noted earlier, strong evidence of one type of racial discrimination continues in the application of the death penalty: The lives of white victims are seemingly valued more than the lives of black victims (Sorensen and Wallace 1999). Prosecutors in homicide cases are more likely to impose a first-degree murder charge (the only charge for which the death penalty is allowed), and also to seek the death penalty after conviction, when the victim is white than when the victim is black. Further, among defendants indicted for first-degree murder, death sentences from juries are also more likely when the victim is white than when the victim is black.

The evidence is less consistent for continuing, harsher treatment of black defendants once the race of the victim is held constant. Some studies find black defendants more likely to be indicted for first-degree murder and also to receive the death penalty eventually, but some studies don't find this difference. When this difference is found, the combination of black offender–white victim is much more likely than other combinations to be charged with first-degree murder, to have the death penalty sought by prosecutors, and to receive death sentences after conviction. Several scholars conclude that discrimination on the basis of the *defendant's* race has declined or even disappeared after *Furman*, but discrimination on the basis of the *victim's* race has continued (Baldus, Woodworth, and Pulaski 1990).

Figures from perhaps the best study of racial discrimination in the death penalty underscore the difference that the victim's race makes. David C. Baldus and colleagues (1990) studied 594 murder cases from Georgia. Before they controlled for legally relevant variables such as the number of *aggravating factors* (evidence of clear premeditation, committing the murder during the course of committing other felonies), the authors found that prosecutors sought the death penalty in 45 percent of the cases with white victims but in only 15 percent of the cases with black victims. Combining the race of the victim and of the defendant, they found that prosecutors sought the death penalty in 58 percent of the black defendant–white victim cases; 38 percent of white defendant–white victim cases; and only 15 percent of black defendant-black victim cases. Juries imposed the death penalty in 57 percent of cases with white victims but only 42 percent of cases with black victims.

After controlling for legally relevant factors, the racial disparities stemming from the victim's race increased: In cases with white victims, prosecutors were five and one-half times more likely to seek the death penalty and juries were seven times more likely to impose it. The authors concluded that the race of the victim had a "potent influence" on the likelihood of the death penalty (p. 185). Interestingly, they also found this influence greater in cases where the number of aggravating factors was neither very high nor very low. In this middle range of cases, where the murders were neither the most terrible nor the least terrible, prosecutors and juries are most likely to take the victim's race into account as they decide to seek or impose the death penalty. Although the authors didn't note it, their finding supported the liberation hypothesis outlined earlier.

In a similar study of 300 capital murders in South Carolina involving the commission of aggravating felonies, Raymond Paternoster (1984) found that prosecutors sought the death penalty in 107 of these cases. When Paternoster investigated why these cases were so chosen, he found that, in cases with white victims, prosecutors were two and one-half times more likely than in those with black victims to seek the death penalty. However, cases with black offenders were not more likely than those with white offenders to have the death penalty sought. In black offender–white victim cases, prosecutors sought the death penalty 49.5 percent of the time; in white offender–white victim cases, 37.5 percent; and in black offender–black victim cases, only 11.3 percent. Thus when blacks were the offenders, prosecutors were more than four times as likely to seek the death penalty when whites were victims than when blacks were victims.

Paternoster concluded that "victim-based racial discrimination is evident in prosecutors' decisions to seek the death penalty" (p. 471). Again supporting the liberation hypothesis, this discrimination was greater in those cases involving fewer aggravating felonies. Moreover, in cases with white victims, prosecutors tended to seek the death penalty when there was only one aggravating felony; in cases with black victims, prosecutors were likely to seek the death penalty only when there was more than one aggravating felony. Thus murders of blacks had to be more appalling for the death penalty to be sought.

The Quality of Legal Representation of Capital Defendants

Another criticism of the death penalty addresses the quality of legal representation of capital defendants (Perez-Pena 2000). Recall that almost all criminal defendants are poor and receive inadequate legal representation. This is no less true for defendants facing the death penalty. Capital cases are extraordinarily complex and can cost at least $250,000 to defend. Most public defenders and assigned counsel simply aren't equipped to handle them, especially when they've often never litigated a capital case before, and often spend only a few days on the case. They thus don't raise evidentiary and other issues at trial that may be grounds for later appeals, and they certainly don't have the funds and other resources to mount an effective defense in the first place. In many states their pay is also inadequate. For example, Mississippi pays attorneys assigned to capital cases only $1,000 in fees, whereas private attorneys would charge much more than $100 an hour.

Similar problems affect the appeals process after conviction in a capital case. Because most defendants given the death penalty cannot afford to hire private counsel to launch an appeal, they must rely on counsel assigned by the state for appeals at the state level. Once again, these counsel are usually not as capable of handling death penalty appeals as more experienced, and much more expensive, private counsel. Once appeals are denied by state courts, the defendant's only recourse lies in the federal courts. At this level, public funding for defense counsel is not available. The defendant thus must usually rely on volunteer attorneys, but there are very few attorneys willing to serve in this capacity. Those that do volunteer their time usually don't have the resources to put forward the best appeal possible.

Sometimes defense attorneys in death penalty cases are downright incompetent or corrupt. Some fail to present witnesses or evidence, and some have even fallen asleep during the trials of their clients. Others have questionable legal credentials: In one death penalty case, the attorney was a former leader of the Ku Klux Klan, and in another case the attorney was facing disbarment at the same time the trial of his client was occurring. According to various studies, 25 percent of Kentucky death row inmates were represented by attorneys who were later disbarred or who resigned to avoid this fate; 13 percent of Louisiana defendants who had been executed were represented by attorneys who had been disciplined for various kinds of misconduct; and 33 defendants sentenced to death in Illinois had lawyers who were later disbarred or suspended (Berlow 1999; Johnson 2000; Perez-Pena 2000).

In short, defendants facing the death penalty receive inadequate representation at all levels of the legal process even though their lives are at stake. This is especially true in the South, where most death penalty cases occur, as few capable attorneys there are willing to take on capital cases. When they do so, their regular legal practice might suffer because of hostility from the public and other legal professionals.

Wrongful Executions

A final criticism of the death penalty centers on the possibility of wrongful executions. Mistakes do occur in criminal justice, either out of honest errors or downright prejudice. One study estimated that slightly under 1 percent of all felony convictions are mistaken (Huff, Rattner, and Sagarin 1996). If someone is mistakenly found guilty, they can be released from prison once the mistake is discovered. But if that person is executed, he or she can't be brought back to life. Evidence of mistaken convictions abounds. Since 1900, at least 350 defendants have been convicted of potentially capital crimes even though they were innocent. Of these defendants, 139 received the death penalty and 23 were executed (Radelet, Bedau, and Putnam 1992). At least 381 homicide defendants have had their convictions overturned since 1963 because prosecutors presented false evidence or hid evidence they knew would favor the defendant. And more than 80 death-row inmates have been released from prison since *Furman* in 1976 after new evidence, sometimes gathered by college and graduate students, established their innocence. This figure represents more than 1 percent of the 6,000 people sentenced to death since *Furman* and more than 10 percent of the number executed (Berlow 1999).

Why are innocent people sometimes convicted of murder and sentenced to death? According to legal writer Alan Berlow (1999:68), the reasons "range from simple police and prosecutorial error to the most outrageous misconduct, such as the framing of innocent people, and everything in between: perjured testimony, erroneous eyewitness testimony, false confessions (including the confessions of innocent defendants), racial bias, incompetent defense counsel, and overzealous police officers and prosecutors...." Rolando Cruz's case, discussed at the beginning of this chapter, typifies several of these reasons. So does the case of one James Richardson, once on death row in Florida for murdering his seven children. He was freed after 21 years in prison after a file stolen from a prosecutor's office indicated that the prosecutor had concealed evidence of Richardson's innocence and that several witnesses had lied under oath (Berlow 1999). In another case of wrongful conviction, a Pennsylvania woman was sentenced to a life term in a capital case after being found guilty of stabbing a girl who had dated the defendant's boyfriend. A judge set her free because of what he termed "gross prosecutorial misconduct" involving suppressed and altered evidence, perjured testimony, and possible witness-tampering (Marder 1997). In June 2000, Gary Graham was executed in Texas for a 1981 murder. He had been convicted on very thin evidence: the testimony of a single eyewitness whose identification of Graham was contradicted by other witnesses. Graham's court-appointed attorney never even interviewed these other witnesses (Alter 2000).

The possibility of wrongful convictions and executions and other problems in the application of the death penalty have led the American Bar Association and other organizations to call for a moratorium on executions. In 1999 the governor of

◀ *In 1985 Rolando Cruz was convicted of the kidnapping, rape, and murder of a 10-year-old girl. Cruz was sentenced to die by lethal injection, but was freed from prison ten years later after DNA evidence cleared him (and implicated another man, who confessed to the crimes) and revelations of police and prosecutorial misconduct surfaced.*

Nebraska rejected his state legislature's call for a moratorium. In early 2000, however, revelations that 13 innocent men had been put on death row in Illinois led the state's governor, George Ryan, a Republican, to impose a moratorium on executions until it could be established that Illinois death penalty cases were free from error or bias. His action led to calls for moratoriums in other states (Johnson 2000).

 ## SUMMARY AND CONCLUSION

This chapter's focus on the prosecution and punishment of criminals completes our brief overview of the criminal justice system. Many issues were omitted for lack of space, but we did deal with the most important ones for a sociological understanding of crime and criminal justice: The inequality of legal outcomes and the deterrent effects of legal punishment.

In this chapter we saw that structural context often shapes post-arrest legal decision making. In particular, we reviewed the extensive literature on class, racial and ethnic, and gender discrimination in sentencing. We saw that disparities do exist in many jurisdictions and at different stages of the legal process, even if legal factors exert the major influence on sentencing. There is thus evidence here to support both consensus and conflict views of law and criminal justice. Whether the system is fair or not overall is difficult to discern. What I've tried to provide is a sociological lens through which to view the evidence and to help you draw your own conclusions.

The chapter also reviewed the evidence on the deterrent effect of harsher and more certain sentences and reached a rather pessimistic conclusion: "Get tough" approaches offer little hope in reducing crime. This, of course, has been the dominant approach to the crime problem in the last few decades, as politicians continue to compete to show who is toughest on criminals. Amid all the calls for cracking down on criminals, it's easy to forget that the social policy may not always have its desired effects. The best evidence indicates that recent social policy on crime and drugs has failed in its most important professed goal, that of reducing the crime problem.

The United States holds the dubious honor of having one of the highest crime rates in the Western industrial world, even though it also has the highest imprisonment rate of all Western nations and longer prison terms than most of these nations. A quadrupling of imprisonment since 1980 has not lowered the crime rate, and a very punitive war on drugs has neither reduced the drug trade appreciably nor lowered drug use. Instead they have swelled our jails and prisons, cost us billions of dollars that could have been put to better use, and otherwise done much more harm than good. There must be a better way.

We've now come full circle. Near the beginning of the book, in Chapter 2, I tried to show that public opinion on crime and politicians' calls for cracking down on crime have little to do with actual crime rate trends. In following chapters, we looked at explanations of crime and examined its nature and dynamics, and we've just examined the extent of discrimination in the criminal justice system and questioned whether a "get tough" approach is the most promising way to tackle the crime problem. This approach cannot and does not work for several reasons, not the least of which have to do with the sociological causes and nature of criminality that earlier chapters presented. Now that we've reached the end of the book, I will spend a few pages in the final chapter spelling out a sociological prescription for crime reduction.

KEY TERMS

adversary system
arbitrariness
brutalization effect
caseloads
correctional supervision
courtroom work group
deterrence
discretion

in/out decision
incapacitation
incarceration
liberation hypothesis
plea bargaining
repressive law
restitutive law
wrongful execution

STUDY QUESTIONS

1. How does the concept of the courtroom "work group" help us understand why so much plea bargaining occurs? Do you think plea bargaining is good or bad? Why?
2. To what extent does social class affect legal outcomes?
3. To what extent do race and ethnicity affect conviction and sentencing?
4. What is the text's "cautious conclusion" on racial and ethnic discrimination in sentencing?
5. To what extent does legal punishment deter potential criminal behavior?
6. What are the arguments for and against the death penalty? Are you in favor of the death penalty? Why or why not?

INTERNET EXERCISES

The Fortune Society is an organization composed primarily of ex-offenders. It seeks to educate the public about prison life and various issues concerning imprisonment in the United States, and it also seeks to help ex-offenders resume normal lives. Its Web site is at **www.fortunesociety.org**. Go to this site and read through the opening page to get an idea of the Fortune Society's mission and philosophy.

Now click on the **Services** link on the opening page to discover the various services that the Fortune Society provides. How important do you think these services are to help ex-prisoners? Do you think our society is providing enough money and other resources to help ex-convicts? Should additional help to ex-offenders be provided as part of a comprehensive crime control strategy? Would such help be akin to "coddling criminals"? Why or why not?

CONCLUSION:
HOW CAN WE
REDUCE CRIME?

e've reached the end of our journey into the world of sociological criminology. In this world, crime and victimization are rooted in the social and physical characteristics of communities and in the structured social inequalities of race/ethnicity, social class, and gender. While not excusing any criminal's action, our sociological imagination allows us to understand that a person's criminality is just one example of a public issue affecting masses of people. Our sociological imagination also forces us to realize that to reduce crime, its structural and cultural roots must be addressed. Even if we could somehow "cure" all the criminals, new ones would replace them unless the structural and cultural conditions underlying crime were changed.

The need to address these conditions becomes even more paramount when we consider the criminal justice system's inability to reduce the crime problem. As we saw in the last two chapters, increasing the certainty and severity of arrest and punishment offers us only false hopes: The "get tough" approach guiding public policy in the last few decades has had little, if any, impact on the crime rate. Since this approach doesn't work, we need to look to a different type of strategy.

The field of public health offers one such strategy. If we tried to prevent a disease by only curing those having it and not attacking the underlying causes, that disease would certainly continue. Recognizing this, the public health model stresses the need to identify the social and other causes of disease so that efforts can be launched to target these causes (Moore 1995). Unfortunately, our approach to crime hasn't followed this sensible strategy. Instead, our main efforts have focused on "curing" those "afflicted" with crime by arresting as many as possible and putting them behind bars. These efforts might make us feel better and give many people jobs, but they haven't worked and have cost billions of dollars.

In recent years public health experts have turned their attention to violent crime, which they consider a public health problem. They've undertaken important studies to uncover the social causes of violence so that these causes can be addressed by public policy (Friedman 1994; Kellerman 1996). In the spirit of this approach, this chapter offers a sociological prescription for reducing crime.

 ## THE CRIMINAL JUSTICE SYSTEM "FUNNEL"

Before doing so, let's look at one more kind of evidence that underscores the futility of using the criminal justice system to reduce crime. This evidence concerns what is often called the "funnel effect" in the criminal justice system (Mauer 1999). The funnel image comes from the fact that as we move from the number of crimes committed (the top of the funnel) to the number of offenders going to prison or jail (the bottom of the funnel), there's a sharp drop in numbers at every stage of the criminal justice process. This drop occurs because at every stage, as we saw in the last two chapters, decision makers determine whether a crime, or someone suspected of that crime, filters down to the next level. Inevitably, their decisions "kick out" many crimes and suspects from the criminal justice system or at least from consideration for incarceration, so that only a few remain by the time we get to prison and jail at the bottom of the funnel. Let's see how this happens.

As we saw in Chapter 3, less than 40 percent of all victimizations are reported to the police. Of the crimes known to the police, only about 21–22 percent overall are cleared by arrest. What happens to the people arrested? Relatively few are convicted of felonies, and even fewer of these are sentenced to prison or jail. As we saw in Chapter 15, many cases are either dropped for lack of sufficient evidence or,

TABLE 17.1

THE CRIMINAL JUSTICE SYSTEM FUNNEL FOR INDEX CRIME, 1996

TOTAL	VARIABLE
30,933,000	NCVS victimizations
13,493,900	UCR index offenses known to police
2,941,670	UCR index crimes cleared by arrest
470,933	Felony convictions in state and federal courts
318,690	Sentenced to prison or jail

Sources: calculated from Maguire and Pastore 1999; Ringel 1997.

sometimes, plea bargained to a misdemeanor, for which incarceration is unlikely. Of those convicted of a felony, some receive probation and/or fines instead of imprisonment.

Now let's illustrate the criminal justice system funnel with some real data in Table 17.1 for 1996 (the latest year for which all this information was available at the time of writing). The data come from the National Crime Victimization Survey, the Uniform Crime Reports, and various federal reports on the judicial processing of defendants. Only the UCR Index crimes of homicide, rape, aggravated assault, robbery, burglary, larceny, auto theft, and arson are represented in the table. Thus I've excluded simple assaults from the NCVS figure, even though the NCVS reports them; keep in mind that the NCVS itself excludes homicides, commercial burglaries, shoplifting, and other crimes included in the other figures in the table. I've added the number of homicides into the NCVS figure for total victimizations.

As you can see, we start with almost 31 million personal victimizations at the top of the funnel and end up with under 319,000 persons going to prison or jail at the bottom of the funnel. This number of incarcerated offenders represents only about 1 percent of the total number of victimizations reported by the NCVS.

Perhaps the funnel effect for violent crimes is less severe. Let's take a look, then, in Table 17.2 at the funnel effect in 1996 for only the Index violent crimes of homicide, aggravated assault, rape, and robbery. Once again, the NCVS figure in the table excludes simple assaults but includes homicides.

TABLE 17.2

THE CRIMINAL JUSTICE SYSTEM FUNNEL FOR INDEX VIOLENT CRIME, 1996

TOTAL	VARIABLE
3,262,000	NCVS victimizations
1,688,540	UCR index offenses known to police
800,368	UCR index crimes cleared by arrest
170,527	Felony convictions in state and federal courts
132,756	Sentenced to prison or jail

Sources: calculated from Maguire and Pastore 1999; Ringel 1997.

Here we start with about 3.26 million personal violent victimizations at the top of the funnel and end up with less than 133,000 going to prison or jail. This number of incarcerated offenders represents just under 4.1 percent of the total number of victimizations reported by the NCVS. Although the drop throughout the violent crime funnel is a little less severe than the drop for the funnel combining violent and property offenses, it's still quite noticeable.

Besides making you perhaps want to live in a low crime state or even move out of the country, what are the implications of the funnel effect for public policy on crime? One implication is that efforts concentrating on offenders and offenses at the bottom of the funnel will have only a limited impact, if that, on crime. Even if all people convicted of a violent felony each year were sentenced to prison for life, for example, they would still represent only a very small proportion of all people committing such felonies, leaving the crime rate essentially intact. This is true even if each person put into prison had committed more than one crime in a given year and therefore accounted for more than one of the crimes at the top of the funnel.

Suppose you decided you wanted to double the number of people going to prison for felonies. How much would that cost, and would the money be worth it? To answer these questions, let's go back to the data in Table 17.1. Doubling the number of people going to prison or jail would mean that instead of about 1 percent of all victimizations leading to someone being incarcerated, we would now have about 2 percent. How much safer would you feel? Even if the people incarcerated had accounted for five crimes each in a given year, you'd be increasing the proportion of all crimes accounted for by imprisonment from 5 percent to 10 percent. That would still leave 90 percent of all crimes unaccounted for. Would you feel much safer? Even if we tried to "fix" only the violent crime funnel depicted in Table 17.2, doubling the number at the bottom would still leave the vast majority of violent crimes unaccounted for.

How much would it cost to double the small number of people at the bottom of the funnel depicted in Table 17.1 who are incarcerated? To keep things simple, let's assume we would eventually have to double the number of prison cells, since our prisons are already stretched beyond capacity. Since we now have about 1.3 million people in our prisons, that would mean building at least 1,300 more prisons, each containing 1,000 beds. With the cost of each such prison averaging about $100 million or more, the cost of prison construction alone would come to about $130

◀ *Building more prisons will cost the nation billions of dollars but will not reduce crime significantly.*

billion, with another $130 billion or so in interest on construction loans. Since it also costs about $25,000 per year to keep each person in prison, it would eventually cost an extra $32 billion annually, in constant dollars, to house the new prisoners. In recent years, California, Texas, and other states have spent huge sums of money on new prisons to incarcerate more and more offenders. These expenditures have reduced funds for higher education and other uses, and have stretched the states' finances severely (Mauer 1999).

Let's assume further that to double the number of people going to prison each year, it would help to double the number of police. With about 660,000 local police in the United States, each earning an average annual income of about $30,000, the extra salaries alone would come to about $20 billion annually. The additional operating expenses, $55,000 (benefits, equipment, etc.) for each police officer would amount to another $37 billion. We would also have to build new courthouses, hire new prosecutors and other court personnel, and elect or appoint more judges, all at an expense that would easily run into the billions of dollars. We are now up to at least $210 billion in immediate and annual costs, just to double the proportion of victimizations leading to imprisonment from 1 percent to 2 percent. If you were a businessperson, how cost-effective would you consider this expenditure? If you ran your business this way, how long would you stay in business?

As this brief discussion suggests, it might make more sense to concentrate on the top of the funnel instead of on the bottom. This means, of course, focusing more on crime prevention than on crime control. It also means looking to the structural and cultural causes of crime rather than relying on the criminal justice system. This is the view of many criminologists. Elliott Currie (1985:225) says that to reduce crime "we must build a society that is less unequal, less depriving, less insecure, less disruptive of family and community ties, less corrosive of cooperative values." Samuel Walker (1993:514–515) notes, "A sound criminal justice policy begins with a sober respect for the limits of what can be accomplished through the criminal justice system. The first principle is that criminal justice agencies … cannot make significant changes in the level of criminal behavior." He writes elsewhere (Walker 1998:278–279) that "the real solution to the crime problem lies outside the criminal justice system" and he says we must address the "underlying structural conditions"—economic deprivation and problems in communities, families, and schools—that contribute so heavily to the crime problem.

To have any hope of reducing crime significantly, then, we need policies that address its structural and cultural roots. The next section outlines several such policies.

 A SOCIOLOGICAL PRESCRIPTION FOR CRIME REDUCTION

Earlier I advocated a public health approach to violence and other crime. A public health strategy emphasizes the need for prevention. Here the public health community stresses three kinds of prevention: primary, secondary, and tertiary.

Primary prevention "seeks to prevent the occurrence of disease or injury entirely" by focusing on aspects of the social or physical environment that contribute to the disease or injury (Moore 1995:247). Thus public health advocates underscore poverty as a cause of poor health, and toxic dump sites and other environmental hazards as a cause of cancer. A primary prevention approach to crime, then, addresses features of our society, culture, and local communities that contribute to our high crime rates. We discussed many of these features in Chapter 6.

Secondary prevention in the public health model aims to identify practices and situations that put certain individuals at risk for illness or injury. Thus public health advocates emphasize that poor children are especially at risk for serious childhood diseases because they often don't get the vaccinations they need. To address this problem, public health workers champion high-profile government vaccination and public education efforts. A secondary prevention approach to crime, then, addresses the developmental processes, especially those in early childhood, that make crime even more likely among individuals living in criminogenic social environments. We discussed many of these processes in Chapter 7.

Finally, *tertiary prevention* occurs after an illness has begun or an injury has occurred and "seeks to minimize the long-term consequences" of the health problem (Moore 1995:247). When you visit a physician for an illness or injury, the physician is engaging in tertiary prevention. A tertiary prevention approach to crime, then, focuses on preventing recidivism, or repeat offending, by offenders and on protecting society from these offenders. This is sometimes called a "criminal justice approach" and, of course, is how the United States has traditionally responded to crime. Although the last two chapters discussed this approach's limitations, there are some criminal justice-related policies that should be considered.

The following proposals represent a reasonable approach to crime reduction. They rest on the vast body of criminological theory and research presented in previous chapters and are advocated by many highly respected criminologists (Blumstein 1993; Currie 1985; Glaser 1997; Sherman et al. 1998; Short 1997; Skolnick 1995). The proposals are grouped according to three categories: (a) social, cultural, and community; (b) developmental (social processes); and (c) legal and criminal justice. These categories roughly correspond to primary, secondary, and tertiary prevention, respectively.

Physicians' prescriptions sometimes don't cure illnesses immediately or at all, and not every aspect of this sociological prescription for crime reduction may have its intended effects. Some of the proposals will undoubtedly sound like pipe dreams and will be difficult or almost impossible to achieve, either because we don't have the national will or desire to accomplish them, or because the issues they address are intractable. But even some success in achieving these proposals' objectives offers real hope to reduce crime. Most of the proposals speak to street crime in general; some speak to violence against women; a few speak to white-collar crime.

Social, Cultural, and Community Crime Prevention (Primary Prevention)

A primary prevention approach to U.S. crime recognizes the geographical and sociodemographic patterning of street crime outlined in earlier chapters. The most important elements of this patterning are these: (1) serious violent crime in the United States is the highest of all Western nations, while U.S. property crime is among the highest of all Western nations; and (2) serious street crime, both violent and property, in the United States is committed disproportionately by young people, the poor, males, urban residents, and African-Americans. Combining all these characteristics, crime rates are highest among young, poor, urban, African-American men.

If we could wave a magic wand, we could probably reduce crime significantly, including white-collar crime, by giving our country a new value system. This value system would place less emphasis on economic success, individualism, and competition, and more emphasis on cooperation and multiple kinds of success. If Bonger

(1916) and other critics of capitalism are correct (see Chapter 8), our capitalist economic system is responsible for many of the criminogenic values that need to be replaced, and a move to economic or social democracy may be needed to change these values (Simon 1999). While the United States is certainly not likely to become such a society, other industrial and nonindustrial nations, Western and non-Western alike, with lower crime rates all feature value systems that stress community and cooperation (Adler 1983; Clinard 1978; Westermann and Burfeind 1991).

If we had a magic wand, we could also reduce crime significantly by wiping out economic deprivation and racial discrimination. The high degree of economic deprivation in the United States is at least partly responsible for its high crime rate, and economic deprivation and racial discrimination help account for much of the high criminality of urban African-Americans.

Finally, if we could wave a magic wand, we could reduce crime significantly by eliminating the many aspects of masculinity that prompt males to be so much more crime-prone than females. If the male crime rate were as low as the female rate, crime in the United States would probably not be considered a serious problem.

Unfortunately, of course, magic wands don't exist except in the Land of Oz and other fictitious worlds, and we're not likely to overhaul U.S. values, abolish inequality and racial discrimination, and eliminate the worst aspects of masculinity in any of our lifetimes. More practical strategies that address the structural and cultural roots of crime are therefore necessary. The following proposals outline several such strategies.

1. *Undertake social policies to create decent-paying jobs for the poor, especially those in urban communities.* Although the U.S. economy thrived during much of the 1990s and into the new century, the economic situation of people at the bottom of the socioeconomic ladder remained dismal and even worsened (Mishel, Bernstein, and Schmitt 1998). Economic and social policies, therefore, must be developed to address their needs. Here employment policy is crucial. Despite complex results, research documents the connection between unemployment and crime (Freeman 1995; Land, Cantor, and Russell 1995). Currie (1985:263) writes that "a commitment to full and decent employment remains the keystone of any successful anticrime policy." He notes that Western nations with lower violent crime rates than the United States all have much more effective employment policies than the United States does. Employment not only reduces poverty, especially among the economic underclass, it also increases an individual's bond to society and sense of responsibility. If the United States can reduce poverty by enabling more people to work at decent-paying jobs, crime will eventually decrease. Several specific policies to increase employment have been proposed elsewhere (Alperovitz and Faux 1984; Currie 1985). They include large public expenditures for job training and public works jobs, and tax and other incentives for corporations to develop stable employment in urban areas.

2. *Provide government economic aid for people who cannot find work or who find work but still cannot lift themselves out of poverty.* Many of the poor are working poor: They have jobs at or close to the minimum wage, which still leaves them far below the poverty line. Other members of the poor are women with young children. They either can't afford to work because of high daycare costs or are unemployable because they lack a high school degree and/or job skills. Welfare reform that began several years ago has had only mixed results, and several studies indicate that the reform worsened the

lot of many families that were on welfare (Hernandez 1998). If we don't provide for our poor, we're certain to increase the chances that their children will grow up to commit crime (Duke and John 1996).

3. *Take measures to end racial segregation in housing.* Douglas S. Massey and Nancy A. Denton (1993) document the devastating effects that housing segregation, promoted in part by government public housing programs, had on African-Americans during the last few decades. Housing segregation exacerbated their economic distress by trapping them in deteriorating neighborhoods with weakened social institutions and increasing crime rates.

4. *Undertake measures to restore the social integration and strengthen the social institutions of urban neighborhoods.* This proposal stems from social disorganization theory, which has recently received renewed attention. Any measures to strengthen the urban neighborhoods in these respects should concentrate on children and adolescents (Sampson 1995). Examples here would include youth recreation programs; increased involvement of parents in school activities; increased involvement of youths in church-based religious and social activities; and adult–youth mentoring in job skills, hobbies, and other areas.

5. *Reduce housing and population density.* Several studies find that crime is more likely when families live in apartment buildings and public housing projects than when they live more spread apart (Roncek 1981; Sampson and Lauritsen 1994). New public housing for the poor should thus be more dispersed geographically. If they desire, current residents of urban public housing projects and other dense housing should be able to move to more scattered housing.

6. *Reduce urban neighborhood dilapidation.* Several scholars emphasize the physical "incivilities" of urban neighborhoods as a key cause of their high crime rates (Skogan 1990; Stark 1987; Wilson and Kelling 1982). These incivilities include graffiti, broken windows, abandoned buildings, and strewn trash. Such dilapidation prompts nondeviant neighborhood residents to move elsewhere and makes those remaining feel stigmatized and less willing to report victimization to the police. It also encourages potential offenders to commit crime, as they feel the residents "are so indifferent to what goes on in their neighborhood that they will not be motivated to confront strangers, intervene in a crime, or call the police" (Sampson 1995:208). Dilapidation also decreases the odds that children will come to respect the need to obey laws and other social norms. With this evidence in mind, efforts that successfully clean up neighborhoods might reduce crime.

7. *Change male socialization practices so that notions of masculinity move away from violence and other criminogenic attitudes and values.* While we're not likely to change masculinity overnight, it is possible for parents to begin to raise their boys according to a different value system. Parents who try to do this, of course, inevitably face the countervailing influences of violent toy advertising, of violent TV shows and movies, and of their sons' friends raised according to traditional masculine values. Despite these influences, parents' socialization practices do make a difference, and to the extent that they begin to raise their boys away from traditional masculine emphases on violence and economic success, crime will be reduced.

◀ *To the extent that we begin to raise our boys away from the traditional masculine emphasis on violence, violent crime will be reduced.*

8. *Undertake social policies to reduce social and economic inequality between women and men.* To the extent that rape and battering arise from women's economic and social subordination, reducing gender inequality should reduce these crimes. A complete discussion of policies addressing gender inequality is beyond our scope but would include, at a minimum, reducing the gender gap in wages and salaries and increasing career opportunities for women.

Developmental Crime Prevention (Secondary Prevention)

A secondary prevention approach recognizes that serious crime is disproportionately committed by a small group of chronic offenders whose antisocial behavior began before adolescence. They tend to come from economically deprived, dysfunctional families characterized by parents whose relationship with each other and with their children is hostile rather than harmonious; by fathers (and stepfathers and boyfriends) who physically abuse mothers; by parents whose discipline of their children is either too permissive or too coercive; by parents who routinely spank and even physically and/or sexually abuse their children; and by parents with histories of criminality and of alcohol or other drug abuse (Loeber and Farrington 1998). These offenders likely attended run-down, dysfunctional schools with overcrowded classrooms and outmoded books and equipment, and more often than not they got poor grades in these schools and were uninvolved in school activities.

A secondary prevention approach thus recognizes that the seeds of juvenile delinquency and adult crime are planted long before delinquency and crime appear, and that it is absolutely essential to focus prevention efforts on developmental experiences in early childhood that set the stage for later offending. As James Q. Wilson (1995:493), observes, "Prevention, if it can be made to work at all, must start very early in life, perhaps as early as the first two or three years, and given the odds it faces ... be massive in scope."

If we could again wave a magic wand, we would reduce crime by immediately transforming dysfunctional families into the kind advocated by Dr. Benjamin Spock in his classic book, *Baby and Child Care*. We would have parents who treated each other and their children with loving respect; who did not abuse alcohol or other drugs; who supervised their children's behavior, and especially their sons' behavior, carefully without being overbearing; and who disciplined their children firmly but fairly, and with little or no spanking and certainly no physical or sexual abuse. If we could wave a magic wand, we would also immediately transform our schools, especially those in poor, urban communities, into better places of learning.

Although once again we have no magic wand, there are still several practical policies that could help our parents and our schools do a better job of keeping our children from developing antisocial and then delinquent and criminal tendencies (Greenwood 1995; Loeber and Farrington 1998; Sherman et al. 1998). These policies include the following:

9. *Establish well-funded, early childhood intervention programs for high-risk children and their families.* These critical programs should target multiple risk factors and should involve, among other things, preschool education, home visits, and parenting training. A growing amount of evidence indicates that intensive early intervention programs of this nature can reduce later delinquency and other behavioral problems.

10. *Provide affordable, high-quality child care for all parents who need it to work outside the home and flexible work schedules to allow parents to spend more time with children.* These two policies would enable parents to be employed and help ensure that their children have good caretaking. Currently the United States lags behind many European nations that already provide government-sponsored day care and flexible work schedules. Adoption of these policies would reduce structural (unemployment and poverty) and developmental (poor child rearing) problems that create criminality.

11. *Undertake measures to improve the nation's schools, especially in urban areas, where schools are beset by "savage inequalities" (Kozol 1991) that generate criminogenic conditions.* These schools should be thoroughly renovated and much better funded. In many areas, new schools should be built. New schools should be smaller than existing schools, and all schools should have small numbers of students in classes, with heavy involvement of community volunteers. Among other things, such measures will improve students' educational performance, strengthen their commitment to the educational process and their attachment to their teachers, and encourage them to become more involved in school activities. All these achievements should in turn lower their risk for delinquency and later criminality.

12. *Provide prenatal and postnatal nutrition and other health-related services.* To the extent that poor prenatal and postnatal nutrition and other health problems impair children's neurological functioning, their chances increase for antisocial and thus later criminal behavior. U.S. prenatal and postnatal programs are currently inadequate, leaving many poor children at risk for neurological impairment.

13. *Expand the network of battered women's shelters and rape crisis centers.* These establishments have provided an invaluable service for women beaten and/or raped by husbands, boyfriends, and former husbands and boyfriends. However, their numbers and resources are currently inadequate to meet the needs of the millions of women battered or raped each year. Expanding the network of shelters and centers would not only help protect these women from additional abuse but also reduce the likelihood that any children they might have will grow up in violent households.

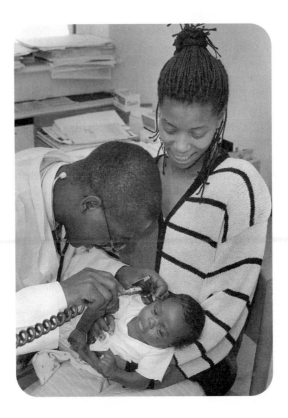

◀ *A developmental focus on early child-hood risk factors will help reduce delinquency and later crime. In this regard, it is essential that we expand prenatal and postnatal nutrition and other health services.*

Criminal Justice Approaches (Tertiary Prevention)

A tertiary approach to crime prevention that is grounded in sociological criminology recognizes the "limits of the criminal sanction," to use Herbert Packer's (1968) famous term. It acknowledges that little if any crime reduction can be achieved by relying on law and criminal justice, and that any crime reduction that can be achieved comes only at a great cost of dollars and threats to civil liberties and civil rights. At the same time, it recognizes that crime is a serious problem and that the public must be kept safe from dangerous offenders. Several of the following criminal justice-based proposals would help make society safer at lower financial, social, and political costs than are true of current strategies. Others might not affect crime rates but at least would raise public trust and confidence in criminal justice and have it operate more in line with democratic ideals.

14. *Reduce reliance on imprisonment and put more emphasis on community corrections.* This model is used by many European nations. The surge in U.S. imprisonment since 1980 has accomplished little but cost us much. Reducing reliance on imprisonment would free up significant dollars for community corrections approaches. There is increasing evidence that these approaches save money, do not lead to more recidivism than imprisonment, and might even lead to less recidivism if they are properly funded and staffed (Palmer 1992). Greater use of these programs would thus save money and keep society at least as safe as, and perhaps a bit safer than, imprisonment. Probation and parole officers should have much smaller caseloads to permit more intensive supervision of offenders released into the community.

Offenders considered for community corrections should be nonviolent drug and property offenders. Nationally, about 25 percent of state prisoners and over 50 percent of federal prisoners, have been convicted of drug offenses, most of them for sale or possession of small amounts of drugs. About one-third of all new prison admissions each year are for nonviolent property offenses such as burglary, larceny, and motor vehicle theft. Many and probably most of these drug and property offenders could be placed into community corrections (without threatening public safety) at a savings of several billion dollars per year, even after paying for their community corrections costs. The dollars saved could be used for employment, early family intervention, or other policies that would reduce crime. For example, the money saved for each offender going into community corrections could fund one preschool teacher who could be involved with five to ten children at high risk for developmental problems. Reducing reliance on imprisonment would also mean that new prison construction could stop, saving tens of billions of dollars in future construction and maintenance costs. These funds could also be reallocated to primary and secondary crime prevention programs.

15. *Prisons and jails should be smaller, overcrowding should be reduced, and other decrepit prison and jail conditions should be improved.* Despite popular belief, conditions in many prisons and jails are substandard (Kappeler, Blumberg, and Potter 2000). Current prison conditions do little to rehabilitate offenders and often make them worse. At a minimum, improving prisons would help reduce the extent to which offenders worsen because of their prison experience—and thus contribute to a safer society. This reform should include the establishment of much better educational, vocational, and other rehabilitation programs in prisons. Despite questions about these programs' effectiveness, they at least appear to work for less serious offenders and would be even more effective were they adequately funded (Johnson 1996; Palmer 1992).

16. *Eliminate "three strikes and you're out" and mandatory imprisonment policies.* These policies have swelled our prisons without lowering the crime rate. Given that criminality declines sharply with advancing age, people sent to prison for life after a third felony stay in prison for many more years after they would have stopped committing crime. In general, many prison terms could be shortened, saving prison costs and reducing prison overcrowding, without endangering public safety (Irwin and Austin 1997).

17. *Consider repealing at least some of the present drug laws.* These laws might do more harm than good, they have unfairly targeted the African-American community, and they have cost billions of dollars in criminal justice expenses. The billions of dollars saved could be redirected to educational and treatment programs designed to prevent drug use from beginning and to halt drug use that has already started. Because of the very legitimate concerns raised by both proponents and opponents of drug decriminalization, a national debate must begin on what drug policies make the most sense.

18. *Eliminate the death penalty.* The death penalty has no general deterrent effect and costs two to three times as much as life imprisonment. It continues to be arbitrary and discriminatory in its application and to put at least some innocent people at risk for death. Philosophically and ethically, serious questions can be raised about the morality of capital punishment in a society that professes to be civilized.

19. *Expand community policing and consider directed police activity in crime "hot spots."* Some evidence indicates that community policing and directed police activity in crime hot spots may reduce crime, and that community policing reduces fear of crime and may help improve the "incivilities" of urban neighborhoods. Because directed patrol may overburden the courts, jails, and prisons and raise civil liberties questions, such activity should be considered carefully before being undertaken.

20. *Increase the hiring of minority and female police officers and develop a "zero tolerance" policy for the hostility and discrimination they now experience from other officers.* This proposal would increase the respect of minority urban residents for the police and strengthen police–community relations. Although the crime-reduction benefit from this proposal may be minimal, a democratic society should not tolerate discrimination among its law enforcement community.

21. *Undertake measures to reduce police brutality and racial profiling.* Police departments should develop zero tolerance for such behaviors and take every step possible to identify and remove the officers responsible for them. Again, these measures might not reduce crime but would at least protect the public from police misconduct and reduce citizen disrespect for and hostility toward the police.

22. *Increase gun control efforts.* The huge number of handguns in the United States is an important reason for our high number of homicides. If we could wave a magic wand and make our handguns disappear, our homicide rates would drop significantly. Without a magic wand, however, there are far too many handguns, and far too many people who want handguns, for these weapons to be eliminated entirely. Given these facts, the best we can do is to undertake policies that limit the supply of handguns for law-abiding citizens and offenders alike, especially youths, and that decrease the chances of gun accidents. Philip J. Cook and Mark H. Moore (1995) discuss several such policies, including (a) heavily taxing guns and ammunition to make them too expensive for at least some people, and especially adolescents, to buy; (b) substantially raising the licensing fee for gun dealers, to reduce their number; (c) requiring that new guns include safety measures to reduce accidental use; (d) increasing community policing to reduce fear of crime and hence citizens' perceptions that they need handguns for protection; and (e) removing guns from homes where domestic violence occurs.

23. *Increase intolerance for white-collar crime and for political corruption.* This will be no easy task. As David O. Friedrichs (1996:357) observes, "It is surely foolish and naive to harbor the illusion that there is an easy solution to the problem of white-collar crime." The same could be said for political corruption. Even so, several policies might help limit white-collar crime and political corruption, including greater media attention to the harm of such crime; the greater expenditure of resources on preventing, detecting, and enforcing current laws; and the development of new laws. More certain punishment, especially imprisonment, for white-collar and governmental offenders might also work. While this "get tough" approach has not been shown to work with common criminals, it may have more of a deterrent effect on potential white-collar and governmental offenders (Friedrichs 1996; Simon 1999). Unfortunately, given the nature of white-collar and government crime, this set of proposals might amount to the fox guarding the chicken coop.

We now stand at a crossroads. Although the economy thrived and crime rates declined during most of the 1990s, conditions for the U.S. poor have not improved and in fact have even worsened. The number of people in the crime-prone 15–25 age group has begun to rise as the baby boom's children come of age. In the meantime, the federal and state governments have implemented huge cutbacks in social services to the poor, whose children will thus be at greater risk for delinquency and later criminality than they already are. Hunger in the United States has been increasing (Revkin 1999). All these changes and actions are setting the stage for an eventual increase in crime. If the United States wanted to ensure that crime would increase, it would do exactly what it has been doing in regard to the poor among us.

Elliott Currie (1985:278) observes that if we intentionally designed a society to be especially violent, it would look much like the one we now have. It would be a society with high rates of inequality and unemployment among the young, which deprives them of participation in community life. It would be a society that allows thousands of jobs to leave whole communities, disrupting their social organization and forcing people to migrate in search of new jobs. It would be a society that promotes "a culture of intense interpersonal competition" and emphasizes material consumption to the degree that many people violate the law to reach this level while others experience anger and frustration over their inability to live up to this lofty standard.

In the same vein, Jeffrey Reiman (1998) notes that if we wanted for some reason to design a criminal justice system that would certainly fail, it would also look very much like the one we now have. It would be a system that bans many consensual behaviors and forces people committed to those behaviors to engage in other types of crime. It would also be a system where arrest, prosecution, and punishment are somewhat arbitrary, and where wealthy individuals and organizations committing quite harmful behaviors generally avoid legal sanctions. Both sets of dynamics, Reiman says, lead to resentment among the relative few who end up under the control of criminal justice officials. Next, it would be a system where the prison experience is more likely to make inmates worse than better, and a system where prisoners learn no marketable skills in prison and have no jobs awaiting them when they leave prison. Finally, it would be a system where ex-offenders are shunned by conventional society, lose their right to vote, can't find work, and otherwise are prevented from reintegrating themselves into the conventional social order.

We live in a society whose fundamental structural and cultural features contribute heavily to our high crime rates. We would also admit that we know that the criminal justice system is not working, and cannot be made to work, to reduce crime. If we are serious about reducing crime, we will undertake some or all of the preventive measures just listed. They may not all succeed, but we certainly cannot do much worse than we have been doing. Dickens, Dostoyevsky, and other great writers remind us that how we treat the poor and the criminals among us is a sign of what kind of a people we are. If we are to be true to our democratic, egalitarian ideals, we must attack the social roots of the crime and victimization that plague us so. Anything else would betray the noble principles on which our nation was founded.

 ## SUMMARY AND CONCLUSION

This chapter has proposed several measures that hold at least some promise for reducing rates of many types of criminal behaviors. The basis for all the proposals is a vast body of research, discussed in earlier chapters, on the structural and cultural causes of crime and victimization.

Back in Chapter 1, I mentioned that one of my key goals was to develop your sociological imagination about crime. I hope I have succeeded. A sociological criminology tells us much about the society in which we live. As C. Wright Mills (1959) observed, the knowledge that the sociological imagination gives us is both terrible and magnificent. Your new sociological imagination about crime may be terrible for indicating the power of the social forces underlying crime and victimization. But I hope it is also magnificent for pointing you to the possibility of changing these forces so that we can, at long last, have a safer society.

KEY TERMS

criminal justice approach

criminal justice funnel

developmental factors

early childhood intervention

primary prevention

public health model

secondary prevention

tertiary prevention

STUDY QUESTIONS

1. About what percent of all serious crime victimizations end up with someone going to prison or jail? How does this criminal justice funnel help us understand what might work or not work to reduce the crime rate?

2. What are any three primary prevention measures that might reduce the crime rate?

3. What are any three secondary prevention measures that might reduce the crime rate?

4. What are any three tertiary prevention measures that might reduce the crime rate?

INTERNET EXERCISES

An excellent report on preventing crime is "Preventing Crime: What Works, What Doesn't, What's Promising," prepared by a team of researchers at the University of Maryland with federal funding. You can access the report at **http://www.preventingcrime.org**. Find the link to the "brief" version of the report and click on it. The report will appear in Adobe Acrobat format.

Go to Page 6 to begin reading about "what works." According to the report, what are two family-related programs that "work" to reduce crime? What are two school-related programs that work? What labor market program works? Now find a list of various programs that don't appear to work. What are any two of these programs?

Read through the rest of the report. Drawing on this report and on what you've learned from your criminology course and from this textbook, what are the five most effective steps that our society could take to prevent and reduce crime in the United States?

GLOSSARY

abnormality an abnormal biological or psychological condition said to be responsible for criminal behavior.

actus reus the actual criminal act of which a defendant is accused.

adversary system the idealized model of the criminal justice process in the United States in which the prosecutor and defense attorney vigorously contest the evidence concerning the defendant's guilt or innocence.

agents provocateurs government agents who pretend to join a dissident group and then try to goad the group into committing violence or other illegal activity.

alien conspiracy model the belief that a small number of Italian-American "families" control organized crime in the United States.

amateur theft property crime committed by unskilled offenders who act when the opportunity arises.

American dream the belief that common people in the United States can become wealthy by working hard.

anomie as developed by Emile Durkheim, a state of normlessness in society in which aspirations that previously were controlled now become unlimited. Robert Merton adapted this term to refer to the gap between the institutionalized goal in the United States of financial success and institutionalized means of working.

arbitrariness refers to the process occurring when legal outcomes are based on prejudice or other nonlegal criteria instead of legal factors such as the seriousness of the crime and the strength of the evidence.

aspirations strong desires or longings. As used in extensions of Merton's anomie theory, aspirations refer to economic and other goals of adolescents that result in frustration when they are not realized.

assault an unlawful attack by one person upon another to inflict bodily injury. Aggravated assault involves a serious injury or the use of a weapon. Simple assault involves only minor injuries and no use of a weapon.

atavism the belief, popularized by Cesare Lombroso, that criminals are born as throwbacks to an earlier stage of evolution.

attachment in Travis Hirschi's social control theory, the degree to which adolescents care about the opinions of conventional others, including parents and teachers, and feel close to them. The greater the attachment, the less the delinquency.

battering physical assaults and other physical abuse committed against a woman by a male intimate.

booster skilled, professional shoplifters who sell their stolen goods to fences or pawn shops.

bourgeoisie as used by Karl Marx and Friedrich Engels, the class in capitalist society that controls the means of production.

bribery the giving or accepting of money or other things of value in return for promises to grant favors to the party giving the bribe.

brothel a house of prostitution.

brutality as a form of police misconduct, the undue or excessive use by police of physical coercion to subdue a suspect or other citizen.

brutalization effect refers to the possibility that executions increase the homicide rate.

caseloads the workload of prosecutors, defense attorneys, and judges.

casino a building used for gambling.

causal order the direction of the relationship between two variables.

child abuse physical violence or sexual misconduct committed against children by their parents or other adults.

chronic offenders a small number of offenders who commit a disproportionate amount of serious crime and delinquency and who persist in their criminality.

civil disobedience the violation of criminal law for reasons of conscience.

classical school a school of thought popular in the eighteenth century in Europe. Its main assumptions were that criminals act rationally and that the severity of legal punishment should be restricted to the degree necessary to deter crime.

climatological as used in discussing the patterning of crime, refers to the variation of crime rates with climate and seasons of the year.

COINTELPRO a secret FBI program, aimed at disrupting and discrediting dissident groups and individuals, that reached its zenith during the 1960s and early 1970s.

collective embezzlement the stealing of company funds by top management. The term was first used to refer to one type of crime that characterized the U.S. savings and loan scandals of the 1980s.

common law the system of law originating in medieval England and emphasizing court decisions and customs.

community policing a style of policing in which police patrol neighborhoods on foot and try to help their residents solve community problems.

concentric zones the division of cities into geographical sectors radiating out from the city's center.

concordance a similarity of criminal behavior and other outcomes between identical twins.

conflict as used in sociology and criminology, refers to a theory that assumes that people disagree on norms and act with self-interest because of their disparate socioeconomic positions.

consensus as used in sociology and criminology, refers to a theory that people agree on norms despite their disparate socioeconomic positions.

constable an official appointed by medieval English nobles to control poaching and otherwise monitor the behavior of people living on the nobles' land.

containment as used in criminology, refers to a theory developed by Walter C. Reckless that stressed the inner and outer conditions that help prevent juvenile delinquency.

conventional social institution structured patterns of behavior and relationships, such as the family, the educational system, and religion.

corporate violence activities or neglect by corporations that lead to injury, illness, or death.

correctional supervision placement in prison, jail, or on probation or parole.

corruption dishonest practices, especially when committed by public or corporate officials.

courtroom workgroup the "team" of prosecutor, defense attorney, and judge, all of whom are said to cooperate to expedite cases.

crackdown the short-term concentration of police resources in a specific neighborhood, usually to control a specific activity, such as drug possession and trafficking.

crime characteristics aspects of a crime such as its location and the typical victim-offender relationship.

crime control the use of the criminal justice system to prevent and punish crime. The "crime control model" refers to the belief that crime control is the primary goal of the criminal justice system.

crime myth a widespread but inaccurate belief about crime.

crime victim any person who unwillingly suffers a completed or attempted crime.

crime wave a sudden and often distorted focus of the news media on one or more types of criminal behavior.

criminal careers the continuation of criminal behavior past adolescence and young adulthood.

criminal intent having the desire to commit a crime.

criminalization the process by which lawful behaviors are turned into criminal ones because of the enactment of new laws.

criminal justice approach the use of the criminal justice system as the primary means to reduce and prevent criminal behavior.

criminal justice funnel the rapid drop from the number of actual crimes committed to the number of offenders incarcerated.

criminogenic crime-causing.

critical perspectives views that challenge traditional understandings and theories of crime and criminal justice.

cultural myths as used in criminology, refers to false beliefs in society that make crimes such as rape and battering more likely.

culture conflict the clash of values and norms between different social groups, especially as it leads the behavior of one group to be branded as criminal.

debunking motif part of the sociological perspective, refers to the challenge sociology poses to conventional understandings of social institutions and social reality.

decision-making processes the ways in which judges and prosecutors determine what happens at various stages of the criminal justice system.

delinquent peers   lawbreaking adolescents with whom a particular adolescent associates.

democratic society   a society in which the people freely elect officials to represent their views and interests and in which they are free from arbitrary government power.

democratic theory   the view that elected officials are to represent the interests of all people in a democracy.

demographic variation   the patterning of criminal behavior according to variables such as age, class, gender, race, and location.

dependent variable   an attitude or behavior that changes because of the influence of an independent variable.

deterrence   in criminology, having a deterrent effect on crime.

deterrence theory   the belief that the threat or application of legal punishment prevents criminal behavior.

developmental factors   aspects of childhood and adolescence that affect the likelihood of crime.

deviance amplification   the process by which official labeling increases the likelihood of deviant behavior.

differential association   Edwin Sutherland's concept for the process by which adolescents become delinquent because they are exposed to more law-breaking attitudes than to law-abiding attitudes.

differential opportunities   conditions or situations that are more or less favorable for the commission of crime.

discordance   a difference in criminal behavior and other outcomes between identical twins.

discretion   latitude in decision-making.

discrimination   treating people committing similar crimes differently because of their race, ethnicity, gender, social class, age, etc.

double burden   the difficulties faced by minority female police officers because of their race and gender.

dowry deaths   murders of women in India and Pakistan because their families could not pay the expected dowry.

dramatization of evil   the process by which deviant labels affect self-images and promote continued deviance.

drift   refers to the intermittent commission of delinquency.

due process   rights granted to criminal defendants by the U.S. Constitution and judicial rulings.

duress   threats or coercion on another to commit a crime.

early childhood intervention   the undertaking of programs in infancy or early childhood to prevent antisocial behavior and other developmental problems.

economic deprivation   poverty and economic inequality.

ego   Sigmund Freud's term for the rational dimension of the personality that develops after the id.

embezzlement   the stealing or misappropriation of funds entrusted to an employee.

encounter   any interaction between a police officer and a citizen.

Enlightenment   an intellectual movement in the seventeenth and eighteenth centuries that challenged medieval religious beliefs.

erotica   written or visual materials dealing with sexual behavior and often intended to arouse sexual desire.

espionage   spying.

exclusionary rule   prohibits evidence from criminal trials that was gathered in violation of judicial rulings and other procedural rules governing the gathering of evidence.

extralegal   refers to race, ethnicity, gender, social class, and other nonlegal factors that may affect arrest, sentencing, and other legal decision-making.

family interaction   behavior and functioning within a family.

family structure   the nature and pattern of statuses in a family.

fear of crime   concern or worry over becoming a crime victim.

felony   a serious criminal offense punishable by a prison term of more than one year.

femicide   the murder of women and girls.

feminism   the belief that women deserve to be men's equals in economic, political, and social power.

fencing   the selling of stolen goods.

focal concerns   Walter Miller's term for beliefs and values said to be characteristic of lower-class males that increase their likelihood of delinquency

forbidden fruit   an attractive but prohibited object or behavior. In the drug legalization debate, the term is used to imply that the illegality of drugs may attract people, and especially adolescents, to use them.

generalize   to apply knowledge of particular cases to other, similar cases.

genital mutilation   the excision of a clitoris.

genocide   the systematic extermination of a category of people because of their race, ethnicity, or religion.

goods   objects the public desires to obtain, several of which are provided by organized crime.

grass-eaters   police who engage in minor bribery and other corruption.

handgun control   efforts to restrict the supply and ownership of handguns.

hate crime   violent or property crimes committed against the person or property of someone because of that person's race, ethnicity, religion, national origin, or sexual orientation.

heredity the genetic transmission of physical characteristics, behavior, and other traits.

homicide the unjustified killing of a human being.

id Sigmund Freud's term for the instinctive, pleasure-seeking dimension of the personality that characterizes infancy.

incapacitation physically preventing a convicted offender from committing a crime; usually refers to incarceration.

incarceration the placing of a convicted offender in prison or jail.

independent variable a sociodemographic characteristic or other trait that influences changes in a dependent variable.

individual characteristics personal traits that influence the likelihood of committing a crime or becoming a crime victim.

inequality the difference in income and wealth between the wealthy and the poor.

in/out decision the determination of whether a convicted offender should be incarcerated.

international comparisons cross-national comparisons of crime rates.

interpersonal violence physically injurious acts committed by one or more people against one or more others.

interracial between two or more races.

intraracial within one race.

IQ intelligence as measured by standardized tests.

Iran-Contra scandal a scandal in the 1980s involving the illegal sale of weapons to Iran and the diverting of funds from that sale to "Contra" rebels in Nicaragua.

joyriding the temporary stealing of a car or other motor vehicle in order to drive or ride in it for thrills.

kinds of people refers to the characteristics of individuals that generate criminality.

kinds of places refers to the structural and physical characteristics of neighborhoods and other locations that generate criminality.

labeling defining a person or behavior as deviant.

learning acquiring attitudes, knowledge, and skills; in criminology, a process by which people become criminals.

left realism an approach to crime developed by radical criminologists in Great Britain; it emphasizes the harm that crime causes and the need to take measures to reduce crime.

legalization the elimination of laws prohibiting certain behaviors, especially public order crimes.

liberation hypothesis the view that racial discrimination in sentencing is more likely for defendants convicted of minor offenses than of serious offenses.

life events changes in one's life that increase or decrease the chances of offending.

lifestyle theory the belief that certain leisure-time and other activities increase the chances of becoming a crime victim.

mala in se refers to behaviors that are wrong in and of themselves.

mala prohibita refers to behaviors that are wrong only because they are prohibited by law.

male dominance the supremacy of men in society.

manslaughter an unjustified killing considered less serious or less blameworthy than murder.

Marxism a set of beliefs derived from the work of Karl Marx and Friedrich Engels that emphasizes the conflict of interests between people based on whether they own the means of production.

masculinity the set of attitudes, values, and behaviors associated with being a male.

mass media modes of communication, such as television, radio, and newspapers.

measurement in criminology, the determination of the frequency of criminal behavior and of the characteristics of offenders and victims.

meat-eaters police who engage in serious forms of corruption.

mens rea a guilty mind; refers to an individual having criminal intent.

misdemeanor a relatively minor criminal offense punishable by less than one year in prison.

moral crusade a concerted effort to prevent and punish behavior considered immoral.

moral development the process by which children and adolescents develop their sense of morality.

morality ethical or virtuous conduct.

more harm than good refers in the drug legalization debate to whether drug laws result in more disadvantages than in more advantages.

muckrakers a group of early twentieth-century U.S. journalists and other social critics of political and corporate corruption and other misconduct.

National Crime Victimization Survey an annual survey of criminal victimization sponsored by the U.S. Department of Justice.

neurotransmitter chemical substances that help neurons transmit impulses to each other across synapses.

news media the members of the mass media transmitting information about current events.

nonviolent pornography sexually explicit materials that do not involve violent acts.

occupational crime crime committed in the course of one's occupation.

organizational crime crime committed on behalf of an organization.

overdramatization the exaggeration by the news media of the frequency and seriousness of violent crime.

patriarchy male supremacy.

patterning the social distribution of criminal behavior according to certain characteristics of locations and of individuals.

peacemaking criminology an approach that combines several humanistic strains of thought to view crime as just one of the many forms of suffering that characterize human existence.

personality aspects of an individual's character, behavior, and other qualities.

phrenology the belief that the size and shape of the skull indicates the propensity for criminal behavior.

pilferage employee theft of workplace items, usually of small value.

piracy robbery at sea.

plea bargaining negotiations between prosecution and defense over the sentence the prosecutor will request in return for a plea of guilty by the defendant.

police sexual violence (PSV) violence committed by police against female suspects or other female civilians.

political trial criminal trials of defendants accused of committing crimes against government.

political violence interpersonal violence committed to achieve a political goal.

politics of victimization refers to the ideological implications of government efforts to help victims of street crime.

positivism the view that human behavior and attitudes are influenced by forces both external and internal to the individual.

premenstrual syndrome symptoms such as severe tension and irritability occurring in the premenstrual phase.

price-fixing the practice where businesses conspire to fix prices on goods and services rather than let the free market operate.

primary deviation the first deviant act that someone commits; in labeling theory, primary deviation is said not to lead often to continued or secondary deviation unless labeling occurs

primary prevention efforts to prevent problems such as disease, injury, or crime by focusing on aspects of the social or physical environment that contribute to these problems.

private troubles individual problems that many people have that they think stem from their own failings or particular circumstances.

professional fraud fraud committed by physicians, attorneys, and other professional workers.

professional theft property crime committed by skilled offenders who carefully plan their offenses.

proletariat as used by Karl Marx and Friedrich Engels, the class in capitalist society that does not control the means of production.

property crime theft and other crime committed against property.

psychoanalytic refers to explanations of human motivation and behavior that derive from the work of Sigmund Freud.

psychological consequences mental and emotional effects; in criminology, particularly from criminal victimization.

public health model an approach to illness, injury, and other problems that emphasizes primary prevention.

public issues social problems resulting from structural and other problems in the social environment.

public opinion the views and attitudes of the public on important social, political, and economic issues.

public policy government efforts to deal with public issues and other societal needs.

racial prejudice unfavorable views toward a certain category of people because of their race.

rape forced or nonconsensual sexual intercourse.

rational choice theory the view that people plan their actions and weigh the potential benefits and costs of their potential behavior.

rationalization a justification or technique of neutralization that minimizes the guilt that criminal offenders may otherwise feel.

reinforcement the rewarding of behavior; a key concept in differential reinforcement theory, which says that criminal behavior and attitudes are more likely to be learned when they are reinforced by friends and/or family.

relative deprivation the feeling that one is less well-off than others.

relativist definition labeling theory's view that deviance is not a property of a behavior, but is rather the result of how others regard that behavior.

religious fundamentalism the belief that the Bible is the actual word of God.

repression government suppression of dissent through violent or legal means.

repressive law Emile Durkheim's term for the punitive type of legal punishment that he thought characterizes traditional societies.

restitutive law Emile Durkheim's term for the compensatory type of legal punishment that he thought characterizes modern societies.

restraint of trade business practices that violate free market principles.

robbery taking or attempting to take something from one or more other people by force or threat of force.

routine activities theory the view that an individual's daily activities can affect his or her chances of becoming a crime victim.

ruling class the capitalist class or bourgeoisie.

seasonal of or relating to the seasons of the year; some crime rates vary from season to season and are thus said to be seasonal.

secondary deviation continued deviance; said by labeling theory to result from the labeling of primary deviance.

secondary prevention the identification of practices and situations that put certain individuals at risk for illness, injury, or criminality, and efforts to address these risk factors.

self-control the restraining of one's impulses and desires.

self-defense violent or other actions committed to protect oneself or others.

self-referral a physician's referral of patients to medical testing laboratories which the physician owns or in which the physician has invested.

self-report studies surveys in which respondents are asked to report about criminal offenses they have committed.

sentencing preferences public views of appropriate legal punishment for given crimes.

seriousness of crime opinions regarding the importance or degree of harm associated with given crimes.

services the performance of activities that the public desires, several of which are provided by organized crime.

sexual assault nonconsensual or forced sexual contact that does not involve sexual intercourse.

shaming social disapproval.

sin a morally improper act.

sneaky thrill crimes offenses committed for the excitement.

snitch an amateur shoplifter.

social bond the connection among individuals or between individuals and social institutions such as families and schools.

social control society's restraint of norm-violating behavior.

social disorganization the breakdown of social bonds and social control in a community or larger society.

social ecology the relationship of people to their environment; in criminology, the study of the influence of community social and physical characteristics on community crime rates.

social inequality the differential distribution of wealth, power, and other things of value in a given society.

social integration the degree to which a community or society is characterized by strong or weak social bonds.

socialization the learning of social norms, attitudes, and values.

social learning the view that individuals learn criminal attitudes and behaviors from others who already hold these attitudes and behaviors.

social organization the pattern of relationships and roles in a society.

social pathology the view that crime and deviance are symptoms of individual and societal sickness.

social structure the pattern of social interaction and social relationships in a group or society; horizontal social structure refers to the social and physical characteristics of communities and the networks of social relationships to which an individual belongs, while vertical social structure refers to social inequality.

social ties social bonds.

sociological criminology the sociological understanding of crime and criminal justice, stressing the importance of social structure and social inequality.

sociological imagination the ability to attribute private troubles to problems in the larger social structure.

sociological perspective the belief that social backgrounds influence individuals' attitudes and behaviors.

somatology the belief that body size and shape influences criminality.

spurious refers to a statistical relationship between two variables that exists only because the effects of a third variable have not been considered.

state-corporate crime cooperation between government agencies and corporations to commit illegal or socially injurious activities.

state terrorism government rule by terror.

status frustration disappointment and feelings of dissatisfaction resulting from the failure to do well in school; said by Albert Cohen to lead to delinquency among lower-class boys.

strain anomie or frustration, stemming from the failure to achieve goals.

structural factors aspects of the social structure.

subculture ways of thinking, feeling, and acting in a given society that are different from those of the larger society.

subculture of violence a set of attitudes, said to characterize poor urban communities, that approve the use of violence to deal with interpersonal problems and disputes.

superego Sigmund Freud's term for the dimension of the personality that develops after the id and ego; this dimension represents society's moral code.

support system the network of tipsters and fences that help burglars carry out their burglaries and dispose of their stolen goods.

surveys questionnaires administered to a set of respondents.

tabula rasa blank slate; refers to the belief that human nature is neutral and can become good or bad because of society's influence.

target hardening efforts to make homes, stores, and other buildings less vulnerable to burglary and other crimes.

technicalities term, often pejorative, used for the rules governing the gathering of evidence against a criminal suspect.

temperament personality.

terrorism the indiscriminate use of violence to intimidate or coerce people in order to achieve social and political goals.

tertiary prevention efforts to treat people already having a problem, such as illness or injury; in criminology, refers to efforts to deal with people who have already committed a crime.

testosterone the so-called male hormone.

theoretical integration the combining of two or more theories to present a more comprehensive explanation of crime.

treason actions designed to overthrow one's government or otherwise weaken it severely.

underclass the group of people living in persistent poverty and unemployment.

underreporting the failure of crime victims to report crimes they've suffered or of respondents in self-report surveys to report crimes they've committed.

Uniform Crime Reports the FBI's annual compilation of crime statistics.

victim-impact statement a written statement by a crime victim that discusses the effects of the victimization and sometimes makes recommendations for sentencing.

victimization the suffering of a crime.

victim-offender relationship refers to whether the victim or offender knew each other before the victimization occurred.

victimology the study of victims and victimization.

victim precipitation activities by an eventual crime victim that initiate or further the events leading to the victim's victimization.

violent crime interpersonal violence, especially homicide, rape, assault, and robbery.

violent pornography sexually explicit materials that depict violence.

Watergate scandal the scandal in the early 1970s that involved illegal activity committed during the 1972 presidential campaign and the subsequent obstruction of justice; the scandal led to several criminal prosecutions and the resignation of President Richard Nixon.

working personality the personality associated with a particular occupation.

wrongful execution an execution of someone who in fact was innocent of the crime for which he or she was convicted.

zero-tolerance policing a style of aggressive policing that calls for making arrests for even minor infractions of the law.

REFERENCES

Abadinsky, Howard. 2000. *Organized Crime*. Belmont, CA: Wadsworth.

Abrams, Robert. 1989. "Protecting Consumers: Unsafe Products Maim and Kill." *Journal of State Government* 62:104–106.

Abramsky, Sasha. 1999. "When They Get Out." *The Atlantic Monthly*: 30–36.

Adams, James. 1995. *Sellout: Aldrich Ames and the Corruption of the CIA*. New York: Viking Press.

Adams, Kenneth and Charles R. Cutshall. 1987. "Refusing to Prosecute Minor Offenses: The Relative Influence of Legal and Extralegal Factors." *Justice Quarterly* 4:595–609.

Adams, Kenneth, Geoffrey P. Alpert, Roger G. Dunham, Joel H. Garner, Lawrence A. Greenfeld, Mark A. Henriquez, Patrick A. Langan, Christopher D. Maxwell, and Steven K. Smith. 1999. *Use of Force by Police: Overview of National and Local Data*. Washington, D.C.: U.S. Department of Justice, National Institute of Justice.

Adler, Freda. 1975. *Sisters in Crime: The Rise of the New Female Criminal*. New York: McGraw-Hill.

Adler, Freda. 1983. *Nations Not Obsessed with Crime*. Littleton, CO: Fred B. Rothman.

Adler, Freda and William S. Laufer, eds. 1995. *The Legacy of Anomie Theory*. New Brunswick, NJ: Transaction.

Adler, Jeffrey S. 1989. "A Historical Analysis of the Law of Vagrancy." *Criminology* 27:209–229.

Adler, Jeffrey S. 1994. "The Dynamite, Wreckage, and Scum in Our Cities: The Social Construction of Deviance in Industrial America." *Justice Quarterly* 11:33–49.

Agnew, Robert. 1985. "Social Control Theory and Delinquency: A Longitudinal Test." *Criminology* 23:47–62.

Agnew, Robert. 1991. "The Interactive Effects of Peer Variables on Delinquency." *Criminology* 29:47–72.

Agnew, Robert. 1992. "Foundation for a General Strain Theory of Crime and Delinquency." *Criminology* 30:47–87.

Agnew, Robert. 1994. "Delinquency and the Desire for Money." *Justice Quarterly* 11:411–427.

Agnew, Robert. 1994. "The Techniques of Neutralization and Violence." *Criminology* 32:555–580.

Agnew, Robert. 2000. "Sources of Criminality: Strain and Subcultural Theories." Pp. 349–371 in *Criminology: A Contemporary Handbook*, edited by Joseph F. Sheley. Belmont, CA: Wadsworth.

Agnew, Robert and D. M. Petersen. 1989. "Leisure and Delinquency." *Social Problems* 36:332–350.

Agnew, Robert and Helene Raskin White. 1992. "An Empirical Test of General Strain Theory." *Criminology* 30:475–499.

Agnew, Robert, Francis T. Cullen, Velmer S. Burton, Jr., T. David Evans, and R. Gregory Dunaway. 1996. "A New Test of Classic Strain Theory." *Justice Quarterly* 13:681–704.

Akers, Ronald L. 1968. "Problems in the Sociology of Deviance: Social Definitions and Behavior." *Social Forces* 46:455–465.

Akers, Ronald L. 1977. *Deviant Behavior: A Social Learning Perspective*. Belmont, CA: Wadsworth.

Akers, Ronald L. 1989. "A Social Behaviorist's Perspective on Integration of Theories of Crime and Deviance." Pp. 23–36 in *Theoretical Integration in the Study of Deviance and Crime: Problems and Prospects*, edited by Steven F. Messner, Marvin D. Krohn, and Allen E. Liska. Albany: State University of New York Press.

Akers, Ronald L. 1991. "Self-Control as a General Theory of Crime." *Journal of Quantitative Criminology* 2:201–211.

Akers, Ronald L. 1992. "Linking Sociology and Its Specialties: The Case of Criminology." *Social Forces* 71:1–16.

Akers, Ronald L. 1997. *Criminological Theories: Introduction and Evaluation*. Los Angeles: Roxbury.

Alaimo, Don. 1990. "Coupon Fraud Said to Have Charity Ties." *Supermarket News*, May 7:48.

Albanese, Jay S. 1996. "Looking for a New Approach to an Old Problem: The Future of Obscenity and Pornography." Pp. 60–72 in *Visions for Change: Crime and Justice in the Twenty-First Century*, edited by Roslyn Muraskin and Albert R. Roberts. Upper Saddle River, NJ: Prentice Hall.

Albanese, Jay S. 2000. "The Mafia Mystique: Organized Crime." Pp. 265–285 in *Criminology: A Contemporary Handbook*, edited by Joseph F. Sheley. Belmont, CA: Wadsworth.

Alexander, P. C. and S. L. Lupfer. 1987. "Family Characteristics and Long-Term Consequences Associated with Sexual Abuse." *Archives of Sexual Behavior* 16:235–245.

Allan, Emilie and Darrel Steffensmeier. 1989. "Youth, Unemployment, and Property Crime: Differential Effects of Job Availability and Job Quality on Juvenile and Young Adult Arrest Rates." *American Sociological Review* 54:107–123.

Allison, Julie A. and Lawrence S. Wrightsman. 1993. *Rape: The Misunderstood Crime*. Thousand Oaks, CA: Sage

Alperovitz, Gar and Jeff Faux. 1984. *Rebuilding America*. New York: Pantheon.

Alter, Jonathan. 1999. "Moving beyond the Blame Game." *Newsweek*, May 17:30.

Alter, Jonathon. 2000. "A Reckoning on Death Row." *Newsweek*, July 3:31.

Ames, Walter L. 1981. *Police and Community in Japan*. Berkeley: University of California Press.

Amir, Menachem. 1971. *Patterns in Forcible Rape*. Chicago: University of Chicago Press.

Anderson, Elijah. 1999. *Code of the Street: Decency, Violence, and the Moral Life of the Inner City*. New York: W. W. Norton.

Anderson, George M. 1987. "A Prisoner for Peace." *America*, October 17:14.

Andrews, Arlene Bowers. 1990. "Crisis and Recovery Services for Family Violence Survivors." Pp. 206–232 in *Helping Crime Victims: Research, Policy, and Practice*, edited by Albert R. Roberts. Newbury Park, CA: Sage.

Andrews, D. A. and James Bonta. 1999. *The Psychology of Criminal Conduct*. Cincinnati: Anderson.

Andrews, James H. 1994. "Health-Industry Fraud Eats Up Billions Yearly." *The Christian Science Monitor*, August 4:3.

Angier, Natalie. 1996. "Variant Gene Tied to a Love of New Thrills." *New York Times*, January 2:1+.

Appel, Adrianne. 2000. "Agencies to Probe W. R. Grace." *Boston Globe*, March 1:B2.

Appel, Adrianne and Neil Swidey. 2000. "Grace Co. Fought Asbestos Label." *Boston Globe*, February 14:A1.

Apple, R. W., Jr. 1999. "Bush Implies He Has Used No Drugs in Last 25 Years." *New York Times*, August 20:A12.

Archer, Dane and Rosemary Gartner. 1984. *Violence and Crime in Cross-National Perspective*. New Haven: Yale University Press.

Armstrong, David. 1999. "U.S. Lagging on Prosecutions." *Boston Globe*, November 16:A1.

Arnold, Bruce L. and John Hagan. 1992. "Careers of Misconduct: Professional Deviance among Lawyers." *American Sociological Review* 57:771–780.

Arnold, Laurence. 1999. "Survey Finds Gambling Woes Could Affect 20 Million in U.S." *Boston Globe*, March 19:A3.

Arnson, Cynthia. 1989. *Crossroads: Congress, the Reagan Administration, and Central America*. New York: Pantheon.

Associated Press. 1994. "Homicide Rate in Young Men Studied." *Boston Globe*, October 14:23.

Associated Press. 1994. "U.S. Reports $1 Billion in Welfare Overpayments in '91." *Boston Globe*, April 12:14.

Associated Press. 1995. "Fraud on Auto Insurers Targeted." *Boston Globe*, May 25:15.

Associated Press. 1995. "Lab Settles Suit on Testing Fraud." *Boston Globe*, May 19:7.

Associated Press. 2000. "Boy, 10, Is Said to Kill Father in Frosting Rift." *Boston Globe*, March 16:A12.

Associated Press. 2000. "Worldwide Look at Violence against Women." January 20.

Auerhahn, Kathleen. 1999. "Selective Incapacitation and the Problem of Prediction." *Criminology* 37:703–734.

Aulette, Judy Root and Raymond Michalowski. 1993. "Fire in Hamlet: A Case Study of a State-Corporate Crime." Pp. 171–206 in *Political Crime in Contemporary America: A Critical Approach*, edited by Kenneth D. Tunnell. New York: Garland.

Austin, James. 1986. "Using Early Release to Relieve Prison Crowding: A Dilemma in Public Policy." *Crime and Delinquency* 32:391–403.

Austin, Roy L. 1978. "Race, Father-Absence, and Female Delinquency." *Criminology* 15:487–504.

Avison, William R. and Pamela L. Loring. 1986. "Population Diversity and Cross-National Homicide: The Effects of Inequality and Heterogeneity." *Criminology* 24:733–749.

Babbie, Earl. 1999. *The Basics of Social Research*. Belmont, CA: Wadsworth.

Bachman, Ronet and Bruce M. Taylor. 1994. "The Measurement of Family Violence and Rape by the Redesigned National Crime Victimization Survey." *Justice Quarterly* 11:499–512.

Bachman, Ronet and Linda E. Saltzman. 1995. *Violence*

against Women: Estimates from the Redesigned Survey. Washington, D.C.: U.S. Department of Justice, Bureau of Justice Statistics.

Bacon, Kenneth H. 1989. "Physicians Who Own Labs Prescribe 45% More Tests on Medicare Patients." *Wall Street Journal*, May 1:B4.

Bailey, James E., Arthur L. Kellerman, Grant W. Somes, Joyce G. Banton, Frederick P. Rivara, and Norman P. Rushforth. 1997. "Risk Factors for Violent Death of Women in the Home." *Archives of Internal Medicine* 157:777–782.

Bailey, William C. 1998. "Deterrence, Brutalization, and the Death Penalty: Another Examination of Oklahoma's Return to Capital Punishment." *Criminology* 36:711–733.

Bailey, William C. and Ruth Peterson. 1999. "Capital Punishment, Homicide, and Deterrence: An Assessment of the Evidence and Extension to Female Offenders." In *Homicide: A Sourcebook of Social Research*, edited by M. Dwaye Smith and Margaret Zahn. Thousand Oaks, CA: Sage.

Baker, Mary Holland, Barbara C. Nienstedt, Ronald S. Everett, and Richard McCleary. 1983. "The Impact of a Crime Wave: Perceptions, Fear, and Confidence in the Police." *Law and Society Review* 17:319–333.

Balbus, Isaac. 1977. *The Dialectics of Legal Repression*. New York: Transaction.

Baldus, David C., George Woodworth, and Charles A. Pulaski. 1990. *Equal Justice and the Death Penalty: A Legal and Empirical Analysis*. Boston: Northeastern University Press.

Balkan, Sheila, Ronald Berger, and Janet Schmidt. 1980. *Crime and Deviance in America: A Critical Approach*. Monterey: Wadsworth.

Bandura, Albert. 1973. *Aggression: A Social Learning Analysis*. Englewood Cliffs, NJ: Prentice Hall.

Bandura, Albert, D. Ross, and S. A. Ross. 1963. "Imitation of Film-Mediated Aggressive Models." *Journal of Abnormal and Social Psychology* 66:3–11.

Bannan, John R. and Rosemary S. Bannan. 1974. *Law, Morality, and Vietnam: The Peace Militants and the Courts*. Bloomington: Indiana University Press.

Bannister, Shelley A. 1993. "Battered Women Who Kill Their Abusers: Their Courtroom Battles." Pp. 316–333 in *It's a Crime: Women and Justice*, edited by Roslyn Muraskin and Ted Alleman. Englewood Cliffs, NJ: Prentice Hall.

Barak, Gregg, ed. 1991. *Crimes by the Capitalist State: An Introduction to State Criminology*. Albany: State University of New York Press.

Barkan, Steven E. 1983. "Jury Nullification in Political Trials." *Social Problems* 31:28–45.

Barkan, Steven E. 1985. *Protesters on Trial: Criminal Prosecutions in the Southern Civil Rights and Vietnam Antiwar Movements*. New Brunswick, NJ: Rutgers University Press.

Barkan, Steven E. 1996. "The Social Science Significance of the O. J. Simpson Case." In *Representing O. J.: Murder, Criminal Justice and Mass Culture*, edited by Gregg Barak. Albany, NY: Harrow and Heston.

Barkan, Steven E. and Lynne L. Snowden. 2001. *Collective Violence*. Needham Heights, MA: Allyn and Bacon.

Barkan, Steven E. and Steven F. Cohn. 1994. "Racial Prejudice and Support for the Death Penalty by Whites." *Journal of Research in Crime and Delinquency* 31:202–209.

Barkan, Steven E. and Steven F. Cohn. 1998. "Racial Prejudice and Support by Whites for Police Use of Force: A Research Note." *Justice Quarterly* 15:743–753.

Barkan, Steven E., Steven F. Cohn, and William H. Whitaker. 1995. "Beyond Recruitment: Predictors of Differential Participation in a National Antihunger Organization." *Sociological Forum* 10:113–134.

Barlow, Hugh D. 2000. *Criminal Justice in America*. Upper Saddle River, NJ: Prentice Hall.

Barnes, Deborah E., Peter Hanauer, John Slade, Lisa A. Beri, and Stanton A. Glantz. 1995. "Environmental Tobacco Smoke: The Brown and Williamson Documents." *JAMA, The Journal of the American Medical Association* 274:248–254.

Barnett, Ola W. and Alyce D. LaViolette. 1993. *It Could Happen to Anyone: Why Battered Women Stay*. Thousand Oaks, CA: Sage.

Baron, Larry and Murray A. Straus. 1987. "Four Theories of Rape: A Macrosociological Analysis." *Social Problems* 34:467–489.

Baron, Larry and Murray A. Straus. 1989. *Four Theories of Rape in American Society: A State-Level Analysis*. New Haven: Yale University Press.

Baron, Robert A. and Paul A. Bell. 1976. "The Influence of Ambient Temperature, Negative Affect, and a Cooling Drink on Physical Aggression." *Journal of Personality and Social Psychology* 33:245–255.

Barrows, Sydney Biddle and William Novak. 1986. *Mayflower Madam: The Secret Life of Sydney Biddle Barrows*. New York: Arbor House.

Barry, Dan. 1996. "Buffeted by Crime, a Long Island Mall Adds Marketing to Law Enforcement." *New York Times*, February 6:B1.

Barry, Kathleen L. 1988. *Susan B. Anthony: Biography of a Singular Feminist*. New York: New York University Press.

Bart, Pauline B. and Eileen Geil Moran, eds. 1993. *Violence against Women: The Bloody Footprints*. Thousand Oaks, CA: Sage.

Bart, Pauline B. and Margaret Jozsa. 1982. "Dirty Books, Dirty Films, and Dirty Data." Pp. 201–215 in *Take Back the Night: Women on Pornography*, edited by Laura Lederer. New York: Bantam.

Bartlett, Ellen. 1995. "Crime and Fear Haunt New S. Africa." *Boston Globe*, May 28:1.

Bartol, Curt R. 1999. *Criminal Behavior: A Psychological Approach*. Upper Saddle River, NJ: Prentice Hall.

Baskin, Deborah R. and Ira Sommers. 1993. "Females' Initiation into Violent Street Crime." *Justice Quarterly* 10:559–583.

Baskin, Deborah R. and Ira B. Sommers. 1998. *Casualties of Community Disorder: Women's Careers in Violent Crime*. Boulder: Westview Press.

Bass, Alison. 1992. "Mental Health Chief in Eye of Storm." *Boston Globe*, March 15:18.

Bass, Alison. 1993. "Gun Ownership Tied to Homicide Risk: Murder Peril Found Higher in Armed Homes." *Boston Globe*, October 7:3.

Bastian, Lisa. 1995. *Criminal Victimization 1993: National Crime Victimization Survey—Bulletin*. Washington, D.C.: U.S. Department of Justice, Bureau of Justice Statistics.

Bastian, Lisa D. and Marshall M. DeBerry. 1994. *Criminal Victimization in the United States, 1992*. Washington, D.C.: U.S. Department of Justice, Bureau of Justice Statistics.

Baumer, Terry L. 1985. "Testing a General Model of Fear of Crime." *Journal of Research in Crime and Delinquency* 22:239–256.

Bayley, David H. 1991. *Forces of Order: Policing Modern Japan*. Berkeley: University of California Press.

Bayley, David H. 1994. *Police for the Future*. New York: Oxford University Press.

Bayley, David H. 1996. "Lessons in Order." Pp. 3–14 in *Criminology: A Cross-Cultural Perspective*, edited by Robert Heiner. Minneapolis/St. Paul: West.

Beattie, J. M. 1986. *Crime and the Courts in England, 1660–1800*. Princeton: Princeton University Press.

Beccaria, Cesare. 1819 [1764]. *On Crimes and Punishment*. Translated by Edward D. Ingraham. Philadelphia: Philip H. Nicklin.

Beck, Allen J. and Christopher J. Mumola. 1999. *Prisoners in 1998*. Washington, D.C.: U.S. Department of Justice, Bureau of Justice Statistics.

Becker, Howard S. 1963. *Outsiders: Studies in the Sociology of Deviance*. New York: Free Press.

Beckett, Katherine. 1994. "Setting the Public Agenda: 'Street Crime' and Drug Use in American Politics." *Social Problems* 41:425–447.

Bedau, Hugo Adam, ed. 1998. *The Death Penalty in America: Current Controversies*. New York: Oxford University Press.

Belknap, Michal R. 1978. *Cold War Political Justice: The Smith Act, the CIA, and American Civil Liberties*. New York: Greenwood Press.

Bellah, Robert N., Richard Madsen, William M. Sullivan, Ann Swidler, and Steven M. Tipton. 1985. *Habits of the Heart: Individualism and Commitment in American Life*. Berkeley: University of California Press.

Bellair, Paul E. 1997. "Social Interaction and Community Crime: Examining the Importance of Neighbor Networks." *Criminology* 35:677–701.

Belluck, Pam. 1998. "Juice-Poisoning Case Brings Guilty Plea and a Huge Fine." *New York Times*, July 24:A12.

Beneke, Tim. 1995. "Men on Rape." Pp. 312–317 in *Men's Lives*, edited by Michael S. Kimmel and Michael A. Messner. Boston: Allyn and Bacon.

Bennett, Richard R. and James P. Lynch. 1990. "Does a Difference Make a Difference: Comparing Cross-National Crime Indicators." *Criminology* 28:153–181.

Bennett, Richard R. and Jeanne M. Flavin. 1994. "Determinants of Fear of Crime: The Effect of Cultural Setting." *Justice Quarterly* 11:357–381.

Bennett, Richard R. and P. Peter Basiotis. 1991. "Structural Correlates of Juvenile Property Crime: A Cross-National, Time-Series Analysis." *Journal of Research in Crime and Delinquency* 28:262–287.

Bennett, Richard R. and R. Bruce Wiegand. 1994. "Observations on Crime Reporting in a Developing Nation." *Criminology* 32:135–148.

Benson, Michael L. and Elizabeth Moore. 1992. "Are White-Collar and Common Offenders the Same? An Empirical and Theoretical Critique of a Recently Proposed General Theory of Crime." *Journal of Research in Crime and Delinquency* 29:251–272.

Berce, Yves Marie. 1990. *History of Peasant Revolts: The Social Origins of Rebellion in Early Modern France*. Ithaca: Cornell University Press.

Bergen, Raquel Kennedy. 1996. *Wife Rape: Understanding the Response of Survivors and Service Providers*. Thousand Oaks, CA: Sage.

Berger, Peter L. 1963. *Invitation to Sociology: A Humanistic Perspective*. Garden City, NY: Anchor Books.

Berger, Ronald J., Patricia Searles, and Charles E. Cottle. 1991. *Feminism and Pornography*. New York: Praeger.

Bergman, A., R. M. Larsen, and B. Mueller. 1986. "Changing Spectrum of Serious Child Abuse." *Pediatrics* 77:113–116.

Berk, Richard A. 1993. "What the Scientific Evidence Shows: On the Average, We Can Do No Better Than Arrest." Pp. 323–336 in *Current Controversies on Family Violence*, edited by Richard J. Gelles and Donileen R. Loseke. Newbury Park, CA: Sage.

Berk, Richard A., Robert Weiss, and Jack Boger. 1993. "Chance and the Death Penalty." *Law and Society Review* 27:89–110.

Berke, Richard L. 1995. "Christian Coalition Unveils 'Suggestions'." *New York Times*, May 18:A11.

Berlow, Alan. 1999. "The Wrong Man." *The Atlantic Monthly*, November:66–91.

Bernard, Thomas J. 1984. "Control Criticisms of Strain Theories: An Assessment of Theoretical and Empirical Adequacy." *Journal of Research in Crime and Delinquency* 21:353–372.

Bernard, Thomas J. 1987. "Testing Structural Strain Theories." *Journal of Research in Crime and Delinquency* 24:262–290.

Bernard, Thomas J. 1990. "Angry Aggression among the 'Truly Disadvantaged.'" *Criminology* 28:73–96.

Bernard, Thomas J. and Jeffrey B. Snipes. 1996. "Theoretical

Integration in Criminology." *Crime and Justice: A Review of Research* 20:301–348.

Bernstein, Carl and Bob Woodward. 1974. *All the President's Men*. New York: Simon & Schuster.

Berrigan, Daniel. 1970. *The Trial of the Catonsville Nine*. Boston: Beacon Press.

Berrigan, Philip. 1998. "Fighting for Disarmament." *Tikkun*, May–June:23–24.

Berry, Bonnie. 1994. "The Isolation of Crime, Law, and Deviance from the Core of Sociology." *The American Sociologist* 25:5–20.

Bertram, Eva and Kenneth Sharpe. 1997. "War Ends, Drugs Win: Resisters Say We're Fighting the Wrong Battles." *The Nation*, January 6:11–14.

Biderman, Albert D. and Albert J. Reiss, Jr. 1967. "On Exploring the 'Dark Figure' of Crime." *Annals of the American Academy of Political and Social Science* 374:1–15.

Biderman, Albert D. and James P. Lynch. 1991. *Understanding Crime Incidence Statistics: Why the UCR Diverges from the NCVS*. New York: Springer-Verlag.

Binder, Arnold and James W. Meeker. 1988. "Experiments as Reforms." *Journal of Criminal Justice* 16:347–358.

Birch, James W. 1984. "Reflections on Police Corruption." Pp. 116–122 in *'Order under Law': Readings in Criminal Justice*, edited by Roberg G. Culbertson. Prospect Heights, IL: Waveland Press.

Bishop, Ed. 1993. "Reporters Ignore Context of Crime, Says Criminologist." *St. Louis Journalism Review* 23:1+.

Black, Donald. 1980. "The Social Organization of Arrest." Pp. 151–162 in *Police Behavior: A Sociological Perspective*, edited by Richard J. Lundman. New York: Oxford University Press.

Black, George. 1993. *Black Hands of Beijing: Lives of Deviance in China's Democracy Movement*. New York: John Wiley.

Blalock, Hubert. 1967. *Toward a Theory of Minority-Group Relations*. New York: John Wiley.

Blau, Peter M. and Judith R. Blau. 1982. "The Cost of Inequality: Metropolitan Structure and Violent Crime." *American Sociological Review* 47:114–129.

Block, Alan A. and Frank R. Scarpitti. 1985. *Poisoning for Profit: The Mafia and Toxic Waste in America*. New York: Morrow.

Blumberg, Abraham S. 1967. *Criminal Justice*. Chicago: Quadrangle.

Blumberg, Mark. 1994. "Police Use of Excessive Force: Exploring Various Control Mechanisms." Pp. 110–126 in *Critical Issues in Crime and Justice*, edited by Albert R. Roberts. Thousand Oaks, CA: Sage.

Blumberg, Rae Lesser. 1979. "A Paradigm for Predicting the Position of Women: Policy Implications and Problems." In *Sex Roles and Social Policy*, edited by Jean Lipman-Blumen and Jessie Bernard. London: Sage.

Blumberg, Rhoda Lois. 1991. *Civil Rights: The 1960s Freedom Struggle*. Boston: Twayne.

Blumstein, Alfred. 1993. "Making Rationality Relevant—The American Society of Criminology 1992 Presidential Address." *Criminology* 31:1–16.

Blumstein, Alfred. 1993. "Racial Disproportionality of U.S. Prison Populations Revisited." *University of Colorado Law Review* 64:743–760.

Blumstein, Alfred. 1995. *Youth Violence, Guns, and Illicit Drug Markets*. Washington, D.C.: U.S. Department of Justice, National Institute of Justice.

Blumstein, Alfred and Jacqueline Cohen. 1980. "Sentencing of Convicted Offenders: An Analysis of the Public's View." *Law and Society Review* 14:223–261.

Blumstein, Alfred J., Jacqueline Cohen, and David P. Farrington. 1988. "Criminal Career Research: Its Value for Criminology." *Criminology* 26:1–35.

Blumstein, Alfred J., Jacqueline Cohen, J. A. Roth, and Christy A. Visher. 1986. *Criminal Careers and "Career Criminals."* Washington, D.C.: National Academy Press.

Bohm, Robert M. 1982. "Radical Criminology: An Explication." *Criminology* 19:565–589.

Bohm, Robert M. 1993. "Social Relationships That Arguably Should Be Criminal although They Are Not: on the Political Economy of Crime." Pp. 3–29 in *Political Crime in Contemporary America: A Critical Approach*, edited by Kenneth D. Tunnell. New York: Garland.

Boisjoly, Russell, Ellen Foster Curtis, and Eugene Mellican. 1992. "Ethical Dimensions of the Challenger Disaster." Pp. 111–136 in *Corporate and Governmental Deviance: Problems of Organizational Behavior in Contemporary Society*, edited by M. David Ermann and Richard J. Lundman. New York: Oxford University Press.

Bolt, Robert. 1962. *A Man for All Seasons*. New York: Random House.

Bonczar, Thomas P. and Allen J. Beck. 1997. *Lifetime Likelihood of Going to State or Federal Prison*. Washington, D.C.: U.S. Department of Justice, Bureau of Justice Statistics.

Bonger, Willem. 1916. *Criminality and Economic Conditions*. Translated by H. P. Horton. Boston: Little, Brown.

Booth, Alan and D. Wayne Osgood. 1993. "The Influence of Testosterone on Deviance in Adulthood: Assessing and Explaining the Relationship." *Criminology* 31:93–117.

Bordo, Susan. 1993. *Unbearable Weight: Feminism, Western Culture, and the Body*. Berkeley: University of California Press.

Boritch, Helen and John Hagan. 1990. "A Century of Crime in Toronto: Gender, Class, and Patterns of Social Control, 1859–1955." *Criminology* 28:567–599.

Bowers, William. 1993. "Capital Punishment and Contemporary Values: People's Misgivings and the Court's Misperceptions." *Law and Society Review* 27:157–175.

Bowers, William J. and Glenn Pierce. 1980. "Deterrence or

Brutalization: What Is the Effect of Executions?" *Crime and Delinquency* 26:453–484.

Box, Steven. 1981. *Deviance, Reality, and Society*. London: Holt, Rinehart, and Winston.

Boyd, William. 1995. "Death of a Writer." *The New Yorker*, November 27:51–55.

Bradwell v. Illinois, 86 U.S. [16 Wall.] 130 [1873]

Brady, James. 1993. "The Social Economy of Arson: Vandals, Gangsters, Bankers, and Officials in the Making of an Urban Problem." Pp. 211–257 in *Crime and Capitalism: Readings in Marxist Criminology*, edited by David F. Greenberg. Philadelphia: Temple University Press.

Brain, Paul Frederic. 1994. "Hormonal Aspects of Aggression and Violence." Pp. 173–244 in *Understanding and Preventing Violence: Biobehavioral Influences*, vol. 2, edited by Albert J. Reiss, Jr., Klaus A. Miczek, and Jeffrey A. Roth. Washington, D.C.: National Academy Press.

Braithwaite, John. 1981. "The Myth of Social Class and Crime Reconsidered." *American Sociological Review* 46:36–47.

Braithwaite, John. 1984. *Corporate Crime in the Pharmaceutical Industry*. London: Routledge & Kegan Paul.

Braithwaite, John. 1989. "Criminological Theory and Organizational Crime." *Justice Quarterly* 6:333–358.

Braithwaite, John. 1989. *Crime, Shame, and Reintegration*. Cambridge: Cambridge University Press.

Braithwaite, John. 1995a. "Transnational Regulation of the Pharmaceutical Industry." Pp. 299–327 in *White-Collar Crime: Classic and Contemporary Views*, edited by Gilbert Geis, Robert F. Meier, and Lawrence M. Salinger. New York: Free Press.

Braithwaite, John. 1995b. "White Collar Crime." Pp. 116–142 in *White-Collar Crime: Classic and Contemporary Views*, edited by Gilbert Geis, Robert F. Meier, and Lawrence S. Salinger. New York: Free Press.

Braithwaite, John. 1997. "Charles Tittle's Control Balance and Criminological Theory." *Theoretical Criminology* 1:77–97.

Braithwaite, John and Stephen Mugford. 1994. "Conditions of Successful Reintegration Ceremonies: Dealing with Juvenile Offenders." *British Journal of Criminology* 34:139–171.

Branfman, Fred. 1972. *Voices from the Plain of Jars: Life Under an Air War*. New York: Harper & Row.

Bray, Hiawatha. 1996. "Stalled at the Gate: Confusion Over New Law, Suit Slow US Crackdown." *Boston Globe*, February 24:19.

Brenda, Brent B. 1997. "An Examination of a Reciprocal Relationship between Religiosity and Different Forms of Delinquency within a Theoretical Model." *Journal of Research in Crime and Delinquency* 34:163–186.

Brennan, Patricia A., Sarnoff A. Mednick, and Jan Volavka. 1995. "Biomedical Factors in Crime." Pp. 65–90 in *Crime*, edited by James Q. Wilson and Joan Petersil-

ia. San Francisco: Institute for Contemporary Studies Press.

Bridges, George S. 1987. "An Empirical Study of Error in Reports of Crime and Delinquency." Pp. 180–194 in *From Boy to Man, from Delinquency to Crime*, edited by Marvin E. Wolfgang, Terence P. Thornberry, and Robert M. Figlio. Chicago: University of Chicago Press.

Bridges, George S. and Robert D. Crutchfield. 1988. "Law, Social Standing and Racial Disparities in Imprisonment." *Social Forces* 66:699–724.

Bridges, George S., Robert D. Crutchfield, and Edith E. Simpson. 1987. "Crime, Social Structure and Criminal Punishment: White and Nonwhite Rates of Imprisonment." *Social Problems* 34:345–361.

Briere, John and Neil Malamuth. 1983. "Self-Reported Likelihood of Sexually Aggressive Behavior: Attitudinal versus Sexual Explanations." *Journal of Research in Personality* 17:315–323.

Brinton, Howard H. 1952. *Friends for 300 Years*. New York: Harper & Row.

Brock, Peter. 1968. *Pacifism in the United States, from the Colonial Era to the First World War*. Princeton: Princeton University Press.

Brock, Peter. 1968. *Pioneers of the Peaceable Kingdom*. Princeton: Princeton University Press.

Brod, Harry. 1995. "Pornography and the Alienation of Male Sexuality." Pp. 393–404 in *Men's Lives*, edited by Michael S. Kimmel and Michael A. Messner. Boston: Allyn and Bacon.

Broder, David S. 1999. "Lessons of 'Six Safer Cities.'" *Washington Post*, March 24:A27.

Brodeur, Paul. 1985. *Outrageous Misconduct: The Asbestos Industry on Trial*. New York: Pantheon Books.

Broehl, Wayne G., Jr. 1964. *The Molly Maguires*. Cambridge: Harvard University Press.

Broidy, Lisa and Robert Agnew. 1997. "Gender and Crime: A General Strain Theory Perspective." *Journal of Research in Crime and Delinquency* 34:275–306.

Brown, Julie Knipe. 1997. "FBI Dumping City's 96–97 Crime Stats." *Philadelphia Daily News*, October 20:1.

Brown, M. Craig and Barbara D. Warner. 1995. "The Political Threat of Immigrant Groups and Police Aggressiveness in 1900." Pp. 82–98 in *Ethnicity, Race, and Crime: Perspectives Across Time and Place*, edited by Darnell F. Hawkins. Albany, NY: State University of New York Press.

Brown, Richard Maxwell. 1989. "Historical Patterns of Violence." Pp. 23–61 in *Violence in America: Protest, Rebellion, Reform*, vol. 2, edited by Ted Robert Gurr. Newbury Park, CA: Sage.

Brown, Richard Maxwell. 1990. "Historical Patterns of American Violence." Pp. 4–15 in *Violence: Patterns, Causes, Public Policy*, edited by Neil Alan Weiner, Margaret A. Zahn, and Rita J. Sagi. San Diego: Harcourt Brace Jovanovich.

Browne, Angela. 1987. *When Battered Women Kill*. New York: Free Press.

Browne, Angela. 1993. "Violence against Women by Male Partners: Prevalence, Incidence, and Policy Implications." *American Psychologist* 48:1077–1087.

Browne, Angela. 1995. "Fear and the Perception of Alternatives: Asking 'Why Battered Women Don't Leave' Is the Wrong Question." Pp. 228–245 in *The Criminal Justice System and Women: Offenders, Victims, and Workers*, edited by Barbara Raffel Price and Natalie J. Sokoloff. New York: McGraw-Hill.

Browning, Sandra Lee and Liqun Cao. 1992. "The Impact of Race on Criminal Justice Ideology." *Justice Quarterly* 9:685–701.

Brownmiller, Susan. 1975. *Against Our Will: Men, Women, and Rape*. New York: Simon & Schuster.

Bruce, Marino A., Vincent J. Roscigno, and Patricia L. McCall. 1998. "Structure, Context, and Agency in the Reproduction of Black-on-Black Violence." *Theoretical Criminology* 21:29–55.

Brydensholt, H. H. 1992. "Crime Policy in Denmark: How We Managed to Reduce the Prison Population." In *Prisons around the World: Studies in International Penology*, edited by Michael K. Carlie and Kevin I. Minor. Dubuque, IA: William C. Brown.

Buckley, William F., Jr. 1994. "Ka-Pow! He's Famous." *National Review*, April 18:62–63.

Bullough, Vern L. 1980. *Sexual Variance in Society and History*. Chicago: University of Chicago Press.

Bullough, Vern L. and Bonnie Bullough. 1977. *Sin, Sickness, and Sanity: A History of Sexual Attitudes*. New York: New American Library.

Bullough, Vern L. and Bonnie Bullough. 1987. *Women and Prostitution: A Social History*. Buffalo, NY: Prometheus.

Bunch, William. 1999. "Survey: Crime Fear Is Linked to TV News." *Philadelphia Daily News* March 16:A1.

Burgess, Robert L. and Ronald L. Akers. 1966. "A Differential Association-Reinforcement Theory of Criminal Behavior." *Social Problems* 14:128–147.

Buriel, R., S. Calzada, and R. Vasquez. 1982. "The Relationship of Traditional Mexican-American Culture to Adjustment and Delinquency among Three Generations of Mexican-American Male Adolescents." *Hispanic Journal of Behavioral Sciences* 4:41–55.

Burns, James MacGregor and Stewart Burns. 1992. *A People's Charter: The Pursuit of Rights in America*. New York: Knopf.

Bursik, Robert J., Jr. 1984. "Urban Dynamics and Ecological Studies of Delinquency." *Social Forces* 69:393–413.

Bursik, Robert J., Jr. 1986. "Delinquency Rates as Sources of Ecological Change." Pp. 63–74 in *The Social Ecology of Crime*, edited by James M. Byrne and Robert J. Sampson. New York: Springer-Verlag.

Bursik, Robert J., Jr. 1988. "Social Disorganization and Theories of Crime and Delinquency: Problems and Prospects." *Criminology* 26:519–551.

Bursik, Robert J., Jr. 1989. "Political Decisionmaking and Ecological Models of Delinquency: Conflict and Consensus." Pp. 105–117 in *Theoretical Integration in the Study of Deviance and Crime*, edited by Steven F. Messner, Marvin D. Krohn, and Allen E. Liska. Albany, NY: State University of New York Press.

Bursik, Robert J., Jr. 2000. "Property Crime Trends." Pp. 215–231 in *Criminology: A Contemporary Handbook*, edited by Joseph F. Sheley. Belmont, CA: Wadsworth.

Bursik, Robert J., Jr. and Harold G. Grasmick. 1993a. "Economic Deprivation and Neighborhood Crime Rates, 1960–1980." *Law & Society Review* 27:263–283.

Bursik, Robert J., Jr. and Harold G. Grasmick. 1993b. *Neighborhoods and Crime: The Dimensions of Effective Community Control*. New York: Lexington Books.

Burt, Martha R. and Bonnie L. Katz. 1984. "Rape, Robbery, and Burglary: Responses to Actual and Feared Victimization with Special Focus on Women and the Elderly." *Victimology* 10:325–358.

Burton, Velmer S., Jr. and R. Gregory Dunaway. 1994. "Strain, Relative Deprivation, and Middle-Class Delinquency." Pp. 70–95 in *Varieties of Criminology: Readings from a Dynamic Discipline*, edited by Gregg Barak. Westport, CT: Praeger.

Bushnell, Rebecca W. 1988. *Prophesying Tragedy: Sign and Voice in Sophocles' Theban Plays*. Ithaca: Cornell University Press.

Bushnell, Timothy. 1991. *State Organized Terror: The Case of Violent Internal Repression*. Boulder: Westview Press.

Butterfield, Fox. 1992. "Studies Find a Family Link to Criminality." *New York Times*, January 31:A1.

Butterfield, Fox. 1994. "A History of Homicide Surprises the Experts: Decline in U.S. Before Recent Increase." *New York Times*, October 23:16.

Butterfield, Fox. 1995. "California's Courts Clogging Under Its 'Three Strikes' Law." *New York Times*, March 23:A1.

Butterfield, Fox. 1998. "As Crime Falls, Pressure Rises to Alter Data." *New York Times*, August 3:A1.

Butterfield, Fox. 2000. "Cities Reduce Crime and Conflict without New York-Style Hardball." *New York Times*, March 4:A1.

Button, James. 1989. "The Outcomes of Contemporary Black Protest and Violence." Pp. 286–306 in *Violence in America: Protest, Rebellion, Reform*, vol. 2, edited by Ted Robert Gurr. Newbury Park, CA: Sage.

Buzawa, Eve S. and Carl G. Buzawa. 1993. "The Scientific Evidence Is Not Conclusive: Arrest Is No Panacea." Pp. 337–356 in *Current Controversies on Family Violence*, edited by Richard J. Gelles and Donileen R. Loseke. Newbury Park, CA: Sage.

Bynum, Tim. 1981. "Parole Decision Making and Native Americans." Pp. 75–87 in *Race, Crime, and Criminal Justice*, edited by R. L. MacNeely and Carl E. Pope. Beverly Hills: Sage.

Bynum, Tim S. and Raymond Paternoster. 1984. "Discrimination Revisited: An Exploration of Frontstage and Backstage Criminal Justice Decision Making." *Sociology and Social Research* 69:90–108.

Bynum, Tim S., Gary W. Cordner, and Jack R. Greene. 1982. "Victim and Offense Characteristics: Impact on Police Investigative Decision-Making." *Criminology* 20:301–318.

Cain, Maureen and Alan Hunt, eds. 1979. *Marx and Engels on Law*. New York: Academic Press.

Calavita, Kitty and Henry N. Pontell. 1990. "'Heads I Win, Tails You Lose': Deregulation, Crime and Crisis in the Savings and Loan Industry." *Crime and Delinquency* 36:309–341.

Cameron, May Owen. 1964. *The Booster and the Snitch: Department Store Shoplifting*. New York: Free Press.

Camil, Scott. 1989. "Undercover Agents' War on Vietnam Veterans." Pp. 319–333 in *It Did Happen Here: Recollections of Political Repression in America*, edited by Bud Schultz and Ruth Schultz. Berkeley: University of California Press.

Canter, Rachelle. 1982. "Family Correlates of Male and Female Delinquency." *Criminology* 20:149–167.

Cantor, David and Kenneth C. Land. 1985. "Unemployment and Crime Rates in the Post-World War II United States: A Theoretical and Empirical Analysis." *American Sociological Review* 50:317–332.

Cao, Liqun, Anthony Adams, and Vickie J. Jensen. 1997. "A Test of the Black Subculture of Violence Thesis: A Research Note." *Criminology* 35:367–379.

Caputi, Jane and Diana E. H. Russell. 1992. "Femicide: Sexist Terrorism against Women." Pp. 13–21 in *Femicide: The Politics of Woman Killing*, edited by Jill Radford and Diana E. H. Russell. New York: Twayne.

Carey, Gregory. 1994. "Genetics and Violence." Pp. 21–58 in *Understanding and Preventing Violence: Biobehavioral Influences*, vol. 2, edited by Albert J. Reiss, Jr., Klaus A. Miczek, and Jeffrey A. Roth. Washington, D.C.: National Academy Press.

Caspi, Avshalom. 2000. "The Child Is Father of the Man: Personalities Continuities from Childhood to Adulthood." *Journal of Personality and Social Psychology* 78:158–172.

Caspi, Avshalom, Bradley R. Entner Wright, Terrie E. Moffitt, and Phil A. Silva. 1998. "Early Failure in the Labor Market: Childhood and Adolescent Predictors of Unemployment in the Transition to Adulthood." *American Sociological Review* 63:424–451.

Caspi, Avshalom, Bill Henry, Rob McGee, Terrie E. Moffitt, and Phil A. Silva. 1995. "Temperamental Origins of Child and Adolescent Behavior Problems: From Age 3 to Age 15." *Child Development* 66:55–68.

Caspi, Avshalom, Terrie E. Moffitt, Phil A. Silva, Magda Stouthamer-Loeber, Robert F. Krueger, and Pamela S. Schmutte. 1994. "Are Some People Crime-Prone? Replications of the Personality-Crime Relationship across Countries, Genders, Races, and Methods." *Criminology* 32:163–195.

Centerwall, Brandon S. 1989. "Exposure to Television as a Cause of Violence." *Public Communication and Behavior* 2:1–59.

Cernkovich, Stephen A. 1978. "Value Orientations and Delinquency Involvement." *Criminology* 15:443–458.

Cernkovich, Stephen A. and Peggy C. Giordano. 1979. "On Complicating the Relationship between Liberation and Delinquency." *Social Problems* 26:467–481.

Cernkovich, Stephen A. and Peggy C. Giordano. 1987. "Family Relationships and Delinquency." *Criminology* 25:295–321.

Cernkovich, Stephen A. and Peggy C. Giordano. 1992. "School Bonding, Race, and Delinquency." *Criminology* 30:261–291.

Cernkovich, Stephen A., Peggy C. Giordano, and Meredith D. Pugh. 1985. "Chronic Offenders: The Missing Cases in Self-Report Delinquency Research." *Journal of Criminal Law and Criminology* 76:705–732.

Chacón, Richard. 1998. "Questions Raised on Campus Crime." *Boston Globe*, February 8:A1.

Chaiken, Jan M. 2000. "Crunching Numbers: Crime and Incarceration at the End of the Millennium." *National Institute of Justice Journal*, January:10–17.

Chaiken, Jan M. and Marcia R. Chaiken. 1982. *Varieties of Criminal Behavior*. Santa Monica, CA: Rand Corporation.

Chaiken, Jan M. and Marcia R. Chaiken. 1990. "Drugs and Predatory Crime." Pp. 203–239 in *Drugs and Crime*, vol. 13, *Crime and Justice*, edited by Michael Tonry and James Q. Wilson. Chicago: University of Chicago Press.

Chaiken, Jan M., Michael W. Lawless, and Keith A. Stevenson. 1975. "The Impact of Police Activity on Subway Crime." *Urban Analysis* 3:173–205.

Chambliss, William J. 1964. "A Sociological Analysis of the Law of Vagrancy." *Social Problems* 12:67–77.

Chambliss, William J. 1973. "The Saints and the Roughnecks." *Society* 11:24–31.

Chambliss, William J. 1988. *On the Take: From Petty Crooks to Presidents*. Indianapolis: Indianapolis University Press.

Chambliss, William J. 1989. "State-Organized Crime." *Criminology* 27:183–208.

Chambliss, William J. and Robert Seidman. 1982. *Law, Order, and Power*. Reading, MA: Addison-Wesley.

Chamlin, Mitchell B. 1991. "A Longitudinal Analysis of the Arrest-Crime Relationship: A Further Examination of the Tipping Effect." *Justice Quarterly* 8:187–199.

Chappell, Duncan, Gilbert Geis, Stephen Schafer, and Larry Siegel. 1971. "Forcible Rape: A Comparative Study of Offenses Known to the Police in Boston and Los Angeles." Pp. 169–193 in *Studies in the Sociology of Sex*, edited by James M. Henslin. New York: Appleton Century Crofts.

Chermak, Steven. 1994. "Crime in the News Media: A Refined Understanding of How Crimes Become News." Pp. 95–129 in *Media, Process, and the Social Construction of Crime*, edited by Gregg Barak. New York: Garland.

Chesney-Lind, Meda. 1995. "Girls, Delinquency, and Juvenile Justice: Toward a Feminist Theory of Young Women's Crime." Pp. 71–88 in *The Criminal Justice System and Women: Offenders, Victims, and Workers*, edited by Barbara Raffel Price and Natalie J. Sokoloff. New York: McGraw-Hill.

Chesney-Lind, Meda and Randall G. Sheldon. 1992. *Girls, Delinquency, and Juvenile Justice*. Pacific Grove, Ca: Brooks/Cole.

Chilton, Roland, Victoria Major, and Sharon Propheter. 1998. "Victims and Offenders: A New UCR Supplement to Present Incident-Based Data from Participating Agencies." Paper presented at annual meeting of American Society of Criminology, November, Washington, D.C..

Chiricos, Ted, Michael Hogan, and Marc Gertz. 1997. "Racial Composition of Neighborhood and Fear of Crime." *Criminology* 35:107–129.

Chiricos, Theodore G. 1987. "Rates of Crime and Unemployment: An Analysis of Aggregate Research Evidence." *Social Problems* 34:187–213.

Chiricos, Theodore G. and Charles Crawford. 1995. "Race and Imprisonment: A Contextual Assessment of the Evidence." Pp. 281–309 in *Ethnicity, Race, and Crime: Perspectives across Time and Place*, edited by Darnell F. Hawkins. Albany, NY: State University of New York Press.

Chiricos, Theodore G. and Gordon P. Waldo. 1970. "Punishment and Crime: An Examination of Some Empirical Evidence." *Social Problems* 18:200–217.

Chiricos, Theodore G. and Gordon P. Waldo. 1975. "Socioeconomic Status and Criminal Sentencing: An Empirical Assessment of a Conflict Proposition." *American Sociological Review* 40:753–772.

Chiricos, Theodore G. and Miriam A. Delone. 1992. "Labor Surplus and Punishment: A Review and Assessment of Theory and Evidence." *Social Problems* 39:421–446.

Chomsky, Noam. 1988. *The Culture of Terrorism*. Boston: South End Press.

Chomsky, Noam and Edward S. Herman. 1979. *The Washington Connection and Third World Fascism*. Boston: South End Press.

Chong, Dennis. 1991. *Collective Action and the Civil Rights Movement*. Chicago: University of Chicago Press.

Christenson, Ron. 1986. *Political Trials: Gordian Knots in the Law*. New Brunswick, NJ: Transaction.

Christopher Commission. 1991. *Report of the Independent Commission on the Los Angeles Police Department*. Los Angeles: City of Los Angeles.

Churchill, Ward and Jim Vander Wall. 1990. *Agents of Repression: The FBI's Secret Wars against the American Indian Movement and the Black Panther Party*. Boston: South End Press.

Clark, Gerald R. 1971. "What Happens When the Police Strike." Pp. 58–76 in *Crime and Criminal Justice*, edited by Donald R. Cressey. Chicago: Quadrangle.

Clark, John P. and Richard C. Hollinger. 1983. *Theft by Employees in Work Organizations*. Washington, D.C.: U.S. Department of Justice, National Institute of Justice.

Clark, Walter Van Tilburg. 1940. *The Ox-Bow Incident*. New York: Random House.

Clarke, James W. 1982. *American Assassins: The Darker Side of Politics*. Princeton: Princeton University Press.

Clarke, Ronald V. and Patricia M. Harris. 1992. "Auto Theft and Its Prevention." Pp. 1–54 in *Crime and Justice: A Review of Research*, vol. 16, edited by Michael Tonry. Chicago: University of Chicago Press.

Clarke, Stevens H. and Gary G. Koch. 1976. "The Influence of Income and Other Factors on Whether Criminal Defendants Go to Prison." *Law and Society Review* 11:57–92.

Clelland, Donald and Timothy J. Carter. 1980. "The New Myth of Class and Crime." *Criminology* 18:319–336.

Clemente, F. and M. B. Kleiman. 1977. "Fear of Crime in the United States: A Multivariate Analysis." *Social Forces* 56:519–531.

Clemetson, Lynnette and T. Trent Gegax. 1998. "The Abortion Wars Come Home." *Newsweek*, November 9:34.

Clinard, Marshall B. 1964. "The Theoretical Implications of Anomie and Deviant Behavior." In *Anomie and Deviant Behavior*, edited by Marshall B. Clinard. New York: Free Press.

Clinard, Marshall. 1978. *Cities with Little Crime: The Case of Switzerland*. Cambridge: Cambridge University Press.

Clinard, Marshall B. and D. J. Abbott. 1976. "Community Organization and Property Crime: A Comparative Study of Social Control in the Slums of an African City." Pp. 186–206 in *Delinquency, Crime, and Society*, edited by James F. Short. Chicago: University of Chicago Press.

Clinard, Marshall B. and Peter C. Yeager. 1980. *Corporate Crime*. New York: Free Press.

Clinard, Marshall B. and Richard Quinney. 1973. *Criminal Behavior Systems*. New York: Holt, Rinehart and Winston.

Clinard, Marshall B. and Robert F. Meier. 1995. *Sociology of Deviant Behavior*. Fort Worth: Harcourt Brace.

Cloward, Richard A. and Lloyd E. Ohlin. 1960. *Delinquency and Opportunity: A Theory of Delinquent Gangs*. New York: Free Press.

Coakley, Tom. 1994. "Robbery Threatens a Lifetime of Memories." *Boston Globe*, June 2:27, 35.

Cobban, Helena. 1985. *The Palestinian Liberation Organisation: People, Power, and Politics*. Cambridge: Cambridge University Press.

Cochran, John K., Mitchell B. Chamlin, and Mark Seth. 1994. "Deterrence or Brutalization? An Impact Assessment of Oklahoma's Return to Capital Punishment." *Criminology* 32:107–134.

Cochran, John K., Peter B. Wood, and Bruce J. Arneklev. 1994. "Is the Religiosity-Delinquency Relationship

Spurious? A Test of Arousal and Social Control Theories." *Journal of Research in Crime and Delinquency* 31:92–123.

Cockburn, Alexander. 1990. "The Fate of the Panthers." *The Nation*, July 2:6–7.

Cockburn, Alexander and Jeffrey St. Clair. 1998. *White-out: The CIA, Drugs and the Press*. New York: Verso.

Cohen, Albert K. 1955. *Delinquent Boys: The Culture of the Gang*. New York: Free Press.

Cohen, Carl. 1971. *Civil Disobedience: Conscience, Tactics, and the Law*. New York: Columbia University Press.

Cohen, Richard M. and Jules Witcover. 1974. *A Heartbeat Away: The Investigation and Resignation of Spiro T. Agnew*. New York: Viking Press.

Cohen, William S. 1994. "Gaming the Health Care System: Billions of Dollars Lost to Fraud & Abuse Each Year." Senate Special Committee on Aging.

Cohen, William S. and George J. Mitchell. 1988. *Men of Zeal: A Candid Inside Story of the Iran-Contra Hearings*. New York: Viking Press.

Cohn, Steven F., Steven E. Barkan, and William A. Halteman. 1991. "Punitive Attitudes Toward Criminals: Racial Consensus or Racial Conflict?" *Social Problems* 38:287–296.

Cole, David. 1999. "Doing Time In Rehab: Drug Courts Keep Addicts Out of Jail." *The Nation*, September 30:30.

Cole, David. 1999. "The Color of Justice." *The Nation*, October 11:12–15.

Cole, Richard. 1995. "Profit Fuels the Burning of America." *Bangor Daily News*, September 14:1.

Coleman, James W. 1987. "Toward an Integrated Theory of White Collar Crime." *American Journal of Sociology* 93:406–439.

Coleman, James W. 1995. "Respectable Crime." Pp. 249–269 in *Criminology: A Contemporary Handbook*, edited by Joseph F. Sheley. Belmont, CA: Wadsworth.

Coleman, James William. 1998. *The Criminal Elite: Understanding White-Collar Crime*. New York: St. Martin's Press.

Collins, James J. 1989. "Alcohol and Interpersonal Violence: Less Than Meets the Eye." Pp. 49–67 in *Pathways to Criminal Violence*, edited by Neil Alan Weiner and Marvin E. Wolfgang. Newbury Park, CA: Sage.

Collins, Randall. 1994. *Four Sociological Traditions*. New York: Oxford University Press.

Colvin, Mark and John Pauly. 1983. "A Critique of Criminology: Toward an Integrated Structural-Marxist Theory of Delinquency Production." *American Journal of Sociology* 89:513–551.

Conklin, John. 1972. *Robbery and the Criminal Justice System*. Philadelphia: Lippincott.

Conley, Darlene J. 1994. "Adding Color to a Black and White Picture: Using Qualitative Data to Explain Racial Disproportionality in the Juvenile Justice System." *Journal of Research in Crime and Delinquency* 31:135–148.

Conlon, Michael. 1999. "Study Links Prenatal Smoking to Offspring's Criminal Actions." *Philadelphia Inquirer*, March 15:A1.

Connell, Christopher. 1993. "Guns' Toll on Youth Cited." *Boston Globe*, November 26:3.

Connell, Evan S. 1988. *Son of the Morning Star: Custer and the Little Bighorn*. New York: Harper & Row.

Connell, Robert W. 1995. *Masculinities*. Berkeley: University of California Press.

Conquest, Robert. 1990. *The Great Terror: A Reassessment*. New York: Oxford University Press.

Consumer Reports. 1985. "Fords in Reverse." *Consumer Reports*, September:520–523.

Consumer Reports. 1992. "Wasted Health Care Dollars." *Consumer Reports*, July:435–448.

Consumer Reports. 1993. "Are Auto Insurers Serious About Fighting Fraud?" *Consumer Reports*, January:7.

Cook, Fred J. 1982. *The Great Energy Scam: Private Billions vs. Public Good*. New York: Macmillan.

Cook, Philip J. 1986. "The Relationship between Victim Resistance and Injury in Noncommercial Robbery." *Journal of Legal Studies* 15:405–416.

Cook, Philip J. 1991. "The Technology of Personal Violence." Pp. 1–72 in *Crime and Justice: A Review of Research*, vol. 14, edited by Michael Tonry. Chicago: University of Chicago Press.

Cook, Philip J. and Jens Ludwig. 1997. *Guns in America: National Survey on Private Ownership and Use of Firearms*. Washington, D.C.: U.S. Department of Justice, National Institute of Justice.

Cook, Philip J. and Mark H. Moore. 1995. "Gun Control." Pp. 267–294 in *Crime*, edited by James Q. Wilson and Joan Petersilia. San Francisco: Institute for Contemporary Studies Press.

Cooper, Helene. 1996. "A Question of Justice: Do Prosecutors Target Minority Politicians?" *Wall Street Journal*, January 12:A1.

Corley, Charles J., Stephen Cenkovich, and Peggy Giordano. 1989. "Sex and the Likelihood of Sanction." *Journal of Criminal Law and Criminology* 80:540–556.

Cornish, Derek B. and Ronald V. Clarke, eds. 1986. *The Reasoning Criminal: Rational Choice Perspectives on Offending*. New York: Springer-Verlag.

Cose, Ellis. 1990. "Turning Victims into Saints: Journalists Cannot Resist Recasting Crime into a Shopworn Morality Tale." *Time*, January 22:19.

Coston, Charisse Tia Maria. 1992. "The Influence of Race in Urban Homeless Females' Fear of Crime." *Justice Quarterly* 9:721–729.

Coughlin, Ellen E. 1994. "Pathways to Crime." *The Chronicle of Higher Education* 40:A8–A9.

Coughlin, Ellen K. 1994. "Mean Streets Are a Scholar's Lab." *Chronicle of Higher Education*:A8–A9, A14.

Covington, Jeannette. 1986. "Self-Esteem and Deviance:

The Effects of Race and Gender." *Criminology* 24:105–138.

Cowan, Alison Leigh. 1992. "Milken to Pay $500 Million More in $1.3 Billion Drexel Settlement." *New York Times*, February 18:A1.

Cressey, Donald R. 1969. *Theft of the Nation: The Structure and Operations of Organized Crime in America*. New York: Harper & Row.

Cressey, Donald R. 1971 [1953]. *Other People's Money: A Study in the Social Psychology of Embezzlement*. Belmont, CA: Wadsworth.

Critchley, Thomas A. 1972. *A History of Police in England and Wales*. Montclair, NJ: Patterson Smith.

Cromwell, Paul. 1994. "Burglary: The Burglar's Perspective." Pp. 35–50 in *Critical Issues in Crime and Justice*, edited by Albert R. Roberts. Thousand Oaks, CA: Sage.

Cromwell, Paul and Karen McElrath. 1994. "Buying Stolen Property: An Opportunity Perspective." *Journal of Research in Crime and Delinquency* 31:295–310.

Crutchfield, Robert D., George S. Bridges, and Susan R. Pitchford. 1994. "Analytical and Aggregation Biases in Analyses of Imprisonment: Reconciling Discrepancies in Studies of Racial Disparity." *Journal of Research in Crime and Delinquency* 31:166–182.

Cullen, Francis T. and Michael L. Benson. 1993. "White-Collar Crime: Holding a Mirror to the Core." *Journal of Criminal Justice Education* 4:325–347.

Cullen, Francis T., Bruce G. Link, and Craig W. Polanzi. 1982. "The Seriousness of Crime Revisited: Have Attitudes toward White-Collar Crime Changed?" *Criminology* 20:83–102.

Cullen, Francis T., William J. Maakestad, and Gray Cavender. 1987. *Corporate Crime under Attack: The Ford Pinto Case and Beyond*. Cincinnati: Anderson.

Cullen, Francis T., Bruce G. Link III, Lawrence F. Travis, and John F. Wozniak. 1985. "Consensus in Crime Seriousness: Empirical Reality or Methodological Artifact?" *Criminology* 23:99–118.

Cullen, Kevin. 1996. "Sides Push to Restore Irish Truce: No Accord on How to Proceed." *Boston Globe*, February 12:1.

Curran, Daniel J. and Claire M. Renzetti. 1994. *Theories of Crime*. Boston: Allyn and Bacon.

Curran, Daniel J. and Sandra Cook. 1993. "Growing Fears, Rising Crime: Juveniles and China's Justice System." *Crime and Delinquency* 39:296–315.

Currie, Elliott. 1985. *Confronting Crime: An American Challenge*. New York: Pantheon.

Currie, Elliott. 1994. *Reckoning: Drugs, the Cities, and the American Future*. New York: Hill and Wang.

Curtius, Mary. 1994. "Report Blasts Global Abuse of Women's Rights." *Boston Globe*, March 8:2.

Dabbs, James and Robin Morris. 1990. "Testosterone and Antisocial Behavior in a Sample of 4,462 Men." *Psychological Science* 1:209–211.

Dailey, Suzanne. 1995. "Blacks in South Africa Turn to Vigilantes as Crime Soars." *New York Times*, November 27:1.

D'Alessio, Stewart J. and Lisa Stolzenberg. 1998. "Crime, Arrests, and Pretrial Jail Incarceration: An Examination of the Deterrence Thesis." *Criminology* 36:735–761.

Dalton, Katharina. 1961. "Menstruation and Crime." *British Medical Journal* 2:1752–1753.

Daly, Kathleen. 1987. "Discrimination in the Criminal Courts: Family, Gender, and the Problem of Equal Treatment." *Social Forces* 66:152–175.

Daly, Kathleen. 1989. "Gender and Varieties of White-Collar Crime." *Criminology* 27:769–794.

Daly, Kathleen. 1994. *Gender, Crime, and Punishment*. New Haven: Yale University Press.

Daly, Kathleen and Meda Chesney-Lind. 1988. "Feminism and Criminology." *Justice Quarterly* 5:497–538.

Daly, Kathleen and Rebecca L. Bordt. 1995. "Sex Effects and Sentencing: An Analysis of the Statistical Literature." *Justice Quarterly* 12:141–175.

Daly, Martin and Margo I. Wilson. 1988. *Homicide*. Hawthorne, NY: Aldine de Gruyter.

Daniele, Elizabeth. 1993. "Fraud: Fighting the Invisible Enemy." *Insurance and Technology*, June:47–50.

Darnton, John. 1993. "Does the World Still Recognize a Holocaust?" *New York Times*, April 25:E1.

Datesman, Susan K., Frank Scarpitti, and Richard Stephensen. 1975. "Female Delinquency: An Application of Self and Opportunity Theories." *Journal of Research in Crime and Delinquency* 12:107–122.

Davies, Peter. 1973. *The Truth about Kent State: A Challenge to the American Conscience*. New York: Farrar, Straus, Giroux.

Davis, James Kirkpatrick. 1992. *Spying on America: The FBI's Domestic Counterintelligence Program*. New York: Praeger.

Davis, Kingsley. 1937. "The Sociology of Prostitution." *American Sociological Review* 2:744–755.

Davis, Nanette J. 1981. "Prostitutes." Pp. 305–313 in *Deviance: The Interactionist Perspective*, edited by Earl Rubington and Martin S. Weinberg. New York: Macmillan.

Davis, Nathaniel. 1985. *The Last Two Years of Salvador Allende*. Ithaca, NY: Cornell University Press.

Davis, Robert C. and Barbara E. Smith. 1994. "The Effects of Victim Impact Statements on Sentencing Decisions: A Test in an Urban Setting." *Justice Quarterly* 11:453–469.

Dawson, John M. and Patrick A. Langan. 1994. *Murder in Families*. Washington, D.C.: U.S. Department of Justice, Bureau of Justice Statistics.

DeBenedetti, Charles and Charles Chatfield. 1990. *An American Ordeal: The Antiwar Movement of the Vietnam Era*. Syracuse: Syracuse University Press.

Decker, Scott H. 1993. "Exploring Victim-Offender Relationships in Homicide: The Role of Individual and Event Characteristics." *Justice Quarterly* 10:585–612.

Decker, Scott and Carol Kohfeld. 1985. "Crimes, Crime Rates, Arrests, and Arrest Ratios: Implications for Deterrence Theory." *Criminology* 23:437–450.

Decker, Scott, Richard Wright, and Robert Logie. 1993. "Perceptual Deterrence among Active Residential Burglars: A Research Note." *Criminology* 31:135–147.

Decker, Scott, Richard Wright, Allison Redfern, and Dietrich Smith. 1993. "A Woman's Place Is in the Home: Females and Residential Burglary." *Justice Quarterly* 10:143–162.

DeFleur, Lois B. 1975. "Biasing Influences on Drug Arrest Records: Implications for Deviance Research." *American Sociological Review* 40:88–103.

DeKeseredy, Walter S. and Martin D. Schwartz. 1991. "Left Realist Criminology: Strengths, Weaknesses and the Feminist Critique." *Crime, Law and Social Change* 15:51–72.

Delaney, Joan. 1993. "Handcuffing Employee Theft." *Small Business Reports*, July:29–37.

Dembner, Alice. 1995. "College in Furor Over Singapore Leader's Visit." *Boston Globe*, July 21:19.

Dembo, Richard and Linda E. Williams, eds. 1993. *Drugs and Crime*. Lanham, MD: University Press of America.

Deming, Richard. 1977. *Women: The New Criminals*. Nashville: Thomas Nelson.

Derber, Charles. 1996. *The Wilding of America: How Greed and Violence Are Eroding Our Nation's Character*. New York: St. Martin's Press.

Devitt, Tiffany. 1992. "Media Circus at Palm Beach Rape Trial." *EXTRA!* (publication of FAIR, Fairness and Accuracy in Reporting), Special Issue, pp. 9–10, 24.

Devitt, Tiffany and Jennifer Downey 1992. "Battered Women Take a Beating from the Press." *EXTRA!* (publication of FAIR, Fairness and Accuracy in Reporting), Special Issue, pp. 14–16.

Diamond, Irene. 1982. "Pornography and Repression: A Reconsideration." Pp. 335–351 in *The Criminal Justice System and Women: Offenders, Victims, and Workers*, edited by Barbara Raffel Price and Natalie J. Sokoloff. New York: Clark Boardman.

Diani, Mario and Donnatella Della Porta. 1999. *Social Movements: An Introduction*. Oxford: Blackwell.

Dibacco, Thomas V. 1993. "When Alcohol Was a Controlled Substance, Illegal Use Soared." *Washington Post*, April 20:WH14.

Dickey, Walter J. and Pam Stiebs. 1998. *"Three Strikes": Five Years Later*. Washington, D.C.: Campaign for an Effective Crime Policy.

Dobash, R. Emerson and Russell P. Dobash. 1979. *Violence against Wives: A Case against the Patriarchy*. New York: Free Press.

Dobash, R. Emerson and Russell P. Dobash. 1992. *Women, Violence and Social Change*. New York: Routledge.

Dobash, Russell P., R. Emerson Dobash, Margo Wilson, and Martin Daly. 1992. "The Myth of Sexual Symmetry in Marital Violence." *Social Problems* 39:71–91.

Dockery, Douglas W. 1994. "An Association between Air Pollution and Mortality in Six U.S. Cities." *JAMA, Journal of the American Medical Association* 271:818J.

Doleschal, Eugene. 1979. "Crime: Some Popular Beliefs." *Crime and Delinquency* 25:1–8.

Domhoff, G. William. 1998. *Who Rules America: Power and Politics in the Year 2000*. Mountain View, CA: Mayfield.

Donnerstein, Edward, Daniel Linz, and Steven Penrod. 1987. *The Question of Pornography: Research Findings and Policy Implications*. New York: Free Press.

Dorsen, Norman and Leon Friedman. 1973. *Disorder in the Courts*. New York: Pantheon.

Dorsey, Tina L. and Marianne W. Zawitz. 1999. *Drugs and Crime Facts*. Washington, D.C.: U.S. Department of Justice, Bureau of Justice Statistics.

Doty, C. Stewart. 1994. "The KKK in Maine was not OK." *Bangor Daily News*, June 11–12:xx.

Dowdy, Eric. 1994. "Federal Funding and Its Effect on Criminological Research: Emphasizing Individualistic Explanations for Criminal Behavior." *The American Sociologist* 25:77–89.

Dowie, Mark. 1977. "Pinto Madness." *Mother Jones*, September/October:18–19, 32.

Downes, David. 1996. "The Case for Going Dutch: The Lessons of Post-War Penal Policy." Pp. 243–253 in *Criminology: A Cross-Cultural Perspective*, edited by Robert Heiner. Minneapolis/St. Paul: West.

Downie, Leonard, Jr. 1972. *Justice Denied: The Case for Reform of the Courts*. Baltimore: Penguin.

Dugdale, Richard. 1877. *The Jukes: A Study in Crime, Pauperism, Disease, and Heredity*. New York: G. P. Putnam's Sons.

Duke, Paul. 1991. "IRS Excels at Tracking the Average Earner but Not the Wealthy." *Wall Street Journal*, April 15:1.

Duke, Steven B. and Richard St. John. 1996. "Cutting Welfare Could Spark a Crime Explosion." *Boston Globe*, January 16:13.

Duncan, Otis Dudley. 2000. "Gun Use Surveys: In Numbers We Trust?" *The Criminologist* 25:1–7.

Durant, Will and Ariel Durant. 1961. *The Age of Reason Begins*. New York: Simon & Schuster.

Durkheim, Emile. 1933 [1893]. *The Division of Labor in Society*. London: Free Press.

Durkheim, Emile. 1947 [1915]. *The Elementary Forms of Religious Life*. Translated by Joseph Swain. Glencoe, IL: Free Press.

Durkheim, Emile. 1952 [1897]. *Suicide*. Translated by John Spaulding and George Simpson. New York: Free Press.

Durkheim, Emile. 1962 [1895]. *The Rules of Sociological Method*. Edited by Steven Lukes. New York: Free Press.

Durkheim, Emile. 1983 [1901]. "Two Laws of Penal Evolution." Pp. 102–132 in *Durkheim and the Law*, edited by Steven Lukes and Andrew Scull. New York: St. Martin's Press.

Duster, Troy. 1995. "The New Crisis of Legitimacy in Controls, Prisons, and Legal Structures." *The American Sociologist* 26:20–29.

Dworkin, Andrea. 1989. *Pornography: Men Possessing Women*. New York: Norton.

Dwyer, Jim. 1994. *Two Seconds Under the World: Terror Comes to America: The Conspiracy Behind the World Trade Center Bombing*. New York: Crown.

Edelhertz, Herbert. 1970. *The Nature, Impact and Prosecution of White-Collar Crime*. Washington, D.C.: U.S. Department of Justice, Law Enforcement Assistance Administration.

Eden, Dov. 1990. "Pygmalion without Interpersonal Contrast Effects: Whole Groups Gain from Raising Manager Expectations." *Journal of Applied Psychology* 75:394–398.

Edgerton, Robert. 1976. *Deviance: A Cross-cultural Perspective*. Menlo Park, CA: Cummings.

Egeland, Byron. 1993. "A History of Abuse Is a Major Risk Factor for Abusing the Next Generation." Pp. 197–208 in *Current Controversies on Family Violence*, edited by Richard J. Gelles and Donileen R. Loseke. Newbury Park, CA: Sage.

Ehrenreich, Barbara. 1994. "Oh, Those Family Values." *Time*, July 18:62.

Ehrenreich, Barbara and Deirdre English. 1979. *For Her Own Good: 150 Years of the Experts' Advice to Women*. Garden City, NY: Anchor Books.

Eijken, Ton. 1995. "The Netherlands: Surveys Provide Insight into Crime." *CJ Europe* 5:1+.

Einstadter, Werner and Stuart Henry. 1995. *Criminological Theory: An Analysis of Its Underlying Assumptions*. Fort Worth: Harcourt Brace.

Eisenstein, James and Hebert Jacob. 1977. *Felony Justice: An Organizational Analysis of Criminal Courts*. Boston: Little, Brown.

Eisenstein, Zilah. 1979. *Capitalist Patriarchy and the Case for Socialist Feminism*. New York: Monthly Review Press.

Elias, Marilyn. 1994. "A Third of Women Hit by Male Partner." *USA Today*, July 7:10.

Elias, Norbert. 1978 [1939]. *The Civilizing Process: The History of Manners*. New York: Urizen.

Elias, Robert. 1986. *The Politics of Victimization: Victims, Victimology, and Human Rights*. New York: Oxford University Press.

Elias, Robert. 1990. "Which Victim Movement? The Politics of Victim Policy." Pp. 226–250 in *Victims of Crime: Problems, Policies, and Programs*, edited by Arthur J. Lurigio, Wesley G. Skogan, and Robert C. Davis. Newbury Park, CA: Sage.

Elias, Robert. 1993. *Victims Still: The Political Manipulation of Crime Victims*. Newbury Park, CA: Sage.

Elliott, Delbert S. 1994. "Serious Violent Offenders: Onset, Developmental Course, and Termination—The American Society of Criminology 1993 Presidential Address." *Criminology* 32:1–21.

Elliott, Delbert S. and Harwin Voss. 1974. *Delinquency and Dropout*. Lexington, MA: Lexington Books.

Elliott, Delbert S. and Suzanne S. Ageton. 1980. "Reconciling Race and Class Differences in Self-Reported and Official Estimates of Delinquency." *American Sociological Review* 45:95–100.

Elliott, Delbert S., David Huizinga, and Suzanne S. Ageton. 1985. *Explaining Delinquency and Drug Use*. Beverly Hills: Sage.

Elliott, Delbert S., Suzanne S. Ageton, and Rachelle J. Canter. 1979. "An Integrated Theoretical Perspective on Delinquent Behavior." *Journal of Research in Crime and Delinquency* 16:3–27.

Ellis, Lee. 1982. "Genetics and Criminal Behavior." *Criminology* 20:43–66.

Engelman, Robert. 1993a. "How Does the Environment Affect Your Health?" *Safety & Health* 147:27–30.

Engelman, Robert. 1993b. "Japan Leads U.S. in Safety." *Safety and Health*, April:38–41.

Engels, Friedrich. 1926. *The Peasant War in Germany*. New York: International Publishers.

Engels, Friedrich. 1993 [1845]. "The Demoralization of the English Working Class." Pp. 48–50 in *Crime and Capitalism: Readings in Marxist Criminology*, edited by David F. Greenberg. Philadelphia: Temple University Press.

Erez, Edna and Pamela Tontodonato. 1992. "Victim Participation in Sentencing and Satisfaction with Justice." *Justice Quarterly* 9:393–417.

Erickson, Maynard L. and Jack P. Gibbs. 1978. "Objective and Perceptual Properties of Legal Punishment and the Deterrence Doctrine." *Social Problems* 25:253–264.

Ericson, Richard V., Patricia M. Baranek, and Janet B. L. Chan. 1991. *Representing Order: Crime, Law, and Justice in the News Media*. Toronto: University of Toronto Press.

Ermann, M. David and Richard J. Lundman. 1978. "Deviant Acts by Complex Organizations: Deviance and Social Control at the Organizational Level of Analysis." *Sociological Quarterly* 19:56–67.

Ermann, M. David and Richard J. Lundman. 1992. "Overview." Pp. 3–43 in *Corporate and Governmental Deviance: Problems of Organizational Behavior in Contemporary Society*, edited by M. David Ermann and Richard J. Lundman. New York: Oxford University Press.

Estes, Ken and Mike Brubaker. 1994. *Deadly Odds: Recovery from Compulsive Gambling*. New York: Simon & Schuster.

Estrich, Susan. 1987. *Real Rape*. Cambridge: Harvard University Press.

Evans, Sandra S. and Joseph E. Scott. 1984. "The Seriousness of Crime Cross-Culturally: The Impact of Religiosity." *Criminology* 22:39–59.

Evans, T. David, Francis T. Cullen, R. Gregory Dunaway, and Velmer S. Burton, Jr. 1995. "Religion and Crime Reexamined: The Impact of Religion, Secular Controls, and Social Ecology on Adult Criminality." *Criminology* 33:195–224.

Evans, T. David, Francis T. Cullen, Velmer S. Burton, Jr., R. Gregory Dunaway, and Michael L. Benson. 1997. "The Social Consequences of Self-Control: Testing the General Theory of Crime." *Criminology* 35:475–501.

Fagan, Jeffrey and Angela Browne. 1994. "Violence between Spouses and Intimates: Physical Aggression between Women and Men in Intimate Relationships." Pp. 115–292 in *Understanding and Preventing Violence: Social Influences*, vol. 3, edited by Albert J. Reiss, Jr. and Jeffrey A. Roth. Washington, D.C.: National Academy Press.

Faison, Seth. 1995. "China's Anti-Graft Drive Grows; So Does Graft." *New York Times*, August 10:A3.

Faludi, Susan. 1991. *Backlash: The Undeclared War against American Women*. New York: Crown.

Farnworth, Margaret. 1984. "Male-Female Differences in Delinquency in a Minority-Group Sample." *Journal of Research in Crime and Delinquency* 21:191–213.

Farnworth, Margaret and Michael J. Leiber. 1989. "Strain Theory Revisited: Economic Goals, Educational Means, and Delinquency." *American Sociological Review* 54:263–274.

Farnworth, Margaret, Raymond H. C. Teske, Jr., and Gina Thurman. 1991. "Ethnic, Racial, and Minority Disparity in Felony Court Processing." Pp. 54–70 in *Race and Criminal Justice*, edited by Michael J. Lynch and E. Britt Patterson. New York: Harrow and Heston.

Farnworth, Margaret, Terence P. Thornberry, Marvin D. Krohn, and Alan J. Lizotte. 1994. "Measurement in the Study of Class and Delinquency: Integrating Theory and Research." *Journal of Research in Crime and Delinquency* 31:33–61.

Farrell, Bill and Larry Koch. 1995. "Criminal Justice, Sociology, and Academia." *The American Sociologist* 26:52–61.

Farrell, Ronald A. and Victoria Lynn Swigert. 1978. "Prior Offense as a Self-Fulfilling Prophecy." *Law and Society Review* 12:437–453.

Farrington, David P. 1986. "Age and Crime." Pp. 189–250 in *Crime and Justice: An Annual Review of Research*, vol. 7, edited by Michael Tonry and Norval Morris. Chicago: University of Chicago Press.

Farrington, David P. 1998. "Individual Differences and Offending." Pp. 241–268 in *The Handbook of Crime and Punishment*, edited by Michael Tonry. New York: Oxford University Press.

Fazlollah, Mark. 1997. "11 More Cleared Due to Scandal." *Philadelphia Inquirer*, March 25:A1.

Federal Bureau of Investigation. 1999. *Crime in the United States: 1998*. Washington, D.C.: Federal Bureau of Investigation.

Feeley, Malcolm M. 1979. "Perspectives on Plea Bargaining." *Law and Society Review* 13:199–209.

Feimer, S., F. Pommersheim, and S. Wise. 1990. "Marking Time: Does Race Make a Difference? A Study of Disparate Sentencing in South Dakota." *Journal of Crime and Justice* 13:86–102.

Feldberg, Michael. 1980. *The Turbulent Era: Riot and Disorder in Jacksonian America*. New York: Oxford University Press.

Felson, Marcus. 1998. *Crime and Everyday Life: Insights and Implications for Society*. Thousand Oaks, CA: Pine Forge Press.

Felson, Richard B. and Henry J. Steadman. 1983. "Situational Factors in Disputes Leading to Criminal Violence." *Criminology* 21:59–74.

Felson, Richard B. and Marvin Krohn. 1990. "Motives for Rape." *Journal of Research in Crime and Delinquency* 27:222–242.

Felson, Richard B. and Steven F. Messner. 1998. "Disentangling the Effects of Gender and Intimacy on Victim Precipitation in Homicide." *Criminology* 36:405–423.

Fenster, Jim. 1994. "Nation of Gamblers." *American Heritage* 45:34–45.

Ferdinand, Theodore. 1970. "Demographic Shifts and Criminality: An Inquiry." *British Journal of Criminology* 10:169–175.

Ferraro, Kathleen J. 1995. "Cops, Courts, and Woman Battering." Pp. 262–271 in *The Criminal Justice System and Women: Offenders, Victims, and Workers*, edited by Barbara Raffel Price and Natalie J. Sokoloff. New York: McGraw-Hill.

Filipov, David. 1995. "Moscow War on Crime Turns Futile." *Boston Globe*, June 5:1.

Finkelhor, David. 1979. *Sexually Victimized Children*. New York: Free Press.

Finkelman, Paul. 1981. "The Zenger Case: Prototype of a Political Trial." Pp. 21–42 in *American Political Trials*, edited by Michal Belknap. Westport, CT: Greenwood Press.

Fischbach, Ruth L. and Barbara Herbert. 1997. "Domestic Violence and Mental Health: Correlates and Conundrums within and across Cultures." *Social Science & Medicine* 45:1161–1176.

Fishbein, Diana H. 1996. "The Biology of Antisocial Behavior." Pp. 26–38 in *New Perspectives in Criminology*, edited by John E. Conklin. Boston: Allyn and Bacon.

Fishbein, Diana. 1998. "Building Bridges." *ACJS Today* 17:1–5.

Fisher, Bonnie S., John J. Sloan, Francis T. Cullen, and Chunmeng Lu. 1998. "Crime in the Ivory Tower: The Level and Sources of Student Victimization." *Criminology* 36:671–710.

Fisher, Lawrence M. 1992. "Accusation of Fraud at Sears; Auto Repair Shops Cited by California." *New York Times*, June 12:C1.

Fishman, Gideon and Simon Dinitz. 1989. "Japan: A

Country with Safe Streets." Pp. 111–126 in *Advances in Criminological Theory*, vol. 1, edited by William S. Laufer and Freda Adler. New Brunswick, NJ: Transaction.

Fishman, Mark. 1978. "Crime Waves as Ideology." *Social Problems* 25:531–543.

Fitzpatrick, Kevin M., Mark E. La Gory, and Ferris J. Ritchey. 1993. "Criminal Victimization among the Homeless." *Justice Quarterly* 10:353–368.

Fletcher, George P. 1988. *A Crime of Self-Defense: Bernhard Goetz and the Law on Trial*. New York: Free Press.

Fletcher, Michael A. 2000. "We Seem to Be Winning the War on Crime. But How?" *Washington Post*, January 16:F1.

Fogelson, Robert M. 1971. *Violence as Protest: A Study of Riots and Ghettos*. Garden City, NY: Anchor.

Fortgang, Erika. 1999. "How They Got the Guns." *Rolling Stone*, June 10:51–52.

Fox, James A. and Jack Levin. 1991. "Homicide against the Elderly: A Research Note." *Criminology* 29:317–327.

Fox, James Alan and Marianne W. Zawitz. 1998. *Homicide Trends in the United States*. Washington, D.C.: U.S. Department of Justice, Bureau of Justice Statistics.

Fox, Stephen R. 1989. *Blood and Power: Organized Crime in Twentieth-Century America*. New York: Morrow.

Fradkin, Philip L. 1989. *Fall Out: American Tragedy*. Tucson: University of Arizona Press.

Francis, David R. 1994. "States May Not Find Jackpot in Gambling." *The Christian Science Monitor*, March 11:11.

Frank, Nancy K. and Michael J. Lynch. 1992. *Corporate Crime, Corporate Violence: A Primer*. New York: Harrow and Heston.

Frankfurter, Felix and Roscoe Pound. 1922. *Criminal Justice in Cleveland*. Cleveland: The Cleveland Foundation.

Franklin, James L. 1995. "Ex-Episcopal Aide Talks of $2.2M Loss." *Boston Globe*, May 2:6.

Frantz, Joe E. 1979. "The Frontier Tradition: An Invitation to Violence." Pp. 101–119 in *Violence in America: Historical and Comparative Perspectives*, edited by Hugh Davis Graham and Ted Robert Gurr. Beverly Hills: Sage.

Freeman, Michael. 1994. "Networks Doubled Crime Coverage in '93, Despite Flat Violence Levels in U.S. Society." *Mediaweek* 4:4.

Freeman, Richard B. 1995. "The Labor Market." Pp. 171–191 in *Crime*, edited by James Q. Wilson and Joan Petersilia. San Francisco: Institute for Contemporary Studies Press.

Friedman, Jane M. 1993. *America's First Woman Lawyer: The Biography of Myra Bradwell*. Buffalo: Prometheus Books.

Friedman, Leon. 1971. *The Wise Minority*. New York: Dial Press.

Friedman, Lucy N. 1994. "Adopting the Health Care Model to Prevent Victimization." *National Institute of Justice Journal*:16–19.

Friedrichs, David O. 1996. *Trusted Criminals: White Collar Crime in Contemporary Society*. Belmont, CA: Wadsworth.

Frieze, Irene Hanson, S. Hymer, and M. S. Greenberg. 1987. "Describing the Crime Victim: Psychological Reactions to Rape." *Professional Psychology Research and Practice* 18:222–315.

Frohmann, Lisa. 1997. "Convictability and Discordant Locales: Reproducing Race, Class, and Gender Ideologies in Prosecutorial Decisionmaking." *Law & Society Review* 31:531–555.

Fyfe, James J. 1983. "The NIJ Study of the Exclusionary Rule." *Criminal Law Bulletin* 19:253–260.

Fyfe, James J. 1988. "Police Use of Deadly Force: Research and Reform." *Justice Quarterly* 5:165–205.

Fyfe, James J. 1993. "Police Use of Deadly Force: Research and Reform." Pp. 128–142 in *Criminal Justice: Law and Politics*, edited by George F. Cole. Belmont, CA: Wadsworth.

Fyfe, James J., David A. Klinger, and Jeanne M. Flavin. 1997. "Differential Police Treatment of Male-on-Female Spousal Violence." *Criminology* 35:455–473.

Gallagher, Carole. 1993. *Nuclear Ground Zero: The Secret Nuclear War*. Cambridge: MIT Press.

Gammage, Jeff. 1997. "Baltimore Forges a Different Course on Drug Abuse." *Philadelphia Inquirer*, December 29:A1.

Gamson, William A. 1990. *The Strategy of Social Protest*. Belmont, CA: Wadsworth.

Garbarino, James. 1989. "The Incidence and Prevalence of Child Maltreatment." Pp. 219–261 in *Family Violence*, vol. 11, *Crime and Justice: A Review of Research*, edited by Lloyd Ohlin and Michael Tonry. Chicago: University of Chicago Press.

Gardner, Carol Brooks. 1990. "Safe Conduct: Women, Crime, and Self in Public Places." *Social Problems* 37:311–328.

Gardner, Saundra. 1994. "Real Domestic Tragedy Continues." *Bangor Daily News*, June 29:A9.

Gargan, Edward A. 1993. "For Many Brides in India, a Dowry Buys Death." *New York Times*, December 30:A4.

Garland, David. 1990. *Punishment and Modern Society: A Study in Social Theory*. Chicago: University of Chicago Press.

Garofalo, James. 1987. "Reassessing the Lifestyle Model of Criminal Victimization." Pp. 23–42 in *Positive Criminology*, edited by Michael Gottfredson and Travis Hirschi. Newbury Park, CA: Sage.

Garofalo, James. 1990. "Crime and the Mass Media: A Selective Review of Research." Pp. 322–327 in *Violence: Patterns, Causes, Public Policy*, edited by Neil Alan Weiner, Margaret A. Zahn, and Rita J. Sagi. San Diego: Harcourt Brace Jovanovich.

Garofalo, James and David Clark. 1992. "Guardianship

and Residential Burglary." *Justice Quarterly* 9:443–463.

Garofalo, James and M. McLeod. 1989. "The Structure and Operations of Neighborhood Watch Programs in the United States." *Crime and Delinquency* 35:326–344.

Garrow, David J. 1981. *The FBI and Martin Luther King, Jr.* New York: Penguin Press.

Gatrell, V. A. C. 1994. *The Hanging Tree: Execution and the English People 1770–1868*. New York: Oxford University Press.

Geis, Gilbert. 1979. *Not the Law's Business: An Examination of Homosexuality, Abortion, Prostitution, Narcotics, and Gambling in the United States*. New York: Schocken.

Geis, Gilbert. 1987. "The Heavy Electrical Equipment Antitrust Cases of 1961." Pp. 124–144 in *Corporate and Governmental Deviance: Problems of Organizational Behavior in Contemporary Society*, edited by M. David Ermann and Richard J. Lundman. New York: Oxford University Press.

Geis, Gilbert. 1992. "White-Collar Crime: What Is It?" Pp. 31–52 in *White-Collar Crime Reconsidered*, edited by Kip Schlegel and David Weisburd. Boston: Northeastern University Press.

Geis, Gilbert. 1995. "White-Collar Crime." Pp. 213–221 in *Readings in Deviant Behavior*, edited by Alex Thio and Thomas Calhoun. New York: HarperCollins.

Geis, Gilbert, Paul Jesilow, Henry Pontell, and Mary Jane O'Brien. 1985. "Fraud and Abuse of Government Medical Benefit Programs by Psychiatrists." *American Journal of Psychiatry* 142:231–234.

Gelbspan, Ross. 1991. *Break-Ins, Death Threats and the FBI: The Covert War against the Central America Movement*. Boston: South End Press.

Gellene, Denise. 1994. "No Easy Fix for Auto Body Repair Fraud." *Los Angeles Times*, July 22:D3.

Gelles, Richard J. 1978. "Violence toward Children in the United States." *American Journal of Orthopsychiatry* 48:580–592.

Gelsthorpe, Loraine and Allison Morris. 1988. "Feminism and Criminology in Britain." *British Journal of Criminology* 28:93–110.

Gentry, Cynthia. 1991. "Pornography and Rape: An Empirical Analysis." *Deviant Behavior* 12:277–288.

Germain, David. 2000. "Shipping Workers Held in Stolen Oscar Caper." *Bangor Daily News*, March 21:C1.

Gerth, Hans and C. Wright Mills, eds. 1946. *From Max Weber: Essays in Sociology*. New York: Oxford University Press.

Giancola, Peter. 1999. "Alcohol: The Aggression Elixir?" *The HFG Review* 3:25–29.

Gibbons, Don C. 1992. "Talking About Crime: Observations on the Prospects for Causal Theory in Criminology." *Criminal Justice Research Bulletin* 7:1–10.

Gibbons, Don C. 1994. *Thinking about Crime and Criminals: Problems and Issues in Theory Development in Criminology*. Englewood Cliffs, NJ: Prentice Hall.

Gibbs, Jewelle Taylor. 1992. "Young Black Males in America: Endangered, Embittered, and Embattled." Pp. 50–66 in *Men's Lives*, edited by Michael S. Kimmel and Michael A. Messner. New York: Macmillan.

Gibbs, Jewelle Taylor and Joseph R. Merighi. 1994. "Young Black Males: Marginality, Masculinity and Criminality." Pp. 64–80 in *Just Boys Doing Business? Men, Masculinities and Crime*, edited by Tim Newburn and Elizabeth A. Stanko. London: Routledge.

Gil, David G. 1979. *Violence against Children*. Cambridge: Harvard University Press.

Gilbert, Martin. 1987. *The Holocaust: A History of the Jews of Europe during the Second World War*. New York: Henry Holt and Company.

Gilligan, Carol. 1982. *In a Different Voice: Psychological Theory and Women's Development*. Cambridge: Harvard University Press.

Gilmore, David D. 1990. *Manhood in the Making: Cultural Concepts of Masculinity*. New Haven: Yale University Press.

Ginger, Ray. 1949. *Eugene V. Debs: A Biography*. New York: Collier.

Giordano, Peggy C., Stephen A. Cernkovich, and Meredith D. Pugh. 1986. "Friendships and Delinquency." *American Journal of Sociology* 91:1170–1202.

Giradet, Evelyne. 1999. "Survey: 1 in 4 Angry at Work." *Boston Globe*, August 11:D6.

Glaser, Daniel. 1956. "Criminality Theories and Behavioral Images." *American Journal of Sociology* 61:433–444.

Glaser, Daniel. 1997. *Profitable Penalties: How to Cut Both Crime Rates and Costs*. Thousand Oaks, CA: Pine Forge Press.

Glassner, Barry. 1999. *The Culture of Fear: Why Americans Are Afraid of the Wrong Things*. New York: Basic Books.

Glover, Scott and Matt Lait. 2000a. "Police in Secret Group Broke Law Routinely, Transcripts Say." *Los Angeles Times*, February 10:A1.

Glover, Scott and Matt Lait. 2000b. "Beatings Alleged to Be Routine at Rampart." *Los Angeles Times*, February 14:A1.

Glueck, Sheldon and Eleanor Glueck. 1950. *Unraveling Juvenile Delinquency*. New York: Commonwealth Fund.

Glueck, Sheldon and Eleanor Glueck. 1968. *Delinquents and Nondelinquents in Perspective*. Cambridge: Harvard University Press.

Goddard, Henry H. 1912. *The Kallikak Family: A Study in the Heredity of Feeblemindedness*. New York: Macmillan.

Gold, David A., Clarence Y. H. Lo, and Erik Olin Wright. 1975. "Recent Developments in Marxist Theory of the Capitalist State, Part I." *Monthly Review* 27:29–43.

Goldberg, Debbie. 1997. "Crime on Campus: How Safe Are Students?" *Washington Post*, April 6:R1.

Golding, William. 1954. *Lord of the Flies*. London: Coward-McCann.

Goldman, Henry. 1997. "N.Y. Crime Crackdown Is Drawing Fire." *Philadelphia Inquirer*, January 1997:A1.

Goldman, Jessica L. 1994. "Arresting Abusers Would Reduce Domestic Violence." Pp. 94–101 in *Violence against Women*, edited by Karin L. Swisher and Carol Wekesser. San Diego: Greenhaven Press.

Goldstein, Amy. 1999. "Theory Ties Abortion to Crime Drop." *Washington Post*, August 10:A9.

Goldstein, Robert Justin. 1978. *Political Repression in Modern America: 1870 to the Present*. Cambridge: Schenkman.

Goldston, James. 1990. *A Year of Reckoning: El Salvador a Decade after the Assassination of Archbishop Romero*. New York: Americas Watch Committee.

Goode, Erica. 1999. "*Roe v. Wade* Resulted in Unborn Criminals, Economists Theorize." *New York Times*, August 20:A1.

Goode, Erich. 1984. *Drugs in American Society*. New York: Knopf.

Goode, Erich. 1994. *Deviant Behavior*. Englewood Cliffs, NJ: Prentice Hall.

Goode, Erich. 1999. *Drugs in American Society*. New York: McGraw Hill.

Goodell, Charles. 1973. *Political Prisoners in America*. New York: Random House.

Goodman, Ellen. 1999. "Linking Crime, Abortion Rates Makes Everyone Queasy." *Boston Globe* August 15:F7.

Goodstein, Lynne. 1992. "Feminist Perspectives and the Criminal Justice Curriculum." *Justice Quarterly* 3:165–181.

Gordon, Margaret T. and Stephanie Riger. 1989. *The Female Fear*. New York: Free Press.

Gottfredson, Michael R. 1986. "Substantive Contributions of Victimization Surveys." Pp. 251–287 in *Crime and Justice: An Annual Review of Research*, vol. 7, edited by Michael Tonry and Norval Morris. Chicago: University of Chicago Press.

Gottfredson, Michael R. and Travis Hirschi. 1986. "The True Value of Lambda Would Appear to Be Zero: An Essay on Career Criminals, Criminal Careers, Selective Incapacitation, Cohort Studies, and Related Topics." *Criminology* 24:213–234.

Gottfredson, Michael R. and Travis Hirschi. 1988. "Science, Policy, and the Career Paradigm." *Criminology* 26:37–55.

Gottfredson, Michael and Travis Hirschi. 1990. *A General Theory of Crime*. Stanford: Stanford University Press.

Gottfredson, Stephen D. and Don M. Gottfredson. 1994. "Behavioral Prediction and the Problem of Incapacitation." *Criminology* 32:441–474.

Gould, Stephen Jay. 1981. *The Mismeasure of Man*. New York: W. W. Norton.

Gove, Walter R., ed. 1980. The *Labeling of Deviance: Exploring a Perspective*. Beverly Hills: Sage.

Gove, Walter R., Michael Hughes, and Michael Geerken.

1985. "Are Uniform Crime Reports a Valid Indicator of the Index Crimes? An Affirmative Answer with Minor Qualifications." *Criminology* 23:451–501.

Graber, Doris A. 1980. *Crime News and the Public*. New York: Praeger.

Graham, Nanette and Eric D. Wish. 1994. "Drug Use among Female Arrestees: Onset, Patterns, and Relationships to Prostitution." *Journal of Drug Issues* 24:315–329.

Grasmick, Harold G. and Anne L. McGill. 1994. "Religion, Attribution Style, and Punitiveness toward Juvenile Offenders." *Criminology* 32:23–46.

Grasmick, Harold G., Robert J. Bursik, Jr., and Bruce J. Arneklev. 1993. "Reduction in Drunk Driving as a Response to Increased Threats of Shame, Embarrassment, and Legal Sanctions." *Criminology* 31:41–67.

Grasmick, Harold G., Charles R. Tittle, Robert J. Bursik, Jr., and Bruce J. Arneklev. 1993. "Testing the Core Empirical Implications of Gottfredson and Hirschi's General Theory of Crime." *Journal of Research in Crime and Delinquency* 30:5–29.

Gray, Francine du Plessix. 1970. *Divine Disobedience: Profiles in Catholic Radicalism*. New York: Knopf.

Green, Gary S. 1987. "Citizen Gun Ownership and Criminal Deterrence: Theory, Research, and Policy." *Criminology* 25:63–81.

Green, Gary S. 1993. "White-Collar Crime and the Study of Embezzlement." *Annals of the American Academy of Political and Social Science* 525:95–106.

Green, Lorraine. 1995. "Cleaning Up Drug Hot Spots in Oakland, California: The Displacement and Diffusion Effects." *Justice Quarterly* 12:737–754.

Green, Robert. 1999. "Tampa Shooting Spree Leaves 5 Dead, 3 Injured." *Boston Globe*, December 31:A3.

Greenberg, David F. 1977. "Delinquency and the Age Structure of Society." *Contemporary Crises* 1:66–86.

Greenberg, David F. 1993. "Introduction." Pp. 1–35 in *Crime and Capitalism: Readings in Marxist Criminology*, edited by David F. Greenberg. Philadelphia: Temple University Press.

Greenberg, Jerald. 1990. "Employee Theft as a Reaction to Underpayment Inequity: The Hidden Cost of Pay Cuts." *Journal of Applied Psychology* 75:561–568.

Greene, Jack R. and Steven Mastrofski, eds. 1988. *Community Policing: Rhetoric or Reality?* New York: Praeger.

Greenfeld, Lawrence A. and Steven K. Smith. 1999. *American Indians and Crime*. Washington, D.C.: U.S. Department of Justice, Bureau of Justice Statistics.

Greenfeld, Lawrence A. and Tracy L. Snell. 1999. *Women Offenders*. Washington, D.C.: U.S. Department of Justice: Bureau of Justice Statistics.

Greenfeld, Lawrence A., Michael R. Rand, Diane Craven, Patsy A. Klaus, Craig A. Perkins, Cheryl Ringel, Greg Warchol, Cathy Maston, and James Alan Fox. 1998. *Violence by Intimates: Analysis of Data on Crimes* by Current or Former Spouses, Boyfriends, and Girl-friends. Washington, D.C.: U.S. Department of Justice, Bureau of Justice Statistics.

Greenhouse, Steven. 1999. "National Guard Is Called to Quell Trade-Talk Protests." *New York Times*, December 1:A1.

Greenwood, Peter W. 1995. "Juvenile Crime and Juvenile Justice." Pp. 91–117 in *Crime*, edited by James Q. Wilson and Joan Petersilia. San Francisco: Institute for Contemporary Studies Press.

Griffin, Susan. 1971. "Rape: The All-American Crime." *Ramparts*, September:26–35.

Griffiths, Richard. 1991. *The Use of Abuse: The Polemics of the Dreyfus Affair and Its Aftermath*. New York: St. Martin's Press.

Groth, A. Nicholas. 1979. *Men Who Rape: The Psychology of the Offender*. New York: Plenum Press.

Grunwald, Michael. 1994. "Crime Takes Its Toll on Quality of Daily Life." *Boston Globe*, April 2:19, 22.

Grunwald, Michael. 1997. "Mavericks in the War on Drugs." *Boston Globe*, November 12:A1.

Grunwald, Michael and Michael Kranish. 1995. "Victim Search Nears End; Bombing Toll Reaches 144." *Boston Globe*, May 4:1.

Gurr, Ted Robert. 1989a. "Historical Trends in Violent Crime: Europe and the United States." Pp. 21–54 in *Violence in America*, vol. 1, *The History of Crime*, edited by Ted Robert Gurr. Newbury Park, CA: Sage.

Gurr, Ted Robert. 1989b. "Political Terrorism: Historical Antecedents and Contemporary Trends." Pp. 201–230 in *Violence in America*, vol. 2, *Protest, Rebellion, Reform*, edited by Ted Robert Gurr. Newbury Park, CA: Sage.

Gusfield, Joseph R. 1963. *Symbolic Crusade: Status Politics and the American Temperance Movement*. Urbana, IL: University of Illinois Press.

Gustin, Joseph, et al. 1999. *National Household Survey on Drug Abuse: Population Estimates 1998*. Washington, D.C.: Substance Abuse and Mental Health Services Administration, U.S. Department of Health and Human Services.

Guthrie, Mary. 1993. "Rip-Offs; Firms Target Employee Thefts." *Los Angeles Times*, January 5:D1.

Haberman, Clyde. 2000. "More Blood, More Cause to Be Uneasy." *New York Times*, March 17:B2.

Haberman, Clyde. 2000. "When Doing Wrong Isn't Wrong-doing." *New York Times*, February 27:section 4, p. 3.

Hacker, Andrew. 1992. *Two Nations: Black and White, Separate, Hostile, Unequal*. New York: Scribner's.

Hagan, Frank E. 1989. "Espionage as Political Crime? A Typology of Spies." *Journal of Security Administration* 12:19–36.

Hagan, John. 1974. "Extra-legal Attributes and Criminal Sentencing: An Assessment of a Sociological Viewpoint." *Law and Society Review* 8:357–383.

Hagan, John. 1990. "The Pleasures of Predation and Disrepute." *Law & Society Review* 24:165–177.

Hagan, John. 1991. "Destiny and Drift: Subcultural Preferences, Status Attainments, and the Risks and Rewards of Youth." *American Sociological Review* 46:567–582.

Hagan, John. 1992. "The Poverty of a Classless Criminology—The American Society of Criminology 1991 Presidential Address." *Criminology* 30:1–19.

Hagan, John. 1993. "Introduction: Crime in Social and Legal Context." *Law & Society Review* 27:255–262.

Hagan, John. 1993. "The Social Embeddedness of Crime and Unemployment." *Criminology* 31:465–491.

Hagan, John. 1994. *Crime and Disrepute*. Thousand Oaks, CA: Pine Forge Press.

Hagan, John, ed. 1989. *Structural Criminology*. New Brunswick, NJ: Rutgers University Press.

Hagan, John and Celesta Albonetti. 1982. "Race, Class, and the Perception of Criminal Injustice in America." *American Journal of Sociology* 88:329–355.

Hagan, John and Holly Foster. 2000. "Making Corporate and Criminal America Less Violent: Public Norms and Structural Reforms." *Contemporary Sociology* 29:44–53.

Hagan, John and Marjorie S. Zatz. 1985. "The Social Organization of Criminal Justice Processing Activities." *Social Science Research* 14:103–125.

Hagan, John and Ruth Peterson. 1995. "Criminal Inequality in America: Patterns and Consequences." Pp. 14–36 in *Crime and Inequality*, edited by John Hagan and Ruth D. Peterson. Stanford: Stanford University Press.

Hagan, John and Ruth Peterson, eds. 1995. *Crime and Inequality*. Stanford: Stanford University Press.

Hagan, John, John Simpson, and A. R. Gillis. 1987. "Class in the Household: A Power-Control Theory of Gender and Delinquency." *American Journal of Sociology* 92:788–816.

Hagedorn, John M. 1994. "Neighborhoods, Markets, and Gang Drug Organization." *Journal of Research in Crime and Delinquency* 31:264–294.

Hall, E. and A. Simkus. 1975. "Inequality in the Types of Sentences Received by Native Americans and Whites." *Criminology* 13:199–222.

Hall, Jerome. 1952. *Theft, Law, and Society*. Indianapolis: Bobbs-Merrill.

Hall, Robert T. 1971. *The Morality of Civil Disobedience*. New York: Harper & Row.

Halperin, Morton. 1977. *The Lawless State: The Crimes of the U.S. Intelligence Agencies*. New York: Penguin Press.

Halverson, Guy. 1991. "Businesses Fight Coupon Fraud." *The Christian Science Monitor*, December 12:8.

Hamilton, Andrea. 1995. "Gay Groups Are Spied Upon, FBI Data Show." *Boston Globe*, May 16:3.

Hamilton, V. Lee and Steven Rytina. 1980. "Social Consensus on Norms of Justice: Should the Punishment Fit the Crime?" *American Journal of Sociology* 85:1117–1144.

Hamm, Mark S. 1995. *American Skinheads: The Criminology and Control of Hate Crime.* Westport, CT: Praeger.

Hamm, Mark S., ed. 1994. *Hate Crime: International Perspectives on Causes and Control.* Cincinnati: Anderson.

Hampton, R. L. 1987. "Race, Class and Child Maltreatment." *Journal of Comparative Family Studies* 18:113–126.

Hardt, Robert H. and Sandra Peterson-Hardt. 1977. "On Determining the Quality of the Delinquency Self-Report Method." *Journal of Research in Crime and Delinquency* 14:247–261.

Harrell, Adele V. and George E. Peterson, eds. 1992. *Drugs, Crime and Social Isolation: Barriers to Urban Opportunity.* Lanham, MD: University Press of America.

Harring, Sidney L. 1993. "Policing a Class Society: The Expansion of the Urban Police in the Late Nineteenth and Early Twentieth Centuries." Pp. 546–567 in *Crime and Capitalism: Readings in Marxist Criminology,* edited by David F. Greenberg. Philadelphia: Temple University Press.

Harris, Anthony R. and James A. W. Shaw. 2000. "Looking for Patterns: Race, Class, and Crime." Pp. 129–163 in *Criminology: A Contemporary Handbook,* edited by Joseph F. Sheley. Belmont, CA: Wadsworth.

Harrison, Ann. 1999. "Mitnick Gets 46-Month Term." *Computerworld,* August 16:16.

Harrison, Judy. 2000. "Police Say Instrument Thefts Could Be Connected." *Bangor Daily News,* March 17:B2.

Hart, Jordana and Francie Latour. 1999. "Serial Killer Theory Downplayed." *Boston Globe,* November 2:B1.

Harvey, William B. 1986. "Homicide among Young Black Adults: Life in the Subculture of Exasperation." Pp. 153–171 in *Homicide among Black Americans,* edited by Darnell F. Hawkins. Lanham, MD: University Press of America.

Hawkins, Darnell F. 1983. "Black and White Homicide Differentials: Alternatives to an Inadequate Theory." *Criminal Justice and Behavior* 10:407–440.

Hawkins, Darnell F. 1987. "Beyond Anomalies: Rethinking the Conflict Perspective on Race and Criminal Punishment." *Social Forces* 65:719–745.

Hawkins, Darnell F. 1990. "Explaining the Black Homicide Rate." *Journal of Interpersonal Violence* 5:151–163.

Hawkins, Darnell F. 1994. "The Analysis of Racial Disparities in Crime and Justice: A Double-Edged Sword." Pp. 48–50 in *Enhancing Capacities and Confronting Controversies in Criminal Justice,* edited by Tom Hester, Yvonne Boston, Linda N. Ruder, Helen A. Graziadel, and Benjamin H. Renshaw III. Washington, D.C.: U.S. Department of Justice, Bureau of Justice Statistics.

Hawkins, Darnell F. 1995. "Ethnicity, Race, and Crime: A Review of Selected Studies." Pp. 11–45 in *Ethnicity, Race, and Crime: Perspectives across Time and Place,* edited by Darnell F. Hawkins. Albany, NY: State University of New York Press.

Hay, Douglas. 1975. "Property, Authority and the Criminal Law." Pp. 17–63 in *Albion's Fatal Tree: Crime and Society in Eighteenth-Century England,* edited by Douglas Hay, Peter Linebaugh, John G. Rule, E. P. Thompson, and Cal Winslow. New York: Panetheon Books.

Heeren, John W. and David Shichor. 1993. "Faculty Malfeasance: Understanding Academic Deviance." *Sociological Inquiry* 63:49–63.

Hegar, Rebecca L., Susan J. Zuravin, and John G. Orme. 1994. "Factors Predicting Severity of Physical Child Abuse Injury: A Review of the Literature." *Journal of Interpersonal Violence* 9:170–183.

Heimer, Karen and Stacy De Coster. 1999. "The Gendering of Violent Delinquency." *Criminology* 37:277–317.

Held, David. 1991. *Political Theory Today.* Stanford: Stanford University Press.

Helfer, R. and C. Henry Kempe, eds. 1979. *The Battered Child.* Chicago: University of Chicago Press.

Hemenway, David. 1997. "Survey Research and Self-Defense Gun Use: An Explanation of Extreme Overestimates." *Journal of Criminal Law and Criminology* 87:1430–1445.

Henderson, Wade. 1991. "Police Brutality Is a National Crisis." Pp. 23–29 in *Police Brutality,* edited by William Dudley. San Diego: Greenhaven Press.

Henggeler, Scott. 1989. *Delinquency in Adolescence.* Newbury Park, CA: Sage.

Henry, Frank and Susanne Chomicki. 1990. "Violence against Children: The Pharmaceutical Industry." Pp. 61–76 in *The Victimology Handbook: Research Findings, Treatment, and Public Policy,* edited by Emilio Viano. New York: Garland.

Hentig, Hans Von. 1948. *The Criminal and His Victim: Studies in the Sociobiology of Crime.* Hamden, CT: Archon Books.

Hepburn, John. 1984. "Occasional Criminals." Pp. 73–94 in *Major Forms of Crime,* edited by Robert Meier. Beverly Hills: Sage.

Hepburn, Mary. 1993. "Prostitution: Will Legalisation Help?" *British Medical Journal* 307:1370–1371.

Herbert, Bob. 2000. "At the Heart of the Diallo Case." *New York Times,* February 28:A23.

Herbert, Steve. 1998. "Police Subculture Reconsidered." *Criminology* 36:343–369.

Hernandez, Raymond. 1998. "Most Dropped from Welfare Don't Get Jobs." *New York Times,* March 23:A1.

Herrnstein, Richard J. and Charles Murray. 1994. *The Bell Curve: Intelligence and Class Structure in American Life.* New York: Free Press.

Hersh, Seymoure M. 1970. *My Lai 4: A Report on the Massacre and Its Aftermath.* New York: Random House.

Hershkowitz, Leo. 1977. *Tweed's New York: Another Look.* Garden City, NY: Anchor.

Hertzberg, Hendrik. 1999. "Comment: Gore's Greatest Bong Hits." *The New Yorker,* February 7:31–32.

Hester, Marianne. 1992. "The Witch-Craze in Sixteenth- and Seventeenth-Century England as Social Control of Women." Pp. 27–39 in *Femicide: The Politics of Woman Killing*, edited by Jill Radford and Diana E. H. Russell. New York: Twayne.

Hicks, Karen M. 1994. *Surviving the Dalkon Shield IUD: Women v. the Pharmaceutical Industry*. New York: Columbia University Teachers College Press.

Hilts, Philip J. and Glenn Collins. 1995. "Documents Disclose Philip Morris Studied Nicotine's Effect on Body." *New York Times*, June 8:1.

Hindelang, Michael J. 1974. "Moral Evaluation of Illegal Behaviors." *Social Problems* 21:370–385.

Hindelang, Michael J. 1978. "Race and Involvement in Common Law Personal Crimes." *American Sociological Review* 43:93–109.

Hindelang, Michael J. 1981. "Variations in Sex-Race-Age-Specific Rates of Offending." *American Sociological Review* 46:461–474.

Hindelang, Michael J., Travis Hirschi, and Joseph Weis. 1979. "Correlates of Delinquency: the Illusion of Discrepancy between Self-Report and Official Measures." *American Sociological Review* 44:995–1014.

Hirschi, Travis. 1969. *Causes of Delinquency*. Berkeley: University of California Press.

Hirschi, Travis. 1979. "Separate and Unequal Is Better." *Journal of Research in Crime and Delinquency* 16:34–37.

Hirschi, Travis and Michael Gottfredson. 1987. "Causes of White-Collar Crime." *Criminology* 25:949–974.

Hirschi, Travis and Michael J. Hindelang. 1977. "Intelligence and Delinquency: A Revisionist Review." *American Sociological Review* 42:571–587.

Hirschi, Travis and Rodney Stark. 1969. "Hellfire and Delinquency." *Social Problems* 17:202–213.

Hobbes, Thomas. 1950 [1651]. *Leviathan*. New York: Dutton.

Hobbs, Dick. 1994. "Mannish Boys: Danny, Chris, Crime, Masculinity and Business." Pp. 118–134 in *Just Boys Doing Business? Men, Masculinities and Crime*, edited by Tim Newburn and Elizabeth A. Stanko. London: Routledge.

Hobson, Barbara Meil. 1987. *Uneasy Virtue: The Politics of Prostitution and the American Reform Tradition*. New York: Basic.

Hoffman, Bruce. 1993. "Terrorism in the United States: Recent Trends and Future Prospects." Pp. 220–225 in *Violence and Terrorism*, edited by Bernard Schechterman and Martin Slann. Guilford, CT: Dushkin.

Hoffman, Jan. 1998a. "Some Officers Are Skirting Miranda Restraints to Get Confessions." *New York Times*, March 29:A1.

Hoffman, Jan. 1998b. "As Miranda Rights Erode, Police Get Confessions from Innocent People." *New York Times*, March 30:A1.

Hoffmann, John P. and Felicia Gray Cerbone. 1999. "Stressful Life Events and Delinquency Escalation in Early Adolescence." *Criminology* 37:343–373.

Holden, Constance. 1992. "Health Official Falls, Lands in NIMH." *Science* 255:1207.

Holmes, Ronald M. 1991. *Sex Crimes*. Thousand Oaks, CA: Sage.

Holt, Andrew. 1993. "Controlling Employee Theft." *CMA—The Management Accounting Magazine*, September:16–19.

Hood, Jane C. 1995. "'Let's Get a Girl': Male Bonding Rituals in America." Pp. 307–311 in *Men's Lives*, edited by Michael S. Kimmel and Michael A. Messner. Boston: Allyn and Bacon.

Hooton, Earnest A. 1939a. *The American Criminal: An Anthropological Study*. Cambridge: Harvard University Press.

Hooton, Earnest A. 1939b. *Crime and the Man*. Cambridge: Harvard University Press.

Hopkins, Andrew. 1975. "On the Sociology of Criminal Law." *Social Problems* 22:608–619.

Horne, Florence. 1993. "The Issue Is Rape." in *It's a Crime: Women and Justice*, edited by Roslyn Muraskin and Ted Alleman. Englewood Cliffs, NJ: Prentice Hall.

Horney, Julie. 1978. "Menstrual Cycles and Criminal Responsibility." *Law and Human Behavior* 2:25–36.

Horney, Julie, D. Wayne Osgood, and Ineke Haen Marshall. 1995. "Criminal Careers in the Short Term: Intra-Individual Variability in Crime and Its Relation to Local Life Circumstances." *American Sociological Review* 60:655–673.

Horney, Karen. 1973. "The Problem of Feminine Masochism." In *Psychoanalysis and Women*, edited by J. Miller. New York: Brunner/Mazel.

Horowitz, Ruth and Anne E. Pottieger. 1991. "Gender Bias in Juvenile Justice Handling of Seriously Crime-Involved Youths." *Journal of Research in Crime and Delinquency* 28:75–100.

Howe, Robert F. 1989. "4th Contractor Pleads Guilty to 'Ill Wind' Charges." *Washington Post*, December 9:A3.

Hoyt, Charles A. 1981. *Witchcraft*. Carbondale, IL: Southern Illinois Press.

Hoyt, Dan R., Kimberly D. Ryan, and Ana Mari Cauce. 1999. "Personal Victimization in a High-Risk Environment: Homeless and Runaway Adolescents." *Journal of Research in Crime and Delinquency* 36:371–392.

Huang, W. S. Wilson and Michael S. Vaughn. 1996. "Support and Confidence: Public Attitudes toward the Police." Pp. 31–45 in *Americans View Crime and Justice: A National Public Opinion Survey*, edited by Timothy J. Flanagan and Dennis R. Longmire. Thousand Oaks, CA: Sage.

Huebner, Hans F. 1993. *Endorphins, Eating Disorders, and Other Addictive Behaviors*. New York: Norton.

Huff, C. Ronald, Arye Rattner, and Edward Sagarin. 1996. *Convicted but Innocent: Wrongful Conviction and Public Policy*. Thousand Oaks, CA: Sage.

Huffington, Arianna. 1999. "This Is Two-Tiered Justice:

Bush's Dilemma Calls Attention to the Hypocrisy of a System in Which the 'Haves' Routinely Get Off Easier." *Los Angeles Times*, August 24:B7.

Huizinga, David H., Scott Menard, and Delbert S. Elliott. 1989. "Delinquency and Drug Use: Temporal and Developmental Patterns." *Justice Quarterly* 6:419–455.

Humphreys, Laud. 1970. *Tearoom Trade: Impersonal Sex in Public Places*. Chicago: Aldine.

Humphries, Drew, John Dawson, Valerie Cronin, Phyllis Keating, Chris Wisniewski, and Jennine Eichfeld. 1995. "Mothers and Children, Drugs and Crack: Reactions to Maternal Drug Dependency." Pp. 167–179 in *The Criminal Justice System and Women: Offenders, Victims, and Workers*, edited by Barbara Raffel Price and Natalie J. Sokoloff. New York: McGraw-Hill.

Hunt, Dana E. 1990. "Drugs and Consensual Crimes: Drug Dealing and Prostitution." Pp. 191–202 in *Drugs and Crime*, vol. 13, *Crime and Justice*, edited by Michael Tonry and James Q. Wilson. Chicago: University of Chicago Press.

Hunter, George. 2000. "Boyfriend Charged in Grisly Slaying." *Detroit News*, January 24:B1.

Hutchings, Barry and Sarnoff A. Mednick. 1977. "Criminality in Adoptees and Their Adoptive and Biological Parents: A Pilot Study." Pp. 127–141 in *Biosocial Bases of Criminal Behavior*, edited by Sarnoff A. Mednick and Karl O. Christiansen. New York: Gardner Press.

Incantalupo, Tom. 1993. "Car Buyers Adding Some Heavy Artillery as Car Thieves Get More Aggressive." *Newsweek*, September 26:91.

Inciardi, James A. 1992. *The War on Drugs II*. Mountain View, CA: Mayfield.

Inciardi, James A., ed. 1999. *The Drug Legalization Debate*. Thousand Oaks, CA: Sage.

Inciardi, James A., Dorothy Lockwood, and Anne E. Pottieger. 1993. *Women and Crack-Cocaine*. New York: Macmillan.

Inciardi, James A., Ruth Horowitz, and Anne E. Pottieger. 1993. *Street Kids, Street Drugs, Street Crime: An Examination of Drug Use and Serious Delinquency in Miami*. Belmont, CA: Wadsworth.

Irwin, John and James Austin. 1997. *It's About Time: America's Imprisonment Binge*. Belmont, CA: Wadsworth.

ITAR/TASS News Agency. 2000. "Russia Crime Rate Grows Over 16 Percent in 1999." *ITAR/TASS*, January 18.

Itzin, Catherine, ed. 1992. *Pornography: Women, Violence, and Civil Liberties*. New York: Oxford University Press.

Jackson, Derrick Z. 1994. "Politicians' Crime Rhetoric." *Boston Globe*, October 21:15.

Jackson, Derrick Z. 1997. "No Wonder We're Afraid of Youths." *Boston Globe*, September 10:A15.

Jackson, Derrick Z. 1999. "From New Mexico's Governor, Rare Candor on Drugs." *Boston Globe*, October 13:A19.

Jackson, Derrick Z. 1999. "The Violent Game Called TV News." *Boston Globe*, May 7:A31.

Jackson, Pamela I. 1989. *Minority Group Threat, Crime, and Policing*. New York: Praeger.

Jackson, Patrick G. 1988. "Assessing the Validity of Official Data on Arson." *Criminology* 26:181–195.

Jacob, Herbert. 1978. *Justice in America: Courts, Lawyers, and the Judicial Process*. Boston: Little, Brown.

Jacobius, Arleen. 1995. "California's Three-Strikes Law Gobbling Up Jurors." *ABA Journal* 81:29.

Jacobs, Bruce A. and Richard Wright. 1999. "Stick-Up, Street Culture, and Offender Motivation." *Criminology* 37:149–173.

Jacobs, David and Robert M. O'Brien. 1998. "The Determinants of Deadly Force: A Structural Analysis of Police Violence." *American Journal of Sociology* 103:837–862.

Jacobson, Kristen C. and David C. Rowe. 2000. "Nature, Nurture, and the Development of Criminality." Pp. 323–347 in *Criminology: A Contemporary Handbook*, edited by Joseph F. Sheley. Belmont, CA: Wadsworth.

James, Jennifer. 1982. "The Prostitute as Victim." Pp. 291–315 in *The Criminal Justice System and Women: Offenders, Victims, and Workers*, edited by Barbara Raffel Price and Natalie J. Sokoloff. New York: Clark Boardman.

Janofsky, Michael. 1999. "A Governor Who Once Dabbled in Drugs Says War on Them Is Misguided." *New York Times*, August 22:16.

Janus, Samuel S. and Cynthia L. Janus. 1993. *The Janus Report on Sexual Behavior*. New York: Wiley.

Jarjoura, G. Roger. 1993. "Does Dropping Out of School Enhance Delinquent Involvement? Results from a Large-Scale National Probability Sample." *Criminology* 31:149–171.

Jeffery, C. Ray. 1993. "Genetics, Crime, and the Cancelled Conference." *The Criminologist* 18:1+.

Jeffery, C. Ray. 1994. "Biological and Neuropsychiatric Approaches to Criminal Behavior." Pp. 15–28 in *Varieties of Criminology: Readings from a Dynamic Discipline*, edited by Gregg Barak. Westport, CT: Praeger.

Jenkins, Patricia H. 1997. "School Delinquency and the School Social Bond." *Journal of Research in Crime and Delinquency* 34:337–367.

Jenkins, Philip. 1988. "Myth and Murder: The Serial Killer Panic of 1983–85." *Criminal Justice Research Bulletin* 3:1–7.

Jenness, Valerie. 1993. *Making It Work: The Prostitutes' Rights Movement*. New York: Aldine DeGruyter.

Jenness, Valerie and Kendal Broad. 1997. *Hate Crimes: New Social Movements and the Politics of Violence*. Hawthorne, NY: Aldine de Gruyter.

Jensen, Arthur R. 1969. "How Much Can We Boost IQ and Scholastic Achievement?" *Harvard Educational Review* 39:1–123.

Jensen, Gary F. and Maryaltani Karpos. 1993. "Managing Rape: Exploratory Research on the Behavior of Rape Statistics." *Criminology* 31:363–385.

Jesilow, Paul, Gilbert Geis, and Henry Pontell. 1991. "Fraud by Physicians against Medicaid." *JAMA, The Journal of the American Medical Association* 266:3318–3322.

Jesilow, Paul, Gilbert Geis, and Mary Jane O'Brien. 1985. "Is My Battery Any Good? A Field Test of Fraud in the Auto Repair Business." *Journal of Crime and Justice* 8:1–20.

Jesilow, Paul, Henry N. Pontell, and Gilbert Geis. 1993. *Prescription for Profit: How Doctors Defraud Medicaid.* Berkeley: University of California Press.

Johan, Sara Lee. 1994. *Domestic Abusers: Terrorists in Our Homes.* Springfield, IL: Charles C. Thomas.

Johnson, Dirk. 1995. "Congressman in Sex Case Will Resign." *New York Times,* September 2:5.

Johnson, Dirk. 2000. "Illinois Governor Hopes to Fix a 'Broken Justice.'" *New York Times,* February 19:A7.

Johnson, Hillary and Francine G. Hermelin. 1995. "The Truth about White-Collar Domestic Violence." *Working Woman,* March:54–61.

Johnson, Richard E. 1979. *Juvenile Delinquency and Its Origins: An Integrated Theoretical Approach.* Cambridge: Cambridge University Press.

Johnson, Richard E. 1986. "Family Structure and Delinquency: General Patterns and Gender Differences." *Criminology* 24:65–84.

Johnson, Robert. 1996. *Hard Time: Understanding and Reforming the Prison.* Belmont, CA: Wadsworth.

Johnson, Weldon T., Robert E. Petersen, and L. Edward Wells. 1977. "Arrest Probabilities for Marijuana Users as Indicators of Selective Law Enforcement." *American Journal of Sociology* 83:681–699.

Johnston, David. 1993. "Secretary of Commerce Faces His Toughest Test." *New York Times,* October 3:15.

Johnston, David. 1994. "White House Gets Espy to Leave the Cabinet." *New York Times,* October 9:E2.

Johnston, Henry P. 1914. *Nathan Hale, 1776: Biography and Memorials.* New Haven: Yale University Press.

Jones, David A. 1986. *History of Criminology: A Philosophical Perspective.* New York: Greenwood Press.

Jones, James H. 1981. *Bad Blood: The Tuskegee Syphilis Experiment.* New York: Free Press.

Josephson, Matthew. 1962. *The Robber Barons: The Great American Capitalists, 1861–1901.* New York: Harcourt, Brace, & World.

Joutsen, Matti and Norman Bishop. 1994. "Noncustodial Sanctions in Europe: Regional Overview." Pp. 279–292 in *Alternatives to Imprisonment in Comparative Perspective,* edited by Ugljesa Zvekic. Chicago: Nelson-Hall.

Joy, L. A., M. M. Kimball, and M. Zabrack. 1986. "Television and Children's Aggressive Behavior." In *The Impact of Television: A Natural Experiment in Three Communities,* edited by Tannis MacBeth Williams. New York: Academic Press.

Judson, George. 1994. "Some Indians See a Gamble with Future in Casinos." *New York Times,* May 15:E5.

Kahn, Helen. 1986. "GAO Study Lists Remedies for Ford Park-Reverse Problem." *Automotive News,* June 23:39.

Kallet, Arthur. 1933. *100,000,000 Guinea Pigs: Dangers in Everyday Foods, Drugs, and Cosmetics.* New York: Vanguard Press.

Kamen, Paula and Steve Rhodes 1992. "Reporting on Acquaintance Rape." *EXTRA!* (publication of FAIR, Fairness and Accuracy in Reporting), Special Issue, p. 11.

Kaminer, Wendy. 1992. "Feminists against the First Amendment." *The Atlantic,* November:110–116.

Kanarek, Robin B. 1994. "Nutrition and Violent Behavior." Pp. 515–539 in *Understanding and Preventing Violence: Biobehavioral Influences,* vol. 2, edited by Albert J. Reiss, Jr., Klaus A. Miczek, and Jeffrey A. Roth. Washington, D.C.: National Academy Press.

Kandel, Denise and Mark Davies. 1991. "Friendship Networks, Intimacy, and Illicit Drug Use in Young Adulthood: A Comparison of Two Competing Theories." *Criminology* 29:441–469.

Kandel, Elizabeth and Sarnoff A. Mednick. 1991. "Perinatal Complications Predict Violent Offending." *Criminology* 29:519–529.

Kanin, Eugene J. 1970. "Sex Aggression by College Men." *Medical Aspects of Human Sexuality,* September:28ff.

Kaplan, Carl S. 1999. "Report Questions Government Efforts against Computer Crime." *New York Times,* August 20. Retrieved August 20, 1999 (http://www.nytimes.com/library/tech/99/08/cyber/cyberlaw/20law.html).

Kaplan, Howard B. 1980. *Deviant Behavior in Defense of Self.* New York: Academic Press.

Kappeler, Victor E., Mark Blumberg, and Gary W. Potter. 2000. *The Mythology of Crime and Justice.* Prospect Heights, IL: Waveland Press.

Karmen, Andrew. 1990. *Crime Victims: An Introduction to Victimology.* Belmont, CA: Wadsworth.

Karmen, Andrew. 1995. "Women Victims of Crime: Introduction." Pp. 181–196 in *The Criminal Justice System and Women: Offenders, Victims, and Workers,* edited by Barbara Raffel Price and Natalie J. Sokoloff. New York: McGraw-Hill.

Karmen, Andrew A. 2000. "Victims of Crime: Issues and Patterns." Pp. 165–185 in *Criminology: A Contemporary Handbook,* edited by Joseph F. Sheley. Belmont, CA: Wadsworth.

Kastor, Elizabeth. 1994. "The Worst Fears, the Worse Reality." *Washington Post,* November 5:A1.

Katz, Jack. 1988. *Seductions of Crime: Moral and Sensual Attractions of Doing Evil.* New York: Basic Books.

Katz, Jack. 1991. "The Motivation of the Persistent Robber." Pp. 277–306 in *Crime and Justice: A Review of Research,* vol. 14, edited by Michael Tonry. Chicago: University of Chicago Press.

Katz, Janet and William J. Chambliss. 1995. "Biology and Crime." Pp. 275–303 in *Criminology: A Contemporary*

Handbook, edited by Joseph F. Sheley. Belmont, CA: Wadsworth.

Kaufman, Michael. 1998. "The Construction of Masculinity and the Triad of Men's Violence." Pp. 4–17 in *Men's Lives*, edited by Michael S. Kimmel and Michael A. Messner. Boston: Allyn and Bacon.

Keen, Judy. 1994. "One Cannot Feel Safe Anyplace." *USA Today*, January 25:1A–2A.

Kellerman, Arthur. 1996. *Understanding and Preventing Violence: A Public Health Perspective*. Washington, D.C.: Office of Justice Programs, National Institute of Justice.

Kellerman, Arthur L. et al. 1993. "Gun Ownership as a Risk Factor for Homicide in the Home." *New England Journal of Medicine* 329:1084–1092.

Kelley, Matt. 1999. "Governor Discusses Drug Legalization." *Bangor Daily*, News October 5:A7.

Kelling, George L. and Catherine M. Coles. 1998. *Fixing Broken Windows: Restoring Order and Reducing Crime in Our Communities*. New York: Free Press.

Kelling, George L., Tony Pate, Duane Dieckman, and Charles Brown. 1974. *The Kansas City Preventive Patrol Experiment*. Washington, D.C.: The Police Foundation.

Kempf, Kimberly L. 1993. "The Empirical Status of Hirschi's Control Theory." Pp. 143–185 in *New Directions in Criminological Theory*, vol. 4, *Advances in Criminological Theory*, edited by Freda Adler and William S. Laufer. New Brunswick, NJ: Transaction.

Kempf, Kimberly L. and Roy L. Austin. 1986. "Older and More Recent Evidence on Racial Discrimination in Sentencing." *Journal of Quantitative Criminology* 2:29–48.

Kendrick, Walter M. 1987. *The Secret Museum: Pornography in Modern Culture*. New York: Viking.

Kenney, Dennis J. and James O. Finckenauer. 1995. *Organized Crime in America*. Belmont, CA: Wadsworth.

Kenny, Anthony John Patrick. 1983. *Thomas More*. New York: Oxford University Press.

Kerner Commission. 1968. *Report of the National Advisory Commission on Civil Disorders*. New York: Bantam.

Kerr, Peter. 1993. "'Ghost Riders' Are Target of an Insurance Sting." *New York Times*, August 18:A1.

Kessell, Doug. 2000. "Two Brewer Teens Arrested in Car Burglaries." *Bangor Daily News*, March 17:B3.

Kessler, Ronald. 1988. *Spy versus Spy: Stalking Soviet Spies in America*. New York: Scribner's.

Keve, Paul W. 1992. "The Costliest Punishment." *Federal Probation* 56:11–15.

Kilpatrick, Dean, B. Saunders, L. Veronen, C. Best, and J. Von. 1987. "Criminal Victimization: Lifetime Prevalence, Reporting to Police, and Psychological Impact." *Crime and Delinquency* 33:479–489.

Kimmel, Michael S. and Michael A. Messner, eds. 1998. *Men's Lives*. Boston: Allyn and Bacon.

King, Martin Luther, Jr. 1969. "Letter from Birmingham City Jail." Pp. 72–89 in *Civil Disobedience: Theory and Practice*, edited by Hugo Adam Bedau. New York: Pegasus.

Kirchheimer, Otto. 1961. *Political Justice: The Use of Legal Procedure for Political Ends*. Princeton: Princeton University Press.

Kirkham, George L. 1984. "A Professor's 'Street Lessons'." Pp. 77–89 in *'Order under Law': Readings in Criminal Justice*, edited by Robert G. Culbertson. Prospect Heights, IL: Waveland Press.

Kitman, Jamie Lincoln. 2000. "The Secret History of Lead." *The Nation*, March 20:11–44.

Klaus, Patsy A. 1994. The Costs of Crime to Victims. Washington, D.C.: U.S. Department of Justice, Bureau of Justice Statistics.

Klaus, Patsy A. 1999. *Carjackings in the United States, 1992–96*. Washington, D.C.: U.S. Department of Justice, Bureau of Justice Statistics.

Klaus, Patsy A. 2000. *Crimes against Persons Age 65 or Older, 1992–97*. Washington, D.C.: U.S. Department of Justice, Bureau of Justice Statistics.

Kleck, Gary. 1981. "Racial Discrimination in Criminal Sentencing: A Critical Evaluation of the Evidence with Additional Evidence on the Death Penalty." *American Sociological Review* 46:783–805.

Kleck, Gary. 1991. *Point Blank: Guns and Violence in America*. Hawthorne, NY: Aldine de Gruyter.

Kleck, Gary. 1995. "Guns and Violence: An Interpretive Review of the Field." *Social Pathology* 1:12–47.

Kleck, Gary. 1997. *Targeting Guns: Firearms and Their Control*. Hawthorne, NY: Aldine de Gruyter.

Kleck, Gary and M. Gertz. 1995. "Armed Resistance to Crime: The Prevalence and Nature of Self-Defense with a Gun." *Journal of Criminal Law and Criminology* 85:150–187.

Klein, Dorie. 1973. "The Etiology of Female Crime." *Issues in Criminology* 8:3–30.

Klier, John and Shlomo Lambroza. 1992. *Pogroms: Anti-Jewish Violence in Modern Russian History*. Cambridge: Cambridge University Press.

Klinger, David A. 1994. "Demeanor or Crime? Why 'Hostile' Citizens Are More Likely to Be Arrested." *Criminology* 32:475–493.

Klockars, Carl B. 1979. "The Contemporary Crises of Marxist Criminology." *Criminology* 16:477–515.

Klotter, John C. and Terry D. Edwards. 1998. *Criminal Law*. Cincinnati: Anderson.

Knapp Commission. 1973. *Knapp Commission Report on Police Corruption*. New York: George Braziller.

Knox, Richard A. 1995. "AMA: Tobacco Firm Lied about Risks." *Boston Globe*, July 14:1.

Kohlberg, Lawrence. 1969. *States in the Development of Moral Thought and Action*. New York: Holt, Rinehart and Winston.

Kong, Dolores and Matthew Brelis. 1995. "Binge Drinking Lures Many College Freshmen, Study Says." *Boston Globe*, April 6:1.

Koppel, Herbert. 1987. *Lifetime Likelihood of Victimization*.

Washington, D.C.: U.S. Department of Justice, Bureau of Justice Statistics.

Kornhauser, Ruth. 1978. *Social Sources of Delinquency*. Chicago: University of Chicago Press.

Koss, Mary P., Christine A. Gidycz, and Nadine Wisniewski. 1987. "The Scope of Rape: Incidence and Prevalence of Sexual Aggression and Victimization in a National Sample of Higher Education Students." *Journal of Consulting and Clinical Psychology* 52:162–170.

Kovandzic, Tomislav V., Lynne M. Vieraitis, and Mark R. Yeisley. 1998. "The Structural Covariates of Urban Homicide: Reassessing the Impact of Income Inequality and Poverty in the Post-Reagan Era." *Criminology* 36:569–599.

Kozol, Jonathan. 1991. *Savage Inequalities: Children in America's Schools*. New York: Crown.

Krahn, Harvey, Timothy F. Hartnagel, and John W. Gartrell. 1986. "Income Inequality and Homicide Rates: Cross-National Data and Criminological Theories." *Criminology* 24:269–295.

Kramer, Ronald C. 1992. "The Space Shuttle Challenger Explosion: A Case Study of State-Corporate Crime." Pp. 214–243 in *White-Collar Crime Reconsidered*, edited by Kip Schlegel and David Weisburd. Boston: Northeastern University Press.

Kraska, Peter B. and Victor E. Kappeler. 1995. "To Serve and Pursue: Exploring Police Sexual Violence against Women." *Justice Quarterly* 12:85–111.

Kratcoski, Peter C. and Duane Dukes, eds. 1995. *Issues in Community Policing*. Cincinnati: Anderson.

Krauss, Clifford. 1996. "Police Say Commander Falsified Crime Data." *New York Times*, October 26:A1.

Krisberg, Barry and James F. Austin. 1993. *Reinventing Juvenile Justice*. Newbury Park, CA: Sage.

Krivo, Lauren J. and Rudth D. Peterson. 1996. "Extremely Disadvantaged Neighborhoods and Urban Crime." *Social Forces* 75:619–650.

Krohn, Marvin. 2000. "Sources of Criminality: Control and Deterrence Theories." Pp. 373–399 in *Criminology: A Contemporary Handbook*, edited by Joseph F. Sheley. Belmont, CA: Wadsworth.

Krohn, Marvin D. and James L. Massey. 1980. "Social Control and Delinquent Behavior: An Examination of the Elements of the Social Bond." *The Sociological Quarterly* 21:529–543.

Kruttschnitt, Candace. 1994. "Gender and Interpersonal Violence." Pp. 293–376 in *Understanding and Preventing Violence: Social Influences*, edited by Albert J. Reiss, Jr. and Jeffrey A. Roth. Washington, D.C.: National Academy Press.

Kruttschnitt, Candace, Jane D. McLeod, and Maude Dornfeld. 1994. "The Economic Environment of Child Abuse." *Social Problems* 41:299–315.

Kruttschnitt, Candace, Linda Heath, and David A. Ward. 1986. "Family Violence, Television Viewing Habits, and Other Adolescent Experiences Related to Violent Criminal Behavior." *Criminology* 24:235–267.

Kuhl, Stefan. 1994. *The Nazi Connection: Eugenics, American Racism, and German National Socialism*. New York: Oxford University Press.

Kuper, Leo. 1985. *The Prevention of Genocide*. New Haven: Yale University Press.

Kurtz, Howard. 1997. "The Crime Spree on Network News." *Washington Post*, August 12:D1.

Kurz, Demie. 1993. "Physical Assaults by Husbands: A Major Social Problem." Pp. 88–103 in *Current Controversies on Family Violence*, edited by Richard J. Gelles and Donileen R. Loseke. Newbury Park, CA: Sage.

Kushner, Gary Jay. 1993. "Meat Safety under Fire: E. Coli Outbreak Prompts Renewed Calls for Meat Inspection Reform." *Food Processing*, April:17–20.

Lab, Steven F. and J. David Hirschel. 1988. "Climatological Conditions and Crime: The Forecast Is …?" *Justice Quarterly* 5:281–299.

Labaton, Stephen. 1993. "Surgeon General Suggests Study of Legalizing Drugs." *New York Times*, December 8:A23.

Lacayo, Richard. 1996. "Law and Order." *Time*, January 15:49–54.

LaFree, Gary D. 1980. "The Effect of Sexual Stratification by Race on Official Reactions to Rape." *American Sociological Review* 45:842–854.

LaFree, Gary D. 1985. "Official Reactions to Hispanic Defendants in the Southwest." *Journal of Research in Crime and Delinquency* 22:213–237.

LaFree, Gary D. 1989. *Rape and Criminal Justice: The Social Construction of Sexual Assault*. Belmont, CA: Wadsworth.

LaFree, Gary and Katheryn K. Russell. 1993. "The Argument for Studying Race and Crime." *Journal of Criminal Justice Education* 4:273–289.

LaFree, Gary, Kriss A. Drass, and Patrick O'Day. 1992. "Race and Crime in Postwar America: Determinants of African-American and White Rates, 1957–1988." *Criminology* 30:157–188.

LaGrange, Randy L. and Kenneth F. Ferraro. 1989. "Assessing Age and Gender Differences in Perceived Risk and Fear of Crime." *Criminology* 27:697–720.

LaGrange, Teresa C. and Robert A. Silverman. 1999. "Low Self-Control and Opportunity: Testing the General Theory of Crime as an Explanation for Gender Differences in Delinquency." *Criminology* 37:41–72.

Lambert, Wade. 1992. "Milken Wins Early Release from Prison; Time to Be Served Is Cut by 2 Years; His Aid to Prosecutors Cited." *Wall Street Journal*, August 6:A3.

Land, Kenneth C., David Cantor, and Stephen T. Russell. 1995. "Unemployment and Crime Rate Fluctuations in the Post-World War II United States." Pp. 55–79 in *Crime and Inequality*, edited by John Hagan and Ruth D. Peterson. Stanford: Stanford University Press.

Landau, Simha F. and Daniel Fridman. 1993. "The Seasonality of Violent Crime: The Case of Robbery and Homicide in Israel." *Journal of Research in Crime and Delinquency* 30:163–191.

Lane, Roger. 1980. "Police and Crime in Nineteenth-Century America." Pp. 1–52 in *Crime and Justice: An Annual Review*, vol. 2, edited by Michael Tonry and Norval Morris. Chicago: University of Chicago Press.

Lane, Roger. 1986. *Roots of Violence in Black Philadelphia, 1860–1900.* Cambridge: Harvard University Press.

Lane, Roger. 1989. "On the Social Meaning of Homicide Trends in America." Pp. 55–79 in *Violence in America*, vol. 1, *The History of Crime*, edited by Ted Robert Gurr. Newbury Park, CA: Sage.

Larson, Richard C. 1975. "What Happened to Patrol Operations in Kansas City? A Review of the Kansas City Preventive Patrol Experiment." *Journal of Criminal Justice* 3:267–297.

Latour, Francie. 2000. "Low Murder Rate Lauded." *Boston Globe*, January 1:B1, B7.

Lattimore, Pamela K., Richard L. Linster, and John M. MacDonald. 1997. "Risk of Death among Serious Young Offenders." *Journal of Research in Crime and Delinquency* 34:187–209.

Laub, John H. and Robert J. Sampson. 1988. "Unraveling Families and Delinquency: A Reanalysis of the Gluecks' Data." *Criminology* 26:355–380.

Laub, John H. and Robert J. Sampson. 1993. "Turning Points in the Life Course: Why Change Matters to the Study of Crime." *Criminology* 31:301–325.

Lauritsen, Janet L., Robert J. Sampson, and John H. Laub. 1991. "The Link between Offending and Victimization among Adolescents." *Criminology* 29:265–291.

Lea, John and Jock Young. 1984. *What Is to Be Done about Law and Order?* New York: Penguin.

Leary, Warren E. 1992. "Struggle Continues Over Remarks by Mental Health Official." *New York Times*, March 18:34.

LeDoux, J. and R. Hazelwood. 1985. "Police Attitudes and Beliefs Toward Rape." *Journal of Police Science and Administration* 13:211–220.

Lee, Gary A. 1995. "U.S. Energy Agency Radiation Tests Involved 9,000, Study Says." *Washington Post*, A13.

Lefcourt, Robert, ed. 1971. *Law against the People.* New York: Vintage.

Lefkowitz, Monroe, Leonard D. Eron, Leopold O. Walder, and L. Rowell Huesmann. 1977. *Growing Up to Be Violent: A Longitudinal Study of the Development of Aggression.* New York: Pergamon.

Lehigh, Scot. 1995. "Attitude toward Cocaine Shifts." *Boston Globe*, March 23:29.

Lemert, Edwin M. 1951. *Social Pathology.* New York: McGraw-Hill.

Lemert, Edwin M. 1953. "An Isolation & Closure Theory of Naive Check Forgery." *Journal of Criminal Law, Criminology, and Applied Science* 44:301–304.

Leonard, Eileen B. 1982. *Women, Crime, and Society: A Critique of Criminology Theory.* New York: Longman.

Leonard, Eileen. 1995. "Theoretical Criminology and Gender." Pp. 54–70 in *The Criminal Justice System and Women: Offenders, Victims, and Workers*, edited by Barbara Raffel Price and Natalie J. Sokoloff. New York: McGraw-Hill.

Lesieur, Henry R. and Michael Welch. 2000. "Vice Crimes: Personal Autonomy versus Societal Dictates." Pp. 233–263 in *Criminology: A Contemporary Handbook*, edited by Joseph F. Sheley. Belmont, CA: Wadsworth.

Lessenberry, Jack. 1994. "A Crime Mortifies Detroit: Attack on Rosa Parks Stirs Feelings of Outrage, Embarrassment." *Boston Globe*, September 2:3.

Lester, Will. 1995. "Ex-Prosecutor to Help U.S. Case on Cali Lawyers." *Boston Globe*, July 4:3.

Levi, Michael. 1992. "White-Collar Crime Victimization." Pp. 169–192 in *White-Collar Crime Reconsidered*, edited by Kip Schlegel and David Weisburd. Boston: Northeastern University Press.

Levi, Michael. 1994. "Masculinities and White-Collar Crime." Pp. 234–252 in *Just Boys Doing Business? Men, Masculinities and Crime*, edited by Tim Newburn and Elizabeth A. Stanko. London: Routledge.

Levine, Adeline. 1982. *Love Canal: Science, Politics, and People.* Lexington, MA: Lexington Books.

Levine, James. 1976. "The Potential for Crime Over-reporting in Criminal Victimization Surveys." *Criminology* 14:307–330.

Levy, Clifford J. 1994. "Postmaster Admits Theft of $870,000 from Service." *New York Times*, December 1:B6.

Levy, Clifford J. 1995. "Russian Emigres Are among 25 Names in Tax Fraud in Newark." *New York Times*, August 8:1.

Levy, Steven and Bard Stone. 2000. "Hunting the Hackers." *Newsweek*, February 21:38–44.

Lewin, Tamar. 1993. "Rape and the Accuser: A Debate Still Rages on Citing Sexual Past." *New York Times*, February 12:B16.

Lewin, Tamar. 2000. "Racial Discrepancy Found in Trying of Youths." *New York Times*, February 3:A14.

Lewis, Dan A. and Greta Salem. 1986. *Fear of Crime: Incivility and the Production of a Social Problem.* New Brunswick, NJ: Transaction.

Lewis, Paul. 1993. "Rape Was Weapon of Serbs, U.N. Says." *New York Times*, October 20:A1.

Lewis, Paul. 1995. "Rights Groups Say Shell Oil Shares Blame." *New York Times*, November 11:5.

Lewis, Paul. 1996. "Nigeria's Deadly War: Shell Defends Its Record." *New York Times*, February 13:1.

Lewis, Raphael. 2000. "Man's Arrest Allays Fears in Wellesley." *Boston Globe*, March 5:B1.

Lewontin, Richard C., Steven P. R. Rose, and Leon J. Kamin. 1984. *Not in Our Genes: Biology, Ideology, and Human Nature.* New York: Pantheon.

Liazos, Alexander. 1972. "The Poverty of the Sociology of Deviance: Nuts, Sluts, and Perverts." *Social Problems* 20:103–120.

Libbey, Patricia and Rodger Bybee. 1979. "The Physical Abuse of Adolescents." *Journal of Social Issues* 35:101–126.

Lichtblau, Eric. 2000. "Older Americans Less Likely to Be Victims of Violent Crime." *Los Angeles Times*, January 10:A1.

Liebow, Elliott. 1967. *Tally's Corner*. Boston: Little, Brown.

Liebow, Elliott. 1993. *Tell Them Who I Am: The Lives of Homeless Women*. New York: Free Press.

Lilienfeld, David E. 1991. "The Silence: The Asbestos Industry and Early Occupational Cancer Research—A Case Study." *American Journal of Public Health* 81:791–800.

Lindsey, Robert. 1984. "Officials Cite a Rise in Killers Who Roam U.S. for Victims." *New York Times*, January 22:1+.

Liska, Allen E. and Mark D. Reed. 1985. "Ties to Conventional Institutions and Delinquency: Estimating Reciprocal Effects." *American Sociological Review* 50:547–560.

Liska, Allen E. and Mitchell B. Chamlin. 1984. "Social Structure and Crime Control among Macrosocial Units." *American Journal of Sociology* 98:383–395.

Liska, Allen E. and William Baccaglini. 1990. "Feeling Safe by Comparison: Crime in the Newspapers." *Social Problems* 37:360–374.

Liska, Allen E., Joseph J. Lawrence, and Andrew Sanchirico. 1985. "Fear of Crime as a Social Fact." *Social Forces* 60:760–771.

Littner, Ner. 1973. "Psychology of the Sex Offender: Causes, Treatment, Prognosis." *Police Law Quarterly* 3:5–31.

Lizotte, Alan J., James M. Tesoriero, Terence P. Thornberry, and Marvin D. Krohn. 1994. "Patterns of Adolescent Firearms Ownership and Use." *Justice Quarterly* 11:51–73.

Locke, John. 1979 [1690]. *An Essay Concerning Human Understanding*. New York: Oxford University Press.

Lockhart, Lettie L. 1987. "A Reexamination of the Effects of Race and Social Class on the Incidence of Marital Violence: A Search for Reliable Differences." *Journal of Marriage and the Family* 49:603–610.

Loeber, Rolf and David P. Farrington, eds. 1998. *Serious and Violent Juvenile Offenders: Risk Factors and Successful Interventions*. Thousand Oaks, CA: Sage.

Loeber, Rolf and Magda Stouthamer-Loeber. 1986. "Family Factors as Correlates and Predictors of Juvenile Conduct Problems and Delinquency." Pp. 29–149 in *Crime and Justice: An Annual Review of Research*, vol. 7, edited by Michael Tonry and Norval Morris. Chicago: University of Chicago Press.

Loeber, Rolf and Marc LeBlanc. 1990. "Toward a Developmental Criminology." Pp. 375–473 in *Crime and Justice: An Annual Review of Research*, vol. 12, edited

by Norval Morris and Michael Tonry. Chicago: University of Chicago Press.

Loftin, Colin and David McDowall. 1981. "'One with a Gun Gets You Two': Mandatory Sentencing and Firearms Violence in Detroit." *Annals of the American Academy of Political and Social Science* 455:150–167.

Loftin, Colin, David McDowall, Brian Wiersema, and Talbert J. Cottey. 1991. "Effects of Restrictive Licensing of Handguns on Homicide and Suicide in the District of Columbia." *New England Journal of Medicine* 325:1085–1101.

Lombroso, Cesare. 1876. *The Criminal Man (L'uomo Delinquente)*. Milan: Hoepli.

Lombroso, Cesare. 1920 [1903]. *The Female Offender*. New York: Appleton.

Loya, F., James A. Mercy, and associates. 1985. *The Epidemiology of Homicide in the City of Los Angeles, 1970–79*. Los Angeles: University of California at Los Angeles and Centers for Disease Control.

Luckenbill, David F. 1977. "Criminal Homicide as a Situated Transaction." *Social Problems* 25:176–186.

Ludwig, Jens, Greg J. Duncan, and Paul Hirschfield. 1999. "Urban Poverty and Juvenile Crime: Evidence from a Randomized Housing-Mobility Experiment." Evanston, IL: Joint Center for Poverty Research.

Luke, Peter. 1990. "Games People Shouldn't Play; State Lotteries Take from the Poor and Give to the Rich." *Washington Monthly*, February, pp. 49–50.

Lundman, Richard J. 1993. *Prevention and Control of Juvenile Delinquency*. New York: Oxford University Press.

Lundman, Richard J. 1996. "Demeanor and Arrest: Additional Evidence from Previously Unpublished Data." *Journal of Research in Crime and Delinquency* 33:306–323.

Lurigio, Arthur J. and Patricia A. Resick. 1990. "Healing the Psychological Wounds of Criminal Victimization: Predicting Postcrime Distress and Recovery." Pp. 50–68 in *Victims of Crime: Problems, Policies, and Programs*, edited by Arthur L. Lurigio, Wesley G. Skogan, and Robert C. Davis. Newbury Park, CA: Sage.

Lynam, Donald, Terrie E. Moffitt, and Magda Stouthamer-Loeber. 1993. "Explaining the Relation between IQ and Delinquency: Class, Race, Test Motivation, School Failure, or Self-Control?" *Journal of Abnormal Psychology* 102:187–196.

Lynch, Colum. 1995. "Amnesty International Faults Rwanda War Crimes Tribunal." *Boston Globe*, April 6:14.

Lynch, James P. and David Cantor. 1992. "Ecological and Behavioral Influences on Property Victimization at Home: Implications for Opportunity Theory." *Journal of Research in Crime and Delinquency* 29:335–362.

Lynch, James. 1995. "Crime in International Perspective." Pp. 11–38 in *Crime*, edited by James Q. Wilson and Joan Petersilia. San Francisco: Institute for Contemporary Studies Press.

Lynch, Michael J., ed. 1997. *Radical Criminology*. Brookfield, VT: Dartmouth.

MacCoun, Robert and Peter Reuter. 1998. "Drug Control." Pp. 207–238 in *The Handbook of Crime and Punishment*, edited by Michael Tonry. New York: Oxford University Press.

Macionis, John J. 2000. *Society: The Basics*. Upper Saddle River, NJ: Prentice Hall.

MacKinnon, Catharine A. 1982. "Feminism, Marxism, Method, and the State: An Agenda for Theory." *Signs* 7:515–544.

Maguire, Kathleen and Ann L. Pastore, eds. 1995. *Sourcebook of Criminal Justice Statistics—1994*. Washington, D.C.: U.S. Department of Justice, Bureau of Justice Statistics.

Maguire, Kathleen and Ann L. Pastore, eds. 1999. *Sourcebook of Criminal Justice Statistics*. Retrieved November 1999 (http://www.albany.edu/sourcebook).

Maguire, Mike. 1982. *Burglary in a Dwelling*. London: Heinemann.

Maher, Lisa and Richard Curtis. 1995. "In Search of the Female 'Gangsta': Change, Culture, and Crack Cocaine." Pp. 147–166 in *The Criminal Justice System and Women: Offenders, Victims, and Workers*, edited by Barbara Raffel Price and Natalie J. Sokoloff. New York: McGraw-Hill.

Majors, Richard and Janet Mancini Billson. 1992. *Cool Pose: The Dilemmas of Black Manhood in America*. New York: Lexington Books.

Males, Mike A. 1999. *Framing Youth: 10 Myths about the Next Generation*. Monroe, ME: Common Courage Press.

Mandelbaum, Paul. 1999. "Dowry Deaths in India." *Commonweal*, October 8:18ff.

Mann, Coramae Richey. 1990. "Black Female Homicide in the United States." *Journal of Interpersonal Violence* 5:176–201.

Mann, Coramae Richey. 1993. *Unequal Justice: A Question of Color*. Bloomington: Indiana University Press.

Mann, Coramae Richey. 1995. "Women of Color and the Criminal Justice System." Pp. 118–135 in *The Criminal Justice System and Women: Offenders, Victims, Workers*, edited by Barbara Raffel Price and Natalie J. Sokoloff. New York: McGraw-Hill.

Marder, Dianna. 1997. "'Rigged' Murder Conviction Is Tossed." *Philadelphia Inquirer*, April 22:A1.

Marks, Patricia. 1990. *Bicycles, Bangs, and Bloomers: The New Woman in the Popular Press*. Lexington, KY: University Press of Kentucky.

Marks, Peter. 1994. "A Victim of Crime Battles the Criminal Justice System." *New York Times*, March 15:B5.

Marshall, Linda L. and Patricia Rose. 1990. "Premarital Violence: The Impact of Family of Origin Violence, Stress, and Reciprocity." *Violence and Victims* 5:51–64.

Martin, Marie Alexandrine. 1994. *Cambodia: A Shattered Society*. Berkeley: University of California Press.

Martin, Patricia Yancey and Robert A. Hummer. 1995.

"Fraternities and Rape on Campus." Pp. 141–151 in *Readings in Deviant Behavior*, edited by Alex Thio and Thomas Calhoun. New York: HarperCollins.

Martin, Sandra L., Amy Ong Tsui, Kuhu Maitra, and Ruth Marinshaw. 1999. "Domestic Violence in Northern India." *American Journal of Epidemiology* 150:417–426.

Martin, Susan E. 1990. *On the Move: The Status of Women in Policing*. Washington, D.C.: Police Foundation.

Martin, Susan E. 1994. "'Outsider within' the Station House: The Impact of Race and Gender on Black Women Police." *Social Problems* 41:383–400.

Martinez, James. 1993. "Two Life Sentences Awarded: While Attackers Go to Prison, Man Set Ablaze Starts Anew." *Bangor Daily News*, October 23–24:35.

Marvell, Thomas B. and Carlisle E. Moody. 1995. "The Impact of Enhanced Prison Terms for Felonies Committed with Guns." *Criminology* 33:247–281.

Marvell, Thomas B. and Carlisle E. Moody. 1996. "Specification Problems, Police Levels, and Crime Rates." *Criminology* 34:609–646.

Marx, Gary T. 1974. "Thoughts on a Neglected Category of Social Movement Participant: The Agent Provocateur and the Informant." *American Journal of Sociology* 80:402–422.

Marx, Karl. 1993 [1887]. "Crime and Primitive Accumulation." Pp. 45–48 in *Crime and Capitalism: Readings in Marxist Criminology*, edited by David F. Greenberg. Philadelphia: Temple University Press.

Marx, Karl and Friedrich Engels. 1962 [1848]. "The Communist Manifesto." Pp. 44 in *Marx and Engels: Selected Works*, vol. 2. Moscow: Foreign Language Publishing House.

Massey, Douglas S. and Nancy A. Denton. 1993. *American Apartheid: Segregation and the Making of the Underclass*. Cambridge: Harvard University Press.

Massey, Douglas S., Andrew B. Gross, and Kumiko Shibuya. 1994. "Migration, Segregation, and the Geographic Concentration of Poverty." *American Sociological Review* 59:425.

Mastrofski, Stephen D. 2000. "The Police in America." Pp. 405–445 in *Criminology: A Contemporary Handbook*, edited by Joseph F. Sheley. Belmont, CA: Wadsworth.

Mather, Lynn M. 1973. "Some Determinants of the Method of Case Disposition: Decisionmaking by Public Defenders in Los Angeles." *Law and Society Review* 8:187–215.

Matsueda, Ross L. 1988. "The Current State of Differential Association Theory." *Crime and Delinquency* 34:277–306.

Matsueda, Ross L. 1989. "The Dynamics of Moral Beliefs and Minor Deviance." *Social Forces* 68:428–457.

Matsueda, Ross L. 1992. "Reflected Appraisals, Parental Labeling, and Delinquency: Specifying a Symbolic Interactionist Theory." *American Journal of Sociology* 97:1577–1611.

Matsueda, Ross L. and Karen Heimer. 1987. "Race, Family Structure and Delinquency: A Test of Differential Association and Social Control Theories." *American Sociological Review* 52:826–840.

Matsueda, Ross L. and Kathleen Anderson. 1998. "The Dynamics of Delinquent Peers and Delinquent Behavior." *Criminology* 36:269–308.

Matthews, Nancy A. 1989. "Surmounting a Legacy: The Expansion of Racial Diversity in a Local Anti-Rape Movement." *Gender & Society* 3:518–532.

Matthews, Roger and Jock Young, eds. 1992. *Issues in Realist Criminology*. London: Sage.

Matza, David. 1964. *Delinquency and Drift*. New York: Wiley.

Matza, Michael. 1997. "Auditors to Eye Penn's Campus-Crime Data." *Philadelphia Inquirer*, June 9:A1.

Matza, Michael, Crag R. McCoy, and Mark Fazlollah. 1998. "Panel to Overhaul Crime Reporting." *Philadelphia Inquirer*, December 9:A1.

Matza, Michael, Craig R. McCoy, and Mark Fazlollah. 1999. "Major Crimes Climb in Phila.: Top Police Officials Say the 9 Percent Increase Simply Reflects More Accurate Reporting, Not a Surge in Violence." *Philadelphia Inquirer*, January 17:A1.

Mauer, Marc. 1999. *Race to Incarcerate*. New York: New Press.

Mawby, Rob and Sandra Walklate. 1994. *Critical Victimology: International Perspectives*. London: Sage.

Maxfield, Michael G. 1989. "Circumstances in Supplementary Homicide Reports: Variety and Validity." *Criminology* 27:671–695.

Mayer, Martin. 1990. *The Greatest Ever Bank Robbery: The Collapse of the Savings and Loan Industry*. New York: Charles Scribner's Sons.

Mayhew, Pat and Jan J. M. van Dijk. 1997. *Criminal Victimisation in Eleven Industrialised Countries: Key Findings from the 1996 International Crime Victims Survey*. The Hague: Justitie, Wetenschappelijk Onderzoeken Documentatiecentrum.

McCaghy, Charles H. and Timothy A. Capron. 1994. *Deviant Behavior: Crime, Conflict, and Interest Groups*. New York: Macmillan.

McCaghy, Charles H. and Timothy A. Capron. 2000. *Deviant Behavior: Crime, Conflict, and Interest Groups*. Needham Heights, MA: Allyn and Bacon.

McCall, Nathan. 1994. *Makes Me Wanna Holler: A Young Black Man in America*. New York: Random House.

McCarthy, Bill. 1995. "Not Just 'For the Thrill of It': An Instrumentalist Elaboration of Katz's Explanation of Sneaky Thrill Property Crimes." *Criminology* 33:519–538.

McCarthy, Bill, John Hagan, and Todd S. Woodward. 1999. "In the Company of Women: Structure and Agency in a Revised Power-Control Theory of Gender and Delinquency." *Criminology* 37:761–788.

McCord, Joan. 1991a. "Family Relationships, Juvenile Delinquency, and Adult Criminality." *Criminology* 29:397–417.

McCord, Joan. 1991b. "Questioning the Value of Punishment." *Social Problems* 38:167–179.

McDowall, David and Brian Wiersema. 1994. "The Incidence of Defensive Firearm Use by U.S. Crime Victims, 1987 through 1990." *American Journal of Public Health* 84:1982–1984.

McDowall, David, Alan J. Lizotte, and Brian Wiersema. 1991. "General Deterrence through Civilian Gun Ownership: An Evaluation of the Quasi-Experimental Evidence." *Criminology* 29:541–559.

McDowell, Edwin. 1992. "34 States Using Gambling as Alternative to Taxation." *New York Times*, June 12:A8.

McGee, Jim. 1995. "Drug Smuggling Industry Is Built on Franchises." *Washington Post*, March 26:A1.

McGovern, George S. and Leonard F. Guttridge. 1972. *The Great Coalfield War*. Boston: Houghton Mifflin.

McGrory, Brian. 1994. "Easy-Going Image, Violent Acts." *Boston Globe*, June 19:12.

McGrory, Brian. 1996. "'Zero-Tolerance' Policing in Houston: No Crime Too Small." *Boston Globe*, January 2:1.

McMullan, John L. and Peter D. Swan. 1989. "Social Economy and Arson in Nova Scotia." *Canadian Journal of Criminology* 31:281–308.

McNamara, Robert S. and Brian VanDeMark. 1995. *In Retrospect: The Tragedy and Lessons of Vietnam*. New York: Times.

Mears, Daniel P., Matthew Ploeger, and Mark Warr. 1998. "Explaining the Gender Gap in Delinquency: Peer Influence and Moral Evaluations of Behavior." *Journal of Research in Crime and Delinquency* 35:251–266.

Meddis, Sam Vincent. 1993. "'Brutalized' Public Lives with Growing Fear." *USA Today*, October 28:6A.

Meddis, Sam Vincent and Dennis Cauchon. 1994. "Community Looks within for Solutions." *USA Today*, January 6:1, 2.

Mednick, Sarnoff A., William F. Gabrielli, Jr., and Barry Hutchings. 1987. "Genetic Factors in the Etiology of Criminal Behavior." Pp. 74–91 in *The Causes of Crime: New Biological Approaches*, edited by Sarnoff A. Mednick, Terrie E. Moffitt, and Susan Stack. New York: Cambridge University Press.

Meier, Robert F. and Gilbert Geis. 1997. *Victimless Crime: Prostitution, Drugs, Homosexuality, and Abortion*. Los Angeles: Roxburty.

Meier, Robert F. and James F. Short, Jr. 1995. "The Consequences of White-Collar Crime." Pp. 80–104 in *White-Collar Crime: Classic and Contemporary Views*, edited by Gilbert Geis, Robert F. Meier, and Lawrence M. Salinger. New York: Free Press.

Meier, Robert F. and Terance D. Miethe. 1993. "Understanding Theories of Criminal Victimization." Pp. 459–499 in *Crime and Justice: A Review of Research*, edited by Michael Tonry. Chicago: University of Chicago Press.

Meltz, Barbara F. 1995. "The Unsparing Rod." *Boston Globe*, April 27:A1.

Menard, Scott and Barbara J. Morse. 1984. "A Structuralist Critique of the IQ-Delinquency Hypothesis." *American Journal of Sociology* 89:1347–1378.

Menzies, Robert. 1992. "Beyond Realist Criminology." Pp. 139–156 in *Realist Criminology: Crime Control and Policing in the 1990s*, edited by John Lowman and Brian D. MacLean. Toronto: University of Toronto Press.

Merton, Robert K. 1938. "Social Structure and Anomie." *American Sociological Review* 3:672–682.

Merton, Robert K. 1957. *Social Theory and Social Structure*. Glencoe, IL: Free Press.

Messerschmidt, James W. 1986. *Capitalism, Patriarchy, and Crime: Toward a Socialist Feminist Criminology*. Totowa, NJ: Rowman and Littlefield.

Messerschmidt, James W. 1993. *Masculinities and Crime: Critique and Reconceptualization of Theory*. Lanham, MD: Rowman and Littlefield.

Messerschmidt, James W. 1997. *Crime as Structured Action: Gender, Race, Class, and Crime in the Making*. Thousand Oaks, CA: Sage.

Messner, Steven F. and Richard Rosenfeld. 1997. *Crime and the American Dream*. Belmont, CA: Wadsworth.

Meyrowitz, Elliott L. and Kenneth J. Campbell. 1992. "Vietnam Veterans and War Crimes Hearings." Pp. 129–140 in *Give Peace a Chance: Exploring the Vietnam Antiwar Movement*, edited by Melvin Small and William D. Hoover. Syracuse: Syracuse University Press.

Michalowski, Raymond J. and Susan M. Carlson. 1999. "Unemployment, Imprisonment, and Social Structures of Accumulation: Historical Contingency in the Rusche-Kirchheimer Hypothesis." *Criminology* 37:217–249.

Miczek, Klaus A., Allan F. Mirsky, Gregory Carey, Joseph DeBold, and Adrian Raine. 1994. "An Overview of Biological Influences on Violent Behavior." Pp. 1–20 in *Understanding and Preventing Violence: Biobehavioral Influences*, vol. 2, edited by Albert J. Reiss, Jr., Klaus A. Miczek, and Jeffrey A. Roth. Washington, D.C.: National Academy Press.

Mieczkowski, Thomas M. 1996. "The Prevalence of Drug Use in the United States." *Crime and Justice: A Review of Research* 20:349–414.

Miedzian, Myriam. 1991. *Boys Will Be Boys: Breaking the Link between Masculinity and Violence*. New York: Doubleday.

Miethe, Terance D. 1982. "Public Consensus on Crime Seriousness: Normative Structure or Methodological Artifact?" *Criminology* 20:515–526.

Miethe, Terance D. 1987. "Stereotypical Conceptions and Criminal Processing: The Case of the Victim-Offender Relationship." *Justice Quarterly* 4:571–593.

Miethe, Terance D. and Gary R. Lee. 1984. "Fear of Crime among Older People: A Reassessment of the Predictive Power of Crime-Related Factors." *Sociological Quarterly* 25:397–415.

Miethe, Terance D. and Robert F. Meier. 1990. "Opportunity, Choice, and Criminal Victimization: A Test of a Theoretical Model." *Journal of Research in Crime and Delinquency* 27:243–266.

Miethe, Terance D., Mark C. Stafford, and J. Scott Long. 1987. "Social Differentiation in Criminal Victimization: A Test of Routine Activities/Lifestyle Theories." *American Sociological Review* 52:184–194.

Milavsky, J. Ronald. 1988. *TV and Violence*. Washington, D.C.: U.S. Department of Justice, National Institute of Justice.

Milavsky, J. Ronald, H. H. Stipp, R. C. Kessler, and W. S. Rubens. 1982. *Television and Aggression: A Panel Study*. New York: Academic Press.

Milgram, Stanley. 1974. *Obedience to Authority*. New York: Harper & Row.

Mill, John Stuart. 1892 [1859]. *On Liberty*. London: Longmans, Green.

Miller, J. L., Peter H. Rossi, and Jon E. Simpson. 1986. "Perceptions of Justice: Race and Gender Differences in Judgments of Appropriate Prison Sentences." *Law and Society Review* 20:313–334.

Miller, Jerome G. 1996. *Search and Destroy: African American Males in the Criminal Justice System*. New York: Cambridge University Press.

Miller, Jody. 1998. "Gender and Victimization Risk among Young Women in Gangs." *Journal of Research in Crime and Delinquency* 35:429–453.

Miller, Jody. 1998. "Up It Up: Gender and the Accomplishment of Street Robbery." *Criminology* 36:37–66.

Miller, Susan L. 1993. "A Critique of Gottfredson and Hirschi's General Theory of Crime: Selective (In)Attention to Gender and Power Positions." *Women and Criminal Justice* 4:115.

Miller, Susan L. and LeeAnn Iovanni. 1994. "Determinants of Perceived Risk of Formal Sanction for Courtship Violence." *Justice Quarterly* 11:281–312.

Miller, Walter B. 1958. "Lower-Class Culture as a Generating Milieu of Gang Delinquency." *Journal of Social Issues* 14:5–19.

Millet, Kate, ed. 1973. *The Prostitution Papers*. New York: Avon.

Mills, C. Wright. 1943. "The Professional Ideology of Social Pathologists." *American Journal of Sociology* 49:165–180.

Mills, C. Wright. 1959. *The Sociological Imagination*. London: Oxford University Press.

Milne, John. 1995. "Tough Campus Test: Saying 'No' to Drink." *Boston Globe*, April 2:1.

Minor, W. William. 1981. "Techniques of Neutralization: A Reconceptualization and Empirical Examination." *Journal of Research in Crime and Delinquency* 18:295–318.

Mintz, Morton. 1985. *At Any Cost: Corporate Greed,*

Women, and the Dalkon Shield. New York: Pantheon Books.

Mintz, Morton. 1992. "Why the Media Cover up Corporate Crime: A Reporter Looks Back in Anger." *Trial* 28:72–77.

Mirowsky, John and Catherine E. Ross. 1995. "Sex Differences in Distress: Real or Artifact?" *American Sociological Review* 60:449–468.

Mishel, Lawrence, Jared Bernstein, and John Schmitt. 1998. *The State of Working America, 1998–99.* An Economic Policy Institute Book. Ithaca, NY: ILR Press.

Mitford, Jessica. 1969. *The Trial of Dr. Spock.* New York: Knopf.

Moffitt, Terrie E. and Avshalom Caspi. 1999. *Findings about Partner Violence from the Dunedin Multidisciplinary Health and Development Study.* Washington, D.C.: U.S. Department of Justice, National Institute of Justice.

Moffitt, Terrie E., Ronald R. Lynam, and Phil A. Silva. 1994. "Neuropsychological Tests Predicting Persistent Male Delinquency." *Criminology* 32:277–300.

Moffitt, Terrie E., G. L. Brammer, Avshalom Caspi, J. P. Fawcett, M. Raleigh, A. Yuwiler, and Phil A. Silva. 1998. "Whole Blood Serotonin Relates to Violence in an Epidemiological Study." *Biological Psychiatry* 43:446–457.

Mokhiber, Russell. 1988. *Corporate Crime and Violence: Big Business Power and the Abuse of Public Trust.* San Francisco: Sierra Club Books.

Molla, Tony. 1994. "The Sting." *Motor Age,* March:4.

Monkkonen, Eric. 1981. *Police in Urban America, 1860–1920.* New York: Cambridge University Press.

Montgomery, Lori. 1995. "In Chicago, Study Raises Hopes, Fears." *Philadelphia Inquirer,* December 27:1+.

Moore, David W. 1994. "One in Seven Americans Victim of Child Abuse." *The Gallup Poll Monthly,* May:18–22.

Moore, Mark H. 1989. "Actually, Prohibition Was a Success." *New York Times,* October 16:A15.

Moore, Mark H. 1995. "Public Health and Criminal Justice Approaches to Prevention." Pp. 237–262 in *Building a Safer Society: Strategic Approaches to Crime Prevention,* vol. 19, *Crime and Justice: A Review of Research,* edited by Michael Tonry and David P. Farrington. Chicago: University of Chicago Press.

Moore, Samuel K. 1999. "Vitamins Makers Settle U.S. Civil Suit for $1.17 Billion." *Chemical Week,* November 10:15.

Moran, Richard. 1977. "Awaiting the Crown's Pleasure: The Case of Daniel M'Naughton." *Criminology* 15:7–26.

Moran, Richard. 1981. *Knowing Right from Wrong: The Insanity Defense of Daniel McNaughton.* New York: Free Press.

Moran, Richard. 1995. "More Police, Less Crime, Right? Wrong." *New York Times,* February 27:A15.

Morash, Merry. 1986. "Gender, Peer Group Experiences, and Seriousness of Delinquency." *Journal of Research in Crime and Delinquency* 23:43–67.

Morash, Merry and Meda Chesney-Lind. 1991. "A Reformulation and Partial Test of the Power-Control Theory of Delinquency." *Justice Quarterly* 8:347–377.

Moreland, Alvin 1994. "Employee Misconduct Is Surveyed." *Supermarket News,* April 4:14.

Morenoff, Jeffrey D. and Robert J. Sampson. 1997. "Violent Crime and the Spatial Dynamics of Neighborhood Transition: Chicago, 1970–1990." *Social Forces* 76:31–64.

Morgan, Robin. 1977. *Going Too Far.* New York: Random House.

Morreim, E. Haqui. 1989. "Conflicts of Interest: Profits and Problems in Physician Referrals." *JAMA, Journal of the American Medical Association* 262:390–394.

Morris, Allison. 1987. *Women, Crime, and Criminal Justice.* New York: Basil Blackwell.

Mosse, George L. 1975. *Police Forces in History.* Beverly Hills: Sage.

Moyers, Bill. 1988. *The Secret Government: The Constitution in Crisis.* Cabin John, MD: Seven Locks Press.

Moynihan, Daniel P. 1965. *The Negro Family: The Case for National Action.* Washington, D.C.: U.S. Department of Labor.

Mueller, G. O. W. 1990. "Whose Prophet Is Cesare Beccaria? An Essay on the Origins of Criminological Theory." Pp. 1–14 in *Advances in Criminological Theory,* vol. 2, edited by William S. Laufer and Freda Adler. New Brunswick, NJ: Transaction.

Muller, Mike. 1982. *The Health of Nations: An Investigation of the Pharmaceutical Industry's Exploitation of the Third World for Profit.* London: Faber and Faber.

Mullins, Wayman C. 1993. "Hate Crime and the Far Right: Unconventional Terrorism." Pp. 121–169 in *Political Crime in Contemporary America: A Critical Approach,* edited by Kenneth D. Tunnell. New York: Garland.

Mustaine, Elizabeth Ehrhardt and Richard Tewksbury. 1998. "Predicting Risks of Larceny Theft Victimization: A Routine Activity Analysis Using Refined Lifestyle Measures." *Criminology* 36:829–857.

Musto, David F. 1999. *The American Disease: Origins of Narcotic Control.* New York: Oxford University Press.

Myers, Martha A. 1990. "Economic Threat and Racial Disparities in Incarceration: The Case of Postbellum Georgia." *Criminology* 28:627–656.

Myers, Martha A. 1995. "Gender and Southern Punishment after the Civil War." *Criminology* 33:17–46.

Myers, Martha A. 1995. "The New South's 'New' Black Criminal: Rape and Punishment in Georgia, 1870–1940." Pp. 145–166 in *Ethnicity, Race, and Crime: Perspectives Across Time and Place,* edited by Darnell F. Hawkins. Albany, NY: State University of New York Press.

Myers, Martha A. 2000. "The Social World of America's Courts." Pp. 447–471 in *Criminology: A Contemporary Handbook,* edited by Joseph F. Sheley. Belmont, CA: Wadsworth.

Myers, Martha A. and Susette M. Talarico. 1987. *The Social Contexts of Criminal Sentencing*. New York: Springer-Verlag.

Nadelmann, Ethan A. 1992. "Drug Prohibition in the United States: Costs, Consequences, and Alternatives." Pp. 299–322 in *Drugs, Crime, and Social Policy: Research, Issues, and Concerns*, edited by Thomas Mieczkowski. Boston: Allyn and Bacon.

Naffine, Ngaire. 1987. *Female Crime: The Construction of Women in Criminology*. Sydney: Allen and Unwin.

Nagin, Daniel S. 1998. "Criminal Deterrence Research at the Outset of the Twenty-First Century." *Crime and Justice: A Review of Research* 23:1–42.

National Center for Health Statistics. 1999. *Healthy People 2000: Review, 1998–99*. Hyattsville, MD: Public Health Service.

Naughton, Keith and Evan Thomas. 2000. "Did Kayla Have to Die?" *Newsweek*, March 13:24–29.

Navasky, Victor S. 1980. *Naming Names*. New York: Viking Press.

Nazian, Florence. 1990. *Why Genocide? The Armenian and Jewish Experiences in Perspective*. Ames: Iowa State University Press.

Nelan, Bruce W. 1995. "Crime and Punishment: Yeltsin and His Critics Vie for the Title of Law-and-Order Champion." *Time*, March 20:54.

Nelkin, Dorothy. 1993. "The Grandiose Claims of Geneticists." *Chronicle of Higher Education*, March 3:B1–B3.

Nelsen, Candice, Jay Corzine, and Lin Huff-Corzine. 1994. "The Violent West Reexamined: A Research Note on Regional Homicide Rates." *Criminology* 32:149–161.

Nelson, James F. 1994. "A Dollar or a Day: Sentencing Misdemeanants in New York State." *Journal of Research in Crime and Delinquency* 31:183–201.

Neuborne, Ellen. 1994. "Fearful Shoppers Play it Safe." *USA Today*, June 2:1B–2B.

New York Times. 1991. "Corporate Tax Cheating Seen." *New York Times*, April 18:C6.

New York Times. 1993. "3 Teen-agers Sent to Prison for Burning Black Churches." *New York Times*, December 5:24.

New York Times. 1993. "349,000 Caesareans in '91 Called Unnecessary." *New York Times*, April 23:A16.

New York Times. 1995. "'A Prized American Privilege.'" *New York Times*, January 23:A13.

Newburn, Tim and Elizabeth A. Stanko, eds. 1994. *Just Boys Doing Business: Men, Masculinities and Crime*. London: Routledge.

Newman, Graeme. 1976. *Comparative Deviance: Perception and Law in Six Cultures*. New York: Elsevier.

Newman, Graeme and Pietro Marongiu. 1990. "Penological Reform and the Myth of Beccaria." *Criminology* 28:325–346.

Nickerson, Collin. 1994. "Canada, US Share Much, but Part Ways on Crime." *Boston Globe*, September 4:1,24.

Nobiling, Tracy, Cassia Spohn, and Miriam DeLone. 1998. "A Tale of Two Counties: Unemployment and Sentence Severity." *Justice Quarterly* 15:459–485.

Noble, Kenneth B. 1995. "Many Complain of Bias in Los Angeles Police; Black Officers Cite Unkept Promises." *New York Times*, September 4:6.

Noggle, Burl. 1965. *Teapot Dome: Oil and Politics in the 1920s*. New York: Norton.

Nordheimer, Jon. 1992. "Arson Rises in Northeast Recession." *New York Times*, May 31:23.

Norland, Stephen, Neal Shover, William E. Thornton, and Jennifer James. 1979. "Intrafamily Conflict and Delinquency." *Pacific Sociological Review* 22:223–237.

Oates, Stephen B. 1983. *The Fires of Jubilee: Nat Turner's Fierce Rebellion*. New York: New American Library.

O'Brien, Robert M. 1991. "Sex Ratios and Rape Rates: A Power-Control Theory." *Criminology* 29:99–114.

O'Brien, Robert M. 2000. "Crime Facts: Victim and Offender Data." Pp. 59–83 in *Criminology: A Contemporary Handbook*, edited by Joseph F. Sheley. Belmont, CA: Wadsworth.

O'Carroll, Patrick W. and James A. Mercy. 1989. "Regional Variation in Homicide Rates: Why Is the West So Violent?" *Violence and Victims* 4:17–25.

O'Carroll, Patrick W., Colin Loftin, John B. Waller, Jr., David McDowall, Allen Bukoff, Richard O. Scott, James A. Mercy, and Brian Wiersema. 1991. "Preventing Homicide: An Evaluation of the Efficacy of a Detroit Gun Ordinance." *American Journal of Public Health* 81:575–580.

Ogle, Robbin S., Daniel Maier-Katkin, and Thomas J. Bernard. 1995. "A Theory of Homicidal Behavior among Women." *Criminology* 33:173–193.

Oil Daily. 1993. "3 Firms Agree to Pay $77 Million in Lawsuit." *The Oil Daily*, January 12:3.

O'Kane, James M. 1992. *The Crooked Ladder: Gangsters, Ethnicity, and the American Dream*. New Brunswick, NJ: Transaction.

O'Leary, K. Daniel. 1993. "Through a Psychological Lens: Personality Traits, Personality Disorders, and Levels of Violence." Pp. 7–30 in *Current Controversies on Family Violence*, edited by Richard J. Gelles and Donileen R. Loseke. Newbury Park, CA: Sage.

Orcutt, James D. and J. Blake Turner. 1993. "Shocking Numbers and Graphic Accounts: Quantified Images of Drug Problems in the Print Media." *Social Problems* 40:190–206.

Ordway, Rennee. 1995. "Relaxation Spas Perplex Officials." *Bangor Daily*, News May 26:1.

O'Reilly, Kenneth. 1983. *Hoover and the Un-Americans: The FBI, HUAC, and the Red Menace*. Philadelphia: Temple University Press.

Ortega, Suzanne T. and Jessie L. Myles. 1987. "Race and Gender Effects on Fear of Crime: An Interactive Model with Age." *Criminology* 25:133–152.

Packer, Herbert L. 1964. "Two Models of the Criminal

Process." *University of Pennsylvania Law Review* 113:1–68.

Packer, Herbert L. 1968. *The Limits of the Criminal Sanction*. Stanford: Stanford University Press.

Packer, Herbert L. 1993. "Two Models of the Criminal Process." Pp. 14–27 in *Criminal Justice: Law and Politics*, edited by George F. Cole. Belmont, CA: Wadsworth.

Pagelow, Mildred Daley. 1994. "Wives, Not Husbands, Are Battered." *Bangor Daily News*, July 8:A13.

Palmer, Ted. 1992. *The Re-Emergence of Correctional Intervention*. Beverly Hills: Sage.

Paltrow, Lynn. 1990. "When Becoming Pregnant Is a Crime." *Criminal Justice Ethics* 9:41–47.

Pan, Philip P. 2000a. "Landlords Owe Sewer Bills." *Washington Post*, March 14:B1.

Pan, Philip P. 2000b. "Slumlord Crackdown Hurts Renters First." *Washington Post*, March 15:B1.

Park, Robert E., Ernest W. Burgess, and Roderick McKenzie. 1925. *The City*. Chicago: University of Chicago Press.

Parker, Karen F. and Patricia L. McCall. 1999. "Structural Conditions and Racial Homicide Patterns: A Look at the Multiple Disadvantages in Urban Areas." *Criminology* 37:447–477.

Parker, L. Craig. 1996. "Rising Crime Rates in the Czech Republic." Pp. 15–20 in *Criminology: A Cross-Cultural Perspective*, edited by Robert Heiner. Minneapolis/St. Paul: West.

Parker, Robert Nash. 1989. "Poverty, Subculture of Violence, and Type of Homicide." *Social Forces* 67:983–1007.

Parker, Robert Nash. 1995. "Bringing 'Booze' Back In: The Relationship between Alcohol and Homicide." *Journal of Research in Crime and Delinquency* 32:3–38.

Parker, Robert Nash and Doreen Anderson-Facile. 2000. "Violent Crime Trends." Pp. 191–213 in *Criminology: A Contemporary Handbook*, edited by Joseph F. Sheley. Belmont, CA: Wadsworth.

Paschall, Mallie J., Robert L. Flewelling, and Susan T. Ennett. 1998. "Racial Differences in Violent Behavior among Young Adults: Moderating and Confounding Effects." *Journal of Research in Crime and Delinquency* 35:148–165.

Passas, Nikos. 1990. "Anomie and Corporate Deviance." *Contemporary Crises* 14:157–178.

Paternoster, Raymond. 1984. "Prosecutorial Discretion in Requesting the Death Penalty: A Case of Victim-Based Racial Discrimination." *Law and Society Review* 18:437–478.

Paternoster, Raymond. 1987. "The Deterrent Effect of Perceived Certainty and Severity of Punishment: A Review of the Evidence and Issues." *Justice Quarterly* 42:173–217.

Paternoster, Raymond. 1991. *Capital Punishment in America*. New York: Lexington.

Paternoster, Raymond and Lee Ann Iovanni. 1989. "The Labeling Perspective and Delinquency: An Elaboration of the Theory and an Assessment of the Evidence." *Justice Quarterly* 6:379–394.

Paternoster, Raymond and Paul Mazerolle. 1994. "General Strain Theory and Delinquency: A Replication and Extension." *Journal of Research in Crime and Delinquency* 31:235–263.

Paternoster, Raymond and Sally Simpson. 1993. "A Rational Choice Theory of Corporate Crime." Pp. 37–58 in *Routine Activity and Rational Choice*, vol. 5, *Advances in Criminological Theory*, edited by Ronald V. Clarke and Marcus Felson. New Brunswick, NJ: Transaction Books.

Patterson, E. Britt. 1991. "Poverty, Income Inequality, and Community Crime Rates." *Criminology* 29:755–776.

Patterson, E. Britt and Michael J. Lynch. 1991. "Bias in Formalized Bail Procedures." Pp. 36–53 in *Race and Criminal Justice*, edited by Michael J. Lynch and E. Britt Patterson. New York: Harrow and Heston.

Payne, Les. 1991. "Police Brutality against Blacks Is a National Crisis." Pp. 36–37 in *Police Brutality*, edited by William Dudley. San Diego: Greenhaven Press.

Peffley, Mark, Todd Shields, and Bruce Williams. 1996. "The Intersection of Race and Crime in Television News Stories: An Experimental Study." *Political Communication* 13:309–327.

Peltier, Leonard. 1989. "War against the American Nation." Pp. 213–229 in *It Did Happen Here: Recollections of Political Repression in America*, edited by Bud Schultz and Ruth Schultz. Berkeley: University of California Press.

Pepinsky, Harold E. and Paul Jesilow. 1984. *Myths That Cause Crime*. Cabin John, MD: Seven Locks Press.

Pepinsky, Harold E. and Richard Quinney, eds. 1991. *Criminology as Peacemaking*. Bloomington: Indiana University Press.

Perez-Pena, Richard. 2000. "The Death Penalty: When There's No Room for Error." *New York Times*, February 13:WH3.

Perrow, Charles. 1986. *Complex Organizations: A Critical Essay*. New York: Random House.

Pertman, Adam. 1995. "Burden Seen Shifting to Simpson's Defense: Athlete's Image Tarnished over Time." *Boston Globe*, January 22:1,10.

Pertman, Adam. 1995. "Fuhrman's Raw, Racist Remarks Heard on Tapes." *Boston Globe*, August 30:1+.

Peters, S. D., G. E. Wyatt, and David Finkelhor. 1986. "Prevalence." In *A Sourcebook on Child Sexual Abuse*, edited by David Finkelhor, S. Araji, L. Baron, Angela Browne, S. D. Peters, and G. E. Wyatt. Beverly Hills: Sage.

Petersilia, Joan. 1983. *Racial Disparities in the Criminal Justice System*. Santa Monica: Rand Corporation.

Petersilia, Joan, Peter Greenwood, and Martin Levin. 1978. *Criminal Careers of Habitual Felons*. Washington, D.C.: National Institute of Law Enforcement and Criminal Justice.

Peterson, Horace C. and Gilbert C. Fite. 1957. *Opponents of War, 1917–1918*. Madison: University of Wisconsin Press.

Peterson, Ruth D. and Lauren J. Krivo. 1999. "Racial Segregation, the Concentration of Disadvantage, and Black and White Homicide Victimization." *Sociological Forum* 14:465–493.

Peterson, Ruth D. and William C. Bailey. 1991. "Felony Murder and Capital Punishment: An Examination of the Deterrence Question." *Criminology* 29:367–395.

Peterson, Ruth D. and William C. Bailey. 1992. "Rape and Dimensions of Gender Socioeconomic Inequality in U.S. Metropolitan Areas." *Journal of Research in Crime and Delinquency* 29:162–177.

Peterson, Ruth D., Lauren J. Krivo, and Mark A. Harris. 2000. "Disadvantage and Neighborhood Violent Crime: Do Local Institutions Matter?" *Journal of Research in Crime and Delinquency* 37:31–63.

Petrik, Norman D., Rebecca E. Petrik Olson, and Leah S. Subotnik. 1994. "Powerlessness and the Need to Control." *Journal of Interpersonal Violence* 9:278–285.

Pfuhl, Edwin H., Jr. 1983. "Police Strikes and Conventional Crime: A Look at the Data." *Criminology* 21:489–503.

Phillips, David P. 1983. "The Impact of Mass Media Violence on U.S. Homicides." *American Sociological Review* 48:560–568.

Phillips, Julie A. 1997. "Variation in African-American Homicide Rates: An Assessment of Potential Explanations." *Criminology* 35:527–559.

Pierce, Glenn L. and William J. Bowers. 1981. "The Bartley-Fox Gun Law's Short-Term Impact on Crime." *Annals of the American Academy of Political and Social Science* 455:120–137.

Pincher, Chapman. 1987. *Traitors: The Anatomy of Treason*. New York: St. Martin's Press.

Piquero, Alex R. and Matthew Hickman. 1999. "An Empirical Test of Tittle's Control Balance Theory." *Criminology* 37:319–341.

Plummer, Carol A. 1993. "Prevention Is Appropriate, Prevention Is Successful." In *Current Controversies on Family Violence*, edited by Richard J. Gelles and Donileen R. Loseke. Newbury Park, CA: Sage.

Pogrebin, Mark, Eric Poole, and Amos Martinez. 1992. "Accounts of Professional Misdeeds: The Sexual Exploitation of Clients by Psychotherapists." *Deviant Behavior* 13:229–252.

Polk, Kenneth. 1991. Review of *A General Theory of Crime* by Michael R. Gottfredson and Travis Hirschi. *Crime and Delinquency* 37:575–581.

Polk, Kenneth. 1994. *When Men Kill: Scenarios of Masculine Violence*. Cambridge: Cambridge University Press.

Pollak, Otto. 1950. *The Criminality of Women*. Philadelphia: University of Pennsylvania Press.

Polsby, Daniel D. 1994. "The False Promise of Gun Control." *The Atlantic Monthly*, March:57–70.

Pontell, Henry N. 1984. *A Capacity to Punish: The Ecology of Crime and Punishment*. Bloomington: Indiana University Press.

Pontell, Henry N. and Kitty Calavita. 1993. "The Savings and Loan Industry." Pp. 203–246 in *Beyond the Law: Crime in Complex Organizations*, vol. 18, *Crime and Justice: A Review of Research*, edited by Michael Tonry and Albert J. Reiss, Jr. Chicago: University of Chicago Press.

Pontell, Henry N., Kitty Calavita, and Robert Tillman. 1994. "Corporate Crime and Criminal Justice System Capacity: Government Response to Financial Institution Fraud." *Justice Quarterly* 11:383–410.

Pope, Carl and Todd Clear. 1994. "Editors' Introduction." *Journal of Research in Crime and Delinquency* 31:132–134.

Pope, Carl and W. Feyerherm. 1992. *Minorities and the Juvenile Justice System*. Rockville, MD: U.S. Department of Justice, Office of Juvenile Justice and Delinquency Prevention.

Porterfield, Austin L. 1946. *Youth in Trouble: Studies in Delinquency and Despair, with Plans for Prevention*. Fort Worth, TX: Leo Potishman Foundation.

Potter, Gary W. 1994. *Criminal Organizations: Vice, Racketeering, and Politics in an American City*. Prospect Heights, IL: Waveland Press.

Potter, Gary W. and Victor E. Kappeler, eds. 1998. *Constructing Crime: Perspectives on Making News and Social Problems*. Prospect Heights, IL: Waveland Press.

Preble, Edward and John J. Casey. 1969. "Taking Care of Business: The Heroin User's Life on the Street." *International Journal of Addictions* 4:1–24.

Preston, Ivan L. 1994. *The Tangled Web They Weave: Truth, Falsity, and Advertisers*. Madison: University of Wisconsin Press.

Pritchard, David. 1986. "Homicide and Bargained Justice: The Agenda-Setting Effect of Crime News on Prosecutions." *Public Opinion Quarterly* 50:143–159.

Pritchard, David and Dan Berkowitz. 1993. "The Limits of Agenda-Setting: The Press and Political Responses to Crime in the United States, 1950–1980." *International Journal of Public Opinion Research* 5:86–91.

Public Health Reports. 1998. "Health Ranks Fifth on Local TV News." *Public Health Reports* 113:296–297.

Pulaski, Mary Ann S., ed. 1980. *Understanding Piaget: An Introduction to Children's Cognitive Development*. New York: Harper & Row.

Quindlen, Anna. 1993. "Gynocide." *New York Times*, March 10:A15.

Quindlen, Anna. 1994. "Sex for Sale." *New York Times*, November 26:15.

Quinn, Thomas. 1998. "Restorative Justice: An Interview with Visiting Fellow Thomas Quinn." *National Institute of Justice Journal*, March: 10–16.

Quinney, Richard. 1974. *Critique of Legal Order: Crime Control in Capitalist Society*. Boston: Little, Brown.

Radelet, Michael L., Hugo Adam Bedau, and Constance

E. Putnam. 1992. *In Spite of Innocence: Erroneous Convictions in Capital Cases*. Boston: Northeastern University Press.

Rafter, Nicole Hahn. 1997. *Creating Born Criminals*. Urbana, IL: University of Illinois Press.

Raloff, J. 1989. "Bladder Cancer: One in Four Due to Jobs." *Science News* 136:230.

Rand, Michael R. 1994. *Guns and Crime*. Washington, D.C.: U.S. Department of Justice, Bureau of Justice Statistics.

Randall, Donna. 1995. "The Portrayal of Business Malfeasance in the Elite and General Media." Pp. 105–115 in *White-Collar Crime: Classic and Contemporary Views*, edited by Gilbert Geis, Robert F. Meier, and Lawrence M. Salinger. New York: Free Press.

Randall, Melanie and Lori Haskell. 1995. "Sexual Violence in Women's Lives: Findings from the Women's Safety Project, a Community-Based Survey." *Violence against Women* 1:6–31.

Randall, Willard Sterne. 1990. *Benedict Arnold: Patriot and Traitor*. New York: Morrow.

Rankin, Joseph H. and L. Edward Wells. 1990. "The Effect of Parental Attachments and Direct Controls on Delinquency." *Journal of Research in Crime and Delinquency* 27:140–165.

Rankin, Joseph H. and L. Edward Wells. 1994. "Social Control, Family Structure, and Delinquency." Pp. 97–116 in *Varieties of Criminology: Readings from a Dynamic Discipline*, edited by Gregg Barak. Westport, CT: Praeger.

Rankin, Joseph H. and Roger Kern. 1994. "Parental Attachments and Delinquency." *Criminology* 32:495–515.

Ransdell, Eric. 1995. "The World's Most Murderous Country: In South Africa, Economic Hardship Has Triggered an Explosion of Violent Crime." *U.S. News & World Report*, August 21:44.

Rasche, Christine E. 1988. "Minority Women and Domestic Violence: The Unique Dilemmas of Battered Women of Color." *Journal of Contemporary Criminal Justice* 4:150–171.

Rasmussen, David W. and Bruce L. Benson. 1994. *The Economic Anatomy of a Drug War: Criminal Justice in the Commons*. Lanham, MD: Rowman & Littlefield.

Ray, Jo-Ann. 1987. "Every Twelfth Shopper: Who Shoplifts and Why?" *Social Casework* 68:234–239.

Reckless, Walter C. 1961. "A New Theory of Delinquency and Crime." *Federal Probation* 25:42–46.

Reckless, Walter C., Simon Dinitz, and Ellen Murray. 1956. "Self-Concept as an Insulator against Delinquency." *American Sociological Review* 21:744–756.

Reed, Ishmael. 1991. "Tuning Out Network Bias." *New York Times*, April 9:A11.

Reibstein, Larry. 1997. "NYPD Black and Blue." *Newsweek*:64–68.

Reiman, Jeffrey. 1998. *The Rich Get Richer and the Poor Get Prison: Ideology, Class, and Criminal Justice*. Boston: Allyn and Bacon.

Reiss, Albert J. 1951. "Delinquency as the Failure of Personal and Social Controls." *American Sociological Review* 16:196–207.

Reiss, Albert J., Jr. 1980a. "Officer Violations of the Law." Pp. 253–272 in *Police Behavior: A Sociological Perspective*, edited by Richard J. Lundman. New York: Oxford University Press.

Reiss, Albert J., Jr. 1980b. "Police Brutality." Pp. 274–296 in *Police Behavior: A Sociological Perspective*, edited by Richard J. Lundman. New York: Oxford University Press.

Reiss, Albert J., Jr. and Jeffrey A. Roth, eds. 1993. *Understanding and Preventing Violence*. Washington, D.C.: National Academy Press.

Rennison, Callie Marie. 1999. *Criminal Victimization 1998: Changes 1997–98 with Trends 1993–98*. Washington, D.C.: U.S. Department of Justice, Bureau of Justice Statistics.

Renzetti, Claire M. 1993. "On the Margins of the Malestream (or, They Still Don't Get It, Do They?): Feminist Analyses in Criminal Justice Education." *Journal of Criminal Justice Education* 4:219–234.

Resick, Patricia A. 1990. "Victims of Sexual Assault." Pp. 69–86 in *Victims of Crime: Problems, Policies, and Programs*, edited by Arthur J. Lurigio, Wesley G. Skogan, and Robert C. Davis. Newbury Park, CA: Sage.

Reuters. 1995. "China Detains Three in Roundup." *Boston Globe*, May 21:21.

Revkin, Andrew C. 1999. "Welfare Policies Alter the Face of Food Lines." *New York Times*, February 26:A1.

Reynolds, Barbara. 1994. "If Civil Rights Legend Rosa Parks Isn't Safe, Who Is?" *USA Today*, September 2:11A.

Reynolds, Pam. 1987. "Thousands Are Locked in with the Danger." *Boston Globe*, March 29:A18.

Rezendes, Michael. 1993. "Jackson Urges Blacks to Wage War on Crime." *Boston Globe*, November 6:1,4.

Rhodes, William, Stacia Langenbahn, Ryan Kling, and Paul Scheiman. 1997. *What America's Users Spend on Illegal Drugs, 1988–1995*. Washington, D.C.: Office of National Drug Control Policy.

Richlin, Amy, ed. 1992. *Pornography and Representation in Greece and Rome*. New York: Oxford University Press.

Riggs, David S. and Dean G. Kilpatrick. 1990. "Families and Friends: Indirect Victimization by Crime." Pp. 120–138 in *Victims of Crime: Problems, Policies, and Programs*, edited by Arthur J. Lurigio, Wesley G. Skogan, and Robert C. Davis. Newbury Park, CA: Sage.

Riksheim, Eric and Steven M. Chermak. 1993. "Causes of Police Behavior Revisited." *Journal of Criminal Justice* 21:353–382.

Ringel, Cheryl. 1997. *Criminal Victimization 1996: Changes 1995–96 with Trends 1993–96*. Washington, D.C.: U.S. Department of Justice, Bureau of Justice Statistics.

Robinson, Paul H. 1984. *Criminal Law Defenses*. St. Paul, MN: West.

Rodden, Bonny. 1977. "Hung Jury in Second Protest Trial." *Stanford Daily*, July 29:1.

Rohter, Larry. 1999. "Colombia Tries, Yet Cocaine Thrives." *New York Times*, November 20:A6.

Roncek, Dennis W. 1981. "Dangerous Places: Crime and Residential Environment." *Social Forces* 60:74–96.

Roncek, Dennis W. and Pamela A. Maier. 1991. "Bars, Blocks, and Crimes Revisited: Linking the Theory of Routine Activities to the Empiricism of 'Hot Spots.'" *Criminology* 29:725–753.

Rorabaugh, W. J. 1995. "Alcohol in America." Pp. 16–18 in *Drugs, Society, and Behavior, Annual Editions*, edited by Erich Goode. Guilford, CT: Dushkin.

Rose, Dina R. and Todd R. Clear. 1998. "Incarceration, Social Capital, and Crime: Implications for Social Disorganization Theory." *Criminology* 36:441–479.

Rosecrance, John D. 1988. *Gambling without Guilt: The Legitimation of an American Pastime*. Pacific Grove, CA: Brooks/Cole.

Rosen, Lawrence. 1985. "Family and Delinquency: Structure or Function?" *Criminology* 23:553–573.

Rosen, Marie Simonetti. 1995. "A LEN Interview with Prof. Carl Klockars of the University of Delaware." Pp. 107–114 in *Annual Editions: Criminal Justice 95/96*, edited by John J. Sullivan and Joseph L. Victor. Guilford, CT: Dushkin.

Rosenbaum, Dennis P. 1988. "Community Crime Prevention: A Review and Synthesis of the Literature." *Justice Quarterly* 5:323–395.

Rosenbaum, Jill Leslie. 1987. "Social Control, Gender, and Delinquency: An Analysis of Drug, Property and Violent Offenders." *Justice Quarterly* 4:117–142.

Rosenbaum, Jill Leslie and James R. Lasley. 1990. "School, Community Context, and Delinquency: Rethinking the Gender Gap." *Justice Quarterly* 7:493–513.

Rosenthal, J. A. 1988. "Patterns of Injury Severity in Physical Child Abuse." *Journal of Social Service Research* 1:63–76.

Rosenthal, Robert and Lenore Jacobson. 1968. *Pygmalion in the Classroom*. New York: Holt.

Rosoff, Stephen M., Henry N. Pontell, and Robert Tillman. 1998. *Profit without Honor: White-Collar Crime and the Looting of America*. Upper Saddle River, NJ: Prentice Hall.

Ross, Edward A. 1965 [1907]. *Sin and Society: An Analysis of Latter-Day Iniquity*. Gloucester, MA: P. Smith.

Rossi, Peter H., Emily Waite, Christine E. Bose, and Richard E. Berk. 1974. "The Seriousness of Crime: Normative Structure and Individual Differences." *American Sociological Review* 39:224–237.

Roth, Jeffrey A. 1994. *Firearms and Violence*. Washington, D.C.: U.S. Department of Justice, National Institute of Justice.

Roth, Jeffrey A. 1994. *Psychoactive Substances and Violence*. Washington, D.C.: U.S. Department of Justice, National Institute of Justice.

Rovner, Julie. 1999. "Clinton Signs Away Tobacco Industry Settlement Money." *The Lancet* 353:1867ff.

Rowe, David C. and David P. Farrington. 1997. "The Familial Transmission of Criminal Convictions." *Criminology* 35:177–201.

Rubenstein, Richard E. 1970. *Rebels in Eden: Mass Political Violence in the United States*. Boston: Little, Brown and Company.

Rubinstein, Jonathan. 1980. "Cop's Rules." Pp. 68–78 in *Police Behavior: A Sociological Perspective*, edited by Richard J. Lundman. New York: Oxford University Press.

Rusche, George S. and Otto Kirchheimer. 1939. *Punishment and Social Structure*. New York: Columbia University Press.

Russell, Diana. 1975. *The Politics of Rape: The Victim's Perspective*. New York: Stein and Day.

Russell, Diana E. H. 1984. *Sexual Exploitation: Rape, Child Sexual Abuse, and Harassment*. Beverly Hills: Sage.

Russell, Diana E. H. 1990. *Rape in Marriage*. Bloomington: Indiana University Press.

Russell, Diana E. H., ed. 1993. *Making Violence Sexy: Feminist Views on Pornography*. New York: Teachers College Press.

Russell, Diana E. H. and Nancy Howell. 1983. "The Prevalence of Rape in the United States Revisited." *Signs* 8:688–695.

Ryan, William. 1976. *Blaming the Victim*. New York: Vintage Books.

Saad, Lydia and Leslie McAneny. 1995. "Black Americans See Little Justice for Themselves: And Most Believe Simpson Not Guilty." *The Gallup Poll Monthly*, March:32–35.

Sacco, Vincent F. and Holly Johnson. 1990. *Patterns of Criminal Victimization in Canada*. Ottawa: Statistics Canada.

Sahagun, Louis. 1998. "On a Navajo Reservation, the Problem of Violence Rivals That in Large Cities." *Philadelphia Inquirer*, January 12:A1.

Samborn, Randall. 1994. "Opinion Divided on Rape Shield; Fractious Appeals Ruling." *The National Law Journal*, January 24:13.

Samborn, Randall. 1995. "Fairchild's Sudden Fall Ends with Drop of a Gavel; Former Head of Winston and Strawn Earns 24 to 30 Months for Embezzlement." *National Law Journal*, January 9:A11.

Sampson, Robert J. 1985. "Structural Sources of Variation in Race-Age Specific Rates of Offending across Major U.S. Cities." *Criminology* 23:647–673.

Sampson, Robert J. 1995. "The Community." Pp. 193–216 in *Crime*, edited by James Q. Wilson and Joan Petersilia. San Francisco: Institute for Contemporary Studies Press.

Sampson, Robert J. 1997. "Neighborhoods and Violent

Crime: A Multilevel Study of Collective Efficacy." *Science* 277:918–924.

Sampson, Robert J. and Dawn Jeglum Bartusch. 1999. *Attitudes toward Crime, Police, and the Law: Individual and Neighborhood Differences.* Washington, D.C.: U.S. Department of Justice, National Institute of Justice.

Sampson, Robert J. and Jacqueline Cohen. 1988. "Deterrent Effects of the Police on Crime: A Replication and Theoretical Extension." *Law and Society Review* 22:163–189.

Sampson, Robert J. and Janet L. Lauritsen. 1990. "Deviant Lifestyles, Proximity to Crime, and the Offender-Victim Link in Personal Violence." *Journal of Research in Crime and Delinquency* 27:110–139.

Sampson, Robert J. and Janet L. Lauritsen. 1994. "Violent Victimization and Offending: Individual-, Situational-, and Community-Level Risk Factors." Pp. 1–114 in *Understanding and Preventing Violence,* vol. 3, *Social Influences,* edited by Albert J. Reiss, Jr. and Jeffrey A. Roth. Washington, D.C.: National Academy Press.

Sampson, Robert J. and John H. Laub. 1993. *Crime in the Making: Pathways and Turning Points through Life.* Cambridge: Harvard University Press.

Sampson, Robert J. and William Julius Wilson. 1995. "Toward a Theory of Race, Crime, and Urban Inequality." Pp. 37–54 in *Crime and Inequality,* edited by John Hagan and Ruth D. Peterson. Stanford: Stanford University Press.

Samuels, David. 1999. "The Making of a Fugitive." *New York Times Magazine,* March 21: 46ff.

Sanday, Peggy Reeves. 1981. "The Socio-Cultural Context of Rape: A Cross-Cultural Study." *Journal of Social Issues* 37:5–27.

Savage, David G. 1994. "Basic 'Right' to Own Gun Yet to Stand Up in Court: Law Professors Say Public Has Been Misled by NRA." *Bangor Daily News,* June 17:A1, A2.

Schafer, Stephen. 1974. *The Political Criminal.* New York: Free Press.

Scheer, Robert. 1999. "A Whole Lot of Us Need to Come Clean." *Los Angeles Times,* August 24:B7.

Scheingold, Stuart A. 1984. *The Politics of Law and Order: Street Crime and Public Policy.* New York: Longman.

Scherer, Ron. 1995. "Sports Gambling Rolls into the Schoolrooms of Suburbia." *The Christian Science Monitor,* May 19:3.

Schlesinger, Philip, Howard Tumber, and Graham Murdock. 1991. "The Media Politics of Crime and Criminal Justice." *British Journal of Sociology* 42:397–420.

Schmidt, Joan and Elena Williams. 1999. "When All Else Fails, Try Harm Reduction." *American Journal of Nursing* 99:67–70.

Schmidt, William E. 1993. "Libya Says Flight 103 Suspects Can Be Tried in Scotland." *New York Times,* September 30:A6.

Schneider, Alison. 1999. "Why Professors Don't Do More to Stop Students Who Cheat." *The Chronicle of Higher Education January,* 22:A8–A10.

Schneider, Keith. 1993a. "A Longtime Pillar of Government Now Aides Those Hurt by Its Bombs." *New York Times,* June 9:A8.

Schneider, Keith. 1993b. "Military Spread Nuclear Fallout in Secret Tests." *New York Times,* December 16:A1.

Schreck, Christopher J. 1999. "Criminal Victimization and Low Self-Control: An Extension and Test of a General Theory of Crime." *Justice Quarterly* 16:633–654.

Schultz, Bud and Ruth Schultz, eds. 1989. *It Did Happen Here: Recollections of Political Repression in America.* Berkeley: University of California Press.

Schur, Edwin M. 1973. *Radical Nonintervention.* Englewood Cliffs, NJ: Spectrum.

Schwartz, Jerry. 1993. "The Airline Ticket Settlement: Don't Expect Big Benefits." *New York Times,* March 27:30.

Schwartz, Martin D. 1987. "Gender and Injury in Spousal Assault." *Sociological Focus* 20:61–75.

Schwartz, Martin D. 1995. "Date Rape on College Campuses." Pp. 135–140 in *Readings in Deviant Behavior,* edited by Alex Thio and Thomas Calhoun. New York: HarperCollins.

Schwartz, Richard D. and Jerome H. Skolnick. 1962. "Two Studies of Legal Stigma." *Social Problems* 10:133–142.

Schwendinger, Herman and Julia Schwendinger. 1974. *Sociologists of the Chair.* New York: Basic Books.

Schwendinger, Julia R. and Herman Schwendinger. 1983. *Rape and Inequality.* Newbury Park, CA: Sage.

Scott, Donald W. 1989. "Policing Corporate Collusion." *Criminology* 27:559–587.

Scott, Joseph E. and Steven J. Cuvelier. 1987. "Violence in Playboy Magazine: A Longitudinal Analysis." *Archives of Sexual Behavior* 16:279–288.

Scully, Diana. 1995. "Rape Is the Problem." Pp. 197–215 in *The Criminal Justice System and Women: Offenders, Victims, and Workers,* edited by Barbara Raffel Price and Natalie J. Sokoloff. New York: McGraw-Hill.

Seeger, Pete. 1989. "Thou Shalt Not Sing." Pp. 13–21 in *It Did Happen Here: Recollections of Political Repression in America,* edited by Bud Schultz and Ruth Schultz. Berkeley: University of California Press.

Sege, Irene. 1994. "Don't Do Away with Dolls." *Boston Globe,* December 15:73, 74.

Seidman, David and Michael Couzens. 1974. "Getting the Crime Rate Down: Political Pressure and Crime Reporting." *Law & Society Review* 8:457–493.

Sellin, Thorsten. 1938. "Culture Conflict and Crime." New York: Social Science Research Council.

Sellin, Thorsten and Marvin E. Wolfgang. 1964. *The Measurement of Delinquency.* New York: Wiley.

Sennott, Charles M. 1995. "Rights Groups Battle Burning of Women in Pakistan." *Boston Globe,* May 18:1, 24.

Serio, Joe. 1997. "Russian Crime Threatens Foreign Investment." *Crime and Justice International,* April:10–12.

Seuss®, Dr. 1961. *The Sneetches and Other Stories*. New York: Random House.

Shannon, Lyle W. 1988. *Criminal Career Continuity: Its Social Context*. New York: Human Sciences Press.

Shapiro, Deane H., Jr., Barton J. Blinder, Jennifer Hagman, and Steven Pituck. 1993. "A Psychological 'Sense-of-Control' Profile of Patients with Anorexia Nervosa and Bulimia Nervosa." *Psychological Reports* 73:530–541.

Shaprio, Susan P. 1990. "Collaring the Crime, Not the Criminal: Liberating the Concept of White-Collar Crime." *American Sociological Review* 55:346–365.

Sharlitt, Joseph. 1989. *Fatal Error: The Miscarriage of Justice that Sealed the Rosenbergs' Fate*. New York: Scribner's.

Shaw, Clifford R. and Henry D. McKay. 1942. *Juvenile Delinquency and Urban Areas*. Chicago: University of Chicago Press.

Shaw, Jan. 1994. "Who Steals, Who Doesn't." *Business Journal*, February 28:25–26.

Shelden, Randall G. 1982. *Criminal Justice in America: A Sociological Approach*. Boston: Little, Brown.

Sheldon, William. 1949. *Varieties of Delinquent Youth*. New York: Harper & Row.

Sheley, Joseph F. 2000. "Shaping Definitions of Crime." Pp. 33–55 in *Criminology: A Contemporary Handbook*, edited by Joseph F. Sheley. Belmont, CA: Wadsworth.

Sheley, Joseph F. and C. D. Ashkins. 1981. "Crime, Crime News, and Crime Views." *Public Opinion Quarterly* 45:492–506.

Sheley, Joseph F. and John J. Hanlon. 1978. "Unintended Consequences of Police Decisions to Enforce Laws: Implications for Analysis of Crime Trends." *Contemporary Crises* 2:265–275.

Shenon, Philip. 1994. "Overlooked Question in Singapore Caning Debate: Is the Teen-Ager Guilty?" *New York Times*, April 17:6.

Shenon, Philip. 1995. "Singapore, the Rope, and Frayed Relations." *New York Times*, March 19:E2.

Shepard, Paul. 1997. "Attacking Black-on-Black Crime." *Philadelphia Inquirer*, April 9:A3.

Sherman, Lawrence W. 1980. "Causes of Police Behavior: The Current State of Quantitative Research." *Journal of Research in Crime and Delinquency* 17:69–100.

Sherman, Lawrence W. 1986. "Policing Communities: What Works?" Pp. 343–386 in *Crime and Justice: A Review of Research*, vol. 8, edited by Albert J. Reiss, Jr. and Michael Tonry. Chicago: University of Chicago Press.

Sherman, Lawrence W. 1990. "Police Crackdowns: Initial and Residual Deterrence." Pp. 1–48 in *Crime and Justice: A Review of Research*, vol. 12, edited by Michael Tonry and Norval Morris. Chicago: University of Chicago Press.

Sherman, Lawrence W. 1992. *Policing Domestic Violence: Experiments and Dilemmas*. New York: Free Press.

Sherman, Lawrence W. 1995. "General Deterrent Effects of Police Patrol in Crime 'Hot Spots': A Randomized, Controlled Trial." *Justice Quarterly* 12:625–648.

Sherman, Lawrence W. and Dennis P. Rogan. 1995. "Effects of Gun Seizures on Gun Violence: 'Hot Spots' Patrol in Kansas City." *Justice Quarterly* 12:673–693.

Sherman, Lawrence W. and Ellen G. Cohn. 1989. "The Impact of Research on Legal Policy: The Minneapolis Domestic Violence Experiment." *Law and Society Review* 23:117–144.

Sherman, Lawrence W. and Richard A. Berk. 1984. "The Specific Deterrent Effects of Arrest for Domestic Assault." *American Sociological Review* 49:261–272.

Sherman, Lawrence W., Patrick R. Gartin, and Michael E. Buerger. 1989. "Hot Spots of Predatory Crime: Routine Activities and the Criminology of Place." *Criminology* 27:27–55.

Sherman, Lawrence W., Denise C. Gottfredson, Doris L. MacKenzie, John Eck, Peter Reuter, and Shawn D. Bushaway. 1998. *Preventing Crime: What Works, What Doesn't, What's Promising*. Washington, D.C.: Office of Justice Programs, National Institute of Justice.

Shichor, David. 1985. "Male/Female Differences in Elderly Arrests." *Justice Quarterly* 2:399–414.

Shipman, Pat. 1994. *The Evolution of Racism: Human Differences and the Use and Abuse of Science*. New York: Simon & Schuster.

Shoemaker, Donald J. 1996. *Theories of Delinquency: An Examination of Explanations of Delinquent Behavior*. New York: Oxford University Press.

Short, James F. 1997. *Poverty, Ethnicity, and Violent Crime*. Boulder: Westview Press.

Short, James F. and Fred L. Strodtbeck. 1965. *Group Process and Gang Delinquency*. Chicago: University of Chicago Press.

Short, James F., Jr. and F. Ivan Nye. 1957. "Reported Behavior as a Criterion of Deviant Behavior." *Social Problems* 5:207–213.

Shover, Neal. 1973. "The Social Organization of Burglary." *Social Problems* 20:499–514.

Shover, Neal. 1991. "Burglary." Pp. 73–113 in *Crime and Justice: A Review of Research*, vol. 14, edited by Michael Tonry. Chicago: University of Chicago Press.

Shover, Neal and Andrew L. Hochstetler. 2000. "Crimes of Privilege." In *Criminology: A Contemporary Handbook*, edited by Joseph F. Sheley. Belmont, CA: Wadsworth.

Shover, Neal, Greer Litton Fox, and Michael Mills. 1994. "Long-Term Consequences of Victimization by White-Collar Crime." *Justice Quarterly* 11:75–98.

Silva, Phil A. and W. R. Stanton, eds. 1996. *From Child to Adult: The Dunedin Multidisciplinary Health and Development Study*. Auckland, New Zealand: Oxford University Press.

Silverman, Milton Morris, Philip R. Lee, and Mia Lydecker. 1982. *Prescription for Death: The Drugging of the Third World*. Berkeley: University of California Press.

Simon, David R. 1999. *Elite Deviance*. Boston: Allyn and Bacon.

Simon, Rita James. 1975. *Women and Crime*. Lexington, MA: Lexington Books.

Simons, Ronald L., Chyi-In Wu, Rand D. Conger, and Frederick O. Lorenz. 1994. "Two Routes to Delinquency: Differences between Early and Later Starters in the Impact of Parenting and Deviant Peers." *Criminology* 32:247–275.

Simpson, Sally S. 1989. "Feminist Theory, Crime, and Justice." *Criminology* 27:607–631.

Simpson, Sally S. 1991. "Caste, Class, and Violent Crime: Explaining Difference in Female Offending." *Criminology* 29:115–135.

Simpson, Sally S. and Lori Elis. 1995. "Doing Gender: Sorting Out the Caste and Crime Conundrum." *Criminology* 33:47–81.

Simpson, Sally S., Anthony R. Harris, and Brian A. Mattson. 1995. "Measuring Corporate Crime." Pp. 115–140 in *Understanding Corporate Criminality*, edited by Michael B. Blankenship. New York: Garland.

Sinclair, Upton. 1990 [1906]. *The Jungle*. New York: New American Library.

Sitton, Lea. 1994. "Regulating Guns as Consumer Product Gains Backers." *Philadelphia Inquirer*, April 1:A1, A8.

Skogan, Wesley G. 1986. "Fear of Crime and Neighborhood Change." Pp. 203–229 in *Communities and Crime*, edited by Albert J. Reiss and Michael Tonry. Chicago: University of Chicago Press.

Skogan, Wesley G. 1987. "The Impact of Victimization on Fear." *Crime and Delinquency* 33:135–154.

Skogan, Wesley G. 1989. "Social Change and the Future of Violent Crime." Pp. 235–250 in *Violence in America*, vol. 1, *The History of Crime*, edited by Ted Robert Gurr. Newbury Park, CA: Sage.

Skogan, Wesley. 1990. *Disorder and Decline: Crime and the Spiral of Decay in American Neighborhoods*. New York: Free Press.

Skogan, Wesley G. and Michael G. Maxfield. 1981. *Coping with Crime: Individual and Neighborhood Reactions*. Beverly Hills: Sage.

Skogan, Wesley G. and Susan M. Hartnett. 1999. *Community Policing, Chicago Style*. New York: Oxford University Press.

Skolnick, Jerome H. 1968. "Coercion to Virtue: The Enforcement of Morals." *Southern California Law Review* 41:588–641.

Skolnick, Jerome H. 1994. *Justice without Trial: Law Enforcement in Democratic Society*. New York: Macmillan.

Skolnick, Jerome H. 1995. "What Not to Do about Crime—the American Society of Criminology 1994 Presidential Address." *Criminology* 33:1–15.

Skolnick, Jerome H. and David H. Bayley. 1986. *The New Blue Line: Police Innovation in Six American Cities*. New York: Free Press.

Skorneck, Carolyn. 1992. "683,000 Women Raped in 1990, New Government Study Finds." *Boston Globe*, April 24, 1992:1, 32.

Skrzycki, Cindy. 1994. "The Feds' Plan to Check the Meat Has Food Groups Beefing." *Washington Post*, December 16:B1.

Slattery, Thomas J. 1994. "Canadian Mood May Boost Anti-Fraud Push." *National Underwriters Property & Casualty-Risk & Benefits Management*, July 11:31.

Smith, Brent L. and Kelly R. Damphousse. 1998. "Terrorism, Politics, and Punishment: A Test of Structural-Contextual Theory and the 'Liberation Hypothesis.'" *Criminology* 36:67–92.

Smith, Carolyn and Terence P. Thornberry. 1995. "The Relationship between Childhood Maltreatment and Adolescent Involvement in Delinquency." *Criminology* 33:451–481.

Smith, Douglas A. 1986. "The Neighborhood Context of Police Behavior." Pp. 313–341 in *Crime and Justice: A Review of Research*, vol. 8, edited by Albert J. Reiss, Jr. and Michael Tonry. Chicago: University of Chicago Press.

Smith, Douglas A., Christy A. Visher, and Laura A. Davidson. 1984. "Equity and Discretionary Justice: The Influence of Race on Police Arrest Decisions." *Journal of Criminal Law and Criminology* 75:234–249.

Smith, M. Dwayne. 1990. "Patriarchal Ideology and Wife Beating: A Test of a Feminist Hypothesis." *Violence and Victims* 5:257–274.

Smith, M. Dwayne. 1992. "Variation in Correlates of Race-Specific Urban Homicide Rates." *Journal of Contemporary Criminal Justice* 8:137–149.

Smith, M. Dwayne. 2000. "Capital Punishment in America." Pp. 621–643 in *Criminology: A Contemporary Handbook*, edited by Joseph F. Sheley. Belmont, CA: Wadsworth.

Smith, Tom W. 1997. "A Call for a Truce in the DGU War." *Journal of Criminal Law and Criminology* 87:1462–1469.

Smolowe, Jill. 1994. "A High Price to Pay." *Time*, December 19:59.

Sniffen, Michael J. 1999. "Serious Crimes Plunge 10%." *Bangor Daily News*, November 27:A1.

Sommers, Ira, Jeffrey Fagan, and Deborah Baskin. 1994. "The Influence of Acculturation and Familism on Puerto Rican Delinquency." *Justice Quarterly* 11:207–228.

Sorensen, Jon and Donald H. Wallace. 1999. "Prosecutorial Discretion in Seeking Death: An Analysis of Racial Disparity in the Pretrial Stages of Case Processing in a Midwestern County." *Justice Quarterly* 16:559–578.

Sorensen, Jonathan R., James W. Marquart, and Deon E. Brock. 1993. "Factors Related to Killings of Felons by Police Officers: A Test of the Community Violence and Conflict Hypotheses." *Justice Quarterly* 10:417–440.

Southern Poverty Law Center. 1994a. "Anti-Immigrant Violence Rages Nationwide: White Supremacists Exploiting Fear of Immigrants." *Intelligence Report*:1+.

Southern Poverty Law Center. 1994b. "The Hidden Victims: Hate Crime against American Indians Under-Reported." *Intelligence Report*:1+.

Southern Poverty Law Center. 1994c. "White Supremacists Exploit King Holiday." *Intelligence Report*:3, 29.

Soyinka, Wole. 1995. "Nigeria Waits." *The Nation*, December 4:692–693.

Spangler, Todd. 2000. "Pa. Gunman Kills 2, Wounds 3 Seriously." *Boston Globe*, March 2:A9.

Spears, Jeffrey W. and Cassia C. Spohn. 1997. "The Effect of Evidence Factors and Victim Characteristics on Prosecutors' Charging Decisions in Sexual Assault Cases." *Justice Quarterly* 14:501–524.

Spitzer, Steven. 1975. "Toward a Marxian Theory of Deviance." *Social Problems* 22:638–651.

Spofford, Tim. 1988. *Lynch Street: The May 1970 Slayings at Jackson State College*. Kent, OH: Kent State University Press.

Spohn, Cassia and Jeffrey Spears. 1996. "The Effect of Offender and Victim Characteristics on Sexual Assault Case Processing Decisions." *Justice Quarterly* 13:649–679.

Spohn, Cassia and Jerry Cederblom. 1991. "Race and Disparities in Sentencing: A Test of the Liberation Hypothesis." *Justice Quarterly* 8:305–327.

Spohn, Cassia and Julie Horney. 1991. "'The Law's the Law, but Fair Is Fair': Rape Shield Laws and Officials' Assessments of Sexual History Evidence." *Criminology* 29:137–161.

Spohn, Cassia, John Gruhl, and Susan Welch. 1987. "The Impact of Ethnicity and Gender of Defendants on the Decision to Reject or Dismiss Felony Charges." *Criminology* 25:175–192.

Sprinkel, Elizabeth A. 1993. "Insurance Fraud in America: A Growing Problem for Everyone." *Compensation and Benefits Management* 9:51–56.

Stack, Steven. 1987. "Publicized Executions and Homicide, 1950–1980." *American Sociological Review* 52:532–540.

Stafford, Mark C. and Omer R. Galle. 1984. "Victimization Rates, Exposure to Risk, and Fear of Crime." *Criminology* 22:173–185.

Stanford, Sally. 1966. *The Lady of the House*. New York: G. P. Putnam.

Staples, Robert. 1982. *Black Masculinity: The Black Male's Role in American Society*. San Francisco: Black Scholar Press.

Stark, Rodney. 1987. "Deviant Places: A Theory of the Ecology of Crime." *Criminology* 25:893–911.

Stark, Rodney and William Sims Bainbridge. 1996. *Religion, Deviance, and Social Control*. New York: Routledge.

Statistics Canada. 1999. *The Daily*. Ottawa: Statistics Canada.

Statistics, Bureau of Justice. 1999. *Crime Facts at a Glance*. (http://www.ojp.usdoj.gov/bjs/glance.htm#Crim).

Steffens, Lincoln. 1904. *The Shame of the Cities*. New York: McClure, Phillips.

Steffensmeier, Darrell. 1980. "Sex Differences in Patterns of Adult Crime, 1965–77: A Review and Assessment." *Social Forces* 58:1080–1108.

Steffensmeier, Darrell J. 1986. *The Fence: In the Shadow of Two Worlds*. Totowa, NJ: Rowman & Littlefield.

Steffensmeier, Darrell. 1989. "On the Causes of 'White-Collar Crime': An Assessment of Hirschi and Gottfredson's Claims." *Criminology* 27:345–358.

Steffensmeier, Darrell and Cathy Streifel. 1991. "The Distribution of Crime by Age and Gender Across Three Historical Periods—1935, 1960, 1985." *Social Forces* 69:869–894.

Steffensmeier, Darrell and Emilie Allan. 2000. "Looking for Patterns: Gender, Age, and Crime." Pp. 85–127 in *Criminology: A Contemporary Handbook*, edited by Joseph F. Sheley. Belmont, CA: Wadsworth.

Steffensmeier, Darrell and Miles D. Harer. 1991. "Did Crime Rise or Fall During the Reagan Presidency? The Effects of an 'Aging' U.S. Population on the Nation's Crime Rate." *Journal of Research in Crime and Delinquency* 28:330–359.

Steffensmeier, Darrell and Miles D. Harer. 1999. "Making Sense of Recent U.S. Crime Trends, 1980 to 1996/1998: Age Composition Effects and Other Explanations." *Journal of Research in Crime and Delinquency* 36:235–274.

Steffensmeier, Darrell, Jeffery Ulmer, and John Kramer. 1998. "The Interaction of Race, Gender, and Age in Criminal Sentencing: The Punishment Cost of Being Young, Black, and Male." *Criminology* 36:763–797.

Steffensmeier, Darrell, John Kramer, and Cathy Streifel. 1993. "Gender and Imprisonment Decisions." *Criminology* 31:411–446.

Stengel, Richard. 1989. "When Brother Kills Brother: Black-on-Black Violence." Pp. 112–118 in *Crime in the Streets and Crime in the Suites: Perspectives on Crime and Criminal Justice*, edited by Doug A. Timmer and D. Stanley Eitzen. Boston: Allyn and Bacon.

Stephens, Richard C. 1992. "Psychoactive Drug Use in the United States Today: A Critical Overview." Pp. 1–31 in *Drugs, Crime, and Social Policy: Research, Issues, and Concerns*, edited by Thomas Mieczkowski. Boston: Allyn and Bacon.

Stets, Jan E. and Murray A. Straus. 1990. "Gender Differences in Reporting Marital Violence and Its Medical and Psychological Consequences." Pp. 151–165 in *Physical Violence in American Families: Risk Factors and Adaptations to Violence in 8,145 Families*, edited by Murray A. Straus and Richard J. Gelles. New Brunswick, NJ: Transaction.

Stewart, James B. 1991. *Den of Thieves*. New York: Simon & Schuster.

Stone, Andrea, Erin Einhorn, and Margaret Litvin. 1994. "Women Who Become Statistics." *USA Today*, July 13:3A.

Stone, Isidor F. 1989. *The Trial of Socrates*. New York: Anchor.

Straus, Murray A. 1980. "Victims and Aggressors in Marital Violence." *American Behavioral Scientist* 23:681–704.

Straus, Murray A. 1991. "Discipline and Deviance: Physical Punishment of Children and Violence and Other Crime in Adulthood." *Social Problems* 38:133–154.

Straus, Murray A. 1993. "Physical Assaults by Wives: A Major Social Problem." Pp. 67–87 in *Current Controversies on Family Violence*, edited by Richard J. Gelles and Donileen R. Loseke. Newbury Park, CA: Sage.

Straus, Murray A. 1994a. *Beating the Devil Out of Them: Corporal Punishment in American Families*. New York: Lexington Books.

Straus, Murray A. 1994b. "State-to-State Differences in Social Inequality and Social Bonds in Relation to Assaults on Wives in the United States." *Journal of Comparative Family Studies* 25:7–24.

Straus, Murray A. and Christine Smith. 1990. "Violence in Hispanic Families in the United States: Incidence Rates and Structural Interpretations." Pp. 341–367 in *Physical Violence in American Families: Risk Factors and Adaptations to Violence in 8,145 Families*, edited by Murray A. Straus and Richard J. Gelles. New Brunswick, NJ: Transaction.

Straus, Murray A. and Richard J. Gelles. 1986. "Societal Change and Change in Family Violence from 1975 to 1985 as Revealed by Two National Surveys." *Journal of Marriage and the Family* 48:465–479.

Straus, Murray A., Richard J. Gelles, and Suzanne Steinmetz. 1980. *Behind Closed Doors: Violence in the American Family*. New York: Doubleday.

Strossen, Nadine. 1995. *Defending Pornography: Free Speech, Sex, and the Fight for Women's Rights*. New York: Scribner's.

Styron, William. 1967. *The Confessions of Nat Turner*. New York: Random House.

Sudetic, Chuck. 1995. "Gambling Finds Haven in Temples." *New York Times*, May 7:45.

Sudnow, David. 1965. "Normal Crimes: Sociological Features of the Penal Code in a Public Defender's Office." *Social Problems* 12:255–276.

Sullivan, Peggy S. 1989. "Minority Officers: Current Issues." Pp. 330–340 in *Central Issues in Policing*, edited by Roger G. Dunham and Geoffrey P. Alpert. Prospect Heights, IL: Waveland Press.

Surette, Ray. 1998. *Media, Crime, and Criminal Justice: Images and Realities*. Belmont, CA: Wadsworth.

Sutherland, Edwin H. 1937. *The Professional Thief*. Chicago: University of Chicago Press.

Sutherland, Edwin H. 1939. *Principles of Criminology*. 3d ed. Philadelphia: Lippincott.

Sutherland, Edwin. 1940. "White-Collar Criminality." *American Sociological Review* 5:1–12.

Sutherland, Edwin H. 1947. *Principles of Criminology*. 4th ed. Philadelphia: Lippincott.

Sutherland, Edwin H. 1949. *White Collar Crime*. New York: Holt, Rinehart, and Winston.

Suttles, Gerald. 1968. *The Social Order of the Slum*. Chicago: University of Chicago Press.

Sutton, Charlotte D. and Richard R. Woodman. 1989. "Pygmalion Goes to Work: The Effects of Supervisor Expectations in a Retail Setting." *Journal of Applied Psychology* 74:942–950.

Swearington, M. Wesley. 1995. *FBI Secrets: An Agent's Expose*. Boston: South End Press.

Sykes, Gresham M. and David Matza. 1957. "Techniques of Neutralization: A Theory of Delinquency." *American Sociological Review* 22:664–670.

Taft, Philip and Philip Ross. 1990. "American Labor Violence: Its Causes, Character, and Outcome." Pp. 174–186 in *Violence: Patterns, Causes, Public Policy*, edited by Neil Alan Weiner, Margaret A. Zahn, and Rita J. Sagi. San Diego: Harcourt Brace Jovanovich.

Tak, Peter J. P. 1994. "Community Service Sentence in the Netherlands." Pp. 305–319 in *Alternatives to Imprisonment in Comparative Perspective*, edited by Ugljesa Zvekic. Chicago: Nelson-Hall.

Takagi, Paul. 1974. "A Garrison State in a 'Democratic Society'." *Crime and Social Justice* 1:27–33.

Tannenbaum, Frank. 1938. *Crime and the Community*. Boston: Ginn.

Tappan, Paul W. 1947. "Who Is the Criminal?" *American Sociological Review* 12:96–102.

Tarbell, Ida M. 1904. *The History of the Standard Oil Company*. New York: McClure, Phillips.

Tarde, Gabriel. 1912 [1890]. *Penal Philosophy*. Translated by Rapelje Howell. Boston: Little, Brown.

Taylor, Ian, Paul Walton, and Jock Young. 1973. *The New Criminology: For a Social Theory of Deviance*. London: Routledge and Kegan Paul.

Taylor, Ralph B. and Jeanette Covington. 1988. "Neighborhood Changes in Ecology and Violence." *Criminology* 26:553–589.

Taylor, Ralph B. and Jeanette Covington. 1993. "Community Structural Change and Fear of Crime." *Social Problems* 40:374–397.

Television Digest. 1991. "Price-Fixing Settlement Reached by Nintendo, FTC, and Attorneys Gen. of 50 States." *Television Digest*, October 28:15.

Tennenbaum, Daniel. 1977. "Personality and Criminality: A Summary and Implications of the Literature." *Journal of Criminal Justice* 5:225–235.

Teret, Stephen P. et al. 1998. "Support for New Policies to Regulate Firearms: Results of Two National Surveys." *The New England Journal of Medicine* 339:813–818.

Terry, Don. 1994. "Woman's False Charge Revives Hurt for Blacks." *New York Times*, November 6:12.

Thomas, Charles W. and Donna M. Bishop. 1984. "The Effect of Formal and Informal Sanctions on Delinquency: A Longitudinal Comparison of Labeling and Deterrence Theories." *Journal of Criminal Law and Criminology* 75:1222–1245.

Thomas, Charles W., Robin J. Cage, and Samuel C. Foster. 1976. "Public Opinion on Criminal Law and Legal Sanctions: An Examination of Two Conceptual Models." *Journal of Criminal Law and Criminology* 67:110–116.

Thomas, Gordon. 1989. *Journey into Madness: The True Story of Secret CIA Mind Control and Medical Abuse*. New York: Bantam.

Thomas, William I. and Dorothy Swaine Thomas. 1928. *The Child in America: Behavior Problems and Programs*. New York: Knopf.

Thomas, William I. and Florian Znaniecki. 1927. *The Polish Peasant in Europe and America*. Vol. 2. New York: Knopf.

Thompson, E. P. 1975. *Whigs and Hunters: The Origin of the Black Act*. London: Allen Lane.

Thoreau, Henry D. 1969. "Civil Disobedience." Pp. 27–48 in *Civil Disobedience: Theory and Practice*, edited by Hugo Adam Bedau. New York: Pegasus.

Thornberry, Terence P. 1987. "Toward an Interactional Theory of Delinquency." *Criminology* 25:863–891.

Thornberry, Terence P. 1989. "Reflections on the Advantages and Disadvantages of Theoretical Integration." Pp. 51–60 in *Theoretical Integration in the Study of Crime and Deviance: Problems and Prospects*, edited by Steven F. Messner, Marvin D. Krohn, and Allen E. Liska. Albany: State University of New York Press.

Thornberry, Terence P., Melanie Moore, and R. L. Christenson. 1985. "The Effect of Dropping Out of High School on Subsequent Criminal Behavior." *Criminology* 23:3–18.

Thornberry, Terence P., Alan J. Lizotte, Marvin D. Krohn, Margaret Farnworth, and Sung Joon Jang. 1994. "Delinquent Peers, Beliefs, and Delinquent Behavior: A Longitudinal Test of Interactional Theory." *Criminology* 32:47–83.

Thornberry, Terence P., Carolyn A. Smith, Craig Rivera, David Huizinga, and Magda Stouthamer-Loeber. 1999. *Family Disruption and Delinquency*. Washington, D.C.: U.S. Department of Justice, Office of Juvenile Justice and Delinquency Prevention.

Thornton, Robert Y. and Katsuya Endo. 1992. *Preventing Crime in America and Japan: A Comparative Study*. Armonk, NY: M. E. Sharpe.

Tibbetts, Stephen G. and Alex R. Piquero. 1999. "The Influence of Gender, Low Birth Weight, and Disadvantaged Environment in Predicting Early Onset of Offending: A Test of Moffitt's Interactional Hypothesis." *Criminology* 37:843–877.

Tieger, Todd. 1981. "Self-Rated Likelihood of Raping and Social Perception of Rape." *Journal of Research in Personality* 15:147–158.

Tillman, Robert and Henry N. Pontell. 1992. "Is Justice 'Collar-Blind'?: Punishing Medicaid Provider Fraud." *Criminology* 30:547–573.

Tilly, Charles. 1989. "Collective Violence in European Perspective." Pp. 62–100 in *Violence in America: Protest, Rebellion, Reform*, vol. 2, edited by Ted Robert Gurr. Newbury Park, CA: Sage.

Tittle, Charles R. 1980. *Sanctions and Social Deviance: The Question of Deterrence*. New York: Praeger.

Tittle, Charles R. 1995. *Control Balance: Toward a General Theory of Deviance*. Boulder, CO: Westview Press.

Tittle, Charles R., Mary Jean Burke, and Elton F. Jackson. 1986. "Modeling Sutherland's Theory of Differential Association: Toward an Empirical Clarification." *Social Forces* 65:405–432.

Tittle, Charles R., Wayne J. Villemez, and Douglas A. Smith. 1978. "The Myth of Social Class and Criminality: An Empirical Assessment of the Empirical Evidence." *American Sociological Review* 43:643–656.

Tjaden, Patricia and Nancy Thoennes. 1998. *Prevalence, Incidence, and Consequences of Violence against Women: Findings from the National Violence against Women Survey*. Washington, D.C.: U.S. Department of Justice.

Tjaden, Patricia and Nancy Thoennes. 1999. "Prevalence and Incidence of Violence against Women: Findings from the National Violence against Women Survey." *The Criminologist* 24:1+.

Toby, Jackson. 1980. "The New Criminology Is the Old Baloney." Pp. 124–132 in *Radical Criminology: The Coming Crises*, edited by James A. Inciardi. Beverly Hills, CA: Sage.

Tolnay, Stewart E. and E. M. Beck. 1995. *A Festival of Violence: An Analysis of Southern Lynchings, 1882–1930*. Urbana: University of Illinois Press.

Tonry, Michael. 1994. *Malign Neglect: Race, Crime, and Punishment in America*. New York: Oxford University Press.

Tracy, Paul E. and James Alan Fox. 1989. "A Field Experiment on Insurance Fraud in Auto Body Repair." *Criminology* 27:589–603.

Tracey, Paul E., Jr., Marvin E. Wolfgang, and Robert M. Figlio. 1990. *Delinquency Careers in Two Birth Cohorts*. New York: Plenum Press.

Tremblay, Pierre. 1986. "Designing Crime: The Short Life Expectancy and the Workings of a Recent Wave of Credit Card Bank Frauds." *British Journal of Criminology* 26:234–253.

Triplett, Ruth A. and G. Roger Jarjoura. 1994. "Theoretical and Empirical Specification of a Model of Informal Labeling." *Journal of Quantitative Criminology* 10.

Tucker, Jalie A. 1999. "From Zero Tolerance to Harm Reduction." *National Forum (Journal of Phi Kappa Phi honor society)* 79:19–24.

Tunnell, Kenneth D. 1990. "Choosing Crime: Close Your Eyes and Take Your Chances." *Justice Quarterly* 7:673–690.

Tunnell, Kenneth D., ed. 1993a. *Political Crime in Contemporary America: A Critical Approach*. New York: Garland.

Tunnell, Kenneth D. 1993b. "Prologue: The State of Political Crime." Pp. xi–xix in *Political Crime in Contemporary America: A Critical Approach*, edited by Kenneth D. Tunnel. New York: Garland.

Tunnell, Kenneth D. 1996. "Let's Do It: Deciding to Commit a Crime." Pp. 246–258 in *New Perspectives in Criminology*, edited by John E. Conklin. Boston: Allyn and Bacon.

Turk, Austin T. 1969. *Criminality and Legal Order*. Chicago: Rand McNally.

Turk, Austin T. 1982. *Political Criminality: The Defiance and Defense of Authority*. Beverly Hills: Sage.

Turk, Austin T. 1991. "Seductions of Criminology: Katz on Magical Meanness and Other Distractions." *Law and Social Inquiry* 16:181–194.

Turner, A. 1981. "The San Jose Recall Study." Pp. 22–27 in *The National Crime Survey: Working Papers*, vol. 1; *Current and Historical Perspectives*, edited by Robert G. Lehnen and Wesley G. Skogan. Washington, D.C.: U.S. Department of Justice: Bureau of Justice Statistics.

Turpin, James. 1999. "Restorative Justice Challenges Corrections." *Corrections Today*, October:60–62.

U.S. Bureau of the Census. 1998. *Statistical Abstract of the United States: 1998*. Washington, D.C.: U.S. Government Printing Office.

U.S. News & World Report. 1982. "Corporate Crime: The Untold Story." *U.S. News & World Report*, September 6:25.

Unnever, James D. and Larry A. Hembroff. 1988. "The Prediction of Racial/Ethnic Sentencing Disparities: An Expectation States Approach." *Journal of Research in Crime and Delinquency* 25:53–82.

Urschel, Joe. 1994. "Yes, There's Spouse Abuse, But …" *USA Today*, June 30:11A.

van Dijk, Jan and Kristiina Kangaspunta. 2000. "Piecing Together the Cross-National Crime Puzzle." *National Institute of Justice Journal* 272:34–41.

van Dijk, Jan and Pat Mayhew. 1993. "Criminal Victimization in the Industrialized World: Key Findings of the 1989 and 1992 International Crime Surveys." In *Understanding Crime: Experiences of Crime and Crime Control*, edited by Anna Alvazzi del Frate, Ugljesa Zvekic, and Jan van Dijk. Rome: United Nations Interregional Crime and Justice Research Institution.

Van Dijk, Jan J. M., Pat Mayhew, and Martin Killias. 1991. *Experiences of Crime across the World: Key Findings from the 1989 International Crime Survey*. Duventer: Kluwer Law and Taxation Publishers.

Vance, Carole S. 1993. "Feminist Fundamentalism—Women against Images." *Art in America* 81:35–38.

Vandiver, Margaret and David Giacopassi. 1997. "One Million and Counting: Students' Estimates of the Annual Number of Homicides Occurring in the U.S." *Journal of Criminal Justice Education* 8:135–143.

Vandivier, Kermit. 1987. "Why Should My Conscience Bother Me?" Pp. 103–123 in *Corporate and Governmental Deviance: Problems of Organizational Behavior in Contemporary Society*, edited by M. David Ermann and Richard J. Lundman. New York: Oxford University Press.

Vaughan, Diane. 1983. *Controlling Unlawful Organizational Behavior: Social Structure and Corporate Misconduct*. Chicago: University of Chicago Press.

Veblen, Thorstein. 1953 [1899]. *The Theory of the Leisure Class: An Economic Study of Institutions*. New York: New American Library.

Venturelli, Peter J., ed. 1994. *Drug Use in America: Social, Cultural, and Political Perspectives*. Boston: Jones & Bartlett.

Verhovek, Sam Howe. 1999. "Seattle Police Chief Resigns in Aftermath of Protests." *New York Times*, December 8:A13.

Viano, Emilio C. 1990. "Victimology: A New Focus of Research and Practice." Pp. xi–xxiii in *The Victimology Handbook: Research Findings, Treatment, and Public Policy*, edited by Emilio C. Viano. New York: Garland.

Vincentnathan, S. George. 1995. "Social Reaction and Secondary Deviance in Culture and Society: The United States and Japan." Pp. 329–347 in *The Legacy of Anomie Theory*, vol. 6, *Advances in Criminological Theory*, edited by Freda Adler and William S. Laufer. New Brunswick, NJ: Transaction.

Visher, Christy A. 1983. "Gender, Police Arrest Decisions, and Notions of Chivalry." *Criminology* 21:5–28.

Visher, Christy A. 2000. "Career Offenders and Crime Control." Pp. 601–619 in *Criminology: A Contemporary Handbook*, edited by Joseph F. Sheley. Belmont, CA: Wadsworth.

Vold, George. 1958. *Theoretical Criminology*. New York: Oxford University Press.

Vold, George, Thomas Bernard, and Jeffrey B. Snipes. 1998. *Theoretical Criminology*. New York: Oxford University Press.

Volkman, Ernest. 1994. *Spies: The Secret Agents Who Changed the Course of History*. New York: John Wiley.

Wald, Matthew L. 1997. "U.S. Warned Film Plants, Not Public, About Nuclear Fallout." *New York Times*, September 30:A16.

Wald, Matthew L. 1998. "Honda and Ford Are Fined Millions." *New York Times*, June 9:A1.

Waldholz, Michael. 1989. "Warm Bodies; Doctor-Owned Labs Earn Lavish Profits in a Captive Market." *Wall Street Journal*, March 1:A1.

Walker, Lenore E. 1984. *The Battered Woman Syndrome*. New York: Springer.

Walker, Lenore E. and Angela Browne. 1985. "Gender and Victimization by Intimates." *Journal of Personality* 53:179–195.

Walker, Samuel and Molly Brown. 1995. "A Pale Reflection of Reality: The Neglect of Racial and Ethnic

Minorities in Introductory Criminal Justice Textbooks." *Journal of Criminal Justice Education* 6:61–83.

Walker, Samuel, Cassia Spohn, and Miriam DeLone. 2000. *The Color of Justice: Race, Ethnicity, and Crime in America*. Belmont, CA: Wadsworth.

Walker, Samuel. 1980. *Popular Justice: A History of American Criminal Justice*. New York: Oxford University Press.

Walker, Samuel. 1993. "Putting Justice Back into Criminal Justice: Notes for a Liberal Criminal Justice Policy." Pp. 503–516 in *Criminal Justice: Law and Politics*, edited by George F. Cole. Belmont, CA: Wadsworth.

Walker, Samuel. 1994. *Sense and Nonsense about Crime and Drugs: A Policy Guide*. Belmont, CA: Wadsworth.

Walker, Samuel. 1998. *Sense and Nonsense about Crime and Drugs: A Policy Guide*. Belmont, CA: Wadsworth.

Walklate, Sandra. 1992. "Researching Victims of Crime: Critical Victimology." In *Realist Criminology: Crime Control and Policing in the 1990s*, edited by John Lowman and Brian D. MacLean. Toronto: University of Toronto Press.

Wall Street Journal. 1994. "Bentsen Creates Task Force in Bid to Fight Tax Fraud." *Wall Street Journal*, April 21:C14.

Wallman, Joel. 1999. "Serotonin and Impulsive Aggression: Not So Fast." *The HFG Review* 3:21–24.

Walsh, James. 1994. "The Whipping Boy." *Time*, May 2:80.

Walters, Glenn D. 1992. "A Meta-Analysis of the Gene-Crime Relationship." *Criminology* 30:595–613.

Walters, Glenn D. and Thomas W. White. 1989. "Heredity and Crime: Bad Genes or Bad Research?" *Criminology* 27:455–485.

Warchol, Greg. 1998. *Workplace Violence, 1992–96*. Washington, D.C.: U.S. Department of Justice, Bureau of Justice Statistics.

Ward, Dick. 1995. "Vietnam: The Criminal Justice Challenge of Moving toward a Market Economy." *CJ International* 11.

Warner, Barbara D. and Glenn L. Pierce. 1993. "Reexamining Social Disorganization Theory Using Calls to the Police as a Measure of Crime." *Criminology* 31:493–517.

Warner, Bob. 1997. "In 25 Years, One Other City Has Had Crime Counts Tossed." *Philadelphia Daily News*, October 21:1.

Warr, Mark. 1985. "Fear of Rape among Urban Women." *Social Problems* 32:238–250.

Warr, Mark. 1990. "Dangerous Situations: Social Context and Fear of Criminal Victimization." *Social Forces* 68:891–907.

Warr, Mark. 1993. "Parents, Peers, and Delinquency." *Social Forces* 72:247–264.

Warr, Mark. 1998. "Life-Course Transitions and Resistance From Crime." *Criminology* 36:183–215.

Warr, Mark. 2000. "Public Perceptions of and Reactions to Crime." Pp. 13–31 in *Criminology: A Contemporary Handbook*, edited by Joseph F. Sheley. Belmont, CA: Wadsworth.

Warr, Mark and Mark Stafford. 1991. "The Influence of Delinquent Peers: What They Think or What They Do?" *Criminology* 29:851–866.

Warr, Mark, Robert F. Meier, and Maynard L. Erickson. 1983. "Norms, Theories of Punishment, and Publicly Preferred Penalties for Crimes." *Sociological Quarterly* 24:75–91.

Warshaw, Robin and Andrea Parrot. 1995. "The Contribution of Sex-Role Socialization to Acquaintance Rape." Pp. 152–160 in *Readings in Deviant Behavior*, edited by Alex Thio and Thomas Calhoun. New York: HarperCollins.

Wauchope, Barbara and Murray A. Straus. 1990. "Physical Punishment and Physical Abuse of American Children: Incidence Rates by Age, Gender, and Occupational Class." Pp. 133–148 in *Physical Violence in American Families: Risk Factors and Adaptations to Violence in 8,145 Families*, edited by Murray A. Straus and Richard J. Gelles. New Brunswick, NJ: Transaction Books.

Weber, Tom. 1995. "Some Push for Violence as Cure for Violence." *Bangor Daily News*, March 6:B1.

Webster's Ninth New Collegiate Dictionary. 1983. S.v. "myth."

Weiner, Neil Alan, Margaret A. Zahn, and Rita J. Sagi. 1990. "Introduction: What Is Violence?" Pp. xi–xvii in *Violence: Patterns, Causes, Public Policy*, edited by Neil Alan Weiner, Margaret A. Zahn, and Rita J. Sagi. San Diego: Harcourt Brace Jovanovich.

Weis, Joseph G. 1976. "Liberation and Crime: The Invention of the New Female Criminal." *Crime and Social Justice* 6:17–27.

Weisburd, David and Kip Schlegel. 1992. "Returning to the Mainstream: Reflections on Past and Future White-Collar Crime Study." Pp. 352–365 in *White-Collar Crime Reconsidered*, edited by Kip Schlegel and David Weisburd. Boston: Northeastern University Press.

Weiss, Mike. 1984. *Double Play: The San Francisco City Hall Killings*. Reading, MA: Addison-Wesley.

Welles, Chris. 1989. "America's Gambling Fever." *Business Week*, April 24:112–117.

Wellford, Charles F. and Ruth A. Triplett. 1993. "The Future of Labeling Theory: Foundations and Promises." Pp. 1–22 in *New Directions in Criminological Theory*, vol. 4, *Advances in Criminological Theory*, edited by Freda Adler and William S. Laufer. New Brunswick, NJ: Transaction.

Wells, Joseph T. 1994. "The Billion Dollar Clip." *Internal Auditor*, October:32–37.

Wells, L. Edward and Joseph H. Rankin. 1988. "Direct Parental Controls and Delinquency." *Criminology* 26:263–285.

Wells, Susan J. 2000. "When It's Nobody's Business But

Your Own: Identity Fraud Is Tough to Combat." *New York Times*, February 13:BU11.

Wenger, Morton G. and Thomas A. Bonomo. 1993. "Crime, the Crisis of Capitalism, and Social Revolution." Pp. 674–688 in *Crime and Capitalism: Readings in Marxist Criminology*, edited by David F. Greenberg. Philadelphia: Temple University Press.

West, Candace and Don H. Zimmerman. 1987. "Doing Gender." *Gender and Society* 1:125–151.

Westermann, Ted D. and James W. Burfeind. 1991. *Crime and Justice in Two Societies: Japan and the United States.* Pacific Grove, CA: Brooks/Cole.

Westley, William A. 1970. *Violence and the Police.* Cambridge: MIT Press.

White, Jacquelyn W. and John A. Humphrey. 1995. "Young People's Attitudes Toward Acquaintance Rape." Pp. 161–168 in *Readings in Deviant Behavior*, edited by Alex Theo and Thomas Calhoun. New York: HarperCollins.

Whyte, William Foote. 1943. *Street Corner Society: The Social Structure of an Italian Slum.* Chicago: University of Chicago Press.

Wiatrowski, Michael D., David B. Griswold, and Mary K. Roberts. 1981. "Social Control Theory and Delinquency." *American Sociological Review* 46:525–541.

Widom, Cathy Spatz. 1989. "Child Abuse, Neglect, and Violent Criminal Behavior." *Criminology* 27:251–271.

Widom, Cathy Spatz. 1992. *The Cycle of Violence.* Washington, D.C.: U.S. Department of Justice, National Institute of Justice.

Widom, Cathy Spatz. 1996. *The Cycle of Violence Revisited.* Washington, D.C.: U.S. Department of Justice, National Institute of Justice.

Widom, Cathy Spatz. 2000. "Childhood Victimization: Early Adversity, Later Psychopathology." *National Institute of Justice Journal*, January:2–9.

Widom, Cathy Spatz and Hans Toch. 1993. "The Contribution of Psychology to Criminal Justice Education." *Journal of Criminal Justice Education* 4:251–272.

Wilbanks, William. 1987. *The Myth of a Racist Criminal Justice System.* Monterey: Brooks/Cole.

Wildavsky, Aaron B. 1981. *The Politics of Mistrust: Estimating American Oil and Gas Resources.* Beverly Hills: Sage.

Wilkie, Curtis. 1995. "Miss. Flogging Debate Opens Old Wounds." *Boston Globe*, February 21:1.

Wilkinson, Karen. 1974. "The Broken Home and Juvenile Delinquency: Scientific Explanation or Ideology?" *Social Problems* 21:726–739.

Williams, Frank P., Marilyn D. McShane, and Ronald L. Akers. 2000. "Worry About Victimization: An Alternative and Reliable Measure for Fear of Crime." *Western Criminology Review* 2(2). <http://wcr.sonoma.edu/v2n2/williams.html>.

Williams, Franklin P., III. 1980. "Conflict Theory and Differential Processing: An Analysis of the Research Literature." Pp. 213–232 in *Radical Criminology: The Coming Crises*, edited by James A. Inciardi. Beverly Hills: Sage.

Williams, Kirk R. and Robert L. Flewelling. 1988. "The Social Production of Criminal Homicide: A Comparative Study of Disaggregated Rates in American Cities." *American Sociological Review* 53:421–431.

Williams, Scott. 1994. "ABC Special Takes the Scare out of Life." *Boston Globe*, April 20:72.

Wilson, James. 1999. *The Earth Shall Weep: A History of Native America.* New York: Atlantic Monthly Press.

Wilson, James Q. 1995. "Crime and Public Policy." Pp. 489–507 in *Crime*, edited by James Q. Wilson and Joan Petersilia. San Francisco: Institute for Contemporary Studies Press.

Wilson, James Q. and Barbara Boland. 1978. "The Effect of the Police on Crime." *Law and Society Review* 12:367–390.

Wilson, James Q. and George L. Kelling. 1982. "Broken Windows: The Police and Neighborhood Safety." *Atlantic Monthly*, March:29–38.

Wilson, James Q. and Richard J. Herrnstein. 1985. *Crime and Human Nature.* New York: Simon & Schuster.

Wilson, Margo I. and Martin Daly. 1992. "Who Kills Whom in Spouse Killings? On the Exceptional Sex Ratio of Spousal Homicides in the United States." *Criminology* 30:189–215.

Wilson, William Julius. 1987. *The Truly Disadvantaged.* Chicago: University of Chicago Press.

Wisotsky, Steven. 1995. "A Society of Suspects: The War on Drugs and Civil Liberties." Pp. 129–134 in *Drugs, Society, and Behavior, Annual Editions*, edited by Erich Goode. Guilford, CT: Dushkin.

Witkin, Gordon. 1994. "Should You Own a Gun?" *U.S. News & World Report*, August 15:24–30.

Witt, Karen De. 1994. "Many in U.S. Back Singapore's Plan to Flog American Youth." *New York Times*, April 5:A4.

Wokutch, Richard E. and Josetta S. McLaughlin. 1992. "The U.S. and Japanese Work Injury and Illness Experience." *Monthly Labor Review* 115:3–11.

Wolfe, Alan. 1973. *The Seamy Side of Democracy: Repression in America.* New York: David McKay.

Wolfgang, Marvin E. 1958. *Patterns in Criminal Homicide.* Philadelphia: University of Pennsylvania Press.

Wolfgang, Marvin E. 1972. "Cesare Lombroso (1835–1909)." Pp. 232–291 in *Pioneers in Criminology*, edited by Hermann Mannheim. Montclair, NJ: Patterson Smith.

Wolfgang, Marvin E. and Franco Ferracuti. 1967. *The Subculture of Violence.* London: Social Science Paperbacks.

Wolfgang, Marvin E., Robert M. Figlio, and Thorsten Sellin. 1972. *Delinquency in a Birth Cohort.* Chicago: University of Chicago Press.

Wolfgang, Marvin E., Robert M. Figlio, Paul E. Tracy, and Simon I. Singer. 1985. *The National Survey of Crime Severity.* Washington, D.C.: U.S. Department of Justice.

Women's Wear Daily. 1989. "Tinsely Pleads Guilty He Stole $2.3M from Evyan." *Women's Wear Daily*, October 2:14.

Wordes, Madeline, Timothy S. Bynum, and Charles J. Corley. 1994. "Locking Up Youth: The Impact of Race on Detention Decisions." *Journal of Research in Crime and Delinquency* 31:149–165.

Worrall, A. and Ken Pease. 1986. "Personal Crime against Women: Evidence from the 1982 British Crime Survey." *The Howard Journal* 25:118–124.

Wright, Bradley R. Entner, Avshalom Caspi, Terrie E. Moffitt, and Phil A. Silva. 1999. "Low Self-Control, Social Bonds, and Crime: Social Causation, Social Selection, or Both?" *Criminology* 37:479–514.

Wright, James D. and Peter H. Rossi. 1986. *Armed and Considered Dangerous: A Survey of Felons and Their Firearms*. New York: Aldine.

Wright, James D. and Teri E. Vail. 2000. "Guns, Crime, and Violence." Pp. 577–599 in *Criminology: A Contemporary Handbook*, edited by Joseph F. Sheley. Belmont, CA: Wadsworth.

Wright, James D., Joseph F. Sheley, and M. Dwayne Smith. 1995. "Kids, Guns, and Killing Fields." Pp. 115–120 in *Readings in Deviant Behavior*, edited by Alex Thio and Thomas Calhoun. New York: HarperCollins.

Wright, Keven N. 1985. *The Great American Crime Myth*. Westport, CT: Greenwood Press.

Wright, Richard A. 1992. "From Vamps and Tramps to Teases and Flirts: Stereotypes of Women in Criminology Textbooks, 1956 to 1965 and 1981 to 1990." *Justice Quarterly* 3:223–236.

Wright, Richard T. and Scott Decker. 1994. *Burglars on the Job: Streetlife and Residential Break-ins*. Boston: Northeastern University Press.

Wu, W. A., K. Steenland, D. Brown, V. Wells, J. Jones, P. Schulte, and W. Halperin. 1989. "Cohort and Case-Control Analyses of Workers Exposed to Vinyl Chloride: An Update." *Journal of Occupational Medicine* 31:518–523.

Wykes, Alan. 1964. *The Complete Illustrated Guide to Gambling*. Garden City, NY: Doubleday.

Yisheng, Dai. 1995. "China: Expanding Economy and Growing Crime." *CJ International* 11:9–16.

Yllo, Kersti A. 1993. "Through a Feminist Lens: Gender, Power, and Violence." Pp. 47–62 in *Current Controversies on Family Violence*, edited by Richard J. Gelles and Donileen R. Loseke. Newbury Park, CA: Sage.

Young, Cathy. 1994. "Gender Terrorism?" *Boston Globe*, January 29:19.

Young, Jock. 1986. "The Failure of Criminology: The Need for a Radical Realism." Pp. 4–30 in *Confronting Crime*, edited by Roger Matthews and Jock Young. Beverly Hills: Sage.

Young, Jock. 1992. "Realist Research as a Basis for Local Criminal Justice Policy." Pp. 34–72 in *Realist Criminology: Crime Control and Policing in the 1990s*, edited by John Lowman and Brian D. MacLean. Toronto: University of Toronto Press.

Young, Vernetta D. 1992. "Fear of Victimization and Victimization Rates among Women: A Paradox?" *Justice Quarterly* 9:419–441.

Zahn, Gordon C. 1970. "The Berrigans: Radical Activism Personified." *Catholic World*, December:125–130.

Zatz, Marjorie S. 1987. "The Changing Forms of Racial/Ethnic Biases in Sentencing." *Journal of Research in Crime and Delinquency* 24:69–92.

Zatz, Marjorie S., Carol Chiago Lujan, and Zoann K. Snyder-Joy. 1991. "American Indians and Criminal Justice: Conceptual and Methodological Considerations." Pp. 100–112 in *Race and Criminal Justice*, edited by Michael J. Lynch and E. Britt Patterson. New York: Harrow and Heston.

Zawitz, Marianne W., ed. 1992. *Drugs, Crime, and the Justice System: A National Report from the Bureau of Justice Statistics*. Washington, D.C.: U.S. Department of Justice, Bureau of Justice Statistics.

Zigler, E., C. Taussig, and K. Black. 1992. "Early Childhood Intervention: A Promising Preventative for Juvenile Delinquency." *American Psychologist* 47:997–1006.

Zimbardo, Philip G. 1972. "Pathology of Imprisonment." *Society* 9:4–8.

Zimring, Franklin E. 1998. *American Youth Violence*. New York: Oxford University Press.

Zimring, Franklin and Gordon Hawkins. 1995. *Incapacitation: Penal Confinement and the Restraint of Crime*. New York: Oxford University Press.

Zimring, Franklin E. and Gordon Hawkins. 1995. *The Search for Rational Drug Control*. New York: Cambridge University Press.

Zimring, Franklin E. and Gordon Hawkins. 1997. *Crime Is Not the Problem: Lethal Violence in America*. New York: Oxford University Press.

Zimroth, Peter L. 1974. *Perversions of Justice: The Prosecution and Acquittal of the Panther 21*. New York: Viking Press.

Zipperer, John. 1994. "Against All Odds." *Christianity Today*, November 14:58–61.

Zuckoff, Mitchell. 1999. "Homicides Haunt Baltimore." *Boston Globe*, December 18:A1.

PHOTO CREDITS

NAME INDEX

SUBJECT INDEX

Critical perspectives on crime (*cont.*)
  critique of, 224–26
  evaluation of, 226
Croats, 362–63
Cruz, Rolando, 471, 503
Cultural goals, 156
Cultural myths, 282–85
  battering, 283–85
  rape, 282–83
Culture conflict, 218
Culture Conflict and Crime (Sellin), 218
Customs, 13–14
Cyber crime (computer crime), 337–38
Czech Republic, crime rate in, 151

Dalkon Shield IUD, 347–48
Dark figure of crime, 57, 60
Day care, 516
Days of Rage, 384
DDT, 350
Death penalty, 44, 45–46, 309, 489, 492, 497–503, 518
  arbitrariness and racial discrimination in application of, 499–501
  cost of, 497–98
  general deterrence and, 498
  quality of legal representation and, 501–2
  wrongful executions and, 502–3
Debunking motif, 5
Defense attorneys, 472, 473, 475
Defense industry, 342
Dehumanization, 393
Delinquency
  girls' lives and, 231
  integrated model of, 199–202
  IQ and, 132
  "life course" development of, 59–60
  middle-class, 72, 157, 159
  peer relations and, 178–79
  sexual abuse and, 231
  social control theory of, 187–97
Delinquent Boys (Cohen), 162–63
Delta Airlines, 340
Democratic National Convention, 372
Democratic theory, 22–23
Demographic variation, 96. *See also* Age; Gender; Race and ethnicity; Social class
Denmark, imprisonment in, 491
Dependent variable, 12
Descent of Man (Darwin), 114
Deterrence theory, 113, 287–90, 458, 460–63, 495–96, 498
Deviance
  historical views on, 6–7

normalcy of, 137
relativity of, 128, 135
Deviance amplification, 210, 213
Deviant lifestyles, victimization and, 95–96
Deviant places, theory of, 153–54
Dialectical Marxism, 222, 224
Diallo, Amadou, 435
Diet and nutrition, 125–26
Differential association theory, 7, 175–80, 184, 353
Differential enforcement, 454
Differential identification theory, 180–81
Differential opportunities, 67, 167–68
Differential processing, 209
Differential reinforcement theory, 182, 184
Direct civil disobedience, 386
Directed police patrol, 458–59
Discipline, 191–92. *See also* Punishment
Discordance, 120
Discretionary justice, 449–50
Discrimination. *See* Race and ethnicity
Disintegrative shaming, 213, 215
Disruption, government, 367–70
Diversion movement, 213, 214
Division of labor, 476
Dogs, as crime deterrent, 319–20
Domestic violence. *See* Battering; Rape
Dominican Republic, 366
Double standard, 456
Dowry deaths, 273
Draft board raids, 389–90
Dramatization of evil, 210
Dreyfus Affair, 391
Drift theory, 184–87
Dropping out, 164
Drug courts, 416–17
Drug laws, repealing, 518
Drug use. *See* Illegal drug use
Drug war. *See* War on drugs
Due process, 27
Due Process model, 436–38
Dunedin Multidisciplinary Health Development Study, 136
Du Pont family, 428
Duress, 15
DWB (Driving While Black), 453

Early childhood intervention, 515–16
Eastman Kodak, 373
Eating disorders, 109
Ecological evidence for police discrimination, 455
Economic costs, of victimization, 98–99

Economic deprivation, 353, 513
  child abuse and, 294
  crime relationship, 150–53, 159–60, 166
  drug abuse and, 405–6
  homicide rates and, 247, 248–49
  illegal drug use and, 430
  property crime and, 315–16
  prostitution and, 430
Ectomorphs, 119
Education, 70, 71, 162–64, 192, 233
Egalitarian households, 232
Ego, 130
Egoism, 221
Eighth Amendment to the Constitution, 499
Elderly
  fear of crime and, 37
  victimization and, 86
Eli Lilly and Company, 347
Elite deviance. *See* White-collar crime
El Salvador, 364
Embezzlement, 300, 301, 330–31, 352–53
  collective, 332
Employee theft, 330–31
Employment policy, 513
Endomorphs, 118–19
English Convict, The (Goring), 117
Enlightenment, 110–12
Entrapment, 16
Environmental pollution, 349–50
Equal treatment hypotheses, 230
Erotica, 423
Erratic discipline, 191
Espionage, 362, 390–91
Essay Concerning Human Understanding, An (Locke), 182
Ethnic cleansing, 363
Eugenics movement, 129
Evil, dramatization of, 210
Evil woman hypotheses, 230, 455–56
Evolution, 114
Exclusionary rule, 464
Experimentation, unethical and illegal, 361, 372–73
Experiments, research, 11
Expert opinion, 23
External pressures and pulls, 183
Extortion, 426
Extralegal factors, 208–9, 212. *See also* Gender; Race and ethnicity; Social class

Face-to-face interviews, 10
Factual guilt, 478
False advertising, 341
Family, 189–92
  discipline and supervision, 191–92
  income, 85–86, 278, 279

Police (*cont.*)
  women and people of color as, 466–68, 519
  working personality of, 441–49
  zero-tolerance policing, 459, 461, 465, 519
Policing, aggressive, 459–60
Polish immigrants, 148
Polish Peasant in Europe and America, The (Thomas and Znaniecki), 148
Political assassination, 385–86
Political corruption, 337, 361, 375–77, 519
Political crime, 8, 358–95
  crime against government, 379–91
    civil disobedience, 15, 360, 386–90
    mass political violence, 380–86
  crime by government
    hate crimes, 129, 361, 377–79
    political corruption, 361, 375–77
    political repression and human rights violations, 361, 362–72
    state-corporate crime, 373–75
    unethical and illegal experimentation, 361, 372–73
  defining, 360–62
  reducing, 393–94
  social patterning of, 392–93
Political opportunity theory, 391
Political prisoners, 370
Political protest, 218
Political repression, 361, 362–72
Political trials, 370
Political violence, 238
Pollution, 349–50
Population density, reducing, 514
Population size, fear of crime and, 36
Pornography, 419–24
  on the Internet, 429
  violent, 11
Positivism, 6, 114–15, 206
Post-traumatic stress disorder (PTSD), 99–100
Poverty, 71, 72, 150. *See also* Economic deprivation
Power-control theory, 232–33
Power groups, 217
Power-threat theory, 455, 477
Predatory crime, 94–95
Pregnancy
  and birth complications, 126, 128–29
  drug abuse and, 407
Prejudice, sentencing preferences and, 44–45. *See also* Race and ethnicity
Premarital sex, 398–99
Premeditated murder, 239
Premenstrual syndrome (PMS), 123–25

Preoperational period, 131
President's Commission on Law Enforcement and the Administration of Justice, 28
Pressing, 111
Price fixing, 340–41
Price gouging, 341
Primary deviation, 210–11, 212
Primary prevention, 511, 512–15
Principles of Criminology (Sutherland), 175
Prior record, 483, 486
Prisoners, political, 370
Prisons. *See also* Imprisonment
  development of, 112
  reform of, 518
Private troubles, 4, 5
Probation, 491
Procedural justice, 436
Professional criminals, 258, 305–6, 311
Professional fraud, 332–33
Prohibition, 413, 428
Project on Human Development in Chicago Neighborhoods, 127
Proletariat, 217
Property crime, 53, 298–323, 495–96
  age and, 302
  arson, 239, 301, 302, 305, 317–18
  burglary, 300, 302, 305
    decision making in, 308
    social organization of, 306–7
    support system, 306, 307, 314–15
  costs of, 308–10
  defining, 300–301
  explaining, 313–18
  extent of, 301–2
  forgery and fraud, 300, 301, 310–13
  gender and, 65–66, 303–5, 306–7
  larceny, 300–301, 302, 305, 310
  motor vehicle theft, 300, 301, 302, 305, 310, 314, 320–21
  patterning of, 302–5
  race and ethnicity and, 69, 305
  reducing, 319–21
  shoplifting, 301, 303–5, 317–18
  social organization of, 305–8
  victimization rates for, 62
Prosecutors, 472, 473, 474–76
Prostitution, 42, 54, 399, 407, 417–19, 420, 426
Psychoactive drugs, 400, 402, 409
Psychoanalytic theory, 130–31
Psychological costs, of victimization, 99–100
Psychological explanations of criminal behavior, 2, 108, 109, 130–38
  critique of, 135–38
  intelligence, 132–33

Milgram and Zimbardo experiments, 138, 144–45
  moral development, 131–32
  psychoanalytic theory, 130–31
  research in New Zealand, 135, 136
  temperament (personality), 133–35
Public defenders, 473, 474
Public health model, 508, 511
Public issues, 5
Public opinion, 21–47
  accuracy of beliefs, 23, 24–34
  on fear of crime. *See* Fear of crime
  public policy and, 22–24
  on punishment, 43–45
  on seriousness of crime, 41–43, 45
Public order crimes, 218, 396–433
  gambling, 398, 424–26
  illegal drug use, 42, 399–417
    arrest practices, 454–55, 489–90
    contemporary U.S. use, 401–5
    crime connection, 408–10
    economic deprivation and, 405–6
    explaining, 405–7
    gender and, 406–7
    in history, 400–401
    international, 429
    legalization debate, 410–16
    organized crime and, 428
  organized crime, 426–30
    alien conspiracy model and myth, 428–30, 431
    history of, 426–28
    Prohibition and, 413, 428
    reducing, 430–31
  overview of, 398–99
  pornography, 419–24
  prostitution, 42, 399, 407, 417–19, 420, 426
Puerto Ricans, 384
Puffery, 341
Punishment, 7, 191, 476–96. *See also* Imprisonment
  crime seriousness and, 41–42
  impact on crime, 492–96
  public attitudes toward, 43–45
  social class and, 478–79
Punishment and Social Structure (Rusche & Kirchheimer), 476
Punitive discipline, 191
Puritans, 377, 424
Purse snatching, 300
Pygmalion effect, 210

Quakers, 377, 387

Race and ethnicity. *See also* African-Americans
  arrest practices and, 450–55
  battering and, 279–80